LIVES OF ENGLAND'S
REIGNING AND
CONSORT QUEENS

LIVES OF ENGLAND'S REIGNING AND CONSORT QUEENS

England's History
through the Eyes of its Queens

The Companion For

LIVES OF ENGLAND'S MONARCHS
The Story of Our American English Heritage

Published by AUTHORHOUSE
2005, Re-issued 2011

H. Eugene Lehman

Ph.D. Stanford University
Professor Emeritus, University of North Carolina Chapel Hill, USA

authorHOUSE®

AuthorHouse™
1663 Liberty Drive
Bloomington, IN 47403
www.authorhouse.com
Phone: 1-800-839-8640

First published by AuthorHouse   10/07/2011

ISBN: 978-1-4634-3057-3 (sc)
ISBN: 978-1-4634-3056-6 (hc)
ISBN: 978-1-4634-3055-9 (ebk)

Library of Congress Control Number: 2011912500

Printed in the United States of America

This book is printed on acid-free paper.

Table of Contents

DEDICATION

For the encouragement and interest expressed throughout
preparation of

Lives of Reigning and Consort Queens of England:
England's History through the Eyes of its Queens

My sincere thanks with appreciation to

Dorothea Claire Lehman Leonard
And
Michael Philip Gates

Cover graphics:

The *Royal Heraldic Shield of Great Britain* of King George I,
redrawn, and *St. George Chapel and Windsor Castle*, photograph
by the author.

AUTHOR'S SPECIAL USAGE

This informs the reader of conventions used in the narrative text:

The term *Queen Consort* is used generically throughout this text to identify the wives of reigning kings. Therefore, the use of the term does not imply that the title 'Queen Consort' was officially conferred by an act of Parliament, as was the case in some instances.

Standard double quotation marks set off statements that are true to original meaning, but they may not be *verbatim*, as when rendered into Modern English from archaic or foreign tongues. Translation may modify the syntax or grammar from the style of the original.

Single quotation marks set off quotations within quotations; on occasion, they are also used to enclose conjectural remarks of uncertain origin, or occasionally in substitution of Italics for words or phrases.

The major authority used for dates on lives and reigns of monarchs is Alison Weir, *Britain's Royal Families,* Pimlico Press, Random House, London 1996. The disagreements on dates given in works of other authors, when they do occur, are of insufficient importance in the present work to warrant challenge or debate.

Historical data given here are selected to illuminate personalities. The biographical chapters are written to stand as independent accounts, which may be read in any order one chooses. Therefore, events are often revisited with different emphasis to reflect ways they were experienced by other contemporary individuals.

These biographical narratives attempt to re-create lives from a day long past. Only fleeting attention is given to concurrent developments in economics, sociology, technology, humanities, or natural sciences.

The author is responsible for opinions and interpretations expressed, and regrets the presence of factual and mechanical errors that remain in the text.

With expectation that one will have a good read, let us now proceed to the banquet before us.

H. Eugene Lehman, Chapel Hill, NC, USA, 2011.

PREFACE

Intent and Format

THIS BOOK, *Lives of Reigning and Consort Queens of England: England's History through the Eyes of its Queens,* is a factual narrative on lives of Norman, Plantagenet, Tudor, Stuart, Hanover, and Windsor queens covering almost a millennium of English history—from the Norman Conquest of 1066 to the life of present Queen Elizabeth II. The biographical portraits start at the close of the Dark Ages and continue into Modern Time. The book gives a view into life as daily living and courtly customs as they moved from an age far removed from the present toward the way of life we know today.

Here, over fifty women take turns as wives or as ruling monarchs at center stage in England's dramatic past. Facts on lives of these women are drawn from many sources. Through these women, one sees England's history unroll.

Eight queens in this starring cast were *Queens Regnant* who ruled (or tried to rule) in her own right. Major events in their lives were documented in this book's companion volume *Lives of England's Monarchs.* The lives of reigning queens reviewed again in the present work are:

> *Empress Matilda, Lady Jane Grey, Queen Mary I, Queen Elizabeth I, Queen Mary II, Queen Anne, Queen Victoria, and Queen Elizabeth II.*

Emphasis here, however, is on Queens Consort wives and occasional 'favorites' of England's kings who follow the Norman Conquest of 1066:

Norman Dynasty: *Matilda of Flanders, Matilda of Scotland, and Matilda of Boulogne.*

Plantagenet Dynasty: *Eleanor of Aquitaine, Berengaria of Navarre, Joan of Gloucester, Isabelle of Angoulême, Eleanor of Provence, Eleanor of Castile, Marguerite of France, Isabella of France, Philippa of Hainault, Anne of Bohemia, Isabella of Valois, Joanna of Navarre, Katherine of Valois, Margaret of Anjou, Elizabeth Woodville, and Anne Neville of Warwick.*

Tudor Dynasty: *Elizabeth of York, Katherine of Aragon, Anne Boleyn, Jane Seymour, Anne of Cleves, Katherine Howard, and Katherine Parr.*

Stuart Dynasty: *Anne of Denmark, Henrietta Maria of France, Katherine of Braganza, Anne Hyde, and Maria Beatrice of Modena.*

Hanover Dynasty: *Sophia Dorothea of Celle, Caroline of Brandenburg-Ansbach, Charlotte of Meckenburg-Strelitz, Maria Anne FitzHerbert, Caroline of Brunswick, Dorothea Bland, and Adelaide of Saxe-Meiningen.*

Saxe-Coberg-Gotha—Windsor Dynasty: *Alexandra of Denmark, Mary of Teck, Wallis Warfield, and Elizabeth Bowes-Lyon.*

Even though these women were at center stage, and participated in major events in the time history allotted to them, the names of most of them are unfamiliar to all but serious students of English history.

As exceptions to this generalization, the names of Eleanor of Aquitaine, Wallis Warfield, and the six wives of Henry VIII usually are recognized by a majority of readers. However, most readers will not recall the name, or remember a single event associated with any other noble lady named above. True, some persons with college textbook familiarity with English history will recall that 'this-or-that' consort was the mother of 'this-or-that' heir apparent, but other than that, little is remembered of them.

The *Introduction* to *Lives of Reigning and Consort Queens of England* gives an overview of England's history from prehistoric time to the Norman Conquest in AD 1066. It gives readers elements of Celtic, Roman, Dark Age, and Saxon English history. These events set the stage for the Norman Conquest, and the rise of medieval Manorial Feudalism, which was the common way of life in Western Europe's Middle Ages. Medieval values and customs were far different than those held fit and proper today, but they have echoes that survive now in the 21st century.

The body of the text falls into seven sections, which follow the dynasties that have ruled England from Saxon to Modern Times:

Dynasty I.   Saxon Wessex Earl-King Dynasty (802-1066)
Dynasty II.   Norman Dynasty (1066-1154)
Dynasty III. Plantagenet Dynasty (1066-1485)
Dynasty IV.   Tudor Dynasty (1485-1603)
Dynasty V.   Stuart Dynasty (1603-1714)
Dynasty VI.   Hanover Dynasty (1714-1901)
Dynasty VII. Saxe-Coburg-Gotha—Windsor Dynasty
              (1901-present)

The introduction to each dynasty includes a genealogical table that lays out the hereditary lineage for the ruling sovereigns in the dynasty.

The body of the text is made up of forty-one chronological *Reign Chapters*. Each is an essay, which begins with a summary of major events in the reign of the ruling monarch. That summary provides the background against which the queen consort's life is played out. Her life is told informally to reveal her individual nature and personality. The term *narrative* in titles implies that the text is written in a nontechnical style to give a pleasant read, but one that also is a factual account of important events in each reign. Chapters are written as independent biographies; accordingly, they may be read in any order the reader chooses.

Life data on kings and queens are selected from many reference sources; personalities are illuminated; decisive events are emphasized; causes are explained; reigns are made memorable as part of an unfolding tapestry of time.

When, a ruling monarch had more than one wife (as was the case with Henry VIII who had six queens consort) the chapter is composed as a sequence of biographical memoirs, one for each wife of the ruling monarch.

An *Index* of major persons and historic events is provided for the reader's convenience.

INTRODUCTION

ENGLAND
BEFORE THE NORMAN
CONQUEST (1200 BC–AD 1066)

Prehistoric and Celtic British Isles
(c. 12,000 BC–48 BC)

THE LAST great Pleistocene ice age began about seventy-five millennia ago. At its peak, c. 20,000 BC, total land surfaces of the British Isles were under an ice sheet that covered all Northern Europe. As huge Arctic and Antarctic polar ice caps extracted water from the oceans, sea level dropped by two hundred to three hundred feet below its present level, so that the British Isles became a peninsula of Continental Europe. Later, as climate warmed and glaciers receded, the British Isles again became ice-free. Plants and animals from the European Continent slowly re-colonized newly exposed land. Around 12,000 to 8,000 BC waves of human inhabitants migrated across a land bridge at the present Straits of Dover, which connected the British peninsula to Europe. The Dover land bridge to England still existed until about 6,500 BC. Celts, the dominant ethnic Caucasian Race in Central Europe, used the Dover Land Bridge to enter the peninsula of Britain. Originally, the Celtic tribes were hunter-gatherers. By 4,500 BC, England was again separated by water from the Continent at the Strait of Dover, and Celts developed agriculture in fertile valleys of southern Britain. English archaeologists have found domestic pottery that was made around 3,500 BC. The megalithic constructions at Stonehenge, and elsewhere in Britain and Ireland, date from around 3,200 to 1,500 BC. These artifacts are variously described as evidences for religious or astronomical inventions, but little is really known of motivations that led to their construction.

By 3,000 BC, smelting of copper and tin in southwestern England was well advanced. A lively trade in these two metals, both of which are important in the manufacture of bronze, was well underway between Britain and Mediterranean civilizations. Britain, the primary supplier of tin from extensive deposits in Cornwall, was important in development of the European Bronze Age, which lasted from 3,200 BC to 1,200 BC. The Iron Age began, at a time roughly contemporaneous with Tutankhamen in Ancient Egypt's 18th dynasty, when the Hittites in Asia Minor first used charcoal as a means for working iron ores. Smelting of iron was practiced in Western Europe around 1,000 BC, and reached England around 800 BC.

The Celtic homeland was the Rhine River valley, but evidences indicate that, during the sixth to third centuries BC, Celts spread through much of west central Europe, and borrowed from cultures as far east as Asia Minor. Incursions of Celtic Jutes from Denmark, and Frisians from the northern border islands of Holland, periodically crossed the North Sea to colonize England. For half a millennium, the island continued on its independent way without other major cultural or ethnic exchanges with Europe.

Present day descendants of the original Celts of the British Isles are the Gaelic of Ireland, the Manx of the Isle of Man, the Highland Scots (the Picts) of Scotland, and the Britons who took over what is now England and Wales. Today major survivors of original Celtic Britons exist in endemic populations throughout England, but they persist chiefly in Wales, Devon, Cornwall, the Channel Islands of Jersey and Guernsey, as well as the peninsula of Brittany in France.

Roman Conquest and Rule of Britannia
(c. 56 BC-AD 476)

CELTIC LANDS (Roman Gaul) initially included much of present France and Spain. Midway into the 1st century BC, Rome showed minor interest in the islands they called Britannia, named for the savage natives that inhabited the islands. Firsthand knowledge of Britons by the civilized world of Rome came with a tentative exploration of the island by Julius Caesar in 56-54 BC. Caesar judged it unwise to continue any attempt to conquer the unruly Britons. He thought them to be inherently so savage as to be beyond benefit from civilizing blessings Rome could give them. After the departure of Caesar, the Britons enjoyed savage Druid domesticity for almost a century, before Emperor Claudius (40-48 AD) attempted to conquer the islands. By 78 AD, Rome had conquered all lands presently known as England and Wales. They became the protectorate colony of the Roman Empire known as *Britannia*, or the *Western March*. Britannia was the outermost western colony of the Roman Empire.

The colonial relationship of Britannia to Rome lasted for about 300 years, and reached its peak during the reign of Hadrian (AD 117-138). During that period, Roman legions built amphitheaters, and baths with heated water. Civic centers with piped water and sewage disposal systems existed at Winchester, London, Gloucester, York, Lincoln, Colchester, St. Albans, and other locations. Excellent roads connected Roman fortifications and cities. Hadrian's Wall 72 miles in length stretched across the narrow neck of the island in AD 122-126. The wall served as a line of defense against invasion from Scottish Picts along Britannia's northern border. Britannia did not include Ireland or Scotland. Hadrian's Wall is evidence that Rome had no intent, at that time, to expand its control of the British Isles into Scotland.

Under Roman rule, Britannia enjoyed peace, tranquility, and civil order under the *Pax Romana* (the Peace of Rome) that included the *Codex Militaris* (Roman Military Law), which established standards for the administration of justice in all Imperial Provinces. A high level of cultural literacy prevailed in Roman Britain that was not equaled again for the next thousand years.

The decline of Imperial Rome began after the death of Hadrian in AD 138. A succession of incompetent emperors deprived the empire of wise moral leadership. The governors were military generals who were only interested in acquisition of personal wealth and power. The collapse of Imperial Rome accelerated rapidly after Alaric and his Visigoths invaded, and sacked the City of Rome in AD 406-410. Repeated attacks by barbarian tribes further weakened Roman authority. Invasion of northern Italy by Attila and his Mongol Huns in AD 451-452 threatened destruction of Rome. Pope Leo I, however, persuaded Attila to spare the city.

The date AD 476 marks the deposition of Romulus Augustus, the last nonbarbarian emperor. That date is often taken as the close of the Ancient Classical Age. During the desperate times that followed the fall of Imperial Rome, Christian monasteries kept feeble flames of literacy burning throughout the wreckage of an empire that had once been the model for stability, and learning in the Western World.

The Collapse of Civility
after the fall of Rome
(c. AD 450-600)

THE MIDDLE AGES cover the millennium that comes between the fall of Rome in the 5th century, and the discovery of the New World at the end of the 15th century (roughly from AD 450 to 1500). The first half of the Middle Ages (the six hundred years from AD 450 to 1050) is popularly called as the Dark Ages. That age is the Anglo-Saxon Period in English History. It began with the arrival in Kent of the Saxon brothers Hengist and Horsa in 446, and ended with the Norman Conquest of 1066.

The revolutionary disruption of continuity in government that followed the fall of Rome led to vast social changes throughout its former Imperial Provinces. The former conquerors were now the conquered. In only three generations—in less than a century—citizens of Rome no longer enjoyed the security of common laws, or of agencies for protection of public comfort and tranquility. Barbarian chieftains conquered provinces, and exploited the land for immediate gain. The new rulers had little experience with, or appreciation for literacy and life under rules of law. These barbarians came from the north, south, and east. They quickly dismantled the classic Roman Empire in a remorseless sequence of Goth, Ostrogoth, Vandal, Frank, Lombard, Norse, and German invasions.

The victors briefly established their own concepts of law, but each period of domination rarely lasted more that one ruler's life span. Most of the ragtag ruffians had previously experienced little more of civilized living than hunter gathering, marauding, and fermenting poor quality beer. Moreover, they had no skilled subordinates able to administer delegated authority, and no trained accountants capable of keeping financial records essential for collection of taxes, and no organized militia able to maintain a peacetime government. The lack of consistency in government was quickly followed by a decline in industry, a collapse in commerce, a drop in wealth of the masses, and the loss of a tax base capable of supporting any stable system of central authority.

Anarchy replaced government by law. Ancient cultural traditions were abandoned, and soon forgotten. It is sad but true that, although the rise of civilization is exceeding slow, neglect of learning for only three generations will see ancient culture disappear, traditions for justice vanish, and racial legends of a valiant past die.

Coincident with the fall of Rome, the most serious loss was a general decline in literacy among the masses. Incessant war impoverished the land, and little surplus wealth remained beyond bare minimal creature needs for survival. As time passed, scholars died, academies closed, and few tutorials remained for the education of students who could assume scholarly leadership for instruction in later generations. As wise just leadership in government declined throughout Europe, the light of learning flickered out. Scarcely two generations after the fall of Rome, few persons in ruling classes, and no common men remained who could either read or write. Consequently, written records for the first two centuries in the Dark Ages are almost nonexistent.

The death knell for scholarship tolled in 529 when Emperor Justinian the Great closed the Platonic Academy in Athens. That institution (for over eight centuries, from 387 BC until AD 529) had been the major center of learning in the Classical Age. In strict conformity with religious correctness in the Early Church, Justinian ordered that documents irrelevant to the Christian Canon should be consigned to flames. After the 4th century, nothing remotely resembling a university existed in all Western Europe until the University of Bologna was founded five centuries later in 1088. Humanistic works on literature, art, and science, which were unrelated to religion or war, would not begin to reappear again until the Italian Renaissance reignited the flame for secular scholarship in the 13th and 14th centuries.

Rise of Christianity in England
(c. AD 325-734)

DURING THE 5th to 11th centuries AD (known as The Dark Ages), most literate persons were priests or mendicant friars trained in monasteries. They were the clerks and scribes that wrote or copied all written records that have come down to us from that intellectually blighted time. Monasteries in Ireland, Scotland, Wales, and England played an important part in recording and preserving information on Britain in the Dark Ages; therefore, passing credit is given to them here.

Church records report that St. Patrick, the Patron Saint of Ireland, was a native Briton who was educated in France circa AD 430. As a Bishop, with the blessing of Pope Leo the Great, he went to Ireland to evangelize the Druid natives. By AD 445, St. Patrick had founded the Archbishopric of Armagh the Mother Church of Ireland. By the time of St. Patrick's death in AD 461, all Ireland had been Christianized, and it has remained so ever since.

St. Kenneth of Scotland brought Christianity from Celtic Ireland to Scotland. In the 6th century, he founded St. Andrews Monastery of Fife (now only a stately ruin). The Church of St. Andrews was a major center for Scottish learning in the Middle Ages. The Archbishop of St. Andrews was the primate for church authority in Scotland.

In the 8th century, St. Dyfed (David) the Patron Saint of Wales established a monastery at the westernmost tip of Wales at the site of the present St. David's Cathedral. The Welsh fiercely resisted Saxon domination, and defended their native Celtic tongue, culture, and Arthurian legends.

St. George the Patron Saint of England is less firmly grounded in historic fact than are St. Patrick of Ireland, St. Dyfed of Wales, and St. Kenneth of Scotland. According to legend, St. George was a soldier of the Roman Legion that occupied England around 300 AD. Legend credits St.

George with slaying a dragon that threatened to carry off the daughter of the King of Kent.

Christianity in southern England was largely independent of the Irish tradition spread by followers of St. Patrick. Archbishop Augustine of Canterbury (not to be confused with the great St. Augustine of Hippa), with about forty Benedictine friars from Italy, arrived in Kent in AD 597. He founded an Abbey at Canterbury that for all time remained the Mother Church of England.

The churches of Ireland, Scotland, Wales, and England provided major centers for literacy and scholarship in Western Europe during the Dark Ages. The greatest name of those trained at Canterbury is the Benedictine monk known to history as The Venerable Bede. For most of his life, Bede served at the Monastery of Jarrow in northern England near Durham. His major work, *The Ecclesiastical History of the English People*, is the primary historical resource for information on England in the Dark Ages. It covered the period from AD 597 until the time of Bede's death in AD 734.

The Benedictine tradition at Canterbury attracted and trained many monks who went out to evangelize all England and much of Germanic Europe. St. Boniface an Anglo-Saxon Benedictine monk was educated at Canterbury. He Christianized savage tribes in Germany and Holland, but finally lost his own life at the hands of fierce intractable Friesland natives to Dutch islands in the North Sea.

Manorial Social Organization in the Dark Ages (c. AD 600-800)

THE SOCIOPOLITICAL *manorial system* arose between 600 and 800 in Europe during the Dark Ages, and became the way of life in Western Europe. Pope Leo III stabilized early nationalism with the election and coronation of Charlemagne as Emperor of the Holy Roman Empire on Christmas Day AD 800. The empire called *Christendom* was a consortium of principalities and kingdoms in Western Europe that recognized the Pope in Rome to be its religious leader.

The first two centuries of the Dark Ages (AD 500 to 700) were characterized primarily by illiterate anarchy and vandalism. After marauders had taken everything else of worth, the only thing of value that remained for exploitation was agricultural land. In keeping with the adage, *it is a poor parasite that destroys its host*, the despoilers who had subdued an area, soon realized that their advantage lay in secure peace and stability in their domains. Only by providing extended periods of tranquility over a succession of growing seasons could their serfs work the land, plant seeds, harvest crops, and allow their flocks and herds to undergo natural increase. Without extended periods free of vandalism, the overlord could have little expectation of profit from his conquests. With its motivation based on economic greed, a modicum of peace, stability, and civility gradually returned to Europe.

The term *manor* broadly refers to all lands and estates controlled by an overlord. More specifically, manor came to mean the fortified great house, or the castle of the *Lord of the Manor* (a title later shortened to Lord). More often than not, the lord managed his manor with the aid from enslaved serfs and hired brigands.

The following oversimplified outline shows how, between 700 and 1000 AD, a simple manorial system gave rise to feudal hierarchies of powerful aristocratic landowners, and later led to the beginning of nationalism in Western Europe.

Resident serfs on the manor were born into a permanent state of servitude. A serf's lot was difficult. Nevertheless, the lord of the Manor gave his serfs the blessing of protection from traveling bands of marauders. In the evolving manorial system, lords of a manor gave each serf a fief of land for his personal use. As determined by their overlord's generosity in disposing of his available arable land, fiefs were of variable size. Customarily, a serf farmed his own fief of land with little outside interference.

Freeborn peasants who lived outside a manor saw the protection gained through association with a manor house, and they occasionally volunteered to become vassals of the lord of the manor. Vassalage entailed a contract of mutual advantage for the lord and freeborn peasants. The lord, on his part, agreed to protect his serfs and vassals from pillage and plunder by wandering raiders in times of peace. In times of war, the lord would give his serfs and vassals haven within the fortified great manor house.

Freeborn peasants who agreed to be vassals to the overlord were required to swear an oath of fealty. In effect, the oath said, 'I am your loyal man in times of peace and war; I place my farm in your manor in exchange for your protection.' Fealty required a pledge to give military aid whenever needed (usually not more than 40 days of military service per year). Vassal peasants also were assessed an annual scutage (an agreed on tax) as a percentage of his farm's yield for the year. Thus, medieval scutage was somewhat like the system called *share cropping* in the rural South after the American Civil War. In the contract of fealty between lord and freeborn vassal, one can see roots of the ingrained tradition in English Common Law that gave all freemen the right to approve taxation imposed on them from above.

At first, the manorial system was local, and involved only peasants in a small hamlet with only a few dozen families. For added safety, peasant homes clustered together near their lord's manor house. During daytime, serf and vassal peasants worked outlying fields. Common pastures were shared for grazing cows, pigs, and sheep. Peasants and serfs of a manor returned at night to their dwellings near the great house for mutual protection. The manorial system provided a modest level of welcome peace, security, and social intercourse for peasants, and a reliable source of income for the lord of the manor.

The advantage of the manorial system was widely appreciated. Lands controlled by a lord gradually increased as surrounding peasants elected to join the manor, and share its protective benefit. However, more often, vassalage was coerced, and was not voluntary, because lords frequently used military force to enlarge their estates. Later, *vassalage* came to embody the meaning of indentured slavery.

Anglo-Saxon England in the Dark Ages (c. AD 450-1050)

ROMAN LEGIONS departed from Britannia soon after AD 410, and anarchy prevailed almost immediately. Many minor Celtic chieftains battled for control of local lands. By AD 450, affairs had fallen into such a state of disarray that Vortigren, a Celtic governor of Kent, in despair, invited the Rhineland Saxon brothers, Hengist and Horsa, to come to Kent to help restore order in Britannia. The brothers were the vanguard of hoards of Angles, Saxons, Franks, Jutes, Frisians, and Danes who followed. They took over the land in *The Anglo-Saxon Invasion*. Native Celtic Britons retreated into northern and western fringes of the island—to Scotland, Wales, Devon, and Cornwall—or to leave Britannia entirely. Some escaped to the Isle of Mann in the Irish Sea, others went to Channel Islands of Jersey or Guernsey, and others went to the peninsula of Brittany on the French mainland.

Thereafter, Britannia became Anglo-Saxon England. Around AD 500, the legendary King Arthur Pendragon, (with his sword Excalibur, and accompanied by the knights of the Round Table, the traitor Mordred, Queen Guinevere, Sir Lancelot, Gawain, and all the rest) made a last futile stand against the Saxon horde at Camelot, possibly at Carmarthen, Wales, but anywhere (or nowhere) in England. At Arthur's death, according to Welsh tradition, the magician Merlin pushed Arthur's funeral barque out on the Irish Sea, and prophesied that, "Some day, King Arthur, 'our once and future King,' will return to free the land from the Saxon horde." Legend says that King Arthur and Queen Guinevere were buried in Glastonbury near Bath, Somerset. The Arthurian legend dates from the close of the Roman Britannia period—its time setting is coequal in age with the legend of St. George killing a dragon—however, most scholars agree that the Arthurian Legend is a fictitious creation by the Middle French author Chrétien de Troyes.

The Saxons repelled later outside invaders, but they were themselves barbarians, and the source of internal strife and woe for England. The last vestiges of Roman literacy and culture vanished entirely during the Saxon period. Saxon England was without central governance for over three hundred years. England, early in the 6th century, was described in the Old English *Epic of Beowulf*. Beowulf was a young Saxon hero, who defeated the dragon, Grendel (it seems, dragons may have been a common nuisance in England during the Dark Ages). Victorious Beowulf became king, and lived on to be the hero of song and story in a place of fear and terror in the 'Foggy Fens of ye Merry Olde Anglesland.'

By AD 550, many clans of invading Saxon settlers claimed small domains throughout England, and defended them as their own realms. Chaotic anarchy ruled. Vestiges of that time persist in England today in the names of dozens of towns, cities, and shires in which abbreviation of Saxon words are of common occurrence. For example, in Old Saxon-German—*ham*, meant home or village; *ton* meant blockade or fortress, but came to mean *town* or *city; shire* referred to a feudal estate or manor. By extrapolation, present names on the land, such as, *Nottinghamshire*, means it is the place where the ancient Notte family had its home fortress, and lived in its manor house. The common suffix-*chester* (and its degraded forms,—*cester*,—*caster*, and even—*ster*) persists in the names of many English cities as relics of the Saxon word, *chest*, which then, as now, meant strongbox, and by extension, it included the sense of fortress. Thus, Win-*chester*, Glou-*cester*, Lan-*caster*, and Dun-*ster* are durable reminders that their present locations long ago were the fortress strongholds that gave refuge in times of war to the ancient Saxon tribes of Winne, Glower, Lanne, and Dunne.

As many as a thousand Saxon mini-kingdoms existed in England in AD 600. The chief of its family clan ruled each of them. This social order in many ways was similar to tribal societies of Native American Indians when Columbus arrived in the New World. Over the next century, neighboring village-tribes in Saxon England united for common protection into larger assemblies. Finally, seven major Saxon counties evolved. They are collectively the *Heptarchy of Saxon Kingdoms*. They are the Provinces or Counties of Kent, Mercia, Anglia, Northumbria, Essex, Sussex, and Wessex, (where the suffix,—*sex*, is an abbreviation of *Saxon*, as in: Essex = East Saxony, Sussex = South Saxony, Wessex = West Saxony). All seven of the Saxon Heptarchy persist as major historic and current Counties of England.

Kent was the first Saxon kingdom to acquire a central governor titled Thane or Earl. Next after Kent to acquire a titled chieftain lord was Essex, then Sussex, Mercia, Northumbria, and finally Wessex. For each of the seven ruling noble families, there is a lineage of Earl-Kings. Most go back, with various degrees of certainty, to the 6th Century. Although a ruling house governed each county in the Heptarchy, there was little cooperative aid among the counties to repel repeated predatory invasion from Scotland, Norway, and from the especially savage Jutes of Denmark. At this time the, so-called, *Danegeld*, a bribe, was paid to Denmark to forestall invasion.

Rise of the Feudal System
(c. AD 800-1000)

THE MEDIEVAL feudal system accompanied the expansion of manorial estates. Feudalism is most easily visualized as a hierarchy of fiefs and vassalage in which lords at lower levels became vassals to a higher-ranking overlord. In this way, manors increased in size from hamlets, to villages, to cities, to counties, to provinces, to states, and, finally, to nations. The lord of a city-state was titled, *Baron*; the lord of a county was titled *Count* (in England Earl); the lord of a province was titled *Duke*; the lord of an independent nation was titled *Prince*, or *King*. The title *Marquess* (in France, *Marquis*) derives from the Roman custom of referring to outposts of empire as *marches*. Marquess in England was originally reserved for the lord of a border county or province: the person with a title of Marquess had responsibility for defending his lord's manor from foreign invasion. The status of Marquess was below that of Duke, but above Count/Earl and Baron. Often, but not necessarily, barons were vassals of an earl; earls were vassals of a duke; dukes were vassals of a prince or king, who may have been a vassal of the Holy Roman Emperor.

Growth of manorial feudalism in the Middle Ages led directly to the rise of European city-states, counties, dukedoms, and autonomous states called principalities or kingdoms. At each ascending feudal level, vassals at lower ranks were required to *pledge fealty* (loyalty) to the overlord immediately above them. The overlord, to whom a vassal pledged fealty, was titled his *Liege lord*. Fealty was binding for life by an oath taken on a sacred relic of saints, or on the Sign of the Cross (as on the hilt of a sword traditionally shaped as a cross). Vassals at all levels were required to give so-called, *homage,* to their overlord as proof of subservience to him. Homage usually entailed kneeling and holding one's hands together, as in prayerful supplication, while the overlord held the vassal's hands between his, and said something to the effect, 'I accept you as my loyal subject and vassal.' Following the ritual of homage, the overlord assigned the vassal a fief of land (often multiple estates) suitable for the vassal's noble rank. The titled vassal then possessed authority to collect scutage (taxes levied against peasants of the fief) from his estate. Scutage provided income for the exalted lifestyle enjoyed by titled nobility in feudal systems. The services given by noble vassals to their Liege lord, in addition to payment of scutage, included a promise to provide a specified number of knights in full armor for use by the overlord at times when the homeland was under attack, or in case of wars of aggression against outlying estates.

The feudal system evolved unique characteristics in different parts of Europe as regions individually struggled for national identity. In the following account, attention is on the Norman feudal system introduced into Anglo-Saxon England by William Duke of Normandy. Many consequences of feudalism are evident throughout England's history. Relics of feudalism persist, even today, in present concepts of nobility, primogeniture, and social status.

Rise of Chivalry and Knighthood (c. AD 1000-1200)

CHIVALRY AND knighthood were late outgrowths of feudalism. During the feudal period, endless internecine struggles to enlarge land holdings led to improved military tactics. Characteristic of late medieval warfare was widespread use of mounted knights clothed in protective armor. Knights replaced foot soldiers as the major means of waging war. Chivalry and knighthood came into being, as formalized martial games devised by titled men of the privileged classes. They were the only ones who could afford a suit of armor and a stable of many horses. Battles were bloody, but performed in compliance with the strict etiquette of chivalry; that is, by formally proscribed acceptable ways in which battles were fought.

Knighthood was the lowest rank of nobility. It was always earned by personal merit, and was never a hereditary right. During the height of the feudal period (c. AD 1000 to 1300), knighthood was a highly prized goal for noblemen at all ranks. Above all, a knight was a brave and loyal horseman in armor. His military apprenticeship was in personal service to an established warrior knight. Training for knighthood began at age seven or eight as a fetch-and-carry *page*. Then, at age twelve, the apprentice advanced to *varlet* (later, valet), and learned to use and care for arms and armor. As a teenage youth, the cadet became an *esquire* (squire), and served as shield bearer in actual battle. Finally, when he was ready for investiture, and was dubbed *knight* in solemn ceremony.

The knight pledged an oath to be loyal, until death, to his Liege lord—to be brave in battle, to be devoted to the Church, and to defend his personal honor by being 'chivalrous' in all things. To be chivalrous (from French meaning, *like a horseman*) was somewhat similar to the American cowboy's romantic fiction called, *The Code of the West*. To be a *perfect chivalrous knight* meant that one would observe all rules of chivalry: a knight (somewhat like a 'boy scout') was devout, honest, trustworthy, loyal, brave, a protector of women, the weak, and the poor. He would faithfully observe the courtesies due to fealty and title.

Following investiture, the knight received the title, *Sir*, and a fief from his Liege lord that permitted him to live in a manner fitting his newly elevated social status. Knights were above the highest of the common gentry, but they were lowest of the nobility. By gaining knighthood, younger sons in noble families could gain a fief and title of their own, which, otherwise, was denied to them by the practice of inheritance by primogeniture.

Chivalry reached its peak during the Crusades. Those military campaigns were a series of eight or more attempts to wrest Jerusalem from the Infidel between 1095 and 1291. Military aspects of knighthood declined when the English longbow was perfected in the 14th Century. Knighthood remained an honorable title. However, it became little more than a personal demonstration of athletic prowess in tournaments at carnival festivals. Eventually, knighthood was granted for any service of merit to an overlord.

Contrary to congenital ingrained British tradition, King Arthur and his Knights of the Round Table came fully 500 years before, as the saying goes, 'chivalry and knighthood were in flower.'

Primogeniture Inheritance of Titles and Estates (c. AD 1200-1400)

THE SYSTEM of inheritance by primogeniture is one in which the eldest surviving legitimate son (or, if no sons, then the eldest daughter) inherits all titles, estates, and property of value, whereas, younger siblings inherit little or nothing.

The dominant principle governing inheritance of feudal estates in noble houses of England was primogeniture. It developed in response to a need for continuity of fealty between the liege lord and his vassals over successive generations. When a senior vassal died, his overlord could not let properties of the senior vassal be divided into many small portions among his many descendants. It was much to the overlord's advantage to make certain that the fief awarded to each of his vassals would pass as a block to a single descendant in each following generation.

Accompanying the issue of primogeniture was the serious matter of deciding legitimacy of descent. Importance lay in an ability to decide exactly which one (possibly among many offspring, often by different mothers) should be declared the rightful heir to inherit noble titles and estates. The Church cooperated in solving this matter by making 'legitimacy to inherit' dependant on the *Sacrament of Holy Matrimony*. Beginning around the 11th Century, it became increasingly difficult for bastard offspring (ones lacking a marriage blessing by the Church) to inherit titles and estates. By the 13th Century, formal church marriage had become so firmly established that, in 1208, Pope Innocent IV added *Matrimony* as the eighth official Catholic Sacrament (previously, the seven traditional sacraments were: Baptism, Confirmation, Eucharist, Confession, Penance, Extreme Unction at death, and Ordination for Holy Orders of priest and bishop).

Social Hierarchy in Medieval England (c. AD 600-1500)

DURING THE Middle Ages, irrespective of whether one was a commoner or of noble birth, people were born to the social status they would keep for life. Few could rise above the rank into which their parents had been born before them. The general belief prevailed that Divine Ordination decided what one's station in life would be.

That is, just as the king had a divine right to rule, so also, the serf's rightful place was to serve.

Church and State were united in maintaining that God's Will determined that a person's social rank should be the same as that of their parents before him. To aspire to rise above one's station at birth was a minor venial sin. The nobility enthusiastically endorsed the divinely ordained social order, but common men grudgingly accepted it.

The English social hierarchy that came down to present day England is essentially unchanged from the social ranks recognized a millennium ago. The following ranks defined the social position a person held by birth, marriage, and State or Church appointment.

1. *Royalty, or Royal Status*: this rank was reserved for persons in direct line of descent from a ruling Prince, King, or Emperor. Ruling monarchs and their family members were addressed: Your Majesty, Your Highness, or Your Grace.

2. *Nobility, or Noble Status*: this rank included the titled aristocracy below the ranks of emperor, king, and prince. In England, nobility formed the *Peerage,* and the members had the right for membership in the House of Lords. The nobility enjoyed the generic courtesy titles: Lord or Lady. The descending ranks in nobility (wives in parenthesis):

Duke (Duchess), Marquess (Marchioness), Earl (Countess), Viscount (Viscountess), Baron (Baroness).

Knighthood was the lowest aristocratic title, but knights were not lords. A knight's title was Sir (the title for his wife was Dame). Knighthood was an earned title, granted for life, but was not hereditary.

3. *Common Status*: included here were all persons lacking honorary or hereditary titles. However, commoners had a hierarchy of five social ranks that have been widely recognized since medieval times:

3a. *Gentry Status or Genteel Class*: these commoners enjoyed the titles of respect: Gentleman, Burgess, Mister, or Master (their wives, Mistress, or the abbreviation, Mrs.). The right of passage into the Rank of Gentry was by approval of a *Family Coat of Arms* by the Office of Heraldry, a government agency entrusted with approval of legitimacy for admission to the rank of gentry. The gentry were comprised of upper middle class persons of refinement, respectability, education, good manners, comfortable financial means, demonstrable achievement, and recognized respect in the community. Royal appointments or election to public office usually went to gentry. The gentry was an upwardly mobile group. Many of the gentry had connections by birth or marriage to titleless younger sons and daughters of the Peerage. Therefore, many gentry (as the saying goes) 'were to the manor born.' Because most gentry had wealth, social status, and contact with sources of power, they were the commoners who held positions of respect, responsibility, or leadership in industry, public office, and Church ordination. Ordinarily, persons of the gentry did not dirty their hands in manual work. For present interests, it is relevant to point out that, during much of English history, the *Landed Gentry* was the only segment among commoners that was enfranchised to vote for representatives in the House of Commons. Not until the first Reform Act of 1832, for the first time, the right to vote was extended to larger segments of commoners below the rank of gentry.

b). *Professions, artisans, craftsmen, and merchant classes*: these were middle class persons who worked for wages. *Professionals* were literate and educated for lower ranks of public service: doctors, lawyers, pedagogues, lower clergy, and clerks. *Artisans and craftsmen* were apprenticed workers trained in skilled trades: architecture, masonry, metallurgy, carpentry, ironmongery, leatherwork, masonry, pottery, weaving, etc. *Merchants* were small and large businessmen who traded in manufactured goods.

c). *Peasant (yeoman, yokel, churl, and villain) class*: these were persons of the lower middle class who worked with their hands. They got dirty doing public tasks that needed much strength, but little training or special skill. They included many landholders who toiled as farmers, fishermen, and miners. They did public work of all kinds, and many of them served as foot soldiers in militia. They often were poor, semiliterate, ill mannered, but were able hard workers; they were the 'salt of the earth.' Largely, the colonial citizenship of the English colonies in the New World was of peasant or gentry origin—as such, President Washington said that the only suitable title for the President of the United States is *Mister*.

d). *Servant class*: these usually were uneducated, unskilled, freeborn persons who were hired for services in homes of gentry and peerage.

e). *Serfs*: these persons were born into a state to permanent servitude in a manor estate: a status from which there was no legal means of escape. During the reign of Edward IV (146-483), serfdom was abolished for native-born Englishmen.

It is estimated that the number of individuals at recognized levels of England's stratified social hierarchy in the 13th and 14th Centuries was:

Numbers in Social Strata of the total English population:
Royalty or Royal status 15-30
Higher Nobility (Duke, Marquess, Earl) 75-150
Lesser Nobility (Baron, Knight) 500-2,000
Gentry (Commoners with a Coat of Arms) 5,000-10,000
Professions, trades, and merchant class 200,000-500,000
Freemen peasants (yeomen, yokel, churl, villain) . . . 2-3 million
Servant class and serfs . . . . 1 million
Total population of England . . . . 3-4 million

Even though the Church supported the view that, *It is God's will that all mankind should accept the station in life inherited at birth*, that admonition did not prevent persons at every level in the social hierarchy from trying to climb above the rank to which one was born.

At all social levels, families tried to marry daughters to husbands who had higher ranks than their own. However, for men, effort and individual merit were avenues whereby sons advanced up the scale from serf, to servant, to peasant farmer, to tradesman, to professional, to gentry, or to titled nobility. Then, as now, personal ability, hard work, creative initiative, education, and individual ambition was recognized and rewarded.

The higher levels of power and wealth for commoners came with literacy and education. Those opportunities in the Middle Ages came to talented individuals in tutorials provided by abbeys and monasteries sponsored by the Church. During most of the Middle Ages, only through the Church were persons of common birth able to acquire the education prerequisite to gaining national power and influence in government. Thus, most Chancellors (the highest office of public service in England) were of gentry birth, and they also usually were ordained priests or bishops of the Church.

Social Status of Women
in Medieval England
(c. AD 800-1600)

THE MEDIEVAL social and legal status of women always placed them in a subordinate relationship to men. The medieval attitude on the inferior status of women derived its legal support from the Biblical Book of Genesis, Chapter 2, which gives the Biblical story of Adam and Eve. Thus, the Biblical legend of Eve being formed from Adam's rib was precedent for medieval law governing the relationship between man and wife.

In the biblical account of God's creation, Eve was an afterthought improvised as consolation for Adam's loneliness. The Book says that on the sixth day of Creation, God created Adam in God's own image from dust. After all birds and beasts of the field were produced for man's use, God finally got around to making Eve from Adam's rib while he slept. Adam awakened and understood that Eve was 'bone from my bone and flesh from my flesh.' Adam accepted Eve as his companion and helpmate, and 'they were as one flesh.' Adam was head of their common household with authority over Eve. However, Adam was given responsibility for supervising Eve, because her judgment was flawed for having conspired with the Serpent to eat the forbidden fruit that caused mankind's fall from grace, and exile from the Garden of Eden.

The medieval wife (from lowest serf, to gentry, to knight, to earl, to duke, and even to king) was treated as a chattel of her husband. The man, as head of household, generally exercised full legal authority over all property that a wife brought with her into marriage.

Civil rights of women, and customs governing inheritance by women in Europe varied from country to country. English laws governing a woman's legal rights in the Middle Ages were far more liberal than those in most

European nations. In many Continental countries, Salic law prevailed. It only recognized inheritance of noble titles and estates through male lines of descent. In Salic law, morganatic marriage was the rule; in morganatic marriages, a wife of lower rank than her husband retained her birth status, and she was not raised by marriage to the higher rank of her husband.

In England, morganatic marriage was outlawed—English wives, by marriage, always gained the title and social status of her husband. English custom (in contrast with the continental Salic legal system), traditionally, permitted eldest daughters without a surviving male sibling to inherit noble titles and estates.

Recognition of the medieval conditions for living summarized in these pages provide a basis for appreciating the historical and cultural settings in which the following narratives of England's kings and queens take place.

DYNASTY I

THE SAXON WESSEX DYNASTY
(AD 802–1066)

The Saxon Earl-King Heptarchy in Britain

TRADITIONALLY, EARL-KINGS of Wessex (beginning in 802 with Egbert) ruled England up to the Norman Conquest of 1066. Egbert Earl of Wessex aggressively expanded his authority over the entire Saxon Heptarchy. By 827, he was able to demand homage from the other six Saxon counties, which were self-proclaimed 'kingdoms'. In so doing, he became the first 'King of all Saxon England.' Between 850 and 900, Alfred the Great Earl-King of Wessex (a grandson of Egbert) unified south central Anglo-Saxon England. Under Alfred, stability and uniformity in Common Law increased. Alfred's greatest service to history, however, lay in creation of the *Anglo-Saxon Chronicle*. It is a historical record compiled from many sources on the history of England. The Chronicle begins with the departure of Romans around the sixth century, and continues into the ninth century. It intermittently received additional contributions well into the twelfth century. The Chronicle is the primary historical resource for information on Anglo-Saxon England.

A Saxon limited Parliament called *The Witan* was an assembly of Saxon Thanes (the Earl-Kings and nobles of the Heptarchy). The Witan collectively elected an overlord to be *King of all England*—he was said to be 'the equal, but first, among the seven Saxon Earls.' The earl-king's main function was to raise militia from all counties, and then to serve as commander-in-chief in defense against invasions from Scandinavia. Witan election of Saxon kings was pragmatic, and always favored potentially strong military leaders. Only secondarily was the choice of a king based on bloodline inheritance. Even so, following the death of Alfred the Great in 899, the Witan customarily elected the Earl of Wessex (Alfred's descendants) to be king. Edward the Confessor was the last in Alfred's line of descent to be elected King of Saxon England. Edward was a devoutly religious Christian, who founded Westminster Abbey near London. He later was canonized in 1161 by Pope Alexander III, and became St. Edward the Confessor—the 'National Saint of England.'

Edward the Confessor died in January 1066, but he left no male heir. Unwisely and without Witan approval, he had promised to bequeath the Kingdom of England to Duke William of Normandy, who was possibly his second or third cousin. In the autumn of 1065 when Edward the Confessor was known to be dying, the Saxon Witan met, and repudiated William of Normandy's claim to become King of England. The Witan decided that the only person fit to rule was, Harold, Son of Godwin Earl of Wessex. He was elected to be their king and supreme military general, with the title, King Harold II of Saxon England. He was charged with responsibility for repelling invasion by outside contenders for the crown of Saxon England.

Harold II was a brother-in-law of Edward the Confessor, whose wife Edith was Harold's sister. Otherwise, Harold had no royal hereditary claim to the crown of England. When Edward died on January 5, 1066, Harold II of Wessex became the last Saxon king, but he reigned for less than a year. He was killed at the Battle of Hastings on October 14, 1066.

With their leader slain, the Saxons fell back in disarray, and Duke William with his Norman knights won the day. The Battle of Hastings ended six centuries of Anglo-Saxon rule in England. Only three months later on Christmas day 1066, the Norman duke was crowned King William I of England.

The Saxon Wessex Dynasty Lineage (802-1066)

THE LINEAGE given here summarizes the royal chronology for Anglo-Saxon Kings of England during the last 250 years of the Dark Ages. Names of ruling Saxon Earl-Kings are given in bold type. Dates in parenthesis give duration of reigns. When known, the names of wives are included when they are also mothers of a following reigning monarch. Numbers in parenthesis give names of offspring in chronological order, but only offspring are given who later reigned.

Egbert, first Earl-King of Wessex wife Raedburh (reign, 37 years, 802-839), parents of—

> **Ethelwulf**   (reign, 19 years, 839-858) married Osburh, parents of—
>> (1) **Ethelbald** (reign, 2 years, 858-860)
>> (2) **Ethelbert** (reign, 6 years, 860-866)
>> (3) **St. Ethelred I** (reign, 5 years, 866-871)
>> (4) **Alfred the Great** (reign, 28 years, 848-899) married Aelhswith, parents of—
>>> (1) **Edward the Elder** (reign, 26 years, 899-925) married Edgifu, parents of—
>>>> (1) **Athelstan** (reign, 14 years, 925-939)
>>>> (2) **Edred** (reign, 9 years, 946-955)
>>>> (3) **Edmund I, the Elder, the Magnificent** (reign, 7 years, 939-946) married Aelfgifu, parents of—
>>>>> (1) **Edwy, the Fair** (reign, 4 years, 955-959)
>>>>> (2) **Edgar the Peaceful** (reign, 16 years, 59-975) married Aelfthryth, parents of—
>>>>>> (1) **Edward the Martyr** (reign, 4 years, 975-978)
>>>>>> (2) **Ethelred II, the Unready** (reign, 38 years, 978-1013) married Aelfgifu, parents of—
>>>>>>> (1) **Edmund II Ironside** (reign, 1/2 year, 1016), married Algitha, parents of—
>>>>>>>> (1) **Edward the Confessor** (reign, 24 years, 1042-1066),

married Edith of Wessex (a
sister of Harold II of Wessex),
no issue.

(2) Matilda of Scotland married
Henry I of England, parents
of—

> **Empress Matilda** married
> Geoffrey (Plantagenet) of
> Anjou, parents of—
>> Henry   Plantagenet
>> (Henry   II   of   the
>> Plantagenet Dynasty)

(3) Edward the Aetheling (heir
to the throne, but did not
reign), father of—

> (1) Edgar   the   Aetheling
> (heir   to   the   throne,
> but Duke William of
> Normandy usurped his
> right to rule), no issue.

Harold II ab Godwin (reign, January to October, 1066), the last Saxon King of
England was not descended from Alfred the Great.

Danish Kings of Saxon England who ruled before the Norman Conquest:
Svein (Forkbeard) I   [preceded and then followed Saxon King Ethelred II,
the Unready] (reign, December 25. 1013-February 3, 1014), father of—
> **Canute I the Great**   [preceded by Saxon King Edmund Ironside]
> (reign, c. October 18, 1016-November 12, 1035), father of—
>> **(1) Harald Harefoot** (reign, November 12, 1035-March
>> 17,1040), no issue.
>> **(2) Canute II, Harthacanute** (reign, March 17, 1040-June
>> 8, 10420 [followed by Saxon King Edward the
>> Confessor], no issue.

End of Dynasty I. The Saxon-Wessex Kings; continue with Dynasty II:
The Norman Lineage, Reign 1. King William I.

DYNASTY II

THE NORMAN DYNASTY
REIGN 1 THROUGH 4 (1066–1154)

The Norman Conquest of
Anglo-Saxon England in 1066

WILLIAM DUKE of Normandy's claim on England's crown was based, in part, on the fact that he was distantly related to Edward the Confessor, the Saxon King of England. However, his more legitimate claim was based on an event that happened in 1054 when Harold of Wessex was shipwrecked on the shore of Normandy. Harold was rescued, and then imprisoned by his host, Duke William of Normandy. To secure his release, Harold was required to swear an oath that he would support Duke William's claim for the crown of Saxon England after sickly King Edward the Confessor died. Harold did not intend to honor this pledge, but, to his consternation, he learned that he had been tricked into making his oath on a chest that concealed bones of a saint. By all medieval rules of jurisprudence, the saint's bones made his oath irrevocably binding. When Harold returned to England, he protested that his oath had been obtained by trickery—the work of the Devil himself—therefore his oath was void.

That is the way things rested until Edward the Confessor died on January 5, 1066. Since no royal Saxon-Wessex heir was on hand who had credible military leadership ability to defend the Saxon homeland, rulers in Norway, Denmark, and Normandy hoped to take command of England.

Harold Earl of Wessex was the foremost Saxon warrior of his age. Even though he lacked royal ancestry, the Witan (the Saxon ruling parliamentary body) chose him to be king in hope that he could forestall foreign invasion.

King Harald Hardrada of Norway struck first with an invasion fleet on the North Sea coast of Northumbria. Harold II of Wessex raced north to counter Hardrada's attack. In the Battle of Stamford Bridge near York (September 25, 1066), Harold II defeated Harald Hardrada, and prevented Norwegian domination of England.

Only three days later on September 28, William Duke of Normandy landed on the Channel Coast of East Sussex near Hastings with a miniscule invading army of fewer than three thousand Norman knights. Harold hurried south from Northumbria with his battle fatigued Saxon troops. On October 14, 1066, a battle was joined at Hastings. It lasted the full day. At sundown, a count of the dead included Harold II of Wessex. With the Saxon leader slain, the smaller band of Norman knights quickly defeated the homeland Saxon militia. Duke William and his Norman knights won the day, and, thereby, ended the 600 year Saxon period in English history.

Harold's common-law wife Aldgyth Swanneshals (Edith Swanneck), with whom he had four sons and two daughters, was an observer at the Battle of Hastings. She identified Harold's body among the fallen and testified that he was dead. A stone memorial near Battle Abbey at Hastings marks the place where Harold is believed to have fallen. Harold's body was moved to Waltham Abbey in Essex for burial.

Harold of Wessex was the last Anglo-Saxon King of England. His line did not contribute to later monarchies of England. His Queen Aldgyth (Edith) of Mercia married Harold only a few months before the Battle of Hastings. Their only son, Harold, Jr. (there may have been twins), was born posthumously three months after his father's death at Hastings. Queen Aldgyth and her infant son escaped to exile in France. The last record of their survival is dated 1075. What finally became of them is uncertain.

After his victory at the Battle of Hastings, William of Normandy, leading fewer than three thousand Norman knights, moved north parallel to the coast. He took Dover, but avoided confrontation with Saxon residents on his way to Canterbury. He terrorized Stigand Archbishop of Canterbury into giving his blessing for Duke William to continue to Westminster to claim the crown. Along his way to London, Duke William showed skill as a military tactician by overcoming superior opposition with his small group of invaders. To achieve this, he bypassed towns with minimum confrontation. However, when he arrived on the south bank of the Thames opposite London, he devastated the land in a demonstration to citizens of London that he could be ruthless. By this ploy, he terrified the Saxon nobles, and the gates of London opened. Thus, London fell without a whimper to the Norman Conqueror and his paltry band of raiders, and he was offered the crown.

After William accepted fealty from citizens of London, he continued southeast to Winchester the Saxon capital of England. William took possession of the court at Winchester, and the Saxon lords accepted him without opposition in November 1066. William received fealty from Dowager Queen Edith of Wessex wife of Edward the Confessor who then represented royal Saxon authority. Her sworn fealty, more than any other act, legitimized Duke William's claim to the crown of England in eyes of his Saxon subjects. William gave Edith royal respect in her honored status as Dowager Queen. She lived in ease at Winchester until her death in 1075, when she was buried in Westminster Abbey with great honor.

Duke William returned from Winchester to London, and only three months after the Battle of Hastings, he was crowned King William I of England in Westminster Abbey on Christmas Day, 1066.

After the Battle of Hastings, the Saxon Witan met, and chose Edgar the Aetheling to be the King of Saxon England. Edgar the Aetheling (Aetheling in Saxon-German meaning, *Prince of Royal blood*, i.e., *The Heir Apparent*) was the only remaining legitimate male descendant of Alfred the Great who had claim on the Saxon throne. Edgar was a grandson of Saxon King Edmund Ironside II, and was a grandnephew of Edward the Confessor. However, Edgar was not crowned, and he never reigned.

Although he was in name the King of all England, it took two decades for Duke William, of Normandy to subdue Saxon England. His conquest was a relentless exercise of will and purpose. At each step in his progress across England, he built strongholds to secure his rule. The Anglo-Saxon Chronicle reports that 'hundreds of castles were constructed' throughout the land. One must downscale first impressions of what that frenzy of castle building actually entailed. The Norman fortifications were stockade constructions that were similar to those hastily built in frontier Colonial America to protect settlers during Indian Wars of the 18th Century.

With a few exceptions (such as the White Tower of London and original keeps at Windsor and Colchester that were built of stone), most Norman castles erected during King William's conquest of England were rude fortifications made of wood and earth. Usually, they were built on high ground outside crossroad Saxon villages. They were hurriedly erected with Saxon slave labor, and served the Norman invaders as emergency habitation for storage of food and military supplies, or as prisons and places of refuge at times of Saxon rebellion. Typically, the 'castle' fortresses consisted of an inner keep that was surrounded by two or three concentric steeply banked earthwork rings, which were crowned by ten to twelve foot high wooden palisades. A moat, fifteen to twenty feet wide separated the castle walls from low ground surrounding them. A single bridge across the moats to a gate through the wall provided access to inner regions of the fort. Bridges in times of attack could be raised to block access to the interior keep. These stockade forts were designed to last about twenty to thirty years; after which, they were repaired or abandoned. Only rarely were the original fortifications replaced by stone and mortar, and then, only at strategically important places. Only earthen moats and footings of walls now mark locations for most of the 'hundreds of castles' constructed by Normans during the 11th Century domination of Saxon England.

The Norman Conquest transferred wealth, power, and authority from the defeated Saxons to an aristocracy of titled Norman-French invaders. Normans occupied all positions of real power. However, native Saxon Englishmen continued to man the oars that drove the Ship of State. Usually, the common man's lot in England remained much the same as before the Conquest. Depending on one's outlook today on events from the distance of a thousand years, one may conclude: either, the Norman invasion was a good thing, or it was an act of total vandalism. Both views have been documented at great length. Everyone will agree that the Norman Conquest ended the Dark Ages, and began a distinctly new medieval phase in English History—one that continues to be of interest today.

The Norman knights who fought for Duke William of Normandy were as hungry for wealth and power as was King William, himself. His knights individually and collectively were always a threat to the authority of King William and to the Norman Dynasty he founded. King William gave fiefs of land that had been wrested from Saxon Thanes as payoff to the knights who fought for him in subduing Saxon England. In his conquest of Saxon England, Duke William of Normandy brought the feudal system that had evolved in his Duchy of Normandy. However, as King of England, he added his own improvisations to the feudal system he set up in Saxon England.

King William knew from firsthand experience that trouble could arise when an overlord grants his vassals large fiefs of land in perpetuity. In order to avoid that error, William kept title to all conquered English lands in his own hand as 'crown property.' He made all fiefs to his nobles contingent on demonstrable loyalty to his crown. Noble titles and estates were valid only at the king's discretion—they could be revoked as easily as created—the king could give and take at will. In addition, King William, prudently saw that when multiple fiefs were given to a noble, the fiefs would be small, disconnected, and scattered over wide areas. Thereby, he prevented individuals from acquiring sufficiently large personal domains that would permit them to challenge authority of his crown.

The Norman Dynasty Lineage, Reign 1 Through 4 (1066-1154)

THIS LINE includes Kings William (The Conqueror) I, William II, Henry I, Stephen, and Empress Matilda (the mother of Henry Plantagenet King Henry II).

Norman legitimacy to rule England was by right of conquest, not heredity. Duke William of Normandy was distantly related to Saxon King Edward the Confessor, but no royal genetic ties connected the Saxon Wessex Earl-Kings to the Norman Dynasty.

Names of reigning Norman English monarchs are given in bold type. Dates in parenthesis give duration of reigns. Wives or Queen Consort names, when known, are included only when they are also mothers of a following reigning monarch. Numbers in parenthesis give offspring in chronological order; however, only offspring are shown that figure conspicuously in events discussed in the present treatment of English history.

Roloph (Richard) I Duke of Normandy, father of—
Richard II Duke of Normandy, father of—
Robert the Devil Duke of Normandy and Herletta of Falaise, parents of—

Reign 1. King William I The Conqueror (1066-1087) married his Queen Consort Matilda of Flanders, parents of—

(1) Robert Curthose, father of—
William Clito, no issue.

(2) **Reign 2. King William II Rufus** (1087-1100), not married, no issue.

(4) **Reign 3. King Henry I** (1100-1135) married Queen Consort Matilda of Scotland, parents of—

Empress Matilda (not crowned) married Count Geoffrey Plantagenet, parents of Henry II Plantagenet.

Continue with Dynasty III. The Plantagenet Lineage.

(3) Adela and husband Stephen of Blois (the Elder), parents of—

Reign 4. King Stephen I (1135-1154) married Queen Consort Matilda of Boulogne, parents of—

William, Count of Boulogne; he made no claim on the crown of England.

End of the Norman Dynasty; continue with Dynasty III. The Plantagenet Lineage.

REIGN I

KING WILLIAM I THE CONQUEROR

AND

QUEEN CONSORT MATILDA OF FLANDERS

Summary of the Reign of King William I (Reign 1066-1087)

> King William I: life dates c. 59/60 years, b. 1027/28-d. September 9, 1087; Duke of Normandy 52 years, July 3, 1035-September 9, 1087; King of England 21 years, December 25, 1066-September 9, 1087.

K ING WILLIAM I of England was the hereditary Duke of Normandy. He held his title in fealty to the King of France. William I is known in English history, as the *Conqueror*, or as *The Bastard King*. He was the illegitimate son of Robert Duke of Normandy and the commoner Arleta (or Herleva) daughter of Fulbert the Tanner of Falaise, Normandy. Duke Robert willed Normandy to his bastard son when William was six or seven years old. In his youth before he invaded England in October 1066, William was hardened in twenty-eight years of battle in defense of his title as Duke of Normandy.

Edward the Confessor Saxon King of England was without an heir when he died on January 5, 1066. Before his death, the Saxon Parliament (called the Witan) had elected Harold Earl of Wessex as its designated king to follow Edward the Confessor as ruler of the Saxon Heptarchy. In addition, three non-Saxons claimed the throne of England: Tostig Godwinson Earl of Northumbria, Harald Hardrada King of Norway, and William Duke of Normandy.

In short order following Edward the Confessor's death, Tostig was defeated, and driven into exile in Scotland. Hardrada was defeated and killed by Harold of Wessex in the battle of Stamford Bridge near York on September 25, 1066; after which, William of Normandy remained the only serious foreign contender for the crown of Saxon England. Duke William of Normandy took the throne of England by defeating Saxon King Herald II of Wessex at the battle of Hastings on October 14, 1066. Duke William was crowned King of England on December 25, 1066, and he ruled for twenty-one years.

As King of England, William I conquered and subdued most of England, but he failed to defeat Wales and Scotland. He built the Tower of London as his own castle stronghold in London. He also built the original fortress at Windsor, and other castles that were scattered elsewhere around England as necessity required. He established a feudal system of government in which all lands were permanently held as crown property. Fief estates were leased out in fealty to the titled Norman nobles who came with him to help in subduing the Saxon Island.

Late in his reign of twenty-one years, King William I ordered an inventory of all England called the *Domesday Book*. The Domesday Book was used as a basis for assessing taxes, for recruiting military duty, and for making land grants in fealty. William was a strong ruthless but fair king, who established foundations for present law and government within accepted principles of 11th century feudalism. The Domesday Book has been the legal starting point for registry of deeds on land ownership in England.

Duke William married Matilda of Flanders around 1051/52. She was crowned Queen of England in Winchester Cathedral in 1068. William and

Matilda had nine or ten children. Two of them, William Rufus and Henry Beauclerc, became King William II and King Henry I of England.

William I died on September 9, 1087 of internal wounds he received at Mantes, France, when his horse stumbled, and threw him to the ground. He is buried in St. Stephen's Abbey, which he founded at Caen near Rouen, Normandy.

King William's second son William Rufus followed the Conqueror to the throne of England on September 9, 1087 as King William II.

Narrative of Queen Consort Matilda of Flanders

Queen Matilda of Flanders: life dates c. 51/52 years, b. 1031/32-d. November 2, 1083; Duchess wife of Duke William of Normandy c. 31 years, c. b. 1052-November 2, 1083; Queen Consort of King William I c. 15 years, May 11, 1068-November 2, 1083.

IN THE Middle Ages, French speaking Flanders (now, Belgium) and German-speaking Holland were major components of a collection of city-states and dukedoms loosely referred to as the Low Countries. In the 11th century, the capital city of Flanders was Bruges (named from an Old Norse word meaning, *bridge*; in German Brügge). At that time, all Europe was just emerging from the sociopolitical system of manorial feudalism characteristic of the Dark Ages. Paris, London, and lesser urban centers such as Bruges was entering what is popularly called the Age of Chivalry—a time when society was sharply stratified into ranks of nobility and commons—a time when battles were fought according to strict rules of etiquette in hand-to-hand combat between knights clad in suits of armor on horseback. Commoners served their liege lords, but did little fighting, because they were neither learned in niceties of conduct for combat, nor could they afford armor and horses.

Bruges in the 11th century was situated at the mouth of the Schelde River, which then opened directly on the North Sea. Bruges was the most important port in northern Europe. It enjoyed brisk commerce fed by excellent local crafts of weaving, embroidery, and lace making. Trade enriched the local Flemish population to a level not realized outside Mediterranean Europe. Bruges reached its peak development in the 14th century, and with its canals and waterways, was called *The Venice of the North*. In the 10th and 11th centuries, Counts of Flanders were enriched with import duties and taxes on industry. They spent freely to transform Bruges into a cultural center unsurpassed in Western Europe. Bruges was nearly the equal of Paris in population and wealth. Bruges lost its prominence in world trade when its harbor silted in, and Antwerp replaced it as the major Low Country port of commerce.

Matilda of Flanders grew to maturity in the superior atmosphere of riches and sophistication of avant-garde 11th century Bruges. She was the second child and eldest daughter of Count Baldwin V of Flanders, and Princess Adela Capet of France, a sister of the King Henry I of France. Matilda was born in c. 1031/33, probably at Bruges, possibly at Lille, Flanders. It is often reported that (by maternal descent through seven generations) she was related to Saxon King Alfred the Great. She was given the best education available for women at the time, but it did not include reading or writing. Those skills were reserved for men going into service of the Church. She was proficient in womanly arts of weaving and embroidery. A contemporary chronicler said of her, "She was the pearl of beauty, the perfection of goodness, and the mirror of womanly accomplishments. She nobly patronized learning, and, with queenly hand, encouraging the arts and refinements of the times." She was famed for her needlework, a craft viewed as an important accomplishment for ladies of rank in the Middle Ages.

Her friends knew Matilda as Maud. She was a petite girl of sixteen, and only four feet two inches tall, when twenty year old burly robust William the Bastard Duke of Normandy came 'a-courtin' from Rouen to Bruges with his intent to propose marriage to Matilda.

William was the illegitimate son, and the only heir of Duke Robert of Normandy and his 'common-law wife' Arletta, daughter of Fulbert the Tanner of Falaise, Normandy. When William was a small child of six or seven, Duke Robert went on pilgrimage to the Holy Land (from which he never returned). However, before he left, he placed his son William in wardship with the King of France. King Henry I of France agreed to be responsible for the boy's protection and education in manly arts of war. Duke Robert also required his Norman liegemen to swear an oath of fealty to his child William as his rightful heir to the Dukedom of Normandy. As a growing boy, William remained in the French court through childhood and adolescence. The French king underwrote William's title as Duke of Normandy. However, after gaining his majority at eighteen, Duke William was required to raise militia, and defend his title with military force on several occasions. With some uncertainty about his ability to defend his title as Duke of Normandy, William went to Bruges (probably in 1047) with intent to marry Matilda of Flanders.

William was a brawny youth about six feet tall and just out of his teens when he first proposed marriage to Matilda of Flanders. She rejected him with arch contempt. At the time, she was infatuated with the Saxon ambassador from Winchester in Flanders. His name was Earl Brihtric Meaw, a man described as 'so fair his hair was said to be as white as snow.' However, Earl Meaw had no interest in adolescent diminutive Matilda.

William persisted in courting Matilda, but Matilda was not impressed. She refused Duke William's proposal with the statement that, in effect, said, "I am far too noble of birth to marry a mere bastard, even if he does claim to be a duke." Her father Count Baldwin also refused to permit Matilda to consider marriage to William, because William's hold on Normandy was far too tenuous to assure permanence.

William protested vigorously. In anger, he said that, in addition to being the true Duke of Normandy, Edward the Confessor had named him to be his heir to all Saxon England. Matilda laughed at him, and taunted, "Mighty words—easily spoken, and, verily proof not of greatness, nor valor . . . [You] the doubtful Duke of Normandy will also be Monarch of England? An excellent joke, truly! But, should not my cousin, better say, 'Emperor of all Christendom' as well?'"

Matilda's scorn enraged William. What happened next is disputed. One account reports that, on the spot, William knocked Matilda to the ground, kicked her a few times, and then dragged her around the palace floor by her long golden braids. Another account says that William rode off in rage, but returned another day to accost Matilda, who was riding a horse on her return from Sunday Mass. Wherewith, William pulled her off her horse. She fell into a mud puddle. There in the courtyard, he kicked her, and dragged her around by her braids. Duke William's violent disrespect for his daughter vexed Count Baldwin mightily. He threatened to call out his guards to slay William on the spot. At that point, Matilda pled with her father to let William depart uninjured. Without additional violence, William continued to woo Matilda for the next five years. She eventually relented, and agreed to accept him.

Duke William and Lady Matilda were married in 1052 or 1053 in Normandy. However, the Archbishop of Rouen denied legitimacy for the marriage, because they were second cousins, a relationship that fell within proscribed degrees of consanguinity. They continued to live together as man and wife, but petitioned Pope Leo IX in 1068/69 to grant them special dispensation to wed. Their marriage was approved, but both were required to found an abbey as penance. William founded the Abbey of St. Stephen at Caen near Rouen, Normandy. Matilda's penance was the Abbey aux Dames, Caen. Both abbeys are in existence today, and William and Matilda, at the end of their lives, were buried in the abbey each founded.

The marriage in 1052/53 worked out remarkably well. William and Matilda were a devoted couple. Both were noted for possession of commanding imperial tempers. The precise number of William and Matilda's offspring is in question. They had a total of nine, and possibly, ten children (4 sons and 5 or 6 daughters. Four of their children are involved in later aspects of England's history:

> Robert Curthose (c. 1051/4—February 10, 1134): the eldest son's nickname meant, 'short pants,' for the small stature he inherited from his mother. He inherited the Duchy of Normandy from his father. Robert was father of William Clitus, pretender to the throne of England during the reign of Henry I.
>
> William Rufus (c. 1056—August 2, 1100): the nickname of the Conqueror's second son translates 'William the Red,' for his florid complexion and red hair. In his will, the Conqueror gave England to Rufus who became King William II (reign 1087-1100).
>
> Adela (c. 1062—March 3, 1138): the Conqueror's youngest daughter married Count Stephen (the Elder) of Blois. They were the parents of King Stephen of England (reign, 1135-1154).
>
> Henry Beauclerc (c. 1068/69—December 1, 1135): the nickname of the Conqueror's youngest son referred to the fact that he was educated and literate—the first English king who could read and write. He was trained

for the clergy, and expected to become a bishop, and make his fortune from the collection plate; he become King Henry I (reign 1100-1135).

King William I is believed to have been faithful to Matilda throughout most of their married lives. However, that may not be true after 1075, when William and Matilda for a time were alienated. Late in life, Matilda sided with their eldest son Robert Curthose when he attempted to wrest Normandy from his father. On all other occasions, Matilda actively supported her husband in all his adventures. On his part, the Conqueror recognized her loyal assistance by having her crowned as his Queen Consort of England at Winchester Cathedral in 1068.

Matilda filled her first decade of their marriage (1052-1062) by bearing children while William stabilized control of his Duchy of Normandy. Matilda was an intelligent decisive sensible woman. She had seen how her father had strengthened and enriched Flanders with public works that improved port facilities and roads. These public acts promoted commerce and wealth in Flanders. Matilda advised William on advantages from building bridges, roads, and general port services. These strengthened his control of civil government in Normandy. Under Duke William's leadership, Normandy steadily rose in prestige among the provinces of France. William also gained experience as a domestic administrator and as a canny military leader in times of war.

William aspired to be King of Saxon England long before 1064 when Edward the Confessor's health was failing and had no heir. A decade earlier as a young man, William went to Winchester in Wessex to visit his cousin Edward the Confessor. William obtained a pledge then from Edward that he (William of Normandy) was heir to the throne of Saxon England.

On the strength of that promise, Duke William began preparations for his invasion of England in 1064, fully two years before Edward the Confessor's death. William hoped that the Saxon people would peacefully accept him. However, if they resisted, he was prepared to use force to secure the crown of England. Duke William's invasion strategy included recruitment of many knights from Normandy, Flanders, and Brittany. The knights were promised spoils of war in the form of estates taken from defeated Saxon thanes.

Matilda assisted William in his preparation to invade England by persuading her father Count Baldwin V of Flanders to provide ships for the invasion effort. William's invasion fleet consisted of several hundred small coastal vessels. The flagship of William's fleet named, *Mora*, was secretly paid for by Matilda. The Mora was the most advanced and splendidly equipped ship of its time. As an omen of victory, a figurehead of a golden bowman was on the prow.

The year 1066 was a year for the return of Halley's comet. It was first seen in autumn of 1165, only shortly before Edward the Confessor's death in January 1166. William took the comet to be his omen as 'an arrow in the sky' for great events to come—a talisman for his successful invasion of England. Duke William's preparations for his invasion of England were complete by late July 1066, but unfavorable winds delayed crossing the English Channel from Calais to Sussex until the end of September. William crossed the English Channel, and landed safely on English soil at the end of September 1066. He had two weeks to get his forces firmly entrenched on English soil, before King Harold II Thane of Wessex brought his Saxon army down from York, and organized them for battle at Hastings on October 14, 1066. The battle lasted all day. The dead at sundown included Harold II of Wessex. Without a leader, the Saxons accepted defeat, and Duke William of Normandy was crowned King of England a little over two month later on Christmas Day, 1066.

Before William departed for his conquest of England, he appointed Matilda to be his regent with power to rule his Duchy of Normandy. Duchess Matilda remained in Rouen when the invasion of England began. Legend says that she was praying in a chapel in Rouen when she first heard of the great victory at Hastings. She rejoiced, and ordered that the chapel in Rouen be renamed, *Notre Dame de Bonnes Nouvelles* (which still exists), in memory of the good news she received there. Matilda governed Normandy with competent authority and diplomatic skill. No threat arose to challenge her regency in Duke William's absence.

Much of the time following the Norman victory at Hastings, Matilda remained in France. She served as regent in control of his Duchy of Normandy during William's long absences, which were required for him to subdue Saxons in his new English domain. She supervised the collection of taxes and gathered the military supplies needed for William's conquest of England. On some occasions, Matilda accompanied William to England as was the case in 1068, when she was crowned Queen Consort of England at Winchester on Whitsuntide after Easter in 1168. She was still in England when her youngest son Henry Beauclerc (later Henry

I), was born in Yorkshire in the following winter. That unplanned event proved to be a boon to Henry when he became king. Having been born on English soil made Henry acceptable to his Saxon subjects, and allowed him to present himself as one of them—*a native born Englishman*.

Around 1077, after William and Matilda's eldest son Robert Curthose had matured into an ambitious militant young man, William and Matilda for a time were alienated. Matilda supported her first and favorite son Robert Curthose when he challenged his father, and demanded permission to take his mother's place as regent of Normandy. William reluctantly granted that wish, and for a time, Robert Curthose was regent for the Duchy of Normandy. Robert soon became dissatisfied with being subservient to his father, and demanded as his birthright that he be made Duke of Normandy. In outrage, King William I refused, and he swore to give up none of his estates until death awarded them to his heirs.

Robert rebelled in 1080. He organized insurgents to capture Rouen in an effort take complete control of the Duchy of Normandy. Matilda exhausted her own wealth in support of her son's effort to take his patrimony before his father's death. When William learned of the rebellion, he first appointed his favorite son William Rufus as regent of England, and then returned to Normandy to take personal control over the duchy from his rebellious son Robert. King William then attacked Robert Curthose who had major support from the king of France. Robert was defeated, and the rebellion was suppressed. Robert fled to sanctuary in France, but William followed him with armed force. Robert was captured from hiding in Gerberoi Abbey in 1080. King William imprisoned him in England, to isolate him from the disloyal insurgents in Normandy who supported the Robert Curthose's rebellion.

William and Matilda had a chilly relationship after Robert's insurrection was put down. William resented Matilda's disloyalty in favoring her son over her husband. In particular, he resented the fact that Matilda had sold the jeweled gifts he had given her at their wedding, and that the money was given to Robert to finance his effort to overthrow his father.

William and Matilda lived separately during the last years of their marriage: he in England, she in Normandy. A peace agreement, of sorts, was established between William and Matilda when William again appointed Matilda as his regent of Normandy. Matilda resumed control over the duchy until close to the end of her life in 1083. During these years, a relationship of goodwill was established sufficiently for Matilda to arrange a truce in the quarrel between King William the Conqueror and his eldest son Robert Curthose.

A few months before the end of her life, Matilda developed an illness of unknown nature that took her strength, and depressed her spirit. Late in autumn of 1083, William in England was told that, if he wished to see Matilda before her death, he must return immediately to Normandy. William arrived at her bedside on the day she died November 2, 1083.

After Matilda died, William became unpredictably autocratic. Some attribute this adverse change in his character to the loss of Matilda's moderating influence on his tempestuous nature. Saxons in England suffered greatly from the unpredictable ruthless rule they received from their Norman conqueror in the last years of King William's reign.

Aside from ordering construction of the Tower of London, Windsor Castle, and other fortresses, King William's most enduring act as conqueror of Saxon England was in ordering an inventory of all property in England. The record called *The Domesday Book* was completed in 1086, only a year before William's death. It marked the beginning of legal records for ownership of property in England. For historians it remains a gold mine of information on English life in the 11th century.

William lived four more years after Matilda died. His death was accidental, and occurred when his horse stumbled, and threw him to the ground while he was trying to suppress a rebellion at Mantes near Rouen in 1087. From the fall, he suffered internal injuries that took his life. At the time, many knights of the court surrounded him, but upon his unexpected death, they hastened away to secure their estates in Normandy and England. Left alone, the body of the Conqueror was stripped of clothing and wealth. His body, nearly naked, was taken for burial to St. Stephen's Abbey, Normandy. There, his body was forced into a stone coffin already at hand. The casket was much too small for his great body, which was bent double, and broken, so it could fit into the cramped space.

William and Matilda are buried at the abbeys they founded in Normandy. The remains of William the Conqueror are in the Abbey of St. Stephen, Caen. Matilda of Flanders tomb is in the Abbey aux Dames, Caen. Their graves were vandalized during the Huguenot Reformation in the 16th century. Only a single thighbone known to be of King William's body remains in the tomb bearing his name. The size of the bone verifies William's height to be, as declared in life, about five feet ten inches tall. Much of Matilda's skeleton survives, but Vandals took all rich jewels buried with her. She lived to about fifty-two years of age, and was Queen of England for fifteen years (1068-1083). Matilda of Flanders was the smallest of all English Queens, being only four feet two inches tall.

The life of Matilda of Flanders gives insight into the role of noble women in the 11th century. Most biographies of women of rank in the Middle Ages usually represent them as little more than a means of providing their husbands with heirs. Matilda's life as Countess of Flanders, Duchess of Normandy, and Queen of England provides a remarkably vivid example of the important and diverse roles women of title and ability could wield at the dawn of civilized history near the end of the Europeans Dark Ages. Her strong secondary supporting roles for her William the Conqueror makes her an important actor in possibly the most transforming, and determining event in English History—the defeat of Saxon England by the Norman Conquest.

Matilda's primary claim to fame through time, however, has rested on the repeated fiction that she was the primary artisan who created the Bayeux Tapestry, an embroidery on linen over two hundred feet long that depicts in cartoon style the events in the life of Duke William of Normandy in his conquest of England.

The French Bayeux Tapestry

CONTROVERSIAL FRENCH tradition maintains that Queen Matilda was responsible for creating the Bayeux Tapestry, an embroidery on linen 18 inches wide and 223 feet long, which depicts events pertaining to the Norman Conquest. No other wall hanging approaching this scale survives from before the 14th Century.

Traditionally, tapestry is understood to be a pattern woven into fabric on a loom. The so-called, *Bayeux Tapestry*, does not meet this requirement for it is a pattern of colored woolen yarns embroidered on a woven linen sheet. The length is composed of eight panels stitched together, and it is missing an end piece of uncertain original length. The existing pattern begins with Edward the Confessor sitting on his royal Saxon Throne and it ends with William the Conqueror's triumphant defeat of Harold in the

Battle of Hastings on October 14, 1066. Legends stitched on the canvas along its length explain actions going on below.

Scholarship points to King William's half-brother Bishop Odo of Bayeux, Normandy to be the person who probably commissioned the tapestry, but its actual fabrication is contested. In France, it is attributed to William's Queen Matilda of Flanders. It is referred to as *Tapisserie de la Reine Mathilde.* She may have actually worked on the project, but as Queen of England and regent Duchess of Normandy, it is inconceivable that she was artisan for the entire project. It is more probable that she supervised the efforts of a battalion of Flemish and French needle workers.

Viewing the fabric as a whole reinforces judgment that its design was by a single original draftsman. The drawing on linen probably was hastily sketched by a talented artist, who was actually present at Hastings. The cartoon was filled in with colored wool with meticulous care. Details of battle depicted on the canvas reveal authentic violence, which suggests that the artist was a witness familiar with military events; therefore, he most likely was a man. It is known that the work was completed by 1077, because the tapestry was consecrated in that year and displayed in the Bayeux Cathedral of Notre Dame.

The Tapestry was preserved in Bayeux Cathedral for 400 years, until the beginning of the French Revolution in 1792. During those centuries, it attracted little attention and was preserved in safety for posterity. For the past two centuries, its survival has been threatened by every war that France endured: the French Revolution, Napoleonic Wars, World Wars I and II. On each occasion it, was safely squirreled away into hiding from foreign and domestic military vandals, only to be returned to Bayeux Cathedral in times of peace. It can be seen today in its own display room at the tourist attraction, *Centre Guillaume le Conquerant*, Bayeux, France.

It is a rare treasure of handicraft from almost a millennium ago. The tapestry is much the largest work of its kind known to exist from the Middle Ages. However, it lacks the endpiece. What subjects may have been on the lost terminal piece is pure conjecture; it may have shown King William's coronation in London on Christmas day, 1066, and who knows what else?

The English Copy of the Bayeux Tapestry

ENGLISH STUDENTS of the Bayeux Tapestry, who seek to find evidence for it as a product of English craftwomanship, have pointed out that peculiarities in Latin names and phrases stitched into the work suggest Anglo-Saxon linguistics, and that, therefore, it must be a product of English needle work. The following is a footnote on the tapestry that is related to the strong feeling of identity the English people have for the Bayeux Tapestry as a relic of their own past.

The Museum of Reading in Berkshire possesses a full scale handmade replica of the Bayeux Tapestry in France known as *Britain's Bayeux Tapestry*. Thirty-five seamstresses of Leek, Staffordshire created it in 1885. They felt that England should have a Bayeux Tapestry of its own. The project was initiated, and carried to completion by the effort of Elizabeth Wardel. Her husband Thomas Wardel enhanced authenticity of the copy. He was an industrial dyer who researched the subject, and was able to recreate authentic mineral and vegetable dyes used in the 11th century. Thereby, the copy accurately duplicates in substance and hue the colored wools of the original. Eight shades for each primary and secondary color, and of muted intermediate tones created from madder (russet & orange), woad (blues & greens), weld (yellows & browns), walnut (dusky & grays), and others.

When *Britain's Bayeux Tapestry* was first shown in 1885, at what was later to become the Victoria and Albert Museum, London marvelled, but later ridiculed it as a huge effort wasted on *just a copy*.

Over a century has now passed since Britain's Bayeux Tapestry was created. Time alone has a way of transforming ridicule in the present into honor for the past—one often sees beer mugs and saddle stirrups from ancient times become honored treasure behind glass—thus, as time goes by, praise and worth may also come to *Britain's Bayeux Tapestry*.

REIGN 2

KING WILLIAM II

Summary of the Reign of King William II
(1087-1100)

King William II: life dates c. 40/44 years, c. b. 1956/60-d. August 2, 1100; King of England & Duke of Normandy 13 years, September 9, 1087-August 2, 1100; William II was not married and had no queen consort or heirs.

KING WILLIAM II never married. He was the second and favorite son of King William I. He was called William Rufus for his strawberry blond hair and florid complexion. He had a stocky build, and was described as stubborn, short tempered, bull-like in appearance, and full of blustering bravado. His rage came and went with such intensity that his tantrums often left him incoherent and stuttering in rage. He indulged in robust sports, jousting, and hunting. He excelled in all aspects of chivalry, was blamed for cruelty, and praised for bravery. On an occasion when crossing the North Sea in a fearful storm, a sailor expressed terror of perishing in the raging sea, but William calmed his men by saying, "Have no fear. I never heard of a king who was drowned." Even his worst enemies admitted that in all things that William attempted, "The whole world seemed to smile upon him. Even the wind and sea obeyed his command."

King William the Conqueror's will gave England to William Rufus, and he came to the throne in 1087 at about the age of thirty. His father's will gave Normandy to William's older brother Robert Curthose, but Robert claimed all his father's English holdings as well. The two brothers competed for the title, King of England, from 1087 until 1095. Norman knights in England were almost equally divided in their support of the two brothers. In the conflict, Archbishop Lanfranc of Canterbury was a major supporter of William Rufus who was successful in his final effort to gain the throne of England.

In the judgment of history, King William Rufus can be credited with few, if any, useful innovations in English Common Law or Government. However, affairs of State in England and Normandy retained stability throughout his reign. Recent historians, in attempts to be evenhanded, credit William Rufus with being a responsible steward in government of England (which he inherited from his father), and of Normandy, which he bought from his brother Robert.

King William II is credited with building Westminster's Great Hall, a building that is almost seventy feet wide and over two hundred feet long. The original hall burned down a century later in the reign of King John, but was replaced in the reign of Richard II. England uses the Great Hall for pomp and circumstance on occasions for recognition of peers and commoners, and for other public functions: for example, Westminster's Great Hall was the site for the trial of Charles I, at which he received the sentence of death for crimes against the State in 1649.

The favorite pastime of William Rufus was hunting stags in New Forest, a royal game preserve created by his father that was located north of Winchester. While hunting there on a late summer day in 1100, William was accidentally killed by an arrow shot by Walter Tyrell, an associate who was hunting with him. The memorial *Rufus Stone* marks the place in New Forest said to be where William II fell. After King William Rufus's accidental death, he was carried in a wheelbarrow to Winchester Cathedral, with his blood dribbling along the way. He was buried there with minimum ecclesiastic formality.

King William Rufus's eulogy by Archbishop Anselm included the disparaging statement, "Everything that was hateful to God, and to righteous men was the daily practice in this land during his reign. Therefore, he was hated by his people, and was abhorrent to God . . . He died in the midst of his sins without repentance or atonement for his evil deeds."

William II was buried at the base of one of the towers of Winchester Cathedral. When the tower fell only a few years later, its collapse was viewed as an act of God's displeasure at William's burial in Holy Ground. William died without an heir in the prime of life at age 42/44.

Following the death of King William II on August 2, 1100, his younger brother Henry Beauclerc acceded the throne in 1100 as King Henry I.

REIGN 3

KING HENRY I

AND

QUEEN CONSORT MATILDA OF SCOTLAND

AND

QUEEN CONSORT ADELA OF LOUVAIN

Summary of the Reign of King Henry I (Reign 1100-1135)

King Henry I: life dates c. 66/67 years, b. 1068/69-d. December 1, 1135; King of England 35 years, August 3, 1100-December 1, 1135.

KING HENRY was the youngest son of King William I and Queen Matilda of Flanders. He was born in Yorkshire in the winter of 1068/69. Henry ascended the throne of England after his brother King William II died in 1100. King Henry was known by the name *Henry Beauclerc*, which translates as, 'Henry able scribe' and refers to the fact that he was literate. Indeed, he was the first King of England who could read and write. As the Conqueror's youngest of four sons, Henry was not expected ever to inherit a substantial estate. Therefore, he was given a classical education as preparation for ordination in the priesthood, since it was thought that he would become a bishop or archbishop in the Church.

Part of the rich tapestry of English legend relates that, when William the Conqueror was near death, he beckoned his youngest son Henry to approach him, and then said, "Thy elder brothers will go before thee. Robert shall have Normandy. William shall have England. But thou shalt inherit all my honors, and excel both thy brethren in riches and power."

After his brother King William Rufus was killed in a hunting accident in New Forest near Winchester, Henry Beauclerc quickly consolidated his claim to be king of England by ingratiating himself with Church authorities. However, King Henry I nearly lost the throne of England to his eldest brother Robert Curthose. Robert was on his way back from the First Crusade in the Holy Land when he learned of his brother William's death. Robert immediately laid claim to Normandy and to all England as well. Over a period of about five years, the brothers Duke Robert and King Henry competed for rule of England and Normandy. Eventually, Henry defeated Robert, and claimed all England and Normandy for himself. King Henry imprisoned Duke Robert in England for the remainder of his brother's life.

King Henry I was politically astute, and an excellent manager of affairs of State. He is credited with completing the conquest of England, and with stabilizing Norman rule in England after the Conquest. Like his father The Conqueror, King Henry I kept all powers of government, and the title to all English land in his own hands. Fiefs given to his vassal lords and knights remained valid only so long as the lords remained loyal to his crown. Henry's major contribution to English government was standardization of a uniform system for administration of justice, and collection of taxes throughout the land. In this manner, the concept of 'Common Law' became standard in England. Henry also created a standing cadre of advisors called *The King's Bench*. Its members were assigned authority for different government functions. Below his 'Bench,' Henry created a hierarchy of public servants and clerics of humble Saxon birth who kept records of taxes and public expenditures. These agents advised the king on matters relating to all aspects of finance, debts, and judicial judgments pertaining to wealth in all parts of the nation. Henry's Bench became a lasting feature of English government later known as the *Privy Council*. It is significant that his use of Saxon underlings in stabilizing English government, served him well—Saxons felt that, again, they were governing themselves.

By cruel feudal standards, King Henry's rule was a model of firm fairness. His Saxon subjects called him *The Lion of Justice* for setting up a uniform system of laws across the land. His rule was autocratic, and exceedingly harsh. However, unlike his older brother King William Rufus, Henry did not have an appetite for pointless sadistic cruelty. By the end of his reign, England was described as being so safe "A maid could travel from London to Durham, with a reticule of gold in her bosom, without fear of molestation along the way."

King Henry's Queen Consort was Matilda of Scotland, a Saxon princess descended of Alfred the Great. Henry's birth in England and his marriage to Princess Matilda legitimized his rule in the eyes of his defeated Saxon subjects. King Henry and Queen Matilda had a single surviving child called the Empress Matilda, to whom Henry willed his crown.

After Queen Matilda's death in 1118, Henry I married his second wife, Queen Consort Adela of Louvain, but they were without issue.

Henry I died on December 1, 1135 at Saint Denis in Lyons, Normandy. His body was returned to England, and buried at Reading Abbey, which he founded in Berkshire. The Abbey and his tomb were destroyed around 1543, during dismantling of the monasteries in the reign of Henry VIII.

Following the death of Henry I, his daughter Empress Matilda contested the right to rule England with her cousin Stephen of Blois. The contested reign (1135-1154) is generally called *The Anarchy*, a time when an effective central government in England was lacking for nineteen years.

Narrative of Queen Consort
Matilda of Scotland

Queen Matilda of Scotland: life dates c. 38/41 years, b. 1077/80-d. May 1, 1118; first Queen Consort of King Henry I, 18 years, November 11, 1100-May 1, 1118.

MATILDA, THE first wife of Henry I, was the daughter of King Malcolm Canmore III of Scotland. He is the same 'Malcolm' who replaced Macbeth in Scottish history, and who appears in Shakespeare's play *Macbeth*. Matilda's mother was St. Margaret of Wessex a daughter of Saxon King Edmund Ironside, and a sister of the uncrowned Saxon pretender king Edgar the Aetheling, who would have succeeded Edward the Confessor, had not William the Conqueror defeated Harold II at Hastings in 1066. Matilda of Scotland was the preeminent Saxon Princess of her time. Matilda was descended by eight generations from Alfred the Great. It is through her (and Matilda of Flanders, King Henry's mother) that the present Royal House of Windsor traces its ancestry back to Saxon King Alfred the Great.

Matilda was born at Dunfermline, Scotland. She was christened, Eadgyth/Edith (in Saxon meaning, *Fortune in Battle*). At her christening, Robert Curthose the eldest son of William the Conqueror was her godfather. Queen Matilda of Flanders was present and probably stood as her godmother. As a child, Edith was described as beautiful, with blond hair and blue eyes. Later in life, Edith changed her name to Matilda (in Norman French, meaning, *Victory in Battle*). The change in name was made to avoid criticism by the Norman court, since all Normans detested everything Saxon.

As small children, Matilda and her younger sister Mary were moved to Romsey Abbey to protect them from Norman invaders. The Abbess Christina their aunt supervised their early education in reading, writing, Latin, and French. Later, for additional safety, the children were moved from Romsey Abbey to Wilton Abbey in the interior of England near Salisbury.

Matilda left Wilton Abbey around 1093 when she was twelve or thirteen years old. Her noble birth, as daughter of the King of Scotland, and granddaughter of the Saxon King of England, made her the most highly esteemed Saxon heiress in England. Custom ruled that by the age of twelve she was of marriageable age. She received several legitimate proposals for marriage from titled lords in England, but she rejected them all. Archbishop Anselm of Canterbury recommended that, for their greater security, Matilda and her sister must return to sanctuary at Wilton Abbey. He feared the princesses might be kidnapped and forced into unwanted marriage by ruthless Norman knights. Matilda was at Winton Abbey when Henry Beauclerc, the youngest son of King William the Conqueror and Matilda of Flanders, came with his offer of marriage.

Almost immediately after being crowned King Henry I of England in August 1100, Henry Beauclerc proposed marriage to Matilda of Scotland, as a means of making his accession to the English throne acceptable to his Saxon subjects. He petitioned Archbishop Anselm for approval of the marriage. However, a problem arose from the fact that Matilda had been reared and educated in a convent. Many believed that she had taken vows of chastity to be a nun. If that were true, she could not legally marry anyone.

Henry requested an immediate ruling on the matter in September 1100, but Archbishop Anselm refused to act alone, because the issue was of great significance for legitimacy of heirs to the throne. Therefore, Anselm called a council of bishops to rule on the matter. Matilda testified that she had only "appeared to be a novice in order to protect herself from lust of the Normans," and that she had never taken vows to be a nun. The council of bishops accepted her sworn testimony, and ruled that Matilda had permission to marry.

King Henry I and Princess Matilda were married, and she was crowned at Westminster Abbey on November 11, 1100. Although her given name at birth was Edith, Archbishop Anselm of Canterbury crowned her as Queen Matilda. Her marriage to Henry I was diplomatically important for the domestic tranquility of England by uniting the Norman, Saxon, and Scottish royal houses. Through Matilda's father, she was related to kings of Scotland. Through her grandfather Edmund Ironside (a half-brother of Edward the Confessor), she was directly related to the long line of Saxon Kings of England. The descendants of Henry and Matilda would thereby unite the houses of Normandy, Scotland, and England. This made Henry the overwhelming Saxon favorite among Norman contenders for the crown of England.

Shortly after King Henry's marriage to Matilda of Scotland, he faced the return of his brother Robert Curthose who claimed all England and Normandy. King Henry had insufficient time to extract oaths of fealty from his English and Norman noble lords. By rules of feudalism, the nobles were still free agents after William II died. King Henry's marriage to Saxon Princess Matilda was applauded by Saxons, but deplored by the Norman peerage in England. The people of England split about equally in giving their support to Robert Curthose Duke of Normandy and to Henry Beauclerc King of England. Henry, however, had additional support from Archbishop Anselm and the Church, which was enough to swing the balance of power to his favor in England.

In peaceful, but exceedingly tense negotiations between the two brothers, agreement was reached in 1101; Robert would get Normandy. Henry would keep England. Henry would also pay a scutage tax of £ 2,000 per year for assurance that Robert would stay out of England. The treaty was only a truce. The brothers understood that the contest would begin again, whenever one brother felt strong enough to force his will upon the other. During the next six years of contested rule, Queen Matilda often served as regent at head of government when Henry was occupied in defense of his realm. During the period of truce between the sons of William the Conqueror, Robert Curthose ruled his Dukedom of Normandy, but he ruled in a haphazard, cruel, and capricious manner that earned him little loyalty from his Norman subjects. Robert also made a nuisance of himself in England by threatening Channel port cities with invasion.

By 1106, Henry I was ready to counterattack. In that year, Henry invaded Normandy. He soon defeated, captured, and imprisoned his older brother Robert Curthose. Robert was confined in various prisons for twenty-eight years at various locations, but chiefly in Cardiff Castle, Wales, where he remained until his death at the age of eighty. Henry is criticized for his lack of brotherly love, but there is no question that Robert Curthose, if free and with the primogeniture right to rule, he would have been an ever-present threat to Henry who wore the crown. With defeat and capture of Robert Curthose, Henry secured his position as King of England, and by conquest, Henry also became Duke of Normandy. In this manner, all estates of King William the Conqueror remained intact during the reign of King Henry I. His reign lasted thirty-five years until 1135.

Winchester in Wessex had always been the traditional capitol of Saxon England. However, Queen Matilda chose to establish her court in Westminster adjacent to London. Queen Matilda of Scotland's preference for London persuaded Henry to build Westminster Palace for his queen. Thereafter, London has always been the recognized capitol of England.

Henry and Matilda had four children (2 daughters and 2 sons), but only the eldest daughter survived their parents:

> Edith/Adelaide (1102-1167), Empress Matilda
> William Adelin (1103-1120), the heir apparent
> Richard (?-1120)
> Euphemia (?) died in childhood.

The two sons, William Adelin and Richard, as young men, drowned when the *White Ship* went aground, and sank at Barfleur harbor on November 25, 1120. The young royals were partying when the accident occurred. A single servant survived to report that only he of the drunken party survived. Legend reports that, after the loss of his two sons, the heirs to his throne, King Henry I never smiled again to the end of his life.

Only the eldest daughter Princess Edith/Adelaide (born in February 1102) outlived her parents. She spent her life as Duchess of Normandy in attempts to gain recognition as Queen of England. She is known to history as *Empress Matilda*, or as *Lady of the English*. She married Emperor Henry V of Germany and the Holy Roman Empire. After the emperor's death, she married, Count Geoffrey Plantagenet of Anjou. Empress Matilda and Geoffrey of Anjou were the parents of Henry Plantagenet (later, Henry II of England).

Queen Matilda of Scotland often accompanied Henry on his frequent progresses through the country. She had a mellowing influence on King Henry's treatment of his Saxon subjects. She is remembered most kindly for kneeling in the dust before her husband to make a plea for mercy for citizens of a besieged Saxon village. The citizens had rebelled and were barricaded against Henry's troops. King Henry I had sworn an oath that, when the siege was finally broken, he would execute them all. On pleas from his queen, Henry relented and lives of the villagers were spared. For this and other acts of similar kindness Queen Matilda is known in English history as *Good Queen Maud*.

Queen Matilda of Scotland was the first fully literate and scholarly Queen of England. She corresponded with spiritual and secular leaders of her time including Archbishop Anselm, Pope Paschal II, Abbot Thurgot of Durham, Bishop Ivo of Chartres, Bishop Hildebert de Lavardin, and Emperor Henry V of the Holy Roman Empire. Many of her letters exist in archives of abbeys and cathedrals in Flanders and France. The majority of Queen Matilda's existing letters were written to Archbishop Anselm during his exile. Her persuasive diplomacy was of major importance in resolving the disagreements between her husband and the archbishop that enabled Anselm to return to England as Archbishop of Canterbury in 1106. Anselm was her religious mentor and intellectual friend.

Matilda's court was noted for refinement and learning as a refuge where poets, musicians, and learned persons were welcome. In her own right, Queen Matilda was a very wealthy woman, and the owner of extensive estates that she inherited from her parents, or acquired as dower rights as Queen of England. Her religious devotion and personal wealth permitted her to make generous bequests to many abbeys, convents, and churches. Queen Matilda was noted for piety and service. She walked to church barefoot at Lent and washed the feet of the poor on Maundy Thursday before Easter. She gave generously to the poor, and cared for the sick.

At age thirty-eight Queen Matilda died on May 1, 1118 at Westminster Palace, and was buried in Westminster Abbey. She was nominated for sainthood, but, instead of being canonized, she was beatified as, 'Matilda of Blessed Memory.' Her greatest contribution to English history rests on her sponsorship of William of Malmesbury's *Gesta Regum Anglorum*, a major historical reference on Saxon England, which was published shortly after her death.

After the death of his Queen Matilda of Scotland, Henry I married Adela of Louvain in hope of getting a male heir to continue his dynasty, but no issue from their union replaced his sons lost on the White Ship.

Narrative of Queen Consort Adela of Louvain

Queen Adela of Louvain: life dates c. 48 years, b. 1103-d. April 23, 1151; second Queen Consort of King Henry I c. 14 years, February 2, 1121-December 1, 1135.

ADELA (also called Adeliza) was a daughter of Count Geoffrey I of Louvain and Countess Ida of Namur. She was an attractive girl of good family, who at age sixteen or seventeen years married Henry I on February 2, 1121 when he was fifty-three. Although his marriage to Adela lasted over thirteen years, and was in expectation of having a legitimate son, there was no issue from his second marriage.

Little is recorded of Adela during her reign as queen consort. She did not play a significant role in government or court, as her predecessor had done. Suggestions have been made that she may have encouraged scholarship and literature in a minor way. After Henry died in 1135, Adela retired to the Wilton Abbey in Salisbury in mourning for a few years.

During King Stephen's reign, which followed the death of Henry I, Adela married William d'Aubigny in 1139. He had been a chief advisor to Henry I, and supported King Stephen during the civil war that dominated the nineteen-year conflict between King Stephen and Empress Matilda. King Stephen created William d'Aubigny Earl of Arundel and Earl of Lincoln for his support. Adela, however, is suspected of being a supporter of Empress Matilda, because Adela gave sanctuary to Matilda when she returned from France to England to claim the crown of England her father had promised her.

Adela of Louvain and William d'Aubigny had seven children (4 sons and 3 daughters), all survived to adulthood. After William died, Adela returned to Flanders. With her queen's dowry, she became a generous benefactor of the Affligem Abbey in Brabant, Belgium. She lived out her life at the abbey, and was buried in the abbey church next to her father, Duke Godfrey I of Leuvain. Her grave was destroyed during the French Revolution in 1798. Among her long line of Arundel descendants was her grandson, William III Earl of Arundel, one of the twenty-five signers of Magna Carta. The Earldom of Arundel is the oldest continuously existing noble title in England.

Illegitimate Offspring of Henry I

KING HENRY I was not faithful to his two queens. He acknowledged twenty-six illegitimate offspring by numerous mistresses—thirteen were by six known mothers, and the remaining thirteen children were born of undocumented liaisons. Henry I had more bastards than any other English king, including notoriously unfaithful Charles II, who acknowledged only a dozen bastards.

All surviving illegitimate offspring if King Henry I took honored places in society. Many carried the surname FitzHenry or FitzRoy (meaning, Henry's son, or King's son), and at least ten were male.

Two minor points of interest relate to the marriages and illegitimate offspring of King Henry I: First, there is no answer to the question of why—over a period of about thirteen years of marriage—Henry was unable to father offspring with his second wife Adela of Louvain. The purpose of the marriage was to have a male heir, but they had no children even though both Henry and Adela were proven capable of procreation. The fault may rest with Henry, rather than Adela. Their marriage covered King Henry's years from 53 to 67. If one considers it a time of rapid aging under stress of constant conflict, poor nutrition, and that few lived to see fifty, Henry would have been considered to be an old, old man during his second marriage.

Second, by 1135, the Church and Popes had strengthened rules for inheritance to such a degree that matrimony sanctified by the Church had become mandatory for inheritance of noble and royal landed estates. Only three-quarters century previously, King Henry's grandfather Duke Robert the Devil of Normandy had successfully passed the Duchy of Normandy to his illegitimate son King William the Conqueror (the bastard father of Henry I). Henry I had nine or ten recognized illegitimate male offspring ready on hand, yet he did not see fit to nominate even one of them to inherit his domains. At the time of his death, King Henry I had only one legitimate surviving child, the Princess Edith/Adelaide, known to history as, Empress Matilda.

Thus, it is apparent that by the 12th century, legitimacy through Church sanctioned marriage had become a rigid requirement, the lack of which prohibited bastards from inheriting estates and realms. This restriction against bastardy would cause problems later when legitimacy was challenged in reigns of several English monarchs including Edward V, Henry VII, Mary I and her sister Elizabeth I, also the succession following the reign of Charles II.

REIGN 4

THE ANARCHY OF EMPRESS MATILDA

AND

KING STEPHEN

Summary of the Contested Reign
(1135-1154)

THE PERIOD 1135 to 1154 covers the contested reign of Empress Matilda and Stephen of Blois. The time was of unrelieved civil war when as two grandchildren of William the Conqueror competed for the throne in England. Both Empress Matilda and Stephen of Blois had clouded credentials for inheritance of the English crown, because their lineages were flawed by inheritance through a female line of descent: Empress Matilda was the daughter of Henry I. Stephen's legitimacy to rule came through his mother Adela the youngest daughter of William the Conqueror.

Saxon tradition permitted women to inherit royal titles and estates, but Norman custom followed Salic law, which allowed inheritance of royal and noble titles only through unbroken male lines of descent. For Normans, the Saxon practice was an abhorrent alien custom, one not respected by a majority of invading Norman nobles who held title to estates in England.

For these reasons, Empress Matilda the daughter of King Henry I was the preferred contender for the crown with the native Saxons in England, but she was barely tolerated by a majority of the titled Norman aristocracy that wielded power over the defeated Saxons. Stephen's legitimacy was tainted by its derivation through a female parent, but because Stephen was a man, he easily won fealty from many titled lords who detested the idea of being ruled by a woman.

Thus, from 1135 to 1154, the Norman and Saxon nobility in England was almost equally divided, but vacillating in their support of bids for the crown by the first cousins Empress Matilda and Stephen of Blois.

In the years of anarchy that followed the death of Henry I, neither Empress Matilda nor Stephen of Blois gained ascendancy for long. For almost two decades, the people of England faced a crisis of uncertainty and indecision as to whom it owed allegiance. The common people despaired that the justice and peace of former authoritarian rule by Saxon and Norman kings would ever return to the blighted land. Chronicles of the time said, "God and Christ slept, and the Saints have forsaken us."

Narrative of Empress Matilda

Empress Matilda: life dates 65 years, February 7, 1102-September 10, 1167; Empress of the Holy Roman Empire c. 11 years, January 7, 1114-May 23, 1125; contested reign to be Queen of England 17 years, December 22, 1135-October 25, 1154.

EMPRESS MATILDA was christened Edith; later, her name was changed to Adelaide, and finally to Matilda. She was the eldest and only surviving legitimate child of Henry I and his Queen Matilda of Scotland. In 1114 at the age of twelve, Princess Matilda married Emperor Henry V of the Holy Roman Empire. Emperor Henry V was in no direct way involved in English history. Most of his reign as emperor was consumed in an ongoing conflict between the Emperor of the Holy Roman Empire and a succession of popes over authority to nominate, and consecrate bishops of the Church. Although Henry and Matilda were married for a little over a decade, no children were born of this union. Matilda chose to keep the title Empress after Emperor Henry V died.

In 1128, King Henry I of England gave his daughter Matilda in marriage to Geoffrey Plantagenet Count of Anjou, Touraine, and Maine. The marriage was a political move designed to secure the southern border of Normandy, which shared a common border with Anjou. The marriage outraged his daughter. Empress Matilda who resented her second marriage, which demoted her from empress to a mere countess. She was twenty-six, and her second husband Geoffrey of Anjou, was only fifteen. The differences between them in age and temperament made the marriage intolerable for both bride and groom.

The marriage of Empress Matilda and Geoffrey Plantagenet was a stormy union punctuated by long periods of separation. Even so, they had three children:

> Henry Plantagenet Count of Anjou, Touraine, and Maine (later
>   King Henry II of England)
> Geoffrey Count of Nantes
> William Count of Poitou

Count Geoffrey Plantagenet of Anjou also had several illegitimate children by several mistresses. He died suddenly from a fever in 1151, and was buried at St. Julian's Cathedral in Le Mans, Maine. His eldest son Henry Plantagenet then inherited his father's major titles and estates.

After his second marriage to Adela of Louvain failed to produce a legitimate male heir, and shortly before his death in 1135, King Henry I of England announced that his daughter Empress Matilda was his heir to succeed him as Queen Regnant of England and as Duchess of Normandy. Before his death, Henry I also required the leading noblemen of the realm to swear fealty to her, and to support her claim for the crown of England. This precautionary step was taken to assure the succession of his only surviving legitimate heir to his estates of England and Normandy.

Empress Matilda was at her estate in Anjou when she learned of her father's unexpected death on December 1, 1135, and that her cousin Stephen of Blois had usurped her crown in England. Matilda hastened to Rouen to secure her title as Duchess of Normandy. Problems in Normandy persisted for two years, and prevented her from returning to England to assert her claim to be Queen of England. In frustration, Matilda appealed to Pope Innocent II, who gave her his blessing, and reassured her that, indeed, she was the rightful ruler and Queen of England. Although Empress Matilda was never crowned in England, the pope's endorsement greatly strengthened her claim to be the legitimate contender for England's crown.

However, the pope had previously also given diplomatic recognition to Stephen who continued as the usurper King of England. Stephen soon demonstrated that he had no gift for ruthless leadership required of a Norman king in the 12th Century. His timid incompetence lost him the respect of those who at first had supported him.

In two years, Empress Matilda raised a sizeable militia in Normandy that permitted her return in force to England in 1137. She succeeded in recruiting additional Saxon support in western Saxon counties. The Saxons viewed her to be one of their own, because Empress Matilda was a daughter of the Saxon Princess Good Queen Maud. Gloucester on the Welsh border became Empress Matilda's center for insurrection against Stephen, who tried to rule from London. She led her followers to a major victory at the Battle of Lincoln on February 2, 1141. Matilda captured Stephen, and imprisoned him in Bristol. Empress Matilda briefly claimed the crown, and took the title *Lady of the English*. At that point, many knights defected from Stephen, and gave their support to Matilda, and recognized her as Queen of England.

However, the advantage from her victory lasted only a few months, because Matilda failed to consolidate her authority in England. Her imperious highhanded manner and arbitrary favoritism alienated many knights who previously supported her cause. Many knights changed sides again, and gave their allegiance back to Stephen. She was defeated at the Battle of Winchester in 1141, and Stephen returned to power after which he was crowned for the second time in London.

The years of this contested reign was a time of continuous strife. Neither side held power for any appreciable time. History records that, on one occasion when Matilda was Stephen's prisoner, she escaped in disguise as a corpse strapped to a catafalque on its way for burial in Holy Ground. However, the wagon rolled on beyond the church, and continued on down the road to Gloucester, where she was returned to safety among her own men. On another occasion, she was imprisoned at Oxford, but escaped (like Grimm's Princess Rapunzel) by climbing down a tower in dark of night and escaping in mid winter while snow covered the ground. She was camouflaged in a white cape, and scampered across snow covered fields, waded icy streams, and finally arrived in safety again at Gloucester.

Stephen was also periodically captured. His Queen Matilda of Boulogne raised troops in France to work for his release. On one occasion, a treaty resulted in an exchange of prisoners: King Stephen was exchanged for Empress Matilda's bastard half-bother Robert FitzRoy Earl of Gloucester, who was Matilda's indispensable chief military strategist. Essentially the same sequence of upsets in fortune was repeated in 1146 when Matilda again captured and imprisoned Stephen. However, he soon escaped, and for the third and last time, he was crowned King of England in 1146.

It was not until 1147 that a stalemate was reached when Empress Matilda's chief military aid Robert FitzRoy died, and troubles in Normandy again required her immediate return to France. At that time, her eldest son fourteen year old Henry Plantagenet raised a small army of mercenaries in Normandy to invade England and to continue the harassment of King Stephen.

Finally, in 1153, Matilda and Stephen signed a truce called the Treaty of Westminster. In it, they agreed that Stephen could reign as King of England for the duration of his life, but that Matilda's son Henry Plantagenet Count of Anjou would inherit the throne of England after Stephen's death. Stephen died a year later, and Henry Plantagenet at age twenty-one became King Henry II of England on December 19, 1154.

Empress Matilda survived until 1167. Her life was filled with disappointment and frustration, but history grants her the honor of being, *The Mother of the Plantagenets*—that she cannot be denied. She died at Notre Dame du Pré, Rouen, Normandy, and was buried in the Abbey de Bec. However, she was later reinterred at Rouen Cathedral in 1847. Empress Matilda's epitaph reads:

> *Great by Birth, Greater by Marriage, Greatest in her Offspring:*
> *Here lies Matilda, the daughter, wife, and mother of Henry.* *

* The closing cryptic phrase in the epitaph: "*daughter, wife, and mother of Henry,*" makes reference to the facts that she was: the *daughter* of King Henry I of England, the *wife* of

Emperor Henry V of the Holy Roman Empire, and the *mother* of Henry Plantagenet King Henry II of England.

Narrative of King Stephen

King Stephen of Blois: life dates c. 58 years, b. 1096/97-d. October 25, 1154; King of England 19 contested years, December 22, 1135-October 25, 1154.

KING STEPHEN was born in c. 1096/97 at Blois in central France. He was the son of Count Stephen (the Elder) of Blois, and Adela, youngest surviving daughter of William the Conqueror. Stephen was a favorite in court in the last decade in the reign of King Henry I of England. Those years included the time when King Henry required Stephen, and all titled nobility to swear allegiance in support of the rights of his daughter the Empress Matilda to inherit his English throne.

Stephen was with King Henry I in Lyons, Normandy when Henry suddenly died from indigestion on December 1, 1135 (said to be from stuffing himself on steamed lampreys). Stephen later asserted that King Henry, on his deathbed, had made him his heir to the English crown.

Immediately after Henry I died, Stephen hired a ship in Boulogne to cross the Strait of Dover to England, and then hastened to Westminster where he claimed the state treasury. Nobles in London accepted Stephen's claim that he was King Henry's heir. He was proclaimed King of England on December 22, and was crowned king on December 26, 1135. Stephen's wife Matilda of Boulogne came to England a year later, and was crowned Queen of England at Westminster on Easter Sunday in 1136.

Stephen's contested reign from 1139 to 1154 was a period of anarchy without any effective central government. Today, after 900 years, Stephen's reign is still judged the worst period England ever knew. Stephen's indecisive need to please everyone, more than any willful destructive act, was responsible for the anarchy of his reign.

Stephen reigned ineffectively and intermittently for nineteen years, until his death on October 25,1154. Stephen died at Faversham Abbey in Dover, Kent. He is buried there with his wife Matilda of Boulogne at the abbey they founded. Their tombs were destroyed during the reign of Henry VIII in the despoiling of monasteries around 1543.

If any lesson in government is gleaned from a study of Stephen and Matilda's time, it is that a very good person, such as Stephen surely was, can be a very poor king. Any government, irrespective of how arbitrary or autocratic it may be, is better than no government at all. Left to themselves, on the whole, people are governed by self-interest, and cannot be counted on to make personal sacrifice for the common good. As Machiavelli would later show, the moral qualities that make a person admirable at the individual level have little in common with the pragmatic decisiveness that is needed for leadership by heads of states.

After the death of King Stephen in 1154, Empress Matilda's son Henry Plantagenet succeeded to the throne in 1154 as King Henry II. His Saxon subjects received him as king with great public approval.

Narrative of Queen Consort Matilda of Boulogne

Queen Matilda of Boulogne: life dates c. 47/50 years, b. 1102/05-d. May 3, 1152; Queen Consort of King Stephen c. 17 years, December 22, 1135-May 3, 1152.

BOULOGNE, FRANCE is a port city south of Calais that was of modest importance for fishing and shipping throughout the Middle Ages. Matilda of Boulogne was the only child of Count Eustace III of Boulogne and Mary of Scotland (a younger sister of Queen Matilda of Scotland, wife of King Henry I). Matilda of Boulogne was a first cousin of Empress Matilda, since they both shared Malcolm III of Scotland and Margaret of Wessex as grandparents. Matilda of Boulogne was an heiress to great wealth who possessed castles and estates in France and England. She married Count Stephen of Blois II (the Younger), who was a grandson of William the Conqueror by the Conqueror's youngest daughter Adele of Normandy.

Stephen of Blois benefited greatly from his marriage to Matilda of Boulogne. Their union had been negotiated by Henry I and took place in 1125. In the same year that Matilda's father died, she became Countess of

Boulogne in her own right. Stephen and Matilda had five children (3 sons and 2 daughters), but only the youngest two, William and Marie, survived their parents. Stephen also acknowledged illegitimate Gervais of Blois, who was born several years before his marriage to Matilda.

Records of the time say that Stephen was a popular and agreeable young man. His married life with Matilda of Boulogne was one of mutual affection and respect. Stephen was a brave chivalrous knight, and was well liked for his amiable kindly easygoing disposition. However, he was a weak and ineffectual leader. Stephen's Queen Consort Matilda of Boulogne played an important supporting role for Stephen during the civil war that plagued his reign. Throughout Stephen's feckless attempts to rule, his Queen Matilda was much admired for her courageous assistance and good judgment. She recruited armed support in France, and planned strategies for Stephen's escape when Empress Matilda captured him at critical phases in the controversy between the two contenders for the throne. After Empress Matilda's departure to France in 1147, Stephen was crowned king of England for the third time. Stephen and his Queen Matilda of Boulogne founded a monastery at Faversham, Kent in gratitude for the fragile peace that lasted until the end of Stephen's reign.

Stephen of Blois and Matilda of Boulogne had one surviving son, Count William of Boulogne who does not figure further in English history. He abdicated all claim to the crown of England in preference for being the uncontested Count of Boulogne, which he inherited after death of his admirable mother.

Stephen's cause failed almost immediately after his queen Matilda of Boulogne died in 1152. She was buried at Faversham Abbey that she and Stephen founded. A year after Matilda of Boulogne died, the Treaty of Westminster (also called, Treaty of Wallingford) was signed between Stephen and Empress Matilda only a year before Stephen died in 1154.

In agreement with articles in the Treaty of Westminster, after Stephen's death, Henry Plantagenet, the son of Geoffrey Plantagenet and Empress Matilda, succeeded to the throne as King Henry II of England on October 25, 1154.

Conclusion to the Norman Dynasty

The Norman Dynasty of English kings lasted for eighty-eight years (1066-1154), and included the reigns of William I, William II, and Henry I, and a period of civil strife contested by Stephen of Blois and Empress Matilda.

IT BEGAN with William the Conqueror's successful bid to take command of Saxon England, and continued with reigns of his second and fourth sons, King William II (William Rufus), and King Henry I (Henry Beauclerc), who finished the task of conquering Saxon England. However, in the contested reign of the last Norman rulers Stephen of Blois and Empress Matilda, almost all progress achieved by the first three Norman kings over seventy years came to naught.

The Norman dynasty ended with England in desperate disarray, as two of the Conqueror's grandchildren competed for rule of England. Neither of them had natural ability to lead or govern. At no time in the interval between 1135 and 1154 did either contestant for the crown have enough support to ensure an ongoing stable government. With a lack of strong leadership at the top, civil law collapsed. The country regressed quickly into conditions of anarchy that were in every way equivalent to those experienced in depths of the Dark Ages.

Characteristic of the time, the earls and dukes who held personal fiefs were left to their own devices to establish autonomous authority over their vassals without oversight or restraint from the king. During the reign of anarchy by Stephen and Matilda, capricious *Manorial Justice* by local overlords replaced the *Common Law* that characterized reigns of former Norman kings. Property laws were replaced by vandalism, famine, and pillage. Property at all levels was unprotected. Agriculture and industry collapsed. People longed for return of the security and peace they enjoyed in the reign of King Henry I, whom they called *The Lion of Justice.*

The period of the Norman Dynasty was a time of general mutual dislike between the Norman conquerors and the conquered Saxons. However, during this time, much of what would become the traditional unique English way of life came into being. The Norman period was a time when Saxon England was dominated by despised foreign invaders from France. It ended with what many history buffs concede was the real beginning of English history.

In 1153, King Stephen and Empress Matilda agreed that Matilda's son Henry Plantagenet Duke of Anjou, Touraine and Maine, and Duke of Normandy would inherit the throne of England after Stephen's death. Fortunately for England, Henry Plantagenet the founder of the Plantagenet Dynasty was ready to take command. He was a true leader, and one of the most gifted innovators in government that ever served England as its king.

DYNASTY III

THE PLANTAGENET DYNASTY
REIGN 5 THROUGH 18 (1154–1485)

The Plantagenet Dynasty Patriarch
Count Geoffrey of Anjou

THE PLANTAGENET dynastic title in English history identifies the English kings descended for 331 years directly from Count Geoffrey of Anjou nicknamed Geoffrey Plantagenet. The Plantagenet Kings are Henry II, Richard I, John, Henry III, Edward I, Edward II, Edward III, Richard II, Henry IV, Henry V, Henry VI, Edward IV, Edward, V, and Richard III.

The *Plantagenet* title for this dynasty comes from the French name for a coarse sedge called *planta genista*, which was used by peasants in the Middle Ages in making brooms. Geoffrey of Anjou usually wore a sprig of the sedge in his hat. That habit gave him the nickname Geoffrey 'Plantagenet.'

Geoffrey Plantagenet was the eldest son of Count Fulk V of Anjou and Countess Eremburga of Maine-Touraine. The Counts of Anjou were among the most noble and colorful in France. Family tradition claimed descent from the witch Mélusine. In legend, she was a contemporary of sorceress Morgan le Fay and the magician Merlin of King Arthur fame. Mélusine was a daughter of Satan, and she is said to have married the incomparably handsome first Count of Anjou. They had several children. When Mélusine attended Mass, she always slipped away before communion was celebrated. However, on one occasion, she was unable to leave the church, and when the Host was raised for the miracle of transubstantiation to generate the presence of Christ, Mélusine vanished in a puff of smoke. She was never seen again. Therefore, the frequent irrational capricious behavior of English monarchs is readily understood, because all later reigning kings and queens of England are in the Anjevin bloodline of Geoffrey Plantagenet and his ancient maternal ancestor Mélusine.

Geoffrey Plantagenet was a perfect knight. He was young, handsome, dashing, gallant, and brave. Geoffrey, called 'Plantagenet le Beau,' was handsome, and was described as redheaded, good-humored, shrewd, and courageous. He had great charm, but he also had a cold calculating side that made him a formidable adversary. By the age of fifteen, Geoffrey had defended his title to Anjou so successfully that King Henry I of England contracted him to marry his daughter Empress Matilda, the recently widowed wife of Emperor Henry V of the Holy Roman Empire. By the marriage of Empress Matilda to the Count of Anjou, King Henry I hoped to secure the southern boundary of his province of Normandy, which bordered on Anjou.

Empress Matilda and Geoffrey Plantagenet were married in 1128. The groom was just fifteen, and the bride was twenty-six years old. Their differences in age and personality made the marriage extremely uncongenial. Even so, the Empress Matilda and Geoffrey Plantagenet had three children; the eldest was Henry Plantagenet, who founded the Plantagenet Dynasty when he became King Henry II of England in 1154. Geoffrey also had several illegitimate children by several mistresses.

When King Henry I died in 1135, Empress Matilda inherited the titles Queen of England and Duchess of Normandy from her father. At the same time, her husband Count Geoffrey of Anjou gained by marriage the title Duke of Normandy, but he did not also become the King of England.

Geoffrey Plantagenet died suddenly from a fever in 1151, and was buried at St. Julian's Cathedral in Le Mans, Maine. On his father's death in 1151, Henry Plantagenet inherited all his father's French titles and estates. In agreement with articles in the Treaty of Westminster signed in 1153 by his mother Empress Matilda and King Stephen of England, Henry Plantagenet also became King Henry II of England in 1154 when King Stephen died.

A final note on Geoffrey Plantagenet relates that his heraldic banner of chivalry was a shield with two lions (or leopards). His grandson, Richard I the Lionheart added a third lion to his personal standard that he carried into the Third Crusade. Forever after, *three lions rampant* have graced the heraldic arms of England, the United Kingdom, and the British Empire.

Henry Plantagenet, founder of the Plantagenet Dynasty, was the eldest son of Count Geoffrey Plantagenet of Anjou and Empress Matilda. The Plantagenet Dynasty lasted for 331 years (1154-1485), and dominated England in the High Middle Ages from the 12th to 15th centuries. The Plantagenet Dynasty ended as the English Renaissance began with the Tudor Dynasty that followed in 1485. Traditionally, the Plantagenet Dynasty is subdivided into three historic parts:

1. The *Angevin Plantagenet lineage,* Reign 5 through 12 (1254-1399)
2. The *Lancaster Plantagenet lineage,* Reign 13 through 15 (1399-1461)
3. The *York Plantagenet lineage,* Reign 16 through 18 (1461-1485)

In the Angevin Plantagenet lineages given below, the names of reigning monarchs are given in bold type with the number for each reign. Dates in parenthesis give duration of reigns. Queen Consort names are included when they are also mothers of a following reigning monarch. Numbers in parenthesis give offspring in chronological order; however, only offspring are shown that figure conspicuously in events discussed in the present treatment of English history.

Dynasty IIIa.
The Angevin Plantagenet Lineage
Reign 5 through 12 (1154-1399)

THIS LINE includes Kings Henry (Plantagenet) II, Richard I, John, Henry III, Edward I, Edward II, Edward III, and Richard II.

The Angevin kings reigned for 245 years. The Angevin Plantagenet line descended directly from Henry Plantagenet (King Henry II). His parents were the Empress Matilda (daughter of King Henry I) and Geoffrey Plantagenet, Count of Anjou—from whence comes the *Angevin* name. With one exception, all kings in The Angevin Line followed one another by strict rules of primogeniture—eldest surviving sons followed reigning fathers. The single exception is King John, who (as shown below) usurped the throne from his nephew Arthur Duke of Brittany who was the rightful heir,

Dynasty II. The Norman Lineage:

Reign 3. King Henry I (1100-1135) and his Queen Consort Matilda of Scotland, parents of—
> **Empress Matilda** (not crowned) and her husband Count Geoffrey Plantagenet of Anjou, parents of—
>> Henry II Plantagenet
>> Continue with Dynasty III-1, The Angevin Plantagenet Lineage—Reign 5.
>> Henry II Plantagenet

The Beginning of Dynasty III-1. The Angevin Plantagenet Lineage:

Reign 5. Henry Plantagenet Henry II (1154-1189) married Queen Consort Eleanor of Aquitaine, parents of—
> (1) **Reign 6. Richard I, the Lionheart (1189-1199)** married Queen Consort Berengaria of Navarre, no issue.
> (2 Geoffrey of Brittany, father of—
>> (1) Arthur of Brittany (rightful heir to the throne), murdered by King John, no issue.

(2) Eleanor the Pearl or Fair Maid of Brittany, imprisoned by King John, no issue.

(3) **Reign 7. John** (1199-1216) married Queen Consort Isabella of Angoulême, parents of—

Reign 8. Henry III (1216-1272) married Queen Consort Eleanor of Provence, parents of—

Reign 9. Edward I (1272-1307) married Queen Consort Eleanor of Castile, parents of—

Reign 10. Edward II (1307-1327) married Queen Consort Isabella of France, parents of—

Reign 11. Edward III (1327-1377) married Queen Consort Philippa of Hainault, parents of—

(1) Edward, the Black Prince married Joan of Kent, parents of—

Reign 12. Richard II (1377-1399) married Queen Consort Anne of Bohemia, no issue

End of Dynasty IIIa. The Angevin Plantagenet Lineage; continue with Dynasty IIIb. The Lancaster-Plantagenet Lineage, **Reign 13. Henry IV.**

REIGN 5

KING HENRY II

AND

QUEEN CONSORT ELEANOR

OF AQUITAINE

Summary of the Reign of King Henry II (Reign 1154-1189)

King Henry II: life dates 56 years, b. March 5, 1133-d. July 6, 1189; King of England 35 years, October 25, 1154-July 6, 1189.

KING HENRY II (Henry Plantagenet Count of Anjou) is first of the eight Angevin Plantagenet Kings of England. He was the eldest of three sons of Empress Matilda and Geoffrey Plantagenet Count of Anjou, Touraine, and Maine. Henry inherited his father's estates in 1151. His marriage to Eleanor of Aquitaine in 1152 added her vast holdings in southern France to his realm. On the death of King Stephen in 1154, Henry became King of England. This gave Henry Plantagenet holdings that reached from Scotland to the Pyrenees in northern Spain. At the age of twenty-one, he was the greatest ruling prince in Europe. Henry Plantagenet's reign lasted 35 years, until his death at age fifty-six in 1189.

Henry Plantagenet became King Henry II of England after nineteen years of misrule (1135-1154), during which King Stephen and Henry's mother Empress Matilda competed for the throne of England. King Henry II faced a nation in anarchy when he became king. Nobles in England administered their estates in whatever way they chose without respect for royal authority. Youthful King Henry had remarkable capacities for leadership, organization, and administration. In short order, he reasserted the crown's supreme authority over all his noble and common subjects. He chose legal administrators without regard to noble rank from persons of good repute among the governed. The Common Law Henry created was modeled on that of his grandfather King Henry I. However, he also devised legal and governmental improvisations of his own that stabilized a uniform code of laws throughout England, Many of his devices for government far outlived his own reign. Most important of his legal innovations were: *Trial by Jury* and *Appellate Courts*, both continued to be central aspects in administration of justice under English Common Law. His basic system for administration was the beginning of legal president for law, as practiced in England ever since.

The greatest popular remembrance of King Henry II unfortunately relates to the shameful assassination of Thomas à Becket Archbishop of Canterbury in the Cathedral in 1170. On that occasion, four of King Henry's knights, who mistakenly thought they were doing their king's will, murdered the Archbishop as he prayed at the altar in the Cathedral. Henry is blamed unjustly for Becket's death.

Henry II married his Queen Consort, Eleanor Duchess of Aquitaine, in 1152. Two sons of Henry II and Eleanor of Aquitaine became kings of England after death of their father King Henry II: King Richard I, known as The Lionheart, and King John, known as John Lackland. King Henry II, Eleanor of Aquitaine, and Richard the Lionheart are buried at Fontevraud Abbey, Chinon, Anjou.

Following the death of Henry II Plantagenet in 1189, Richard the Lionheart succeeded his father as King Richard I.

Narrative of Queen Consort Eleanor of Aquitaine

Queen Eleanor of Aquitaine: life dates c. 81/82 years, b. 11212/22-d. April 1, 1204; Duchess of Aquitaine 67 years, April 9, 1137-April 1, 1204; Queen Consort of Louis VII of France 15 years, August 1, 1137-March 21, 1152; Queen Consort of King Henry II of England 35 years, October 25, 1154-July 6, 1189; Dowager Queen of England 15 years, July 6, 1189-April 1, 1204.

ELEANOR OF Aquitaine was born around 1122 in Bordeaux or Guienne, Gascony, a province of Aquitaine in southern France. She was the elder of two daughters of Duke William X of Aquitaine and Poitou and Eleanor of Rochefaucauld. In the 12th century, Aquitaine was the largest and richest wine producing region, and the culturally most enlightened province in France. Aquitaine and Poitou together were almost one-third the size of modern France. Duke William made sure that his two daughters received the best education in courtly manners available.

Eleanor was fifteen in 1137 when her father Duke William set out on pilgrimage to Compostela, Spain to do penance on Easter at the Shrine of Saint James the Apostle. Before reaching the shrine, Duke William was fatally stricken with a sudden illness (possibly appendicitis), and he died shortly after making a will that left his title and entire estate to his eldest daughter Eleanor. Overnight, teenage Duchess Eleanor was the most sought after heiress in France. She was decisive, intelligent, and stubborn. She was literate, and had mastered Latin. She enjoyed music, was a dancer of grace, and enthusiastically enjoyed all vigorous sports popular at court, including riding and the hunt. Eleanor was often called, 'the great beauty of her age,' but no contemporary written or graphic picture exists to give insight on her real appearance.

Duke William's will named King Louis VI of France as Eleanor's guardian. Louis was given the responsibility of finding a suitable husband for his young marriageable charge. Louis promptly solved this problem by marrying Eleanor to his son the Dauphin (who shortly would become Louis VII of France). This solution was of great advantage to both the bride and groom. Eleanor soon became Queen of France, and the Dauphin doubled his personal land holdings. The young couple married with great pomp in the Cathedral of Saint André in Bordeaux, Gascony (Aquitaine capital city) on July 22, 1137. The Dauphin became King Louis VII in the same year as his marriage to Eleanor.

At first, his vivacious bride infatuated young King Louis VII. He granted her every wish, and forgave her every indiscretion. However, from the beginning, Eleanor was unpopular and poorly received by the court in Paris. She disdained Parisian court etiquette, and was accused of being a willful, nonconforming, free spirit who often dressed in mannish peasant clothing. Like an uncouth country bumpkin, she often "swore worse than crudely" in open court. Eleanor was accused of lacking the manners suitable for the Queen of France, the person who should lead in a fashionable society.

The young king and queen were of dissimilar temperament. Louis was devout, scholarly, and conservative. His fame as King Louis VII of France's fame in France rests on founding the University of Paris, building Notre Dame Cathedral, and on his incompetent management of military matters in the Second Crusade.

Eleanor was a *bon vivant* party girl. Even so, Louis and Eleanor remained married for fifteen years (1137-1152). During that time, Eleanor had two daughters, but no sons:

> Marie de Capet Countess de Champagne (1145-1198)
> Alix de Bois Countess de la Vexin (1151-1198)

Gradually King Louis's affection for Queen Eleanor paled, and his patience wore thin. Their incompatible union was destined to end in acrimony and divorce.

Ten years into their marriage, Louis decided to lead French troops in the Second Crusade (1147-1149). He had no leadership experience, no appreciation for the importance of authoritative discipline, ordnance supply, and no native mental capacity to make or execute logical tactical decisions. A Second Crusade news report said, "From the moment the Crusaders entered Asia Minor, the Crusade went badly. The German army was massacred, and the French, with what remained of the Germans, then march on in an increasingly disorganized fashion towards Antioch . . . with faith that God's hand would lead the way to victory . . . [but] no aid came from Heaven, except that battles stopped when night fell."

Eleanor accompanied the French army to Asia Minor as nominal leader of the Aquitaine contingent of the French army. Eleanor was of no help in advancing the cause of wresting Jerusalem from the Infidel. She spiced things up with unseemly behavior for of a Queen of France on foreign soil. On many occasions, she behaved in an outrageous scandalous manner. Gossip reported that she spent a full night in the tent of the Egyptian Sultan Saladin (but that is unlikely, because he would have been only ten or eleven years old at the time). Worse, she imperiously claimed the right to command her own Aquitaine troops. When she was denied that function, Eleanor gave authority over Aquitaine troops to her uncle Raymond of Antioch. Raymond detested King Louis, and opposed him at every turn. In desperation, Louis finally imprisoned Eleanor to prevent any further mischief, but that only alienated her Aquitaine army. Thereafter, her army gave only lackluster support to orders from France.

Thus, discord and incompetence captured defeat from every opportunity for a French victory. With such inept Christian opponents, the Islamic Egyptian Infidels could not fail to win the Second Crusade. Jerusalem and the Holy Land were successfully spared Christian domination. In every diplomatic and military sense, the Second Crusade was a disastrous failure for King Louis of France.

Louis and Eleanor were estranged before the Crusade began. By the time Louis admitted to failure of his Jerusalem adventure, and was ready to return to France in 1149, Louis and Eleanor were embittered, hostile, and mutually in favor of divorce. The royal entourage returned to Paris in 1150, and negotiations for separation and divorce began almost immediately. Pope Eugenius III decided that, as a means of avoiding an appearance of scandal, the cause for annulment of the royal marriage would be consanguinity. Louis and Eleanor were third cousins-once removed—a remote hereditary proximity usually ignored as a valid incestuous basis for denying marriage.

The pope annulled the royal marriage in March 1152. Louis hoped to keep title to Eleanor's Aquitaine estate as part of his dower right for marriage to Duchess Eleanor. However, a codicil in the will of Eleanor's father Duke William X of Aquitaine said, "Aquitaine will remain an independent Duchy through the life of Duchess Eleanor, and may only be transferred to France in the event the Duchess and Dauphin have a male heir, who, thereby, will unite in blood the title to Aquitaine and Capet estates." Eleanor and Louis VII had two daughters, but no sons. On that ground, the pope ruled against Louis's claim for Aquitaine. Moreover, since their union was annulled (not divorced), in eyes of law and the Church, Louis and Eleanor had never been married; therefore, their two daughters were illegitimate.

Eleanor kept her title, Duchess of Aquitaine, until her death at age c. 82 in 1204. At that time, King Philip Augustus of France (Louis's son by a second wife), renewed his father's claim for Aquitaine, and he succeeded in swindling Eleanor's incompetent youngest son King John of England of all his continental territories.

A contributing factor that hastened the annulment of the royal marriage between Louis VII of France and his queen Eleanor of Aquitaine was a torrid affair between Queen Eleanor and Count Henry Plantagenet, which had been openly flaunted in Paris for over a year.

Count Geoffrey Plantagenet, Henry Plantagenet's father, died in 1151, and his eldest son Henry inherited the title Count of Anjou, Maine, and Touraine. Count Henry, in compliance with feudal custom, went to Paris to pledge fealty to French King Louis VII. After performing the necessary courtesies with the king, Henry stayed in Paris to enjoy sporting life at court. Auburn haired Henry Plantagenet had much of his father in him. He was handsome, dashing, gallant, and brave. His kinsman Sir Peter de Blois described Henry in youth as having "keen gray eyes, red hair, a restless temperament, towering rage that came and went like a summer storm . . . [but] when he was at peace, there was great sweetness in his eyes."

When seventeen year old Count Henry Plantagenet met twenty-nine year old Queen Eleanor at court, they immediately charmed one another. They soon were involved in a tempestuous, poorly concealed, romantic affair that soon became gossip in every court in Europe. Henry and Eleanor were married on Whitsuntide, May 18, 1152, less than two months after Eleanor's final release from marriage to King Louis VII. Eleanor brought as her dowry to Henry, the provinces of Poitou, Gascony, and Aquitaine, which were a compact unit of counties in southwestern France. The wine-growing region around Bordeaux alone was of immense economic value, and the total area of her estates exceeded those of the King of France.

After his marriage to Eleanor of Aquitaine, Henry petitioned the King Louis VII of France (Eleanor's Liege lord and former husband) that Eleanor's French estates should be transferred outright to himself on grounds that, "A woman cannot be expected to have enough good sense to rule." Neither King Louis VII nor Duchess Eleanor of Aquitaine was persuaded by Henry Plantagenet's ungracious suggestion.

As will be seen, Eleanor retained personal title to all her French estates throughout her life.

After King Stephen of England died in 1154 (in keeping with the Treaty of Westminster signed in 1153 by Stephen and Henry Plantagenet's mother, the Empress Matilda), Henry and Eleanor went to London to claim the English crown. Both Henry Plantagenet and Eleanor of Aquitaine were crowned at Westminster Abbey a few days before Christmas in 1154.

Eleanor and Henry were deeply passionately in love in early years of their stormy marriage, which lasted for thirty-seven years, during which eight children were born:

> William (1153-1156), died in childhood
> Henry the Young King (1155-1183)
> Richard the Lionheart (1157-1199), later King Richard I
> Geoffrey Duke of Brittany (1158-1186)
> Matilda Duchess of Saxony (1156-1189)
> Eleanor Queen of Castile (1162-1214)
> Joan Queen of Sicily (1165-1199)
> John Lackland (1166-1216), later King John

In middle years of his reign, King Henry II and Queen Eleanor drifted apart. However, from the start, Henry was never a faithful husband. Indeed, his bastard son Geoffrey of York was born within weeks of birth of his first legitimate son Prince William. Eleanor, who was a sophisticated woman of the world, apparently accepted King Henry's infidelity with equanimity. She took responsibility for the care, wellbeing, and education of the bastard Geoffrey of York, while he grew to maturity in court with her own children who were his half-siblings. Eleanor may have looked out for Henry's other bar sinister offspring as well.

As might be expected of two persons who are much alike—both were born to great wealth and power, and both had incisive intelligent bossy temperaments—that Eleanor's marriage to Henry Plantagenet was contentious. Neither Henry nor Eleanor had a gift for subordination to anyone. Eleanor was a realist who admitted, "My marriage to Henry was a much happier one than my marriage to Louis [who was] more suited to being a Monk than a husband."

After her youngest child John Lackland was born in 1166, it is probable that Henry II and Eleanor no longer shared a marriage bed. In that year, Henry's notorious affair with Rosamond Clifford 'in her flowered bower at Woodstock' became common gossip. It is often stated as fact that Henry's affair with Rosamond catalyzed Eleanor's departure to Aquitaine in 1167. Great theater depicts Eleanor flouncing off to Southern France in high dudgeon, but in fact, her departure probably was with amiable consent from Henry. He had the good grace to supply an armed escort, and to provision the ships that transported her goods safely back to Bordeaux and Poitiers. Therefore, it is probably only legend that says, "Cruel Eleanor gave Sad Rosamond the choice of a dagger, or a draught of poison, as a way out of her shame."

After Eleanor returned to her French estates in Aquitaine, she established a colorful court of her own at Poitiers. It played an important part in advancing instrumental music and poetry, known to literary history as the style of *Courts of Love*. The parlor game, Courts of Love, invented by Eleanor for amusement of her guests was a stylized romantic make believe, in which guests took sides. One team pled the case for true love. The other team prosecuted false betrayal. A mock jury of several men and women chosen from among the guests heard arguments, and rendered judgment. All was done for amusement with emphasis on wit, exaggerated emotion, incredible excuses, absurd logic, and low innuendo. These court charades lasted for centuries well into the reign of Queen Elizabeth I.

Courts of Love, out of which grew the elaborate feudal etiquette of Courtly Love, was a romantic fiction of knights in shining armor, who rescued beautiful chaste maidens from the clutches of evil overlords. Ballads of great sentimentality were composed that told a sad tale—*one cannot be married to, and be in love with, the same person at the same time*—wildly popular songs of chivalry were recited to an accompaniment of doleful plinky-plunky music played on lutes, flutes, and tambourines. Troubadours traveled from court to court, singing and playing their wares. They were patriarchs of theatrical entertainers who have delighted us in music halls, pubs, and nightclubs ever since.

In addition to the impact Eleanor's Courts of Love clearly had on music, poetry, and theater, the unique importance of Eleanor's fictional courts may be that they popularized the idea of *trial by jury*. If one leaps ahead to the reign of King Richard I The Lionheart, when Eleanor was regent of England during Richard's absence on the Third Crusade, and during his captivity afterwards (around 1190-1194), Eleanor is credited with often using juries composed of commoners to help her decide whether to release persons imprisoned during the reign of King Henry II. In these serious legal trials, Eleanor charged jurors with the discovery of guilt or innocence of the accused. Is it not possible that Eleanor adapted her romantic Courts of Love (which had been invented for amusement of guests in her drawing rooms at Poitiers and Bordeaux) to serious legal trials in England, when Eleanor charged jurors to decide guilt or innocence of the accused? English courts of Common Law, however, credit Henry Plantagenet with being the originator of *trial by jury* in English Common Law—as Thomas Jefferson said, "Trial by Jury is the greatest defender of justice ever invented."

Eleanor enjoyed about eight years in Aquitaine with all freedoms of a ruling monarch. During much of the time, her children freely moved between England and Southern France. Prince Richard (known as the Lionheart), the second of her surviving sons, spent much of his youth enjoying the climate and cultural advantages of his mother's court. He was educated at Poitiers, where chivalry in its highest form was brought to flower. Richard, although alienated from his father, was always his mother's favorite. Eleanor promised he would inherit her Aquitaine estates. Her promise created the problem that would end Eleanor's merry days of freedom in Aquitaine.

A few years after Eleanor left England for Aquitaine, King Henry II embarked on a futile effort in 1170 to win loyalty from his four contentious sons, by giving them land inheritances before he died. This was done in mistaken hope that their gratitude would assure loyal support from his sons for the rest of King Henry Plantagenet's life. The eldest son, Prince Henry the 'Young King' was made Co-King of England and Co-Duke of Normandy in 1170. However, Henry II retained full command of both estates. His second son Prince Richard had previously alienated his father, so Richard was omitted from his father's planned bequests. King Henry provided for his third surviving son Prince Geoffrey, by negotiating his marriage of State in 1181 to Constance Duchess of Brittany who held the title to the province of Brittany in her own name. By this means, Geoffrey became Duke of Brittany. The youngest son Prince John, who was only four years old, was his father's favorite. King Henry decided to give Aquitaine to John. However, Eleanor refused to honor the bequest, and insisted that she had promised to give Aquitaine to Richard. Thus, Prince John was not given title to any great estate; therefore, he became known to history as *John Lackland.*

The conflict between King Henry II and Queen Eleanor was an example of unrelenting purpose frustrated by implacable resistance. Nothing would persuade Eleanor to surrender Aquitaine. Early in 1173, Prince Henry (called 'the Young King') rebelled against his father, and went to France to organize a revolt against his father. Eleanor encouraged her sons, Princes Richard and Geoffrey, who were in Aquitaine, to support their older brother's insurrection against their father Henry II. She was on her way to Paris to raise mercenaries for her son's treasonous adventure, when Henry Plantagenet's militia captured her. King Henry spirited Eleanor away to a secret hiding place on the Continent (possibly at Caen or Rouen in Normandy). Her whereabouts were unknown for over a year. In mid summer 1174, she was openly transported as a prisoner to England. Eleanor remained a captive of King Henry II for sixteen years, until his death 1189.

During Eleanor's imprisonment, she was given all courtesies and comforts suitable for her status as Queen of England. However, she was severely restricted in where and when she could move around England. King Henry's whim decided what castle she would occupy at a given time. Usually, she was permitted to be present in court at Windsor or Westminster at Christmas and Easter, but she was only rarely in court on lesser feast days. She had rare contact and conversation with her sons.

During the years 1166-1189, Henry faced increasing opposition and rebellion from his sons. They continued in efforts to increase control over French estates they claimed. Henry stoutly resisted their attempts to rob him of power, and usually he was successful in keeping authority in his own hands. Princes Henry and Geoffrey died before their father. Princes Richard and John joined forces with Philip II Augustus of France to conspire traitorously to defeat their father. In King Henry's last days, he could not raise enough troops in England to defeat the combined strength of his sons and the King of France. Henry retreated north from Poitiers to Tours in hope of gaining a secure refuge in Anjou, his ancestral patrimony that always remained loyal to him. However, he was overtaken and captured by Philip Augustus before he gained sanctuary. Richard and John then forced their father King Henry II to pay homage to King Philip

II Augustus as his Liege lord. Thus, all Henry's estates in France were acknowledged as fiefs, which Henry held only at discretion of the French king.

Only a few days later, on July 6, 1189, Henry II died at ancient Chinon Castle in the Loire Valley of central France. His surviving legitimate sons Richard and John deserted him. Only his bastard son Geoffrey Plantagenet of York was present to bid him the long goodbye. King Henry said to Geoffrey, "Baseborn indeed have my other children shown themselves to be. You alone are my only true son . . . Let things go now as they may . . . Shame, shame on a conquered king. I care no more for myself, or for this world." Henry Plantagenet then turned his face to the wall and died. King Henry II, one of England's greatest kings, is buried in Fontevrault Abbey, Chinon, Anjou.

Richard the Lionheart was in Normandy when he learned of his father's death, and that, as the eldest surviving prince, he had inherited all his father's estates. Richard was King of England, Duke of Normandy, Count of Anjou, Torraine, and Maine.

One of the first things Richard did as King of England was to issue an order for the release of his mother Eleanor of Aquitaine from imprisonment in England. She was freed and restored to all honors due the Dowager Queen Mother of the king. She entered London with great rejoicing from the crowd that greeted her. As prelude to Richard's coronation at Westminster, Eleanor received the oaths of fealty from nobles of the realm, in the name of her son King Richard I.

Eleanor was sixty-seven or sixty-eight when Richard came to the throne in 1189. She was directly involved in most government activities in England during the decade of his reign (1189-1199). Much of the time, Eleanor served as King Richard's regent or viceroy. Many state documents of the time carry her signature, "Eleanor, by God's grace, Queen of England." Most of her official acts, judged in the context of her time, earn praise and little censure.

Eleanor's regency is remembered most favorably for her defense of King Richard the Lionheart's English and French realm, and for her successful fund raising for Richard's Third Crusade. Eleanor acted for England in negotiating the treaty for Richard's ransom and release when he was a prisoner of Leopold V of Austria, and he was later sold to Holy Roman Emperor Henry VI of Germany. She raised troops in England and

Normandy to thwart Philip II Augustus of France and Richard's deceitful younger brother Prince John Lackland, when they plotted to steal Richard's kingdom while he was a prisoner in Austria and Germany.

Unexpected death came to Richard the Lionheart on April 6, 1199. It came with a random crossbow arrow shot by a boy on a battlement of Chalus Castle that hit Richard between neck and shoulder. England was at war with France, and King Richard's death created a crisis for succession to the English crown. The Law of Primogeniture recognized that King Richard's rightful heir was his thirteen year old nephew Arthur of Brittany, son of his deceased brother Duke Geoffrey of Brittany. However, at that critical time, England's chief military commanders decided that the fate of the nation could not to be entrusted to teenage Arthur of Brittany. Eleanor gave her consent, and the crown was given to Prince John Lackland in misplaced belief that he had military ability, like that possessed by his illustrious father and older brother Richard the Lionheart. History's judgment is that John Lackland was probably the worst king England ever suffered.

After King John came to the throne in 1199, his inept efforts in diplomacy and war were no match against the shrewd scheming of King Philip II Augustus of France. He had been King John's former friend and conspirator against his father King Henry II, and his brother King Richard I. Philip Augustus was able to alienate all France against King John of England by pointing out that John had usurped Normandy, Anjou, and Brittany from Duke Arthur of Brittany, who was their rightful ruler. By 1204, John lost even Normandy, which was England's hereditary birthright from the Conqueror. Only Bordeaux and Gascony near the Spanish border remained in English hands.

Eleanor worked tirelessly for almost fifteen years to support her two reigning sons: King Richard and King John. She tirelessly tried to protect their French estates, but finally in 1204, with the fall of Rouen and loss of even Normandy, 82 year-old Dowager Queen Eleanor of Aquitaine died on April 1, 1204. Those with her said she died of a broken heart for King John's loss of his French estates, and for collapse of the empire, she and Henry Plantagenet had created for their heirs.

Eleanor of Aquitaine is buried between her husband King Henry Plantagenet, and her beloved son, King Richard the Lionheart, in Fontevraud Abbey, Chinon, Anjou. At pivotal points in history, she was queen of France and later Queen and Regent of England. She was mother of England's King Richard I and King John. History remembers her with honor, admiration, and amusement. She is one of the great ladies of history—one of the wealthiest, powerful, and influential personalities of the Middle Ages.

REIGN 6

KING RICHARD I

AND

QUEEN CONSORT BERENGARIA OF NAVARRE

Summary of the Reign of King Richard I (Reign, 1189-1199)

King Richard I: life dates 42 years, September 8, 1157-April 6, 1199; King of England 10 years, July 6, 1189-April 6, 1199.

KING RICHARD I (always known as the *Lionheart*, or in France as *Richard Coeur de Lion*) was the eldest surviving son of King Henry II and Queen Eleanor of Aquitaine. Richard was born at Beaumont Palace, Oxfordshire in 1157. After the death of his father Henry II in 1189, he succeeded as King of England, Duke of Normandy, and Counts of Anjou, Touraine, and Maine. King Richard I was one of England's most colorful charismatic kings, but he did almost nothing for his island kingdom. Even so, his English subjects always held Richard in high esteem. His mother

Eleanor of Aquitaine supervised his education in the enlightened court at Poitiers, where chivalry flowered most brightly. He was a good amateur musician, and a recognized poet of popular ballads. Richard was over six feet tall, had blue eyes, golden wavy hair, and was distinguished for handsome appearance, for courtly manners, and for amiable informality in his dealings with persons irrespective of their rank. He was the model of a true *Knight-errant*, and was hugely popular wherever he wandered. Without question, Richard was the best military leader in 12th century Western Europe.

King Richard's reign of ten years was overshadowed by the role he played in leading the Third Crusade. However, he failed in that effort to defeat Saladin the Sultan of Egypt, and he was unable to liberate the Holy Land from the Infidel. The first years of his reign (1189-1192) were consumed by activities in the Third Crusade. On King Richard's return from Jerusalem, Leopold Duke of Austria captured and imprisoned him, and then traded him to King Henry IV of Germany Emperor of the Holy Roman Empire. Richard was finally ransomed at enormous cost to his English subjects. It is during the period of his captivity in Germany that the legend of Robin Hood and his Merry Men of Sherwood Forest is set. These fictional outlaws valiantly opposed *Bad King John,* and raised money for the ransom of *Good King Richard.*

Aside from being born in England, Richard only returned to England as an adult for his two coronations. The first came soon after the death of King Henry II in 1189. The second coronation came in 1194 after his ransom from prison in Germany. On both of those occasions, his stay in England was brief, as he focused his efforts on raising taxes to support his military adventures on the Continent. Richard called England his *Milk Cow*. On one occasion he said, "If I could have found a buyer, I would have sold London itself." During the last six years of his reign, Richard attempted to stabilize rule in his far-flung estates in England, Normandy, and Aquitaine.

Richard married Berengaria of Navarre on May 12, 1191 in Cyprus while on his way to the Third Crusade in the Holy Land. No issue came from the marriage, and it may never have been consummated. Berengaria lived for thirty-one years after Richard died. She died on December 23, 1230, and was buried: first, at the L'Espan Abbey, and later was reinterred at Le Mans Cathedral, France.

No evidence exists that King Richard's reign made any lasting contribution to the progress of English Common Law. However, the Lionheart continues to hold his own as the very model for amethyst tinted romantic feudal chivalry. King Richard I died prematurely at age forty-two on April 6, 1199. He was buried with his father Henry II, at Fontevrault (or Fontevraud) Abbey, Chinon, Anjou. His mother, Eleanor of Aquitaine, was buried later between father and son at the Abbey.

Following the death of King Richard I, his only legitimate surviving younger brother, John Lackland, usurped the crown from the rightful heir, his nephew Arthur of Brittany. John Lackland was crowned King John of England on May 27, 1199.

Postscript: Richard the Lionheart was born to die in a flamboyant heroic event of chivalry. However, fate intervened, and his death came otherwise. Richard met his end during a pause in a siege of Chalus Castle near Limoges, France. All was quiet; armed men were at ease; siege engines rested; nothing disturbed the end of day. At evensong and setting sun, Richard strolled among his men. A crossbow arrow, shot aimlessly from the battlement by a mere boy, lodged in Richard's neck above his left shoulder. The arrow was removed carelessly. Blood poisoning and gangrene followed. About a fortnight later, Richard died on April 6, 1199-April 6 is still celebrated in France, as: *The day an ant killed the Lion King.*

Narrative of Queen Consort Berengaria of Navarre

Queen Berengaria of Navarre: life dates c. 59/65 years, b. 1165/70-d. December 23, 1230; Queen Consort of Richard I c. 8 years, May 12, 1191-April 6, 1199; Dowager Queen of England 31 years, April 6, 1199-December 23, 1230.

BERENGARIA WAS the fourth of five children and the eldest daughter of King Sancho VI of Navarre and Blanche of Castile. Berengaria was born some time between 1165 and 1170 at a peaceful interval in Navarre's turbulent history. Her father, called Sancho the Wise, provided an enlightened cultural environment for his growing family. Berengaria probably was literate, and was taught to appreciate the poetry and music of regional Provençal troubadours.

Princess Berengaria was described as "dark of hair and eye, petite, intelligent, and a fine musician . . . in all things, a suitable consort for a king." From this brief statement, one can visualize a typical girl of Spanish or Basque descent. Ambrose the Minstrel, a contemporary witness who saw her in life, said that Berengaria was 'elegant and prudent.' Another contemporary described her as having 'probity' (which Webster says is, 'an admirable quality of upright integrity and rectitude'). However, 'elegance, prudence, and rectitude' are hardly the words one expects from troubadours, who were noted for glib words of extravagant praise routinely flung about to earn generous gratuities for their blatant flattery. The modest faint praise used to describe Berengaria suggests that the truth about her appearance is that, at best, she was 'plain.' Even so, a later balladeer referred to her as 'Ravishingly beautiful Berengaria,' another said she was the 'Fairest in the land,' but these descriptions were made on hearsay long after her death.

Romantic accounts report that Berengaria instantly fell hopelessly in love with Richard the Lionheart, when he came to joust in a tournament at Navarre's capital Pamplona in 1175. If Richard and Berengaria did meet on that occasion, their age differences (he over 25, she only 10 or 11) probably generated only indifference, not love. It is certain that their union, sixteen years later, in 1191 was a marriage of State, not of sentiment.

Shortly after Richard came to the throne, after the death of his father King Henry II in 1189, Queen Eleanor of Aquitaine chose Berengaria to be King Richard's bride. Eleanor's decision was entirely political. The small Kingdom of Navarre shared a border with Eleanor's southernmost Aquitaine province of Gascony—it is always prudent to have nations on one's borders, with their friendship assured by ties of marriage. Eleanor's negotiations and dower agreements with Navarre for the marriage of Richard and Berengaria were not completed until the summer of 1191. At that time, Richard was occupied with organizing the armies of Christendom for the Third Crusade (1189-1192).

The Holy Land had been secure in Christian hands for almost fifty years following the First Crusade, but Jerusalem had been under Infidel control since 1145, following the Second Crusade led by King Louis VII of France, which failed to liberate the city. In 1187, Saladin the Sultan of

Egypt took control of Jerusalem. In that year, Pope Gregory VIII called for a Third Crusade to free the Holy Sepulcher on the Mount of Olives, and Church of the Nativity in Bethlehem from Infidel hands.

King Richard of England and King Philip Augustus of France were at war when they received the call for a new crusade. They immediately signed a truce, and agreed to join forces to retake the Holy Land. The Third Crusade is often called the *Crusade of the Three Kings*: Richard the Lionheart of England, Philip II Augustus of France, and Frederick Barbarossa of the Holy Roman Empire. However, at the 3rd Crusade's conclusion, only Richard the Lionheart remained as Commander-in-Chief of the multinational forces of Christendom in Asia Minor.

Richard appointed his mother, Eleanor of Aquitaine, to be regent in charge of his English and Continental domains. In her capacity as regent, Eleanor finalized King Richard's royal marriage. She traveled to Pamplona, Navarre in 1191, and completed dower arrangements there. Richard agreed to terms of the marriage contract. He viewed Berengaria's dower as an additional means of financing his swashbuckling military campaign. His coronation in London in September 1189 had delayed his departure to the Crusade for over a year. When the complex dower agreement was signed, Richard was at Portofino on the Mediterranean coast in Northern Italy. He was immersed in gathering his army and supplies for transport by water to the Holy Land. By the spring of 1191, he could no longer be delayed by trifling distractions such as his own marriage.

With the marriage agreement signed and sealed, Eleanor, who was almost seventy, accompanied Berengaria by land from Navarre, through the Pyrenees, across Provence, to Portofino for the planned wedding. However, when they arrived, Richard had already departed by sea for Cyprus. The royal ladies hurried over the Alps, then continued to Brindisi, on the heel of the Italian boot, in hope of intercepting Richard there. However, at Brindisi, they learned that the Crusaders were still assembled in Sicily. Wherewith, Eleanor chartered a ship, and went by water to Sicily, and arrived at Messina on March 30, 1191. In Messina, they stayed with Eleanor of Aquitaine's widowed daughter Queen Joanna of Sicily. Eleanor wanted King Richard's marriage to be performed promptly, but foot-dragging Richard protested that Lent was not a correct time to celebrate a royal wedding.

Sicilian peasants soon tired of feeding and housing the undisciplined Crusaders from England and France. After two months, the uninvited foreign visitors had depleted the land of food resources, had gravely disrupted the peace, and they were no longer welcome. Richard prudently decided to load his men and military supplies on a flotilla of over one hundred small ships, and to proceed to Antioch in Asia Minor.

Eleanor, Joanna, and Berengaria, left to their own devices, agreed that Eleanor should return to England and Normandy for the important task of raising money for the Crusade. Joanna and Berengaria, in hope of overtaking Richard, hired a ship, and headed east to Cyprus. Their ship went aground in the shallow harbor at Limassol, where Isaac Comnenus Emperor of Cyprus threatened them with capture for ransom. Then (as in a Penny Dreadful Thriller), Richard arrived just in time to overthrow Comnenus, and declare himself King of Cyprus. Joanna firmly told her brother Richard that he could delay no longer in marrying Berengaria—to postpone further would irreparably damage her reputation. The Archbishop of Cyprus finally married reluctant Richard to patient Berengaria on May 12, 1191. The archbishop also declared them King and Queen of Cyprus.

Richard and Berengaria were at last properly married. However, just at that moment, word came from Antioch that Frederick Barbarossa had died by drowning in chest-high water in the Saleph River in the German army's approach to Antioch in Turkey. Barbarossa was dressed in full armor when his horse shied, and he was thrown into the river. No vassals were on hand to help him rise from the shallow water; so he drowned: in a manner of speaking, his protective armor 'done him in.' Barbarossa's German Army originally consisted of twenty thousand armed nights, and five times more aids and noncombatant camp followers. In all, less than five thousand Germans survived.

Clearly, Richard was urgently needed in Antioch. With admirable haste, King Richard's entire English and French party hastened from Cyprus to the Levant to join Philip Augustus of France and Leopold of Austria who waited for King Richard I in Antioch. The siege of Acre soon followed, and was the first real victory for the Armies of God. After the city fell, thousands of its inhabitants were massacred in the name of *The Prince of Peace*. By so doing, Christianity earned the undying hatred of Islam.

Dysentery and typhoid have defeated more armies than battles. So it was, too, with the Third Crusade, where thousands succumbed to pestilence of all kinds. King Philip of France was stricken, but he survived.

Philip returned to France only a few weeks after the fall of Acre in 1191. Berengaria and Joanna lingered on in a Saracen palace in ravaged Acre for several months. Finally, Richard ordered both women to return to France in September 1192. Berengaria and Joanna stopped briefly in Rome, Marseilles, and Provence, before they finally arrived in Paris shortly before Christmas 1192.

Berengaria took permanent residence in France: first at Poitiers in Aquitaine, later at Chinon and Le Mans in Anjou. While Berengaria waited for Richard's return, she diligently worked to raise money for his battles in Palestine. Aside from that scrap of information, Berengaria vanished from historic records for five years.

Richard and his dwindling troops continued from Acre, to Jaffa, and then to Jerusalem. He won a few small victories, but Sultan Saladin outmaneuvered him. He never permitted King Richard's Crusaders to win a decisive battle. Richard once saw domes in distant Jerusalem, but realized his war could never be won. Late in 1192, the Third Crusade inconclusively flickered out.

Richard decided to return to England overland through Italy, Austria, Germany, and Normandy. He traveled in disguise as a peasant, and reached the Danube before he was recognized for openly wearing his fabulous jeweled coronation ring.

King Leopold of Austria had been Richard's companion in arms in the Third Crusade only a few months before, but he captured Richard, and secretly imprisoned him at Dürnstein Castle on the Danube. Leopold later traded Richard to Emperor Henry IV of the Holy Roman Empire, who held Richard captive for two years. Finally, Richard was ransomed by England, and released in February 1194. Richard returned from Germany to England for his second English coronation at Winchester Cathedral on April 16, 1164. Eleanor had the place of high honor at the coronation. Berengaria was not invited to attend, even though she was available at Chinon in central France.

Richard remained in England only a few weeks after his second coronation before returning to France. He never set foot in England again, but he delegated regent authority for government in England to his mother Eleanor of Aquitaine, and to Hubert de Walter. In Normandy, Richard resumed war with Philip Augustus in France. That conflict continued to the end of Richard's reign in 1199.

In the remaining five years of his reign, Richard only rarely saw or communicated with Berengaria. Richard never seemed to have time or inclination to enjoy her company. To the contrary, it is said that Richard "disported himself with evil companions" such that Pope Celestine III dispatched a monk to chastise and warn Richard, saying, "Remember the destruction of Sodom, and abstain from illicit acts . . . mend your ways, and return to your queen." In compliance, Richard spent Christmas with Berengaria at Poitiers in 1195. After that brief encounter, Richard was off again for more battles with Philip Augustus. It is probable that he never saw his wife after 1195.

Richard died at age 42 on April 6, 1199 from blood poisoning after receiving a minor wound. His mother Eleanor of Aquitaine attended him when he died, and organized his funeral at the Plantagenet vault in the Fontevraud Abbey near Chinon in Anjou. Berengaria was less than a half-day ride away in Angers, but was not invited to be present or take part in last rites for her husband.

After King Richard's death, Dowager Queen Berengaria faced difficult times that amounted to abject poverty. Her pension as Dowager Queen of England was not paid during the seventeen year reign of King John (1199-1116), which followed the reign of his brother Richard I. Berengaria never set foot in England while she was Queen of England, but she traveled to London more than once as Dowager Queen. Even so, she had no success in collecting her pension. Instead, King John claimed all her dower properties in England for himself, which denied Berengaria even a place to stay when she was in England.

Berengaria, with no one to defend her, fared little better in France. She retired to a shabby castle on the outskirts of Le Mans in Maine. Previously, she had many land holdings in Normandy, Anjou, and Maine, but Philip II Augustus of France declared them all spoils of war from his endless conflict with King Richard. Philip let Berengaria retain title only to tiny Abbaye de l'Epau, which was in a rundown suburb of Le Mans. She lived in poverty at the abbey for almost three decades until King John died in 1216. Circumstances improved for chronically neglected and impoverished Berengaria, when King John's ten year old son Henry III came to the throne in England in 1216. He honored England's responsibilities to its former queen. From 1220 until her death in 1230, Berengaria regularly received her Dowager Queen pension that transformed her into a woman of means.

With her new wealth, Berengaria became benefactress of the Cistercian Order in Le Mans. She joined it as a novice, and became a nun in its convent. Her generous donations paid for rebuilding the Abbaye de l'Epau. The abbey was near completion at close of Berengaria's life on December 23, 1230. Berengaria was buried there, and her grave is marked:

La Dame Abbess de l'Epau

The abbey still exists, but the tomb and skeleton thought to be Berengaria's, were moved to St. Julien Cathedral in Le Mans in the 19th century. On the Le Mans tomb is an effigy described by one observer as representing "a veiled young woman, not of great beauty, with unbound hair befitting a bride, but not of a wife or widow, and wearing a jeweled crown, and flowing gown caught up with a rich girdle."

The few known facts about Berengaria of Navarre raise questions: What was the real nature of her marriage to Richard the Lionheart? What was the basis for Richard the Lionheart's indifference to Berengaria? Does the effigy on her tomb show the real face and appearance of Berengaria?

The simple fact is that Berengaria was chosen by Eleanor of Aquitaine to be the wife of her son Richard the Lionheart. Berengaria married Richard in 1191, when he was thirty-six, and she was in around twenty-two years-of-age. Judged against custom of the time, their marriage came surprisingly late in life for them both. Royal and noble first weddings in the Middle Ages usually came in one's middle teens, to assure production of several heirs (preferably male warriors), who would continue the dynastic estate. Richard and Berengaria's marriage lasted eight years, until King Richard's death in 1199. Even though she had many remaining potential childbearing years, Berengaria did not marry again, and she had no recorded children or stillbirths. This suggests that Berengaria possibly was barren.

However, it is also possible that her marriage to Richard was never consummated. Incredible as that may be, it may be true. Before and during their entire marriage, Richard showed only disinterested unconcern for Berengaria. Many historians conclude that Richard's indifference to his wife signifies that the Lionheart had a deviant sexual orientation. Documented records of Richard's adolescent infatuation and behavior also suggest that he may have had an underlying homosexual attraction for young Prince

Philip Augustus of France, when the two princes were teenage friends in the French court in Paris. A similar innuendo is offered for adult King Richard's very close bond of friendship during the Third Crusade with his squire, the minstrel Blondel. Blondel is credited with discovering the location of Richard when he was imprisoned by Leopold of Austria at impregnable Schloss Dürnstein, located high above the Danube before the raging river leaves the Wachau (Nibelungengau) Gorge, and begins its quiet meander across the eastern plain to Vienna. However, that fog of gay gossip conflicts with Richard having at least one, and possibly two, illegitimate offspring, so a reasonable assumption is that Richard probably was of ambivalent bisexual orientation.

Yet, the most obvious explanation for Richard's persistent neglect of a husband's marital duties is never mentioned. The simple truth probably was that Richard and Berengaria may have been incompatible. Many maxims refer to mysteries underlying personal choice in mates: *there is no accounting for taste; love sees imperfect as perfect; one never understands what he/she sees in her/him—et ad infinitum.*

Richard and Berengaria's marriage was arranged, and was not a union of personal choice. It is not a stretch of imagination to suppose that Richard may simply have reacted strongly against Berengaria's manners and appearance. History gives us Richard—*a six-foot tall blond blue-eyed charmer*, who is presented with Berengaria—*a small bride of Mediterranean coloring, with black hair and eyes.* Contrary to notoriously flawed popular wisdom, opposites do not always attract one another; more often, *like attracts like*. How many times does the simple statement, "Sorry, she/he is just not my type!" frustrate matchmakers?

Therefore, the lack of cohabitation by Richard and Berengaria might be attributed to the lack of attraction of one to the other. Yet, a dislike for his wife would need to be exceedingly strong (to be an aversion bordering on revulsion) for Richard to forgo all prospect of having a legitimate heir of his own to inherit his crown and titles. The desire for an heir, or heirs, compels men of any sexual persuasion, gay, or straight, to marry and have children of their own. Thus, all speculation about causes for the estrangement between Richard and Berengaria will continue to challenge imagination and remain uncertain.

As a historical personality, Berengaria of Navarre is one of the least clearly visualized queens in English history. She left little mark on colorful events of her time. She lived among persons who, unquestionably, were among England's best remembered personalities: Richard the Lionheart and Eleanor of Aquitaine. Berengaria also was present at many historical events that have been thoroughly documented. Yet, she played one of the least recorded roles in history.

Where facts are few, speculation abounds. That applies to Queen Berengaria. Her main claim to fame now comes in occasional questions in crossword puzzles, and television quiz shows that ask: Who was the only English queen who never set foot in England?

Postscript: The story of Richard and Berengaria's marriage was fictionalized in an acclaimed successful 1935 film, *The Crusades*, which provided lengthy film footage that was later incorporated into a BBC series on English history in the 1960s. Neither the movie nor BBC television programs made claim for historical accuracy, but they certainly implied as much by not saying it really was just romantic fiction. The motion picture starred tall Nordic blue-eyed Loretta Young as Berengaria, and Caribbean swarthy hirsute Henry Wilcoxon as Richard the Lionheart—it was a classic example of what can be expected of a casting department's ability to turn history topsy-turvy—history records the Lionheart as a blond, and Berengaria as brunette.

Loretta Young was a breathtakingly lovely statuesque blond. She took pride in being remembered for her roles as Berengaria. One wonders: Should not Spanish petite brunette Berengaria also have a right to be remembered as looking like blond stately Nordic Loretta Young?

REIGN 7

KING JOHN

AND

FIRST WIFE JOAN OF GLOUCESTER

AND

QUEEN CONSORT ISABELLE

OF ANGOULÊME

Summary of the Reign of King John Lackland (Reign, 1199-1216)

King John: life dates 50 years, b. December 24, 1166-d. October 19, 1216; King of England 17 years, April 6, 1199-October 19, 1216.

KING JOHN was the youngest surviving son of King Henry II and Queen Eleanor of Aquitaine. John was born at Beaumont Palace, Oxford, in 1166. After the death of his brother King Richard the

Lionheart in 1199, John succeeded to the throne as King of England, Duke of Normandy, Duke of Brittany, and Count of Anjou and Maine. He reigned for seventeen years, until his death (possibly by poisoning) in 1216, and was buried in Worcester Cathedral.

King John was usually called John Lackland, because his father King Henry II failed to give any titled estate to his youngest son. Later, John was ridiculed by the name *John Softsword*, for his disastrously inept management of troops during his wars with France. As a child, John was a spoiled brat, and as king, he was one of the worst rulers in England's history. He was cruel, avaricious, capricious, deceitful, and unfair to everyone with whom he dealt. It is believed that he stabbed, with his own hand, his twelve year old nephew Arthur of Brittany, who by primogeniture should have inherited the crown on King Richard I the Lionheart's death.

King John's reign was a masterpiece of incompetent misrule. Everything he attempted was done poorly. He lost most of his French estates to King Philip II Augustus of France. He alienated his own English nobility, and was forced to sign *Magna Carta*, a document that severely limited powers of his crown. John alienated the Church so severely that Pope Innocent III excommunicated him, and placed an Interdict on all England, which denied Holy Sacraments to the entire realm. To lift the religious bans and to avoid Magna Carta, John paid homage to the Pope, which made all England a fief of Rome. This so angered his English nobility that they demanded John's abdication, but John refused. Civil war followed and English barons invited Prince Louis Capet (son of Philip II Augustus of France) to invade England. The civil rebellion forced John to leave London with the royal treasury. When John tried to cross a mud flat at the Wash, the wagon bearing the national treasure was lost in the North Sea on the incoming tide—none of the wealth was recovered—John was distressed by his loss, and collapsed. He was taken to Swinstead Abbey, where he died. King John may have been poisoned by mushroom soup served to him by one of the monks. Fortunately, everyone was absolved of King John's death, when Stephen Langton Archbishop of Canterbury reminded God, "*No one can be all bad who did King John in.*" King John was buried at Worcester Cathedral where his tomb and effigy remain.

King John's first marriage in 1189 to Joan (Isabel) of Gloucester was without issue. The marriage ended in annulment/divorce in 1199 on grounds of consanguinity. His second marriage to Queen Consort Isabella of Angoulême in 1200 produced five surviving children (2 sons and 3 daughters); the eldest son became Henry III. After John died in 1216, Isabella of Angoulême returned to France, and married Hugh de Lusignan et La Marche. They had nine surviving children, all were half-siblings of future King Henry III. Isabella died at age fifty-eight, and was buried at the Plantagenet mausoleum at Fontevrault Abbey, Rouen, France.

Following death of King John on October 19, 1216, his eldest son Prince Henry ascended the throne in 1216 as King Henry III.

Narrative of Joan (Isabel) of Gloucester First wife of John Lackland

Queen Joan (Isabel) Countess of Gloucester: life dates c. 43 years, b. 1170/1183-d. October 14, 1217; first wife of John Lackland (before he became King John) 10 years, August 29, 1189-annulled/divorced, 1199; Countess of Gloucester wife of Geoffrey de Mandeville 2nd Earl of Essex c. 3 years, January 23, 1214-c. 1216/17; wife of Hubert de Burgh 1st Earl of Kent 1 month, September 1217-October 14, 1217.

Joan (Isabel) Countess of Gloucester is also known by the given names: Isabel, Joanna, Hadwiga, Hawise, Avis, and Eleanor. In most historic references, she is called *Isabel of Gloucester*, but here the name, *Joan*, is used to avoid confusion, since King John's second queen was also named Isabelle: Isabelle of Angoulême.

JOAN OF Gloucester's parents were William FitzHenry 2nd Earl of Gloucester and Hawise de Beaumont of Leicester. Her father's holdings were among the greatest in England. Joan's date of birth is highly uncertain. It occurred sometime between 1170 and 1183. She was youngest of three daughters who had no surviving brothers. Thus, Joan was entitled to no more than one-third of her parent's estates, but even at that fraction, her anticipated inheritance was great. Joan's marriage to Prince John Lackland was arranged by his father King Henry II as a means of providing his youngest son with a suitable grand estate through marriage to one of the richest heiresses in England. Joan's two older sisters married well, and King Henry persuaded them to sell him their Gloucester shares, after which Henry transferred them to his son John. By this circuitous means, John Lackland gained the title, Earl of Gloucester.

Joan of Gloucester was the wife of John Lackland for ten years, but no children or stillbirths were recorded from it. The marriage was annulled/divorced by John only a few weeks after he became King John. Therefore, although Joan of Gloucester was the first wife of King John Lackland, she usually is not credited with ever having the status of Queen Consort of England; however, nominally, Joan was Queen Consort for a few weeks before the marriage ended with annulment approved by Pope Boniface VIII on grounds of consanguinity.

Joan and John were full second cousins by descent from their common great-grandfather, Henry I. John's grandmother was the Empress Matilda, the only legitimate surviving child of Henry I. Joan's grandfather was Robert FitzHenry the eldest bastard son of Henry I. Puzzling complications arise from uncertainty about Joan's date of birth. The marriage contract for Joan and John was agreed upon in 1174, but the marriage did not take place until fifteen years later in August 1189. Royal marriages usually were arranged at very young ages for political expediency. It is possible that Joan was married as a three or four year old child. If that were true, the marriage probably was not consummated until Joan had reached childbearing age in the last years of her marriage to John Lackland.

History is essentially silent on the subject of what John and Joan's domestic life was like in the ten years they were married. Their second cousin relationship was well known from the beginning, and was of no concern to anyone before John suddenly demanded separation and divorce almost immediately after his unanticipated coronation as King of England in May 1199. The religious grounds for their separation may have been that the Church originally approved the marriage between John and Joan without a right to have offspring, which would have been incestuous cohabitation. When one considers King John's grasping greedy nature, it is possible that he removed Joan to get a greater dowry from a richer new queen consort.

However, most likely of all, the hasty marriage annulment came because John suddenly became infatuated with beautiful young Isabelle of Angoulême who would become his second queen.

Typical of John Lackland's venal nature, he kept the title *Earl of Gloucester* after the annulment from Joan. He collected taxes from her Gloucester estates for almost fifteen years after their separation. His meanness of spirit prevented Joan from marrying again until early in 1214. King John refused permission for Joan to marry Geoffrey de Mandeville 2nd Earl of Essex until she gave him (King John) a bribe equal to her dower gift to her new groom.

Joan's second marriage lasted a little over two years before her second husband Geoffrey died late in 1216, or early in 1217. Joan's third marriage took place in September 1217 to Hubert de Burgh 1st Earl of Kent, but it ended only a month later by Joan's own death on October 14, 1217. She was buried at Canterbury Cathedral.

No children are recorded for any of Joan's three marriages. Little is known of the personal life of Joan (Isabel) of Gloucester in her second and third marriages. She appeared fictitiously (with her alternate name *Hawise*) in the tale of Robin *Hood*, which was written over a century later. Her walk-on role in English history is little remembered or recorded.

Narrative of Queen Consort Isabelle of Angoulême

Queen Isabelle of Angoulême: life dates c. 58 years, b. 1186/8-d. May 31, 1246; Queen Consort of King John 16 years, August 24, 1200-October 19, 1216; wife of Count Hugh X de Lusignan of La Marche c. 26/29 years, 1217/20-June 5, 1246.

ISABELLE OF ANGOULÊME was the only child of Aymer de Taillefer Count of Angoulême and Alix de Courtenay, a great-granddaughter of King Louis VI of France. Isabelle's date of birth is contested, and it falls between 1183 and 1188—the last of those years is most often cited. As Aymer's only child, Isabelle was destined to inherit the title to the County of Angoulême. Isabelle heiress of Angoulême was affianced at a very young age to Hugh de Lusignan, the heir to the adjacent independent County of La Marche. In anticipation of that marriage, Isabelle had been sent to La Marche to be educated in the court of Hugh's father Count Hugh

IX de Lusignan. Their union was favorably anticipated by the people of Angoulême and La Marche, but the marriage was frustrated when Isabelle accepted King John of England's proposal, and they were married on August 24, 1200 in Bordeaux, Gascony, about a year after John's marriage to his first wife, Joan (Isabel) of Gloucester was annulled.

Isabelle of Angoulême and King John were mismatched in age and temperament. Isabelle was about fourteen years old, and John was thirty-three. Everyone acknowledged Isabelle's great beauty. Throughout Europe, she was called the *Fair Maid of Angoulême*. Later French historians called her *Helen of the Middle Ages*. However, English chronicles refer to Queen Isabelle of Angoulême as the *Jezebel of England*.

John Lackland probably met Isabelle for the first time in May 1199, shortly after his coronation as King of England. All reports say that he was immediately smitten with Isabelle's youthful loveliness. His infatuation was total, and he was besotted with passion to possess her. Questionable accounts say that John physically abducted Isabelle, and spirited her away to Bordeaux, where they were married on August 24, 1200. She was crowned Queen of England at Westminster Abbey later that year.

Little is known of Isabelle's own feelings at the time of her whirlwind courtship and marriage to John Lackland. She may have been dazzled with the thought of being Queen of England, but she probably was underwhelmed with the thought of John as her husband. A contemporary described John as "small of stature, with the appearance of a toad, and the nature of a weasel." Isabelle probably made comparison between middle aged King John and her former fiancé, seventeen year old Hugh de Lusignan, and arrived at conclusions unfavorable to John.

The domestic life of King John and Queen Isabelle was characterized by mutual infidelity, distrust, dislike, and contempt. It is understatement to describe their marriage as a dysfunctional tempestuous failure. However, the sixteen-year marriage of King John to Isabelle of Angoulême produced five children (2 sons and 3 daughters):

> Henry of Winchester (October 1, 1207-November 16, 1272),
> > later King Henry III of England)
> Richard Earl of Cornwall (January 5, 1209-April 2, 1272), later
> > King of Germany and Holy Roman Emperor
> Joan Queen of Scots (July 22, 1210-March 4, 1238)

Isabelle Empress of the Holy Roman Empire (1214?-December
1, 1241)
Eleanor Countess of Pembroke (1215?-April 13, 1375)
In addition: King John was the father of a dozen known
bastards.

Lives of the royal children were exemplary, but their parent's domestic life
was deplorable. John and Isabelle had volatile violent tempers. Both had
been spoiled as the favorite child of wealthy powerful parents. Both were
strong-willed, and accustomed to having their own way in everything.
Neither of them could bear contradiction or opposition. John's ingrained
qualities of deceit, greed, cruelty, vindictiveness, and a total lack of concern
for feelings of others made him the least liked of all English kings. Both
John and Isabelle were strongly sexed, promiscuous, and indiscrete. On
one occasion, John executed a lover of Isabelle, and hanged his body over
her bed as a warning for her to be more circumspect in future behavior.
Finally, in 1214, John imprisoned Isabelle, and she remained in detention
until his death two years later.

King John's feckless reign approached its end with the nation in
rebellion. He was humiliated in the summer of 1215 when his nobles
forced him to sign *Magna Carta*. The Charter stripped him of a monarch's
absolute power, and led to civil war. Mercenaries from France soon invaded
the counties of Kent and Essex, and they were bent on making England a
province of France.

When King John died on October 18, 1216, his ten year old son Prince
Henry became King Henry III. He inherited a bankrupt nation mortally
threatened by civil and foreign wars. Immediately after King John died,
Queen Isabelle was released from prison on orders of the new king her
son. She was present when her son was crowned in Gloucester on October
28, 1216. King John had lost the royal treasury shortly before his death;
therefore, Isabelle's own gold crown was used in the coronation of her son.
The regency headed by William the Marshall Earl of Pembroke ruled the
child-king's government. The Marshall drove the defeated French out of
England, and restored order by 1220.

Isabelle was less than thirty years old, when her eldest son Henry
was crowned King of England in 1216. A year later, Isabelle's childhood
fiancé Count Hugh X de Lusignan et La Marche, came to England. Hugh
and Isabella were married in May 1217. Isabelle and Hugh remained in

England until the political situation in England was again stable. They returned to France in 1220. Some accounts say that the English court accepted Isabelle's departure as good riddance, but other accounts imply that her departure was in response to a command for her exile. Whatever her reason may have been for leaving, she never returned to England.

When Isabelle returned to France with her husband Hugh de Lusignan, she was Dowager Queen of England and Countess de La Marche et Angoulême. She was thirty-two or thirty-three years old, and was still a very handsome woman. However, by that time her former county of Angoulême in France was no longer independent. Angoulême was now a fief of Philip II Augustus the King of France who had confiscated it, along with all other properties in France formerly claimed by King John: namely, Brittany, Normandy, Anjou, Maine, Touraine, Poitou, Limosine—even Aquitaine, which King Philip Augustus gobbled up immediately after Queen Eleanor of Aquitaine died in 1204.

Almost everything of the French domain of Henry Plantagenet and Eleanor of Aquitaine was now in French hands; Gascony alone in southernmost France remained under English control.

Hugh and Isabelle returned to Charroux the capital of La Marche, and lived out nineteen years of married life there. Their union was a romantic conclusion to a standard love story—*boy meets girl; boy loses girl; boy gets girl; they live happily ever after*. All indications suggest that Isabelle and Hugh were sincerely in love, and that Isabelle was a discrete faithful wife. They had nine surviving children (some reports say eleven, 5 sons and 4 daughters):

> Hugh XI de Lusignan (1221-1250), Count of La Marche
> Aymer de Valence (1222-1260), Bishop of Winchester
> Agnes se Lusignan (1224-1269), Countess of Surrey
> Guy de Lusignan (1225-1264)
> Geoffrey de Lusignan (1226-1274)
> William de Valelnce (1228-1296). Earl of Pembroke
> Marguerite de Lusignan (1229-1288)
> Isabella de Lusignan (1234-1250)

Toward the end of Isabelle's life, she was accused of treasonous plotting against King Louis IX of France (later canonized as Saint Louis). The nature of her plotting may have been associated with the Cathars, an aberrant Christian sect that was persecuted in southern France around that time. Whatever the cause of her treason or heresy may have been, Isabelle sought sanctuary in the Abbey of Fontevraud near Chinon in Anjou in 1244. She remained there for two years until her death on May 31, 1246.

During the last year of her life, Isabelle was deeply depressed about her many youthful indiscretions. On her deathbed as her penance for sins she had committed in life, she insisted on burial in a common grave outside the Abbey. Years later during a visit to the traditional Plantagenet mausoleum at Fontevrault, her son Henry III learned of his mother's common grave. He requested that her remains be moved for burial inside the mausoleum to a suitable tomb placed near those of his uncle Richard the Lionheart, and his grandparents Henry Plantagenet and Eleanor of Aquitaine. Finally at peace, Queen Isabelle of Angoulême still lies there in the Plantagenet mausoleum.

Epilogue on Isabelle of Angoulême: The closing page to Isabelle's life bears on her children with Hugh de Lusignan. The estate she and Hugh possessed in La Marche was far too small to provide suitable livelihood for their nine surviving children who were half-siblings of King Henry III of England. He willingly accepted responsibility to be their benefactor. Their eldest son Hugh in 1249 inherited his fathers titles, and became Hugh XI de Lusignan Count de La Marche et Angoulême, and he remained in France. His remaining eight siblings moved to England in search of fortune from their half-brother, King Henry III. Henry greeted them with extravagant gifts of property and noble titles. The English nobility rebelled against King Henry's lavish nepotism, and a civil war called the *Simon de Montfort Rebellion* almost cost Henry III his throne.

Consequences for England
of King John's Marriage to
Isabelle of Angoulême

KING JOHN paid dearly in gratifying his passion for the 'Fair Maid of Angoulême,' His marriage to her set in motions a chain of events that, in less than four years, robbed England of all its French estates, save Gascony. Angoulême was a small independent region in France, which was almost surrounded by Aquitaine. Only a narrow corridor to the northeast of Angoulême abutted on the county of La Marche. La Marche was a fief of the King of France, and it served France as an important armed border state that opposed Aquitaine.

Dowager Queen Eleanor of Aquitaine opposed all moves by Angoulême to increase its alliance with France. Eleanor viewed with alarm discovery that Isabelle, heiress of Angoulême, was affianced at a very young age to marry Hugh de Lusignan, heir to the independent and potentially threatening county of La Marche. Isabelle heiress of Angoulême as a small child had been sent to La Marche to be educated in its court. Hugh de Lusignan was about five years older than Isabelle. The two children had been reared together in anticipation of their eventual marriage at a suitable age.

King John Lackland's interference blocked the Angoulême-La Marche marriage contract, which would have united the noble families and lands of Angoulême and La Marche. This infuriated the fathers of the children. Count Aymer de Taillefer of Angoulême and Count Hugh IX de Lusignan of La Marche petitioned King Philip II Augustus of France for redress for King John's insulting illegal breach of their prior marriage contract.

King John, who was also the Duke of Normandy, was therefore a vassal of the King of France. As such, he was required to get prior permission from the French King to wed a titled heiress of France. Philip Augustus ordered John to appear before the French court, to answer for his calumny, but John steadfastly refused to go to Paris. King John's impulsive marriage to Isabelle of Angoulême had ignored important feudal etiquette.

Philip Augustus was jubilant. He quickly acted under feudal law to reclaim, all lands ruled by John who was Duke of Normandy, Duke of Brittany, and Count of Poitou. Philip declared John Lackland's estates in France to be forfeit. Normandy, Brittany, and all Aquitaine except Gascony in southernmost France were confiscated as property of the French crown. In an instant, Philip's French estates doubled in size. Philip's diplomatic coup was a source of national pride that united all nobility of France against England.

France and England immediately declared war, but King John had no military ability. By 1204, King John lost English holdings in France that had been part of the Plantagenet Empire ruled by his father Henry II, and brother, Richard I. Only Gascony in southern France remained in English hands. As his brother Richard the Lionheart once said, "My brother John Lackland is not made of the stuff to conquer nations, and create a kingdom.

REIGN 8

KING HENRY III

AND

QUEEN CONSORT ELEANOR

OF PROVENCE

Summary of the Reign of Henry III
(Reign 1216-1272)

King Henry III: life dates 65 years, b. October 1, 1207-d. November 16, 1272; King of England 56 years, October 18/19, 1216-November 16, 1272.

DURING HIS life, King Henry III was known as Henry of Winchester, but he is better remembered in history as, *Henry the Builder.* He was the eldest son of King John and Isabella of Angoulême, and was born at Winchester Castle, Hampshire in 1207. As a barely ten year old lad, he succeeded to the throne under exceedingly precarious conditions following the death of his father King John in 1216. Civil war divided the realm; France had invaded England; half of the rebellious nobility of England had defected, and supported the invaders; the Scots and Welch attacked the Midlands; mercenaries hired by King John demanded pay, and the royal treasury was bare.

Until the king reached age seventeen, rule of the realm was under regents appointed by nobles. The first and most important of them was William the Marshall, the greatest knight of the Middle Ages. Many English nobles had defected to support the French invasion of England. The Marshall's first acts were to reissue Magna Carta, and promise amnesty to all nobles, if they would swear fealty to King Henry III. He then superbly led English forces against the French, and successfully drove them out of England in less than two years.

Henry III began his personal rule in 1224 when he was seventeen, but affairs of State under Henry rapidly deteriorated. King Henry III was a reckless spendthrift, and his main fault lay in poor judgment about use of limited available resources. He placed great value on his reputation for being the most generous prince in Christendom. He pushed the realm into bankruptcy. Finally, in 1258, the English nobility refused to pay the taxes needed to fund Henry's many costly projects.

Simon de Montfort, a brother-in-law of the king, organized the English noblemen in opposition to the king. De Montfort captured, imprisoned the king, and usurped royal power. He called an assembly of the barons, which is known as the *First Great Council*. Its membership consisted of representative nobles and landed gentry. The Council met at Oxford, and passed *The Provisions of Oxford* in 1258, a document second only to Magna Carta as a landmark event in the evolution of English Common Law. The Great Council ordered King Henry and his son Crown Prince Edward to sign its Provisions, which re-stated the limits that Magna Carta had placed on the monarch's powers, but it also required the king to call periodic Councils comprised of nobility and elected land-owing gentry chosen from throughout the land. Later Councils would have power to approve all new laws on assessment of taxes, on the transfer of ownership of property, and on administration of justice. The Provisions of Oxford is the document that first set in motion representative parliamentary procedures for government in England. Although subsequent Great Councils were held during the reign of King Henry III, they came during the regency of Prince Edward, who correctly receives the honor of creating the parliamentary system of government in England.

King Henry III was a weak ineffectual king, but he must be credited with having a refined taste in art and architecture. At huge national expense, Henry employed hundreds of builders and stone cutters to repair, improve, and preserve the best of English Gothic architecture, including the cathedrals at Wells, Lincoln, Peterborough, Winchester, and Salisbury, which were rebuilt, repaired, or enlarged during his reign. Westminster Abbey was rebuilt after it burned down, and was neglected during King John's reign. For these services to the realm, he is known as *Henry the Builder*. Henry was a scholarly, generous, well-intentioned aesthete. His profound concern for literacy and learning is seen in the charters he gave for founding Oxford and Cambridge Universities.

Henry married his Queen Consort Eleanor of Provence in 1236. They had four surviving children. Their eldest son Edward Longshanks served as regent during his father's final years, and he became King Edward I after his father's death in 1272.

Henry III died after a reign of 56 years. His was the fourth longest reign in English history. The length of his reign is surpassed only by reigns of King George III, Queen Victoria, and Queen Elizabeth II. Henry III was buried in the recently restored Westminster Abbey beside his patron saint Edward the Confessor. His Queen Eleanor lived until June 21, 1291, and was buried at ancient Almesbury Abbey, Wiltshire: a favored burial place of Saxon kings.

Following the death of King Henry III, his eldest son, Prince Edward Longshanks, ascended the throne in 1272 as King Edward I.

Narrative of Queen Consort Eleanor of Provence

Queen Eleanor of Provence: life dates c. 68 years, b. 1223-d. June 26, 1291; Queen Consort of Henry III 36 years, January 14, 1236-November 16, 1272; Dowager Queen of England 19 years, November 16, 1272-June 26, 1291.

ELEANOR OF Provence was a daughter of Count Raimond de Berenger IV of Provence and Countess Beatrix de Savoy. Eleanor probably was born in 1223 in Aix-en-Provence in southern France, where the presence of hot springs had made it a favorite vacation spa since Roman times. Eleanor was the second of four sisters, all of whom became queens by marriage: Queen Marguerite married King Louis IX of France; Queen Eleanor married King Henry III of England; Queen Sanchia married Henry's brother Richard Emperor of the Holy Roman Empire; Queen Beatrice married King Charles I of Sicily.

In 1236, Eleanor married Henry III, the son of King John Lackland of England and Isabelle of Angoulême. The marriage was diplomatically arranged, and it is almost certain that Eleanor and Henry had not met before their wedding took place at Canterbury Cathedral on January 14, 1236. She was crowned queen six days later in Westminster Abbey on January 20, 1236.

In 1236, Eleanor probably was between twelve and fourteen years old and Henry was twenty-nine. Henry was of stocky medium build, and probably was not over five feet seven inches tall. No description exists of Eleanor, except that she was often described as beautiful, or 'exceeding fair.' That, however, explains little, since queens always set standards of fashion for their age, and they regularly got high marks for their appearance. However, the probability that Eleanor was truly beautiful is supported by the fact that several accounts remark on the exceptional beauty of all four daughters of handsome Count Raimond de Berenger, and of the great beauty of their mother Beatrix de Savoy. True beauty of the Provençal sisters would help to account for Count Raimond's extraordinary success in marrying his four daughters to kings.

Eleanor of Provence's first responsibility as Queen of England was to bear male children, and thereby to assure perpetuation of the royal

Plantagenet dynasty. She accomplished that with the birth of Edward Longshanks in 1239. Motherhood greatly strengthened King Henry's affections for Queen Eleanor, and amplified her status in court. Eleanor and Henry III were an affectionate royal couple, and totally devoted to their children. They had nine children, of whom four survived to maturity:

> Edward Longshanks, King Edward I of England (June 17, 1239-July 7, 1307)
> Margaret Queen of Scots (September 29, 1240-February 26, 1275)
> Beatrice Duchess of Brittany (June 25, 1242-March 24, 1275)
> Edmund Crouchback Duke of Lancaster (January 16, 1245-June 5, 1296)

> Note: it is incorrect to think that *crouchback* had reference to a physical deformity. In idiomatic Middle English, the term *crouchback* was derived from Latin 'crux,' meaning that Edmund had been on Crusade; therefore, he was entitled to wear *The Cross* on his back. Edmund Crouchback was the father of Dukes Thomas and Henry of Lancaster, the brothers who played central roles in future reigns of Edward II and Edward III.

Queen Eleanor and her husband King Henry III had a strong sense of personal loyalty to their respective blood-relatives. His family loyalty would be the underlying cause for major problems Henry met in his long reign of fifty-six years (1216-1272).

It is recalled that after Henry's father, John Lackland, died in 1216, Henry's mother Isabelle of Angoulême returned to France and secondly married Hugh X de Lusignan the Count of La Marche. They had at least nine surviving offspring, all were half-siblings of King Henry III. *Lusignans* is the collective name given to these Louisgnan-Angoulême relatives of the king. Eight of King Henry's Lusignan half-brothers and sisters immigrated to England in expectation of enrichment from their half-brother's generosity. All were welcomed, and several received noble titles or positions of power: William de Valence was created Earl of Pembroke, and Aymer de Valence became Bishop of Winchester. They were exceedingly unpopular with the English nobility for preempting positions of power and influence in court.

When Queen Eleanor of Provence arrived in England, she observed the favors King Henry had given to his Lusignan relatives. She invited her Savoy relatives to come to England to seek wealth and honored positions in her husband's court. Henry could not deny his queen's requests. Her impecunious French relatives became known in England as the *Savoyards*. King Henry showered them with wealth and positions: Peter de Savoy was made Earl of Richmond, and Boniface de Savoy was appointed Archbishop of Canterbury.

King Henry and Queen Eleanor were of very different temperament. Henry was devout, easygoing, and he wanted to please everyone. In particular, he was generous to a fault to his own, and to his wife's relatives. In contrast to her husband, Eleanor was strong-willed aggressive, and bent on accumulating as much wealth, position, and power for herself as was possible. However, Eleanor depended on Henry's favor, because she had no wealth or power of her own. She assiduously cultivated Henry's affection, and usually was able to control the course of their lives. Everything Queen Eleanor undertook displayed wasteful ostentation, or a total lack of concern for the public good of England. In addition to exhibiting unparalleled greed, she openly held England in contempt as a country of bumpkins and yokels without culture.

Queen Eleanor ingratiated her status with King Henry by encouraging him in his plans for grand scale building, and renovation of castles and cathedrals throughout England. Among his many architectural triumphs of building in stone were Salisbury Cathedral, and the restoration of Westminster Abbey, which had burned during his father's reign. He also authorized additions to the Tower of London, Windsor Castle, and the royal Palace of Westminster.

Eleanor was a domineering woman, but Henry had faith in her loyalty, and great respect for her managerial ability. This was made abundantly clear by Henry naming Eleanor in his will as keeper of crown wealth and castles in trust for their children. Henry also appointed Eleanor regent during his absence to France in 1253 until 1254. Eleanor honored the trust Henry placed in her, and she worked tirelessly for his best interests. However, Eleanor unwisely, encouraged him to defy restrictions placed on his royal prerogative by Magna Carta. He suffered oppositions from the barons when he openly opposed restraints on his royal authority that had been firmly established in English legal president since the reign of Henry Plantagenet.

In the years 1254 to 1258, the king and queen's Lusignan and Savoyard relatives endlessly bickered and squabbled, as they competed for personal gain with no concern for wellbeing of the realm. Native English nobles became ever more enraged by rampant court nepotism. They blamed the king for soaring taxes levied to support the host of pushy obnoxious foreign relatives of the king and queen.

The barons charged the king's commissioners with embezzlement, and mismanagement of national affairs. They railed that their right to positions of power and wealth had been usurped by a host of contemptuous incompetent foreigners. Open hostility in 1258 led the barons to force Henry to sign the Provisions of Oxford. It made King Henry surrender his independent power to create taxes. Taxes in the future would require approval by a 'King's Council' of fifteen elected peers, who would meet three times a year to review, and approve government policies: namely, to give approval for public appointments, to approve use of taxes, and for administration of crown properties. The English lords showed intense irritation for the greedy squabbling of Lusignan-Savoyard interlopers by adding a new law that prevented the king from making any government appointments to foreigners without prior approval by the King's Council made up of English lords. The Provisions of Oxford set in motion events that eventually led to the British parliamentary form of government known today.

Finally, in 1264, the English nobility openly opposed the crown in the *Simon de Montfort Rebellion,* also called the *Second Baron's War,* or *Revolt of the Barons* of 1264-1265 (cf., the First Baron's War of 1215-1217 forced King John to sign Magna Carta).

Simon de Montfort VI Earl of Leicester was a brother-in-law of King Henry III. Throughout the de Montfort revolt, Queen Eleanor gave loyal support to her husband by raising funds for hiring French mercenaries to fight against insurgent forces led by Simon de Montfort. However, this effort by the queen was of little service, because the troops she gathered never arrived in England. Early in the controversy, the King and Crown Prince Edward were captured at the Battle of Lewes (1264), and held under house arrest as prisoners, first, at Wallingford, and later, at Kenilworth Castle. Tables were turned a year later at the Battle of Eversham (August 4, 1265). In that battle, Simon de Montfort was defeated, and killed through excellent leadership on the field of battle by Prince Edward Longshanks. King Henry III was not a man of war. His imprisonment during the Revolt of the Barons permanently impaired his ability to rule. After the Battle of Eversham, Crown Prince Edward served as regent vested with powers of the king until Henry III died in 1272.

Eleanor was a strong-willed decisive woman who never shied from advising her husband Henry III on matters of State. During Prince Edward's regency (1265-1272), Dowager Queen Mother Eleanor tried to control her favorite son, but Prince Edward steadily moved to distance himself from his mother's influence, and from tribal goals of his mother's Savoyard relatives. Although, Prince Edward rebelled against interference of his mother and her family, he recognized her abilities and loyal efforts to preserve his royal rights during the de Montfort struggle. The mother and son always remained on civil terms, even though disagreement often divided their personal desires. When conflict of interest came between them, Queen Eleanor of Provence's family loyalties always kept her Savoyard relatives foremost in mind, whereas Prince Edward consistently tended to favor his father's Lusignan family.

During much of her reign as Queen Consort of Henry III, Eleanor was thoroughly hated by her English subjects. It is even reported that common Londoners once showed their dislike for her, and their lack of respect for their queen by throwing foul refuse on her barge as it passed under London Bridge. However, as she gradually faded from public attention as dowager queen, public opinion improved greatly for Eleanor during her retirement years at Amesbury Abbey. Through it all, she retained cordial relationships with her children. She also took responsibility for rearing her grandchildren: namely, the children of Edward I and of his brother, Edmund Crouchback. On occasion, her son King Edward I even invited her opinion on matters of State.

Dowager Queen Eleanor's importance in government waned to extinction after Prince Edward Longshanks became king in his own right in 1272. Dowager Queen Eleanor retired to, or was ordered to enter the convent in Amesbury Abbey near Salisbury. Eleanor survived her husband King Henry III by almost twenty years. In her last six years, she was "a humble nun at the Benedictine Convent of Amesbury." In retirement after 1284, Eleanor guarded her dowager queen rights, and retained full control of her dower estates. Thus, it may be assumed that she did not immediately take religious vows to become a nun after entering Amesbury

Abbey. Like Henry III, Eleanor became a follower in the *Cult of Edward the Confessor*, and a patron of the Franciscan friars who supported that belief. In her last years, Eleanor was much admired for piety, modesty of dress, and for donations in support of convents and abbeys.

Eleanor of Provence died in her late sixties on June 24, 1291, at Amesbury Abbey where she was buried. She is now almost forgotten. She was a strong, forceful, competent woman of many parts—a credit to her sex—a proper helpmate, and consort of a king. Eleanor was noted for extensive correspondence (nearly 300 of her letters, notes, and records exist) with friends, family, and persons of political importance in foreign lands. She often wrote to her sister, Queen Marguerite of France. Many of her notes and letters deal only with mundane domestic, financial, or political transactions, but they also are evidence of a shrewd mind capable of juggling many ideas, comprehending them, and recognizing their practical applications.

A part of her existing correspondence includes an exchange of letters with Robert Grosseteste Bishop of London (the First Chancellor of Oxford University newly chartered in 1214). Grosseteste is notable for being the first humanist scholar to bring the philosophy of Aristotelian rationalism, and knowledge of Arabic mathematics to the attention of Western Europe. He is most honored in secular learning for anticipating the Renaissance by his aphorism that gave legitimacy to secular scientific study, namely:

Invoke miracles only if there is no other possible natural explanation for a phenomenon.

For Eleanor to have been in correspondence with Grosseteste (albeit only on matters of religion and faith) points to intelligence and awareness of intellectual matters of unusual depth for any person at that time, and even more so for a woman of power and royal status. The life of Eleanor of Provence is illuminating on the way a woman in the Middle Ages played a significant role in events of her time.

REIGN 9

KING EDWARD I

AND

QUEEN CONSORT ELEANOR
OF CASTILE

AND

QUEEN CONSORT MARGUERITE
OF FRANCE

Summary of the Reign of King Edward I
(Reign 1272-1307)

King Edward I: life dates 68 years, b. June 17, 1239-d. July 7,
1307; King of England 35 years, November 16, 1272-July 7,
1307.

KING EDWARD I, the eldest son of Henry III and Eleanor of Provence, was born at Westminster Palace. He was named for his father's patron saint the Saxon King Edward the Confessor. Prince Edward was over six feet tall, and as a young man he was called *Edward Longshanks*, he referred to himself as *The Hammer of Scotland,* but history remembers him as *The Lawgiver.* A contemporary in arms said of Edward, "In youth his hair was silvery blond, while in old age it became a magnificent swan-like white. His forehead was broad, and the rest of his features were regular . . . His long arms were in proportion to his supple body. No man was ever endowed with greater muscular strength for wielding a sword . . . and the length of his legs ensured that he was never dislodged from his seat by the gallop and jumping of his horse."

Edward I was called *The Lawgiver* for creating the first true English Parliament. For it, he ordered that Native English (not Norman French) be spoken in courts of law and Parliament. From his order, 'The King's English' replaced Norman-French as the official language in England. 'The King's English' of Edward I was the Saxon-Norman French patois of Chaucer's Middle English.

When the Simon de Montfort's Rebellion broke out in 1265, the English nobility protested authority of King Henry III with open civil war. Prince Edward Longshanks was placed in command of the king's forces when he was a teenage youth barely seventeen years old. Early in the confrontation, de Montfort captured, and imprisoned King Henry III and Prince Edward Longshanks. While de Montfort was in control, he called an assembly of barons at Oxford, which is known as the *First Great Council.* Its membership consisted of representative nobles and landed gentry. The Council passed *The Provisions of Oxford* in 1258, which severely limited powers of the king. It stated that the king would be required to get approval from the Council before taxes could be levied, before monies were spent, before new laws were enacted, and before rules for justice were changed. The king and prince were required to sign the document.

Edward soon escaped, and he led the king's loyal troops to victory at the Battle of Eversham. De Montfort's opposing forces were decisively beaten, and Simon de Montfort was killed. Without de Montfort's leadership, the civil war ended. However, King Henry III was so traumatized by imprisonment during the civil war that his mind failed. Prince Edward became regent for the realm at the age of seventeen. He ruled for seven years as regent from 1265 until his father's death in 1272 before he became King Edward I.

Edward I is correctly given credit for initiating the English Parliamentary System to English government. Edward recognized merit in de Montfort's *Provisions of Oxford*, and adopted its methods for limiting the king's prerogatives by a representative government of elected nobility and landed gentry with power to approve/reject taxation and new rules of law. As regent, Prince Edward invited an assembly called the Great Council to meet at Marlborough in 1267. At the assembly, Edward reissued Magna Carta and announced that similar councils would meet often. They would have representation from the three levels of chivalry: namely, the *king's appointees, titled nobility,* and *landed gentry*. These representatives were antecedents respectively for the *Privy Council, House of Lords*, and *House of Commons.*

King Edward's administrative system also provided England with the first written framework for statutory law. Edward recognized that stability in government depended on honoring legal precedent. That is, laws must continue until amended or repealed. Edward decreed that the system of laws set forth by his great-grandfather Henry Plantagenet II would be the starting point for precedent in English Law.

Great councils were regular events during the reign of King Edward I. Thus, in spite of Simon de Montfort's personal defeat, his ideas for an elected democratic government live on in English and American representative forms of rule by law. King Henry Plantagenet II and King Edward Longshanks are co-authors for legal priority in English Common Law. The service of King Edward I to English Common Law justifies his name, *Edward the Lawgiver.*

Edward Longshanks was handsome, decisive, athletic, a gifted military tactician, and totally committed to justice for the common good of England. No picture or effigy of Edward I exists. Only word descriptions by contemporaries tell us that he was tall, handsome, athletic, and always in the prime of life, never in senile old age. He tirelessly tried but failed to unite England, Wales, and Scotland. Edward Longshanks was loved by his English subjects, but was hated by the Welsh and Scots.

Edward I reined a total of 35 years. He died at age 68 in 1307 while on campaign against Scotland. He is buried at Westminster Abbey. An inscription on his unadorned tomb reads, *Malleus Scotorum* (The Hammer of Scotland).

Prince Edward married Princess Eleanor of Castile when he was 15, and she was 10 years of age. They had sixteen children, most of them girls, but only one of their four sons survived childhood. He was Edward of Caernarvon who became King Edward II. Queen Eleanor of Castile died on November 28, 1290, and was buried in Westminster Abbey.

After Eleanor died, Edward I married his second Queen Consort, Marguerite of France in 1299. They had two sons and a daughter. Queen Marguerite outlived Edward for ten years. She died in 1318, and was buried at Greyfriars Church, London, which was destroyed by fire in 1666.

After the death of Edward I in 1307, his eldest surviving son Edward of Carnarvon succeeded as King Edward II.

Narrative of Queen Consort Eleanor of Castile

Queen Eleanor of Castile: life dates c. 49 years, b. 1241-d. November 28, 1290; first Queen Consort of Edward I c. 28 years, November 16, 1254-November 28, 1290.

ELEANOR OF CASTILE, was the second of five children of King Ferdinand III of Castile et León and his second wife Countess Jeanne of Ponthieu et Dammartin. Eleanor was born most likely at Burgos, Castile in 1241. Her Spanish name, *Leonora Infanta de Castile* is correct only in the broad sense when *infanta* is used in synonymy with *princess*—she was not heiress to her father's crown of Castile.

The marriage of Prince Edward Longshanks of England and Princess Eleanor of Castile was negotiated as part of a peace treaty that settled a border dispute between kings Henry III of England and Alfonso X of Castile over title to Gascony. Gascony, with its rich vineyard country surrounding the port city of Bordeaux, was the last English territory of any importance on the European Continent. When Castile attacked and tried to occupy Gascony in 1252, Henry III declared war on Castile. He sent thirteen year old Crown Prince Edward to Gascony for military instruction in arts of war. The desultory conflict lasted for two years until peace was restored in 1254 by a treaty approved by Alfonso X and Henry III.

In addition to settling border disputes, the treaty also authorized marriage between Henry's eldest son Edward Longshanks and Alfonso's half-sister, Eleanor of Castile. The treaty diplomatically transferred Castile's spurious claim for Gascony to England as part of Eleanor's dowry to Prince Edward. The treaty also approved a military alliance between England and Castile in the event of war with France.

It is unlikely that Edward ever met Eleanor of Castile before their wedding took place on November 16, 1254 at the Abbey de Santa Maria la Real de Las Huelgas in Burgos the capital of Castile. Edward was fifteen and Eleanor was ten years old, and the diplomatically arranged marriage was one of history's great matches of true affection and fidelity. Their marriage lasted for thirty-six years until Eleanor died in 1290. During that time, they were almost inseparable, and there is no evidence that Edward, as prince or king, was ever unfaithful to her.

Almost immediately after the wedding, Eleanor was sent to London for education in the court of Henry III. However, Prince Edward remained on police duty in Gascony for two more years before he returned to England at the age of eighteen in 1256. The couple did not live together as husband and wife until Eleanor reached fourteen, an age considered suitable for childbearing. However, her first child was not born until 1264 when she was twenty. Eleanor had a total of sixteen pregnancies and births (but only 5 daughters and 1 son (Edward of Caernarvon) reached maturity):

> Eleanor Countess of Bar (June 18, 1269-August 29, 1298)
> Joan of Acre Countess of Hertford (c. 1272-April 23, 1307)
> Margaret Duchess of Brabant (March 15, 1275-c. 1333)
> Mary of Woodstock (March 11/12, 1279-c. 1332)
> Elizabeth Countess of Hereford (April 7, 1282-May 5, 1316)
> Edward of Carnarvon (April 25, 1884-c. 1327), later King
> Edward II of England

At first, common Englishmen did not view the marriage to the Spanish Infanta with enthusiasm. They saw it merely as, yet an another opportunity for even more foreign royal relatives to raid the English treasury. At the time, the English court was overrun with royal French relatives of deceased King Henry III and Dowager Queen Eleanor of Provence. The Lusignan relatives of King Henry III and the Savoyard relatives of Queen Eleanor were all characterized by insatiable greed, which brought the country to Simon de Montfort's Rebellion (see Reign 8 for an explanation of the Lusignan-Savoyard issue).

It is true that Eleanor of Castile brought a few Spanish relatives and friends to England as companions for her own court, but they did not create a diplomatic problem like the one that plagued Henry III when the king and queen's royal relatives provoked civil war. The princess from Spain had the official title: *Leonora la Infanta del Castile*. Its Spanish meaning was a puzzle to English yokels who translated it: *Lioness Elephant of the Castle*—which made no sense—yet it had the foreign sound of high status, and therefore, was accepted as the fitting title for their future queen.

Little is reported on Eleanor's activities from her marriage in 1254 until 1264. History gives Eleanor high marks as a loyal loving wife and mother. Shortly before the beginning of the Simon de Montfort's Rebellion (also called the *Second Barons War*), Eleanor assisted the king's cause by raising troops from her estates in Picardy, France. However, that activity ended after the Battle of Lewes (May 14, 1264) when de Montfort defeated, and captured King Henry and her husband Edward Longshanks. For over a year the king and prince were imprisoned at Wallingford or Kenilworth Castles, but Eleanor was confined at Westminster Palace in London. Edward Longshanks soon escaped, and successfully organized resistance against the rebellious barons. The civil war ended at the Battle of Eversham (August 4, 1265) with the death of Simon de Montfort. After the battle, all imprisoned royalists were released, but after King Henry's imprisonment, his capacity to rule was permanently impaired. Prince Edward Longshanks took command of government the regent head of State until his father's death seven years later.

By 1268, Edward had stabilized mechanics of government in England sufficiently well for him to take part in the eighth Crusade. Louis IX (later Saint Louis) led the adventure, but it went so poorly that Pope Clement X asked Edward to take leadership over of the effort to recover Jerusalem from the Infidels. Edward went to Acre in the Holy Land, and attempted to organize counter attacks against Islam in a last futile effort (sometimes called the ninth Crusade, 1271-1272), but Christendom was apathetic, and unwilling any longer to provide men or supplies needed to continue the effort.

Eleanor accompanied Edward to the Holy Land. She was criticized of being unladylike for associating with crude soldiers in bivouac. She countered the criticism with the reply, "Nothing must part them whom God has joined together . . . . The way to heaven is as near, if not nearer, from Syria as from England or my native Spain."

An anecdote reports that Edward was injured by an assassin's attempt to stab him with a poisoned dagger. Legend (without substantiation) credits Eleanor with saving her husband's life by 'sucking the poison from his wounded arm.' All told, the ninth Crusade was costly waste of life and wealth, and had no lasting importance.

While in Syria, Prince Edward heard of his father's death late in 1272, and that he was now King Edward I. Edward was so confident of the stability of government in England that he delayed return to England until 1274. King Edward I and Queen Eleanor were crowned at Westminster on August 19, 1274.

For the rest of her life, Eleanor accompanied Edward on nearly all his political and military travels at home and abroad. She was with Edward in his Welsh war in 1284 at Caernarvon Castle in Wales when her youngest child Edward was born. After futilely chasing of the Welsh Celts around their rugged hills for almost ten years, King Edward I knew he would never defeat the wily mountain folk by any conventional military tactics. He therefore titled his newborn son *Prince of Wales*, with hope that his Welsh foe could be tricked into accepting his son Edward Prince of Wales as their king when he eventually becomes the King of England. The ruse did not work, but that was the origin for the tradition of calling the Crown Prince of England *The Prince of Wales*.

Household records show that Eleanor loved fine clothes and the amenities of good living. If effigies on tombs have any base in reality, Eleanor's effigy depicts a self-assured regal queen, one who knew and accepted the prerogatives that accompanied her station in life. However, contemporary records fail to show any major influence Eleanor had on affairs of State during the reign of her husband. She occasionally recommended a Spanish female cousin for marriage to an English Lord. She was a circumspect regal hostess. She entertained, and distributed gifts to foreign guests and envoys with condescension and dignity suitable for court custom of the time. She managed the royal house with authority, but did not attempt to impose her will on her husband the king.

King Edward I ruled as well as reigned. He governed strictly with great respect for the law. His lords could not sway the king's administrative judgment, and no evidence exists that Edward ever let his wife meddle in, or influence his authoritarian manner of ruling with decisive justice. Edward was much admired by his subjects. They honored King Edward I with the names *Edward the Lawgiver*, and *England's Justinian*.

Although Wales was never entirely subdued, Edward controlled Wales by 1284. Thereafter, for the last two decades of his reign, the conquest of Scotland occupied most of Edward's time and effort. Eleanor accompanied Edward in his repeated efforts to subdue the redheaded Highland Picts of Scotland. Even though the wild mountain men were often beaten, the Scots never conceded defeat for long.

Eleanor died while following Edward to a Scottish foray in 1290. She had been unwell for some time, but insisted on following the English troops at some distance. She collapsed at a village near Lincoln, where she received Last Rite Sacraments, and died on November 28, 1290 at age forty-nine. Her body was taken to St. Catherine's Priory in Lincoln in preparation for burial. Her viscera, except heart, were embalmed, and kept at Lincoln Cathedral. Her heart was buried in Blackfriars Church, London, and her body was buried in Westminster Abbey. On being informed of her death, Edward hurried back from the Scottish border to accompany Eleanor's body back to London.

Events that followed Queen Eleanor's death, and the transport of her body to London gave Eleanor of Castile her most lasting fame. Edward grieved mightily, and ordered that an elaborate wayside memorial to Eleanor be built at the twelve cities where the funeral party stayed overnight in its sad progress back to London for her burial in Westminster Abbey. It took nearly four years to finish the roadside shrines at cities where the cortège stopped: Lincoln, Grantham, Stamford, Geddington, Northampton, Stony Stratford, Woburn, Dunstable, St Albans, Waltham, Westcheap, and Charing.

Almost immediately, the shrines were called *Eleanor Crosses*. Only parts of three original Eleanor Crosses still exist, and they have been modified, or moved from original locations at Geddington, Northampton, and Waltham. The famous one at Charing Cross in central London originally was near present Trafalgar Square, but Puritans demolished the original shrine for being 'idolatrous' in 1647 during the Civil War. Today's Eleanor

Cross at Charing Cross was built anew at its new location in the 19th century.

During the first eighteen years of their marriage (1254-1272), Eleanor of Castile was Crown Princess of England, and during the last eighteen years (1272-1290), she was Queen Consort. However, throughout the thirty-six years of marriage, she was in the shadow of her indomitable stepmother Eleanor of Provence. Eclipsed in that way, Eleanor of Castile failed to make a strong personal mark on history.

During much of her lifetime, her subjects strongly criticized Queen Eleanor of Castile for collecting huge land holdings in England. No one accused her of any dishonesty, but her dealings with sharp moneylenders tarnished her reputation. She bought large properties with aid of unprincipled realtors who used shady practices to separate property from common landholders, and transfer them to Eleanor's royal accounts. Eleanor's personal properties earned more than £2500 yearly in rent. It appears that her husband Edward the Lawgiver approved of his wife's acquisitive activities, possibly because they earned enough financial reward to cover all royal household expenses. Even so, history has been kind to Eleanor of Castile's memory for the admirable support she always gave to her husband, and for the dignity of the court she led.

After Eleanor's death in 1290, Edward remained single until 1299 before he wed again. Evidence that Edward sincerely mourned Eleanor is found in a letter to the Abbot of Cluny Abbey in France (January 1291), where he requested that prayers be said in perpetuity for his wife "whom living we dearly cherished, and whom dead we cannot cease to love."

For thirty-six years, Eleanor of Castile was Queen Consort of strong-willed King Edward I. They were a devoted couple. Their union is credited with being one of the most successful royal marriages of all time.

With his only living son Edward of Caernarvon, and with long life made uncertain by war, and God's unfathomable wrath, Edward I faced his duty, and married Marguerite of France in 1299 nine years after Eleanor's death in hope of siring more sons.

Narrative of Queen Consort Marguerite of France

Queen Marguerite of France: life dates c. 36 years, b. 1282-d. February 14, 1317; second Queen Consort of King Edward I c. 8 years, September 8, 1299-July 7, 1307; Dowager Queen of England 10 years, July 7, 1307-February 14, 1317.

MARGUERITE DE CAPET Princess of France, second wife and child-bride of ageing King Edward I, is surely one of the most forgotten queens consort in English history. Edward was fifty-two when his first wife Eleanor of Castile died in 1290. He had only one living son, Edward of Caernarvon, who was only six years old. Pressure was on the aging king to marry again to secure the succession with as many more sons as possible.

The delay of nine years between the death of King Edward's first wife Queen Eleanor of Castile in 1290, and Edward's second marriage to Princess Marguerite of France in 1299 is usually cited as evidence for Edward's prolonged mourning for his first wife. Further inquiry into the matter, however, shows that negotiations for Edward's second marriage began three years after Eleanor's death, and fully five years before his marriage to Marguerite actually took place. This does not cast doubt on Edward's sincere devotion to his first wife Eleanor, but it does show that, after a reasonable three-year interval for grief, Edward could face Eleanor's demise with equanimity. He was a pragmatic king who understood his nations needs. He faced life, and did what was required of him.

Witnesses of the time said that Princess Marguerite of France "possessed comeliness of person, and showed piety, and religious devotion characteristic of her grandfather, Louis IX of France [Louis was later canonized as Saint Louis]." However, her older sister Blanche was the reigning beauty in Europe. She is known to history as *Blanche la Belle!* A court witness in London reported that, when Edward heard of Blanche's beauty, he was determined to possess her, no matter what the cost. He sent envoys to Paris to negotiate the dowry with Blanche's older half-brother Philip IV who had become King of France when their father died in 1285.

Philip, in recognition of the strong bargaining position he was in, agreed to a marriage between King Edward and his younger sister Blanche: Edward could have Blanche, if Edward would give up England's claim to Gascony—the rich wine growing province of southern France with its maritime capital Bordeaux—which was the last part of Aquitaine still in England's hands. Incredibly, Edward agreed to King Philip's dower conditions.

King Edward I sent his younger brother Edmund Duke of Lancaster to France as envoy to escort Blanche to London. However, in Paris Edmund learned that Blanche had already been given in marriage to Rudolph I of Habsburg King of Bavaria, Poland, and Duke of Austria. King Philip IV of France then calmly proposed that King Edward could have Blanche's younger sister Marguerite. In rage, fifty-five year old King Edward resoundingly refused to accept the eleven year old Princess Marguerite. Edward declared war on France for the breach of his original wedding contract.

The war sputtered on for almost five years with little result. In 1299, Philip and Edward finally agreed on a truce to end the war with the terms: if Edward would accept Marguerite as his wife, Philip would give up French claim to Gascony. Edward accepted the offer, but only after the dowry was further enriched by Marguerite adding £15,000 of her own inheritance from her father Philip III of France.

Therefore, after almost five long years, Princess Marguerite was married and crowned Queen of England at Canterbury on September 8, 1299. She was now sixteen, and Edward was sixty-one years old. Soon after ceremonies of marriage and coronation were complete, Edward rejoined his troops on the Scottish border in his long effort to subdue Scotland. He found the Highland Scottish Picts to be tediously stupid for never understanding when they had been soundly vanquished.

Child-bride Queen Marguerite remained in London for several months after the wedding to familiarize herself with court customs in England. She then travelled north to join her warrior-king husband at Carlisle just south of the Scottish border. Her voluntary choice to join Edward I on the gale buffeted heaths of Cambria delighted him, as a return to as it had been in former times with his beloved first wife Eleanor of Castile. She, too, had accompanied Edward on all his diplomatic and military adventures at home and abroad.

Edward and Marguerite first became respectful friends, and then a devoted affectionate married couple. Their first child Thomas was born in 1300 barely a year after they were married. A second son was born a year later. In all, they had three children (2 sons and 1 daughter):

> Thomas of Brotherton Earl of Norfolk (June 1, 1300-August
> 4, 1338)
> Edmund of Woodstock Earl of Kent (August 5, 1301-March
> 19, 1330), the father of Joan 'The Fair Maid of Kent'—the
> mother of King Richard II
> Eleanor Plantagenet (b. 1306-d. 1311), died in childhood.

The name *Eleanor* for their last child was a surprise to many in court when the explanation said it was in honor of King Edward's first wife Eleanor of Castile. Clearly, naming the child *Eleanor* was evidence that Marguerite understood and respected the abiding affection her husband held for his first wife, and was proof that Marguerite lacked a jealous nature.

The couple, although mismatched in age, was happy and devoted to one another throughout the eight years of their married life. Edward remarked that his new wife was "a pearl of great price." From that followed the custom of referring to Marguerite in her lifetime as, *The Pearl of France.* She possibly had more influence on Edward than did even his first wife Eleanor of Castile. Edward I was noted for a total lack of tolerance for lawbreakers, and for his severe punishment of miscreants. The record shows that many persons guilty of crimes were spared wrath from their king by adjudications that ended with, "Pardoned solely on the intercession of our dearest consort, Queen Marguerite of England."

Edward's sensitivity to Marguerite's feelings was shown when he ordered that a High Mass be said for her sister, Queen Blanche of Bavaria and Poland, who died in 1309 (possibly in childbirth). Marguerite was in deep mourning for the loss of her much-loved older sister. The High Mass ordered for Blanche was of the same dignity as usually was reserved for deaths in the immediate English royal family.

Most records of Marguerite's roles in history stress the important part she constantly played as peacemaker between her husband King Edward I and her half-brother, Philip IV of France. She often also softened tempers in contests between Edward and his son the heir apparent, Edward of Caernarvon. However, in that ongoing confrontation, even Marguerite's temporizing intervention could not repair the stormy acrimonious relationship between the royal father and son.

Marguerite was well liked by children of Edward I by his first wife Eleanor of Castile. They were of Marguerite's own age and generation. She befriended Prince Edward of Caernarvon (later Edward II) who was two years younger than she was, and he gave her a rich jeweled gift as a token of his friendship and affection for her. Marguerite's closest friend became Edward's daughter Mary, a nun in Amesbury Benedictine Abbey, who was a few years older than she. This friendship remained and deepened during the remaining ten years of Marguerite's life after Edward's death, when Sister Mary became Mother Mary Abbess of the Convent of Amesbury Benedictine Abbey.

Marguerite was twenty-six when Edward died in 1307 at age sixty-eight. King Edward I reigned for thirty-five years. He died at Burgh-on-Sands near Carlisle close to the Scottish border while still trying to subdue the Scots. He was buried at Westminster Abbey in an unadorned tomb with only a Latin inscription that reads, *Malleus Scotorum* (Hammer of Scotland). Word descriptions by contemporaries exist, which tell us that he was tall handsome athletic, silver-haired, and always in the prime of life, never in senile old age. Edward I was succeeded by his only surviving son by Queen Eleanor of Castile, Edward of Carnarvon Prince of Wales who became King Edward II in 1307.

Dowager Queen Marguerite never married again. In her late twenties, she was a desirable heiress: she had well over a decade of child-bearing years remaining; her titles were Princess of France and Dowager Queen of England; she had great personal wealth and estates. When asked, why she never married again, she said, "When Noble Edward died, for me, all men died with him."

In retirement, Marguerite lived out her life at the royal residence Marlborough Castle in Wiltshire. She was near her friend and stepdaughter, Mother Mary Abbess at Amesbury Benedictine Abbey. Dowager Queen Marguerite spent her life and immense fortune on charitable works. She died at age thirty-six in 1317. Marguerite was buried at Greyfriars Church, London, which was destroyed in the Great Fire of London in 1666. Legend says that Mother Mary Abbess composed the epitaph on Marguerite's tomb:

Marguerite de Capet,
Princess of France, Queen of England,
Her Life is Without Reproach

Queen Marguerite's most memorable contribution to history comes through her granddaughter, Joan The Fair Maid of Kent. Joan was the daughter of Edmund of Woodstock Earl of Kent, the second son of Edward I and Queen Marguerite. Froissart who chronicled the time said, "[Joan was] the most beautiful woman in all England, and the most loving." Joan married her first cousin Edward 'The Black Prince,' and they were the parents of King Richard II. In her own right, Joan was an important player in history for sponsoring the radical cleric John Wycliffe, who is often called 'The Morning Star of the Reformation.'

REIGN 10

KING EDWARD II

AND

QUEEN CONSORT ISABELLA

OF FRANCE

Summary of the Reign of Edward II
Reign 1307-1327)

King Edward II: life dates c. 43 years, b. April 25, 1284-d. September 21, 1327; King of England 20 years, July 7, 1307-January 20, 1327.

KING EDWARD II, known as Edward of Caernarvon, was the only surviving son of Edward I and Eleanor of Castile. He was born in 1284 at Caernarvon Castle, Wales, and was the first Crown Prince styled Prince of Wales. He succeeded his father King Edward I, and became King Edward II of England in 1307. His reign lasted twenty years. It ended in abdication, and was followed by his murder at Berkeley Castle in 1327. Like his father, Edward of Caernarvon was tall, handsome, physically strong, and able in all knightly activities. There, the similarity between father and son ended. With the possible exception of Henry VI, Edward II was the most thoroughly incompetent king England ever had. The Crown Prince lacked all his father's capacities for military leadership and commitment to good government.

At the coronation of Edward II at Canterbury, his oath required that he continue the exemplary parliamentary system established during the reign of his father King Edward I. The oath included recognition of the right of nobility to approve royal taxation and appointments to high office. However, Edward II consistently ignored Parliament, and he chose to rule independently with advice coming from unfit self-serving personal favorites, who were not of the titled nobility of England.

Edward showed lackluster military ability. At the Battle of Bannockburn on June 24, 1314, he was outmaneuvered, and defeated by smaller Scottish forces led by Robert the Bruce. When defeat was near, Edward deserted his troops, and returned to England. At Bannockburn, Edward lost all lands won during his father's conquests in Scotland. The defeat confirmed independence of the Scottish kingdom, and established Robert the Bruce as father of Scottish independence.

Edward of Caernarvon offended English custom by his frequent association with peasants, by wearing yeoman apparel while working at menial tasks more suitable for farmers and herdsmen than nobility wears, and by frittering away national treasure on aimless pursuits. However, he offended most severely by his effeminate manner, and unseemly affection for young handsome male favorites that he rewarded with great gifts and high noble titles. Piers Gaveston and Hugh le Despenser (the Younger) were his two most notorious favorites. They were removed by execution: the former by assassination, the latter by trial and execution with hanging, drawing, and quartering.

History's criticism and censure of Edward II are nearly universal. He left no worthy legacy in war, in government, or in his private life. His chief claim to fame lies in the unimportant fact that he was born in Wales at Caernarvon Castle and, thereby, he was the first 'Prince of Wales', a title that has usually been awarded to subsequent princes recognized as England's *heir apparent*.

In 1308, Edward II married Isabella of France the eldest daughter of King Philip IV of France. They had four children (2 sons and 2 daughters), but marriage was extremely uncongenial for Queen Isabella. Isabella led a revolt that deposed, and forced King Edward II to abdicate his throne. After Edward's abdication, he was imprisoned at Berkeley Castle near Gloucester. When several Welsh attempts to rescue him failed, Queen Isabella and the regent Roger Mortimer decided that Edward II must die.

He was secretly murdered, probably on September 21, 1327. Edward II was buried at Gloucester Cathedral. A 19th Century historian summed up his life by saying, "The greatest failure of Edward I was his son Edward II." The only success of Edward II was his son, Edward III.

Following the murder of Edward II, his eldest son Prince Edward of Windsor ascended the throne in 1327 as King Edward III. He would be one of England's greatest Warrior Kings.

Narrative of Queen Consort Isabella of France

Queen Isabella of France: life dates c. 63 years, b. 1295-d. August 22, 1358; Queen Consort of King Edward II 20 years, January 28, 1308-January 20, 1327; Dowager Queen of England 31 years, January 20, 1327-August 22, 1358.

QUEEN ISABELLA was the only surviving daughter of Philip IV of France and Joan (Jeanne) of Navarre. She was born in Paris in midyear 1295, and was the eldest sister of three French kings: Louis X (1314-1316), Philip V (1316-1322), and Charles IV the Fair (1322-1328). England and France agreed to the marriage of Isabella of France and Edward of Caernarvon of England when she was still an infant and Edward was about eleven years old. The French purpose behind the diplomatic marriage of State was that, in exchange for Isabella, England would, at long last, surrender its ancient claims to Normandy and Anjou. Those counties of France were part of the no longer extant 'Angevin Empire' created by Henry Plantagenet and Eleanor of Aquitaine. However, rule of those French provinces had actually ended when King John lost them to France by forfeit over a century before.

The royal marriage, although approved by Pope Boniface VII, was delayed for over a decade by endless bickering between the royal parents, Edward I of England and Philip IV of France. As a twelve year old bride, Isabella of France was said to be "The Beauty of Beauties" in France. Even discounting the usual hyperbole of court flattery, it is likely that Isabella was a captivating budding young woman. She came from a family noted for its handsome men and women—her father Philip IV of France was called Philip le Bel (Philip the Fair). A half-year after King Edward I Longshanks died in July 1307, the marriage of Edward II and Isabella of France took place in Paris on January 25, 1308. Prince Edward of Caernarvon was twenty-four and Isabella was twelve or thirteen years old. Isabella was a mere child, innocently unaware of the underlying flaw that would make their union extremely unhappy for her.

From early adolescence, Edward of Caernarvon had exhibited unmistakable evidence of sexual ambivalence bordering on active homosexuality. Prince Edward of Caernarvon as a growing youth was popular in the English court. However, he was so dominated by his father Edward I that he had little self-confidence. Throughout his life, Edward of Caernarvon showed no capacity for leadership. During most of his reign of twenty years, he was manipulated by handsome male favorites who misused their influence for personal gain. Eventually, their insatiable greed destroyed him.

Whatever Isabella's appearance may have been, Edward of Caernarvon showed no romantic interest in her. When he married Isabella, Edward of Carnarvon had been King of England for only six months. He was infatuated with Piers Gaveston, a handsome charming commoner who was an escaped convict from France. The recently crowned king showered Gaveston with many jeweled gifts of great value, created him Earl of Cornwall, and appointed him to be regent of England while Edward was in Paris for his marriage to Isabella.

All nobility in England strenuously disapproved of the honors Edward gave to Gaveston—it was contrary to English custom for the status of regent to be awarded to anyone other than the spouse or a close blood relative of the king. On that occasion, the commoner Piers Gaveston had authority and precedence over all other lords in the land. As holder of the Great Seal, Gaveston was free to make any personal wish into law. He flaunted his authority, and treated the English nobility like serfs. In so doing, he earned their fear, hatred, and contempt. Immediately after the wedding, King Edward II insulted and humiliated his child-bride Isabella, by giving to Piers Gaveston many jeweled gifts he received in France as part of her dowry.

Edward and Isabella's marriage probably was not consummated until she was around fifteen years of age. That is suggested by the birth of their first child in 1312 when Isabella was sixteen. Between 1312 and 1321, four surviving children were born:

> Edward of Windsor (November 13, 1312-June 21, 1327), later
> King Edward III
> John of Eltham Earl of Cornwall (August 15, 1316-September
> 13, 1336)
> Eleanor of Woodstock (June 18, 1318-April 22,1355), later
> Countess of Guelders
> Joanna of the Tower, or 'Joan Makepeace' (July 5, 1321-September
> 7, 1362), later Queen of Scotland

Notwithstanding the sexual ambivalence of King Edward II, all children of Edward and Isabella held their father in high affection as a loving and caring parent. No question was ever raised about their legitimate parentage. Edward II also acknowledged an illegitimate son Adam FitzRoy who served as his esquire in England's disastrous effort to best Robert the Bruce and his Scottish Highlanders at the Battle of Bannockburn in 1314.

For the first thirteen years of their marriage (1308-1321), King Edward II and Queen Isabella had a reasonably circumspect royal married relationship. However, those years were also marked with the king's intermittent, but ever more open infidelity with attractive and often common young men. His favorite Piers Gaveston was assassinated in 1312. However, Hugh Despenser (the Younger), Piers' brother-in-law, soon took Pier's place as the court favorite, and occupied a dominant position in court for over a decade. As the king's favorite, Hugh enjoyed dictatorial power over irresolute and vacillating King Edward. Hugh greedily built a huge personal fortune at government expense, which infuriated the nobility.

It is uncertain what Isabella's feelings for her husband were during the first decade of their marriage, but during the following years, Edward and Isabella were violently estranged. However, for self-protection, she made every effort to hide her feelings by dissembling affection for her husband,

and by giving Hugh Despenser condescending courteous agreement. Her alienation and distrust included fear of imprisonment, fear of physical danger, and even fear of murder at the hand of Edward II or Hugh. Finally, in 1321 when Isabella was in her last pregnancy, she demanded that Edward banish Hugh from court. Edward sent Hugh away, but in less than a year, Edward invited Hugh back.

The turning point for Isabella's troubles came in 1223 when her brother Charles IV of France ordered Edward II to appear in Paris to show fealty, and to pay homage for the French province of Gascony. Although Edward II was granted freedom to delay his fealty and homage for almost a year, he still refused to go to Paris. Charles patience wore thin, and he then declared Gascony forfeit, and no longer an English domain. A state of war existed for almost a year.

Finally, in 1325, Edward decided to send Isabella as his diplomatic envoy to Paris to plead England's suit for a peaceful end to the matter without loss of Gascony to France. Isabella was unable to soften her brother's demands on England, and after a two-month parlay, King Charles IV of France still demanded that Edward pay homage, or he would suffer loss of Bordeaux and Gascony.

Isabella is credited with suggesting the diplomatic solution that temporarily resolved the matter. She proposed that King Edward transfer title for Gascony to their son, Crown Prince Edward of Windsor, so Gascony would remain an English crown property when Prince Edward became King Edward III. The kings of England and France approved the plan. However, the plan required that Prince Edward go to Bordeaux first to receive fealty from citizens of Gascony. He would then as Duke of Gascony proceeded to Paris, and declare homage for Gascony.

The young prince sailed with his mother Queen Isabella to Bordeaux to receive oaths of fealty from his Bordeaux subjects. They continued on to Paris, where, with suitable courtly flamboyance, Prince Edward performed the feudal of homage to his uncle King Charles IV of France.

King Edward II instructed Isabella to return to England with Prince Edward immediately after the homage ceremonies were concluded at Paris in autumn 1325. However, Isabella refused to return while Hugh Despenser remained in London. King Edward refused to exile Hugh, and asked King Charles of France to order Queen Isabella back to England.

Charles IV of France replied, "The queen has come of her own freewill. She may freely return to England when she wishes. She is my sister, and if she prefers to remain here, I refuse to expel her."

In a pet, Edward II immediately ended Isabella's financial support from England. Isabella then turned to her brother Charles for aid. He offered her free occupancy in one of his palaces, but refused to give her financial aid. Isabella remained for a time in France, and her presence in Paris served to attract many English exiles that opposed King Edward II and had fled to France.

When Isabella came as peacemaker envoy to Paris in 1325, she met Roger Mortimer I Earl of March. Roger Mortimer was an English nobleman from the western border between England and Wales. He was the most important expatriate to join Isabella's English coterie in Paris. Mortimer had strongly opposed Edward II and the Despensers from 1318 until 1322, However, in that year, he was captured, tried, found guilty of treason, and awaited death in the Tower of London. Mortimer bribed a jailor to help him escape, and he then fled to France in 1223. In Paris, Mortimer met and offered his services to Isabella. She probably was aware of Mortimer as a premier peer of the realm, but it is uncertain whether she had personal contact with him before their meeting in the French court.

A new irreversible phase in Queen Isabella's life began when she met Roger Mortimer.

With dwindling funds in hand, Isabella left Paris with her son Prince Edward, and moved north to Hainault, Flanders in the company of many English malcontents who followed her to Flanders in 1326. In Flanders, Isabella worked tirelessly to recruit militia for an insurrection to remove Edward II as King of England. Her goal was to place her son Prince Edward of Windsor on the throne. To gain that end, she struck a bargain with Count William III of Hainault: Isabella promised:

> If Count William would supply mercenary fighting men and ships to transport her to England, Crown Prince Edward of Windsor would marry his daughter Philippa of Hainault, who then would become Queen of England when Prince Edward became King Edward III.

Roger Mortimer and Queen Isabella lived openly together as lovers when they moved to Hainault. The two conspired on the plan to depose Edward

II. The plot unfolded flawlessly, and events moved with incredible speed. Isabella, Mortimer, and their Flemish mercenaries invaded England in September 1326. King Edward II had little success in raising troops to repel the invaders. His government and all his popular support collapsed in less than a month. Edward II fled to Wales where, as Prince of Wales, he still enjoyed popularity.

When the invasion to overthrow the king began in September 1326, Hugh Despenser (the Elder) was the focal point for popular opposition to the regime of Edward II. Only two months later, the Despensers, father and son, were captured and executed. Hugh Despenser (the Elder) was hanged on October 27, 1326. The execution of his son Hugh Despenser (the Younger) came on November 24, 1326, by hanging, drawing, and quartering. In keeping with custom of that barbaric time, horses dragged Hugh naked to his execution. First, he was hanged, but cut down before dead; while he was still conscious, the executioner cut off his private parts and threw them into a fire; then his body was cut open, his entrails were pulled out, cut off, and burned; lastly, his beating heart was removed. A chronicle of the event said that, "[With his last breath, just before he died] he gave a great howl much to the delight and merriment of the spectators." After his death, Hugh's head was mounted over a gate to London, and the four parts of his quartered body were placed on posts at crossroad entries to London. Months later, his body parts were abandoned to dogs. His widow piteously asked permission to take his remains for Christian burial, but "only his head, one thighbone, and a few backbones were recovered for her."

The insurrection and civil war ended when Duke Henry of Lancaster captured King Edward II in Wales on November 16. The king was imprisoned in the impregnable Lancaster fortress Kenilworth Castle from November 1326 until April 1327. King Edward II formally abdicated his throne on January 20, 1327, but retained his title, Edward of Carnarvon Prince of Wales. His fourteen year old son Prince Edward of Windsor became King Edward III, and was crowned at Westminster on February 1, 1327.

Queen Isabella and Mortimer secured their control of government by declaring that they were 'Acting Regents' for young King Edward III. By that subterfuge, they became all powerful. Roger Mortimer was the 'actual regent' through his influence over Isabella, and she had total control over her son King Edward III.

Deposed Edward of Carnarvon was an affectionate father who doted on his children, and they all adored him. During his imprisonment at Kenilworth, he pled for permission to share their company, but his captors denied him that simple parental pleasure. In April 1327, Edward was secretly transferred from Kenilworth Castle to a prison cell in Berkeley Castle in Gloucestershire near the Welch border. A few failed attempts were made by Welch loyalists to free Edward, whom they prized as their own Prince of Wales. Then, Roger Mortimer and Queen Isabella decided that, to secure the regime they controlled, Edward of Caernarvon must die.

The general belief is that, on orders from Roger Mortimer and Queen Isabella, Edward of Caernarvon was murdered at Berkeley Castle some time between September 21 and October 11, 1227. Reports of his death are conflicting. Exactly how Edward II died is uncertain.

Edward was interred at Gloucester Cathedral instead of in Westminster Abbey as was usual for English monarchs, because his burial in London might be cause for riot and insurrection. Soon after Edward of Caernarvon's eldest son Edward of Windsor claimed authority to begin his personal rule as Edward III in 1330, he commissioned construction of a splendid alabaster tomb for his father in Gloucester Cathedral. An alabaster effigy of Edward of Carnarvon as a sleeping young knight lies atop the tomb. In Wales, the murdered king was revered as Prince Edward the Martyr, and his tomb became a shrine that attracted penitent pilgrims for many decades. The Edward II tomb and effigy survived the dissolution of monasteries in the reign of Henry VIII, and they remain in pristine condition in Gloucester Cathedral today.

When Edward II was first deposed in 1327, Queen Isabella demanded and received control of the Great Seal, which gave her the power of the monarch. Isabella and Roger Mortimer, although never married, openly lived together, and Roger acted as regent for the realm for the next four years. Mortimer, in his roles as regent, quickly assumed all prerogatives of royalty. He awarded himself huge estates, titles, and governmental powers. Mortimer's greed for wealth and position was unquenchable. Dowager Queen Isabella was only slightly less grasping than her lover. Together they exceeded the misuse of power that led to the rebellion of the barons during the Despenser dominance in the reign of Edward II. As accused regicides, as openly sinful cohabitants, and for other highly autocratic aspects of their regency, Roger and Isabella became as unpopular with the public as were the Despensers and King Edward II whom they deposed.

During his minority years, 1327-1330, the boy-king Edward III watched, waited, and kept council to himself. Custom ruled that Prince Edward would come of age on his eighteenth birthday in 1330. He then could assume the functions of majesty. Common knowledge understood that when Edward reached eighteen, Roger Mortimer's power as regent would vanish. As the king's eighteenth birthday approached, Mortimer kept Edward under strict surveillance. The young king was almost a prisoner in his own court.

Parliament met and was housed at Nottingham Castle for its session in 1330, at which King Edward was expected to assume royal authority. The huge stone castle on a high promontory was a structure of ancient origin with many secret passages that connected public and private rooms. The king's loyal confidants engineered a well-planned clandestine enterprise to apprehend Roger Mortimer and Dowager Queen Isabella. Late on the evening of October 19, 1330, Edward feigned dyspepsia; he excused himself, and departed to unlock a secret passageway that gave access to Roger and Isabella's bedchamber. Later that evening, after a brief skirmish, Roger Mortimer was captured and taken to prison. Isabella pled, "Fair son, have pity on gentle Mortimer."

Next day, Edward of Windsor announced in Parliament that he now claimed the right to rule in his own right as King Edward III. He initially intended to hang Roger Mortimer immediately. However, his levelheaded cousin Duke Henry of Lancaster persuaded him to let due process of law judge, condemn, and set penalty on him. Roger Mortimer was taken from Northampton to prison in the Tower of London. A month later on November 26, 1330, he faced trial by his peers on fourteen charges of misrule, including the murder of King Edward II. Roger was not permitted to defend himself. He was judged "guilty by common knowledge . . . guilty as traitor, and enemy of the king and the realm, to be hanged, drawn, and quartered."

Roger Mortimer was hanged until dead at Tyburn on November 29, 1330, but he was spared the indignity of being beheaded, drawn, and quartered, which was the usual fate for traitors. In his trial, Roger Mortimer received most rights of due process of law. It is uncertain whether (in recognition of his mother's grief) King Edward ordered the modest clemency Hugh received, which reduced his sentence only to hanging. As aftermath of the palace coup by Edward III, a few of Roger's henchmen also were hanged, but there was no punitive blood bath. Edward III pardoned many others; thus, his long reign of fifty years began with justice and moderation.

Dowager Queen mother Isabella was not charged or tried for the murder of Edward II. However, most titles to estates she had taken for herself when she was a powerful co-regent with Roger Mortimer were taken from her. For about two years, she was placed in custody at Windsor Castle. Later, in 1332, Edward III banished his mother from court, but she was permitted to live under the king's supervision on her own estate, Castle Rising, near Norfolk and the Wash on the North Sea. She lived there in relative comfort to the end of her life in 1358. As years passed, her relationship her son King Edward III mellowed. She was often invited to court where she enjoyed the company of a growing number of her grandchildren.

During retirement, Isabella no longer had any influence on her son the king, or on government. She nearly vanished from the political records of her time. There is no evidence, as some legends assert, that she was consumed by guilt, and ended her life in raving madness, or that on stormy nights when gales blow in across the Wash from the North Sea, her wails and groans still echo in corridors and dungeons at Castle Rising. However, she may have had remorse for some of her past actions. Near the end of her life, Dowager Queen Isabella wore the somber habit of a Franciscan Poor Clare nun, an Order noted for vows of contrition, piety, and poverty.

Isabella died on August 22, 1358 in Norfolk. She was buried at Greyfriars Franciscan Church, London with a lavish ceremony provided by her son King Edward III. A Record of her death and burial states that "She was buried in her wedding dress, with the heart of Edward II interred with her." Her tomb was destroyed in the destruction of the abbeys around 1543 in the reign of Henry VIII.

End Note: Isabella of France, the queen consort of much maligned Edward II of England, is the most poorly regarded queen consort in England's history. She is most often referred to by the unflattering title *The She Wolf of France.* Recent historians, in particular Alison Wier, have treated Isabella more gently than has been customary in the past. Isabella is presented more, as one who possessed admirable qualities of leadership and intelligence. Doubt is even cast on her role, if any, in the natural or criminal death of Edward II.

The so-called, *Fieschi Letter,* discovered in 1878 challenges traditional wisdom on the manner of death of King Edward II. The document is a copy of a letter written over a decade after the supposed death of his father Edward II in 1327. The letter is attributed to Manuele de Fieschi Bishop of Vicelli, and addressed to King Edward III of England around 1340. The letter was said to be found in archives of Pope Benedict XII at the Papal Palace, Avignon, France. The letter stated that Edward of Caernarvon escaped from Berkeley Castle by murdering a guard whose body was buried in Gloucester Cathedral in place of the body of Edward II. Edward then escaped to Ireland, and later went to France, where he met Pope Benedict XII in Avignon, before finally moving to Milan, Italy in 1340. Most historians think the 'Fieschi Letter' is a forgery. The scholarly historical consensus on Edward of Caernarvon's death, remains, as originally reported. Namely, Edward II was murdered by suffocation in late September 1327 at Berkeley Castle on orders of Roger Mortimer and Queen Isabella. It is probable that this reasonable and simple account will be argued for many years to come.

As is the case for Richard III, historical rehabilitation of Isabella of France the consort of Edwared of Carnarvon is a daunting task.

REIGN 11

KING EDWARD III

AND

QUEEN CONSORT PHILIPPA

OF HAINAULT

Summary of the Reign Of King Edward III
(Reign 1327-1377)

King Edward III: life dates 65 years, b. November 13, 1312-d. June 21, 1377; King of England 50 years, February 1, 1327-June 21, 1377.

K ING EDWARD III, known as Edward of Windsor, was the eldest son of King Edward II and Isabella of France. He was born in 1312 at Windsor Castle, and was fifteen years old when he came to the throne after the forced abdication of his father Edward II in 1327. Roger Mortimer Earl of March and the king's mother Queen Isabella led an insurrection that deposed his father, and put Prince Edward of Windsor on the throne as King Edward III.

The regency of Roger Mortimer and Queen Isabella governed in the first three years of Edward's reign. Soon after they came to power, they conspired to have the young king's father Edward II murdered. In 1330, Edward III assumed authority to rule. One of his first acts as king was an order for the arrest, trial, and execution of Roger Mortimer for the murder of his father Edward II. Edward III banished his mother Dowager Queen Isabella from court, and for much of her life thereafter, she was confined at Castle Rising in Norfolk for conspiring to kill his father Edward II.

Edward III is one England's great Warrior Kings. He started the Hundred Years War with France in 1337, and personally led the English army to great victory at the Battle of Crécy (1346), and again at the Battle of Poitiers (1356). Among England's gains were the recovery of the French province of Gascony in southern France, and the port city of Calais on the English Channel, which had been forfeited to France in the previous reign. Great wealth came to England from French payment of huge ransoms for the liberation of French lords and knights who had been captured by the English in the long-running conflict.

Edward III enjoyed good fortune in most ventures he undertook. His success in war, diplomacy, and trade enriched the country as never before. In early and middle years of his reign, Edward enjoyed the goodwill of all his people as wealth from France flowed into England. However, near the end of his reign, after the Black Death entered, and decimated Western Europe at mid century, England's fortunes of war sharply declined. Near the end of his reign, the Treaty of Bruges of 1375 returned to France most of its lost territory, and with the French losses, King Edward's popularity sharply declined. By the end of his reign in 1377, England continued to hold only Calais as its last continental possession of any size. The cost of the first thirty years of the Hundred Years War to England and France was bankruptcy for both nations.

Edward III married Philippa of Hainault, Flanders in 1328, and they were married for forty-one years. The marriage was an extraordinarily successful and happy union. They had five surviving sons, but none of them reigned. The major impact of Edward III on English history rests on the turbulent struggle for domination and kingship among descendants of his sons in the fierce internecine Wars of the Roses that ran its course in the century after his death.

Queen Philippa died in 1369, and Edward III died in 1377, after a reign of fifty years. Both are buried in Westminster Abbey

Following the death of Edward III, his grandson Prince Richard of Bordeaux, son of Edward of Woodstock (known to history as 'The Black Prince') succeeded to the throne in 1377 as King Richard II.

Narrative of Queen Consort Philippa of Hainault

Queen Philippa of Hainault: life dates c. 58 years, b. June 14, 1311-d. August 15, 1369; Queen Consort of King Edward III of England 41 years, January 24, 1328-August 15, 1369.

PHILIPPA WAS the second of four daughters of Count William III the Good of Hainault and Holland; her mother was Princess Jeanne de Valois of France. Philippa was born on January 24, 1311 at Valenciennes, Flanders, which now is a part of northern France. The complex maze of intermarriages among noble and royal families shows that Philippa traced descent back to Saxon King Harold II of Wessex who was defeated by William the Conqueror in 1066. Also, Philippa's marriage to Edward III brought back into English royal genealogy a lost connection to descendants from the early English-Norman King Stephen of Blois. His reign is often called 'England's worst of times' for the civil war, anarchy, and widespread famine that characterized most of the nineteen year contested reign of King Stephen and Empress Matilda in the mid 12th century.

A contemporary description of adolescent Philippa noted that "The lady has hair, betwixt blue-black and brown color . . . Her eyes are blackish brown and deep. Her nose is . . . broad at the tip and flattened . . . Her nostrils are also broad and . . . Her lips somewhat full . . . Much like her father, she is brown of skin all over, and in all things she is pleasant." The remark on her 'dark skin' tone has raised a suggestion of Moorish ancestry in Hainault descent.

Philippa was a second cousin of her future husband, Prince Edward of Windsor. He was fifteen and she sixteen when they married on January 24, 1328. A tempest of violent civil war, not of their making, preceded their marriage. A year before their marriage, civil war in England forced Prince Edward of Windsor's father King Edward II of England to abdicate his throne; one week later, the fourteen year old prince was crowned Edward

III on February 1, 1327. Edward III was under age, so rule in England was by a shared regency headed by Roger Mortimer 1st Earl of March who was the lover of Edward's mother the Dowager Queen Isabella. Less than nine months later, probably sometime between September 21 and October 11, Edward II was brutally murdered at Berkeley Castle.

Immediately after the crowning of Edward III, Scotland declared war on England. Regent Roger Mortimer sent boy-King Edward to the Scottish border to halt an invasion of Northumbria and Cambria. The inexperienced youthful king, although eager to win his spurs in battle, had little chance for success against Sir James Douglas (known as 'The Black Douglas') who led the Scots. The king was perilously close to death in a night raid when his equerry stepped in and took a blow that was intended to cleave the young king's skull. The Scots defeated youthful King Edward III, who was forced to surrender all English claims to Scottish lands.

As the year 1327 came to a close, the king's mother Dowager Queen Isabella was under strong pressure to fulfill a commitment she made to Count William of Hainault. She had promised Count William that if he raised mercenaries to fight for the overthrew of Edward II, her son Crown Prince Edward of Windsor, would marry Count William's daughter Philippa, and she would then become the Queen of England.

Count William of Hainault had more than fulfilled his part of the agreement. In addition to support in deposing Edward II, he had also provided military aid to his future son-in-law in the disastrous war led by King Edward III in the summer of 1327 against Scotland.

The wedding of King Edward and Philippa of Hainault took place at York Minster in Yorkshire. Ordinarily, the marriage should have been scheduled in London, but the English court had gathered at York for diplomatic negotiations on a truce to end the border conflict between England and Scotland. The Treaty of Edinburgh-Northampton (revised later as the Treaty of Lincoln) was completed in May 1328 as total capitulation by England. It recognized Scotland as a separate kingdom with Robert the Bruce as its king. To seal the bargain, Edward gave his six year old sister Joanna of the Tower (later know as 'Joan Makepeace') as bride for Prince David, eldest son and heir of Robert the Bruce King of Scotland.

The marriage of Edward and Philippa lasted as a genuinely affectionate and respectful union for forty-one years until her death in 1369. They had fourteen children; nine lived to maturity (5 sons and 4 daughters). The four sons, although never reigning themselves, were ancestors of future kings of England. The surviving sons and daughters of Philippa and Edward III were:

> Edward of Woodstock 'The Black Prince' Duke of Cornwall (June 15, 1330-June 8, 1376), the father of King Richard II.
>
> Isabella Lady Coucy (June 16,1332-October 5, 1382).
>
> Joan Plantagenet (c. 1333/35-September 2, 1348), a teenage victim of the Black Death.
>
> Lionel of Antwerp Duke of Clarence (November 29, 1338-October 7, 1368), the father of Philippa of Clarence, who transmitted her right to reign to her Mortimer descendants in the House of York.
>
> John of Gaunt Duke of Lancaster (March 6, 1340-February 3, 1399), the father of King Henry IV, ancestor of Lancaster Plantagenet Kings.
>
> Edmund of Langley Duke of York (1341-1402), great-great-grandfather of King Edward IV, the ancestor of York Plantagenet Kings.
>
> Mary of Waltham Duchess of Brittany (October 10, 1344-c. 1362).
>
> Margaret of Windsor Countess of Pembroke (July 20, 1346-c. Fall 1361).
>
> Thomas of Woodstock Duke of Gloucester & Earl of Buckingham (January 7, 1355-September 8/9, 1397), the leader of the Lords Appellant who opposed King Richard II.

The first event in which Philippa appeared as a moderating influence on King Edward came in the summer of 1330 at a tournament in London. The event celebrated the birth of their first child Edward of Woodstock. The temporary bleachers built for observers collapsed during the tournament. Philippa was not injured, but Edward vowed to execute all carpenters responsible for building the shaky stands. Philippa, as on many future occasions, pled for pardons of the carpenter's unintended negligence, and they were released. Throughout his reign, King Edward was noted for impatience and a volatile explosive temper. His subjects praised Philippa for gentleness, and for her ability to calm Edward in the service of justice.

Philippa also played a prominent role in promoting cooperation between sheep rearing farmers in England and weavers in the Low Countries. Philippa established a school for weavers in England by bringing Flemish loom makers to Norwich, England to teach the natives how to make and use looms in production of fine English woolens.

Queen Consort Philippa and her husband Edward III are two of England's most admired monarchs. Edward III was a major English medieval warrior king who did much to generate national pride in being English. He was recognized to be the most effective military leader in Europe for his conquests in France during the first half of his long reign. At home, he strengthened Parliament, and restored respect for royal authority with rule by Common Law, which had been carefully built up by his grandfather (Edward I the Lawgiver), but had been severely eroded by mismanagement in the reign of his father (Edward II of Caernarvon). The reign of Edward III and Queen Philippa was a period of elegance and grace, unsurpassed since Roman rule ended in Britannia a millennium before.

England enjoyed its first great success in the Battle of Crécy on August 28, 1346. The French outnumbered Edward's army by a ratio of five to one, but England's Welsh longbow men proved their superiority over French chivalry. At Crécy, French nobility was decimated with little loss to English yeomen who fired their arrows across a wide valley, far out of reach of men on horseback. The Battle of Crécy earned Edward recognition as the greatest military leader of the age. The victory at Crécy was surpassed a decade later by the Battle of Poitiers on September 19, 1356.

Edward III admired the Arthurian legend, which had been rescued from Welsh prehistory in a Latin translation by Geoffrey of Monmouth in 1136. The real King Arthur Pendragon (if indeed he ever existed) lived in Celtic Britannia five centuries before feudal chivalry was imagined. However, King Edward resurrected King Arthur, as a contemporary of Richard the Lionheart—the embodiment of chivalry—just as we visualize King Arthur today. Edward founded the *Order of the Garter* as a latter-day *Arthurian Round Table*, one in which the living of the English court honor themselves by honoring supposed ideals from a fictional romantic past.

The reign of King Edward III is now usually downplayed as flamboyant gallantry with shallow reverence for outmoded rituals of chivalric feudalism. In their own time, Edward and Philippa's subjects saw their king and queen as leaders of the kingdom into a new age of elegance, glory, and prestige. King Edward's England was the envy of all Europe. All Englishmen took pride in a unified Norman-Saxon England. Nobility and commons alike all spoke 'Chaucerian' Middle English. English patriotism would not reach such unified heights, until four centuries later in Queen Victoria's reign.

Jean Froissart, Queen Philippa's secretary, recorded many of her acts of kindness. He wrote a famous tale of the *The Six Burghers of Calais*, which tells of King Edward responding to Queen Philippa's plea for clemency and pardons for six merchants of Calais:

> The Froissart story of *The Six Burghers of Calais*: After the English victory at Crécy in 1346, Edward III laid siege on Calais. The siege lasted for almost a year, by which time citizens of Calais were starving. City leaders petitioned the English king to end the siege with pardons for all citizens of the city.
>
> Froissart said that the King replied, "You will inform the governor of Calais, that the only grace he can expect from me is, that six of the principal citizens of Calais march out of the town, with bare heads and bare feet, with ropes round their necks, and the keys of the town and castle in their hands. These six persons shall be at my absolute disposal, only then will the remainder of the inhabitants of Calais be pardoned."
>
> Six of the highest-ranking gentry men of Calais volunteered to meet Edward's demands as hostages. With full expectation of death, they came to Edward in the manner prescribed: they fell to their knees in the dust, and pled for mercy for themselves, and for the citizens of Calais, saying:
>
> "Most gallant King, see before you six citizens of Calais, who have been capital merchants, and who bring you the keys of the castle and of the town. We surrender ourselves to your absolute will and pleasure, in order to save the remainder of the inhabitants of Calais, who have suffered much distress and misery. Condescend, therefore, out of your nobleness of mind, to have mercy and compassion upon us all."
>
> Edward showed no tendency for clemency until Queen Philippa knelt before him in dust on the street with the six burgers and said, "My loving lord and husband, I have been

faithful to you all our wedded life. As proof of our love, spare the lives of these six of my countrymen."

Edward scowled, then replied, "Lady, I would you had not been here. However, I cannot refuse you. So do as you please with them."

In response to Philippa's plea, Edward granted the six burghers pardons, along with lifting the siege on Calais, without penalty to its citizens.

Philippa's intercession at the siege of Calais earned her permanent gratitude. Calais, forever after, honored Philippa with the title, *Patroness of Calais*.

As footnote to this story, Calais in 1884 commissioned sculptor, August Rodin, to create a commemorative memorial of the six burghers titled *Les Bourgeois de Calais*. Rodin completed the group in 1889, and it was presented to the city in 1895. Now, it occupies a prominent place in a garden near the municipal center in Calais. Bronze copies of the famous group are in Paris, London, New York, Copenhagen, Tokyo, and major art centers elsewhere.

Almost immediately, after the Treaty of Brétagne was signed in 1360, and established a truce in the Hundred Years War, England's fortunes from war from France ended. For a decade, England had enjoyed artificially inflated national wealth. Peace, when it finally came, proved to be an economic calamity. Poverty bred public discontent with all levels of authority from Church and State.

An additional complicating factor of the time was the sudden appearance of the Black Death. It came to Europe and England in 1348 at the middle of Edward's reign. The plague forever changed the feudal world of the Middle Ages. By 1355, fully one-third of all populations in Europe perished in the most dreadful epidemic Western Civilization ever experienced. As death took its toll throughout the land, unemployed soldiers and dispossessed peasants roamed the land in anarchy, and they took what they willed. Everyone everywhere struggled to survive the dreadful conditions that continued to worsen throughout the last half of the 14th Century. With European countries decimated, social, political, economic, and religious turmoil undermined all aspects of conventional medieval life.

Edward and Philippa were married for forty-one of his fifty-year reign. After Philippa's death in 1369, Edward's mind failed, and he lost ability to rule. Edward's eldest surviving son, John of Gaunt Duke of Lancaster served as an able regent for the kingdom at the end of his father's life. In the Treaty of Bruges in 1375, England lost most French land it had won earlier in King Edward's reign, and with the French losses, the king's popularity sharply declined. By the end of Edward's reign in 1377, only Calais remained as an English outpost of importance on the Continent. English and French economies were in a ruinous state. Dwindling wealth, and fading glamour of the war in France, fanned English discontent and rebellion at home.

As Queen Philippa aged, she personified the portly Dutch matron that, indeed, she was. All England honored and genuinely loved her. Queen Philippa was England's 'Queen Mum of the Middle Ages.' English public gave Queen Philippa love that was in contrast to the dislike and even hate some former queen consorts earned. Queen Philippa never flooded the English court with impecunious relatives from her homeland, as many of her predecessors had done. She always enjoyed real affection from her English subjects.

King Edward built the Palace of Sheen on the Thames in southwest London for his beloved wife. Edward and Philippa presided over a court of superior learning and elegance. On one occasion, five kings (albeit, two of them were prisoners) were entertained as guests at the English court. In that climate of intellectual tolerance, at the dawn of the English Renaissance, John Gower and Geoffrey Chaucer enriched Middle English with their writings, and John Wickliffe tweaked to pope's beard with heretical ideas of Church reformation. In Edward's reign, the English language ceased to be a French patois. It came into its own as *English,* the most versatile of all spoken and written tongues.

Near the end of Philippa's life, Queen's College, Oxford was founded and named in respect for her. As she was dying, Queen Philippa asked for an audience with the king, Froissart reported that she said, "My husband, we have enjoyed our long union in peace and happiness. Before we are forever parted in this world . . . I beg you will pay all [my debts to] merchants . . . I beseech you to fulfill all gifts or legacies I have made to churches and to my servants . . . and when it shall please God to call you hence, that you will lie by my side in the cloisters of Westminster Abbey."

King Edward replied, "Dear Lady, all this shall be done."

Queen Philippa died on August 15, 1369 at Windsor Castle at age fifty-eight. Some say her ailment was dropsy (an unspecified edematous condition often caused to kidney failure), but some assert that she was a victim of the Black Death. She is buried in Westminster Abbey in an alabaster tomb commissioned in 1367 by Edward III during her lifetime and completed in 1376. The effigy of Philippa on the tomb is realistic, representing with dignity an aging portly woman, not at all in the customary style of the time that traditionally represented the dead in the bloom of youth. Edward III died on June 21, 1377. He was buried with Queen Philippa in Westminster Abbey.

After Edward III died, his grandson at age ten, Richard of Bordeaux (the only surviving child of Edward of Woodstock, the Black Prince and Joan of Kent) succeeded as King Richard II.

Alice Perrers:
Adventuress and Concubine

THROUGHOUT THEIR marriage, Edward was notoriously unfaithful to Queen Philippa. He had a succession of mistresses, and at least two bore several of his illegitimate offspring. His most notorious mistress was Alice Perrers, Queen Philippa's chief lady-in-waiting. She was the mother of at least four of Edward III's bastards. After Queen Philippa died, Alice took on royal airs, and used power over members of Parliament to enrich her own purse. Negative comments against her include the tale that, as the king lay dying from a stroke at Sheen Palace, she stripped the jeweled rings from his fingers before slithering away. Only by accident, a priest found the king later in the day in time to administer Extreme Unction before he died.

Alice Perrers was the daughter of a Hertfordshire knight, but her surname Perrers may have come from a first husband. She was also known by the name Alice de Windsor for a second husband named William de Windsor. Both of her marriages came before she was lady-in-waiting to

Queen Philippa. She became the mistress of King Edward III around 1369. Edward recognized four of her children as his own. After Queen Philippa's death, Edward gave Alice (or Alice stole) many of Philippa's jewels, and wore them openly at court. She is reputed to have used bribes, and personal influence to force financially favorable legal decisions for herself and her favorites. Parliament expelled Alice from court in 1376 for using witchcraft to influence the king. However, in answer to a request from the infirm king, she soon returned. She was briefly banished again after King Edward's death in 1377. However, she returned, and soon rose to a high social position in court as a person of substantial means. She died in 1400, but lives on as England's most egregiously calculating ambitious scheming and greedy woman of disrepute.

REIGN 12

KING RICHARD II

AND

QUEEN CONSORT ANNE
OF BOHEMIA

AND

QUEEN CONSORT ISABELLA
OF VALOIS

Summary of the Reign of King Richard II
(Reign 1377-1399)

King Richard II: life dates c. 32 years, b. January 6, 1367-d. c.
February 14, 1400; King of England 22 years, June 22, 1377-c.
February 14, 1400.

KING RICHARD II was a grandson of King Edward III, and the only surviving child of Prince Edward of Woodstock ('The Black Prince') and Joan the Fair Maid of Kent. Richard of Bordeaux was born in Gascony while his father was viceroy of that province in southern France. The Black Prince died before Edward III. Therefore, following the death of Edward III, Richard of Bordeaux, who was next in line for the throne, became King Richard II in 1377. Richard inherited the crown as a frail blond ten year old boy.

For the first eight years of his reign, Richard's uncle, John of Gaunt Duke of Lancaster ruled England as regent.

King Richard inherited a nation deeply in debt from nearly forty years of war with France. The conflict now called the Hundred Years War continued intermittently from 1337 until 1453. When Richard came to the throne in 1377, England and France enjoyed a fragile peace created by the Treaty of Bruges signed in 1375. All England suffered despair from the loss of all its earlier winnings of war, save Calais. England and all Europe also suffered from horrors of the Black Death, which had reduced populations in Europe to nearly half after 1350. Anarchy and rebellion challenged authority of Church and State.

The high point in King Richard's reign came when, as a fourteen year old boy, he quieted a peasant revolt led by Wat Tyler in 1381. Richard's intervention spared London burning and massacre. Initial high expectations for Richard's reign were quashed by later imperious acts when he claimed full powers of the throne in 1386 after John of Gaunt's regency ended.

Richard ruled capriciously, and appointed many unqualified favorites to positions of great power. With Richard's approval, they passed and revoked laws to their own advantage, with no regard for presidents of Common Law that had evolved for two hundred years. His imperial acts outraged Parliament.

Five nobles, who called themselves the Lords Appellant, took control of Parliament in 1387-1389—history has called it the *Merciless Parliament*—they usurped the king's authority and immediately executed, exiled, or otherwise removed all King Richard's appointments to high office. Although he was deeply offended, King Richard played a game of mock contrition, acquiescence, and diplomacy with Parliament. By so doing, he slowly rebuilt his political power, and when he was sure of his strength in 1396, he again flouted Parliamentary tradition, and again, justice in courts of law vanished. Richard entered a period of personal misrule known as the *Tyranny of Richard II* that continued from late in 1396 to the end of his reign in 1399.

By 1398, four of the five Lords Appellant, who had offended his vanity and power, were removed by murder, execution, or exile. Of the Lords Appellant, only Henry of Bolingbroke, the eldest son of John of Gaunt remained. He led a revolt of English noblemen against King Richard II in 1399. The king was defeated, captured, and then imprisoned in the Tower of London, before he was forced to abdicate his throne. Following his abdication, Richard was imprisoned on the Lancaster estate at Pontefract Castle in Yorkshire. An official report said that Richard refused to eat rich foods presented to him, and that he committed suicide by starving himself to death. However, most people believed that his Lancaster prisoners starved Richard, and he probably died in mid February 1400 at the age of thirty-two or thirty-three.

At the age of fifteen, King Richard married Anne of Bohemia, daughter of Emperor Charles IV of the Holy Roman Empire. The marriage of Richard and Anne lasted only twelve years before the plague carried Anne away in 1394. Two years after Queen Anne died, Richard married Princess Isabella of Valois who was the eldest daughter of King Charles IV of France.

Richard had no issue from either of his marriages.

Henry of Bolingbroke usurped the crown of King Richard II, and Bolingbroke was crowned King Henry IV of England on October 13, 1399.

Narrative of Queen Consort Anne of Bohemia

Queen Anne of Bohemia: life dates 28 years, b. May 11, 1366-d. June 7, 1394; first Queen Consort of King Richard II 12 years, January 20, 1382-June 7, 1394.

ANNE OF BOHEMIA was the eldest daughter of King Charles IV of Bohemia Emperor of the Holy Roman Empire and his fourth wife

Elizabeth of Pomerania. Anne was born in Prague on May 11, 1366 when her father was sixty-two. He was an erudite aesthete who had been educated in Paris. He was recognized as a scholar fluent in Czech, German, French, Italian, and Latin. After his father (the blind King John of Bohemia) was killed at the Battle of Crécy in 1346, Charles became King of Bohemia and Emperor of the Holy Roman Empire in 1355. Charles IV returned to Bohemia where he made Prague his capital. He spent his life as king and emperor in efforts to modernize Prague on the model of Paris, and to transform it into a center of art and scholarship. One of his first acts was to create the University of Prague in 1348, the first university in Central Europe. Through Charles' patronage, Prague became a major intellectual and cultural center. His reign of thirty years (1348-1378) is credited with being the *Golden Age of Bohemia*, and he is recognized as *Pater Patriae* of what is now the Czech Republic. After his death, that title was awarded to him by acclaim from his adoring people. He was buried at Saint Vitus Cathedral Prague in 1378.

Princess Anne of Bohemia grew up in Prague at the time Prague was at the apogee of its remarkable cultural emergence from the Dark Ages. Princess Anne had many virtues. She was beautiful, cultured, well-read, intelligent, noble, religious, and admired for gentle kindness. She was proficient and literate in Latin, Czech, German, and French. She was far more educated and intellectually alert than was usual for women in the Middle Ages, or of any age.

Richard's marriage to Anne of Bohemia was a departure from earlier English royal marriages. Never had there been an English royal marriage alliance with a Central European royal house. Previous English queens consort were royal or noble heiresses of England, Scotland, the Low Countries, or from provinces of France or Spain. The reason for the novelty of seeking a queen consort from a German-Slavic-Italian country becomes clear by understanding events that were taking place in Western Europe when Richard II came to the throne in 1377. Two events polarized diplomatic relationships between England and Western Europe:

> *First*, was the altercation that history now calls the *Hundred Years War* (1337-1453), by which France and England became hereditary enemies.
>
> *Second*, was the *Great Western Schism* in the Catholic Church (1378-1417), in which the Catholic Church had

elected two popes—Pope Clement VII in Avignon had support
from France, Spain, and the Low Countries—Pope Urban IV
in Rome was supported by England, Italy, and the Holy Roman
Empire of Central Europe.

Thus, both diplomacy and religion denied Richard a bride
from traditional Atlantic European nations—France, Spain, or
the Low Countries. Therefore, Richard's bride must come from
either Italy or Central Europe.

In these polarized circumstances, Richard's trusted Oxford teacher Sir
Simon Burley headed a commission assigned to negotiate a suitable
marriage for young King Richard. A daughter of Viscount Barnabo of
Milan was favored at first, for the handsome dowry that accompanied
her nomination. However, Pope Urban IV in Rome favored Anne of
Bohemia. Anne's marriage to Richard II would strengthen his authority in
the Church by creating a strong alliance between England and the Holy
Roman Empire with its capital in Prague, Bohemia.

Emperor Charles, Anne's father, died when she was only six years old,
and her half-brother became King Wenceslaus IV of Bohemia. Negotiations
for Anne's marriage to child-King Richard II began in 1379.

Both children were twelve years old. Wenceslaus enthusiastically
promoted the alliance with England, but regretted that he would be
unable to provide a suitable dowry for Anne. The Bohemian treasury was
bankrupt occasioned by the lavish expenditures of his father Charles IV in
transforming Prague into a center of culture and learning. Also, recurrent
civil conflicts in administering Bohemian provinces (Luxembourg,
Moravia, Selicia, and annexed parts of Poland and Austria) were a constant
drain on Bohemian finances. Like all Europe, Bohemia suffered crushing
economic depression brought on by the Black Death, which had entered
Italy from the Near East in 1348, and in repeated epidemics, the plague
had eliminated up to half the population throughout Europe.

On receiving the short list of prospective queen consorts for King
Richard, the English Parliament (itself in no better economic health
than Bohemia) rejected impoverished Anne of Bohemia, as providing no
advantage to the realm. Twelve year old King Richard was of a different
mind. He was instantly smitten by the glowing descriptions of Anne's
many virtues—especially her piety and gentle nature. It mattered little

to Richard that Anne was penniless, and spoke no English. Time could correct that.

Against strong opposition from the English nobility and Parliament, Richard commanded that arrangements for his marriage to Anne of Bohemia be finalized. He even agreed to reverse tradition, and give his prospective brother-in-law Emperor Wenceslaus a dowry of 20,000 florins (the equivalent of £13,000 Sterling). Wenceslaus, in lieu of cash, signed a mutually beneficial free trade agreement between England and the Holy Roman Empire.

The marriage contract was finally signed early in 1381, but the Wat Tyler Rebellion (May and June 1381) threatened domestic tranquility in England until the end of July. It delayed plans for the marriage. Finally, by late summer 1381, Anne was ready to depart for London. Parliament was appalled when Emperor Wenceslaus said he could not even afford the expense of a suitable Grand Progress for Anne's move from Prague to England.

England's Parliament refused to underwrite Anne's travel costs. Gallant King Richard agreed to pay for it all from his own pocket—what amounted to a king's ransom—for Anne's leisurely, five hundred mile, six-week junket, from central Europe to the North Sea.

One can visualize her entourage of many priests, clerks, domestic servants, squires, valets, cooks, scullery knaves, and noble ladies-in-waiting—numbering in all over a hundred. They, with necessary luggage, stumbled and grumbled on foot, horseback, and wagon over endless muddy roads, across many creaking bridges, at a ponderous velocity of no more than ten to fifteen miles a day. Her trip required many stops for rest and refreshment of her entourage at castles of her many relatives along the way.

Anne's cavalcade arrived at Brussels in early fall of 1381. It set up temporary residence with Anne's aunt, Duchess Joanna of Brabant, and her uncle Duke Wenceslaus I of Luxembourg. Anne asked them to intervene on her behalf to persuade their cousin Charles IV of France to approve safe transit for Anne's company to Bruges, and then to lift the French blockade on trade between French and English ports. If that were done, Anne would hire ships to transport her party and its voluminous impedimenta to England

Original plans called for Anne to cross the North Sea from Flanders to Kent by Michaelmas, September 29, 1381. However, King Charles of

France withheld approval of their passage from Bruges to England until late November. The first thirty-five years of the Hundred Years War, which had just ended, left deep animosity between France and England. The Treaty of Bruges in 1375 declared a truce between England and France, but the peace was tenuous and still fragile between the two nations. Finally, in the first week of December, Anne's party arrived in Bruges. However, their North Sea crossing in winter was further delayed by foul weather until the first of the year. Anne's party finally arrived, and had unloaded on English soil in the first week of January 1382, just before a North Sea gale wrecked their anchored ships. Anne went to London, and exchanged rings in symbolic marriage with King Richard on January 14. Their formal marriage was at Westminster Abbey on January 20. Anne was crowned Queen Consort two days later on January 22, 1382.

King Richard was just fifteen and Queen Anne a half-year older when they exchanged vows. The royal crown for her coronation was obtained from pawn in London, because all those in the royal treasury were too large for her small head. The Westminster chronicle of the occasion referred to Anne as "a tiny scrap of humanity." Another observer said she was "of comely countenance and courtly demeanor." Festivities, jousting, and tournaments throughout England celebrated the marriage, and her coronation. The January wedding of 1382 was followed in the spring by two elaborate progresses through England to introduce the new queen to her subjects. At great expense, the royal party stayed in abbeys and castles of noble friends.

The marriage of English King Richard to Princess Anne of Bohemia was little welcomed by citizens of England. In the depressed economic time, few English purses jingled, and Anne brought no rich dower with her. All England knew that the new queen's German-speaking Bohemian retinue all expected support at government expense. The foreigners would demand to live in a style equal to, or better than the one, they enjoyed in their homeland. Although common people customarily blamed foreign consort queens for all their king's failings, Anne's genuinely kind and winsome nature soon erased the hostility that greeted her arrival in England.

Anne's first diplomatic triumph came in winning the love of common folk in England almost immediately after her coronation. Wat Tyler's Peasant Rebellion of May and June 1381 had delayed Anne's arrival to England. The uprising was the first challenge by the English commons to royal authority. The peasant revolt was a reaction against an increase in taxes, and protest to laws that limited earning by peasants.

In this uncertain calm after her coronation, Queen Anne proposed to Richard that, in honor of their marriage, she would like him to give amnesty to the peasants of Essex and Kent who had participated in Wat Tyler's rebellion. Richard was smitten by his new bride. He could deny Anne nothing. On learning of their reprieve, the peasants of England rejoiced. When they learned of Anne's intercession on their behalf, she was named, *Good Queen Anne.* This was the first of many occasions in which Queen Anne later pled for mercy for persons unjustly charged with crimes.

Anne's second important conquest was with her mother-in-law Countess Joan the Fair Maid of Kent. Joan was immediately won over on learning that her new daughter-in-law Queen Anne was well informed on philosophy and religion, and that she brought from Prague many printed religious texts, including German gospels. Countess Joan was most impressed by writings of the young priest Jan Huss, who was gaining notoriety for expressions of radical challenge to Church authority. Countess Joan found many beliefs of Jan Huss to be similar to those of John Wycliffe, the radical priest at Oxford who has been called, *The Morning Star of the Reformation*; Countess Joan was Wycliffe's benefactor. Anne and Joan cooperated in having German gospels and religious texts translated into English. Anne was active in sending copies of Wycliffe's essays to Jan Huss in Prague.

Chronicles of the time agree that King Richard's attraction to Princess Anne, at first, was mere teenage infatuation, but their love grew to be unwavering deep affection. The twelve years they were married, without question, were the happiest years of Richard's life. Richard and Anne were adolescent children born to privilege with little understanding for poverty of the masses. Their court engaged in frenzied ostentation at a time when poverty prevailed throughout the land. The Palace of Sheen on the Thames southwest of London, which had been built by his grandfather Edward III, was the center for Richard and Anne's court.

A report gives the breakdown of their annual court expenses, as £9,000 for servants, £15,000 for royal apparel, and £18,000 for food and refreshment. The degree to which the court was out of touch with the English public gains perspective in learning that an annual income of only £5 or £10 a year was thought to be ample for an average family's sustenance.

Shapeless smocks fit for monks and nuns who had taken vows of poverty were not for Anne. She imported extravagant costumes from the Continent that were appropriate for *Mardi Gras*—such garb was never before seen in England (see the note on *Medieval Sumptuary Laws* at the close of this chapter).

The fashions of Anne's court are best visualized today in theatrical period costumes commonly used for Shakespearean productions of *Taming of the Shrew, A Midsummer Night's Dream,* or *All's Well that Ends Well.* Fashionable headdresses commonly towered two feet high, and sported cones or horn-like prominences bedecked with lace, feathers, and flowing veils. Velvet and lace in bright patterns and plaids decorated outlandishly ornate gowns. Stockings were held up with ribbons and bows; high heel shoes with upturned points carried tinkling bells. Elaborate masques and balls were contrived to make the English court the standard for sophisticated entertainment.

The court of Richard and Anne also was famous throughout Europe for its sumptuous food. The first cookbook in the English language dates from 1390 and comes from the chef in Richard's royal kitchen. In it are over two hundred recipes, many for meat and sweet dishes, which give directions for preparing elaborately spiced sauces and pastries that called for ginger, cinnamon, mace, cardamom, curry, and other rare herbs transported overland at great expense from the spice islands of the Far East. The cookbook described (in the quaint phonetic spelling of Chaucerian Middle English) the preparation of *blancmange* (a sweet sauce thickened with wheat flour by simmering then cooling to gel), *flummery* (a hot fruit soup of honey, berries, or figs), *mortrew* (a sweet savory meat stew covered with pastry), *custard* (a sweet or spiced baked omelet-like ancestor of quiche).

Outdoor equestrian activities were popular and Richard, who was so infatuated with Anne that he could hardly bare to have her leave his side, encouraged Anne to take part in sporting events and horseback riding. She met the challenge by having the sidesaddle invented for her use. That awkward contraption remained in vogue through the Victorian Age for women of status who enjoyed riding for pleasure, or for sport in following the hounds. Anne also was instrumental in bringing to England designs for aristocratic carriages from central Europe, to make travel clean and somewhat comfortable to stylish outings at noble palaces.

The first eight years of Richard's reign (1377-1385) were under a regency of the king's uncle John of Gaunt Duke of Lancaster who administered government with power of the monarch. Under Gaunt's regency, Richard was given much freedom of the purse for his extravagant court expenses, but the king was restrained from tampering with the operation of parliamentary government. However, King Richard was a monarchist to the core. He had little respect for any democratic measures that curbed his will. Richard had massive contempt for English Common Law and Parliament.

At the beginning of 1386, Richard turned eighteen, and he was then eligible to rule in his own name. Shortly after his regency ended, John of Gaunt left England and went to Spain in 1386 on a personal venture designed to earn him the title King of Castile. However, that ambition failed, and after two years, Gaunt returned to England at the end of 1389.

In Gaunt's absence Richard ruled without any restraint—the consequence for him and England was disastrous.

With Gaunt's exodus, King Richard's mismanagement of government rapidly extended far beyond personal extravagance in food and costume. The adolescent king appointed favorites to positions of great power. They passed laws to their own advantage that enraged the populace. Richard's inept first attempt to rule lasted only one year. It ended in 1387 with the election of the *Merciless Parliament,* in which a self-appointed group of five noblemen in the House of Lords, who called themselves the *Lords Appellant,* took charge of Parliament. With unseemly dispatch, they removed Richard's appointments to high office. During the trial of the king's great friend and childhood mentor, Sir Simon Burley, Queen Anne pled for his acquittal on bended knee, but even her special entreaties left the stonyhearted Lords Appellant unmoved. Burley and many others of the king's favorites were executed. However, her efforts to gain mercy for the king's men strengthened respect for the queen among the nobility.

King Richard offended the City of London on an occasion in 1392, when the Lord Mayor of London refused to increase the annual crown tariff by £1,000. In rage, Richard revoked London's charter for general trade. That amounted to closing all means of trade for citizens in the city. Queen Anne interceded on The City of London's behalf by bowing down with her head on the floor, pleading piteously for the king to relent. Richard reluctantly reinstated the city charter for trade. Anne had a calming effect on Richard, and a positive influence in making him reflect twice before he acted in anger. Anne only rarely inserted herself into political affairs.

Personal tragedy struck Richard a cruel blow in 1394. After only two days of illness, Queen Anne suddenly died from the Black Death on June 7, 1394. Richard entered a period of profound mourning, and people said, "[He was] wild with grief . . . utterly inconsolable . . . distraught beyond measure . . . and feared he would lose his mind."

King Richard ordered a High Mass for Queen Anne in Westminster Abbey. The entire court was ordered to attend. Richard FitzAlan Earl of Arundel (one of the five Lords Appellant) did not arrive on time, and then he insulted the king by asking permission to leave early "to attend to matters of importance."

In fury, King Richard struck Arundel on the head with such force that he fell bleeding to the floor of the Abbey, The King then ordered Arundel to prison in the Tower of London. Anne's funeral was delayed until the sanctuary could be properly purified, and consecrated to allow the Mass to continue.

For a year after Anne's death, Richard refused to step foot in any room or corridor that Anne had used in Sheen Palace. Sheen had been the favorite home of Edward III and Richard II, but in spring of 1395, Richard issued an order to his master of grounds, "Lay waste and destroy the Manor of Sheen, [including all] the houses and buildings within the moat." The order was carried out down to bare foundations of the great house, including its many outbuildings and barns. Sheen Castle estate lay fallow for a century, until the Crown Property was used by Henry VII to build Richmond Court, the favorite resident of Tudor monarchs.

After Queen Anne's death, King Richard commissioned an elaborate marble tomb to be built to hold his and Anne's bodies. The tomb was decorated with heraldry and saints in *bas-relief,* and was surmounted with two life-size gilded copper effigies in regal dress with scepters, and holding hands; a canopy covered it all. The tomb was installed in Edward the Confessor's Chapel beside the tombs of Richard's grandparents, Edward III and his Queen Philippa.

All was in readiness when Anne died, and her body was interred in Westminster Abbey in June 1399. Anne's effigy shows a small, somewhat dumpy plain woman of no particular beauty or nobility. One wonders, does her effigy truly represent Queen Anne? She was said to be, "The model for beauty, grace, and fashion."

During her life, Queen Anne of Bohemia tirelessly tried to bring out the best elements in her husband's character. The animosity and hate that swirled around Richard did not cling to Anne. She has been cited as an example of an *ambassadorial royal bride*; that is, she was one who transplanted cultural aspects of her home country into customs of her spouse's land. Anne served that function by importing German religious scholarship to England. She was admired for personal bravery in defense of justice for the common man, and for support to many charitable foundations. Of little lasting importance were the contributions she made to fashion in dress, food, and etiquette. Her acts as queen had little lasting effect on England, but her countrymen held her dear. Now after six hundred years, without help from any major writer, Anne of Bohemia remains England's *Good Queen Anne*. Whatever Anne's minor failings may have been, they hurt no one. Anne's virtues were many, and her vices fall among forgivable feminine tendencies to add unnecessary sparkle and merriment to life.

Richard II probably died in mid February 1400 at the age of 32 or 33. He was first buried at King's Langley Dominican Priory at Pontefract Castle, but he was reinterred later in Westminster Abbey with Queen Anne during the reign of King Henry V. Effigies on the tombs are believed to be true-to-life representations of Richard and Anne. Richard's effigy is of a handsome slender youth. His epitaph read:

He threw down whomsoever violated the Royal Prerogative

That statement is a reasonably exact summary of Richard's views on the proper roles of a monarch in government.

Historians are unanimous in giving Richard and Anne unblemished matrimonial records. As one of them put it, "[They were the] ultimate personification of true love and faithfulness in marriage." However, a persistent unanswered question has troubled historians about the reign of King Richard II and his Queen Anne of Bohemia: Why were no children born? Why were no stillbirths reported?

Specters of barrenness and deviant behavior have been raised as possible reasons for their lack of children. However, no convincing factual answer exists for either of those possibilities. One writer has speculated that their marriage was without issue, because "the marriage itself was entirely chaste, and never consummated." Others have suggested that Anne may have been barren, but if so, why did Richard not use that as a legitimate reason for him to seek annulment with Church permission to marry again? Richard never gave any sign of a wish to end their union.

Richard married again about two years after Anne died. His second marriage on October 31, 1396 was to Isabella de Valois of France, but it does not illuminate the question of why King Richard and Queen Anne had no heir. Isabella de Valois was only six years old, and Richard's second marriage was never consummated. His second marriage was part of a political exercise to ensure continuation of peace between England and France.

Richard of Bordeaux and his queen consort Anne of Bohemia were not major actors in the brief time history allotted them. Their cockleshell lives tumbled before an incoming tide of social, political, and theological change beyond anyone's ability to withstand, much less could they be controlled by children who were heirs to privilege and plenty when, as adolescents, they were dropped into what history calls the *Close of the turbulent 14th Century.*

Richard II and Anne of Bohemia had no issue. Two years after Anne died in June 1394, Richard married Princess Isabella of Valois in November 1396.

Narrative of Queen Consort Isabella of Valois

Queen Isabella of Valois: life dates 20 years, b. November 9, 1389-d. September 13, 1409; second Queen Consort of King Richard II 3 years, November 1, 1396-September 30, 1399; Dowager Queen c. 9 years, February 14, 1400-September 13, 1409; Duchess of Orleans, spouse of Duke Charles of Orleans 3 years, June 29, 1406-September 13, 1409.

PRINCESS ISABELLA of Valois was the eldest child of King Charles VI of France and Isabella of Bavaria-Ingolstadt. She was born in Paris on November 9, 1389. At age six, she was married to recently widowed King Richard II of England. The marriage on October 31, 1396 was part of a diplomatic package designed to prolong a truce in the Hundred Years War that was created by the Treaty of Bruges in 1375.

When Richard agreed to the marriage of State with Princess Isabella of Valois, he was in deep mourning for his first wife Anne of Bavaria who had died in June 1396. Isabella was only six years old. His new child-bride was treated as an adopted daughter, in which the consummation of marriage was never contemplated. The tender mutual relationship that developed between Richard and Isabella was entirely that of a deeply affectionate father and daughter, or of a doting uncle for a niece.

Three years later in 1399 when Isabella was nine, Richard embarked on a futile military mission to Ireland. In the king's absence from England, the entire English nobility, led by the king's first cousin Henry of Bolingbroke, rebelled, and forced the king to abdicate. Richard was imprisoned until his death, probably on February 14, 1400, in Pontefract Castle on Bolingbroke's Lancaster estate in Yorkshire. When Richard abdicated, Henry of Bolingbroke Duke of Lancaster was crowned King Henry IV on September 30, 1399.

Isabella's fate was highly uncertain after this brief civil war in England that deposed her husband Richard II. She was removed from her royal residences at Wallingford and Windsor Palaces, and placed for protective custody in care of the Bishop of Salisbury at his palace on the Thames outside London. At first, Henry IV planned to give Isabella in marriage to his son Henry of Monmouth (later, Henry V), but Isabella violently objected to the plan on grounds that she was still in deep mourning for her former husband Richard II. The plans for her marriage to Monmouth were abandoned, and Isabella returned to France in 1402.

Three years later, when she was seventeen, Isabella married her cousin Count Charles d'Angoulême Duc d'Orleans, on June 29, 1406. They had one living daughter, but when Isabella was nineteen, and after only three years into her second marriage, she died in her second childbirth on September 13, 1409. Isabella of Valois was interred, first in the abbey of St. Laumer in Blois, after which in 1624 her body was removed to the Orleans Celestine Monastery in Paris.

Isabella of Valois' minor mark on English history rests mainly on a coincidence: she was the eldest sister of Katherine of Valois, Queen Consort of Henry V—Katherine of Valois' was in succession: Princess of France, Queen of England, mother of King Henry VI, and grandmother of King Henry (Tudor) VII of England.

Medieval Sumptuary Laws

A NOVELTY of the reign of King Richard II and Queen Anne of Bohemia was that *Fashion in Clothing* reared its lovely head.

For centuries in England, clothes worn by men and women alike varied little from century to century. Clothing consisted of four basic elements: *The head* was covered for protection from rain and weather with a cloth or leather cap or cowl (the latter was a hood stitched at the shoulder to a tunic or long-coat). *The upper body* was covered by a loose-fitting tunic (a shirt, with or without sleeves). *A long skirt supported at the waist with a girdle with an attached reticule for carrying personal items covered the lower body of women.* Whereas, *the lower body of men* was enclosed in single-piece close-fitting (long-john-like) hose that covered waist, hips and legs, and supported at the waist by a heavy belt with holsters for a dagger and sword. *The feet,* for inside wear were shod in cloth or leather heelless socks or slippers, but outside the feet were bare or covered in leather leggings with heavy wooden soles to give protection from stones, mud, and filth. These four elements of clothing were often layered to meet temperature requirements of different seasons throughout the year. In addition, scarves, shawls, veils, waistcoats, long coats, and gloves were optional accessories. Clothing was tailored to suit size and function, but all elements of clothing were shapeless and lacked individuality. It is said that a maiden could wear hand-me-down clothing from a great-grandmother, and confidently be in style—*any time* was *every time* in medieval fashion.

However, very great differences in costume centered on materials from which clothing was made. For example, coarse linsey-woolsey was standard for peasants, but silk, satin, or damask identified the clothing for nobility. Wealth has always been evident in attire, but in the Middle Ages, laws also dictated which materials were restricted to different ranks in society. These legally enforced class restrictive conventions in attire were the *Sumptuary Laws*.

In England they reflected the hierarchy of seven social classes: *serfs* (bonded slaves), *peasants—stewards* (free laborers—servants), *artisans—clerks* (skilled craftsmen & professionals), *gentry—esquires* (land holding gentlemen), *lower nobility addressed sir* (knights & barons), *higher nobility addressed lord* (earls & dukes), *royalty* (kings & princes). In England, wives always carried the same social status as one's husband, but that was not the case in most continental countries in which Salic Law denied acquisition of titled status through marriage.

Obviously, the purpose of sumptuary laws was to maintain rigidly the stratified structure of society by making persons of each rank readily identifiable by the clothing one wore, and by administering severe penalties if one did not conform with the dress code appropriate for one's station in life.

Sumptuary laws did not prescribe specific costumes or uniforms to be worn by the respective classes. Instead, the laws merely defined *materials that could not be worn* by classes below a given rank. Thus, cloth with gold and silver thread could not be worn by anyone below royal rank; silk and satin could not be worn by anyone below noble rank; the length of veils and trains on dresses, and height of heels on shoes had specific lengths that could not be exceeded by lower classes.

Ever since the Stone Age, men and women alike have adorned their bodies with ornaments; accordingly, the wearing of necklaces, brooches, rings, buckles, and crowns made of precious or base metals were also prescribed and proscribed by sumptuary laws, as were jewels. Diamonds, rubies, and sapphires were always rare, and were denied those without royal or noble title. Semiprecious amethyst, topaz, garnet, and pearls were not permissible for persons without noble or gentry heraldic title. Finally, no matter what one's wealth might be, commoners not approved for a coat of arms by the Office of Heralds had to make-do with baubles of rock crystal, carnelian, jet, jasper, and jade. Faceting of gemstones would not be practiced until the end of the 15th century. Thus, all medieval jewels, although hand rubbed to cabochon smoothness, were mounted as lackluster pebbles—the huge Black Prince ruby (actually, a crystal of *spinel*, not *corundum*) presently mounted front and center on England's Royal Crown of State is one of these.

Sumptuary laws also restricted the use of certain foods, spices, furs, furniture, and tableware. Indeed, whatever served to define social position was eligible for restriction.

It is natural that sumptuary laws were despised by lower classes, since they flouted all mankind's generic instincts for social climbing.

Conclusion to the Angevin Plantagenet Dynasty

RICHARD II was the last king of the Angevin Plantagenet Dynasty. It began in 1154, and ended 245 years later in 1399. The founder of the Angevin Plantagenet Dynasty was King Henry II (Henry Plantagenet Count of Anjou), who was followed by his lineal descendants: Kings Richard I The Lionheart, John, Henry III, Edward I, Edward II, Edward III, and Richard II.

The Angevin Plantagenet Period ended with the death of Richard II. King Richard had no heir and, had primogeniture been observed after Richard's death, his rightful successor would have been, eight year old Roger Mortimer, 4th Earl of March, grandson of Lionel of Antwerp Duke of Clarence. However, the Mortimers in the Western Marches had neither the political clout, nor inclination to advance their prior rights to the throne at the time Henry of Bolingbroke usurped the crown on October 13, 1399.

Henry of Bolingbroke usurped the crown from his cousin Richard II, and was crowned Henry IV on October 13, 1399. Henry IV was the first in the brief Lancaster Plantagenet Dynasty, which included only Henry IV, Henry V, and Henry VI. The Lancaster Plantagenet Dynasty lasted sixty-two years, from 1399 to 1461.

Rest assured, the Mortimers descended from Lionel Duke of Clarence and Edmund Duke of York would bide their time. Three generations later, Yorkists, who inherited the Mortimer prior claim through marriage, would reopen the issue of, *the right to rule by primogeniture*. The Lancaster-versus-York Wars of the Roses (1453 to 1485), which dominate reigns of Henry VI, Edward IV, Edward V, Richard III, and (to a lesser degree) Henry VII, are bloody internecine attempts to resolve this problem of primogeniture.

DYNASTY IIIb

THE LANCASTER PANTAGENET DYNASTY
REIGN 13 THROUGH 15 (1399–1461)

The Lancaster Plantagenet Dynasty
Patriarch John of Gaunt
Duke of Lancaster

JOHN OF Gaunt Duke of Lancaster was the third surviving son of Edward III and Queen Philippa. Although never king, he was the patriarch of Lancastrian and Tudor kings. Except for the three York Kings (Edward IV, Edward V and Richard III), the Lancaster bloodline is in all English monarchs after Richard II.

John of Gaunt's is recognized in English history by the simple titles *Old Lancaster* or *Time Honored Lancaster*.

Historians have slighted John of Gaunt, possibly because in his own time, the English people held him in disrepute. He was regent for his father Edward III at a desperate time of defeat during the Hundred Years

War while wealth declined in the nation, and hopelessness faced recurrent outbreaks of the Black Death. Now, six hundred years after Gaunt's death, enough time has passed to ignore past prejudice. Old Lancaster, when judged by standards of any age, shines forth as a talented and honorable public servant.

John was born at Ghent, Flanders. The city was about equidistant from Bruges, Antwerp, and Brussels. John's English countrymen always corrupted the city of his birth to *Gaunt*. His birth in Flanders (his mother native land) came while his father pursued an English attack on France in the Hundred Years War. The marine victory over the French at nearby Sluys on the North Sea came a few months after John's birth.

Born in the twilight of chivalry, Prince John was destined to be a warrior prince indoctrinated to accept all concepts of medieval feudal fealty. Prince John was only four years old when his older brother Edward 'The Black Prince' gloriously won his spurs at the age of sixteen in the great English victory at Crécy on August 26, 1346. Ten years later sixteen year old John had his day in battle, as he fought beside the Black Prince at Poitiers on September 19, 1356. Near the end of the reign of Edward III, Gaunt led England's armies in less successful phases of the Hundred Years War. After the Black Prince became viceroy of Gascony, and his health began to fail, Gaunt served as vice-regent of Bordeaux.

As a youth of seventeen, John of Gaunt married Blanche the second daughter of Duke Henry of Lancaster. John of Gaunt and Blanche of Lancaster should have looked for better matches, but they married for love. John of Gaunt, as third surviving son of King Edward III, was too far down in the succession to have any expectation of inheriting great power or wealth from his father King Edward III. Blanche was a second daughter. Therefore, she, too, expected to inherit no great share of the vast Lancaster estate, which eventually went to her older sister Matilda. Neither John nor Blanche could know in advance that the Black Death would take Blanche's father a year after they married, which made Blanche's sister Matilda the Duchess of Lancaster. Nor that only a year later, the plague also would remove Matilda.

With Matilda's death, fate's unpredictable frowns and smiles awarded Blanche the entire Lancaster estate, and she became Duchess of Lancaster in her own right. She was now the richest woman in England. By his marriage to Blanche, her husband Prince John of Gaunt became the Duke of Lancaster—John of Gaunt was now Liege lord over the greatest estate in England. John of Gaunt was known ever after by his title Duke of Lancaster.

It is from their descent from John of Gaunt Duke of Lancaster that the kings Henry IV, Henry V, and Henry VI are known as the Lancaster Plantagenet Dynasty.

As Duke of Lancaster, John of Gaunt had great personal responsibilities for maintaining his estates. In size and location, the Lancaster holdings in northwest England made the Duchy of Lancaster almost an independent principality. The Lancaster lands boasted over thirty castles. In total size, it equaled nearly one-sixth of all England. Many Lancaster estates near the Scottish border constantly required defense from attack. Later in his life, Gaunt played a dominant role as regent (or vice-regent) during the last years of the reign of his father King Edward III, and as regent during the early years in the reign of his nephew Richard II.

John of Gaunt's position, ability, and ambition made him the most powerful, most feared, most hated, and richest man in England. He was blamed for everything that went awry—falling wages, rising taxes, floods, droughts, and even outbreaks of the Black Death—in the public mind, his power to create evil exceeded that of the Devil.

Many of Gaunt's detractors assumed that his personal goal was to wear the crown of England. Nothing in the record supports that view. Direct evidence shows that Gaunt worked loyally for his father King Edward III, and labored equally honorably for his nephew Richard II. Only gossip says that he worked surreptitiously behind the scene to remove Richard II from his throne. History shows that Richard was quite able to do that alone, with no help from anyone.

John of Gaunt served as King Richard's regent until Richard II was eighteen (from 1377 to 1386). During these early years of Richard's rule, Gaunt gave wise counsel that restrained Richard's willful ways. After his regency ended, Gaunt went to Spain in expectation of becoming King of Castile through marriage to Infanta Constance of Castile. Gaunt married Constance, but civil war prevented him from becoming the King of Castile. Gaunt returned to England almost three years later. King Richard II ruled, but Gaunt give him sage advice until Gaunt's death in 1399.

All evidence indicates that Richard loved and trusted Old Lancaster. Gaunt's wise council was almost the only restraint on King Richard to prevent open parliamentary conflict during much of Richards reign. When Richard ruled alone (cf., during Gaunt's absence in Spain, and after Gaunt died), affairs of State went awry. In 1399, the English nobles rebelled; King Richard abdicated, and Henry of Bolingbroke was crowned King Henry IV.

Henry of Bolingbroke was Old Lancaster's eldest son, and the first of Lancaster Plantagenet Dynasty of kings.

> *Note:* John of Gaunt is also a Patriarch of the Tudor Dynasty of English Kings. For that aspect of his life, see Dynasty IV. The Tudor Kings and Queens, Reign 19 through 24 (1485-1603).

The Lancaster Plantagenet Lineage, Reign 13 through 15 (1399-1461)

THE LANCASTER Plantagenet line lasted slightly over sixty years and included the reigns of Kings Henry VI, Henry V, and Henry VI.

Lancaster kings were descended from Edward III by his third son, John of Gaunt Duke of Lancaster. His eldest son Henry of Bolingbroke deposed Richard II, then usurped the crown, and became the first Lancastrian king, Henry IV.

From Dynasty IIIa. The Angevin Plantagenet Lineage:
Reign 11. Edward III (reign, 1327-1377) married Queen Consort Philippe of Hainault, parents of—
> John of Gaunt, Duke of Lancaster (3rd son of Edward III) married Blanch of Lancaster, parents of—

Beginning of Dynasty IIIb. The Lancaster Plantagenet Lineage:
Reign 13. Henry IV (reign, 1399-1413) married Mary de Bohun, parents of—
> **Reign 14. Henry V** (reign, 1413-1422) married Queen Consort Katherine of Valois, parents of—

Reign 15. Henry VI (reign, 1422-1461 & 1470-1471)
married Queen Consort Margaret of Anjou, parents of—
Edward of Westminster Prince of Wales was murdered
and Edward IV, Duke of York, usurped his crown.

End of Dynasty IIIb. The Lancaster Plantagenet Lineage; continue with
Dynasty III-3. The York Plantagenet Lineage.

REIGN 13

KING HENRY IV

AND

FIRST WIFE MARY DE BOHUN

AND

QUEEN CONSORT JOANNA

OF NAVARRE

Summary of the Reign of King Henry IV
(Reign 1399-1413)

King Henry IV: life dates 46 years, b. April 3, 1367-d. March 20, 1413; King of England 14 years, April 30, 1399-March 30, 1413.

K<small>ING</small> H<small>ENRY</small> IV is the first of three Lancastrian Kings (father, son, and grandson) Kings Henry IV, Henry V, and Henry VI.

Henry IV (Henry of Bolingbroke) was the eldest son of John of Gaunt Duke of Lancaster and Blanche Duchess of Lancaster. Henry was born in 1367 at Bolingbroke Castle, Lincolnshire. When his grandfather King Edward III died in 1377, his first cousin Richard of Bordeaux (son of Edward of Woodstock, the 'Black Prince') became King Richard II. His capricious and tyrannical reign lasted until 1399. When John of Gaunt died in February 1399, Richard confiscated the huge Lancaster estate. Henry of Bolingbroke was exiled in France, and when he learned that King Richard had disinherited him, he immediately returned to England from France to reclaim his ancestral Lancaster estate. The English nobility rallied behind Henry, and they encouraged him to usurp the crown from his cousin King Richard, who then was in Ireland attempting to repress a rebellion.

When Richard returned to England, Henry of Bolingbroke led the nobles and forced King Richard to abdicate. With parliamentary approval, Henry of Bolingbroke was crowned King Henry IV. Richard was imprisoned at Pontefract Castle on the Lancaster estate, where he died a few months later (possibly around February 14, 1400) from starvation on orders approved by King Henry.

The fourteen-year reign of Henry IV was one of continual strife as he tried to legitimize his usurped hold on the throne. He faced seditious plots at home, and rebellions on the Welsh and Scottish borders. His domestic involvements did not permit him to pursue the Hundred Years War with France. However, by avoiding confrontation with Parliament, he obtained its support through diplomacy, and he lost no significant amount of royal power. In this cautious way, he restored trust between Crown and Parliament, which had been severely eroded during the tyrannical reign of King Richard II.

The reign of King Henry IV serves as a prelude to the Wars of the Roses. History and fiction are intermingled in Shakespeare's rendering of the reign of Henry IV. In those plays, Falstaff triumphs as a bawdy buffoon, and rowdy Prince Hal (later Henry V) acts the part of a troublesome adolescent rebel against his father King Henry IV. The Bard summed up the reign of Henry IV accurately with the statement, "Uneasy rests the head that wears a crown."

Henry IV and his first wife Mary de Bohun had six surviving children. The eldest was Henry of Monmouth (Shakespeare's Prince Hal) who became King Henry V following his father's death in 1413. Mary de Bohun died before Henry became king; thus, she was never a queen consort. Mary de Bohun was buried at the Church of St Mary de Castro in Leicester.

After Mary de Bohun died, Henry IV married his second wife and Queen Consort Joanna of Navarre; this union had no issue.

The reign of Henry IV lasted 14 years: he died on March 30, 1413, and was buried in Canterbury Cathedral, Kent.

When Henry IV died, his eldest son Prince Henry of Monmouth succeeded to the throne in 1413 as King Henry V.

Narrative of Mary de Bohun the first wife of Henry IV

Mary de Bohun: life dates c. 24 years, b. 1369-d. June 4, 1394; first wife of Henry of Bolingbroke 14 years, July 27, 1380-June 4 1394; she died before he became King Henry IV, therefore, she was his wife, but never his queen consort.

MARY DE Bohun (pronounced, de Boone) was youngest of two daughters of Humphrey de Bohun 7th Earl of Hereford and Joan FitzAlan Countess of Arundel. The Earls of de Bohun, FitzAlan, and Arundel were of ancient nobility. The first Humphrey de Bohun was recorded as an esquire of King Henry I. He supported Empress Matilda and her son Henry Plantagenet in their struggles for the crown. Mary de Bohun probably was born late in 1368, or in early 1369 at Rochford, Essex in southeast England. She and Henry of Bolingbroke were married on July 27, 1380, when Henry was fourteen, and she was scarcely twelve years old. The ceremony occurred at her mother's family estate Arundel Castle on the English Channel east of Portsmouth. By his marriage to Mary de Bohen, he gained the titles, Earls of Hereford, Essex, and Northampton. Later, Henry of Bolingbroke received his title Earl of Darby from King Richard II.

In the 1380s, Henry of Bolingbroke was fourth in line to the throne, and he had no aspirations for the crown of England. His cousin King Richard II was a young married man with a high expectation of having heirs of his own, and they would have precedence in succession to the throne.

Soon after their marriage, Henry of Bolingbroke and Mary de Bohun went to live at Monmouth Castle in southwest England near Wales. Monmouth Castle originally was part of William the Conqueror's Norman defense against Wales. Henry of Monmouth (later, Henry V) the eldest of Henry and Mary's six surviving children were born there. The surviving offspring of Henry of Bolingbroke and Mary de Bohun were:

> Henry of Monmouth Prince of Wales (c. 1386/87-August 312, 1422), later King Henry V, and the hero of the battle of Agincourt
>
> Thomas of Lancaster Duke of Clarence (c. 1388-March 22, 1421)
>
> John of Lancaster Duke of Bedford (June 20, 1389-September 14, 1435)
>
> Humphrey of Lancaster Duke of Gloucester (October 3, 1390-February 23, 1447)
>
> Blanche of Lancaster Electress Palatine (c. 1392-May 22, 1409)
>
> Philippa of Lancaster Queen of Denmark, Sweden, and Norway (June 4, 1394-January 7, 1430)

During the reign of Richard II, Henry of Bolingbroke and his wife Mary were prominent in social activities at court. Incidental records show that they shared a love of music and playing chess. Aside from her significant role as mother of Harry of Monmouth (later Henry V), and of his brothers Thomas, John, and Humphrey, Mary de Bohun leaves little mark on English history.

Mary de Bohun was about twenty-four years old when she died on June 4, 1394 of childbed fever a few days after the birth of her seventh child. Mary de Bohun was buried in St Mary de Castro at Leicester Castle.

Narrative of Queen Consort Joanna of Navarre

Queen Joanna of Navarre: life dates c. 67 years, b. 1370-d. June 10, 1437; Duchess third wife of John V Duke of Brittany 13 years, October 2, 1386-November 1, 1399; Queen Consort second wife of King Henry IV 10 years, February 7, 1403-March 20, 1413; Dowager Queen of England 14 years, March 13, 1413-June 10, 1437.

JOANNA WAS the younger of two daughters of Charles II (the Bad) of Navarre and Jeanne de Valois a daughter of King John II of France. Joanna was born in Pamplona the capital of Navarre around 1370. She was fifteen or sixteen when she became the third wife of John de Montfort (John V, the Valiant) Duke of Brittany on October 2, 1386, when he was almost fifty years old. Duke John served Brittany well by resolving a conflict called the *Breton War of Succession*. It ended in 1364, and settled a dispute between the noble Houses de Blois and de Montfort for hereditary control of the Province of Brittany. When the conflict ended, the House de Montfort prevailed.

In spite of the differences in age between Duke Charles and Princess Joanna, the marriage was congenial. It lasted until John's death fourteen years later on November 1, 1399. They had nine children, of whom seven survived to maturity. Their eldest and second sons, in succession, became Dukes of Brittany after their father's death in 1399. In that year, King Richard II of England exiled Henry of Bolingbroke Duke of Lancaster to France. Joanna's husband Duke John V of Brittany was in Paris, and he responded favorably to Bolingbroke's request for support in his plan to return to England to reclaim his Lancaster estates that had been confiscated by King Richard II. Joanna probably met Henry of Bolingbroke in Paris in 1399 before her husband died later in the same year.

Historians speculate on whether the meeting of Henry and Joanna in Paris in 1399 started a mutual affection that led to their marriage four years later. It is suspected that Bolingbroke (who was now King Henry IV) engineered his second marriage with practical goals in mind. Perhaps, his motive was to gain Brittany as an ally, in the event that England again went to war with France.

Joanna returned from Paris to Brittany after her husband the Duke of Brittany died in November 1399. For over a year, she served as regent for her young son Duke John VI for the Duchy of Brittany. When negotiations began for her marriage to Henry IV of England in 1401, Joanna resigned her regency, and gave control of education and government of her sons to other relatives in Brittany. However, she was free to take her daughters with her to England after her marriage to Henry IV in 1403.

Joanna found the proposal for marriage to Henry of Bolingbroke (now King Henry IV) highly agreeable. However, a religious difficulty blocked the marriage. The *Great Western Schism of the Catholic Church* divided Western Europe into two Catholic camps; Henry of England was in one, and Joanna of Brittany was in the other.

The Western Schism occurred after Pope Gregory XI died in 1376, when two popes were chosen to succeed him: Boniface IX in Rome, and Benedict XIII in Avignon. France was allied with the Pope in Avignon, whereas England supported the Pope in Rome. Each pope referred to the other as the *Heretical Antipope*. Neither pope would agree with the other on any matter. Joanna, with her French connections, gave allegiance to Pope Benedict in Avignon. Henry recognized Pope Boniface in Rome. However, Henry was further tarnished for his support of John Wycliffe of Oxford (Wycliffe was a radical priest whose heretical views had been declared anathema by Pope Gregory XI).

In order that the royal second marriage between King Henry IV and Joanna of Navarre Duchess of Brittany could take place, a resolution to this sticky theological problem was needed.

With deft deception, Joanna gained papal approval for a second marriage by secretly sending agents to Pope Benedict in Avignon to submit a seemingly innocent request for permission to marry anyone whenever she chose. Ignorant of her true motives (to marry King Henry VI of England), Pope Benedict in 1401 gave Dowager Duchess Joanna of Brittany *carte blanche* permission to marry whomever she fancied, whenever she wished.

The royal marriage contract for Henry and Joanna was signed early in 1402. King Henry was thirty-six, and Queen Joanna was thirty-three when they were married by proxy in London on April 3, 1402; then, they were married in person at Winchester Cathedral on February 7, 1403.

Joanna's coronation took place on February 26, 1403. The splendid affair was in full royal regalia. She was crowned alone on a single throne with the ceremonial splendor usually reserved for a reigning monarch. In her right hand was the Orb with Crucifix, and on her head a crown. The special honors given to Joanna clearly showed Henry's respect for his new queen. Henry, never one noted for romantic generosity, awarded his wife an income of £10,000 a year, a generous sum for maintaining a court staffed by as many Bretons as she might choose to bring with her.

The populace in Brittany was enraged by the marriage of their duchess to England's king. In rebellion, the Bretons crossed the Channel to Plymouth, and burned the port city to the ground.

Joanna was thoroughly disliked by citizens in both Brittany and England. In England, the common people criticized her foreign manners, her lofty airs, and her aloof extravagant arrogance. She was accused of greedy attempts to gather land and wealth. She repeatedly pled poverty, and petitioned Parliament for more money to pay her personal debts. She brought many Bretons to England and they all expected support at public expense. However, that was common for all foreign attendants of the queen consort of their kings.

Henry was generous in meeting Joanna's demands, but in most other things, he was famous for tightfisted meanness. In 1404, the economic status of the realm was severely depressed. Parliament demanded that all foreigners be expelled, including almost all the Queen's retinue. Joanna was allowed to keep only her daughters, and a skeleton household crew of Bretons. However, with a return to good times in 1406, Joanna was again permitted to enjoy a pension equal to the one lavished by King Richard II on his beloved consort Good Queen Anne of Bohemia. In the 1406, Joanna's son Duke John IV of Brittany ordered his sisters to return to Brittany. He soon arranged noble French marriages for them.

Joanna and Henry were married for ten years, but (even though both had multiple offspring in first marriages) their second marriage had no issue. Joanna of Navarre was the first widow and mother of many previous children to be crowned Queen Consort of England. This situation would be repeated only once again in the reign of Edward IV by his marriage to Elizabeth Woodville in 1464.

Joanna had a friendly relationship with Henry's children from his marriage to Mary de Bohun. Joanna often took the side of Crown Prince Harry of Monmouth (future King Henry V of England) in his quarrels with his father. However, she carefully avoided showing favoritism for the prince, in fear of antagonizing her husband the king.

The amiable relationship Queen Joanna had with her stepson Prince Henry of Monmouth continued through most of his reign as King Henry V. He gave her all privileges her status as Queen Dowager deserved. King Henry V trusted his stepmother so much that, on at least one occasion, he gave Joanna permission to occupy his royal residence in London. Records show that she may even have served for a time as his regent when he was waging war in France.

Joanna supported cooperation between her son Duke John VI of Brittany and her stepson King Henry V of England, but when the war with France began, Joanna found her personal concerns acutely divided by family ties on both sides in the conflict. The great English victory at Agincourt on October 25, 1415 counted possibly up to 10,000 French casualties, but little over three hundred English died—a thirtyfold difference between victors and vanquished. For days, London was in frenzied ecstasy over the great victory in France. Queen Joanna, as Dowager Queen Consort, performed the role English custom required of her in the celebrations that followed. In stoic silence, she concealed grief for her brother King Charles of Navarre, and for her son-in-law Duke Jean of Alençon the husband of her daughter Marie; both were killed at Agincourt. However, her greatest concern was for the fate of her son Arthur of Brittany who was one of the wounded, captured, and held for ransom by King Henry V.

Arthur's future was uncertain because he had received from Henry V the title Earl of Richmond before the war with France began. In accepting the title, Arthur had pledged fealty to King Henry V. However, by fighting with France against England, Arthur had broken that vow. Now, as a prisoner of Henry V, Arthur's fate was subject to Henry's whim.

Arthur was deprived of his English title, and was held prisoner in England for five years before being released in 1420 when the *Treaty of Troyes* was signed. During the time of Arthur's imprisonment, Joanna was permitted to have conversation with her son only once. Descriptions of that single meeting of mother and son are puzzling and hard to explain. Joanna had last seen her son Arthur, as an eleven year old boy, when he had visited England soon after his mother's marriage to Henry IV in 1403. Twelve years later after Agincourt, Arthur was a full grown fighting man. Joanna decided to have a woman stand in as her proxy for the meeting in court with Arthur. Arthur failed to recognize the proxy substitute, until Joanna resolved the deception by identifying herself. However, she then rebuked Arthur for not recognizing his own mother—only Joanna understood the purpose, if any, of that charade.

After Arthur's ransom and release in 1420, he returned to France, and was a strong supporter of the French monarchy. He also defended and supported the cause of Joan of Arc, until her death as a martyr in hands of the English in 1431. A year before the end of his life, Arthur in his own right became Duke Arthur III of Brittany in 1457.

As dowager queen, Joanna lived quietly on her estates in and near London. The war in France went well for Henry V. His victories over French provinces were consistent and impressive. However, the cost of war brought both France and England to their knees near bankruptcy. King Henry approached his stepmother for a loan to help defray military costs early in 1419, but Joanna refused. She knew that military debts are never repaid. It is hardly a coincident that, in September of that year on trumped-up charges designed to enrich the national treasury, Joanna was accused of witchcraft, sorcery, and treason for "conjuring up forces of evil that endangered the life of the king." Her rich dower estates were confiscated to the crown, and she was confined to her own Pevensey Castle in Sussex until 1422. However, hers was not a frugal existence. Joanna lived well, and entertained guests of high status in State and Church. Occasionally, her guests included earls, dukes, once the Bishop of Winchester, and even the Archbishop of Canterbury. Some guests enjoyed her hospitality for weeks and even months.

The sorcery accusations against her came through false testimony from her Franciscan confessor Friar John Randolf. Part of the phony flapdoodle attending Joanna's witchcraft case made reference to a possibility that she had been "instructed in occult skills by her disreputable father [King Charles II the Bad of Navarre who was] known to have consorted with Spanish Gypsies and heretical Cathars of Aquitaine."

The sorcery case against Joanna was never brought to trial. Indeed, after Parliament took her taxable properties, no more interest was ever again shown in the case. Three years later, near the end of his life in 1422, Henry V showed contrition for appropriating Joanna's properties. He released Joanna from detention; he gave orders for all her dower estates to be returned, and he restored full honor to Joanna as dowager queen. However, because no official charges had been made, or brought to trial, she neither received from Parliament an apology for having wrongly taken her possessions, nor any statement of innocence of sorcery.

Henry V died on August 31, 1422, and his eight month old son Henry of Windsor became King Henry VI. Regents appointed by Parliament ruled England for many years through the minority years of child-King Henry, and long after that in the Wars of the Roses that followed.

In the tempestuous court struggles for power in those years, Joanna of Navarre Dowager Queen of Henry IV lived in quiet comfort outside London. Through it all, she had an amiable association with her grandson-in-law Henry of Windsor (the child-King Henry VI). In an exchange of Christmas gifts, he gave Joanna a tablet with jewels and pearls all mounted in gold as evidence of his affection for the aging dowager queen.

Joanna is credited with exemplary behavior, dignity, and courtly manners. As the regent of Brittany, she demonstrated diplomatic and administrative skills of the highest order. As Queen of England, she enjoyed high favor with both her husband Henry IV, and her son-in-law Harry of Monmouth (later Henry V). In that capacity, she created domestic civility where dissention and acrimony were common.

However, Joanna is usually remembered, only as the barren second wife of Henry IV, and as a sorceress charged with witchcraft.

Joanna died on July 9, 1437 at her estate at Havering-atte-Bower, a village on the eastern edge of London. She is buried in Canterbury Cathedral beside Henry IV.

REIGN 14

KING HENRY V

AND

QUEEN CONSORT KATHERINE OF VALOIS

Summary of the Reign of King Henry V (Reign 1413-1422)

King Henry V: life dates c. 36 years, b. September 16, 1386-d. August 31, 1422; King of England c. 9 years, March 21, 1413-August 31, 1422.

KING HENRY V in his youth was known as Prince Hal and throughout life as Harry of Monmouth. He was the eldest surviving son of King Henry IV and Mary de Bohun, and was born in 1386 at Monmouth Castle, Gwent, Wales. His reign following 1413 was marked by spectacular military successes in France. Henry V was the last and greatest of England's Warrior Kings of the Middle Ages. He is mainly remembered as the hero of the Battle of Agincourt against France in 1415.

That battle is taken as the high point in romantic chivalry. During his brief reign of nine years, Henry V recovered all French estates of his ancestor Henry Plantagenet (Henry II). As part of the spoils of war, Henry V won the hand of Princess Katherine of Valois daughter of Charles VI of France as his bride. He was also made regent of France for the rest of the reign of Charles VI, and was named heir to the throne of France after Charles VI died, but Henry's early death in 1422 prevented him from ever becoming King of France.

Little in the personal life of King Henry V demands admiration. He was ascetic, intolerant, and fanatically bent on taking whatever he wished with little regard for the wellbeing of his subjects or friends. The legacy from his military triumphs in France was disastrous to the welfare of both nations. In France, Henry was judged a curse worse than Attila the Hun, and worthy of being called *Teacher of the Devil* himself. However, England always held Harry of Monmouth in highest esteem. Even so, by the end of his reign of only nine years, the royal cupboards of England and France were bare. The legacy of Henry's valiant victories to England was bankruptcy and discontent.

Unlike his father Henry of Bolingbroke King Henry IV, whose reign was always challenged for usurping the crown from his cousin King Richard II, the personal legitimacy of Henry V to reign was never challenged. However, when Henry of Lancaster usurped the crown, resentment by the York faction of descendants from Edward III led to open conflict between the House of Lancaster and House of York. The internecine civil war called the *Wars of the Roses* began in the reign of Henry VI, the son of Henry V.

Following the death of Henry V, his only son, Prince Henry of Windsor, then only eight months old, succeeded to the throne in 1422 as King Henry VI.

Narrative of Queen Consort
Katherine Of Valois

Queen Katherine of Valois: Life dates 36 years, b. October 27, 1401-d. January 3, 1437; Queen Consort of King Henry V c. 2 years, June 2, 1420-August 31, 1422; Dowager Queen of England c. 15 years, August 31, 1422-January 3, 1437; paramour (common-law wife) of Owen Tudor c. 9 years, c. 1428-January 3, 1437.

KATHERINE OF VALOIS was born at the Palace de St. Pol (Hotel of St. Paul) in Paris on October 27, 1401. She was fifth of six children, and youngest of three daughters of Charles VI (*le Fou*—the Mad) of France and Isabella (*le Mal*—the Bad) of Bavaria. France enjoyed an uneasy peace with England. However, economic wellbeing in France still suffered severely from the Black Death and previous wars. At the beginning of the 15th century, the people in France endured barebones existence, but the insensitive nobility continued merciless taxation of estates to save a semblance of ostentation that they had flaunted in times past.

Although she was a princess of royal blood, Katherine's early life in the French court was an upside down Cinderella tale of dire want and adversity. The Palace de St. Pol had served for years as the royal nursery while princes and princesses were underage children. The royal nursery was described as uninviting, austere, and dismal. No State funds were provided for the children's care. The royal children survived on charity from their unpaid palace servants. The royal princes and princesses were reared in a state of true poverty through neglect by their deplorable parents. Their father King Charles VI was insane, but benevolent. Their mother Queen Isabella was compulsively immoral and sadistic.

King Charles often lapsed into prolonged comatose states, in which he was only dimly aware of his surroundings. The feckless king, on arousing from his usual dreamy state, deplored conditions into which the Palace de St. Pol had fallen. In effect, he chided, 'Mercy me! This palace is a dump. Why is all this garbage strewn about? Why is no one is doing anything to cleaning it up?'

Public criticism accused Queen Isabelle of embezzling huge sums from the national treasury, of immodest disport with her brother-in-law, the Duc d'Orleans, and of having no concern for the welfare of her children.

Economic conditions throughout France were deplorable. In the absence of a steady source of income and domestic supervision, the royal children were housed, clad, and fed no better than the poorest peasants in the land. On one occasion, the negligent queen arranged for the entire royal brood to be abducted, then spirited out of Paris, and delivered to her in Milan. She intended that they would be held as hostages for her protection during her trial on charges of gross impropriety and theft. The children, including the ten year old Dauphin, were recovered, and returned to Paris by a posse led by the Duke of Burgundy. After the royal brood returned from Italy to Paris, the quality of their lives improved modestly when they were individually parceled out to monasteries and convents. For the first time, proper attention was given to creature comforts and education of the children.

When war again broke out with an invasion of Normandy by King Henry V of England in August 1415, Katherine was sent as a fourteen year old novice to the Convent of Poissy. The chivalry of France saw the attack by the English king as an occasion for thrashing the brash young English upstart. From his past well-advertised record for adolescent indolence, the nobility of France knew that Prince Harry of Monmouth was an irresponsible carousing braggart with no experience or ability in arts of war. However, he excelled in tennis, so the King of France sent him a bucket of tennis balls as a coronation present. All France was confident it would crush King Henry V in the impending war. France had a minimum of twenty thousand knights in armor and myriad attendants; whereas, the Island Prince had only five thousand men in arms, and most of them were Welsh peasants with childhood toys called 'longbows.'

Harry of Monmouth used his first two years as King of England to build a strong lean fighting force. As a measure of the single-minded thoroughness in his plans to defeat France, he ordered that every grayling goose in England must forfeit six feathers from each wing, so his Welch bowmen could fletch myriad arrows. Two months after Henry V invaded France—on Friday October 25, 1415, St. Crispin's Day—the decisive victory at Agincourt left almost ten thousand French knights dead or captured—less than three hundred English and Welsh knights died. With the knighthood of France in tatters, Henry used the next five years to vanquish France totally.

After Agincourt, Henry's armies, like a locust hoard, despoiled France. The countryside was reduced to wasteland. Resident peasants burned their fields, and slaughtered their domestic herds to deprive their invaders of sustenance. Wells were poisoned with carcasses of dead animals. Even windmills were deprived of their blades, so potable water was not available for quenching the invader's thirst.

As a ruthless military strategist, King Henry V used the tried-and-true practice of divide-and-conquer. By playing up regional loyalties, Henry skillfully alienated Armagnac Frenchmen in the south against Bergundians in the north. With those two provinces neutralized, he attacked Normandy in the middle. He easily captured Caen, Falaise, and Meaux, and then moved on to the capital city Rouen. Henry V rarely showed citizens of captured cities any mercy. His most egregious act came in the way he subdued Rouen. When non-combatant citizens were expelled from the besieged city for lack of sufficient food for all, Henry refused to give them passage through his encircling army. Over several months, more than twelve thousand women, children, and feeble old men starved between the walled city of Rouen and his siege line. The stench of their decaying bodies fouled the air for miles around. However, Rouen's surrender gave Henry control of Normandy. The military wisdom of Henry's ruthless handling of the siege was shown by what immediately followed the fall of Rouen. The Burgundians, wanted none of Henry's scorched earth treatment, and they sued for peace without battle.

Henry's winning of Normandy and Burgundy placed him in a strong position to dictate victory over all France in 1420. The truce prescribed in the *Treaty of Troyes* was negotiated over a period of many months. It required signatures of approval from reigning dukes and counts of other French provinces. The Treaty of Troyes was an agreement with the primary (but ultimately unsuccessful) intent to end permanently the Hundred Years War. That war was a dynastic conflict between the Royal House of Plantagenet (England) and Royal House of Valois (France) for control of France. The Treaty of Troyes acknowledged Henry V to be the legitimate hereditary heir to the crown of France. However, the treaty specified that Henry would become king of France only after the death of French King Charles VI.

King Henry V demanded even more assurance of his royal status in France. He insisted on having Princess Katherine of Valois for his bride, but the French royal family stoutly refused that demand. Henry's men continued to ravage and devastate the land, until France was brought to its knees. King Charles VI and the French Estates General finally accepted their total humiliation. They agreed to give Henry of Monmouth the hand of Princess Katherine of Valois, so the two royal families would be joined in marriage. In the same stroke, they denied her younger brother Charles the Dauphin the right to rule France. However, history would soon show that, with aid of Joan of Arc, the Dauphin would succeed in being crowned King Charles VII of France on October 21, 1429.

Katherine of Valois and Henry V were wedded on June 2, 1420 at the parish Church of St. John in Paris. One can picture the muted joy of the new Queen of England on marrying the man all France called *Le Tuteur de Diable* (the Devil's own teacher). How different the real occasion must have been, as compared with the adolescent confection written for the same event by Shakespeare in his historical drama, *Henry V*, where Henry woos Katherine with mincing saccharine words:

> Henry: "Fair Katherine, and most fair! Will you agree to teach a soldier terms such as will enter at a lady's ear and plead his love suit to her gentle heart?"
>
> Katherine with lowered eyes and coquette modesty replies: "Your majesty shall mock me; I cannot speak your England."
>
> Henry persists: "Oh fair Katherine, if you will love me soundly with your French heart, I will be glad to hear you confess it brokenly with your English tongue. Do you like me, Kate?"
>
> And so forth.

Shakespeare's prattle between Harry and Kate, albeit suitable for the stage, was totally unlike the real Harry of Monmouth. Shakespeare's imagery for the courtship and marriage of Harry of Monmouth to Princess Katherine is copied in many English histories—a fulsome description of tender romance—*love at first sight and in love forever*—which must be taken as somewhat overblown.

In England, Henry V was thought of as the stand-in for Archangel St. Michael the Sword of God, but in France, Henry V was Lucifer the Devil's

Advocate. When one comprehends the climate of the time, it is probable that the wedding of King Henry V to Princess Katherine of Valois had much in common with a slave auction for a Sultan's harem. Henry was thirty-four and Katherine nineteen when their vows were exchanged. The marriage of State was understood, resented, but thankfully accepted by everyone in France. They knew the key to peace required sacrifice of Princess Katherine to the Devil.

It is well recorded that Henry of Monmouth (before he was King Henry V) first expressed a strong wish to marry Katherine's older sister Isabella. She was the second wife of Richard II who was widowed in 1399. Isabella refused Henry and returned to France where she later married Charles, Duc d'Orleans (the same Duc d'Orleans that Isabella and Katherine's mother seduced).

The Treaty of Troyes was signed in May 1420, and Henry's marriage to Katherine took place in June, but sporadic outbreaks of guerilla revolt continued to disrupt peace in France. For the rest of his life, Henry V was occupied with stamping out rebellion in his conquered lands. However, six months after their marriage, Henry's control of government in France was sufficiently secure for him to take Katherine to London for her coronation at Westminster Abbey on February 23, 1421. London received its new queen Katherine of Valois handsomely with citywide celebrations. Yet, after only three months in England, King Henry was forced to return to France. In life, he never again came back to England. Postwar France required Henry's presence to quell civil outbreaks, and to reassert his regency with brutal force to the end of his life. To this day, what is seen in a Frenchman's mind's eye when he hears the name, Harry of Monmouth or Henry V, is much different than an Englishman's mental image of Prince Hal as a reincarnate Galahad.

Soon after Henry left London for France in June 1421, Katherine was sent to Windsor Castle for her confinement. Her child (Henry of Windsor later Henry VI) was born on December 6, 1421. King Henry V remained in France, and never saw his son. A half-year later, King Henry died on August 31, 1422 from old wounds and dysentery (possibly typhoid fever) contracted during a siege at Meaux. In preparation for the State funeral in London, the body of King Henry V was dismembered, then boiled to delay decay, and reassembled for burial in England. The remains of Henry V were entombed with grand ceremony in the original Lady Chapel at Westminster Abbey.

King Charles VI of France died on October 21, 1422, six weeks after the death of King Henry V of England. Thus, although Henry V ruled France as regent, he did not live to be crowned King of France.

Scarcely four months before his death, Henry V summoned Katherine to attend him at Chateau de Vincennes, Paris. She was with him when he died there a few weeks before his thirty-fifth birthday. On his deathbed, Henry V appointed his brother Duke John of Bedford to be regent of England during his infant son's minority. Henry also requested that his brother John, "Comfort my dear wife, the most afflicted creature living." Duke John faithfully carried out his brother's request, and Katherine was handsomely provided for in her new status as Dowager Queen Mother.

With the deaths of King Henry V of England and of King Charles VI of France, Katherine's eight month old infant son, Henry of Windsor, became the nominal King of England and France. History credits him with being the only person simultaneously to be king of both nations. However, Henry of Windsor never truly ruled either country, so his dual kingship was a hollow distinction. In only seven years of resurgent French nationalism led by Joan of Arc, the Dauphin was crowned King Charles VII of France at Rheims on July 17, 1429.

Queen Katherine was widowed when not quite twenty-one years old. She had been Queen Consort of England for only two years and three months. She was only with her husband for the first year of marriage: namely, from June to June 1420-1421, and briefly at his bedside from May to August 1422 before his death. No one knows what sentiment she held for her husband; however, Henry's will showed that he had admirable concern for his wife's wellbeing when their brief marriage ended.

Katherine remained in London after her husband's State funeral in 1422. It is uncertain whether she stayed in England primarily on court order, or because she wished to stay near her infant son King Henry VI. Because he was a ward of the State, and not under her personal care, some biographers of Queen Katherine infer that she was denied contact with her son during much of his early childhood. Others say that child-King Henry VI had free and frequent contact with his mother. In later life, King Henry VI showed solicitous respect for his mother, as might be expected of one with memories of a doting parent in childhood.

No evidence suggests that Katherine wished to return to France, even though her younger brother Charles VII now ruled France, and France prospered in the absence of her former husband's repressions. France had no love for Katherine. She was seen as the penniless expatriate wife of a despised despot. As Dowager Queen of England, Katherine's prospects for gracious living were excellent. Her independence and material wellbeing in England was far superior to anything she had known before. She had high court status. She owned several fully staffed private residences, and she received a State pension that gave her freedom to do whatever she wished, in whatever way she fancied.

Dowager Queen Katherine's life in London attracted little political attention for five years. Then, unexpectedly, the Parliament of 1427-1428 enacted a unique law that applied solely to her. In effect, it said that 'Queen Katherine can not marry again without the express permission of her son King Henry VI, and even he cannot give that permission until he reached his maturity, and reigned in his own right after age eighteen.' It meant that Dowager Queen Katherine would not be free to wed again before 1439—not for another eleven years! The penalty for marrying Katherine would be that 'Katherine's new husband, without the King's consent to marry, would lose his lands and possessions, but any children born of the marriage would be royal and would not be penalized.'

One wonders—*Why at this time, this tempest in a teapot?*—until one sees the powerful cards Katherine held in the games of power politics that were being played at court during the minority years of King Henry VI.

Dowager Queen Katherine had many powerful assets. Socially she was the *First Lady* of England. She was a French princess of royal blood. She was the widow of England's most honored warrior king. She was the mother of the present king. She was still a stunningly beautiful twenty-six year old woman of proven fecundity with many remaining childbearing years. Moreover, as the Dowager Queen of England, she had great fortune and estates (in actual fact, she was one of two 'queens dowager' in England at that time—the other one was Joanna of Navarre the second wife of Henry VI, the father of Henry V).

What a marriage catch Katherine of Valois would be! In one stroke, her husband would be rich. He would have unmatched status in court, and he would be father-in-law of the king. By that last connection, her husband would be the logical candidate for regency of the realm.

It is not surprising that power-hungry competitors in government would want an effective checkmate to prevent Queen Katherine's remarriage. The ruling by Parliament in 1428 effectively denied Katherine the right to marry for eleven years. She never married again; in nine years, she was dead. Although intensive search has been made to discover proof of Katherine of Valois's second marriage, no written record exists that she ever married her equerry Owen Tudor the Master of Wardrobe who managed her London residence.

The Welshman Owain ap Maredudd ap Tewdwr was openly involved romantically with Dowager Queen Katherine by 1428. He was a Welsh squire of common birth, and his name when translated into English was *Owen Meredith Tudor*, or simply, *Owen Tudor* (born c. 1400—died February 2, 1461). He claimed descent from 12th century Cadwaladr ap Madoc the first Prince of Wales, and from Cadwaladr he was able to extend his ancestry back to the royal blood of King Arthur (if, indeed, Arthur and Guinevere did actually exist). However, it is noteworthy that all Welshmen claim descent from at least one knight of the Round Table.

Sometime between 1429 and 1431, Katherine of Valois moved out of London to her rural residence at Wallingford Castle described as " . . . on a hill surrounded by three motes and most securely fortified by impregnable walls" located about forty miles west of London, and halfway between Reading and Oxford. The Norman castle in Oxfordshire had been a refuge for King Stephen in his conflict with Empress Matilda.

Owen Tudor continued in his service to Dowager Queen Katherine as Squire of Wallingford. They lived quietly in the country for six or seven years, far removed from the growing conflict between the Houses of Lancaster and York that later would be called the Wars of the Roses.

Katherine's years at Wallingford were happy and fulfilling. Finally, she had the means to enjoy domestic comfort in the company of those she loved: that is, with the master of her house Owen Tudor, and a growing family of their illegitimate children.

Almost all English histories refer euphemistically to the *secret marriage of Owen Tudor and Katherine of Valois*, but no written record exists that they ever were formally married. Written records of marriage were universally required for all ranks in society as proof of legitimacy of offspring in order for legitimate children to prove their right to inherit titles and property. Yet, no such written records exist for the children of Owen Tudor and Katherine of Valois. It is certain that they had at least two children; they usually are credited with having four, but it is possible that they had seven offspring. Four children (3 sons and 1 daughter) are usually attributed to Owen Tudor and Katherine of Valois:

Owen Tudor, Jr. (life dates, 1429-1550), a monk at Westminster
Abbey

Edmund Tudor, (1430-1456), created Earl of Richmond by
Henry VI, and legitimized by Parliament in 1453

Jasper Tudor (1431-1495), created Earl of Pembroke and Duke
of Bedford by Henry VI, but never legitimized

Jacena Tudor (birth 1433, death date unknown), died young,
or survived to be a nun

Three uncertain children born after 1433 were attributed
to them; they included two sons and the last one being
a daughter who may have been born in the last year of
Katherine's life. Difficulty with the birth of her last child
possibly caused Katherine's death in 1437.

Of these children, only Edmund and Jasper play any important parts in
later English History. Many historians speculate (mainly on supposed
times of infant births) that Owen and Katherine 'must have been married
as early as 1427, but surely no later than 1433.'

However, in the face of the specific parliamentary ban against
Katherine's remarriage, it is certain that Katherine and Owen never
married in any recognized legal manner. Without prejudice, they may
be thought of as united without sacrament of clergy in a *Common Law
Marriage,* which was surely acceptable in the eyes of God. However, the
cohabitation of Owen and Katherine was not sufficient for Parliament to
confer routine legitimacy on their bastard sons Edmund and Jasper Tudor.
Parliament granted legitimacy to Edmund on his request in 1453 when
he was twenty-three, but Jasper never requested or was given legitimacy
in his lifetime.

One must conclude that all children born to Owen Tudor and
Katherine of Valois were illegitimate issue of a Common Law Marriage.

Katherine was ailing, and possibly pregnant in 1436 when she left
Wallingford to retire for hospice care at Bermondsey Benedictine Abbey
near London. Three days before Katherine died, she prepared a will with
instructions that put her two sons (six and five year old Edmund and
Jasper Tudor) in care of Abbess Katherine de la Pole of Barking Abbey in
London for their care, supervision, and education.

Queen Katherine died on January 3, 1437 in St. Saviour's Priory in
London at age 36. She was buried beside her husband, King Henry V,

in the chantry he ordered built over his tomb in the Old Lady Chapel at Westminster Abbey. Much later, her son King Henry VI added grand alabaster decorations to his mother's tomb.

Katherine of Valois grave was poorly served in following years. Her grandson Henry Tudor (King Henry VII) ordered her tomb removed to create a connecting corridor for his New Lady Chapel to Westminster the Abbey. His chapel was completed in 1503, but Katherine's casket in Westminster Abbey remained open to view for nearly three hundred years. In 1878, Queen Victoria ordered that Queen Katherine of Valois be reinterred with proper dignity with Henry V in Westminster Abbey.

See *Dynasty IV. The Tudor Kings and Queens* for additional information on the lives of Katherine of Valois, Owen Tudor, on their sons Edmund Tudor and Jasper Tudor, and on their grandson Henry Tudor King Henry VII.

REIGN 15

KING HENRY VI

AND

QUEEN CONSORT MARGARET
OF ANJOU

Summary of the Reign of King Henry VI
(Reign 1422-1461 & 1470-71)

King Henry VI: life dates 49 years, b. December 6, 1421-d. May 21, 1471; King of France 11 years, October 21, 1422-October 219, 1453; King of England c. 39 years, August 31, 1422-March 4, 1461, and his 'Readeption' c. 6 months, October 30, 1470-April 11, 1471.

KING HENRY VI of Lancaster began life with high expectations for a reign of brilliant majesty, but less than a half-century later, it ended in abject failure and defeat. He was the only child of England's great warrior King Henry V and Princess Katherine of Valois of France. Henry VI was born on December 6, 1421 at Windsor Castle. Less than nine months later, the infant prince became the only person ever to be the king of both England and France.

Henry of Lancaster succeeded Henry V to the throne of England on August 31, 1422, and reigned in England for thirty-nine years until 1461. He became the nominal King of France on October 21, 1422 when his grandfather Charles VI of France died. Henry of Lancaster was immediately challenged by the French Dauphin Charles of Valois who succeeded in reclaiming his throne, and was crowned King Charles VII of France in Reims on July 17, 1429.

In minor ways, Henry of Lancaster was a patron of scholarship. He founded Eton School, and built King's College Chapel, Cambridge, but he is not credited with doing anything of merit himself. His thirty-nine year reign was wracked by failure in two wars: *The Hundred Years War* ended with total victory for France; the *Wars of the Roses*, an English civil war between the noble Houses of Lancaster and York, which ended in victory for York. In 1461, Edward Duke of York defeated Lancaster forces, and Parliament deposed King Henry VI and accepted Edward of York as king. He was crowned King Edward IV on June 28, 1461. Henry of Lancaster briefly returned to the throne ten years later (October 30, 1470 to April 11, 1471) in what is called the *Readeption of Henry VI*.

Henry VI, unlike his warrior father King Henry V, lacked any ability for political or military leadership. However, he was the best intentioned, religiously devout, ethically motivated, but inept king ever to wear the crown of England. For decades after his death, he was worshiped as a miracle worker. Pope Innocent VIII accepted his nomination for sainthood; that effort died, but is still open.

Henry VI married Margaret of Anjou on April 23, 1445. Their only child Crown Prince Edward of Winchester did not survive his parents. Queen Margaret was the indomitable leader of Lancaster forces in the Wars of the Roses. When York defeated Lancaster decisively at the Battle of Tewksbury on May 4, 1471, Prince Edward of Winchester was captured, and executed after the battle. Henry VI also was taken, and confined in the Tower of London for a time before May 21, 1471, when he, too, was murdered. Queen Margaret was taken, and held prisoner for five years, but she finally was allowed to return to France in 1475. She died on August 32, 1482 at age 52, and was buried at Angers Cathedral in Anjou.

Henry VI was buried, first, in Chertsey Benedictine Abbey in Surrey; later, his body was reburied in St. George's Chapel, Windsor on orders of Henry VII.

The Lancastrian Plantagenet Dynasty in English history ended with the death of Henry VI. The York Plantagenet Dynasty began with King Edward IV.

Narrative of Queen Consort
Margaret of Anjou

Queen Margaret of Anjou: life dates 52 years, b. March 23, 1430-d. August 25, 1482; Queen Consort of King Henry VI c. 16 years, April 23, 1445-March 4, 1461 & October 30, 1470-April 11, 1471; Dowager Queen c. 11 years, May 31, 1471-August 25, 1482.

MARGARET OF Anjou's birth and childhood were coincident with the rise of Joan d'Arc of Dorémy in Lorraine, France, and with the restoration of the Dauphin Charles of Valois who as King Charles VI reclaimed the throne of France from King Henry VI of England in 1429. From then until 1453, England experienced only losses as the French empire of King Henry V collapsed. Finally, only Calais remained fully under English control. Factions of the French nobility vacillated in its attempts to anticipate the winning side in the drawn out struggle between England and France. The Hundred Years War (1337-1453) between the English House of Plantagenet and the French House of Valois ended in complete victory for Valois and France.

Margaret of Anjou was born at a violently unsettled time of revolutionary change in France. Divided provincial loyalties often bred struggles for power that led to civil war, or even anarchy, in many parts of France. She was the third child of René Count of Anjou, Duke of Bar, King of Naples, and titular King of Aragon and Jerusalem. Margaret was born on March 23, 1430 in Pont à Mousson, Lorraine at the home of her mother Isabella the ruling Duchess of Lorraine. Margaret's aunt Marie of Anjou was Queen Consort of Charles VII of France. Thus, Margaret's family connections in French nobility were impeccable, yet as the third child born to her parents, she did not have a noble title in her own right.

Her father René of Anjou was a strong Valois supporter, but his wife's Duchy of Lorraine and neighboring Burgundy had marked sympathy for the English Plantagenets. During Margaret's childhood, her father Count/ Duke/King René was captured, imprisoned, and released several times by Burgundians. In those years, Duchess Margaret educated, and tutored her daughter in court etiquette until she was fifteen years old.

Suddenly in 1444, Margaret was astounded to learn she would be an important 'Pawn of State' in a treaty between France and England. The treaty would be of enormous value to France, and it would make a swindled dupe of England. Margaret's part in the French scam, called the *Truce of Tours,* would make her the Queen of England.

One must step back a few years to see how the Truce of Tours could ever have come about.

> In 1437, sixteen year old King Henry VI of England began his personal rule after his mother Katherine of Valois died. At first, all looked promising. He was mild mannered, pious and scholarly. Most of his days were spent in prayers, and reading philosophical treatises. However, he showed little interest or aptitude for dealing with practical matters of government. Almost immediately, it became clear that he was incapable of mastering matters of any complexity, or of managing affairs of government, or of choosing wise council, or of appointing qualified persons to do essential domestic or diplomatic functions of government. Indecision was his standard method or response to all problems that demand judgment. Any situation that needed prompt action was occasion for his acute mental collapse.
>
> Therefore, in the reign of King Henry VI, all aspects of government in England were in disarray, and the empire in France that his father Henry V had won was quickly eroded. A record from these times summed up the status in England by saying, "England is out of all good governance as our King is simple [silly and stupid], and led only by covetous counsel." Another analysis of the times asserted, "Personal ambition motivated all that served Henry VI . . . Court favorites, who

rose to positions of power, almost immediately became wealthy, unpopular, envied and feared." Well-intentioned King Henry VI remained oblivious of evil intrigue that swirled about him.

By 1444, only two decades after Harry of Monmouth (Henry V) had conquered all France, English mismanagement was close to losing it all. The chief power in Parliament in 1444 was William de la Pole Duke of Suffolk. He was a confused observer of the passing parade who saw English advantage in arranging the *Truce of Tours* with France, because the Truce gave respite from the endless war of attrition in France. The Duke of Suffolk (a former day Neville Chamberlain) went to France, as royal emissary, and proudly negotiated the Truce of Tours. A minor part of the agreement was a contract for the royal marriage of King Henry VI of England to Lady Margaret of Anjou.

At the diplomatic table, Charles VII of France succeeded in persuading Suffolk to agree to a swap. France would give titleless Margaret of Anjou as Queen Consort for King Henry VI of England, if England would surrender its hereditary claims to the French Provinces of Maine, Anjou, and Normandy. England's claim on those estates went back to the 12th century titles of Henry Plantagenet Count of Anjou and Maine and Duke of Normandy. Margaret would go to England without dowry, since she had no major estates of her own.

In England, it was explained "the new queen's dowry was waived because Margaret's beauty and intelligence were so great as to outweigh all the riches in the world."

Charles VII (called the 'Well served') gave up nothing of economic or political value—for a penniless royal niece, he gained uncontested control of three of France's major western provinces.

The *Truce of Tours* is a classic example of 'A farthing buying the Christmas goose.'

Twenty-three-year old King Henry VI married fifteen year old Margaret of Anjou. First, they were joined by proxy engagement and marriage at Tours, France in 1444. They were married in person again on April 23, 1445 at Titchfield Abbey, Hampshire. Titchfield was then, and is now, an unpretentious village between Portsmouth and Southampton. Duke William of Suffolk chose Titchfield for the marriage, because timid King Henry of Lancaster was embarrassed in the presence of women, and he insisted on being costumed as a common squire, so he could see Princess Margaret secretly, and not be thrown into confusion on their first meeting. Margaret of Anjou was not reassured by her first meeting with her proxy-husband. Evidence for Henry of Lancaster's mental instability increased in frequency and severity with time.

King Henry and Queen Margaret were opposites in nature. Henry was a profoundly religious, cautious, timid, vacillating, antisocial aesthete. Margaret was a vain, aggressive, arrogant, outspoken, domineering commander.

Margaret was not significantly involved in matters of State in the first years of their marriage (1445 to 1450). However, she gradually became a power behind the throne, and it was said, "Queen Margaret managed King Henry while he was sane, and she ran the country when he was mad." Margaret was an intensely unpopular queen, and a constant reminder of England's defeat in France.

William de la Pole Duke of Suffolk (who had negotiated the royal marriage contract) was Lord Chamberlain Admiral of England in 1449. In that year, the English garrison in Rouen surrendered the Province of Normandy to France. All England was outraged, and humiliated by the loss of Normandy. Suffolk explained the loss by saying that ceding Normandy back to France was just another part of the Truce of Tours that he forgot to mention when he announced the marriage contract in which England gained Lady Margaret of Anjou as Queen Consort for King Henry VI.

The loss of Normandy created a crisis in government. All blame for the debacle was placed on William de la Pole Duke of Suffolk. Queen Margaret's first conspicuous intervention in government came in a protest to Parliament for its actions against Suffolk. However, Suffolk was deposed, arrested, imprisoned, then tried for treason in May, and banished to France as a traitor. However, in transit across the English Channel he was illegally thrown overboard and drowned. His drowning was blamed on Richard Plantagenet Duke of York, who was responsible for Suffolk's safe transport to exile in France.

More repercussions of the Normandy fiasco reached crisis in Jack Cade's Rebellion, which took place in June and July 1450. Cade submitted to Parliament a written manifesto that expressed widespread public displeasure in the state of incompetence, embezzlement, and lack of justice in England. The Cade rebels looted London, and executed some high officials in King Henry's government. More important, the Cade manifesto openly suggested that England would benefit from the abdication of King Henry VI in favor of his cousin Richard Plantagenet Duke of York. Richard of York was recognized to be the next in succession to the throne. The historic importance of the Cade Rebellion lies in its identifying and naming the major protagonists on the opposing sides before the Wars of the Roses began between the House of Lancaster and House of York.

Queen Margaret protested violently at thought of her husband Henry VI of Lancaster stepping down, and giving his crown to Duke Richard Plantagenet of York. She labeled the Cade proposal 'pure treason.' Margaret's growing influence in government made sure that Jack Cade, and many more of the rebel leaders would be imprisoned and executed.

By midsummer 1453, Bordeaux and all Aquitaine had been surrendered to France. With the Battle of Castillon on July 17, 1453, the Hundred Years War finally came to an ignominious close for England. Save for Calais, all France was lost. Calais, with a twelve mile fortified pale surrounding it, was the only foothold England held on the Continent of Europe. The immediate aftermath of the exile of Suffolk for the loss of French provinces and from the Cade Rebellion was parliamentary disarray. England searched for stable leadership, but for many years, peace and tranquility would be strangers in England as events moved ever closer to civil war.

Henry VI was a scholarly, timid, almost saintly, aesthete, who abhorred social controversy, violence, and vulgarity. When he faced situations of public discord or problems that needed decisive action, he retreated into an inner mental refuge for protection from a harsh world he rejected. He could not be awakened from his coma-like withdrawal, but his behavior during the trances was neither objectionable nor violent. These conditions resembled a profound séance of meditation. On recovery, he was of good mind, but without recall about his time in withdrawal. Courtiers around him referred to his recurring trance-like states as *madness*, and his recovery as *clarity of mind*.

Chronic dissent and turmoil throughout England in 1453 led to Henry's collapse into his first *grand mal foli* (great madness). His attacks came with increasing frequency after 1450, but they never lasted more than a few days. However, the grand mal of July 1453 lasted eighteen months, until mid December 1454. He retreated into a sheltered cloister in his mind where troubles of the world could not intrude. On rare occasions, awareness of the world outside prompted Henry to mumble, "Fie, fie! For shame! Forsooth ye are all to blame."

In July 1453, Queen Margaret petitioned Parliament to be made regent during her husband's madness. Instead, Parliament appointed Richard Plantagenet Duke of York to be regent with the title Lord Protector. Richard of York, as next in line for the crown, expected that by act of God or by Parliament he would soon become King of England, and that only patience was needed for his expectation to become fact.

Then, on October 13, 1453, the only child of Queen Margaret of Anjou was born in the Palace of Westminster. The infant Edward of Westminster (also called Edward of Lancaster) was invested Prince of Wales five months later on March 15, 1454. Thereby, the baby was the acknowledged rightful heir of King Henry VI. The infant Prince of Wales immediately displaced Richard Plantagenet Duke of York as heir apparent to the throne.

Gossip and hanky panky were well established staples at court, so many immediately wondered: Why had eight years passed since Margaret's marriage to Henry in 1445, without any previous pregnancies or miscarriages?

It had long been thought that both King Henry and Queen Margaret were barren. Speculation impugned Henry, as being without either inclination, or physical ability to father a child. Therefore, rumors quickly surfaced that Crown Prince Edward of Westminster was the 'natural child,' a bastard, of an illicit liaison between Queen Margaret and one of her court favorites. Many believed that the infant's true father was either Edmund Beaufort Duke of Somerset, or James Butler Earl of Wiltshire. Both were high in government, and were close friends of Queen Margaret. All in the House of York were convinced of the prince's bastardy.

In December 1454, Henry regained clarity of mind. He was delighted to learn that he was the father of fourteen month old Crown Prince Edward. However, the king had no recollection of being involved in the child's conception. To this day, it is not known whether Crown Prince Edward of Westminster was legitimate.

When Henry recovered in December 1454, Queen Margaret successfully petitioned Parliament to dismiss Richard Duke of York as regent, and let King Henry resume his position at head of state. She again became all-powerful behind the throne. Queen Margaret was the effective leader of Lancaster forces for the first eighteen years of the Wars of the Roses. She was the motivating force behind Lancaster efforts that began with the first Battle of St. Albans (May 22, 1453), and lasted until the Battle of Tewksbury (May 4, 1471), after which Henry VI was murdered, and she was captured and imprisoned.

The Wars of the Roses was a civil war waged between the great royal Houses of Lancaster and York, where the standard for Lancaster bore a red rose, and that of York a white rose. The English people had divided loyalties. They readily saw the distinction between the main contenders. On one side was *Richard Plantagenet* a virile strapping physical Prince of the Blood, with the appearance of a true king, and with proven ability to rule. Opposed to York was Queen Margaret, the bossy French wife of *King Henry VI of Lancaster*, who was a monk-like recluse out of touch with reality, yet a harmless devout ascetic scholar of dubious sanity much of the time.

For five years after the first Battle of St. Albans in 1453, the tide of battle oscillated violently between the opponents. Until 1460, victories generally went to Lancaster. Queen Margaret unwisely made a practice of displaying King Henry in safety off the edge of battle. This presumably was done so citizens could see the true King. Henry was so distraught by the violence of war that, on these occasions, his mind withdrew into a remote recess of consciousness where he mumbled rosaries, and hummed sacred chants, but otherwise he was unaware of all around him. He was in that state of withdrawal, or madness, when York men captured him at the Battle of Northampton in July 10, 1460. He was not harmed, but was taken to the Tower of London for his safekeeping.

The Battle of Northampton was a decisive turning point that favored the House of York.

In the monastic solitude of the Tower of London, Henry VI soon regained consciousness and his full mental powers. Parliament debated the prickly dilemma: Who had the right to be king? Who should be king for the good of the nation?

King Henry was invited with full courtesy for his status as king to address Parliament on the controversy over his, and Richard Plantagenet's right to reign.

King Henry VI, with full mental clarity, addressed Parliament, and said, "My father was king. His father was also the king. I have worn the crown near forty years from my cradle. You have all sworn fealty to me as your sovereign, and your fathers have done the like manner to my father and grandfather. How, then, can my right be disputed?"

However, Parliament knew that Henry was often incapable of ruling, and that in every way, Richard of York was able to govern. King Henry showed willingness to compromise. He agreed that, if he were permitted to reign until his natural death, that the crown could then pass to the Duke of York and his heirs. King Henry VI then returned to protective custody in the Tower of London.

Henry's willingness to compromise in this way has always been taken to be evidence that he did not believe that Edward Prince of Wales was his own true son.

On receiving King Henry's conciliatory proposal, Parliament quickly passed the *Act of Accord* on October 10, 1460. The Act recognized Henry to be the true King, but it reinstated Richard Plantagenet Duke of York as Regent Lord Protector. He would have full power of regency until Henry died, after which he would become the King of England in his own right. The Act of Accord clearly cast doubt on the legitimacy of Crown Prince Edward by denying him the right to follow Henry VI to the throne.

Queen Margaret, with her son Crown Prince Edward, and tattered remnants of Lancaster supporters had taken refuge in Scotland after the disastrous Lancaster defeat in the Battle of Northampton. When she learned of the Act of Accord passed by Parliament in October, Queen Margaret was enraged to the point of madness. The Act disinherited her six year old son Edward of Westminster of his right to be King of England. By casting doubt on his legitimacy, the Act also insulted her personal honor.

Queen Margaret protested "[I am not] the whore of Edmund Beaufort Duke of Somerset, or of James Butler Earl of Wiltshire . . . [Crown Prince Edward of Westminster] is the true son of King Henry VI."

In righteous rage, Queen Margaret promptly moved to organize a Lancaster rebellion against regent Richard Plantagenet Duke of York. For the next decade (1461-1471), Queen Margaret led Lancaster opposition against the Parliament-approved York government in London.

Queen Margaret recruited a motley band of cutthroats, highwaymen, vagabonds, and mercenaries in Wales, Scotland, Northern England, and France to join her forces. She did not hesitate to use merciless authority to order that her York enemies when captured would be executed without trial. That practice outraged ancient courtesies of feudal chivalry, in which honorable warriors taken in battle deserved just treatment as prisoners, and the right to be ransomed with freedom to fight again.

Margaret's first opportunity to challenge the York government came in the Battle of Wakefield on December 30, 1460. Regent Richard Plantagenet Duke of York underestimated his Lancaster opposition, and was soundly defeated. He was killed in the battle, and his son Edmund of Rutland, and their kinsman Richard Neville Earl of Salisbury were captured and executed after the Lancastrian victory. Queen Margaret ordered that the decapitated heads of the three York noblemen be mounted on pikes over the gate at York with a placard that insultingly read, "York looks down on York."

The second Battle of St. Albans on February 12, 1461 was another Lancaster victory. It is notable mainly for a post-battle event that eroded Queen Margaret's reputation further. King Henry was taken to St. Albans by his York jailors, and placed in the shade of a tree with two York guards assigned to protect him as the battle raged around him. It is said that King Henry sang softly to himself unaware of the surrounding turmoil. York fighters retreated in defeat, and left King Henry with the two York guards who protected him throughout the battle. When Lancaster men rescued King Henry, the two York guards were captured. Queen Margaret ordered them to be beheaded as enemy traitors.

This unjust vindictive act by Queen Margaret set a savage president that would be followed by both York and Lancaster armies in later conflicts of the Wars of the Roses. Many prisoners on both sides were executed without trial or hearing as the war raged on.

The death of Richard Plantagenet Duke of York at the Battle of Wakefield in December 1460 raised his eighteen year old son, Edward Earl of March to Duke of York. He immediately swore vengeance against Queen Margaret for the death of his father, brother, and kinsmen.

Edward of York was a blond giant six feet four inches tall—a born leader of men. He claimed for himself all rights that had been given to his father in the Act of Accord. On March 4, 1461, Edward of York declared that he was the true and rightful King of England. Parliament confirmed his claim after the Battle of Towton on March 29, 1461 when Edward of York decisively defeated Lancaster.

Towton was a small village in northern Yorkshire that was accustomed to being buffeted by harsh weather blown in from the North Sea. The Battle of Towton took place on Palm Sunday, March 29, 1461. It is said to have been 'the largest longest bloodiest battle ever fought on English soil.' Each side raised about forty thousand troops, and nearly half of the titled nobility of England was present. Neither side gave quarter, nor were prisoners taken. The weather was unseasonably foul with high wind, sleet, and snow relentlessly blowing in from the North Sea. Fighting began at daybreak, and lasted until midnight. Possibly, thirty thousand died, and Lancaster forces were demolished. King Henry, Queen Margaret, Prince Edward of Westminster, and remnants of Lancaster forces fled for safety, first into Wales, later into Scotland, then to Flanders, and finally to France.

Parliament interpreted the Lancaster flight as tantamount to the abdication for Henry IV. Edward of York was promptly recognized to be the rightful king. He was crowned Edward IV on June 28, 1461. From that date, Edward of York was the only king that was recognized by Parliament, until his death twenty-two years later on April 9, 1483.

After the disaster for Lancaster at Towton in March 1461, Lancastrian nobles that remained in England were stripped of their estates, and were required to make a pledge of good conduct and loyalty to Edward of York as their King Edward IV.

Indomitable Queen Margaret continued for a decade to plot for a return to power: first from Scotland, then Flanders, and later from France. Lancastrian uprisings instigated by Queen Margaret were mainly in northern England, but some skirmishes on the Welch border also disturbed the peace of England. Usually, King Edward IV easily suppressed the uprisings, but they warned of growing discontent in the land. In 1465 at one of these brush fire rebellions, King Henry VI was retaken while he sat under a tree, singing softly, oblivious of all around him. He was confined in the Tower of London for five years until September 1470, all the while treated with kindness and respect.

During her years of exile (1461-1470), Queen Margaret kept her son Crown Prince Edward of Westminster with her and supervised his education. In France, Margaret faced grave financial hardships. She used her persuasive talents to beg and borrow support from all who took pity on her condition. Her loyal followers admired her. One of them said, "We be all in great poverty, yet the queen sustaineth us in meat and drink. Her highness can do no more than she doth."

Many failures had convinced Queen Margaret that she could never succeed in restoring Henry VI to the throne (thereby protecting the inheritance rights of her son) without major help from military strength within England. Richard Neville Earl of Warwick was the most powerful lord in northern England. He was an uncle of Edward IV, and had been central in bringing Edward to the throne. Yet, Richard Neville was now in exile in Calais, having fallen from favor with King Edward IV. The Neville-Warwick estates in northern England had a great tactical advantage by being close to the Scottish border where foreign mercenaries could be gathered, garrisoned, and ready to give support at a moment's notice.

Margaret approached Richard Neville with a proposal: If you will give me aid in deposing Edward IV of York to return Henry VI of Lancaster to his throne, I promise that your daughter Anne Neville will marry my son Prince Edward of Westminster. Then in due course, Anne will become Queen of England.

Warwick found the proposition appealing. It combined reward with revenge. He agreed to proceed with preparations for a secret rebellion designed to evict Edward IV, and restore the throne to Henry VI.

By September 1470, a motley band of Lancaster sympathizers had secretly assembled on the Scottish border. It included foreign mercenaries, Scots and Northumbrian natives under leadership of Richard Neville. Jasper Tudor, a bastard half-brother of King Henry, was counted on to bring more help from disgruntled Welch volunteers. The combined attack on London on September 13, 1470 took Edward IV by surprise.

The *coup d'état* succeeded, but King Edward was able to escape to France, where he took refuge with his brother-in-law Charles Duke of Burgundy.

In London, Richard of Warwick liberated King Henry VI from the Tower, where he had been confined, but had been well treated for five years. Henry VI was reinstalled on October 30, 1470 as faux-king (Henry did not receive Parliament's approval) in what history now calls the *Readeption of Henry VI.*

In keeping with the precontract between Warwick and Queen Margaret, Warwick's fourteen year old daughter Anne Neville married seventeen year old Prince Edward of Westminster at Angers Cathedral in France on or around December 13, 1470.

Clearly, the first phase in Queen Margaret's planned rebellion to take over the government in England was successful. However, she remained in France to recruit more militia that would soon be needed. Edward IV was sure to return with force to regain his crown.

After his exile, Edward IV wasted no time girding for battle. His brother-in-law Charles the Bold Duke of Burgundy gave him great help. They were ready to invade England long before Margaret was ready to send aid to Richard Neville the self-appointed regent in England.

Edward IV landed in force at Ravenspur, Yorkshire in March 1471. Many York loyalists in England joined him on his way to London. On April 14, he met a superior army led by Richard Neville of Warwick near the village of Barnet north of London. Edward opened a surprise attack at dawn in heavy fog. In the confusion of battle, Richard Neville of Warwick was killed. Then, lacking effective leadership, Lancaster forces yielded to York with little loss of men on either side.

Bad weather delayed Queen Margaret's return to England. She landed at Weymouth on the very day of the Battle of Barnet, but her troops were too late to give aid to Warwick.

London surrendered to Edward IV, and King Henry was again placed in custody in the Tower of London.

Queen Margaret and her foreign mercenaries attracted few Lancaster loyalists in England. Three weeks after the defeat at Barnet, Queen Margaret and her eighteen year old son Edward of Westminster led Lancaster forces in the Battle of Tewksbury (May 4, 1471). York defeated Lancaster totally at Tewksbury. Crown Prince Edward of Winchester was taken and executed without trial. Queen Margaret was captured, and held prisoner at various castles, including the Tower of London, for five years.

King Henry VI died on May 21. He was probably executed, but his official death notice said that he died "from melancholy on learning of his son's death." Common belief, however, held that Henry's death was ordered by Edward IV, and was carried out by his brother Duke Richard of Gloucester.

King Henry VI was a gentle devout scholarly ascetic who was sadly miscast by birth to play the aggressor in the struggle for power about which he cared not a fig. As a priest he might have made a great pope—as a King of England, he is among the most incompetent kings England ever had.

The death of her son Edward of Westminster shattered Queen Margaret's hope of restoring his eligibility to inherit the throne. Only Prince Edward, while still living, gave Margaret's life purpose. After five years in prison, King Edward IV permitted Dowager Queen Margaret to return to France as part of the *Treaty of Picquigny* with France. Dowager Queen Margaret owned no personal estates to provide income in France. She was destitute when she arrived in Anjou after her release in 1475. She lived on scant charity from King Louis IX until her death in 1482.

Queen Margaret of Anjou died on August 25, 1482 at age 52 in Château Dampierre, Anjou. She was buried at St. Maurice's Cathedral, Angers in Anjou. Her tomb was spared vandalism in riots of the French Revolution, but her tomb is largely ignored, though surviving to the present day.

Queen Margaret of Anjou—a lioness defending her cub—was never able to understand that the people of England had any right to expect that their king should have attributes of leadership, judgment, and practical acumen, which are essential qualities for rulers of efficient just governments.

If Queen Margaret possessed any ability to compromise, she might have accepted Parliament's Act of Accord, which was based on suggestions made by her peace-loving husband in 1460. She then would have been his Queen Consort enjoying a handsome pension, noble estates, and a high position in court for the rest of her life. Her son Crown Prince Edward would have survived. Henry VI would have recovered his sanity, and he may even have become an important Christian philosopher. Had that come about, everyone would have lived happily ever after.

Ability to compromise could have given Queen Margaret almost everything she desired. Her stubborn effort to protect her son's right to inherit the crown of England created much grief. Had she won, not lost everything, she might be remembered as a valiant *Warrior Queen* who saved the nation. However, she lost everything, and ended life abandoned, unloved, and unmourned.

Considering the death, suffering, and hate Queen Margaret caused by prolonging the Wars of the Roses for a decade, one may ask: Did not fate, indeed, deal Margaret justice?

Conclusion to the Lancaster Plantagenet Dynasty

THE ANGEVIN Plantagenet Dynasty ended when Henry of Bolingbroke, the eldest son of John of Gaunt Duke of Lancaster, usurped the crown from his first cousin, King Richard II.

The Lancaster Plantagenet Dynasty began with Henry of Bolingbroke and lasted for slightly over sixty years (1399 to 1461). It included the father, son, and grandson: Kings Henry IV, Henry V, and Henry VI.

When he usurped the crown, Henry of Bolingbroke was third in line to inherit the throne. Thus, his right to rule as King Henry IV was clouded by the existence of a cousin, Roger Mortimer V Earl of March, with better rights to reign than his own. Had strict rules of primogeniture been followed, Roger Mortimer V Earl of March, a descendant of Lionel of Clarence, should have followed Richard II to the throne.

The civil war (usually called Wars of the Roses) was a contest between the two great Royal Houses of Lancaster and York. Both houses disputed the right of the other to reign. The civil war ended in victory for the House of York.

The house of York based its claim on precedence of birth by descent from the second son of King Edward III, Lionel Duke of Clarence and his fourth son Edmund of Langley I Duke of York. Their conjoined bloodline clearly was superior to that of the House of Lancaster. An explanation for York claims on the crown is given in the introduction to the York Plantagenet Dynasty that follows.

DYNASTY IIIc

THE YORK PLANTAGENET DYNASTY
REIGN 16 THROUGH 18 (1461-1485)

The York Plantagenet Dynasty Patriarchs: Lionel Duke of Clarence and Edmund Duke of York

TANGLED RELATIONSHIPS between Lancaster and York descendants of Edward III underlay causes for the Wars of the Roses.

The House of Lancaster descended from John of Gaunt Duke of Lancaster who was the third son of Edward III. For three decades, England had accepted the Lancaster Kings Henry IV, Henry V, and Henry VI as rightful rulers, even though Henry IV had forcibly usurped the crown from Richard II.

The House of York based its right to rule on simple primogeniture. Throughout the period of Lancaster dominance (1399-1461), descendants from Lionel of Antwerp Duke of Clarence (the second son of Edward III) claimed the right to rule by precedence of birth by descent King Edward III.

To understand the York position, requires a review the York line of descent from Edward III who had five surviving sons, but none became king. The sons of Edward III in chronological order were:

> 1st son, Edward of Woodstock (the 'Black Prince', father of King Richard II)
>
> * 2nd son, Lionel of Antwerp Duke of Clarence (father of Philippa Plantagenet of Clarence, the rightful heiress after Richard II)
>
> ** 3rd son, John of Gaunt Duke of Lancaster (Lancaster patriarch and father of Henry of Bolingbroke, King Henry IV)
>
> * 4th son, Edmund of Langley Duke of York (York patriarch and grandfather of Richard Plantagenet 3d Duke of York)
>
> 5th son, Thomas of Woodstock Duke of Gloucester (no royal descendants)

> * The House of York claim on the crown came by decent from the 2nd and 4th sons of Edward III: 2nd son Lionel of Antwerp Duke of Clarence, 4th son Edmund of Langley Duke of York.
>
> ** The House of Lancaster's hereditary legitimacy to rule rested on descent from only John of Gaunt the 3rd son of King Edward III.

During the sixty-two years of rule by the Lancaster Dynasty (1399-1461), the primogeniture right to rule passed down through descendants of Philippa Plantagenet of Clarence (the daughter of second son Lionel of Antwerp Duke of Clarence) to the first York king, her great-great-grandson King Edward IV. The genealogy of this inheritance is shown by the following lineage, which begins with Edward III of the Angevin lineage:

King Edward III (1327-1377) married Queen Philippa of Hainault, parents of second son—

Lionel of Antwerp Duke of Clarence, father of—

Philippa Plantagenet of Clarence, heiress presumptive married Roger Mortimer III, parents of—

Roger Mortimer *4th Earl of March* heir presumptive, father of—
Anne Mortimer *of March* Countess of Cambridge, heiress presumptive, married Richard of York, Earl of Cambridge, parents of—

Richard Plantagenet Duke of York and *6th Earl of March*, heir presumptive married Cecily Neville, parents of—

King Edward IV Duke of York and *7th Earl of March* and Queen Consort Elizabeth Woodville, parents of—

King Edward V, no issue

Elizabeth of York married Henry Tudor who became King Henry VII

King Richard III Duke of Gloucester married Queen Consort Anne Neville of Warwick, parents of—

Edward of Middleham, died young, no issue.

It will be noted in *Italics* above that the right to rule followed the Roger Mortimer title as *4th Earl of March* down to Edward IV *7th Earl of March*, who was also the Duke of York.

The end of the York Plantagenet Dynasty came with the defeat and death of King Richard III at the Battle of Bosworth Field on August 22, 1485 at the hands of Henry Tudor.

The genealogy shown above passed Philippa of Plantagenet's original claim on the crown of England to the House of York when (as shown above) Anne Mortimer the heiress presumptive married Richard of York Earl of Cambridge.

Their son Richard Plantagenet Duke of York & 6th Earl of March led the York faction in early years of the Wars of the Roses. After Richard Plantagenet's death at the Battle of Wakefield on December 30, 1460, his son Edward 7th Earl of March became the Duke of York. His York forces vanquished Lancaster in 1461, and he became King Edward IV. Edward IV had no surviving sons. His right as heir presumptive by primogeniture descended to his eldest daughter Elizabeth of York.

Henry Tudor, who was the major surviving Lancaster claimant for the crown, became King Henry VII, and was the founder of the Tudor Dynasty.

The marriage of Elizabeth of York to Henry Tudor King Henry VII united in marriage the two major contenders for the throne in the Houses of York and Lancaster. Their marriage ended the Wars of the Roses, and began the Tudor Dynasty in 1485.

The York Plantagenet Lineage, Reign 16 through 18 (1461-1485)

THE YORK Plantagenet Dynasty lasted for only twenty-four years (1461 to 1485), and it included Kings Edward IV, Edward V, and Richard III.

The York kings were victors in the prolonged civil war popularly called *The Wars of the Roses*. The conflict arose from contested reigns by descendants of sons of King Edward III. The following lineage follows the line of descent for Edmund of Langley Duke of York who was the fourth son of King Edward III; it repeats some aspects of the lineage given for Lionel of Antwerp Duke of Clarence, the second son of King Edward III.

From Dynasty IIIa. The Angevin Plantagenet Lineage:

Reign 11. Edward III (1327-1377) and Queen Consort Philippa of Hainault, parents of—

Edmund of Langley 1st Duke of York, fourth son of Edward III, father of—

Richard 3rd Earl of Cambridge married Anne Mortimer (who was heiress presumptive granddaughter of Philippa Plantagenet of Clarence), parents of—

Richard Plantagenet 3rd Duke of York married Cecily Neville, parents of—**Edward IV**

Continue with Dynasty III-3. The York Plantagenet Lineage. Reign 16, Edward IV.

Beginning of Dynasty IIIc. The York Plantagenet Lineage:

(1) **Reign 16. Edward IV** Duke of York (reign, 1461-1483) and Queen Consort Elizabeth Woodville, parents of—

    (1) Elizabeth of York married Henry Tudor Earl of Richmond, who became Henry VII, founder of the Tudor Dynasty.

    (2) **Reign 17. Edward V** (reign, April to June, 1483; the murdered Prince in Tower'), no issue

(2) George Plantagenet, Duke of Clarence (executed for treason), father of—

    George Duke of Warwick, executed by Henry VII, no issue

    Margaret Plantagenet, executed by Henry VIII, mother of—

    Archbishop Reginald de la Pole, no issue

(3) **Reign 18. Richard III** Duke of Gloucester (reign, 1483-1485) and Queen Consort Anne Neville of Warwick, parents of—

    Edward of Middleham, Prince of Wales, died young, no issue.

End of Dynasty III. The Plantagenet Kings and Queens; continue with Dynasty IV. The Tudor Kings and Queens.

REIGN 16

KING EDWARD IV
AND
QUEEN CONSORT ELIZABETH WOODVILLE

Summary of the Reign of King Edward IV
(Reign 1461-1483)

King Edward IV: life dates 41 years, b. April 28, 1442-d. April 9, 1483; King of England 22 years, March 4, 1861-October 31, 1483.

EDWARD OF YORK was the eldest surviving son of Richard Plantagenet Duke of York and 7th Earl of March and his wife Cecily Neville. Edward descended by his father from Lionel Duke of Clarence, and Edmund, Duke of York, and by his mother Cecily Neville, to John of Gaunt through the Katherine Swynford-Joan Beaufort line of descent, albeit, the latter was a minor embarrassment for its questioned legitimacy. By descent from three sons of Edward III (i.e., from Lionel of Clarence,

John of Gaunt, and Edmund of Langley), Edward of York's right to reign was superior to all others.

Edward of York was a robust child who, by his late teens, had grown to six feet four inches tall. He was the tallest of England's monarchs. As an eleven year old child, Edward was present in 1455 with his father Richard Plantagenet at the first Battle of St. Albans. Thereafter, he played active leadership roles in many later battles of the Wars of the Roses. Most notable of them was the Battle of Towton on March 28, 1461 where Lancaster forces were decisively defeated, and he was crowned King Edward IV on June 25, 1461.

Thus, Edward IV became King of England by deposing King Henry VI of Lancaster by conquest, as well as by superior hereditary credentials.

King Edward was a gifted military tactician. He never lost any battle he personally led. He was a handsome blond giant who had great personal charm, and leadership ability in both war and politics. He was respected for bringing stability back to government after decades of mismanagement, and civil strife during initial phases in the Wars of the Roses. English economy thrived to such a degree under his leadership that he was the first king to end his reign without the government in debt. Edward was influential in bringing the printer William Caxton to England. Caxton introduced the new craft of printing with movable type to England that Gutenberg used in printing the first Bible in 1454. Printing in England had a profound effect in advancing the English Renaissance and Reformation. Those great cultural changes in Continental Europe were delayed in England by decades of civil turmoil that accompanied the Wars of the Roses. The Renaissance and Reformation only began in England during reigns of the Tudor Kings Henry VII and Henry VIII.

The reign of Edward IV is not notable for major improvisations in English law, but he was a sociological innovator for ending villeinage, and serfdom for native-born English subjects.

For his queen, Edward IV chose a titleless widow Elizabeth Woodville who had two sons by her first husband Sir John Grey. Edward and Elizabeth had ten children, three of them figure prominently in later events. The eldest daughter Elizabeth of York became the queen consort of Henry VII. The two sons, Edward and Richard, are immortalized as the 'Princes in the Tower' who were murdered by their uncle King Richard III.

Edward IV ruled for 22 years, from 1461 to 1483. He was buried at St. George's Chapel, Windsor. His queen Elizabeth Woodville died in

1492 at St. Savior's Bermondsey Abbey, London, and was buried with Edward VI at St. George's Chapel, Windsor.

Following the death of Edward IV, his eldest son, Edward Prince of Wales, then only 12 years old, briefly became King Edward V. He lost the crown in less than three months to his uncle Richard of Gloucester who became Richard III on June 22, 1483.

Narrative of Queen Consort Elizabeth Woodville

Queen Elizabeth Woodville: life dates c. 55 years, b. 1436/37-d. June 8, 1492; Queen Consort of Edward IV c. 19 years, May 1, 1464-April 9, 1483; Dowager Queen c. 9 years, April 9, 1483-June 8, 1492.

ELIZABETH WOODVILLE (also spelled in contemporary documents: Widvile, Wydvil, and Wydeville) was the eldest of twelve children born to Sir Richard Woodville 1st Earl Rivers of Grafton and Lady Jacquetta of Luxembourg. Both were loyal supporters of the House of Lancaster in the Wars of the Roses. Elizabeth, as a child eight or nine years old, had the brief honor of being a maid-of-honor to Queen Margaret of Anjou in the court of in Henry VI. At age fourteen or fifteen in 1452, she married Sir John Grey of Groby. They had two sons: Thomas (born, c. 1457 and later created the Marquess of Dorset by Edward IV) and Richard (born, c. 1458 and later knighted as Sir Richard Grey). Her husband Sir John Grey was injured while fighting for Lancaster in the Second Battle of St. Albans on February 17, 1461, and he died a few days later. For his service to Lancaster, he was penalized; his properties and estates were declared forfeit to York, and then claimed for the crown by Edward IV. Elizabeth Woodville was a commoner born of gentry, and had no title of her own.

All agreed that Elizabeth was spectacularly beautiful. According to legend, the twenty-five or twenty-six year old widow first conspired to meet twenty-one year old King Edward IV in a way that involved courage and cleverness. She learned of a path Edward often took while hunting. One morning when he came by, she stepped out from behind an oak tree (now a famous tourist attraction called, *Queens Oak* in Northampton) accompanied by her six and five year old sons Thomas and Richard Grey. She accosted the king with a request that properties of her husband Sir John Grey, which had been taken following his death in battle, be returned to her for the benefit of herself and her sons.

Edward was immediately smitten by Elizabeth's natural blond beauty. He heard her plea, and then proposed that an amiable agreement for illicit intimacy could be reached in exchange for granting her request. However, Elizabeth refused Edward's amorous advance. Edward wooed Elizabeth for several months, before they wedded secretly in the village chapel at Grafton (probably on May 1, 1464). The ceremony was without posting of Church bans, or of knowledge by any in the king's extended York family. Never before had a King of England married a common person without title since the Norman Conquest four hundred years before.

Five months later, the marriage between Edward and Elizabeth became known. It created a furor throughout England and all Europe. The king's marriage was considered totally inappropriate. The secretive ceremony alone showed that King Edward was aware of how ill advised the marriage was. A chronicle then reported, "[The marriage was] led by blind affection, and not by the rule of reason . . . When this maryage was first blowen abrode, forren Kyngs and Princes marvelled at it, noble men detested it, the common people grudged, and murmured at it." Members of Edwards York family protested loudly against his marrying a widow with two children. He replied, "By God's blessed Virgin, I am a bachelor, and have some, too! So each of us has proof that neither is likely to be barren."

Elizabeth Woodville was crowned queen on May 26, 1465. Both of her parents, Sir Richard Woodville and Lady Jacquetta of Luxembourg, were present. Her mother's rowdy relatives from Luxembourg who spoke and understood little English marred Elizabeth's marriage. After the wedding, the Luxembourgers caroused with flamboyant heraldry that depicted Elizabeth as the witch 'Mélusine' (the bawdy water-witch daughter of Satan himself). The meaning of the Luxembourg charade was totally lost on the English hosts. The English nobility wondered: Was their new queen in some way involved in dark arts of sorcery? Dame Elizabeth Woodville was accepted as queen, because she was the wife of King Edward, but she never enjoyed the good will of her subjects.

A constant source of irritation brought on by Elizabeth's marriage and coronation as queen came with her alienation of her mother-in-law Cecily Neville the mother of King Edward IV, and a sister of powerful Richard Neville Earl of Warwick who had done much to bring Edward his crown. Before Edward married Elizabeth Woodville, Edward's mother Cecily Neville had been the uncontested *First Lady of the Land*. Edward gave his mother the deference due a queen, and had even conveyed to his mother many land entitlements traditionally awarded to a queen consort. Duchess Cecily could not abide losing precedence in court to a beautiful, but common woman; a woman whose father Sir Richard Woodville was a mere Lancaster knight. Duchess Cecily's demotion below such person as Elizabeth Woodville (whose first husband Sir John Grey had died fighting for Lancaster, which made Elizabeth suspect of being a closet Lancaster, too) was unthinkable, unbearable, and unforgivable.

The generally stated reason for Elizabeth's persistent unpopularity, however, stemmed from Elizabeth's scheming to get noble titles and power into hands of her large family (six brothers and six sisters). She pressured her husband Edward IV to grant noble titles to many of her common relatives. Virtually all noble titles for Elizabeth's brothers and sisters came with marriages forced by King Edward's command on reluctant husbands and wives who held hereditary titles of earl/countess, marquess/marchioness, or duke/duchess. Two of the arranged marriages were most criticized. The marriage of Elizabeth's sixteen year old brother John Woodville to sixty-four year old Katherine Neville Dowager Duchess of Norfolk gave him the title Duke of Norfolk. The marriage of her eight year old sister Katherine Woodville to eleven year old Henry Stafford Duke of Buckingham, a prince of royal blood, gave her the title Duchess of Buckingham.

Elizabeth Woodville's social climbing was nothing new. Indeed, seeking preferment through marriage always had been an underlying ploy for gaining social position and political power in court. Elizabeth committed no breach in etiquette when the king found her to be irresistibly captivating. She committed no crime for using her status as queen to share its benefits with family and friends. Although no sins or crimes were leveled against her, resentment against Elizabeth and her Woodville family steadily grew during her nineteen-year marriage to Edward VI.

The House of York distrust of the Woodville's came from direct support they had given to the House of Lancaster in a variety of ways.

Elizabeth's first husband Sir John Grey was a knight who died in cavalry service for King Henry VI. In addition as a child, Elizabeth had served as maid-of-honor to King Henry's Queen Margaret of Anjou. Her father Sir Richard Woodville had been chamberlain to John of Lancaster Duke of Bedford before he switched sides, and became an aid to King Edward IV of York.

However, those objections were all secondary to Elizabeth's marriage to King Edward for frustrating plans for a political marriage of the King of England with a Princess of France. When the secret marriage of Edward and Elizabeth took place in the village chapel at Grafton, Edward's powerful uncle, Richard Neville Earl of Warwick, was negotiating a royal marriage in France. Elizabeth's misfortune was in having Richard Neville Earl of Warwick as her chief antagonist. Next after the king, Richard Neville Earl of Warwick was the richest and most powerful nobleman of the England. In the conflict between Lancaster and York that finally brought Edward of York his crown, Warwick played the leading military role in defeating the armies of Lancaster. For that great service, Warwick was called *The King Maker*. After Edward became king in 1461, Warwick held the most dominant position of power in government under the king. Warwick enjoyed the king's full confidence, respect, and appreciation for past and continuing services he rendered.

Warwick was at the apex of his personal power in the summer of 1464 when he served as England's envoy to Louis XI (The Spider King of France) to negotiate marriage of Edward IV to the King of France's sister-in-law Princess Bora of Savoy. In the midst of parley at the summit of diplomatic prestige, the preposterous marriage of King Edward to the common nobody, Elizabeth Woodville Grey, a widow with two children and no noble title, became common knowledge in all courts of Europe. The king's emissary Richard Neville Earl of Warwick was incoherently, furiously, wroth beyond measure! That the king would marry a person so far beneath him was incredible. That the king had not informed his viceroy of what he had done was insulting. Proud Warwick's loss of face in international diplomacy was intolerably humiliating. After Elizabeth's marriage to the king, Warwick became bitterly committed to destruction of Elizabeth and her common Woodville relatives.

Elizabeth, through no fault of her own, had gained an unforgiving enemy of great power. The animosity for Elizabeth, and against others of the Woodville clan was echoed throughout the Houses of York and

Neville. It mattered little that its cause was neither of Elizabeth's making, nor in her ability to control.

Gradually over the next few years, Warwick became estranged from the king, and he lost much of his former influence and power in court. Arrogance and wounded feelings of imagined injustice, and the king's lack of gratitude for past services, motivated Warwick's withdrawal from court. He eventually left London, and returned to his estates in the north. Evidence of Warwick's decline in status was most evident in the rise of Sir Richard Woodville (the king's father-in-law) as chief in government in the position Warwick previously held. Warwick's alienation from York moved him to accommodation with his former Lancaster enemies.

Open rebellion against the king reached a peak when Warwick organized a small fray called the Battle of Edgecote Moor on July 26, 1469, In it, several of King Edward's lords were killed, among them was Richard Woodville, Queen Elizabeth's father. Warwick captured and detained King Edward for a time; however, King Edward soon regained his freedom. However, after Edgecote Moor, reconciliation between King Edward and Richard of Warwick was no longer possible, and Warwick fled to exile in France.

In the next year, Queen Margaret of Anjou and Richard Neville of Warwick met in France, and conspired to dethrone King Edward IV, and regain the crown for Henry VI of Lancaster. Warwick's surprise attack against the King Edward's militia in London on September 13, 1470 gave Edward IV scarcely time to make his escape to France. King Edward took refuge with his brother-in-law Charles Duke of Burgundy.

When Edward fled to France, Queen Elizabeth immediately sought sanctuary in Westminster Abbey with her three daughters: Princesses Elizabeth, Mary, and Cecily. The queen knew that she could expect no more mercy from Warwick than he had shown in murdering her father following the Battle of Edgecote Moor.

The queen was heavily pregnant when she entered sanctuary in the Abbey. Elizabeth's child, a prince, was born six weeks later on November 2 1470. The queen named him Edward in honor of his absent father. Prince Edward (later Edward V) was baptized without ceremony in a manner as simple as had he been but a peasant.

After forcing Edward's flight to France, Richard Neville of Warwick liberated King Henry VI from the Tower of London, where he had been held for five years. Warwick reinstalled the pathetic manikin as king on October 30, 1470. His pseudo-rule (in what history now calls the *Readeption of Henry VI*) lasted until Edward's return to England in force on March 14, 1471. By May, Edward had regained his throne, but Elizabeth remained in her Westminster sanctuary until after the defeat of Lancaster in the battle of Tewksbury on May 4, followed by the murder of gentle King Henry VI in the Tower on May 21, 1471.

The next twelve years (1471-1483) were relatively calm. Queen Elizabeth was secure, and her popular husband Edward IV ruled in firm control of government. Their family grew to ten children, (7 girls and 3 boys); eight of them survived to maturity:

> Elizabeth of York (February 11, 1466-February 11, 1503),
>> Queen Consort of Henry VII, mother of Henry VIII, etc.
> Mary of York (August 11, 1467-May 23, 1482), died young
> Cecily of York (March 20, 1469-August 24, 1507), Viscountess
>> Welles
> Edward Prince of Wales (November 2, 1470-c. fall 1483), King
>> Edward V, one of the 'Princes in the Tower'
> Richard Duke of York (August 17, 1473-c. fall 1483), one of
>> the 'Princes in the Tower'
> George Plantagenet (c. march 1477-c, march 1479), died in
>> infancy
> Anne of York (November 2, 1475-November 23, 1511),
>> Countess of Surrey
> Catherine of York (August 14, 1479-Novemner 15, 1527),
>> Countess of Devon
> Bridget of York (November 10, 1480-c. 1517)
> Illegitimate son: Arthur Plantagenet Viscount Lisle (c. 1470-c.
>> 1542)

Suddenly at Easter in 1483, Queen Elizabeth Woodville's world again crashed down when Edward contracted pneumonia or typhoid. Within a week he died on April 9, 1483 at the age of forty-two. However, Edward IV lived long enough to write a will that appointed his younger brother Richard Duke of Gloucester to be the custodian of his eldest son Crown Prince Edward Prince of Wales. The will of King Edward IV also appointed Richard of Gloucester to be *Regent and Protector of the Prince* during the boy's minority until he was eighteen years old when he would be King Edward V with full right to rule.

The will of King Edward IV unambiguously favored the House of York by giving all legal ruling authority to his brother Richard Duke of Gloucester. Queen Elizabeth and the Woodville side of the prince's biological family received no important authority. Edward's will left Queen Elizabeth Woodville with control only over their daughters. Queen Elizabeth knew she was vulnerable to ill will from her York-in-laws. They despised her, and had no enthusiasm for protecting the inheritance of her spawn.

When Edward IV died in London, Crown Prince Edward was twelve years old, and lived at Ludlow Castle on the Welch border under care of his Woodville relatives. Queen Elizabeth sent a courier to her brother Anthony Lord Rivers, with instructions for him to bring his nephew (now King Edward V) immediately to London, where the young king could be housed safely in the Tower of London until his coronation. It took two days for the queen's letter to arrive at Ludlow. The king's uncle Anthony Lord Rivers, his half-brother Sir Richard Grey, and a small party of Woodville attendants set out promptly for London with child-King Edward V. On their way, the Woodville party stopped overnight for lodging at Stony Stratford in Buckinghamshire west of London. Richard Duke of Gloucester intercepted them there, and the two parties shared an amiable evening meal at the hostel.

Next morning, Richard of Gloucester demanded that Lord Rivers give him custody of King Edward V, since he (Richard of Gloucester) was appointed in King Edward's will to be 'Regent and Protector of the Prince.' Prince Edward had grown up with his Woodville kinsfolk, and he was deeply distrustful of his York relatives. Lord Rivers and Richard Grey protested Gloucester's demand, but being without armed force, they were powerless to resist. Because they protested, Richard arrested Rivers and Grey, and sent them to prison in Gloucester's Pontefract Castle, from which they never escaped. They were executed for treason a little over a month later as part of Richard of Gloucester's relentless climb to the throne.

News sped to London of the trouble at Stony Stratford, where Richard of Gloucester opposed Woodville authority over custody of King Edward V. In alarm over what Richard might do, Queen Elizabeth again took sanctuary at Westminster Abbey, taking with her seventeen year old

Elizabeth of York, fifteen year old Cecily, and eleven year old Richard Duke of York. Queen Elizabeth also carried into sanctuary as much wealth as she could bundle together on short notice.

Next day, the Archbishop of York arrived, and reassured the queen by saying, "Madam, be of good comfort. If they crown any other king than your eldest son, whom they have with them, I will on the morrow crown his brother, whom you have with you here. I also, give you the Great Seal, which in likewise as your noble husband gave it to me, so I deliver it to you for the use of your son the King."

The original date for coronation of Edward V was May 4. However, that date was too soon for completion of suitable preparations, so the coronation of King Edward V was rescheduled for June 22, 1483. However, the coronation never took place, for by then, Richard of Gloucester had usurped the crown.

Incredible though it may seem: in less than two months, Parliament decided that Prince Edward and his siblings were illegitimate. Richard of Gloucester was proclaimed King Richard III on June 22. He was crowned king on July 6, 1483.

> Note: The remainder here only follows events that directly affect Queen Elizabeth Woodville and her children in sanctuary. For more information on how Richard of Gloucester accomplished his slight-of-hand substitution of kings, see narratives in chapters on Reign 17. King Edward V, and Reign 18. King Richard III.

Dowager Queen Elizabeth Woodville remained in sanctuary at Westminster Abbey through much of the first year in the reign of Richard III. Her youngest son, nine year old Richard Duke of York was with her in the Abbey. He was the *heir apparent* for his older brother Edward V who was now in the Tower of London as a prisoner of Richard of Gloucester.

Queen Elizabeth was determined to prevent her nine year old son Richard Duke of York from falling into the hands of his uncle Richard Duke of Gloucester.

Richard of Gloucester was equally determined to gain custody of his nephew Prince Richard. Gloucester's first ruse was to tell the Queen that twelve year old "[King Edward V] required the company of his brother, being melancholy without a playfellow." Elizabeth was suspicious and replied to Richard of Gloucester, "Pray God . . . 'The King doth lack a playfellow?' Can none be found to play with him, but only his brother, who hath no wish to play because of sickness?"

Confounded for the moment, Richard of Gloucester cleverly schemed to outwit the Queen Elizabeth Woodville by persuading (possibly by bribing) John Kemp the Archbishop of Canterbury to intercede with the queen. Kemp told Queen Elizabeth that, because the boy was too young to stand trial for a crime, he also was ineligible for protection by sanctuary. Kemp proposed that the queen should give him custody of her son Richard Duke of York for safekeeping in Canterbury Cathedral. Queen Elizabeth, believing that the Archbishop spoke true, and having confidence in his honor, she surrendered her son Richard, to the Archbishop, and prophetically said, "Farewell my sweete sonne. Let me kiss you ere you go, for Gode only knows if we shall ever kiss again."

The Archbishop traitorously delivered Prince Richard to his uncle Richard of Gloucester, who then took him to the Tower of London to join his brother Edward V. The princes never left their prison. The two brothers are forever known to history as *The Princes in the Tower*. Their true fate is uncertain, but it is believed that after Richard of Gloucester became King Richard III, he ordered their murder sometime in September 1483.

Princess Elizabeth of York, the eldest daughter of Edward IV and Queen Elizabeth Woodville, was now the unquestioned prime York candidate for the crown.

Before the end of the year 1483, Lady Margaret Beaufort (the mother of Henry Tudor Earl of Richmond, the major remaining Lancaster contender for the crown) secretly met with Dowager Queen Elizabeth Woodville, who was still in sanctuary at Westminster Abbey. The ladies plotted for the downfall, and destruction of Richard III. They reasoned:

> If the Dowager Queen Elizabeth Woodville's eldest daughter Princess Elizabeth of York would marry Lady Margaret Beaufort's son Henry Tudor Earl of Richmond, then, all York and Lancaster factions that opposed king Richard III could be united in common cause to bring King Richard III down.

The great ladies conspiracy to unite the great Houses of Lancaster and York by a marriage between Princess Elizabeth of York and Henry Tudor of Lancaster was publicly announced in Paris at Christmas in 1483.

Henry Tudor's preparations for invasion of England continued for eighteen months before he successfully challenged, defeated, and killed Richard III at Bosworth Field on August 22, 1485. Henry Tudor became King Henry VII on that date. He married Elizabeth of York five months later on January 18, 1486 at Westminster Abbey.

After the marriage of Henry Tudor and Elizabeth of York in 1485, Dowager Queen Elizabeth Woodville retired to Bermondsey Abbey on the outskirts of London. Thereafter, she rarely took part in events at court. She was forty-eight years old, and even after bearing a dozen children by two husbands, she was still a beautiful woman.

Authorities disagree on whether her retirement was by personal choice, or was on command from her son-in-law King Henry VII. Many suspect that he chose to banish her from court to prevent her meddling in affairs of State. However, distancing herself from court was probably her own choice from a desire to enjoy a life of quiet meditation after her many tempestuous years at the center of turbulent events in reigns of Edward IV and his brother Richard III.

Evidence exists that she had a pious nature, and enjoyed charitable endeavors. Viewed from that perspective, her retirement from court fitted the wishes of one who cherished a private life without confrontation.

Henry VII respectfully gave his mother-in-law Elizabeth Woodville dower palaces suitable for her status in court as Dowager Queen. Evidence for the friendly regard of Henry VII for his mother-in-law is seen in his naming her the Godmother for his first son and heir Arthur Prince of Wales.

Through the rest of her life in the reign of Henry VII, Dowager Queen Elizabeth Woodville received all respect due her station as mother of the reigning queen, and as the Dowager Queen of Edward IV. She gave generous support to Queen's College, Cambridge, which had been founded by her predecessor, Queen Margaret of Anjou.

Dowager Queen Elizabeth Woodville died at age fifty-five on June 8, 1492 at Bermondsey Benedictine Abbey, London. Elizabeth's will shows that she had little personal property to bequeath. Her possessions were all dower rights that, on her death, reverted to the crown. Clearly, she did not use her exalted position to gain great personal wealth. That alone tends to deny her critics, who accused her of insatiable greed. She was buried without ostentation with her husband Edward IV at St. George's Chapel, Windsor. Their tomb was inscribed simply:

King Edward and his Queen, Elizabeth Widville.

Elizabeth Woodville's place in history lacks unanimity in the opinions of competent judges. In her own time, members of the noble Houses of York and Neville despised her, and could see no good in her. Anecdotal legends abound that distort her record, and make true evaluation of her nature difficult. Some extreme views see her as a *Romantic Heroine* (the model of fidelity, propriety, and fortitude). To others, she was a *Gold Digging Vamp* (a single minded venal materialist bent on extracting gain from every opportunity she met). A few see her as a *Sex Goddess* (a vixen that snares, and enchants a gullible king with carnal rewards). However, a moderate assessment sees her as an *Upper middleclass Cinderella* (a many faceted personality that met life's trials with courage, ingenuity, and fortitude). Other opinions abound.

Elizabeth Woodville's historical credits: She was the first Queen Elizabeth of England. She was mother of Queen Elizabeth of York, grandmother of Henry VIII, and great-grandmother of reigning Queen Elizabeth I. Through her son Thomas Grey, Marquess of Dorset, she was great-grandmother of 9-day-Queen, Lady Jane Grey. Through her great-great-granddaughter Mary Queen of Scots, Elizabeth Woodville is also an ancestor of all Stuart, Hanoverian, and Windsor monarchs of England. Elizabeth Woodville shares these genealogical honors with Katherine of Valois the Queen Consort of Henry V, and grandmother of Henry Tudor.

REIGN 17

CHILD-KING EDWARD V
(PRINCE IN THE TOWER)

Summary of the Reign of King Edward V
(Reign, April 9-June 22, 1483)

King Edward V: life dates c. 12/13 years, b. November 2, 1470-d. September/October 1483; King of England less than 3 months, April 9-June 22, 1483.

Since Edward V had no queen consort, this chapter only summarizes his biography.

Edward of Westminster was the eldest son of King Edward IV and Queen Elizabeth Woodville. He was only twelve years old when his father Edward IV died on April 9, 1483. On that date, Prince Edward became King Edward V. He was not married during his short reign of less than three months. However, the prince was precontracted to marry Anne of Brittany when he was ten, and she was only four years old in 1480.

The place in history of King Edward V is notorious in that he was the older of the two sons of Edward IV who were imprisoned in the Tower of London by their uncle Duke Richard of Gloucester. They were never seen again outside its walls after July 1483. What happened to the two, who have always been called *The Princes in the Tower,* is the most contentious mystery in English history. This narrative considers two issues:

> Known facts about the Princes in the Tower
> The assumed fate of the Princes in the Tower of London

The place in history of King Edward V rests entirely on his being the eldest of the two 'Princes in the Tower.' Otherwise, he was merely a pawn whereby Duke Richard of Gloucester became King Richard III.

Known Facts about
the Princes in the Tower

EDWARD V was born in sanctuary of Westminster Abbey on November 2, 1470 while his father Edward IV was briefly exiled in Burgundy. His mother Queen Elizabeth Woodville had taken sanctuary in Westminster Abbey as refuge for herself, and for her children's safety during the half-year while Lancastrian forces were again briefly in control of government during the so-called, *Readeption of Henry VI.* After King Edward IV returned from Burgundy, and had defeated the Lancastrians at the Battle of Tewksbury on May 4, 1471, eight month old Prince Edward was created Prince of Wales in June 1471.

Twelve years later, the prince was at Ludlow Castle on the Welsh border, with members of his mother's Woodville family, when news came of the death of King Edward IV on April 9, 1483. Anthony Woodville Lord Rivers (brother of his mother the queen) and a small company of Woodville retainers set out for London with the prince, who was now King Edward V. He anticipated that he would be crowned about three weeks later on May 4.

The appointment of Richard of Gloucester as the prince's official custodian was much against Dowager Queen Elizabeth Woodville's wish. She and the entire Woodville family were alienated against Duke Richard and the rest of the House of York to which her husband Edward IV belonged. Woodville relatives had reared the young king. He shared their fear of his paternal York relatives. When he as apprehended by Richard of Gloucester, the young king demanded that he be returned to the

Woodville clan. Edward refused to believe that his uncle Lord Rivers, or his half-brother, Sir Richard Grey, were guilty of treason.

Richard of Gloucester was unmoved, and proceeded to London with Edward V in custody. The Lord Mayor and city dignitaries met the young king at London Gate. The entire retinue was clad in black, in deference to the recent death of King Edward IV. Only the prince wore royal purple, so he could be recognized as the new King Edward V. Young Edward was escorted to the Tower of London, and set up in the royal suite with royal dignity, as was the custom for a monarch awaiting coronation. The original date for coronation was May 4, but the date was rescheduled for late June to give more time for suitable preparations to be completed. However, the coronation never took place. By June 22, Richard of Gloucester had already usurped the throne.

Public opinion agreed that young King Edward V should to be in the care and keeping of his paternal uncle Richard of Gloucester. He was a nobleman by birth, and the young king should not to be supervised by his common Woodville relatives. Most nobility in the realm disapproved of the upstart Woodvilles. They expressed a common view, "*You can dress up mules in harness of fine horses, but they're still mules.*"

Nothing was yet amiss in Richard of Gloucester's handling of affairs. However, twelve year old Edward V bitterly resented his uncle Richard of Gloucester for his disrespectful treatment to himself, and for the arbitrary imprisonment of his uncle Anthony Rivers and his half-brother Richard Grey.

The Queen was alarmed when she heard that Richard of Gloucester had seized her son Edward V. She immediately took her other children, including nine year old Richard Duke of York (the king's younger brother), into sanctuary at Westminster Abbey. She believed that her children would be secure out of Richard of Gloucester's grasp in the Abbey. However, in this she was foiled by Gloucester, who prevailed on the Archbishop of Canterbury to convince the queen that Prince Richard would only be safe when he was in the Archbishop's custody. She was betrayed when the Archbishop delivered her son to Richard of Gloucester on June 16. He imprisoned the two princes in the Tower of London, and observers never saw the princes (King Edward V and his brother, Richard Duke of York) after they were last seen playing within the walls in mid July.

Suspicion that King Richard contrived to do away with the two princes reached near certainty on August 27, 1483 when Richard III invested his son Edward of Middleham as Prince of Wales. That was not possible so long as the younger of the two Princes still lived (Prince Richard was the *heir apparent*, and no one else could be Prince of Wales if he still lived).

Most people believed that the Princes in the Tower were secretly murdered on orders of Richard III no later than mid September, nine to eleven weeks after Richard of Gloucester was crowned Richard III on July 6, 1483.

The Assumed Fate of the Princes in the Tower of London

THE MOST convincing account of the Princes brief residence and ultimate deaths in the Tower of London was from a report of the event, twenty years later in, *The Great Chronicle of London*. That documentary record for the city said:

> "The children of King Edward [IV] were seen shooting and playing in the garden of the Tower sundry times . . . but after Easter [1484 nine months later] much whispering was among the people that the King [Richard III] had put the children of King Edward to death."

Dominic Mancini an, Italian diplomat to the court of Richard III, added:

> "[The brothers] were withdrawn into the inner apartments of the Tower, and day by day, began to be seen more rarely behind the bars and windows, till at length they ceased to appear altogether . . . The last of his [King Edward V] attendants whose services the King enjoyed, reported that the young King, like a victim prepared for sacrifice, sought remission of his sins by daily confession and penance, because he believed that death was facing him . . . Whether, however, he has been done away with, and by what manner of death, so far I have not at all discovered."

Thomas More the Chancellor for Henry VIII, author of *Anglica Historia* (c. 1513) on the reigns of Richard III and Henry VII, reported his interviews with contemporary persons of the time, and said that shortly after his coronation on July 6, 1483, Richard III sent a letter to Sir Robert Brackenbury Constable of the Tower that authorized execution of the two Princes, but Brackenbury refused to take action on the matter. Richard then gave orders to Sir James Tyrrell, who "rode sorrowfully to London" to commit the deed. Tyrrell went to the Tower with instructions that keys to the tower should be given to him for one night. Thomas More wrote:

> "Sir James Tyrell devised that they should be murdered in their beds, to the execution whereof he appointed Miles Forest, a fellow fleshed in murder before time, and John Dighton, his own horsekeeper, a big broad, square strong knave. Then, all the others being removed from them, this Miles Forest and John Dighton about midnight, the innocent children lying in their beds, came into their chamber and suddenly covered them with bedclothes so bewrapped them and entangled them, keeping them down by force, the featherbed and pillows hard into their mouths, that within a while, smothered and stifled, their breath failing, they gave up to God their innocent souls into the joys of Heaven, leaving their tormented bodies dead on the bed. Which, after the wretches perceived by the end of struggling and breath, and after long lying still and thoroughly dead, they laid their bodies naked on the bed and fetched Sir James [Tyrell] to see them. Which, upon the sight of them, caused those murderers to bury them at the stayre foote, metely depe in the grounde under a great heape of stones. [Thus, these innocent children were] privately slain and murdered . . . by the cruel ambition of their unnatural uncle [King Richard III] and his dispiteous tormentors."

Thomas More added that Richard spread the rumors of the princes' death in the belief that it would discourage rebellion. Tyrrell is reported to have confessed the murder of the princes, when Tyrell was executed for other crimes in 1502.

Thus, when it occurred, the generally accepted version of the fate of the two princes was that guards in the Tower had smothered them, and had hidden their bodies beneath a staircase. There was little doubt that King Richard III had authorized the heinous crime in his attempt to remove them as legitimate contenders for the crown he had usurped. However, proof is lacking that Richard III was responsible for ordering James Tyrell to arrange the murder of Edward V and his brother Richard of York.

At the time of the princes' demise, common Englishmen were sufficiently hardened by public executions to enjoy the beheading, drawing, and quartering of traitors, but they could not stomach the smothering of two little princes to advance ambition of Duke Richard of Gloucester.

Almost two hundred years after these events took place, during renovation and repairs of the Tower in 1674, the bones of two juvenile humans, and some animal bones were found in a wooden chest under stones beneath a seldom-used staircase in the Tower (exactly as Thomas More had described the deed). Without further evidence, Charles II, then King, immediately assumed that the human skeleton remains were those of The Princes in the Tower who died in 1483. King Charles ordered the bones to be buried in a marble urn with somber dignity in Westminster Abbey.

The urn was opened in 1933, and two medical examiners confirmed that the human skeletal anatomy was consistent in age with that for the twelve and nine year old princes who disappeared in the reign of Richard III. Structural peculiarities in the skeletons agreed with similar anomalies found in bones of other Plantagenets. The medical report concluded that the anatomical facts were consistent with the possibility that the bones were, but not proven to be, the skeletons of the Princes in the Tower.

These circumstantial evidences convince most historians that responsibility for murder of the Princes in the Tower rests firmly on Richard III. However, members of the *Richard III Society* evangelize their belief that history has maligned Richard of Gloucester in charging him with guilt for this, and for other crimes and misdemeanors in his reign.

One of Henry Tudor's first acts as King Henry VII in 1485, after usurping the throne from Richard III, demanded that Parliament restore legitimacy to all children of Edward IV. By this means, his Queen Consort Elizabeth of York (the eldest child of Edward IV and Elizabeth Woodville) would not have a cloud of bastardy besmirch any children born to them.

Legitimacy was of cardinal concern to Henry Tudor. More than enough bastardy existed in his genealogy. Henry's father Edmund Tudor was born a bastard who had to be legitimized by Parliament before he was free to marry Henry's mother, the Venerable Lady Margaret Beaufort. Moreover, her grandfather, John Beaufort was born a bastard of John of Gaunt and his mistress Katherine Swynford, before later being legitimized by Parliament and Pope Boniface IX in 1390.

REIGN 18

KING RICHARD III

AND

QUEEN CONSORT ANNE NEVILLE OF WARWICK

Summary of the Reign of King Richard III (Reign 1483-1485)

> King Richard III: life dates 32 years, b. October 2, 1452-d. August 22, 1485; King of England 2 years, June 26, 1483-August 22, 1485.

RICHARD OF York Duke of Gloucester was the youngest of eight children, and fourth of four sons of Richard Plantagenet Duke of York and Cecily Neville Countess of Westmoreland. His father Richard Plantagenet was the major York protagonist at the beginning of the Wars of the Roses, but after his death in the Battle of Wakefield in 1460, York leadership was taken over by his eldest son Edward who became Edward IV.

Richard of Gloucester was the youngest brother of Edward IV. His enduring claim to notoriety lay in common belief that he usurped his crown from his nephew Edward V, that he contrived an accusation that the prince was illegitimate, and then he devised a secret means for murdering twelve year old Edward V together with his nine year old brother Richard Duke of York. Richard III imprisoned the two sons of Edward IV in the Tower of London, and they were famously known as the *Princes in the Tower*. After two months, the princes were never again seen alive. Richard III was blamed for authorizing their murder. Because Richard III was believed to be responsible for deaths of The Princes in the Tower, he has always been considered the worst of English Kings. Shakespeare depicts Richard III to be the epitome of evil. Even so, the *Richard III Society* in London persists in defending Richard's innocence of any devious roles in the disappearance of the Princes in the Tower.

Richard, Duke of Gloucester was born on October 2, 1452 at Fotheringhay Castle, Northamtonshire. Late in the reign of his brother King Edward IV, Richard was created Duke of Gloucester, and thereafter, he was known as Richard of Gloucester before he became King Richard III. After Parliament, on spurious evidence, ruled the children of Edward IV to be illegitimate, and therefore ineligible to reign, Parliament then recognized Richard to be king on June 26, and he was crowned King Richard III on July 6, 1483.

All was done legally, but public opinion accused Richard of Gloucester of usurping the crown from his nephew Edward V, who was king for less than three months.

The reign of Richard III lasted slightly over two years. He never earned respect and trust from his subjects. His reign was wracked by civil dissent as he tried unsuccessfully to legitimize his crown.

Henry Tudor Earl of Richmond, the major Lancaster contender for the throne, deposed and killed Richard III at the Battle of Bosworth Field on August 22, 1485. After his death, Richard III was buried in Greyfriars Abbey in Leicester, but his tomb was destroyed before 1543 in despoiling of the monasteries during the reign of Henry VIII.

Anne Neville of Warwick was the queen consort of King Richard III. She was his first cousin, and it was her second marriage. Ann's first husband was Prince of Wales Edward of Westminster, the son of Henry VI who was killed after the Battle of Tewksbury in 1471. Anne died of tuberculosis in

1485, and was buried at Westminster Abbey. Richard's only child with Anne Neville was Edward of Middleham (styled Prince of Wales during his father's reign), who was born in 1473, and died in 1484.

Henry Tudor, Earl of Richmond, defeated and killed Richard III at the Battle of Bosworth Field, and then claimed the crown by right of conquest. Henry Tudor ascended the throne as King Henry VII on August 22, 1485.

Narrative of Queen Consort
Anne Neville of Warwick

Queen Anne Neville: life dates 28 years, b. June 11, 1456-d. March 16, 1485; Princess of Wales as wife of Edward of Westminster c. 4 months, December 1470-May 4, 1471; Duchess of Gloucester as wife of Richard of Gloucester 11 years, July 12, 1472-June 22, 1483; Queen Consort of Richard III, nearly 2 years, June 22, 1483-March 16, 1485.

ANNE NEVILLE was the younger of two daughters of Richard Neville Earl of Warwick and his wife Anne de Beauchamp Countess of Warwick. The Warwick title was in her name, and Richard Neville acquired his title (Earl and later, Duke of Warwick) by his marriage to her. Their daughter Anne, who is of central interest here, was a central, but passive figure in the violent events that characterized closing years of the Wars of the Roses.

A reading of Anne's record creates the impression of an agreeable complacent girl who accepted demands made upon her by authoritative persons, such as her father and her second husband Richard III. However, there is little evidence that she personally approved, or opposed actions demanded of her. Anne's image in history is of a person manipulated by events, akin to a leaf drifting on a turbulent stream. This being the case, the following narrative tells of what happened to Anne, but aside from occasional speculation, it is silent on her personal feelings about the roles she was forced to play in a bloody time with ruthless players.

Anne Neville was born on June 11, 1456 at Warwick Castle in Warwickshire, but much of her childhood was spent at Middleham Castle, Yorkshire. The mighty fortress had foundations laid in the 11th century during the reign of William the Conqueror. Over time, the castle was strengthened and improved with twelve-foot thick impenetrable stone walls. By the 15th century, it had three levels for living, and the largest set of dungeon keeps in England. Middleham was an operating military bastion noted for its lack of ostentation in the style of living it provided for family or guests. From Middleham Castle, Anne's father governed his vast northern estates in Warwick, Yorkshire and Northumbria. He commanded the largest personal militia in England, and was accustomed to being obeyed when he ordered those around him to do his bidding, be they vassals or lords.

Anne's father Richard Duke of Warwick, without question, was the richest, most powerful, and most ambitious nobleman in England.

Anne was only a year old when the Wars of the Roses began with the first Battle of St. Albans on May 22, 1455. In that battle, Lancaster forces for the first time were challenged, and defeated by York insurgents led by Anne's father Richard Neville Earl of Warwick. Her uncle Richard Plantagenet Duke of York was the primary York contender for the throne. Richard Plantagenet was killed in a great Lancaster victory at the Battle of Wakefield on December 30, 1460. Wherewith, his eldest son Edward Earl of March became Duke of York, and took leadership for the House of York in the ongoing Wars of the Roses.

Anne lived at Middleham Castle during much of her childhood. Another resident at Middleham then was her cousin Richard of York (later, Duke of Gloucester and King Richard III). He was ten years old when he came to Middleham Castle for military training under direction of his uncle Richard Neville Duke of Warwick. The first cousins lived under the same roof, and surely were familiar with one another. They would be married a decade later, but it is farfetched to speculate on whether future affection (or animosity) between them began in childhood.

Anne Neville was only five years old when Lancaster again was soundly defeated at the Battle of Towton on March 29, 1461. After that, Edward of York (Anne's first cousin) was accepted by Parliament as King Edward IV. Anne's father Richard Neville played a major part in winning the crown for the king his nephew. Richard Neville enjoyed high favor in the court of King Edward IV from 1461 to 1465. However, he later fell from favor with the king.

Anne was thirteen in 1469, when her father went into exile in France after the Battle of Edgecote Moor (July 26, 1469). In that encounter, Richard Neville challenged King Edward IV, and they became embittered enemies. For their safety, Richard's family accompanied him to France, and remained in Calais until 1470. Anne was fifteen when her father and Queen Margaret of Anjou agreed to cooperate in an effort to overthrow King Edward IV.

Their plan called for Richard of Warwick to supply military force in deposing Edward IV. Then, if the enterprise were successful, his daughter Anne would marry Queen Margaret's son Crown Prince Edward of Winchester, and she would become Queen of England when Edward of Winchester eventually became King of England. Warwick accepted Queen Margaret's terms, and give his strongest support in her conspiracy to overthrow King Edward IV.

Queen Margaret and Duke Richard of Warwick recruited an invasion force of Flemish, French, Northumbrian, Welsh, and Scottish troops, and then invaded northern England. His surprise attack succeeded in defeating King Edward IV, who was driven to flight and refuge in Burgundy. Warwick captured London on September 13, 1470, and released King Henry VI from prison in the Tower of London, and he began a pseudo-reign known as the *Readeption of Henry VI*. It lasted from September 1470 until March 1471. History has honored Richard Neville of Warwick with the title, *Warwick the Kingmaker*, for his slight-of-hand elevation of kings Edward IV and Henry VI to the throne in middle years of the Wars of the Roses.

During the so-called Readeption Reign of Henry VI, Queen Margaret remained in Flanders, and kept her son Edward of Westminster (the Lancaster Prince of Wales) with her. Anne Neville was in Calais. The date of the previously agreed upon marriage between Edward of Westminster and Anne Neville is uncertain, but it probably took place at Angers Cathedral on December 13, 1470. At the time, Prince Edward was eighteen and Anne was fourteen or fifteen. The bride and groom remained in Flanders during the half-year readeption of Henry VI. It is unlikely that the marriage was ever consummated.

In March 1471, King Edward IV returned to England with a sizeable military force recruited in Burgundy. On April 14, 1471, Edward IV defeated and killed Richard of Warwick in the Battle of Barnet, and reclaimed his crown as King of England. On the very day, Warwick was defeated and killed at the Battle of Barnet, Queen Margaret, her son Edward of Westminster, and his bride Anne Neville landed in England with armed force recruited to support Warwick. However, they arrived too late to be of assistance to Richard Neville of Warwick who was killed in battle on the same day they landed in England.

History is silent on Anne's reaction on hearing news of her father's death at the Battle of Barnet. One can only guess that she grieved sincerely for her father, whose ambition was to make his daughter Queen of England. Richard of Warwick had no male heir, and his will provided for equal division of his huge estates in Warwick, Yorkshire, and Northumberland to his two daughters, Isabelle and Anne Neville. Both daughters had married exceedingly well: Isabelle Neville married George Plantagenet Duke of Clarence (a younger brother of King Edward IV); Anne Neville was the bride of Lancaster Crown Prince Edward of Westminster.

Two weeks after the Lancaster defeat at Barnet, Queen Margaret of Anjou challenged King Edward IV at the Battle of Tewksbury on May 4, 1471. Lancaster forces were again decisively defeated. Anne's husband Prince Edward of Westminster was captured and executed after the battle (history usually credits Richard of Gloucester with being his executioner).

Anne was only fifteen when she was widowed by the execution of her first husband. Soon after the battle, Anne was also seized and imprisoned in the Tower of London. Her brother-in-law George Plantagenet Duke of Clarence arranged for Anne to be placed in his custody. While Anne was confined in the London residence of her sister and brother-in-law, she served as a scullery maid to keep her presence hidden. However, it is suspected that her confinement in that menial role was part of George of Clarence's intent to hide Anne from his younger brother Richard of Gloucester, because George knew his younger brother longed to marry her. It is thought that George planned to put Anne in a nunnery, where she could be forced to take vows of chastity and poverty. In that event, Anne's half of the huge Warwick estate would revert to her sister Isabelle, George Plantagenet's wife.

After the Battle of Tewksbury, Anne was treated as a traitor for having been married briefly to the Lancaster Prince of Wales Edward of Westminster. However, Anne's cousin Richard of Gloucester was determined to marry her. He discovered Anne's location in his brother's residence, and with King Edward's approval, Richard of Gloucester secured her release, and then spirited Anne into sanctuary at the Church of St. Martin le Grand in London until they could be married.

Richard of Gloucester was only nineteen when he won his spurs in the Battles of Barnet and Tewksbury. In those frays, Richard played a significant role in winning back the crown for his brother King Edward IV. It is believed that Richard was the executioner of both Prince Edward of Westminster and King Henry VI. For Richard's services, King Edward IV gave his younger brother the heiress Anne Neville as his bride. In addition, the king gave Richard the title Duke of Gloucester, and appointed him as his governor of the Northern Shires (including: Northumberland, Cambria, Durham, Yorkshire and border counties). For his excellent management, Edward IV awarded Richard many honors including the titles *Constable of England* and *Lord High Admiral of England*. In all but name, Richard was viceroy for the northern third of England. Richard's management of the vast estate was efficient, fair, and just. People of the northern shires loved Duke Richard, and they remained loyal to him through all his later travails.

Richard Plantagenet Duke of Gloucester and Anne Neville of Warwick were first cousins. They probably were married on July 12, 1472 with royal approval, but without papal dispensation, which usually was required of persons who were first cousins. The newlywed couple immediately departed to live at Anne's ancestral Neville estate, Middleham Castle in Yorkshire.

Anne was now the Duchess of Gloucester and a member of the York royal family. A good case can be made that motives behind the marriage of Richard of Gloucester and Anne Neville was based as much on real tender affection from childhood years spent together, as on Anne's recently acquired great fortune.

Many historians impugne Anne's character and accuse her of insensitivity for marrying Richard of Gloucester, who many believed had, with his own hand, killed her first husband Edward of Westminster. However, one must remember that Anne was ordered into her first marriage as part of the scheme her father Duke Richard Neville of Warwick and Queen Margaret of Anjou made to overthrow Edward IV. There is no evidence to suggest that Anne's first marriage was ever consummated, or that any tender sentiment was part of it. Also, Anne was a prisoner of State after the Battle of Tewksbury. She had no one in power to defend her. She had no option but to follow a court order to marry her cousin Richard of Gloucester. The marriage to the king's youngest brother had real advantage for Anne. By it, she gained some control over her own destiny, and over her enormous personal estate.

The decade 1473-1483 included the most serene and happy married years of Anne's life. These years were spent mainly in Warwick, or at Middleham Castle in Yorkshire. Anne's husband Richard Duke of Gloucester served King Edward IV as governor over much of northern England. Objective accounts from the time credit Richard with being an excellent judicious administrator. Richard earned respect and loyalty of his Yorkshire-Northumbrian people, which lasted long after Richard's personal reputation was destroyed by common belief that, when he was King Richard III, he was responsible for the murder of his nephews The Princes in the Tower.

After her marriage, Anne chose to live in her ancestral home at Middleham and on other estates in Yorkshire. She occasionally returned to London, when court etiquette required her presence. Her health, never robust, steadily declined over the years from what may have been tuberculosis. Richard and Anne's only child, Edward of Middleham, was born in Yorkshire sometime between April 1473 and December 1474. The child was the great joy of Anne's life, but he was weak, in chronic poor health, and he died in his tenth year in 1484.

Anne welcomed her sister Isabelle to join her at Middleham. Isabelle and Anne shared ownership of the vast Warwick estate. Isabelle died after the stillbirth of a third child in January 1477, and Isabelle's husband George Plantagenet Duke of Clarence was executed for treason in 1478. George Plantagenet was a selfish blundering drunkard who was repeatedly involved in conspiracies to overthrow his older brother King Edward IV—history maintains that his means of execution was "by drowning in a butt of Malmsey wine."

After their mother and father died, Anne assumed responsibility for mothering, and rearing the two orphaned children of her sister Isabelle. The children, Margaret Plantagenet and Edward Plantagenet, were born royal with expectations for grand futures, but tragically, they were destined for cruel death; both were imprisoned, and finally executed—Edward by Henry VII, and Margaret by Henry VIII—both for having 'blood too blue and too close to the throne.'

Anne and Richard of Gloucester were in residence at Middleham Castle at Easter when news arrived of the death of King Edward IV on April 9, 1483, and that Richard had been appointed *Regent and Protector of the Prince* for supervision of twelve year old King Edward V in his minority years. Richard immediately departed for London to assume control of government, and to take custody of his nephew Edward V. Anne was not present in court during the whirlwind events that deposed Edward V, and raised her husband to be King Richard III in June 1483. Anne was twenty-seven when she and Richard were crowned in Westminster Abbey on July 6, 1483.

Two months after her coronation, Anne was in Yorkshire when her ten year old son, Edward of Middleham was invested Prince of Wales on September 8, 1483. That ceremony took place at York Minster, not in Westminster Abbey as was customary. The ten year old boy's fragile health made distant travel ill advised. Edward of Middleham's investiture as Prince of Wales was the event that convinced Dowager Queen Elizabeth Woodville, who was in sanctuary in Westminster Abbey, that her sons the Princes in the Tower were dead.

Although rumors about the Princes in the Tower were widespread in court, it is probable that Anne knew little or nothing of the fate of the princes after she became queen (see the chapter on Reign 17. Edward V, which summarizes events associated with the fate of The Princes in the Tower). Richard III did nothing to deny their deaths, and did nothing to absolve himself of responsibility for their presumed murder.

Prince Edward of Middleham lived only into his tenth year. He died suddenly on April 9, 1484 at Sheriff Hutton Castle exactly one year after his uncle King Edward IV died. The boy's death was widely taken to be God's judgment against Richard III for murdering the Princes in the Tower.

Queen Anne died on March 16, 1485, less than a year after the death of her son. Richard grieved and wept openly at her burial in Westminster Abbey.

Only five months after Anne died, Richard lay dead at the hands of Henry Tudor in the Battle of Bosworth Field on August 22, 1485. No one ever questioned the personal bravery of Richard of Gloucester. Richard fought bravely at Bosworth Field. He was the only King of England to be killed in battle. Richard wore a thin circlet of gold as his crown. History tells that, when Richard was struck down, his crown rolled under a hawthorn bush. Lord Thomas Stanley retrieved it, and placed it on Henry Tudor's head, declaring, "Henry Tudor Earl of Richmond is now the true King of England."

Richard's naked body, striped of armor, was carried on a packhorse to Greyfriars Abbey in Leicester. He was buried without holy benediction. During despoiling of the monasteries in the reign of Henry VIII, the tomb of King Richard III was destroyed, and his bones were thrown in the River Soar. Nothing of him remains.

Gentle Queen Anne Neville died of natural causes (said to be tuberculosis) at age twenty-eight at Westminster on March 16, 1485. Few persons of any age have witnessed more turmoil and heartache than she. History credits her with leaving few marks on her own time. She led a tragic life as a pawn of power politics, and holds a place among history's most enigmatic passive personalities.

Anne Neville's unmarked burial place in Westminster Abbey was said to be "near the high altar at the entry to Edward the Confessor's Chapel." In 1960, *The Richard III Society* placed a bronze tablet near the supposed location of her tomb. It is the only memorial for Queen Anne's final resting place. It bears the citation:

> *Anne Neville (1456-1485), Queen of England,*
> *Younger Daughter of Richard, Earl of Warwick, called the*
> *Kingmaker,*
> *Wife of the last Plantagenet King, Richard III*

The reign of Richard III lasted only two years and two months (June 26, 1483-August 22, 1485). He was the last Plantagenet king. It is sad that so illustrious a dynasty would end so ignominiously.

Conclusion to the York Plantagenet Dynasty

THE PLANTAGENET Dynasty consisted of fourteen consecutive male heirs of Count Geoffrey of Anjou, beginning with his son Henry Plantagenet who was England's King Henry II. He began his reign in 1154, and the dynasty ended 331 years later with the death of Richard III on the Bosworth battlefield in 1485. The Plantagenet Kings fall into three groups:

> The Angevin Plantagenet Kings: Henry (Plantagenet) II, Richard I, John, Henry III, Edward I, Edward II, Edward III, and Richard II
>
> The Lancaster Plantagenet Kings: Henry IV, Henry V, and Henry VI
>
> The York Plantagenet Kings: Edward IV, Edward V, and Richard III

The Plantagenet Dynasty had its origin in 12th century Normandy, France during what is often referred to as the High Middle Ages (c. 1000-1250), and it continued to reign in England through the Late Middle Ages (c. 1250-1500). Henry Plantagenet was the personification of a ruler for the feudal age when knighthood and chivalry were coming into flower. Ancient social hierarchies of rank and title resisted evolutionary change. Moves to improve justice and efficiency of government crept at a snails pace through five centuries. In most ways, the mindset of the last Plantagenet was much like that of his progenitors. They were medieval to the end.

Modern Time began with discovery of the new World in 1492. The Tudor Dynasty that followed the Plantagenet Dynasty traced its origins to ancient Celtic ancestry in Wales. The marriage of Henry Tudor Earl of Richmond and Elizabeth of York, the eldest surviving child of Edward IV of York, united the two dynasties in the reign of Henry VII, the first Tudor king.

Their marriage also brought to a close Thirty-two years of internecine civil strife called the Wars of the Roses. The struggle for ascendancy between the House of Lancaster and House of York in the battles of that war took the lives of heirs of many noble houses in England, such that nearly half of the peerage titles in England became extinct for lack of any male survivors.

Henry Tudor was called 'The last hope for Lancaster.' When he became Henry VII, he feared insurgency from all remaining Plantagenets of the House of York. They were seen as threats to survival of his dynasty. Henry VII and his son Henry VIII held all in the House of York in suspicion of treachery and treason. The two Tudor kings systematically restrained, curtailed, or weeded out York Plantagenet blood remaining in England. The majority of remaining Plantagenets fled to Europe, and the few who remained in England were unsuccessful in feeble attempts to displace the firmly entrenched Tudors.

DYNASTY IV

THE TUDOR DYNASTY
REIGN 19 THROUGH 24 (1485–1603)

Patriarchs of the Tudor Dynasty:
John of Gaunt Duke of Lancaster and
Katherine Swynford

THE HOUSE of Lancaster and House of York were united in the marriage of Henry Tudor to Elizabeth of York after he became Henry VII. Except for a few minor challenges from the House of York that followed, their marriage ended the Wars of the Roses. Elizabeth of York had a far, far better hereditary claim to the crown than Henry. She was a true Plantagenet with ancestry that went back directly for eleven generations of kings to Henry II. When Henry Tudor and Elizabeth of York married, many felt that she should be the reigning queen in her own right. However, Queen Elizabeth of York never pursued a personal ambition to wear the crown.

Henry Tudor Earl of Richmond was the founder of the Tudor Dynasty. His father Edmund Tudor was the illegitimate son of Owen Tudor who was the paramour of Dowager Queen Katherine of Valois after her husband Henry V died. Henry Tudor's mother was the Venerable Lady

Margaret Beaufort, a Lancaster great-granddaughter of John of Gaunt and his mistress Katherine Swynford through their illegitimate eldest son John Beaufort, Sr. (Lady Margaret's grandfather), and his son John Beaufort, Jr. (Lady Margaret's father).

Henry Tudor, with illegitimacy conspicuous on both sides of his family, was an improbable slender reed to continue John of Gaunt's line in England's royal succession. Being saddled with two bastard hereditary claims (one great-grandfather, John Beaufort, Sr. on his mother's side of the family, and his illegitimate father Edmund Tudor, on the other) was hardly enough to convince most persons that Henry Tudor would be a serious contender for the throne.

It is relevant that John of Gaunt Duke of Lancaster, before his death acknowledged as his own, John Beaufort and his three other children with Katherine Swynford. Pope Boniface IX affirmed the Royal Charter of Richard II that legitimized the four Beaufort children and their descendants. The original legitimization document placed no restriction on Beaufort descendants, but King Henry IV (the Beaufort's half-brother) added a codicil that denied a right to reign by anyone in the Beaufort-Lancaster line of descent. King Henry IV excluded his Beaufort half-siblings from eligibility to reign, to protect inheritance rights in his own line of descent. However, King Henry IV own line ended with the murder of his grandson Henry VI in the Wars of the Roses in 1471.

The Beauforts married well, multiplied, and were ambitious, but they occupied a nebulous place in court. They had great prestige, wealth, and held high positions, but they resented the ceiling placed over their royal advancement. The restrictive codicil Henry IV made on the Beaufort's right to royal succession was believed to be binding. However, Henry Tudor did not accept that view. He was the last living male descendant of John of Gaunt who had any hope of recovering the crown for the House of Lancaster. Henry Tudor succeeded in regaining the crown, and in founding a dynasty that lasted for three generations.

The Tudor century, 1485-1603, is the most unforgettably dramatic, transforming, and brilliant period in English history. The Tudor story will unfold in following narratives on the reigns of Kings Henry VII, Henry VIII, Edward VI, and Queen Lady Jane, Queen Mary I, and, especially, Queen Elizabeth I.

First, the complex lineages of Henry Tudor from his parents Edmund Tudor and Margaret Beaufort must be reviewed.

Owen Tudor and Queen Katherine of Valois and their Sons Edmund Tudor and Jasper Tudor

OWEN TUDOR and Katherine of Valois have a major place in English history, because they were the parents of Edmund Tudor, and the grandparents of Henry Tudor, the Founder of the Tudor Dynasty who became King Henry VII.

Henry Tudor's grandmother Katherine of Valois was the Queen Consort of King Henry V and the mother of King Henry VI. She was twenty-one years old in 1422 when Henry V died. Her exalted social position as Dowager Queen of England gave her a handsome State pension and rich properties. She was beautiful, and eligible for a second marriage, but she did not marry again. A Parliamentary ruling in 1428 denied Katherine the right to marry for ten years, but she died in 1436 before that restriction expired.

Katherine's royal residence in London was fully staffed and included a Master of Wardrobe who was charged with managing her house. His name was Owen Tudor (born c. 1400-died February 2, 1461). He was without noble title, but claimed descent from legendary King Arthur Pendragon of Celtic fame.

Sometime between 1429 and 1431, Katherine of Valois moved out of London to her rural estate at Wallingford Castle forty miles west of London. Owen Tudor remained in service to Queen Katherine and they shared a common-law marriage relationship without legal status. Their four or more children were born illegitimate. Queen Katherine died on January 3, 1437, probably from complications in her last childbirth.

Owen Tudor and Queen Katherine lived for seven or more years at Wallingford, when, without forewarning, Owen was arrested in 1436 for violating the Parliamentary act that prohibited Katherine from marrying for ten years without the king's consent. Owen was imprisoned in the Tower of London for violating that restriction. Over the next four years, he was twice arrested, tried, released, and acquitted of charges that he had married Dowager Queen Katherine of Valois. His case was finally decided in 1439, with full pardon, and all bail fees cancelled, because no evidence was ever found that he had married Queen Katherine. No paper evidence of their marriage has ever been found. So, one may assume that Owen and

Katherine had a marriage that was good enough for the eyes of God, but not good enough for Parliament to grant their children legitimacy without the king's approval.

After his pardon in 1439, Owen Tudor was a loyal Lancaster henchman in the Wars of the Roses that began in 1455. York militia in the Battle of Mortimer's Cross captured him on February 2, 1461. The Battle was a decisive victory for Edward Duke of York who was crowned King Edward IV five months later on June 28, 1461. Edward ordered that Lancaster prisoners taken in battle who held officer rank were judged traitors, and were sentenced to death by beheading.

On the scaffold, Owen Tudor addressed his ax man with wry Welsh wit, "As this head ye lop, think how oft hap it lain in the lap of a Queen."

Owen's head was posted in Hereford marketplace as warning to Lancaster loyalists of what they risked, should they rebel against King Edward IV of York's authority. Owen Tudor's body parts were collected, and buried in Greyfriars Franciscan Chapel, Hereford. Owen Tudor's blood, and that of his common-law-wife Queen Katherine of Valois, was in their grandson King Henry VII, and in all later monarchs of England.

Before her death in 1437, Katherine of Valois wrote a will that gave her two sons, Edmund Tudor (6 years old) and Jasper Tudor (5 years old), to Abbess Katherine de la Pole of Barking Abbey in London for their care and education.

In essence, the boys were orphans. Their mother Katherine died in 1437, and their father Owen Tudor was in and out of prison until 1441. The boys remained at the Abbey from 1437 to 1442. The Abbess had high family connections with the royal family (her father Michael de la Pole, 2nd Earl of Suffolk had been a strong Lancaster supporter of Henry IV and Henry V). The boys received a sound general education, and had mastered court etiquette in the Abbey school. The Abbess saw fit to introduce them to court in 1442. Twelve year old Edmund Tudor and eleven year old Jasper Tudor were half-brothers of twenty-one year old King Henry VI by having the same mother, Queen Katherine of Valois.

King Henry VI gladly accepted the boys as his closest kin. He treated them as wards of his court from 1442 to 1452. They were part of the king's royal English Lancaster family, even though their relationship to the king was through their French mother, Dowager Queen Katherine—not through Henry V of Lancaster—thus, they lacked true Lancaster blood. Both teenage boys were ennobled in 1452(3?), and given titles. Edmund became Earl of Richmond, and Jasper became Earl of Pembroke. Rich estates were given to match their exalted titled ranks.

At court, Edmund and Jasper Tudor were openly recognized to be illegitimate children of Owen Tudor and Queen Katherine. Edmund petitioned Parliament for legitimization, and he was legitimized in 1453, just before his betrothal to Margaret Beaufort, who was also a ward of the court. She was the heiress of John Beaufort 1st Duke of Somerset. Twenty-five year old Edmund Tudor and twelve year old Margaret Beaufort were married on November 1, 1455 just as the Wars of the Roses began.

Shortly after the first Battle of St. Albans in May 1456, York militia captured Edmund who served as an emissary for King Henry VI. While in prison at Carmarthen Castle in Wales, Edmund became ill (possibly plague), and died on November 1, 1456, exactly one year after his wedding day. Edmund was buried at St. David Cathedral in Pembrokeshire, Wales. Edmund's child-bride Margaret Beaufort was a frail girl of thirteen, and heavily pregnant. She took refuge in the residence of her brother-in-law Jasper Tudor Earl of Pembroke in the mighty Norman fortress Pembroke Castle in far western Wales, which dated back to William the Marshal in the reign of King Henry Plantagenet. Two months later on January 28, 1457 Edmund's son Henry Tudor was born. At birth, the child posthumously inherited his father's title Earl of Richmond. His uncle Jasper Tudor, in essence, adopted the infant Henry Tudor, and took responsibility for protecting, rearing, and educating his nephew for almost three decades, much of the time while they were exiles in Brittany. Without the help of Jasper Tudor at every later phase of his life leading up to, and including the Battle of Bosworth Field, Henry Tudor would never have succeeded in defeating Richard III, and in winning the crown.

Venerable Lady Margaret Beaufort

HENRY TUDOR'S remarkable mother is known to history as the Venerable Lady Margaret Beaufort. She played a major part in bringing Henry Tudor to the throne. Lady Margaret was a great-granddaughter of John of Gaunt and his mistress Katherine Swynford. Lady Margaret descended from their eldest illegitimate son, John Beaufort Sr., and his only son, John Beaufort, Jr., from whom she was the only child. Through much of her life, Lady Margaret Beaufort was a pawn of State. Kings Edward IV and Richard III used Margaret for political advantage by giving her in marriage, in succession, to four great noble families. It is through her marriages that she was able to play a central, but behind the scene, role in political maneuvers that eventually would carry her only child Henry Tudor to the throne as Henry VII. Margaret's four husbands were:

> First marriage in 1450 at the age seven to John de la Pole, Duke of Suffolk; marriage later annulled.
>
> Second marriage in 1455 at age twelve, to Edmund Tudor, Earl of Richmond (the legitimized son of Owen Tudor and Dowager Queen Katherine of Valois). Lady Margaret devoted her life to advancement of their only child, Henry Tudor.
>
> Third marriage in c. 1462 to Henry Stafford Duke of Buckingham, c. 1461. Lady Margaret, prevailed upon Henry Stafford Duke of Buckingham to shift his support from the House of York and to give aid to her son, Henry Tudor, but the planned insurrection was discovered, and Richard III executed Henry Stafford for treason.
>
> Fourth marriage in 1483 almost immediately after Buckingham's execution, King Richard III gave Lady Margaret in marriage to Lord Thomas Stanley Earl of Derby in an attempt to block Margaret's Lancaster influence.

Richard III declared his own son Edward of Middleham to be the new Prince of Wales in August 1483. Shortly after this announcement, Lady Margaret Beaufort secretly met Dowager Queen Elizabeth Woodville, who was in sanctuary in Westminster Abbey. In that meeting, they agreed on the marriage of Henry Tudor and Elizabeth of York, the primary Lancaster and York candidates for the crown. Two years later when Henry Tudor launched his successful attack against Richard III in August 1485, Lady Margaret's husband Lord Thomas Stanley Earl of Derby brought 7,000 men to Bosworth Field in support of King Richard. However, before the battle, Lady Margaret persuaded her husband to withhold his men from battle. This deception changed the balance of power, and Richard III lost the battle, lost his life, and lost his crown. Lord Stanley personally crowned Henry Tudor on Bosworth Field, as King Henry VII.

In these ways, Lady Margaret played a decisive part in this major turning point in English history.

Venerable Lady Margaret was treated with great affection and respect when her son became King Henry VII. She also is remembered as a Renaissance spirit for learned translations of Latin texts into French and English, and as founder of St. Johns College, Cambridge.

Venerable Lady Margaret Beaufort died in 1509, two months after death of her son, King Henry VII, and she is buried with him in Westminster Abbey.

The Tudor Lineage,
Reign 19 through 24 (1485-1603)

THIS LINE includes Kings Henry VII, Henry VIII, Edward VI, and Queens Regnant Jane (Grey), Mary I, and Elizabeth I.

The lineage of Henry Tudor's Queen Consort Elizabeth of York has been given in the York Plantagenet Dynasty (she was the eldest surviving child of King Edward IV Duke of York and his Queen Consort Elizabeth Woodville).

The lineage of Henry Tudor Earl of Richmond's dynastic line comes through two lines of royal descent with very weak connections to the Plantagenet monarchs who preceded him. Henry Tudor's maternal descent came from John of Gaunt Duke of Lancaster and Katherine Swynford (Gaunt's mistress and third wife), and Henry Tudor's paternal descent came from Owen Tudor and Queen Katherine of Valois. Both lines are given below.

In these lineages, the names of reigning monarchs are given in bold type with the number for each reign. Dates in parenthesis give duration of reigns. Queen Consort names are included when they are also mothers of a following reigning monarch. Numbers in parenthesis give offspring in chronological order. However, only offspring are shown that figure conspicuously in events discussed in the present treatment of English history.

A. *The Lancaster-Swynford connection to Henry Tudor Earl of Richmond:*

Reign 11. Edward III (reign, 1327-1377) married Queen Consort Philippa of Hainault, parents of—

John of Gaunt Duke of Lancaster (3rd son of Edward III) married 3d wife, Katherine Swynford, parents of—

Illegitimate (later legitimized) John Beaufort, Sr., father of—

John Beaufort, Jr., father of—

Margaret Beaufort married illegitimate (later legitimized) Edmund Tudor, parents of—

Henry Tudor Earl of Richmond, later became King Henry VII after the defeat of Richard III at Bosworth Field on August 22, 1485.

Continue with the Tudor Lineage—Reign 19. King Henry VII.

B. *The Owen Tudor-Katherine of Valois connection to Henry Tudor Earl of Richmond.*

Owen Tudor and his mistress Queen Katherine of Valois, parents of—

Edmund Tudor married Margaret Beaufort, parents of—

Henry Tudor Earl of Richmond became King Henry VII.

Continue with the Tudor Lineage—Reign 19. King Henry VII.

Dynasty IV. The Tudor Lineage:

Reign 19. King Henry VII Earl of Richmond (1485-1509) married Queen Consort Elizabeth of York (see York-Plantagenet line of descent), parents of—

(1) Arthur Tudor married (1486-1502) married Katherine of Aragon, no issue.

(2) Margaret Tudor (1489-1541) married King James IV of Scotland, parents of—

James V of Scotland married Mary of Guise, parents of—

Mary Queen of Scots married Henry Stewart Lord Darnley, parents of—

Reign 25. King James I of England = James VI of Scotland Continue with Dynasty V. The Stuart Lineage.

(3) **Reign 20. King Henry VIII** (1509-1547) married—

Queen Consort Jane Seymour, parents of—

(1) **Reign 21. King Edward VI** (1547-1553), no issue.

Queen Consort Katherine of Aragon, parents of—

(2) **Reign 23. Queen Mary I** (1553-1558) married King Philip II of Spain, no issue.

Queen Consort Anne Boleyn, parents of—

(3) **Reign 24. Queen Elizabeth I** (1558-1603), no issue.

(4) Mary Tudor (1496-1533) married Charles Brandon Duke of Suffolk, parents of—

Frances Brandon married Thomas Grey, parents of—

Reign 22. Queen Regnant Lady Jane Grey (July 10-19, 1553) married Guildford Dudley, no issue (*Note*: Lady Jane's 9-day reign comes between those of Edward VI and Mary I)

End of Tudor Dynasty; continue with Dynasty V. The Stuart Lineage.

REIGN 19

KING HENRY VII

AND

QUEEN CONSORT ELIZABETH
OF YORK

Summary of the Reign of King Henry VII
(Reign, 1485-1509)

King Henry VII: life dates 52 years, b. January 28, 1457-d. April
21, 1509; King of England 24 years, August 22, 1485-April
21, 1509.

KING HENRY VII was known throughout life as Henry Tudor Earl
of Richmond. He was the son of Edmund Tudor and Lady Margaret
Beaufort. Henry Tudor was born on January 28, 1457 at Pembroke Castle,
Wales. He succeeded to the throne after the defeat and death of Richard
III at the Battle of Bosworth Field on August 22, 1485. After the battle,
Henry Tudor claimed the crown by right of conquest. He was well aware
that his hereditary claim to the crown was, at best, exceedingly fragile.

Throughout his reign, Henry VII, worked to legitimize and stabilize his hold on the crown. He ruthlessly removed most Plantagenets who remained in England, and threatened his right to rule. His reign was stern and stark, but his manner of ruling was admired for its stability after the uncertainty in England during a quarter century of strife during the Wars of the Roses.

Henry was an autocratic tyrant, but England prospered economically during his reign. He was notable for using persons of common birth who had great personal ability to assist him in government. At the end of his reign, the court in England was among the richest in Europe. The Renaissance was just beginning in England at the close of his reign. Overall, he ruled harshly, but well.

Throughout his reign, Henry was almost paranoid in suspecting treachery and sedition on every hand. He feared that someone else—someone with an army no larger than the one that brought him to power—would surprise and overthrow his rule. In order to keep detailed contact with all parts of his realm, he restricted parliamentary authority by creating local Justices of the Peace (a judicial office created during the reign of Edward III, and an element of Common Law in England and America today). The Justices were responsible for collecting taxes, and for administering local courts of law. In addition, they listened for murmurs of public discontent or sedition. Through his Justices, Henry's power was felt in every corner of the land.

The Wars of the Roses reduced the English nobility—fully forty per cent of the noble houses in England became extinct for lack of a surviving male heir—and Henry reclaimed the vacant estates to the crown. Henry Tudor became England's most powerful landholder since the reign of William the Conqueror. Taxes from his estates made Henry Tudor the richest king in Christendom.

His Queen Consort Elizabeth of York was the eldest daughter of Edward IV and Elizabeth Woodville. Henry Tudor and Elizabeth of York were parents of four surviving children who later figured importantly in the English history: Arthur Prince of Wales, Margaret Tudor Queen of Scots, King Henry VIII, Mary Tudor Queen of France and Duchess of Suffolk.

Henry Tudor's reign of 24 years ended with his death at Richmond Palace on April 21, 1509. Henry Tudor's Queen Elizabeth of York died after her last pregnancy on her birthday February 2, 1583. Henry and

Elizabeth were buried in the magnificent Lady Chapel he commissioned for Westminster Abbey.

Following the death of Henry VII, his only surviving son Henry Duke of York succeeded to the throne in 1509 as King Henry VIII.

Narrative of Queen Consort Elizabeth of York

Queen Elizabeth of York: life dates 37 years, b. February 11, 1466-d. February 11, 1503; Queen Consort of King Henry VII 17 years, January 18, 1486-February 11, 1503.

ELIZABETH OF York was eldest of ten children born to Edward IV and his Queen Consort Elizabeth Woodville. After death of her father and her two younger brothers (the 'Princes in the Tower,'—Edward V and Richard of York), she was next in line by primogeniture to inherit the crown. However, her right to rule was negated when Parliament passed an act, *Titulus Regius*, that declared the offspring of Edward IV and Elizabeth Woodville to be illegitimate, and therefore ineligible to reign. Elizabeth of York's illegitimacy was restored by Parliament soon after Henry VII came to the throne before they were married in 1486.

> The hardships experienced by the children of Edward IV were addressed in the chapters on Reign 17 and Reign 18, which dealt respectively with lives of King Edward V and King Richard III and his wife Queen Anne Neville of Warwick. The same events are revisited, with different emphasis, in the following narrative.

Elizabeth of York was born in Westminster Palace on February 11, 1466. Her birth came ten months after her parents Edward IV and Elizabeth Woodville were secretly married on May 1, 1485. Her father was a hugely popular king, but her mother was despised by most of their subjects because Elizabeth Woodville lacked a noble title of her own. She was widely perceived to be a crass ambitious power-grabbing social climber.

Elizabeth of York was the eldest of eight surviving royal siblings. King Edward IV and Queen Elizabeth Woodville treated all their children with indulgent affection.

Elizabeth of York enjoyed a life of privilege from age five to seventeen (1471-1483) as the Princess Royal in the popular court of her father Edward IV. In 1475 when Elizabeth was nine, marriage negotiations were begun for her to become Queen of France through marriage to the Dauphin Charles, later Charles VIII. In expectation that Elizabeth would someday be queen in the most splendid and class-conscious court in Europe, her father took steps to see that she would be suitably prepared for her role at the apex of society. Language tutors were recruited from France, Italy, and Spain. Oxford scholars in Classics were employed to assure that Elizabeth's education would equal the best in reading, writing, and court discourse. Scrivener experts in calligraphy were brought in from the Scriptorium at Westminster Abbey to instruct Elizabeth in formal court writing (here, it is of interest to note that her father, King Edward IV, also first learned to write when his daughter was instructed in the fine art of penmanship). Elizabeth's education was unusual for all women in the 15th century, and much superior to that of most men who were not specifically schooled for the Church.

The England-France marriage contract was approved in 1480. Thereafter, Elizabeth was formally addressed in the London court as *Madam la Dauphine*. However, the marriage never occurred. King Louis XI of France canceled Elizabeth of York's marriage contract with the Dauphin after King Edward IV died in April 1483. His death threw England into a dynastic crisis over the succession in England on who next would become the King of England (see Reign 17 and Reign 18 for summaries on lives of King Edward V and King Richard III).

Elizabeth of York, therefore, did not become the Queen of France, but, as is often remarked by pragmatic observers of 'the passing parade', "that was a good thing," and much to her good fortune. The Dauphin Charles VIII was a silly feeble-minded twit who was so incapable of ruling that his father's will dictated that his older sister Princess Anne be created regent to govern France in his place. In certifying Anne's qualifications to rule, King Louis XI said, "My daughter Anne la Grande Duchesse Bourbon is the least insane woman in France."

The tranquil secure life of ease that Elizabeth enjoyed during childhood and early teenage years ended abruptly following the death of her father

King Edward IV on April 9, 1483. Her younger brother, twelve year old Edward of Westminster, was immediately accepted to be King Edward V. However, (as described in Chapter 17) he reigned for less than three months before his uncle Richard Duke of Gloucester usurped his crown, and became King Richard III.

Only a little over three months after the coronation of Richard III on July 6, the first serious, but abortive, opposition to him came in October 1483. A small Lancaster invasion force organized by Henry Tudor Earl of Richmond and his uncle Jasper Tudor Earl of Pembroke set sail from Brittany in France for Wales. They hoped to join Welsh supporters, and overthrow the regime of Richard III, but an early winter storm prevented the invasion fleet from reaching Wales. Richard III learned of the rebellion, and easily defeated the Welsh insurgents. Although the October 1483 invasion attempt from Brittany failed, it raised Henry Tudor to first rank among those determined to remove King Richard III from his throne. Henry Tudor's successful second attempt was delayed until August 1485.

In late November 1483, Elizabeth of York's mother, Dowager Queen Elizabeth Woodville, who was still in sanctuary in Westminster Abbey, had a clandestine meeting with Henry Tudor's mother Lady Margaret Beaufort. Secretly the noble ladies plotted together for destruction of Richard III. Their plan was simple. They saw that, if the Dowager Queen's daughter Elizabeth of York married Lady Margaret's son Henry Tudor, then all York and Lancaster opposition to Richard III could be united, and all Englishmen who deplored the murder of the Princes in the Tower would desert King Richard, and would help to bring Henry Tudor to the throne.

As a fourteen year old youth, Henry Tudor had fought for Lancaster in the Battle of Barnet in 1471, after which he was forced to flee to Brittany where he lived in exile with his uncle Jasper Tudor. On December 16, 1483, Henry Tudor, now twenty-six years old, openly declared at Rennes, Brittany his intent to invade England, and depose Richard III. At the same time, Henry Tudor said he was in contract to wed Elizabeth of York. Dowager Queen Elizabeth Woodville, who was still in sanctuary in Westminster Abbey with her surviving daughters, gave the union her approval and blessing. She added that, if Elizabeth, for some reason could not wed Henry Tudor, her second daughter, Cecily, would take her place.

Richard III recognized this turn of events as a challenge and call for rebellion against his rule. Henry Tudor's declaration of intent to marry Elizabeth of York elevated her as a threat to his crown.

Elizabeth of York, with her mother Queen Elizabeth Woodville and sisters, stayed in the safety of sanctuary at Westminster Abbey until March 1484. It is unknown what assurances King Richard III gave for their safe return to open court after almost a year in the Abbey. However, soon after the queen and princesses left sanctuary in April, Richard III took steps to prevent Elizabeth of York's marriage to Henry Tudor. King Richard ordered Elizabeth to marry a common knight Sir William Stillington who was the son of Bishop Robert Stillington of Bath and Wells (who notoriously provided evidence for the precontract for marriage of Edward IV to Eleanor Butler that led Parliament to declare all children of Edward IV and Elizabeth Woodville to be bastards; see Reign 18). However, before the marriage of Elizabeth of York to William Stillington took place, Stillington was imprisoned in Normandy, and he perished from "hunger and poverty" some time in 1484-1485.

On March 16, 1485, frail Queen Anne Neville died after a prolonged respiratory complaint that usually was said to be tuberculosis. After his queen died, rumors surfaced that Richard III considered marrying his niece Elizabeth of York. That possibility was so incestuously unacceptable to public will that (if ever contemplated) Richard soon abandoned it.

However, only shortly after Queen Anne Neville's death in March 1485, King Richard imprisoned Elizabeth of York in remote Sheriff Hutton Castle in Yorkshire. Her prison was a secure remote dismal fortress with few amenities for gracious living that King Richard inherited from his wife's Neville-Warwick estates.

During her imprisonment, Elizabeth of York became involved in a clandestine exchange of letters sent to Henry Tudor. They gave assurance of her continued loyalty to their cause, and of her desire that they marry following his eventual successful invasion of England. Henry Tudor had never met his prospective bride Elizabeth of York. Her letters to him were answered in formal expressions of affection and appreciation.

Intermediaries in transmission of the letters between Elizabeth and Henry included the brothers, Lords William Stanley and Thomas Stanley. The brothers were loyal York supporters of Elizabeth's father Edward IV. It is known that Lord Thomas Stanley was not literate, and that on several occasions, he used Elizabeth as his secretary in preparing letters to supporters of Henry Tudor as a way of alerting them if events were moving rapidly to a time when troops would be needed to oppose King Richard in battle.

Scarcely over two years after the reign of Richard III began on July 6, 1483, Henry Tudor's second attempt to invade England, and depose King Richard came in late August 1485. His second invasion attempt was successful. Henry landed with his small Lancaster army at Milford Haven near Pembroke in Wales. He moved toward London, gathering Welsh recruits as he went. Almost immediately, King Richard learned of his presence, and then called for support throughout the land. However, to Richard's dismay, only nine lords brought men to assist their king. Even so, Richard's army was twice as large as Henry Tudor's rabble.

The men supporting Richard, although greater in number, were poor in leadership and morale. The two opponents met near Leicester at Bosworth Field on August 22, 1485. In the battle, King Richard fought bravely. He charged directly at Henry Tudor, and came close enough to kill him with his own sword. However, Henry Tudor's personal standard-bearer stepped in, and took the lethal blow. At the last minute, Lord Thomas Stanley defected from Richard, and withdrew his 7,000 men from the battle. That changed the balance of power to Henry Tudor's favor. King Richard's horse was killed under him, and on foot, he was soon cut down with many mortal wounds. Some came from Henry's own sword. In only a few hours into battle, King Richard III was dead, and Henry Tudor was acclaimed King of England on the battlefield at Bosworth Field.

Although nearly all Plantagenet kings at times led their men into heated conflicts, only Richard III died on the battlefield. Tradition says that Richard was wearing a thin circlet of gold as his crown when he went to Bosworth Field, and that it rolled under a hawthorn blush as he lay dying. Lord Thomas Stanley retrieved the circlet, and placed it on Henry Tudor's head, saying, "Henry Tudor is now true King of England."

As has been emphasized previously in the chapter on the Reign 18. Richard III, Lord Stanley was Henry Tudor's father-in-law, Lady Margaret Beaufort's fourth husband. It is usually inferred that she persuaded Lord Stanley to refrain from supporting Richard in the last moments of the crucial Bosworth battle. However, as has been shown, Elizabeth of York also influenced Lord Stanley, which contributed to her future husband's success that day.

Elizabeth of York was in Sheriff Hutton Castle while she waited out the last months of Richard's reign. While there, she heard of Richard's defeat at Bosworth Field on August 22, 1485. Legend reports "Elizabeth was immediately released from confinement, and was escorted to Leicester where she saw Richard's bloody body when carried through the streets to burial at Greyfriars Abbey." Tradition also maintained that she said (in reference to her brothers the Princes in the Tower), "Uncle, how like you now the slaughtering of my dear brethren?" The legend continued saying "Elizabeth then proceeded on to London, and joined her mother and sisters in residence at Westminster Palace."

This traditional account of events cannot be true. The city of York is about a hundred miles from Leicester. Without modern means of rapid transportation, Elizabeth could not possibly have been both in York to hear of Richard's defeat on Bosworth field, and to have arrived in Leicester on the afternoon of the battle to see Richard's bloody naked corpse, slung over the back of a nag, on its way to burial at Greyfriars Chapel.

The victory for Henry Tudor at Bosworth Field was a major turning point in his life. Since early adolescence, much of Henry Tudor's life had been that of prisoner, or fugitive who narrowly survived endless plots by York to capture and execute him. The single person he trusted absolutely was his uncle Jasper Tudor Earl of Pembroke, who adopted him as an infant following his posthumous birth in Pembroke Castle. Jasper Tudor had protected, educated, and looked out for Henry's wellbeing during most of his life. They shared years of adversity before victory came in 1485. One of the first things Henry did, as king was to create his uncle Duke of Bedford. Jasper Tudor held the highest place among the inner circle of advisors of King Henry for ten years until Jasper's death in 1495; Jasper never asked to be legitimized.

Henry Tudor knew that just to be declared, "Henry Tudor is now true King of England," on the battlefield by his father-in-law Lord Stanley, fell far short of meeting all requirements of being the true king. Parliamentary approval was also required before his aspiration could become fact.

Henry hastened to London. About a week later, he presented his demands to Parliament that included specific requests:

He demanded approval to wear the crown by right of conquest for defeat of Richard III.

He demanded that all children he would have with his intended bride Elizabeth of York would have precedence over all others for inheritance of the crown of England.

He demanded that the act of *Titulus Regius,* which Parliament passed in 1483 that made all children of Edward IV bastards, be deleted and expunged from Parliamentary record.

Approval of these demands made the reign of Richard III false. They restored legitimacy to all children of Edward IV. They legitimized the marriage of King Edward IV and Queen Elizabeth Woodville, and would legitimize Henry's prospective bride Elizabeth of York.

Parliament approved all his demands. Later, Parliament unanimously added to the petition, "[King Henry VII] would pray take the Princess Elizabeth to wife." To which Henry replied, "I am most willing to do so."

After this assurance of Henry's intent to marry her, Elizabeth received all recognition and courtesies appropriate for a Queen Consort. Many assumed that one of Henry's first acts following his victory over Richard III would be marriage to Elizabeth of York. However, this did not take place for several months. King Henry was determined to be king in his own right—he would not take the crown as a petticoat-monarch—his rule would not depend on a wife with better hereditary qualifications to reign than his own.

Henry recognized his indebtedness to Elizabeth for the added strength it lent his coming into power. Nevertheless, Henry never intended to share the power once the crown was firmly on his own head. Elizabeth would be his Queen Consort, not his co-regnant queen. Therefore, to stabilize his claim on the crown as a single monarch, Henry delayed his marriage to Elizabeth until after his own coronation was confirmed at Westminster Abbey on October 30, 1485.

Three months later, when Henry's position on the throne was secure, their marriage took place at Westminster Abbey on January 18, 1486. Thomas Bourchier Archbishop of Canterbury presided. The official chronicle of the wedding gives the first known use of the floral symbolism for the, so-called, *Wars of the Roses,* in stating, "[The Archbishop] by whose hand was tied together the *sweet posy of the red and white roses* in their union [Italics mine]."

Elizabeth of York's coronation took placed on November 25, 1487, fully two years after Henry's coronation, and a year after their first child Prince Arthur was born. King Henry insisted that the child must be born in Winchester. That city was then believed to be the 'Camelot' of King Arthur's legendary court. Henry Tudor claimed descent from King Arthur, and believed his son would fulfill the prophesy made when Arthur's funeral barge was pushed out on the dark waters of the Irish Sea, and magician Merlin said, "Arthur, our once and future king, will return to rule again, and bring peace and profit to all the land."

The marriage of Henry Tudor and Elizabeth of York is always cited as the event that brought together the two major contenders from the Houses of Lancaster and York to the throne of England, and that their marriage, thereby, ended the thirty-plus years of the Wars of the Roses.

However, members of the House of York were less than exuberant about having Elizabeth of York—a hybrid York-Woodville—represent the House of York on the throne. They had participated in the fall of Richard III in expectation that Elizabeth of York would be co-regent, or might even be Queen Regnant, and that bastard-ridden Henry Tudor would be her menial King Consort. They were outraged by his insult to her in delaying their marriage for months, and that when it did finally occur early in 1486, the coronation was done in such a bare-bone pinch-penny way as to add insult to injury.

The simple fact was—in 1486, the royal treasury was bare—Henry had not yet acquired enough personal wealth to put on a royal show of suitable ostentation for a royal marriage of himself as king or of Elizabeth as queen.

The economy boomed as Henry brought peace and rule of law back to the land after three decades of civil strife. However, no one in the House of York was pleased by anything Henry VII did. They were incensed at the two-year delay of Elizabeth's coronation, and that King Henry did not put in a personal appearance when her coronation finally did take place. The chronicle of Elizabeth of York's coronation shows, however, that King Henry, instead of showing disrespect to his wife's coronation, had ordered that she be honored as the sole recipient of honor at the event. He was present, but sat with his mother Lady Margaret Beaufort behind a screen that shielded them from public view during Elizabeth's investiture. In her coronation, Elizabeth's younger sister Cecily of York carried Elizabeth's train, and was said to be "far more beautiful of countenance than her sister the queen."

York nobility was vexed that Henry did not share any royal authority with Elizabeth. They were displeased most of all when they suddenly realized that the House of Lancaster had shrewdly tricked them out of England's Crown—a crown that York had worn for a quarter century. True, Henry Tudor was descended from royal Blood. However, his royal blood was sullied by bastardy on both sides of his family. Henry's father Edmund Tudor was born a bastard of Owen Tudor and Queen Katherine of Valois. His mother Lady Margaret Beaufort was a granddaughter of John Beaufort the eldest bastard son of John of Gaunt and Katherine Swynford. Thus, even though both of his bastard ancestors were later legitimized by Parliament; still, they were bastard born.

It is not surprising, therefore, that almost immediately after Henry VII came to power, several York challenges to his rule surfaced. Four of them involved persons named Lambert Simnel, John de la Pole, Perkin Warbeck, and Edward of Warwick. Henry apprehended all four, and all, except Lambert Simnel, were eliminated by execution or death in battle. All except Edward of Warwick were promoted with financial support from Duchess Margaret of Burgundy, a sister of York kings Edward IV and Richard III. After 1500, no serious York attempts were made to reclaim the crown.

After her marriage on January 18, 1486, Queen Elizabeth of York was an exemplary dutiful wife for Henry VII. Elizabeth is described, as being much like her father Edward IV—tall, blond, and blue-eyed with innate dignity, regal presence, and easy grace in formal greeting—but her countenance was more mannish than radiantly feminine. She did not have the great beauty of her mother Queen Elizabeth Woodville, or of her sister Cecily of York.

The royal marriage immeasurably strengthened Henry's right to rule. Their marriage of State was for political expediency, but it grew into a union of respect, affection, and fidelity. Insofar as Henry's dour pragmatic nature permitted, their union was a loving happy one. Henry's queen was eight years younger than he. She had charm and piety, but none of her mother's domineering qualities. Queen Elizabeth of York was a good wife for Henry, an affectionate mother for their children, and she never participated in the political struggle for authority and power that dominated her husband's twenty-four year reign. In their seventeen years as king and queen together, Elizabeth left few marks on her times, aside from serving with strict propriety as head of court society.

As all queens are criticized, she was chided for always running out of money and for pleading for increases in her allowance. However, her need for more money was not based on feeding a royal vanity. It arose because she was generous to fault in rewarding those who served her, and for her donations to goodly causes. She also incurred major expenses in providing dowries for her sisters Cecily, Anne, and Katherine; they all lacked remunerative estates, since Henry VII awarded them no pensions as members of the royal family.

Queen Elizabeth of York's palace accounts show that, after gifts and charities, she had little remaining for her own use. One account reads that "Her gowns were mended, turned, and . . . newly hemmed . . . for which her tailor was paid 2 pence. She wore shoes which only cost 12 pence, with copper or tin buckles . . . her affectionate subjects brought her trifling offerings of early peas, cherries, chickens, bunches of roses, and posies or other flowers, [which] were very high in proportion to what she paid for her own shoes."

Palace records show that Elizabeth enjoyed playing games of chance, dicing, music, dancing, active sports of archery, hunting, horseback riding, and she kept a kennel for greyhounds. She also kept her own account books of palace expenses written in a firm sure hand.

She may have acquired her bookkeeping practice from King Henry her husband. Henry was known to check and sign approval of national accounts on a routine daily basis. In this practice, Henry adopted the new Florentine system of 'double entry accounting,' which only recently had been invented by Cosimo di Medici in Florence. The device for balancing books by simultaneously recording 'income earned', and 'expenditures paid out,' informed Henry daily on the precise economic status of the crown. Henry was an excellent arithmetician, and personally enjoyed checking his accounts; his initials of approval are present on most Exchequer records dating from his reign. Henry VII is said to be the best businessman and economist ever to have worn the crown of England.

Elizabeth of York's mother, Dowager Queen Elizabeth Woodville, was absent from court during much of her daughter's reign. It is not known whether her absence from court was voluntary, or on orders from king Henry VII. The queen's mother-in-law Lady Margaret Beaufort was Queen Elizabeth's most valued confidant and friend in court. Elizabeth became pregnant almost immediately after her marriage in January 1486. Venerable Lady Margaret Beaufort accompanied the queen for her 'lying in' to Winchester, and stayed with her until the first royal Tudor child, Arthur Prince of Wales, was born on September 20, 1486. He was christened with fanfare and great ceremony at Winchester Cathedral. The queen's mother Dowager Queen Elizabeth Woodville was present as godmother of the prince, and she carried the princeling down the Abbey's majestic aisle to the high altar baptismal font for sprinkling with Holy Water. Their second child was a girl born late in 1489 named Margaret in respect for the king's mother Lady Margaret Beaufort who was the infant girl's godmother. Queen Elizabeth of York bore ten children, of whom four survived to maturity:

> Arthur Prince of Wales (September 20, 1486-April 2, 1502), married Katherine of Aragon, but died young and did not reign
>
> Margaret Tudor (November 28, 1489-October 18, 1541), became Queen Consort of James IV of Scotland, grandmother of Mary Queen of Scots, and great-grandmother mother of King James I of England
>
> Henry Duke of York (June 28, 1491-January 28, 1547), became King Henry VIII, married six wives, and was the father of King Edward VI, Queen Mary I, and Queen Elizabeth I
>
> Mary Tudor (March 18, 1446-June 25, 1533), briefly Queen of France, later Duchess of Suffolk, and grandmother of Queen 'Lady' Jane Grey.

The four surviving children of Henry Tudor and Elizabeth of York were reared at Henry's newly constructed Richmond Palace on the Thames in southwest London. The royal estate had been left fallow since Richard II ordered the former Royal Palace of Sheen destroyed following death of his beloved Queen Anne of Bohemia. The elaborate new royal residence was first occupied in 1501, and named for Henry Tudor's personal title Earl of Richmond. Richmond Palace remained in continual expansion, and renovation as the favorite Tudor family residence through the reigns of all Tudors, including their granddaughter, the incomparable Elizabeth I Regina who died in Richmond Palace.

Henry Tudor is usually criticized for being a stingy money grubbing miser. It is more just to say that, having experienced many youthful years in deprivation, he knew the value of money, and wanted to realize its worth. When he paid for something he wanted its value to be worth every penny paid out. He spent lavishly when he thought an effort was worthwhile; an example is seen in the lavish outlay for the wedding of his son Arthur Prince of Wales to Princess Katherine of Aragon in November 1501. Also, he spared no expense in the construction of his magnificent 'Lady Chapel,' built as an eastern addition to Westminster Abbey in 1503. The chapel was done without financial restraint in the finest Gothic style as dictated by Late Italian Renaissance standards. The Lady Chapel (now called the 'The Henry VII Chapel') was Henry's insurance plan for entry into Heaven.

Henry may not have been familiar with the ideas of his contemporary Niccolò Machiavelli in *The Prince* and *The Arts of War*, but Henry was certainly in sympathy with Machiavelli's ethical aphorisms—"If it benefits the state, it is good; if it weakens or causes harm, it is bad." Also, "It is better for a prince to be feared than loved." King Henry VII had no qualms about using cunning and deceit to gain his ends in government. However, concern for his personal fate for eternity was another matter altogether. The Lady Chapel was his gift to the Virgin Mary. The Chapel was also conceived to be the Tudor Mausoleum.

The great tragedy near the end of Elizabeth of York's life came in the unexpected death of Arthur Prince of Wales on April 2, 1502. It occurred at Ludlow Castle, Wales only a little over four months after the prince's marriage to Katherine of Aragon. King Henry VII and Queen Elizabeth were in residence at Greenwich Palace, London when they learned of the prince's death. Henry and Elizabeth were considerate and attentive to each other in their shared sorrow in loss of their favorite child. Their grief was profound. Queen Elizabeth attempted to comfort Henry with words, "Remember that your mother had . . . no more children, but only you, yet God by his grace has ever preserved you, and brought you where you are now . . . God has left you yet a fair prince and two fair princesses, and we are both young enough [to have more]."

Elizabeth agreed to have another pregnancy in hope that it would yield another male heir. She gave birth on February 2, 1503 to a daughter named Elizabeth, in honor of her mother, Dowager Queen Elizabeth Woodville; the child died on its day of birth. A little over a week after the birth and death of her eighth child, Elizabeth of York died of puerperal fever on her thirty-seventh birthday, February 11, 1503.

King Henry grieved profoundly for his queen. For days, he neither saw nor spoke to anyone. All London went into mourning as the bells of St. Paul's tolled dolefully until Queen Elizabeth of York was finally laid to rest twelve days later. She was the first to be buried in Henry Tudor's Westminster Abbey Lady Chapel.

Henry VII gave his queen a magnificent funeral and splendid burial. The tomb King Henry VII and Queen Elizabeth of York share was ordered before Henry died. The Italian sculptor Pietro Torrigiano of Florence created the tomb with its realistic effigies of King Henry and Queen Elizabeth. The tomb is credited with being the first fully Renaissance work of art in England. Henry and Elizabeth's granddaughters, Queen Mary I and Queen Elizabeth I, and great-granddaughter, Mary Queen of Scots are buried nearby.

Despite the great differences in the natures of Elizabeth of York and Henry VII, evidence from their lives together suggests that their marriage was grounded on deep genuine affection, and a mutual desire to support one another in times of need. Elizabeth was a loyal wife and loving mother. She was a genuinely good admirable person with proven courage, intelligence, and great sympathy for those in need of her help.

By way of contrast, Henry was a genuinely unlovable shrewdly practical, pinch-penny miser, with great intelligence, and an inexorable drive to win his own goals without much concern for what others thought or wanted. As far as one knows, King Henry was entirely faithful to his queen during their marriage, and he was faithful to her memory until his death in 1509.

As a widower, King Henry VII became ever more morose, distrustful, pessimistic, avaricious, guilt-ridden, and irascible. Henry's last years gave little evidence that any of his efforts yielded personal pleasure or satisfactions. All around him trembled at his rage. They longed for former days, when his gentle queen soothed their king's animosity against all mankind.

Elizabeth of York is little remembered for any personal achievements as Queen Consort of Henry VII. Game-show impresarios often point out that she is the only English Queen who was also a daughter, sister, niece, wife, and mother of a reigning King of England. However, she is most remembered for being the mother of Henry VIII, grandmother of Queen Elizabeth I, great-grandmother of Mary Queen of Scots, and great-great-grandmother of King James I.

Gaming room tradition maintains, also, that the likeness of Queen Elizabeth of York's graces all decks of playing cards as the *Queen of Hearts.*

Henry VII died on April 21, 1509, rich as Croesus, feared, and unloved by all, including his imperious profligate son, Henry Duke of York who followed his father on the throne as King Henry VIII.

REIGN 20

KING HENRY VIII

AND

HIS SIX QUEENS CONSORT

KATHERINE OF ARAGON, ANNE BOLEYN, JANE SEYMOUR, ANNE OF CLEVES, KATHERINE HOWARD, AND KATHERINE PARR

Summary of the Reign of King Henry VIII (Reign, 1509-1547)

King Henry VIII: life dates 58 years, b. June 28, 1491-d. January 28, 1547; King of England 38 years, April 21, 1509-January 28, 1547; reign as King of Ireland 5 years, c. 1542-January 28, 1547.

King Henry VIII was the only surviving son of King Henry VII and Queen Elizabeth of York. He was born in 1491 at Greenwich Palace, Kent. During most of his life before coming to the throne, he carried the title Duke of York. Following death of his older brother Arthur Prince of Wales, Henry was heir apparent with the title Prince of Wales. Henry succeeded his father King Henry VII to the throne in 1509, and his reign lasted 38 years until his death at Whitehall Palace, London on January 28, 1547. He was buried with his favorite wife Jane Seymour in St. George's Chapel, Windsor.

As a young man, Henry VIII was known as the *Golden Prince*, and in his advancing years as *Great Harry*. Everything about him was an exaggeration of extremes. By all accounts, he was a king's king—the most formidable ruler of his age in Europe—he was intellectually gifted, a religious scholar, a talented musician, but he had a towering thoroughly selfish ego that brooked no opposition or difference of opinion.

The major impact of King Henry VIII on English government rested on his confrontation with the Pope in Rome that led to creation of an independent Anglican Church of England. This step was taken solely for annulling marriage to his first wife Queen Katherine of Aragon who failed to give him a desired son. Removal of Katherine was a necessary prelude to marriage with his second wife Anne Boleyn, who he hoped would provide a son for him. Henry created himself the head of both Church and State when the Reformation was just beginning in Continental Europe. This set the stage for great conflicts of interest that surfaced during the next two centuries, and created almost insurmountable religious problems for future Tudor and Stuart monarchs of the realm.

The reign of Henry VIII is notable for being the first period in English history that can be identified clearly as both Renaissance and Reformation. The Reformation in England, however, began as a way of solving the king's marital problems, not as a means for making doctrinal change in religious traditions of the Roman Church. The Anglican Church of England began with few doctrinal changes or innovations aside the substitution of the Pope in Rome with the King of England as its supreme head.

The cultural and legal consequences of creating the Anglican Church of England were huge. Placement of all secular and religious power in the realm in hands of the monarch, gave Henry, as king and quasi-pope, a degree of absolute power never before vested in an English monarch. He used his power autocratically to satisfy his own selfish desires, and Henry

VIII deserves no ethical or moral credit for founding the philosophical base of the Anglican Church, as we know it today.

Instead, Henry VIII deserves much condemnation for destruction of the abbey and monastery ecclesiastical foundation of the Catholic Church in England. That act of vandalism was motivated by naked greed—to stuff his own purse with Church riches—in so doing, he destroyed much of England's historical record of the Middle Ages.

Without question, popular claim to fame in history of King Henry VIII rests on his six marriages. The salient points on each of his six Queens Consort are summarized in the following six narratives of this chapter:

> Reign 20-1. Narrative on Queen Katherine of Aragon
> Reign 20-2. Narrative on Queen Anne Boleyn
> Reign 20-3. Narrative on Queen Jane Seymour
> Reign 20-4. Narrative on Queen Anne of Cleves, no issue
> Reign 20-5. Narrative on Queen Katherine Howard, no issue
> Reign 20-6. Narrative on Queen Katherine Parr, no issue

The children of Henry VIII and his three wives Queen Katherine of Aragon, Queen Anne Boleyn and Queen Jane Seymour, who figure in the English Tudor monarchy, are:

> Edward of Cornwall, son of Henry VIII and Jane Seymour; following death of his father, he succeeded to the throne in 1547 as King Edward VI.
> Mary Tudor, daughter of Henry VIII and Katherine of Aragon (after the brief 9-day reign of Lady Jane Grey), Lady Mary succeeded to the throne in 1553 as Queen Mary I.
> Elizabeth Tudor, daughter of Henry VIII and Anne Boleyn, after her half-sister, Mary I died, Lady Elizabeth succeeded to the throne in 1558 as Queen Elizabeth I.

Following the death of his father Henry VIII, his ten year old son Edward of Cornwall ascended the throne in 1547 as King Edward VI.

Reign 20-1.
Narrative of Queen Consort
Katherine of Aragon

See the introduction to Chapter 20 for a summary of the
reign of Henry VIII

Queen Katherine of Aragon: life dates 51 years, b. December
16, 1485-d. January 7, 1536: first Queen Consort of King
Henry VIII until divorce 24 years, June 11, 1509-May 23,
1533.

QUEEN KATHERINE of Aragon's full Spanish name was, *Infanta
Catalina de Aragón y Castilla*, but in English history, her name usually is
abbreviated to Katherine of Aragon. She was the youngest of five children
of Ferdinand II of Aragon and Isabella I of Castile. Both parents were
sovereign monarchs in their Spanish provinces of Aragon and Castile.

The marriage of Ferdinand and Isabella created the unified nation of
Spain. Ferdinand II is celebrated in the history of Spain for his defeat of the
Moors in the Kingdom of Granada in 1492. Katherine's mother Isabella is
most remembered in American history for her financial support of Italian
navigator, Cristóbal, Colón (Christopher Columbus), in his adventure
that led to discovery of the New World. Princess Katherine was also a
great-great-granddaughter of John of Gaunt by his second wife Constance
of Castile. This hereditary link between the English House of Tudor and
the Castile House of Trastámera were equally close to the English throne
in the marriage of Arthur Tudor and Katherine of Aragon.

Katherine was born in 1485 at Palais Loredo, Alcalá de Henares, an
ancient university and religious citadel north of Madrid. Katherine was
small, with red-gold hair, and blue eyes. Those characters are attributed
to her Plantagenet ancestry from John of Gaunt. She received a strong
religious grounding that was a determining aspect of her nature throughout
life. She was proficient in Spanish and French languages, and read Latin
and Greek. She was well educated in Spanish literature, secular history
of Western Europe, as well as on the Latin foundations of Church belief

and Canon law. She was excellently educated for a woman of her time, and exchanged intellectual ideas with contemporary leading scholars. In addition, Katherine was accomplished in needlework, enjoyed games of chance, and delighted in the music and dancing characteristic of Spain.

Katherine grew up in the richest and most powerful court in Europe. Much of her childhood was spent in southern Spain in the Province of Granada, where her mother Queen Isabella set up her own court in the magnificent Alhambra Palace, which for centuries had been the royal residence of Moorish kings. When Elizabeth was only seven years old, Columbus discovered the New World, and the golden riches of Mexico and Peru gave Spain all the power money could buy.

In 1489 at the age of four, Katherine was contracted to marry Arthur Prince of Wales, the barely three year old heir of Henry VII and Elizabeth of York. Her second rate marriage contract into the shaky English House of Tudor was thought to be a fortunate catch for the youngest of four princesses in the Spanish House of Trastámera. In England, King Henry Tudor VII saw the marriage as evidence for his own acceptance among the great royal houses of Europe. It also gave his son Arthur stronger acceptance for having a wife with her own claim to royal legitimacy in England. She was a Plantagenet third-cousin of Henry VII and third-cousin-once-removed of her future husband Arthur Prince of Wales.

Arthur and Katherine were married by proxy on May 19, 1499. In mid summer 1501 at age sixteen, Katherine set out for England with a retinue that included priests, household servants, a troop of protective guardsmen, a bishop emissary of the pope, and many noble Spanish ladies-in-waiting, none of whom, including the princess herself, spoke English. Inclement weather delayed her arrival at Plymouth until October 2, 1501. Soon after her presence in England became known in London, nobles were sent to greet and accompany the Princess of Spain to court. However, in the absence of suitable translators, a conflict of cultures presented such problems of royal etiquette that her arrival in London was delayed for over a month.

Katherine arrived in London on November 10, 1501. Four days later, fifteen year old Prince Albert and sixteen year old Princess Katherine were married at St. Paul's Cathedral, London. The splendid court occasion, at which the Archbishop of Canterbury officiated, was followed by a week of celebration. Henry VII opened his purse to pay for grand banquets, elaborate jousting events, and theatrical extravaganzas at Westminster

Palace. White doves filled the air; ladies of gentle birth hiked up their skirts to avoid rabbits that scurried freely among the crowd; much merriment was enjoyed all around. In the month that followed, many social occasions presented the new Spanish Princess of Wales to the English public. The Lady from Spain made a fine impression, and was well received by the people of England. However, she never learned to speak English without a strong Spanish accent, and the English country folk always referred to her as 'The Spanish Lady.'

At first, Katherine showed hauteur over the rustic reception she received from England's populace, but later she joined the merriment by dancing in the Spanish style, with clicking of bones (castanets), and coy bowing with veils, while her groom cavorted and leaped in the athletic manner favored for frolic and Volta dances in England. She irritated her husband by refusing to ride horseback or attend rude boisterous events like hunting, which she considered unsuitable for a well-bred lady. Throughout her life, Katherine modeled her dress and deportment after the manner she had learned in her mother's court in Spain.

Most characteristic of her nature was steadfast fidelity to the Catholic faith. Her custom was to hear the Mass several times a day. Spanish and Latin remained her favored means of communication. She read constantly to improve her understanding in many subjects that included history, philosophy, and current events. She enjoyed correspondence and discourse with learned persons of the realm. Among them were the philosopher and civil servant Thomas More, Roger Ascham lecturer at Cambridge University, and the eminent Dutch moralist Erasmus of Rotterdam. The latter said, "Catherine loved good literature, which she had studied with success since childhood."

A few weeks after their marriage, the Prince and Princess of Wales moved from London to Ludlow Palace, Wales where they set up their own court. Their popularity and happiness was short-lived. Less than four months after their marriage, Arthur died on April 2, 1502. He was buried in Worcester Cathedral. His brief fatal illness was of unknown nature (possibly plague, tuberculosis, influenza, or the strange, 'sweating illness' often cited in records of the time).

Katherine suddenly was a widow in a foreign land. Her fate and livelihood were solely dependant on the generosity of her father-in-law King Henry VII.

Katherine's father Ferdinand II of Aragon had provided an exceedingly generous dowry to Henry VII for his daughter. Half of it had already been deposited to Henry's account, but miserly King Henry VII had a wish neither to return what had been paid, nor to lose what was still owed. Henry therefore proposed to Ferdinand II that his daughter Katherine remain in England as the prospective bride for Prince Henry Duke of York (later Henry VIII), who now was the heir of Henry VII. Henry Duke of York was only eleven years old, and the marriage would not take place for six or seven years until Prince Henry became of age.

Although the royal parents (King Henry VII and King Ferdinand II) approved the marriage of Prince Henry and Princess Katherine, Pope Julius II was also petitioned to give it his dispensation, because the marriage conflicted with an important biblical proscription against a man marrying his brother's wife:

> Leviticus 20:21, *If a man marries his brother's wife, it is an act of impurity; he has dishonored his brother; they will be childless.*

> As will be seen, although the pope granted the dispensation request, and the marriage did take place, but this issue did not die. It later became the central factor for terminating the marriage of Henry VIII to Katherine of Aragon.

Fourteen months after Arthur died, Katherine became engaged to Henry Duke of York, and he was raised to Prince of Wales. The long delay made certain that Katherine could not be pregnant, and carrying an heir of her first husband Prince Arthur.

Only Katherine was displeased with her engagement to Prince Henry. She had little wish to be married to an eleven year old child six years her junior, even though the lad was called the Golden Prince for his head of bronze auburn hair. For Katherine, the next six years of waiting for Prince Henry to grow to young manhood were exceedingly trying. She had only the empty title of Dowager Princess of Wales, which lacked any taxable estate. Consequently, she was neglected, in poverty, and without an official regular pension from any source.

Characteristically, paltry Henry VII provided funds, too little and too late, to pay for her personal court and staff of Spaniards. They numbered in dozens and depended on her for their maintenance in the foreign land.

She wrote piteous letters to her father describing her dire destitute state, and asked him for money to meet critical living expenses. She even pleaded for permission to return to Spain, but Ferdinand withheld support, and explained that, since he had already provided a handsome dowry, now her father-in-law must take care for her needs.

On March 9, 1509, Katherine wrote in despair to her father that she could no longer abide King Henry's spiteful disregard of her dire straits. Only a month later on April 21, Henry VII died.

King Henry VII had been in declining health for several years from real and imagined causes. Before leaving life, he advised his son Henry Prince of Wales that it would be to his advantage to marry the Spanish princess, so he could keep her rich dowry. Previously, Prince Henry had shown little enthusiasm for marriage to his sister-in-law, even though he had been engaged to her for almost six years. However, Prince Henry was now eighteen, and he was ready to marry Katherine. Ferdinand II paid the rest of Katherine's dowry, and preparations for Katherine's second marriage proceeded quickly.

Six weeks after Henry VII died, Henry VIII and Katherine of Aragon were married on June 11, 1509. The wedding was followed by extravagant court celebrations that reached climax when, in a common ceremony, Henry and Katherine were crowned king and queen on June 24th in Westminster Abbey, with full nobility and high Church officials in attendance. The festivities ended abruptly on June 29, when the young king's grandmother, The Venerable Lady Margaret Beaufort, died in her sixty-sixth year.

The next decade would be the happiest of Katherine's life. Henry professed to be deeply in love with his bride, and his behavior bore out his protestations of affection for her. Katherine was a dutiful and affectionate wife. She earned respect and admiration of her subjects, and was well accepted in court. The respect and confidence King Henry VIII had for his wife Katherine was shown by his appointment of her as regent while he was occupied with a war with France and Scotland in 1512-1514.

Henry began the conflict with the expectation of gaining glory by reopening England's Hundred Years War claims on France. Katherine encouraged Henry in this venture, because it called for cooperation with Spain to bring France down. Katherine, as regent, administered affairs of State competently in England while Henry was away on his unsuccessful saber rattling in France.

The war ended with no gains for England, but more important, Henry received no praise for military or diplomatic skill. Henry, with wounded pride, blamed Katherine for getting him to enter the war. He accused her of acting like an ambassador of Spain. He believed that Queen Katherine had misled him to enter the war with France, because her loyalty to her father King Ferdinand in Spain was greater than her loyalty to him, her husband.

Henry VIII felt that he had been played-the-fool, by having to pay for the entire French fiasco, while Spain sat by to harvest benefit from the military losses of both France and England. Katherine would never regain her husband's confidence, so she, too, was a loser in England's 1512-1514 war with France and Scotland.

Over nine years, Katherine had six (possibly seven) pregnancies. The first, third, and sixth pregnancies ended in stillbirths; the second and fourth produced male infants that seemed to be healthy at birth, but both died in infancy. Only the fifth conception ended in birth of a surviving child; she was the healthy daughter Princess Marry (later Queen Mary I) who was born on February 18, 1516.

A year later, Martin Luther, who posted his 95 Theses at Wittenberg in 1517, ignited a shattering religious controversy within the Church in Rome. It began the Reformation, and the *Edict of Worms* in 1520 excommunicated Martin Luther. King Henry VIII wrote a scholarly rebuttal to Luther's 'Theses'. Henry's rebuttal was entitled, *In Defense of the Seven Sacraments*, of which Katherine strongly approved. Pope Leo X awarded Henry the honorary title, *Defender of the Faith*, an ironic title in view of what Henry would do in creating Church of England a little over a decade later.

By 1515, the Tudor Dynasty had lasted for only thirty years (1485-1515), and the dynasty was exceedingly insecure for lack of a male heir. Henry VIII was impatient to the point of desperation for lack of a surviving son to carry on the Tudor name. Henry's only legitimate heir was Princess Mary. Saxon law permitted women to inherit royal titles and estates, but Norman-French Salic law gave that privilege only to male descendants. England had never had a ruling queen after the Norman Conquest of 1066. Henry had no assurance that England's Parliament would accept Princess Mary as its ruling Queen of England. Moreover, even if Parliament did accept her, her heirs would carry the name of her spouse—his grandchildren by Mary would not bear his Tudor name.

A male heir became an imperative necessity for King Henry VIII. Soon, Henry was convinced that God would not permit Katherine to be his son's mother, because Leviticus 20:21 foretold her barrenness.

Henry was guilt ridden in belief that his marriage to Katherine, his brother Arthur's wife, had violated basic Canon Law. Even though Pope Julius II had approved their marriage, King Henry, a specialist in Cannon Law himself, now felt that Pope Julius had made a fundamental error in his ruling. Henry was convinced that an angry God was punishing him by death of his two healthy sons: the 1st and 2nd Prince Henry Dukes of Cornwall who had died in infancy.

After the last stillbirth on November 10, 1518, Katherine was thirty-three. She still had several remaining childbearing years, but she had no more pregnancies. Henry was twenty-seven years old, in prime of life, a huge man now called 'Great Harry,' and famous for being the handsomest prince in Christendom. During the coming years, he moved ever more strongly in belief that Katherine must be set aside. Only then could he marry a person who was 'suitable in God's eyes' to bear him the son and heir he desperately needed.

Henry dithered on the matter for several years, before he finally took direct action against Katherine. In 1523, Henry secretly sent an emissary to Pope Clement VII with a request to have his marriage to Katherine annulled, on grounds that Pope Julius II had been ill advised on the matter when the marriage was given approval in 1502. The annulment almost certainly would have been approved by Pope Clement VII, had not Pope Julius II given it special dispensation. Since popes almost never annul rulings of previous popes, Pope Clement denied Henry's first petition for an annulment.

King Henry then ordered Katherine, as his obedient wife, to ask for a papal annulment of their marriage, on grounds that she wished to take vows of celibacy, retire to a nunnery, and thereby vacate her place in the royal bedchamber.

Katherine refused to comply; she said, "God hath never called me to a nunnery. I am the King's true legitimate wife, and I will not be held otherwise."

The matter was complicated further in 1524/25 when King Henry became irrationally enamored of one of Queen Katherine's ladies-in-waiting, Anne Boleyn. The affair between Henry VIII and Anne Boleyn was known as the *King's Great Matter.* It dominated court life for almost seven years. It began when Anne was in her early twenties, when she had many years in which to bear sons; whereas, Queen Katherine was approaching forty, and by reasonable expectation, she was close to passing beyond a time when she could expect to have more children.

By 1527 at age thirty-six, Henry ran out of the little patience he ever had. On June 22, he bluntly told Katherine that their marriage was finished. They must separate because they were living in mortal sin that endangered their very salvation. At the same time, King Henry reopened negotiations with Pope Clement VII for annulment of his royal marriage to Queen Katherine of Aragon by sending Chancellor Cardinal Thomas Wolsey as his petitioner.

Wolsey's arguments to the pope included the fact that Pope Pius II had previously approved the marriage in conflict with the explicit proscription against such marriages in Leviticus 20:21: "If a man shall take his brother's wife . . . they shall be childless." Wolsey also pointed out that, in England, Canon Law was traditionally adjudicated in keeping with established English Common Law. Clement then ordered that Cardinal Wolsey and Cardinal Campeggio of the Papal College act together to decide the issue.

A trial began in London at Blackfriars in May 1529, but the trial was manifestly biased against the queen's interest, and she refused to be judged by anything but a Papal decision. The matter was at impasse.

Cardinal Compeggio refused to act as judge, and he returned to Rome.

Nothing happened for half a year, until the king ordered an ecclesiastical court trial to begin in London in autumn 1529. The king was present. Katherine walked in, and knelt before Henry VIII. She presented her case with moving eloquence. Her self-defense presented the following facts:

Katherine insisted that her brief first marriage to Arthur Tudor was never consummated. She entered marriage with King Henry VIII in a pure virginal state. She would never be anything but his true faithful loyal wife. She had borne Henry VIII sons and daughters. She demanded that her case be referred the Pope and his College of Cardinals in Rome.

She then rose to leave the court. The Chief Justice ordered, "Madam, you are called back."

Katherine turned to him, "I hear you well enough." Then to her ladies in attendance, "On, on, go you on, for this is no Court wherein I can have justice."

The pope reversed his earlier decision, and decided that the issue was of sufficient gravity that authority of the Church in Rome alone would addresses it. From the outset, this decision was prejudicial to Henry's desire. Pope Clement, at the time, was a virtual prisoner of Charles V Emperor of the Holy Roman Empire. The Emperor was a son of Joanna of Castile, Katherine's eldest sister, and therefore, he was a nephew of Queen Katherine. Emperor Charles held the Pope hostage in Rome, and he was determined to thwart every effort by King Henry VIII to disgrace his aunt by declaring her marriage illegal. That would name his aunt Queen Katherine a whore, and would make his cousin Princess Mary a bastard.

In March 1, 1530, Pope Clement VII ordered King Henry to recognize Queen Katherine as his rightful queen, and he forbade Henry to marry anyone else, while Katherine was his wife. With that total papal opposition, Wolsey was powerless to win Henry's goal of annulment.

On July 14, 1531, Henry abandoned his queen with resolute determination to get a divorce. Henry VIII never saw Queen Katherine face-to-face again.

King Henry VIII could not accept criticism, contradiction, or outright opposition gracefully. Henry's rage was terrifying. Henry dismissed Wolsey's for his failure to resolve the matter in a way favorable to his wishes. Wolsey died from natural causes in November 1530.

Around this time, Henry set an unswerving course to separate England from all affiliation with the Catholic Church in Rome, and to create his own Church of England, with himself head, "The authority from the Pope in Rome be damned!"

King Henry's denial of authority from Rome created the final break between the king and queen. Early in 1531, Henry banished Queen Katherine from court to Ampthill Castle near St. Albans. She remained there in isolated semi-poverty, and she did not see her daughter Mary until 1533 when her trial was finally settled.

Creation of the Anglican Church moved more slowly than Henry desired. However, in October 1532, Thomas Cranmer was appointed Archbishop of Canterbury for the proposed new Church of England. He had been a Lecturer in Divinity and Canon Law at Cambridge. He received his the new appointment in the Church of England for having advised King Henry that "If University Canon scholars should decide that marriage with a deceased brother's widow was illegal, and if it were proven that Katherine had been married to Prince Arthur, her later marriage to Henry could be declared void by ordinary [English] ecclesiastical courts."

That was all Henry wanted, or needed, from his new church. Parliamentary approval of the Church of England came in November 1534 with passage of *The Act of Supremacy*.

However, even earlier in 1533, Parliament began the annulment trial for Queen Katherine. She did not face impartial judges. All were predisposed to grant whatever the King Henry demanded. Henry and Anne Boleyn had been secretly married (possibly on January 25, 1533), but that ceremony was clearly bigamous, while Katherine was Henry's legitimate wife. New urgent demands on Parliament from the king ordered Parliament to act speedily. Anne Boleyn the king's favorite was now pregnant. Her fetus, the much hoped for royal male heir, must be borne legitimate. Queen Katherine's trial suddenly moved briskly.

Cranmer opened the trial on May 10, 1533. Queen Katherine was permitted no defense. On May 23, Katherine's marriage to Henry was ruled contrary to the Will of God; therefore, it also was unlawful in courts of England. On May 28, the January marriage of Henry VIII and Anne Boleyn was judged valid. On June 1, Anne Boleyn was crowned Queen of England. On September 7, Anne's child was born.

Sadly, the child was not the hoped-for son. She was just a girl. Henry VIII greeted his new daughter with the disparaging comment, "With luck. The next child will be a son." They named her Elizabeth in honor of her deceased grandmother, Elizabeth of York.

Queen Katherine was informed at Ampthill in 1533 of her demotion in status by Parliament from *Queen* to mere *Dowager Princess of Wales*, the latter title was in reference to her first marriage to Prince Arthur Tudor in 1502.

Her emphatic reply to that ruling was, "Go where I may, I am wife of King Henry, and for him I will pray." She forbade all in her reduced household staff to use her official new title—she would respond only to *Queen*—which she legitimately had been, and always would be so long as the Pope did not rule otherwise.

On March 23, 1534, Pope Clement finally acted affirmatively on Katherine's long delayed request for his decision on the legitimacy of her marriage to King Henry VIII. However, it came too late to have any effect in England—by that time, Parliament had ruled Anne Boleyn to be queen. The implementation of Henry's Anglican Communion moved relentlessly forward, and was complete with passage of the *Act of Supremacy* that created the Anglican Church of England in November 1534.

Katherine was ruled in contempt of King, Parliament, and the Church of England for refusing to be styled Dowager Princess of Wales, and for refusing to honor the king's authority, and the sacraments in the manner of the new Anglican Church.

Her residence was moved from time to time to various locations. In April 1534, she was moved to Kimbolton Castle near Peterborough, where she remained until her death less than two years later. In Katherine's words, Kimbolton Castle was a "dank moldy dismal prison," but, by English standards, the castle was as "a house buried in woods with open uplands to east and west, each knoll of which was crowned by either an abbey tower or village spire—a green bright country full of deer and birds and fen wildfowl."

During her time at Kimbolton, Katherine was permitted only a skeleton staff of three ladies-in-waiting, a few household servants, and a priest of the Catholic Church. She was given exceptional permission to have a daily Mass said for her in the manner of the 'Old Devotion.' Katherine lived out her two last years of life, banished from court, and in semi-poverty. King Henry offered to restore both Katherine and her daughter Princess Mary to honored places, if they would recognize Anne Boleyn as his true queen, and accept the religious authority of the Church of England, but both mother and daughter refused to do either.

Princess Mary was now simply 'The Bastard Lady Mary.' She was incarcerated at Hatfield House with minimum budget for comfort and sustenance. The mother and daughter were not permitted to carry on correspondence. However, secret letters were exchanged through trusted couriers. Katherine counseled Mary to be respectful and dutiful to her father's will, but to stay true to their shared Catholic faith. Katherine was Mary's mentor; they were much alike, and were devoted to each other.

During her last two years, Katherine ordered all in her household to refrain from making disparaging statements about King Henry or Queen Anne. Of her rival she said, "Hold your peace. Curse her not, but rather pray for her, for the time is fast coming when you shall have reason to pity her, and lament her case."

Katherine's health deteriorated rapidly after her move to Kimbolton Castle. In his petty way, Henry denied Katherine's deathbed request that she be permitted to see her daughter Mary, or to give Mary her blessing, or to pass to her by hand a few trinkets before she died.

Katherine made out her will in December 1535. She had very little to give away, but asked Henry to pay the bills she owed her servants, and to give to charities her rich robes he withheld when she was banished from court. Her will ended with her last message to Henry VIII, which said:

> "For my part, I pardon you everything, and I wish devoutly
> to pray God that He will pardon you also. For the rest, I
> commend unto you our daughter Mary, beseeching you to be
> a good father unto her, as I have heretofore desired . . . Lastly,
> I make this vow, that mine eyes desire you above all things."
> Katharine the Queen.

At age fifty-one, Queen Katherine died on January 7, 1536 at Kimbolton Castle. By that time, his second queen, Anne Boleyn, had also fallen from favor, and Henry was actively pursuing his third wife Jane Seymour. Reports differ on Henry's response at hearing of Queen Katherine's passing. One account said that Henry mourned her with prayers and the statement, "I would have to her memory one of the goodliest monuments in Christendom." Another said Henry received word of Queen Katherine's death with exceeding ill grace, "When he heard that Queen Katherine was dead, he dressed as a mimer [a clown], and ordered palace festivities to commence." The Spanish ambassador reported, "Henry went mad with delight; he dressed himself from head to foot in yellow damask, and stuck a white feather in his yellow velvet cap."

In the autopsy after Katherine's death, discoloring noted on her heart raised suspicion that Queen Anne Boleyn had conspired to have Queen Katherine poisoned. It is now believed, however, that Queen Katherine died of natural causes, probably from cardiac cancer. Queen Katherine's daughter Lady Mary was not permitted to attend her mother's funeral, which took place late in January at Peterborough Abbey. The ceremony was suitable for a Dowager Princess of Wales, but not for a queen.

It is irony of history, on the day that Queen Katherine was buried at Peterborough Abbey, Queen Anne Boleyn miscarried a four-month male fetus she was carrying. The miscarriage ended her last hope for regaining King Henry's affection.

Queen Katherine of Aragon was buried at Peterborough Cathedral on January 29, 1536. Her English subjects always held her in high esteem and called her *The Spanish Lady*. Her original grave was below ground and still exists. However, during the Dissolution of Monasteries ordered by Henry VIII, which came close after her death, the original monument that marked her grave was destroyed.

Peterborough Abbey was later designated a Diocese Cathedral for the Church of England, and Henry approved handsome renovation and expansion of the Abbey chapel. The renovated Peterborough Cathedral is a masterpiece of English Gothic architecture. Henry's contrition (over the treatment his first wife received) may have stimulated the special consideration that the Abbey later received.

Reign 20-2.
Narrative of Queen Consort
Anne Boleyn

See the introduction to Chapter 20 for a summary of the
reign of Henry VIII

Queen Anne Boleyn: life dates c. 30/35 years, b. 1501/1507-d.
May 129, 1536; second Queen Consort of King Henry VIII 3
years, May 28, 1533-executed May 19, 1536.

ANNE BOLEYN was born at Blickling Hall, Norfolk, and is now believed to have been the second daughter of Sir Thomas Boleyn (or Bullen) and Lady Elizabeth Howard a daughter of Thomas Howard II Duke of Norfolk. Her date of birth is contested as falling between 1501 and 1507. She was small, had dark hair, and eyes, but she was not a great beauty. She was well educated and skilled in courtly graces of singing, dancing, and playing musical instruments, such as the lute, virginal, recorder, and rebec (a primitive bowed string instrument). She was gifted with a vivacious personality and a quick wit that enabled her to advance beyond others of equal appearance, or beyond those in much higher station in life than she possessed. Many accounts of Anne mention that she had a crimson birthmark on her neck and a rudimentary duplicate little finger on her left hand. The latter was cited as evidence of her being a witch in the trumped-up trial that ended her life by beheading at the Tower of London in 1536.

Her father Thomas Boleyn was a commoner employed in military and diplomatic service by King Henry VII. Thomas Boleyn was fluent in several foreign languages including French and Spanish. These abilities made him fit for trusted foreign appointments on the Continent, for which he was knighted in 1509. He remained in service to Henry VIII when he came to the throne after death of his father.

Sir Thomas Boleyn and his family spent much of their time between 1512 and 1521 in Belgium or France, where his children, George, Mary, and Anne were educated and became idiomatically proficient In French. It is probable that this linguistic ability played a significant part in Mary and Anne receiving appointments as lady-in-waiting in the entourage of Princess Mary Tudor (the younger sister of Henry VIII) when she went to Paris in October 1514 to become the Queen Consort of King Louis XII of France. Mary Tudor was eighteen and her husband Louis XII was fifty-two. He died just three months later on January 1, 1515. His young bride, now the Dowager Queen of France, returned to England, and secretly married her childhood truelove, Charles Brandon Duke of Suffolk, who had been sent to Paris to escort her back to England. Their marriage was without the king's required approval. King Henry VIII forgave them, possibly because his youngest sister Mary Tudor was the only person Great Harry ever held in unselfish true affection.

After teenage Dowager Queen Mary Tudor left Paris, both Mary and Anne Boleyn remained in France to complete their educations as ladies-in-waiting to Queen Claude of King Francis I, where they acquired lively reputations in the outer fringes of court life. Mary was notorious for promiscuity (possibly even into the bed of Francis I), and Anne for her acid wit. Sir Thomas Boleyn brought his two tarnished daughters back to England in 1519. They soon became ladies-in-waiting to Queen Katherine of Aragon the queen consort of King Henry VIII. Mary and Anne disdainfully adapted to the religiously conservative London court prescribed by the Spanish queen, who did not countenance the lively sporting life that the girls had been accustomed to in Paris.

Sir Thomas Boleyn gained special attention from King Henry VIII for service he gave in making arrangements for the *Field of Cloth of Gold* tournament of 1520. That celebrated event was the occasion when the two youthful kings (Henry VIII of England and Francis I of France) tried to outspend each other in a pointless farewell to medieval chivalry. All the two kings accomplished was to bankrupt both nations. Mary and Anne Boleyn accompanied Queen Katherine to Calais for the Cloth of Gold festivities. It is possible that both girls first came to the attention of Henry VIII at that occasion.

In 1521, Sir Thomas Boleyn served as diplomatic envoy of Henry VIII to Emperor Charles V of the Holy Roman Empire. The Boleyn family may have accompanied him to Madrid, but it is more likely they remained in England. Anne left court for three years, while negotiations for marriage to the heir of the Earldom of Ormonde was pursued (but failed), followed by another matrimonial effort, this time with the heir to the Earldom of Northumberland, which also failed.

While Anne was away from court, her older sister Mary Boleyn was involved in a torrid affair with King Henry VIII. As one of its benefits, Mary became pregnant, and her father Sir Thomas Boleyn was raised in rank to Viscount Rochford. Mary gave birth to a son on March 4, 1526, and named him Henry of Richmond (the same name was given to another of King Henry's baseborn sons by his mistress Bessie Blount). By virtue of Mary Boleyn's brief preferred place as concubine of the King, her father Viscount Thomas Boleyn was raised to the rank of Earl of Wiltshire when his royal bastard grandson Henry of Richmond was born. King Henry never acknowledged the infant to be his true son. As early as 1524, Mary Boleyn's place as the favorite royal mistress had faded. Henry already had shifted his interest to Mary's younger sister Anne Boleyn.

In 1524, Anne Boleyn returned to court as lady-in-waiting to Queen Katherine of Aragon. Anne was intelligent, witty, vivacious, and supremely ambitious. Most important, she fascinated and was attractive to the king. When their affair started, King Henry, a self-confident swain, expected to have his way with Anne, as was his custom in past dalliances. However, Anne had learned a critical lesson from her sister Mary's brief liaison with the king—never yield to Great Harry's desires without having a wedding band on your finger—Anne would not submit to the king's entreaties, and she said to him, "I would rather lose my life than my honor." Her opposition to his will only increased Henry's desire to possess her.

By 1525, Anne Boleyn was the sole romantic obsession of King Henry VIII. For the next nine years, Anne Boleyn was the unflagging object of infatuation for Henry VIII, but she was consistently adamant in saying that she would only bed with him as his wife and queen.

By then, Henry was set on siring his next son legitimately. To do that, he knew he must marry Anne Boleyn, but first, he must remove his Queen Katherine of Aragon. Henry's desire to be rid of Queen Katherine and to make Anne his queen was widely gossiped, and was called *The King's Great Matter.*

In 1527, Henry told Queen Katherine that their marriage was over, and that he had set his course for divorce or annulment of their marriage. Cardinal Thomas Wolsey advised against an annulment, but the king, true to character, insisted on charging ahead. Anne Boleyn's great animosity toward Wolsey stemmed from his opposition to the divorce. Wolsey was unable to get the Pope's approval of annulment. Anne's favored position with the king empowered her to bring about Wolsey's downfall. Wolsey was on his way to prison in the Tower of London, and he surely would have been executed for treason, but, for the Grace of God, he died of natural causes before he arrived in London. On his deathbed in 1530, Wolsey said, "Had I served God as diligently as I have done the King, He [God] would not have given me over in my grey hairs."

The dickering with Pope Clement for annulment continued for six years until 1532 when Pope Clement VII finally declared Katherine of Aragon to be the true queen of England. In September of that year, Anne was publicly acknowledged the king's favorite when King Henry created her Marchioness of Pembroke. It is suspected that the title was awarded to Anne in Henry's appreciation that she had finally become his 'secret wife.'

Finally, in January 1533, the king and court knew Anne was with child. King Henry was convinced it would be the son he long desired. Therefore, a legitimate marriage to Anne must be an accomplished fact before the child was born. With that pressing urgency, the King announced that he would separate the English Church from the Catholic Church in Rome.

Chancellor Thomas Cromwell, previously a professor of Canon Law at Cambridge, gave legal advice for the drafting of the *Act of Supremacy*, which in 1534 created the Anglican Church with the king as head of both

Church and State. In creating the Anglican Church, the Act of Supremacy also made allegiance to the Church of Rome treasonous.

With no wasted time, Thomas Cranmer was appointed the first Archbishop of Canterbury for the new Church of England. The Archbishop hoped that England would soon be a part of the new Reformation Movement that was sweeping Continental Europe. Cranmer was aware that the king's favorite Anne Boleyn was of much the same mind. However, her separatist sympathies were based more on spite, than on profound intellectual conviction, because only the pope's authority stood between her and her title as queen.

The royal marriage of King Henry and Anne Boleyn took place on January 25, 1533. King Henry's marriage to Queen Katherine of Aragon was annulled on May 23, 1533. Anne Boleyn was crowned Queen Consort on June 1, 1533. The royal baby daughter named Elizabeth was born on September 7, 1533.

The King had not endured seven years of conflict for just a girl (who became the incomparable Queen Elizabeth I). Anne's next child must be a boy. In the two years following the birth of Princess Elizabeth, Anne had three failed pregnancies; the first two were stillbirths; the last was a miscarriage of the male child Henry desired.

When Anne became queen, she was determined to outdo in ostentation everything her predecessor Queen Katherine of Aragon had done. Anne's palace staff numbered nearly three hundred. Her court was crowded with an excess of maids-in-waiting, priests, coachmen, guards, cooks, laundry staff, and household servants.

Queen Anne's marriage to King Henry almost immediately shattered Anne's relationship with the king. He soon tired of Anne's extravagant demands for clothes, jewels, and means for lavish renovation of many royal residences. Henry even chided Anne for referring to Lady Mary (his daughter by Queen Katherine) as 'That Cursed Bastard.'

Anne was unable to check her acid wit, or her flashes of sarcastic temper. Queen Anne's undoing came, when her caustic nature took on shrew-like managerial qualities common in new wives. Fidelity was not in King Henry's nature. Henry denied anyone the right to criticize his actions, so he was vexed by Anne's tantrums over his infidelities. He also took it to be disloyalty that Anne did not immediately become pregnant and deliver a male heir. Without a son in hand as Henry's heir, Anne was skating on very thin ice.

The two years immediately following separation of the Church of England from Rome were tempestuous for England. Suddenly, all religious certainty of the past was now set adrift. New directives on this-and-that new ways to worship were of almost daily proclamation from Westminster. Understandably, most priests were strongly opposed to the changes King Henry made in creating the Church of England. Priests in the newly established Church remained spiritually loyal to the Pope in Rome. They could not see any virtue in the king's authority over spiritual matters, when it was apparent they were motivated only by passions in his groin. Parliament quickly passed laws that made treasonous any opposition to the king on matters of faith.

Heads rolled off dozens of shoulders, and many devout people immigrated to the Continent, because they would not deny old beliefs, nor could they swear allegiance to their capricious hedonistic venal King Henry VIII, whom they felt lacked a natural gift for dispensing Divine Authority. One of those who lost his head was Henry's Chancellor Thomas More. He could neither declare allegiance to authority of the English Church, nor accept legitimacy of Queen Katherine's divorce, nor accept validity of the king's so-called marriage to Queen Anne Boleyn.

Continental countries were divided in their acceptance of England's Reformation experiment. King Henry's Queen Anne and her daughter Princess Elizabeth were recognized to be legitimate only in the principalities of Venice and Florence, but all other capitals in Europe considered them false pretenders, because the Pope in Rome had previously decreed them to be illegitimate.

Queen Anne's rejection by Catholic Europe merely energized her support for the Reformation that embroiled middle Europe. She supported Martin Luther's rebellion against the Pope at Wittenberg in 1517, and protested Luther's excommunication by the Edict of Worms in 1521. She vigorously supported authority of Henry's Church of England, because the Church of England provided the only basis for the legitimacy of her crown. Anne is credited with encouraging publication of Miles Coverdale's heretical first translation of the Bible into English in 1535. Her motivation for encouraging this Godly work was probably as much to irritate her predecessor, Queen Katherine of Aragon and the entire Catholic World, as for any personal convictions she held on Reformation theology. However, after Anne's execution, leaders of the Reformation in Bohemia, Germany, Switzerland, and France gave the Boleyn girl the status of 'Anne the Martyr.'

Anne apparently never felt secure in her role as queen until Katherine of Aragon died on January 7, 1536. On hearing the news, she said, "Now I am indeed Queen of England." After which she showed vindictive poor taste by joining the celebration of her rival's death.

Anne was an exceedingly unpopular queen in England. The nobility resented her for acquiring exalted status she did not deserve. She offended most acquaintances at one time or another with her unkind sarcastic wit. She offended Parliament by always being an outspoken Francophile that pointed out the superiority of continental innovations and culture. She was feared most for having an unforgiving vindictive nature, and a towering ambition for ever higher social status. She had no trusted friends in court, which would soon be her tragic undoing.

Anne Boleyn's unfortunately had two stillbirths and a final miscarriage in three pregnancies that followed birth of Princess Elizabeth. By late January 1536, Anne suspected that Henry's affections were wandering, when she surprised Henry and his new flame Jane Seymour in a compromising embrace. Anne flew into a hysterical frenzied rage, which was followed by premature miscarriage of an apparently normal four-month male fetus on January 29, 1536. By coincidence, the miscarriage occurred on the very day Queen Katherine of Aragon was buried at Petersburg Abbey.

Anne's last pregnancy and miscarriage was the male child Henry so desperately desired. Anne never again enjoyed Henry's favor. After two-and-a-half years of marriage to Anne, the self-indulgent king had tired of her, and he had set his course to be rid of Anne, and to acquire his third queen, Jane Seymour.

Many opportunists who feared Great Harry, but wanted to stay in his favor joined Anne's many enemies in court. They turned against the unpopular queen when she fell from royal favor. Chief among her enemies was Chancellor Thomas Cromwell, who had served Henry flawlessly in coercing Parliament to approve Henry's marriage to Anne less than three years before. Cromwell now served his tyrannical king by fabricating a false case for treason against Anne with charges from which there was no avenue of escape.

From the beginning, Henry vetoed the idea of divorce—experience with that course of action against his first wife Katherine of Aragon had a track record of being far too slow—a charge of treason simplified shortcuts in law, and its results could be fast and final.

In late April 1536, an acquaintance of Anne, the poet Mark Smeaton, was arrested and tortured into giving false incriminating testimony against Anne of incest with her brother George Boleyn, and of adultery with Sir Henry Norris, and of treasonous plotting by witchcraft against the king's life. The accused were not permitted to present defense. They were found guilty, and were executed at Tyburn by hanging, drawing, and quartering. Several others were accused, but were not judged guilty.

A few days later on May 2, Anne's grandfather Thomas Howard II Duke of Norfolk arrested Anne. He escorted her to the Tower of London, where she was charged with the crimes of incest, adultery, and treason. Two weeks later, Anne and her brother George went on trial. Both pled innocent, but both were ruled guilty on all charges. Anne and George's grandfather Lord Thomas Howard read the verdict and sentence of his grandchildren, which said they were " . . . to be burnt or beheaded at the King's pleasure." Henry immediately signed Anne's death warrant to be by beheading.

When Anne heard her sentence, she closed her eyes and clasped her hands in prayer, "Oh Father, Creator, Thou, who art the way truth and life, knowest if I deserve this death."

Anne's brother George Boleyn Viscount Rochford was executed in the Tower on May 17. Anne expected that she would die the next day. In the following hours, she had moments of great calmness, then mirth with witty jokes. Then, occasions punctuated by hysterical weeping, and prayers that often ended, "Jesu, have mercy on me." Or with a satirical aside, "This is too good for me." Next, she was laughing and wailing. At times of calmness she gave directions for care of her daughter Elizabeth, who was now three years old. Anne even sent an apology to the king for her previous disrespect to his daughter, Lady Mary.

It is hard to account for the wit, satire, sarcasm, or what she may have hoped to gain from her final entreaty to the king, which read, "Commend me to his Majesty and tell him he hath ever been constant in his career of advancing me from a private gentlewoman. He made me a Marchioness and a Queen, and now he hath left no higher degree of honor—he gives my innocence the Crown of Martyrdom."

Anne's grandfather Thomas Howard Duke of Norfolk's performance on this occasion was designed to save his own neck from guilt by association.

His actions give evidence for the absolute despotic power Henry VIII held over his subjects.

On the day before her execution, Archbishop Cranmer gave Anne absolution and Last Rites Sacrament. On his own initiative, Cranmer ruled that Anne's marriage to King Henry was null and void—presumably in an effort to provide a means for Anne to escape execution—for, if never married, she could not be guilty of adultery to the king. However, this had no effect on delaying the remorseless course of action already in motion.

Tradition maintains that Anne requested an expert French swordsman to be her executioner. His arrival from Calais delayed the execution a full day, until mid afternoon on May 19. As royalty, Anne was given the courtesy of a private execution at which few were present. Most were of high status in Parliament, but a few were her ladies-in-waiting. She dressed in a white cap and cape, over a black gown covering a crimson underskirt. One observer remarked that she was never more beautiful than in her last day in life. Her final speech was in condemnation of no one, but with assertion of her innocence of all charges made against her. She ended with:

> "I pray God save the king and send him long to reign over you, for a gentler nor a more merciful prince there never was . . . to me he was ever a good, a gentle, and sovereign lord . . . Thus, I take my leave of the world and of you all, and I heartily desire you all to pray for me. O Lord have mercy on me, to God I commend my soul."

She removed her cap, and then famously said, "I have heard say my executioner is very good and I have a very slender neck." After which, she put her hands around her throat and gave a high nervous laugh.

Some reports assert that a lady-in-waiting put a blindfold over her eyes before Anne put her head on the block. However, another describes her last moments as refusing to have her eyes covered. The swordsman was discomfited by her eyes focused on his face, but her head turned when she heard steps of someone approaching from the other side. When she turned away, her head was severed with a single clean blow.

Henry, ever thoughtless of others, had failed to provide a coffin for her. Her head and body were placed in a plain chest at hand. The rude casket was transferred to the Chapel of St. Peter ad Vinclula in the Tower, and interred in an unmarked place on the chapel floor.

For three hundred years, the location of her grave was unknown. Then, in the 19th century, her remains were identified during restoration and repair of the chapel during Queen Victoria's reign. She authorized creation and placement of a bronze marker to identify Anne's grave on the floor of the chapel. It is octagonal and carries at center a shield with the royal arms in high relief; at top, it reads:

Queen Anne Bolenn MDXXXVI.

King Henry's total lack of common humanitarian feeling at the close of Anne's life is shown by his order that a cannon be fired in the Tower when Anne's head hit the ground. That would be a signal for festivities to begin in anticipation of his marriage to Jane Seymour, which took place with unseemly haste next day.

By way of contrast, when Archbishop Thomas Cramer, who married Henry and Anne, heard the cannon rumble, he broke into tears and wept, "She, who was England's Queen on earth, will today become Heaven's Queen."

Cranmer was the only person of high rank in Church or State who attempted to defend Anne when the charges of treason were brought against her. Cranmer protested to the king that the charges must be false, and all England shared Cranmer's belief. Widespread belief held that all trials associated with the fall of Anne Boleyn were sham, and all executions associated with her fall were illegal miscarriage of justice.

Sympathy for Anne grew after her execution. The people of England did not like Queen Anne, but a disregard for legal justice by Parliament and the king was held to be even more reprehensible.

Anne Boleyn has been the subject of endless memorials in the form of books, plays, and even an opera. She was condemned as a heretic by the Catholic Church, and extolled as a defender of the new truth by leaders of the Protestant Reformation. John Foxe in his *Lives of the Martyrs* treated Anne as a martyr of the English Reformation. Without question, Anne Boleyn was the proximal cause that finally led to creation of the Church of England. For that, Anne has been called the 'most influential queen consort in English history.'

However, that view gives Anne a positive causal role in history she hardly deserves. Little evidence emerges from a study of Anne's life to indicate that she was ever motivated by anything more exalted than self-advancement. Her enduring claim to fame in history rests on the irrefutable fact that she was the mother of the incomparable Queen Elizabeth I Regina.

The aftereffect of Anne's death on her daughter Princess Elizabeth was profound. Elizabeth was declared illegitimate when her mother was convicted of treason and beheaded. Elizabeth was immediately downgraded from Princess to 'The Bastard Lady Elizabeth.' That was the only title she enjoyed during much of her impoverished precarious childhood. Fortunately for England, The Royal Bastard was endowed by nature to bring England to the splendid glories of the Elizabethan Age.

Reign 20-3.
Narrative of Queen Consort
Jane Seymour

See the introduction to Chapter 20 for a summary of the
reign of Henry VIII

Queen Jane Seymour: life dates c. 28 years, b. 1508/1509-d. October 24, 1537; third Queen Consort of King Henry VIII until death in childbirth c. 1.5 years, May 30, 1536-October 24, 1537.

EVENTS IN the one-and-a-half year reign of Queen Jane revolved mainly around rapid changes that attended creation of the Church of England in 1534. King Henry VIII had divorced Queen Katherine of Aragon, and married Queen Anne Boleyn in 1533. The new Church came into being as an outgrowth of the necessity for legitimizing the marriage to Anne Boleyn before the birth of their expected offspring, a hoped-for male heir. Unfortunately for Anne, the child was Princess Elizabeth who later became Queen Elizabeth I. Queen Anne Boleyn fell from favor in 1536, and was executed on false charges to make way for his third wife. King Henry VIII and Jane Seymour married in midsummer 1536, at a time of public confusion, turmoil, and dissent over the newly established Church of England.

Jane Seymour was the third of nine children, and eldest of four daughters of Sir John Seymour and Margaret Wentworth. Jane was born at Wulf Hall Manor, Wiltshire in 1508 or 1509. The Seymour family name in England goes back almost to the Norman invasion in the reign of King William I. Family ties link the Seymours as descendants of William the Marshall Earl of Pembroke, the great warrior of fame in reigns of Kings Stephen, Henry Plantagenet, Richard the Lion Heart, and Henry III. Although they were well-established gentry, the Seymour family did not rise to renown before Jane became the object of affection of Henry VIII.

Jane's father Sir John Seymour was part of the company Henry VIII took with him to the Cloth of Gold Tournament in Calais in June 1520. From this association with the king, John Seymour gained an appointment for his daughter Jane as maid-in-waiting for Queen Katherine of Aragon. That court appointment was the social equivalent of admission of his eldest daughter to a select girl's finishing school. To be a maid-in-waiting to the queen opened a favorable opportunity for young ladies of good breeding to meet young noblemen in court, and the appointment often led to advantageous marriage.

Facts relating to Jane's early life are few. Jane was described as being of medium height, pale, fair, by nature calm, modest, and even-tempered, but of only moderate comely beauty. She was proficient in domestic tasks including needlework. Some accounts report that Jane, like Anne Boleyn, was one of the maids-in-waiting who accompanied Princess Mary Tudor to Paris in the summer of 1514, when she become the Queen Consort of King Louis XII of France. Louis died only three months later, and Mary Tudor, the youngest sister of King Henry VIII, returned to England.

However, it is unlikely that Jane Seymour was ever one of Mary Tudor's maids-in-waiting in Paris. Instead, it is almost certain that she had no experience, or education in the French court, as is sometimes stated. A portrait in Versailles by the German painter Hans Holbein (the Younger) titled, *"Maid-of-Honor to Mary of England, Queen of Louis XII of France"* is the basis of that assertion. The portrait is of an unidentified courtier who is often said to be Jane Seymour. The portrait in question is of a fully developed mature maiden, whereas Jane would have been an immature child of not more than eight years old when Mary Tudor left France in 1515. Holbein was noted for accurate renditions of his painted subjects. Holbein's rendition of Jane Seymour in another painting twenty years later, when Jane was queen, bears little resemblance to the picture in the Louvre. Holbein's known picture of Jane Seymour as queen is not flattering. As one observer of the picture, said, "[Holbein depicted Jane Seymour as] a coarse, apathetic-looking woman, with a large face and small features. Her expression is sinister; the eyes are blue; the mouth very small; also the lips thin, and closely compressed; the eyebrows very faintly marked; high cheek bones, and a thickness at the point of the nose." However, since all queens are invariably proclaimed to be great beauties, many descriptions of Jane also say "she was exceeding fair."

One cannot rule out the unlikely possibility that Jane may have finished her education in service to Mary Tudor, or later to Queen Claude in France, but direct evidence from existing records implies that her education was limited to English language, manners, and court etiquette. By any standard, Jane Seymour was poorly educated. She had limited ability to read, and her only known writing skill was that she could pen her signature. Her rudimentary literacy was usual at a time when few men and almost no women could read or write in 16th century England. Only the first and last wife of Henry VIII (Katherine of Aragon and Katherine Parr) had any claim to depth in scholarly learning.

Jane probably became a lady-in-waiting for Queen Katherine of Aragon in 1530, just before the queen was banished from court. Jane continued as lady-in-waiting to Anne Boleyn in her rise to power from 1530 to 1533, and through Anne's reign as queen from 1533 to her execution on May 19, 1536. In Jane's roles as lady-in-waiting to Queen Anne Boleyn, she was able to attract the attention of the King Henry VIII. The poet Thomas Wyatt a diplomat of Henry VIII said that Jane's father introduced her to court "for the express purpose of stealing the King's affections from Queen Anne Boleyn."

In a monarchy, all power flows down from the king to preferred persons he chooses to favor. In the Seymour family, Jane's two brothers and a sister would rise from obscurity to unimagined heights of influence after Henry decided to make Jane his third wife. Jane's elder brother Edward Seymour became Duke of Somerset, and Lord Protector of England. Jane's brother

Thomas Seymour became Baron of Sudeley; he married Queen Katherine Parr after the death of Henry VIII, and then served as Lord High Admiral in the reign of King Edward VI. Jane's sister Elizabeth Seymour was Jane's chief lady-in-waiting. She supervised the palace during Jane's brief reign. Elizabeth Seymour was titled Marchioness of Winchester, and married Gregory Cromwell the son of Chancellor Thomas Cromwell for King Henry VIII.

Most accounts report that King Henry VIII may have met Jane Seymour in court, but had paid little attention to her before their chance meeting away from court in September 1535. The king was on progress through the realm, and routine arrangements were made for the king's party to honor Sir John Seymour by staying with him at his country estate Wulf Hall Manor in Wiltshire for a few days. The itinerary included a few days of hunting in the royal game preserve at nearby Savernake Forest. Wulf Hall Manor was merely a convenient lodging place for the hunting party. The bucolic setting provided by Sir John Seymour apparently was favorable for showing off Jane's demur modest manner to advantage. Her calm qualities had been overshadowed in court by the gaggle of giggling flirtatious coquettes in service to Queen Anne Boleyn. The King clearly had tired of the court dominated by increasingly desperate Queen Anne, who knew she was losing the king's affection, because she had failed to give him the son and heir he so desperately desired.

Jane Seymour acquired most of her experience in court during Anne Boleyn's rise to power. As one of Anne's maids-in-waiting, Jane must have been acutely aware of Anne's towering ambition, and of Anne's determination to remain the favorite of the king. Queen Anne also was aware that most of the silly empty headed flirts, who pretended interest in serving her, were all hypocritically hoping to take her place as next in line for the king's fickle passions.

Jane rose rapidly in the king's favor, after their September meeting at Wulf Hall. An apocryphal anecdote dated from October 1535 points to Queen Anne Boleyn's first identification of Jane Seymour as her future rival. Gossip said that Anne saw a locket with a splendid jewel suspended on a chain around Jane's neck. She demanded that Jane let her inspect the locket. It contained a miniature likeness of the king. Anne then forcibly jerked the locket, broke the chain, and threw it on the floor. Other equally uncertain traditions say that the King offered Jane expensive gifts, but they were always returned as inappropriate evidences of affection while the king was still married to Queen Anne. However, court gossip of Jane's growing favor with the king continued to flourish into the New Year.

The final break between Henry VIII and Queen Anne happened on January 29, 1536. On that day, Anne surprised the King caressing Jane, who was sitting on his lap, and they obviously were enjoying what had become customary inappropriate familiarity. Queen Anne flew into a hysterical rage, which was followed by premature miscarriage of an apparently normal four-month male fetus. If Anne had carried it to full term, the infant son would have been the salvation of her status as the queen of Henry VIII.

After the January miscarriage, Anne was never again in Henry's favor. With only two-and-a-half years of marriage to Queen Anne, the self-indulgent king had tired of her. King Henry set a course to be rid of Queen Anne, and to acquire a new queen. As an expedient for Jane to meet the King privately, Jane's brother, Edward Seymour, and his family were given apartments adjacent to the king at Hampton Court Palace. With that subterfuge, Jane was free to entertain the king secretly in their quarters. However, it is believed that Jane was never a mistress of Henry VIII before Anne Boleyn's execution on May 19, 1536. Therefore, history has granted Jane Seymour the virtue of not dallying with a married man, but it hardly excused her from being an accomplice beneficiary of Anne Boleyn's fall and execution.

Both Henry VIII and Jane Seymour showed a total lack of common humanitarian feeling at the close of Queen Anne Boleyn's life. King Henry ordered that a cannon be fired from the Tower of London when Anne was beheaded. The cannon was a signal for festivities to begin in anticipation of Jane's marriage to the King. Henry was dressed for the hunt at Richmond Palace in southwest London when the cannon boom was heard. He straightaway ordered, "Uncouple the hounds and away." He then galloped off toward Wulf Hall where he arrived at dusk.

Next day on May 20, the day after Anne's execution, King Henry and Jane Seymour, who was dressed in splendid wedding attire, made vows of betrothal and marriage at the Parish Church of Grafton-Burbage. They proceeded in leisurely festive manner to Winchester, then on to London, greeting cheering crowds along the way. Ten days later, they were married again in a grand formal ceremony in London on May 30, 1536. Preparations for those marriage events must have been planned, and in the making for weeks, or even months before the wedding actually took place.

Jane Seymour was declared Queen on June 4. A few days later, Parliament passed the *Second Act of Succession*, which decreed that only offspring of Henry VIII and Jane Seymour would be legitimate heirs to the throne of England. The *Second Act* repealed the *First Act of Succession*, which had named children of Henry VIII and Anne Boleyn to have the same exclusive right of offspring to inherit the crown). A coronation date for Queen Jane was not announced, probably because Henry was unwilling to crown Jane until she had fulfilled her part of their marriage contract; that is, until after she had provided him with a viable male heir. If Jane produced only girls, she would be removed as quickly from the king's bed, as had his first two wives. Above all else, Henry wanted a son! Jane was never crowned Queen of England; she died only a fortnight after the heir Prince Edward (later Edward VI) was born on October 24.

The Seymour family religion was Lollard (the precursor of Puritans). They had hope that the new Church of England, which had just been established by King Henry VIII in 1534, would be a spiritual improvement over the worldly excess that characterized ways of worship in the traditional Catholic Church. Queen Jane's court was Puritanically simple, strict, and conventional in every way. Her court was in sharp contrast with the opulent excesses in the court of her predecessor Queen Anne Boleyn. Dress and jeweled ornaments were limited in Queen Jane's court. Jane appointed her sister, Elizabeth Seymour, to be her chief lady-in-waiting with responsibility for maintaining severe decorum in court.

Queen Jane Seymour is often criticized for having almost no impact on events that marked the middle years in the reign of Henry VIII, while she was queen. However, on July 6, little more than a month after her marriage, Jane suggested to King Henry that he might wish to renew contact with his daughter the Princess Mary. King Henry had no association with Princess Mary since she had been declared illegitimate after he divorced her mother Queen Katherine of Aragon in 1533. Jane Seymour had briefly served as maid-of-honor to Queen Katherine, and she had known Princess Mary as a teenage girl when she was the court favorite. Lady Mary was a grown young woman of twenty when she again became reconciled with her father in 1536. However, Mary's official status as 'The Bastard Lady Mary' remained unchanged.

Queen Jane's reign was brief and, aside from producing Henry's heir Prince Edward (later Edward VI), her impact on English history was slight. The single event in which Jane tried to influence political actions of Henry VIII came in October 1536 two months after her marriage. It involved her plea for clemency in the treatment of prisoners apprehended following a religious insurrection in the northern shires of Lincoln and York, which history later called the *Pilgrimage of Grace.* Queen Jane made her first and only official petition to the king in behalf of those who took part in the rebellion. King Henry's blunt response to Jane was a reprimand. He reminded her of what had happened to former queens who meddled in his affairs, In effect, he said, 'Hereafter, don't worry your pretty little head about matters of Church and State. They are beyond your comprehension and responsibility.'

Queen Jane, who was a first-hand witness to Henry's volatile and heartless rejection of previous queens that displeased him, prudently refrained from any further effort to sway her husband's actions. Records of the time show that, during much of 1537, Jane accompanied the king, and performed the necessary duties of the queen in court events, but her participation in them was passive.

In May 1537, positive evidence from 'quickening in the womb' showed that Jane was with child. The nation rejoiced, and prayers in every parish petitioned for birth a royal son. Jane's condition was given solicitous care, and the queen's apartment at Hampton Court Palace was readied for delivery of her child. In September, she retired to Hampton Court for her lying-in, which continued until October 9. Then, Jane's exceedingly difficult labor began. After the second day, her midwife attendants feared she might die during delivery of the child. They fearfully requested an audience with King Henry to ask his advice on the question: Would the King wish that the mother or the child be given preference, if only one of them could be saved?

Characteristically, King Henry replied, "If you cannot save both, at least let the child live, for other wives are easily found."

On the third day near midnight on October 12, a healthy boy was born. He was the son Prince Edward, who would later be King Edward VI.

King Henry VIII was delirious with joy. He spared no expense in celebrating the birth of his son. Many cannon were fired from the Tower of London, and church bells carried word of birth of a royal heir throughout the land. London remained in festival mood for days. With great pageantry, Archbishop Cranmer performed Prince Edward's baptism on October 15 in the King's Chapel at Hampton Court. Since the prince was delivered at midnight just as St. Edward the Confessor's day was beginning, the infant was named Edward in thanks to the saint, to whom prayers throughout the nation had been made, and whose intercession had assured safe delivery of a male heir for the throne. Three days after his baptism on October 18, Parliament proclaimed Prince Edward to be Earl of Caernarvon, Duke of Cornwall, and Prince of Wales.

Queen Jane's delivery of the prince brought her close to death. She was still in perilously fragile health when Henry ordered her to leave her bed, and dress in formal garments. Queen Jane was carried on a litter to witness her infant's Sacrament of Baptism in the Hampton Court Chapel. The prince's twenty-one year old half-sister Princess Mary was his Godmother, and his four year old half-sister Princess Elizabeth (held in arms of the queen's brother Thomas Seymour) presented the oil for anointment. Many nobles in attendance gave the three-day-old prince rich gifts of brocade, gold, and jewels. After the baptismal party left the chapel, it adjourned to the queen's apartment, where an exuberant boisterous celebration continued, hour after hour, until long past midnight. One guest reported that "[The band) made such loud and goodly noise that the like thereof I have never before heard."

The festivities went on until the King Henry tired, and he led the exit from the queen's chambers with a brass band and cymbals playing all the way.

After the baptismal festivities ended, Jane was exhausted, and she never again left her bed. Jane's health declined precipitously. She clung to life for a week, before she was given the Sacrament of Extreme Unction in the manner of the Catholic Church. She died at midnight on October 24, 1537 at Hampton Court. Everyone thought Jane sympathized with the Protestant Puritanism, but she met death in a Catholic ritual.

It is often said that Jane Seymour's death was a consequence of either: a botched attempt at Cesarean birth, or that she expired from puerperal infection following birth of the prince. There is little direct evidence to support either of these suppositions to be the cause of her death.

The simple most likely explanation is that she died from exhaustion, and thoughtless demands placed on her frail body following the difficult birth of her child. As a seriously ill woman who was exhausted by a long delivery, Queen Jane was given no opportunity to rest and regain the strength that was needed for her recovery. Had King Henry granted his queen the consideration for post-natal care that a peasant in a hovel ordinarily would give his wife, most likely, Queen Jane would have survived.

However, as usual for him, Henry VIII acted in his own interests. He gave no thought to the wellbeing of his wife after she had just given him his long-wished-for son. His ecstatic pleasure for having a male heir and need to celebrate was more important than for him to give any thought about what was needed for survival by the infant's mother.

Even so, after Jane's death, the king wore black in mourning for several weeks, and he did not begin marriage plans again for several months.

Jane did not have a will. After Jane died, King Henry repossessed Queen Jane's dower gifts of castles and manor houses. Insofar as King Henry VIII was able, he showed devotion to the memory of Queen Jane. Of his six wives, Jane was his favorite. However, his affection for her was only in appreciation that she had given him a son. One now wonders: If Jane had lived, how long would it have been before the fickle king tired of Jane? When would he have replaced her with yet another short-lived romance?

Historians are divided in their estimations of Jane Seymour's virtues and vices. Her motto, *Bound to Obey and Serve*, agrees with histories usual picture of her, as the 'traditional obedient wife without a flaw' of Henry VIII. However, historical accounts of her brief reign record little other than her passive presence at court events. Her lack of direct involvement, even in conversations, was the stimulus for a contemporary observer to say, "She passed eighteen months of regal court life without uttering a sentence significant enough for preservation."

Another expression of faint praise said, "For the most part, Jane Seymour was unobjectionable."

History has been kind to Jane Seymour, notwithstanding the few biographical facts available on her life. Little can be said of her true nature, but she was not a dumb sheep who guilelessly stumbled into marriage with King Henry VIII. She rose to her position of power in a court riddled by intrigue and ruled by her archrival Queen Anne Boleyn. Jane Seymour must have had some natural talent for intrigue for her to be successful in a corrupt court dedicated to ruthless self-promotion. Almost surely, Jane was a calculating agent who knowingly advanced herself in the king's favor. Jane Seymour did nothing to save Queen Anne Boleyn, even though the accusations against Anne were known to be contrived falsehood. Everyone in court was, at very least, a passive accomplice in Anne Boleyn's execution.

Jane is justly criticized for the heartless insensitivity of her marriage to King Henry VIII, which took place less than a day after Anne was executed. Without Jane's long foreknowledge, Jane's seamstresses could not have had time to stitch, fit, and have Jane's elaborate wedding attire ready for Jane to wear on the morning after Anne's head hit the turf at the Tower of London.

A vacuous evaluation of Jane Seymour might be: *She was not as good as she seems to be, but not as bad as she might have been.*

Jane Seymour was buried in St. George's Chapel at Windsor Castle on November 12, 1537 in a vault Henry VIII had ordered built for his own entombment. Princess Mary was the chief mourner at Queen Jane's funeral. When Henry VIII died a decade later in 1547, he was buried in the tomb with Jane Seymour.

Reign 20-4.
Narrative of Queen Consort
Anne of Cleves

See the introduction to Chapter 20 for a summary of the
reign of Henry VIII

Queen Anne of Cleves: life dates 41 years, b. September 22,
1515-d. July 16, 1557; fourth Queen Consort of King Henry
VIII about 6 months, January 6, 1540-July 9, 1540.

ANNE OF Cleves was the second of three daughters of John III (The Peaceful) Duke of Cleves and Maria Duchess of Jülich-und-Berg. The culture of Cleves was bilingual with its dialects being Flemish-French south of the Rhine and Dutch-German to the north. The ducal palace was north of the Rhine in German Düsseldorf, where Anne was born at the ducal palace on September 15, 1515. At the age of twelve in 1527, she was betrothed to ten year old Francis of Lorraine heir of the Duke of Lorraine, but the contract was broken when other arrangements were made for him to wed Christina of Oldenburg-Denmark.

In German States, little effort was expended on education of women, even on women of noble birth. Thus, Anne's mental achievements were modest and lacking in intellectual depth. However, her training in domestic skills, such as embroidery and needlecraft, were excellent. She could read and write German, but was literate in no other language. She was not trained in singing, or playing any musical instrument. She almost never read books, nor had any interest in philosophy, literature, conversation, or courtly etiquette. All these were desirable in cultured courts of Europe, and were important qualities for a wife of King Henry VIII in England.

Anne was twenty-three, had been once betrothed, but she was now free to contract a marriage when envoys of Henry VIII came to Düsseldorf courting her in the spring of 1439.

It is often said, in support of the fiction that Henry VIII was deeply in love with Jane Seymour, that he waited in mourning for three years before he moved to find a fourth wife. It did take Henry almost three years to marry again, but the search for a fourth wife began only a few weeks after Jane Seymour's death in late October 1537. In January 1538, Henry approached Chancellor Thomas Cromwell stating his urgent need for a wife. He had only one son, Prince Edward of Cornwall, who then was only a few months old. Henry said that he needed more male heirs to assure continuation of his dynasty.

His second and third queens, Anne Boleyn and Jane Seymour, were local English girls that Henry had become enamored of as ladies-in-waiting in the court of a previous queen. Cromwell advised the king to choose Queen Jane's successor from among suitable European heiresses. Preferably, one who would not only serve as his wife, the prospective mother of male heirs, but one who also would provide political advantage to the realm. King Henry approved the plan to seek a queen of foreign origin, provided she was physically beautiful, and that he could approve of her appearance and courtly manners.

Henry sent an ambassador to Paris with an imperious request to the King of France for him to order all marriageable (and hopefully fecund) noble ladies at the rank of countess and higher to assemble to Calais as soon as possible, for King Henry's inspection, approval, and choice.

King Francis I was amused at the idea of all the titled ladies of France being lined up, as in a beauty pageant, but he informed Henry that the manner of his proposal was impossible. Even so, King Henry was free to woo any great lady in France of his choosing in any other way he wished.

Chancellor Cromwell advised King Henry that the usual procedure in such matters was to use diplomatic ambassadors to act as proxy for the king. The king protested, "But how will I know that I will be pleased by the appearance and manners of the one they choose?"

Henry agreed to observe custom, but ordered that his ambassadors could make no official commitment to marriage before he passed approval on a candidate's beauty and sophistication.

Cromwell advised Henry to employ the great German painter, Hans Holbein (the Younger), to submit portraits of candidates for the king's inspection. The painter was instructed to render true likenesses with all warts and smallpox blemishes each candidate might possess.

The great search for the next queen of England began in February 1538 just four months after Queen Jane Seymour's death. Holbein traveled, as required, from court to court, enriching art with likenesses of great ladies of the age. However, the choice of a queen turned out to be far more difficult to conclude than vain Henry VIII imagined it would be at its outset.

Although Henry was king of the great English nation, his reputation among titled women in Europe was severely tarnished; indeed, his record as a husband was abysmal. He was seen to be a monster that disposed of wives with cavalier abandon whenever one displeased him. His first wife, *Katherine of Aragon,* was dumped after twenty-three years, and was allowed to expire in poverty. His second quasi-legitimate bride, *Anne Boleyn,* after less than three years was beheaded on trumped-up charges of witchcraft, incest, and bigamy. His third wife, *Jane Seymour,* was queen for only eighteen months, and she died two weeks after birth of a son, who was widely believed to have been ripped from her body by a botched Cesarean birth previously approved by the infant's Bluebeard father.

Heading Henry's short list of French prospects was a beautiful widow, twenty-one year old Duchess Marie de Lorraine-Guise, mother of two sons by her first husband Duke Louis II of Longueville. Marie de Guise rejected the offer of marriage from Henry VIII in April with the acid remark, "Thank you, but No! I am a grown woman, but I also have a very little neck." The comment to her 'neck' was in sarcastic reference to Anne Boleyn's famous remark, when she said to her executioner "I have a slender neck that should give you little trouble." Marie de Lorraine-Guise (in English history, Mary of Guise) added insult to Henry VIII by marrying his nephew, James V of Scotland on May 18, 1538. Mary of Guise is of interest to English history as the mother of Mary Queen of Scots and grandmother of England's King James I.

Second on Henry's list of candidates was Marie's younger sister Louise de Guise. She, too, firmly rejected Henry's proposal with an assertion that she preferred other suitors. Other French princesses and duchesses let it be known that they were not interested in the English king's proposals of marriage. Most of them were in some degree related to Katherine of Aragon, and they resented Henry's shabby treatment of his first wife.

The disreputable record of King Henry VIII as a husband made any further search for a bride in France, Spain, and Holy Roman Empire futile.

Henry's third prospect was sixteen year old Christina of Oldenburg-Denmark, a grandniece of Katherine of Aragon. She was greatly admired throughout Europe for beauty, cultivation, and intelligence. Hans Holbein painted her portrait as ordered by Henry VIII, but Christina insisted in dressing entirely in black, as if in mourning. She made it perfectly clear to the English Ambassador that she loathed King Henry, and would marry him, only, "If I had two heads, then one would be at the King of England's disposal." Her reference to two heads was an allusion to the beheading of Henry's second wife, Anne Boleyn. She turned Henry down in 1439, and later married Francis I Duke of Lorraine (as a child, he had been betrothed to Anne of Cleves).

By spring 1539, Henry VIII ran out of patience in the yearlong delay in getting a bride. Cromwell felt that time was propitious for the king to seek a spouse who could strengthen England's economic and religious ties with Low Country and Central European Protestant nations.

The Flemish and Dutch Low Countries were noted in the late Middle Ages for excellence in general weaving, and for advanced methods in creation of fine brocades and elaborately decorative tapestries. England was the producer of the best wool in Europe, and Cromwell saw great advantage in protecting economic ties with continental buyers of England's major export product, wool. The Duchy of Cleves was a border state that occupied lands on both sides of the Rhine River between Flanders and Rhineland. Flanders and Cleves enjoyed a long history of textile interdependence with England.

Moreover, many Puritans in England looked forward to a day when the Church of England might be a more active leader in the religious reform movement that was sweeping northern Europe. Duke John III of Cleves was an active sympathizer with the new religious movement led by Martin Luther to reform the Catholic Church, but the Duke of Cleves was more inclined toward accommodation and compromise than toward militant confrontation with the Pope and his College of Cardinals. However, the Duke of Cleves eldest daughter Sybille of Cleves was married to John Frederick I Elector of Saxony, who was the major supporter of the radical heretic priest Martin Luther who had stirred up the religious maelstrom that had challenged the age-old authority of Rome. These connections made Cleves a favorable place to find a bride for the impatient King of England.

Cromwell commissioned Holbein to paint Duke John of Cleves's daughters Anne and Amelia for King Henry's inspection. The portraits were delivered to Henry in July. Chancellor Cromwell and the Puritans in England hoped Henry would select one, of the two Cleves sisters to be his bide.

Hans Holbein's portrait of twenty-three year old Anne showed a front-on countenance of a mature serious woman of average countenance. It presented a mask-like stolid face, in a helmet-like hat, and a body heavily concealed in shawls and quilted robes that masked her body. A fair assessment was that Anne was plain, but otherwise she was of unremarkable appearance. A later portrait of her in profile showed that her nose was large, but acceptable as an aristocratic nose at all levels of society. It is likely that his portrait of Anne of Cleves closely approximated Anne's true unpretentious visage. Henry VIII examined portraits of the two sisters and chose Anne. He let his imagination run wild, and convinced himself that he was madly in love with Anne of Cleves.

Negotiations for the marriage contract began in spring 1539. Anne's brother Duke William of Cleves indicated that he was unable to provide a dowry for his sister. Henry's ambassador said that Henry was so enamored by Anne's portrait that a dowry was unnecessary. Anne's childhood betrothal at age twelve to Francis, heir of the Duke of Lorraine was judged a nonbinding commitment arbitrarily made for children without their knowing consent. Thus, Anne was free of any restrictions on marriage as an adult.

The contract for marriage was approved on September 24, 1539, and signed on October 4/6, 1539 by Anne's brother William, who now was Duke of Cleves, following death of their father in February 1539. The prospect for the marriage of Anne of Cleves to Henry the VIII brought Cromwell's hopes closer to reality for the Church of England to be truly part of the Protestant Reformation. Thus, religion as much as wool finally brought Anne of Cleves to England.

Anne soon completed her preparations for marriage to Henry VIII. She left Düsseldorf in late November with over two hundred attendants. She, with many wagons weighted down with all imaginable attire and domestic impedimenta needed by a royal bride, took three weeks to traverse the two hundred miles from Düsseldorf on the Rhine to Calais on the English Channel. Two weeks of bad weather further delayed Anne's crossing to England.

While awaiting good weather for passage, Anne of Cleves marked time with tutors in futile efforts to learn basic English words and phrases before meeting her bridegroom. Her armada of almost fifty small ships finally landed in England at Deal a few miles north of Dover on December 27, 1539. The Duke of Suffolk and an impressive group of English nobles awaited her arrival to escort her to London.

Her carefully choreographed travel itinerary scheduled a week for traversing the seventy-mile trip. Her comfort was assured by overnight stops at hostels, and a full day of rest at Canterbury, and Rochester along the way. Anne's bridal party planned to arrive in London on January 3, 1540. King Henry and Anne of Cleves would be married on January 4, after which the king and queen would be fêted in a splendid festival with all nobility in command attendance.

The agenda planned for the royal marriage was shattered by King Henry's impetuous decision to surprise Anne, by meeting her in Rochester before she arrived in London. He declared her picture had driven him to madness with desire, and that his surprise greeting would "thus nourish love."

Henry selected a few members of his Privy Council to ride with him. All were in disguise as common yeomen clad in rustic winter garb. This was done so they would not be recognized as they galloped from London through the countryside to Rochester. The first meeting of Henry VIII and Anne of Cleves set a pattern of disaster for their marriage that lasted barely six months, from January 6 to July 9, 1540.

Anne's bridal party was on schedule at the end of their fourth day of travel from Dover. They arrived in Rochester on New Years Eve 1539/40, where Anne and her immediate retinue were housed at the Bishop's Abbey Palace. Records of Henry and Anne's first encounter agree that it occurred unplanned in mid afternoon on New Years Day 1540.

Anne sat in a casement window of the Abbey enjoying New Years festivities in the Abbey courtyard. She was engrossed in watching bull baiting by mastiffs when, suddenly her apartment door burst open, and several coarsely dressed ruffians burst in. Without introduction, their grossly corpulent leader rushed forward, and embraced Anne in a most unseemly familiar manner. Anne was outraged.

Anne repulsed her assailant with unmistakable commands in German, "Halt! Wird gegangen! Weg! Wird gegangen! [Stop! Be gone! Away! Be gone!]." Clearly, she was irritated, but returned to the window to observe the sporting event before she was so rudely interrupted.

The ruffian leader, wroth by the chilly response his amorous advances received, shouted to his associates to follow, as he stormed out.

Anne had no prior knowledge of the king's appearance. After the unruly intruders departed, she was informed that their leader was King Henry. Henry was forty-nine years old. He weighed nearly three hundred pounds, and in his rough garb, presented little by way of charm calculated to sweep a mature noble lady off her feet with love at first sight. Anne's rejection must have bruised Henry's towering ego to the core.

Henry expected to be greeted by an affectionate sylvan elf with a youthful bloom of roses on a winsome face. Alack, instead, he found a broad beamed, sallow cheeked, long faced matron with a big nose, who brayed at him in Low German sounds that offended his ear. In the face of such disappointment and rejection, Henry can hardly be blamed for calling her a "Great Flemish Mare (if, indeed, he ever did)."

Henry returned to Anne's apartment after he changed into royal attire. Anne made an appropriate deep bow, after which German and English interpreters translated their first exchange of formal greeting. They shared no common language. The prospective bride and groom spent the evening together in formal discourse. All was done with appropriate courtly etiquette. Awkward stilted conversation, with many pauses, was carried out through formal court intermediaries. Finally, they bade goodnight.

King Henry departed with his attendants to his own quarters in the Bishop's Palace. Many witnesses reported that, throughout the rest of the evening, Henry repeatedly complained:

> "I like her not. I like her not . . . I see nothing in this woman as men report of her. I marvel that wise men would make such report as they have done . . . Do you think her fair, personable, and beautiful, as report hath been made unto me? I pray, tell me true . . . I see no such thing as hath been shown me of her by pictures and report . . . I like her not. I like her not."

The prelude of mistaken identity cited above may have set the stage, but it was not the determining factor that instantly transformed Henry's infatuation for Anne of Cleves into revulsion. Henry was a superbly educated, sophisticated, vain, self-indulgent *bon vivant*. Anne was a modestly literate, passively obedient, conservative product of a provincial European capital.

Henry wanted a cultivated beautiful siren seductress to be his companion. Through no fault of her own, Anne was unable to fulfill Henry's overpowering need for a flirtatious coquette to be his bride. Anyone with foresight would predict with certainty that the marriage between a hedonist like Henry VIII and the pastoral Anne of Cleves would founder.

Within but a moment, Henry had crashed from euphoria to gloom. Next day he sped back to London to find some way out of his predicament of unrequited love, and a despised marriage.

Henry VIII was incapable of self-criticism. He knew absolutely and irrevocably that he could not bed with Anne. He had been betrayed. How could his trusted servants describe Anne in flattering terms that were denied by first seeing her? Someone was at fault; punishment must fall with a heavy hand on the one who was guilty of this most foul stewardship. No one can know with certainty what another heart will love or hate, but to misjudge King Henry so poorly, made certain that heads would roll before this calamity ended.

After arriving back at Greenwich Palace outside London on January 2, King Henry summoned his best legal and theological advisors to attend him. He ordered them immediately to find a basis for him to cancel his marriage contract with Anne of Cleves.

Their wedding, with great pomp and circumstance, was originally scheduled to occur on January 4. Without any explanation or warning that she was in ill-favor, Anne was ordered to take lodging in Dartford, about ten miles east of Greenwich. She would wait there for a summons to appear in London for her formal presentation at court.

On January 3, Henry assembled his Privy Council at Greenwich and reprimanded Chancellor Thomas Cromwell for engineering this intolerable predicament.

Cromwell defended his actions on grounds that he was no better advised on the beauty of Anne than was the king. He strongly stressed the importance for England to stay in good favor with the block of Central European Reformation Nations led by the king's prospective brother-in-law Frederick Elector of Saxony. Henry was reminded that, since England was out of favor with France, Spain, and the Holy Roman Empire, loss of an alliance with Low Country Protestants would leave England alone without an ally and perilously vulnerable in case war suddenly broke out.

Henry bitterly complained, "If I had known as much before, she would not have come hither. But what remedy now?"

Cromwell replied, "There is no remedy."

On the same day, January 3, appropriate noble courtiers went to Dartford to escort Anne to Blackheath near Greenwich, where a splendid reception was given to introduce Anne to leading English nobles of London. The court then repaired to the King Henry's favorite Greenwich Palace east of London. Next day behind closed doors, Henry's barristers studied the marriage contract minutely in search of a flaw that could justify its cancellation.

They found no escape.

In despair on December 5, Henry conceded defeat and said, "[But] for fear of making a ruffle in the world, and of driving her brother into the arms of the Emperor and the French King, I would not now marry her . . . Now it is too far gone [to delay longer]."

January 6, 1540 was the newly set day for the wedding. The ceremony on the last of the Twelve Days of Christmas took place at Greenwich Palace with Archbishop Cranmer presiding. On way to the chapel, Henry grumbled, "My Lords, if it were not to satisfy the world and my realm, I would not do what I must this day for any earthly thing."

Even now, only the stoniest of hearts fails to weep at the distress of King Henry VIII.

The wedding day festivities lasted from morning until long into night, with many receptions, banquets, masques, and entertainments. Finally, the bride and groom retired to their wedding bed. Anne was totally naïve of what to expect from her husband on the occasion. She had not even bathed in anticipation of any unusual intimacy. Henry found her body odor offensive, and that set the sour mood for his dislike of everything else about her. They did not then, or ever later, engage in any procreative act.

Next morning with hope that the relationship between king and queen had improved, Cromwell asked King Henry, "How does your Grace like the Queen?"

In rage, Henry replied, "Not so pleasant as I trusted to have done . . . I liked her before not well, but now I like her much worse . . . I had neither will nor courage to prove the rest . . . I have left her as good a maid as I found her."

Cromwell heard, and trembled when he saw the king's foul mood and temper. He realized that the king may have bowed to necessity, but he had not abandoned his intention soon to be out of this detested union.

As days passed, the king spoke openly to court favorites of his impotence with his new queen. They knew of his past flagrant infidelities, and therefore, accepted his blame of Anne. Anne's linguistic deficiency in English spared her knowledge that she was the subject of uncouth jokes and cruel ridicule by innuendo. It soon became clear that Henry had no intention, ever, to accept Anne to be his true wife.

On one occasion in open court, he said, "[With this marriage] I will never have any more children for the comfort of the realm." His statement rejected the purpose for the marriage, and for its continuation.

King Henry was single minded in determination to be rid of Anne of Cleves. Even so, as a dutiful husband, he spent many nights in bed with her. He caressed her hand, kissed her, said goodnight, then turned his face to the wall, and slept through the night with nothing else done. He skillfully dissembled to conceal his true emotion, and always treated Anne with the respect and courtesy she deserved as his queen.

His true intent became clear on February 1 when plans for Anne's coronation (originally scheduled for Candlemass on February 2) were cancelled, and no new date was ever set. At about the same time, a majority of Anne's German courtiers and servants were ordered back to Cleves.

For two months, Anne was oblivious that anything was amiss in her marriage. Near the end of February, several of her English ladies-in-waiting informed her that the routine affection the king showed each night was insufficient to assure pregnancy. One of the ladies said, "I think your Grace is still a maid . . . Madam there must be more than this, or it will be long ere we have a Duke of York, which all this realm most desireth."

Anne was horrified when a maid-in-waiting informed her of what more was necessary.

In March, over two months after the wedding, and still with no legal basis for its dissolution, Henry jolted his Council by saying that he was convinced that God considered Anne's precontract to the Duke of Lorraine to be binding. Therefore, his marriage to Anne was false, and could never produce a viable heir.

In this statement, the Council saw a repetition of the long struggle over King Henry's divorce from his first queen Katherine of Aragon. To avoid that, the Privy Council quickly acted to make 'non-consummation of marriage' of itself, an adequate ground for divorce. King Henry did not immediately take advantage of the freedom his Council gave him to put Anne aside. Political repercussions of such an action delayed his hand. He did not know how she, or her brother the Duke of Cleves, or how her brother-in-law Frederick Elector of Saxony would react to the insult, if Anne were divorced.

A month later in April 1540, it became well known in court that King Henry was infatuated with one of Queen Anne of Cleves's ladies-in-waiting. His new love was fifteen year old Katherine Howard, a niece of the Duke of Norfolk, and a cousin of Anne Boleyn whose mother was a Howard.

Queen Anne of Cleves eventually became aware of Henry's true feeling toward her, and that plans were afoot to annul their marriage. Knowing the fate of his former Queen Anne Boleyn, the present Queen Anne of Cleves was gravely alarmed. She was determined to do nothing that would incite the king's anger. He was now forty-nine, and had aged beyond his years. Moreover, he had a great open ulcer on one leg that would not heal; it pained him constantly. Pain leads to anger; anger disturbs judgment. Henry's volatile temper was frightening to behold, and incapable of control.

In apprehension, Anne received an order on June 24 from the king that, henceforth, her residence would be moved from Hampton Court to Richmond Palace in southwest London. Although her accommodations were luxurious, Anne was filled with apprehension as she patiently waited to see what would happen next.

On July 6, a committee of the Privy Council called on Queen Anne at Richmond Palace to request her consent to begin divorce proceedings, which would eventually require a ruling by Parliament and the Church on the matter.

Most reports say that Anne immediately swooned and fell to the floor. She may have visualized a quick trip to the Tower of London to meet an executioner in a precedence set by Queen Anne Boleyn. However, if she did faint, she recovered quickly with full mental instincts for survival.

The councilmen were astonished when Anne immediately said, "I am content to abide by whatever the Church and State judges decide."

On July 9, the Archbishops of Canterbury and York reported their decision. The marriage of King Henry and Anne of Cleves was void on three causes:

> There had been a binding precontract for marriage of Anne with the House of Lorraine.
> Henry had not been given adequate information before his consent to the marriage.
> The marriage had not been consummated,
> Therefore, both King Henry and Lady Anne were free and at liberty to marry again whenever they chose to do so.

On July 12, 1540, Parliament passed an Act of Annulment of marriage of Henry VIII to Queen Anne of Cleves. With it went a petition to the king that he "[Seek a suitable bride] by whom his Majesty might have more store of fruit and succession to the comfort of the realm."

On the same day, deputies from the Privy Council went to Richmond and informed Anne of her divorce. She accepted the annulment gracefully without protest. King Henry was so pleased by Anne's total acquiescence to his will that he generously awarded her an annual pension of £4,000, and gave her three great manors, including Richmond Palace. As a special favor and peace offering, Henry decreed that Anne would be styled *The King's Honored Sister*.

On July 11, Anne of Cleves wrote to the king acknowledging their divorce. She said:

> "Though this case must needs be both hard and sorrowful for me, for the great love which I bear to your most noble

person . . . I neither can nor will repute myself your Grace's
wife considering this sentence and your Majesty's pure and
clean living with me . . . [I am honored] that your Highness
will take me for your sister, for which I most humbly thank
you . . . [I am] Your Majesty's humble sister and servant Anne,
the Daughter of Cleves."

Queen Anne of Cleves was possibly more pleased to get her divorce than
even the king was. A French diplomat reported, "Madam de Cleves has
a more joyous countenance than ever before. She wears many splendid
dresses, and passes the day in games and diversions."

After the annulment, Anne created no political difficulties for Henry.
Instead, she did all in her power to assure peace and equanimity in
England and Cleves. Anne informed her brother William Duke of Cleves,
and brother-in-law, Frederick Elector of Saxony that she was entirely
pleased and content with all aspects of her settlement. She added that she
did not intend to return to Cleves, and that they should not harass her
former husband over the annulment. They accepted her explanation, and
honored her request to avoid conflict with England.

However, Martin Luther was less tolerant of King Henry VIII, and
he was obviously miffed at losing a potential ally in his joust with Rome.
Martin Luther (self-styled God's secretary) said, "Squire Harry thinks he
is God, and can do as he pleases." In this, Great Harry and Friar Luther
were in complete agreement.

With her quaint unique title, *Sister of the King*, Anne was granted
precedence over all nobility with titles of duke, marquess, and earl, but
lower than only the king himself, and the prince and princesses Edward,
Mary, and Elizabeth.

Although Anne of Cleves was welcomed at all court occasions, King
Henry ordered that she should be free to do whatever she wished, and
not be coerced in any way to do anything not of her own choosing. As
the nominal sister of the king, Anne of Cleve's place in English society
was unique. She was allowed to live her life as a private citizen of means
in whatever way she wished. Anne of Cleves lived unobtrusively and
comfortably in London for seventeen more years, outliving Henry and all
his other wives.

Anne had a kind affectionate nature that ingratiated her with all the
king's children. In 1540 when Anne of Cleves was queen, Princess Mary

and Anne of Cleves were of nearly the same age, in mid twenties. Prince Edward was scarcely three years old, and for most-part he was sheltered from infection far away from court. Seven year old Princess Elizabeth, who was much neglected in most of her young life, established the warmest affectionate relationship with Anne of Cleves. After Elizabeth's mother Queen Anne Boleyn fell from favor, Princess Elizabeth was neglected, and survived in impoverished conditions that were grudgingly provided by a miserly Parliament. Before the annulment of Henry VIII from Anne of Cleves, Princess Elizabeth had asked her father for permission to visit her new mother-in-law, but the king refused, He heartlessly ordered that his reply say, "Tell her that she had a mother, so different from this woman [Anne of Cleves], that she ought not to wish to see her." However, after the separation, Anne's request to have Elizabeth as her guest was immediately granted. Princess Elizabeth often spent extended time with Anne of Cleves at Richmond Palace—the palace Elizabeth later always considered to be her home, and in which the great Queen Gloriana chose to die a half-century later.

History has been relentless in picturing Anne of Cleves as possessed of an unimaginative pedestrian mind that King Henry could not abide. History's usual portrait of Anne of Cleves, modeled after the supposed allusion to her by Henry VIII as a *Great Flemish Mare*, is unfair. It is doubted that Henry actually ever made that disparaging remark about Anne of Cleves. Most likely, the quotation attributed to Henry VIII is a fabrication by Horace Walpole in the 18th century.

Evidence from Anne's life after King Henry VIII annulled their marriage, suggests that her intelligence was better than average, that her appearance was even comely, and that she had many pleasant agreeable qualities that King Henry's royal children admired.

After Anne's separation from Henry VIII, their relationship was amiable and cordial. On many occasions, Lady Anne spent pleasant evenings with the king playing cards far into the night. No derogatory references were ever made against Anne's appearance or deportment after her role as queen consort was set aside. After Queen Katherine Howard, Henry's fifth wife, was executed in 1542, the suggestion was made for King Henry to remarry Anne of Cleves.

Anne was a master of diplomatic restraint in speech. She never said a word to suggest that she was anything other than satisfied with all aspects of the annulment of her marriage to Henry VIII. She was astute in appointing a competent financial advisor to manage her affairs. With his help, she became a woman of great wealth. In the main, her tastes were simple; she was financially secure; she had an unassailable social position in court; she lived a life of ease in whatever manner she chose; where can one find stupidity here?

Contrary to Chancellor Thomas Cromwell's hopes, Anne of Cleves exerted no influence on King Henry VIII concerning matters of religion. Her religious pilgrimage through life is curious. She was a Roman Catholic at birth. Then in childhood, she was reared a Lutheran Protestant. In the reign of King Henry VIII, she accepted the Anglican Church of England. In the reign of Edward VI, Anne wore the sober garb of an English Quaker. When Queen Mary I returned England to the faith of Rome, Anne became a Roman Catholic, and was buried in the manner of Roman Catholicism.

Anne's spiritual life went full circle without any apparent mental distress, as she briefly touched all styles of Christian worship. Anne's religious journey may have involved profound philosophical comprehension of complex problems of certainty in matters of faith. However, it is likely that her accommodation to whatever may have been the proximal religion was simply a case of *monkey-see-monkey-do*. Anne had little curiosity, or concern beyond passive acceptance of what others around her thought, or did, or wished done.

Anne chose never to remarry. She remained in England, and lived out the remaining seventeen years of her life in freedom, wealth, and exalted social position. She obviously gloried in her new freedom. Her life was largely spent away from the hurly-burly of London court. She found contentment in ordinary English country ways. She much favored English ale and stout. She enjoyed gambling and games of chance in moderation. As a woman of means, she delighted in dressing well, and in entertaining friends with grace. Her most notable public appearance in later years was at the coronation of Queen Mary I in 1553. On that occasion, she rode on a litter to Westminster Abbey with Princess Elizabeth, who was just twenty. Elizabeth was more honored by Anne's presence, than for herself.

The grace with which Anne of Cleves accepted the winds of fate, which many would have found disastrous, surprised and greatly improved general opinion of her. Esteem for her grew by the gossip free private life she lived after her separation from the king. Anne was admired for her good manners and charitable activities. As an exalted Lady, the common people of England had a great regard for Anne of Cleves, and regretted loss of her as their queen. The general opinion expressed by one of her common subjects was, "[Lady Anne of Cleves is] one of the most sweet, gracious, and humane queens we have had, and we greatly desire her to continue as our queen."

Raphael Holinshed, the historian Shakespeare admired, said of Anne, "[There never were] any quarrels, tale bearings, or mischievous intrigues in her court, and she was tenderly loved by her domestics."

Anne of Cleves will is a testament to her gentle and generous nature. In it, she made bequests to charities, to all who served her, and to the most menial in her household. One of her smallest bequests was to her laundress of £ 4 "that she might pray for us." Anne lacked vindictive meanness of spirit. She was a person of kind and courteous temper without regard to rank.

From 1540 to 1557, Anne of Cleves was witness to the tumultuous reigns of King Henry's Queen Katherine Howard and Queen Katherine Parr, and to the reigns of King Edward VI, Queen Lady Jane Grey, and Queen Mary I. However, her choice was to forego nearly all court life surrounding her. Therefore, Anne of Cleves, aside from the shambles of her marriage to Great Harry, leaves virtually no mark of her own on the history of England.

At the age of almost forty-two, Anne of Cleves was confined to bed following an illness of undetermined nature. She died on July 16, 1557 in the Chelsea Old Palace, a manor house Queen Mary gave her in appreciation for their long friendship. Indeed, Queen Mary persuaded Anne to return to Catholicism. When Anne died, Mary ordered a State funeral for her at which the Bishop of London presided in a Requiem Mass. Anne lay in state for a day before being interred in Westminster Abbey. She was the only one of Henry VIII six queens to be so honored. Additional monuments that have been added in the Abbey since her time now obscure her tomb.

History's portrait of Anne of Cleves ignores the fact that she played cards Fate dealt her with exceeding skill. She lived out her life in great financial ease, with a high social position, and she now lies for eternity in Westminster Abbey among participants in England's greatest glories. The heads of many of her brilliant contemporaries were lopped off, and rolled around her like loose cannon balls on a rocking deck. Who can gainsay the intelligence and diplomatic talent that lay behind Anne of Cleves' docile exterior?

Postscript: A matter of unfinished business in the life of Anne of Cleves is the fate of Chancellor Thomas Cromwell.

On July 10, 1540, the day after the Archbishops of Canterbury and York reported that the marriage of King Henry and Anne of Cleves was void, Henry called his Privy Council and, without any forewarning, the Duke of Norfolk (now the king's favorite) ordered the arrest and imprisonment of Chancellor Thomas Cromwell. He was taken to the Tower of London, and on the same day, a Bill of Attainder was drawn up against him, and sent to Parliament with unspecified charges against Cromwell of heresy and treason. The Bill was approved by Parliament on June 29, and Cromwell was beheaded a month later on July 28, 1540. Cromwell's fall was the price he paid for arranging the despised marriage of Henry VIII to Anne of Cleves.

On the same day in which Cromwell lost his head, Henry VIII married Katherine Howard, and gained his fifth wife. Only eighteen months later, she too, would lose her head.

Reign 20-5.
Narrative of Queen Consort
Katherine Howard

See the introduction to Chapter 20 for a summary of the
reign of Henry VIII

Queen Katherine Howard: life dates c. 17/21 years, b. 1521/25-d. February 13, 1542; fifth Queen Consort of King Henry VIII, c. 18 months, July 28, 1540-February 13, 1542.

KATHERINE HOWARD was the tenth and last child of Lord Edmund Howard and his first wife Joyce Culpeper. Katherine's mother died when she was between three and nine years old. For an indeterminate number of years in early childhood, Dorothy Troyes her fathers second wife, supervised Katherine's life. Most life dates and facts on Edmund Howard and his family are spare and contested. Katherine's place of birth may have been the suburb Lambeth south of the Thames across from Westminster. Her date of birth falls between 1521 and 1525. The most persuasive evidence argues for the date 1525, provided a court record is correct in saying that Katherine was fifteen when she first met Henry VIII in the spring of 1540. Official records show only that she was born sometime before 1527. Katherine Howard was a first cousin of Anne Boleyn, whose mother Elizabeth Howard was a younger sister of Katherine's father.

Katherine Howard's father was the third son of Thomas Howard II Duke of Norfolk. Although, Edmund Howard was of noble birth, he enjoyed few material benefits from his noble origin, because he had no title of his own. He had open access to court, but as a third son, he inherited little wealth. Shortly after King Henry VIII came to the throne in 1509, Edmund Howard was on the outer fringe of court activities. When his niece Anne Boleyn rose to favor with Henry VIII, she was instrumental in getting her uncle Edmund Howard appointed to the lucrative position of Controller of Calais in 1531. Edmund held that position until shortly before his death on March 19, 1539.

The head of the Howard family was Lord Thomas Howard III Duke of Norfolk. He and his aged mother-in-law Agnes Tilney Dowager Duchess of Norfolk played pivotal roles in the tragic life of their niece Katherine Howard.

Around the age of seven to ten, Katherine transferred to the household of her great-grandmother Agnes Tilney Dowager Duchess of Norfolk for education in social graces essential for acceptance in life at court. Dowager Duchess Agnes had a grand manor house at Lambeth on the south bank of the Thames, where she provided housing and education for a dozen or more young men and women of good family, who were her wards. In essence, she sponsored a boarding school for relatives who could not afford to train their children for life in court.

The arrangement provided by the Duchess of Norfolk at Lambeth House School was duplicated many times in great homes of noble families throughout the land. Dowager Duchess Agnes maintained an active social life in court, and was absent from Lambeth for extended periods. Even when she was in residence, she stayed in her apartment at a distant end of the manor, to avoid being disturbed by boisterous socializing in the dormitories set aside for her wards.

The Duchess was never directly involved in the education, or coaching of her wards. She delegated authorities for all activities and discipline at Lambeth House to employed subordinates. Major authority for supervision and education of the wards at Lambeth House was assigned to Lady Jane Parker Viscountess of Rochford, a sister-in-law of Anne Boleyn. Lady Rochford served as headmistress-housemother, for what might be called the *Duchess of Norfolk's Finishing School.*

The dormitory rooms for wards at Lambeth House were subdivided for privacy into individual cubicles set apart by fabric screens. Lady Rochford's presence lent credibility that the 'Lambeth School' was properly set up and staffed to serve its purpose: namely, for her boys and girls to marry well, because all children of noble ancestry must acquire advanced social skills and knowledge of courtly etiquette.

Supervision of wards was lax at Lambeth House because the headmistress Lady Jane Parker of Rochford had little personal commitment to her task. She made few demands for learning, and granted much liberty to her eight to ten charges that ranged in age from eight to eighteen. The wards did only as much as they wished. As a ward at Lambeth House, Katherine Howard was a typical empty-headed preadolescent child with no innate drive to learn anything. She acquired the barest level of literacy in the three to five years she spent at Lambeth House. Katherine was barely able to read, and she was unable to write more than her own name. Throughout her brief life, Katherine was dependent on secretaries to write simple notes or letters for her. Several of her notes were found by powerful enemies who used them to destroy her.

Katherine matured early, and became a charming winsome maiden with a gentle kindly nature. She always wanted to please and to be popular. Inevitably, as Katherine entered young womanhood, she had many friends and beaux at Lambeth House. Her first romance began at age ten or eleven. It involved her music teacher Henry Manox who had been hired to instruct the wards in playing the virginal, harpsichord, and lute. He was an unprincipled knave, who quickly chose Katherine as an object for pleasure. Over a period of months, he introduced her to full body petting. However, even at the tender age of ten or eleven, she was able to deny him total intimacy. By 1538 at age twelve, Katherine had tired of Manox, and she began a more serious relationship with the Dowager Duchess's secretary Francis Dereham. He was literate, and far better educated than most persons who were not associated with the Church. Their relationship as lovers began when Katherine was no more than twelve, and Francis was twenty-one or twenty-two. The affair was recognized by other wards to be a man-and-wife commitment.

Mary Hall, one of the Lambeth House chambermaids, later testified, "In a hundred or more nights, Francis came in late at night, crept through a window in the girl's dormitory, and took his place in Katherine's bed, but he usually left by dawn." Mary added that others in the women's room knew of Francis's visits, and "[They] had little doubt, from the heavy breathing, and squeaking of the mattress ticking, what was going on between Francis and Katherine behind the bed hanging that gave them privacy."

Several of Katherine's associate wards disapproved of her behavior, and warned her, "No good will come from your freedom with Francis. If it became known, you will come to evil days."

It is certain that by the age of twelve, Katherine was no longer sexually naïve. Francis Dereham and Katherine Howard shared a common intent to become officially married as soon as Francis could afford to care for her as his true wife. Katherine and Francis openly referred to each other as husband and wife. Before Francis went for an extended stay in Ireland to seek better employment, he behaved as any husband might do for his beloved spouse. He gave Katherine £100 he had managed to save for her own use if he failed to return. Thus, the relationship of Katherine and Francis Dereham was essentially a common-law-marriage. It lasted as a serious mutual commitment for up to two years, until she left Lambeth House shortly after her father's death in 1539. There can be no doubt that they had a precontract agreement to marry, and that they had exchanged oral vows before they went together to their 'marriage bed.'

The young lover's idyllic plebeian romance ended when Katherine's former swain Henry Manox sent an unsigned note to Dowager Duchess Agnes of Norfolk that informed her of "rampant lechery in her woman's dormitory." To make sure all impropriety ended immediately, Duchess Agnes ordered headmistress Lady Rochford to lock dormitory doors every night.

Lady Rochford locked the doors, but the windows were not secured. Hence, little change resulted from the Duchess's initial agitation. However, when the duchess learned that her secretary Frances Dereham intended to wed her grandniece Katherine Howard, the Duchess firmly told Dereham it could not happen! She said, "The Duke of Norfolk hath sent his niece Katherine to me for training to be consort of an earl or duke, not to be the bride of a common house servant." Dereham was informed that, if the Duke heard of his presumptuous intentions, the Duke would send his varlets to cut Dereham's throat. Dereham was immediately discharged. That, most likely, was what motivated Dereham's sudden departure to Ireland to seek his fortune.

Around mid year 1539 at age fourteen after her father died, Katherine ceased being a ward of Dowager Duchess Agnes at Lambeth House. Then, for the first time, her uncle Thomas Howard Duke of Norfolk took responsibility as Katherine's guardian. He introduced her to court in mid winter 1539/40 as a maid-in-waiting to Queen Anne of Cleves. For that position, Duke Thomas Howard carefully instructed Katherine in ways to capture the attention of the king.

Shortly after entering Queen Anne of Cleves' service in February 1540, Katherine renewed acquaintance with her cousin Thomas Culpeper. He was a handsome personable young man who enjoyed great favor from King Henry VIII. Culpeper was a trusted person in the king's personal employ who served as gentleman valet in the King's Privy Chamber. Katherine and Thomas were often seen together, and by March, many other maids-in-waiting believed that they had become romantically involved.

In April 1540, the court knew that King Henry was inflamed by a new love. The object of king's infatuation was fifteen year old Katherine Howard. Duke Thomas Howard's fortunes rose rapidly as his niece gained favor with the king. Events proceeded at bewildering speed:

> The divorce trial against Anne of Cleves began on June 6, 1540.
>
> The marriage of King Henry and Anne of Cleves was annulled on July 9, primarily on grounds that the marriage had never been consummated.
>
> Both King Henry and Lady Anne of Cleves were free to marry again whenever they chose to do so.
>
> On July 28, 1540, Henry VIII married Katherine Howard, his fifth wife.

On the same day, Chancellor Thomas Cromwell was beheaded
for arranging the despised marriage of Henry VIII to Anne
of Cleves.

Uncharacteristic of his previous formal weddings, King Henry VIII
married Katherine Howard in a private ceremony that was kept secret for
over a week. The marriage took place at the king's private country lodge
Oatlands Manor located a few miles northwest of London near Chertsey.

Queen Katherine Howard was the object of the last grand romance
for King Henry VIII. The post-marriage week had all the trappings of a
modern honeymoon getaway. Henry wanted his first days with Katherine
as his wife to be free from court turmoil. He wanted unlimited time for
them to be together in romantic surroundings.

Coincidentally, on the same day as the royal wedding, Cromwell was
beheaded at Tyburn for his responsibility in arranging the marriage of
King Henry VIII to Queen Anne of Cleves, and Katherine's uncle Duke
Thomas Howard became the Chief Councilor for King Henry VIII.

Queen Katherine was a silly, empty-headed, fifteen year old flirt with
no qualifications for becoming a queen consort. Contemporary writers
uniformly described her as a small, slender, auburn haired sprite. She
was a girl with sweetness of appearance, vivacious personality, but only
modest beauty. A portrait of her painted in 1540/41 by Hans Holbein
(the Younger) shows an ordinary woman in modest attire of no unusual
comeliness. However, all that really mattered was that King Henry was
totally infatuated with his young bride. Her youth, sunny disposition,
enthusiasm to please, and affectionate responsiveness were irresistible to
the fat aging king. He had reached almost fifty years of age, and for him to
be so rejuvenated with the fires of youth made Katherine a jewel beyond
compare.

It is easy to account for Henry's infatuation with teenage Queen
Katherine, but it is quite a different task to understand how she could
respond to King Henry's physical demands. King Henry VIII at age fifty
was ill tempered. He had aged beyond his years, and weighed over twenty
'stone'—nearly 300 pounds. Also, Henry had an open running abscess
(now suspected to have been a syphilis chancre) on his thigh. It would
not heal, and the ulcer gave off a foul smell that offended all around him.
Thus, Henry's image fell far short of being that of a youthful swain likely
to capture the heart of a winsome maid. However, Katherine was able to

convince the king of her true love for him. She pleased him even more by choosing as her motto: *Non autre volonte que la sienne* (No other will than his).

November-April romances do exist, and prove that time alone need not halt the flight of Cupid's arrows.

After their honeymoon at Oatlands Manor, the king and queen returned to Hampton Court where many banquets and fêtes introduced Katherine to court. However, no plans were announced for Katherine's coronation. Her coronation would only come after Katherine had presented the king with a male heir (which never happened).

Katherine delighted in being the center of attraction, and Henry doted on everything she did. He gave her extravagant gifts of jewels and gowns. She danced and flirted with everyone. Henry watched and smiled in seeing how much everyone admired his child bride. Henry had never been so completely happy. Court recorders talked of the king's amiable manner.

All the attention she received soon completely spoiled Katherine. She spent part of her time happily organizing the queen's palace apartment. For this, she recruited the service of Lady Jane Parker Viscountess of Rochford, the headmistress she had known when she was a ward of the Dowager Duchess of Norfolk at Lambeth House. Lady Rochford now had the exalted position of chief lady-in-waiting to the queen. Unfortunately, for them both, Lady Rochford also was a link to Queen Katherine's shady past.

Court festivities ended in late August 1540, and the king and queen set out on a traditional autumn progress through the realm. They stopped for rest and refreshment at stately homes of earls and dukes in midland and northern shires. Along the way, the king and his new queen greeted, and touched hand with their subjects at all levels of society.

The king and queen returned to Hampton Court in London for the Christmas season, where Henry presented Katherine with the most lavish collection of jewels ever reported for a single occasion. Her gifts included ropes of pearls, pendants with diamonds, other great stones, and a lace neckpiece bedecked with diamonds and pearls. The king's contentment with his queen knew no bounds. He could not have been more entranced by Queen Katherine, even if his russet haired pixie had been a premier ballerina dancing the Sugar Plum Fairy.

New Years and Twelfth Night Revels of the Epiphany in 1541 brought all the king's family together. Even Lady Anne of Cleves (the former queen, now titled *The King's Honored Sister*) was on the guest list. She played cards with the king until late one night. The king's eldest daughter, Princess Mary was one of only a few who were not fully won over by Queen Katherine's charm. Princess Mary was nine years older than her new mother-in-law, and was put off by the queen's shallow adolescent devotion to dance, bangles, and gowns.

Katherine's first half-year of marriage to King Henry VIII passed with few ripples to disturb its serenity. The first time King Henry VIII and Queen Katherine were separated for even a day came in early February 1541. In preparation for opening Parliament, Henry went to Westminster for a fortnight to attend meetings with his Privy Council. Katherine remained at Hampton Court. During this interval, gossip about Katherine's life as a ward of Dowager Duchess of Norfolk at Lambeth House surfaced, and, for the first time, her name was linked with her cousin Thomas Culpeper who also was in court as a favorite squire in Henry VIII household staff.

When King Henry returned to Hampton Court in mid February, the court immediately noticed that the king's mood had become testy and moody. He complained that the ulcer on his leg was the source of unremitting pain. The honeymoon was over, but Queen Katherine was still his major joy in life. Allison Weir (*Six wives of Henry VIII*, 1991) described the condition of Henry VIII through Lent 1541, as follows:

"By Shrove Tuesday [the last day before Mardi Gras], he was sunk in apathy, and not interested in any kind of recreation, even music . . . at one point his doctors were in fear for his life. There was little they could do to alleviate his pain, or his depression, and for some weeks, Queen Katherine presided over a court that felt strangely empty . . . masques were held . . . but the King did not attend them. In private, the Queen was dutiful in attending to her husband's needs, yet he was not an easy person to live with at this time. He was melancholy and irascible . . . He could not bear people near him during those weeks, and kept to his rooms, so that the court 'resembled more a private family than a King's train [court]' . . . Henry had had enough. He could not accept his latest setback to his health, or face the fact he was now a prisoner of his aging sickly body.

Queen Katherine could not arouse him from his depression, and he shut his door even against her."

In the Easter season of 1541, Henry Manox, Katherine's music teacher and swain during her days as a ward at Lambeth House, obsequiously approached Queen Katherine with barely concealed blackmail. In effect, he politely said that 'he was sure she would want to employ him in her palace service, because he remembered things she did not want others to know.'

In fear and panic to buy his silence, Queen Katherine employed Henry Manox as a musician for her court. Also, in that spring, Katherine's former affianced lover and common-law husband Francis Dereham appeared, and requested employment in her palace household staff. After Dereham's return from Ireland, Dowager Duchess of Norfolk again employed him, and gave him a letter-of-reference that recommended him for the queen's service. Faced with yet another primary witness to her tarnished past, Queen Katherine employed Dereham as her secretary to buy his silence.

These three appointments from her past—Lady Rochford, Henry Manox, and Francis Dereham—were disastrous errors in Katherine's judgment. Both Manox and Dereham knew tales that could destroy her. By hiring them into her household staff, Katherine invited suspicion that her intent was to cuckold the king.

An additional hazard was her recent dalliance with the king's aid, her cousin Thomas Culpeper. Indeed, by March 1541, Culpeper had completely eclipsed all former romantic rivals for the Queen Katherine's affection. Her relationship with Culpeper was clear when she proudly told him, "Do not worry. I have sufficient knowledge to avoid pregnancy."

Culpeper as a gentleman of the King's Privy Chamber knew the king's moods better than anyone, and he had no wish to risk losing his position in King Henry's favor by adverse gossip about any familiarity with the Queen Katherine.

Sixteen year old Katherine had neither the experience nor intellect to cope with the problems she soon faced. In late March and April 1541, King Henry's health and temperament improved, but court entertainments and activities remained minimal through June and July. For a time, Katherine thought she was pregnant. The king rejoiced, but the false expectation came to naught. In August, the annual autumn progress through the shires was set to celebrate their marriage of a year before. Their travel began with visits to eastern counties where approving subjects greeted the royal party enthusiastically on their way to Yorkshire.

The king and queen were in fine spirits when they returned to Hampton Court on All Saints Eve, October 31, 1541. The king never before seemed more happy and content. He continually referred to his wife as, my *Rose without a thorn*. Next morning at early Mass on All Saints Day, Henry gave a prayer of thanks to God in honor of his wife Katherine. He prayed, "I render thanks to Thee, O Lord, that after so many accidents that have befallen my past marriages, Thou hast been pleased to give me a wife so entirely conformed to my inclinations as I now have."

King Henry intended to decree that all churches in the land make prayers of thanks to God for the his most gracious Queen Katherine, the epitome of married virtue. The king was at the apex of delight with his fifth marriage. He was overwhelmed with gratitude that his advancing years would be blessed by so loving and perfect a companion as his Sweet Kate.

Archbishop Thomas Cranmer saw the king enter the Hampton Court Chapel, and heard the king's prayer of thanks for the perfect wife for his old age. Cranmer cautiously and fearfully gave the king a manuscript that summarized evidences that had been volunteered to him and the Privy Council. The paper gave testimony that the virtue of Queen Katherine was far less than desirable for one in her exalted station in life. The paper indicated that the queen might have been unchaste with several men including Thomas Culpeper, who was in the king's employ, and with Henry Manox and Francis Dereham, who were employed in the queen's household.

King Henry was dumbfounded by the report. He was sure they were malicious fabrications. He ordered Cranmer to study the matter, "You are not to desist until you have gotten to the bottom of this plot to discredit my queen."

Although he was sure of Katherine's innocence, he ordered that Queen Katherine must stay in her palace apartment with only Lady Rochford in attendance until the court of inquiry cleared her. Guards confined Katherine to her suite with Lady Rochford. She was not told why she was confined to quarters. One can only speculate on her terror in wondering—What can the cause be? What should I do? What will I lose, or forfeit?

An understanding of Cranmer's unforeseen challenge to the queen's virtue comes by reviewing the steps that exposed evidence against the queen's character, which began shortly after the royal progress to the shires began in August 1541.

> The case against Katherine Howard began when Archbishop Thomas Cranmer received testimony volunteered by a conservative Quaker named John Lascelles. He reported that, as a young girl, the present queen had behaved in a way unsuitable for the queen's present station in life.
>
> The source of Lascelle's information was Mary Hall, a chambermaid in Lambeth House, when Katherine Howard was a ward there.
>
> Archbishop Cranmer personally questioned Mary Hall. She gave detailed recollections of Katherine flirting with many men. She believed that Katherine had given sexual favors to the music teacher Henry Manox, and to Dowager Duchess of Norfolk's secretary Francis Dereham.
>
> Mary Hall did not think that the Duchess knew of the matter, but she was certain that the headmistress, Lady Jane Parker Viscountess of Rochford, knew how her wards carried on, and that she did little to control the behavior of her wards.
>
> However, all evidence against the queen was hearsay. No witnesses had yet provided direct observations to confirm the allegations made against Katherine.

Cranmer received the king's approval to interrogate all witnesses who might have knowledge of these events. On November 5, Archbishop Cranmer, speaking for the Privy Council, informed the king that they believed all charges made against the Queen Katherine were true. Cranmer pointed out that the queen had employed Manox for her household staff, and more recently, she had appointed Francis Dereham to be her secretary. Cranmer concluded, "She has betrayed you in thought, and, if she had an opportunity, would have betrayed you in deed."

At these words, the king broke down and wept. He never again was seen to have the joy of youth on his face. He was forever after a broken old man.

On the same day Archbishop Thomas Cranmer told the king of this gossip about the queen (November 5, 1541), King Henry went into isolation at Oatlands Manor with only a few chosen friends and servants to attend him. If his queen's guilt should be proven true, Oatlands would provide refuge for the king from the public gossip and personal mortification that was sure to follow.

Soon, Henry's despair gave way to anger, then to self-pity. He sought blame for yet another disastrous marriage. As days went by, the king became more set on finding blame than in proving the queen's innocence, or in showing mercy.

By the end of the first week in November, everyone known to have knowledge of events at Lambeth House when the queen was a ward was arrested and taken to the Tower. They were thoroughly questioned, often under torture.

Manox admitted that he had tried to seduce Katherine, and that he had great personal familiarity with her body, but he denied that they ever had full carnal knowledge of one another.

Dereham openly admitted that he and Katherine were precontracted in marriage, and that they had shared a marriage bed many times, but never after she had married the king.

Interrogators were convinced that the Manox and Dereham testimonies were true. Queen Katherine was informed that Manox and Dereham had given testimony against her. Archbishop Cranmer questioned Queen Katherine who was permitted no council. In despair at thought of her cousin Anne Boleyn losing her life, Queen Katherine collapsed into hysterics, and incoherent sobbing. Her testimony gave such conflicting admissions, and denials of past relationships with Manox and Dereham, that little she said carried conviction. She steadfastly denied ever having a precontract for marriage with Francis Dereham. She swore that, although they did have carnal knowledge, for her, it always was unwelcome rape.

No one told child-Queen Katherine that admission of a precontract for marriage to Dereham was her only route to survival. That admission would cost her the crown, but it would save her life, because her later marriage to the king would be bigamous, and therefore void. An admission to a precontract for marriage would void the legal case for extramarital adultery.

Even worse, at the end of her interrogation, Katherine inadvertently volunteered that her estrangement from Dereham came when he asked her, "Is it true that you plan to marry Thomas Culpeper?" which Katherine denied.

The Katherine's mention of Culpeper's name, alerted Cranmer to follow that unsuspected additional lead in the tangled web that ensnared the queen.

Katherine knew that no mercy could be expected from the court that would judge her. Her only hope was to see the king, and to plead for his mercy in hope that, for their past love, he would pardon her. She saw the king as her only hope for survival. However, Henry refused to see Katherine, possibly because he knew he might weaken, and forgive her.

Whatever Henry's reason may have been, he allowed the wheels of justice to grind on without his intervention. On November 10, the king returned from Oatlands Manor to Hampton Court in London, but he never again saw Katherine face-to-face.

On November 11/13, Katherine was removed from London, and confined in Syon Abbey on the Thames westward from London to prevent her from gaining access to the king. She was treated in accord with her rank, but she was allowed no fine dresses, jewels, or any sort of entertainment. At this time, Lady Rochford the chief lady-in-waiting to the queen was taken to the Tower of London for detailed questioning. An assortment of Katherine's ladies-in-waiting, female servants, and associates were also arrested, and sent to the Tower.

When Agnes Tilney Dowager Duchess of Norfolk, learned of the queen's detention and fall from grace, she realized that she would also soon be under suspicion for neglect in supervision of her wards at Lambeth House. In panic, she immediately confiscated, and burned all records in the office of her former secretary Francis Dereham. By that act, the duchess hoped to destroy all harmful evidence against her, but when Cranmer learned of the burning of Dereham's records, he immediately saw it to be a crime of obstruction of justice. The duchess had self-incriminated herself, and she, too, went to the Tower.

In late November, Cranmer informed the king that he felt there was good reason to believe that his queen had been precontracted in marriage to Dereham, and that annulment of their royal marriage on grounds of bigamy was the best course of action to take.

However, Cranmer also advised the King that, before proceeding with annulment, a few loose ends should be examined on the question of, whether Katherine had committed adultery at any time after her marriage to the king.

For this purpose, Cranmer examined members of the queen's palace staff. He learned that, on more than one occasion, the Queen had spent the better part of a night in the apartment of the queen's chief lady-in-waiting, Lady Rochford, where the Queen illicitly met, and entertained unidentified lovers. Francis Dereham and Thomas Culpeper were now believed to be the queen's active present lovers. Lady Rochford was now seen as the bawd who facilitated Katherine's adultery.

Thus, the Privy Council concluded that Dereham, Culpeper, Lady Rochford, and Katherine, after she became queen, had all committed treason against the king.

On November 22, the public announcement was made that the queen would stand trial before the court of law, with charges that she had led a former "abominable, base, carnal, voluptuous, and vicious life." Until the case was settled, Katherine would not be addressed *Queen*. Her official title would simply be *Lady Katherine*. She remained at Syon House for the next two months.

Only three weeks had passed since the king and queen had returned to Hampton Court from their progress in northern shires. The king at that time had intended to order nationwide prayers of thanks to God for his 'most gracious and virtuous queen,' In only three weeks, the legal case against Katherine's virtue had advanced so far as to strip her of her crown. Foreign ambassadors from Spain and France were at a loss to explain Katherine's precipitous fall from favor.

In the following weeks, convincing evidence against Lady Katherine and her associates continued to build. Culpeper was incriminated of adultery with Katherine by a passionate letter from Katherine to Culpeper that was discovered among Culpeper's possessions. It read, "It maketh my heart to die when I do think that I cannot always be in your company. Come to me when Lady Rochford be here for then I shall be best at leisure to be at your command."

That letter mentioned Lady Rochford, as the accomplice who made her chambers available for assignations, and that she stood guard during the couples many meetings. Under questioning, Lady Rochford testified that intimacies between Queen Katherine and Thomas Culpeper began in the spring of 1541 when the king was morose and indisposed.

When Culpeper was questioned, he admitted tender feelings had been expressed between the queen and himself, and that, on two occasions, they met privately in Lady Rochford's suite. However, he denied that they went farther than exchanging "sweet words." His expressed restraint was not believed.

Parliament passed a retroactive act that made it treasonous to promote an unchaste candidate for marriage to the king. This act incriminated Frances Dereham, Duke Thomas Howard, and Agnes Tilney Dowager Duchess of Norfolk. They surely knew of Katherine's transgressions before she was presented at court, and was promoted as a consort for the king.

On December 1, both Culpeper and Dereham were charged with treason. On December 10, Thomas Culpeper, as a nobleman, was simply beheaded. Francis Dereham a commoner was executed by hanging, drawing, quartering, and beheading. Their heads, on pikes, were displayed on London Bridge until 1546.

With the guilt of Culpeper and Dereham confirmed and paid for by execution, Queen Katherine's fate in similar kind was almost certain.

Katherine, waited with apprehension at Syon Abbey through December and January 1541/42 for the Privy Council and Archbishop Cranmer to render a decision on her fate. Finally, on January 16, since a judgment of guilty was certain, there was no reason to subject the former queen to the indignity of an open trial by jury. A Bill of Attainder was drawn up against her on January 21 citing guilt of treason against the honor of the king. The question of a precontract for marriage by the queen and Dereham was rejected as irrelevant grounds for excusing Katherine's execution. The Bill of Attainder against Katherine made illegal, *the intent to commit treason by adultery with the king's wife*. That was enough to seal Queen Katherine's fate in view of her recent relationship with Thomas Culpeper.

On January 21, 1542, Parliament and king reaffirmed the Act of Attainder against the Queen Katherine. King Henry took no part in any other aspect of Katherine's trial, nor did he respond to her pleas for clemency.

On February 10, Katherine was taken to the Tower of London with moments of hysteria, weeping, and calmness. Next day, the Bishop of London heard her final confession, but she never admitted to betraying the King with Culpeper.

She was sufficiently calm through most of the day before her execution to ask that the block be brought to her, so that she might try it out in advance, so as not to make a bad spectacle on the scaffold. Her wish was granted, as well as her request for the execution to be within the Tower walls, and not open to public view.

On Monday morning, February 13, 1542, the Privy Council and other selected nobles gathered on Tower Green. Katherine was helped to the scaffold. Legend says that she whispered, "I die a queen, but I would rather have died the wife of Thomas Culepper." She made a short speech that ended with a request for prayers for her soul. She put her head on the block, and her neck was severed with one blow of an ax.

An observer remarked, "She had a Godly Christian end."

Her head and body were wrapped in black cloth and carried to the chapel of St. Peter ad Vincula in the Tower of London where she was buried beside Anne Boleyn. The locations of their graves are marked on the floor of the chapel by medallions ordered by Queen Victoria in the 19th century.

Lady Rochford was beheaded after Katherine's body was removed. Two and a half months of imprisonment in the Tower had driven her mad. Parliament passed a special dispensation to permit the execution of an insane person. She was forcibly carried struggling and incoherent to the scaffold where, kicking and howling, after eleven blows, she was finally hacked to death.

Katherine Howard, the fifth wife of Henry VIII, was the least qualified of his six wives to be queen of England. Her reign of eighteen months ended before she had any influence on the course of events that followed. She was best equipped to be a courtesan, not a queen—in that role, she could better have served as England's Madame de Maintenon, Madame de Pompadour, or Madame du Berry. Sadly, Katherine Howard's country was England, not France.

After Katherine Howard's fall, King Henry VIII was a broken man. Yet, the last three and a half years of his life were blessed by marriage to his sixth and best queen, Katherine Parr.

Reign 20-6.
Narrative of Queen Consort
Katherine Parr

See the introduction to Chapter 20 for a summary of the
reign of Henry VIII

Queen Katherine Parr: life dates c. 36 years, b. 1512/14-d.
September 5, 1548; Baroness wife of Lord Edward de Burgh
c. 3 years, c. 1527-1532; Baroness wife of Lord John Neville of
Larimer-Snapes 9 years, c. 1534-1543; sixth Queen Consort of
King Henry VIII c. 3.5 years, July 12, 1543-January 28, 1547;
Dowager Queen and Baroness wife of Sir Thomas Seymour c.
1.5 years, January 28, 1547-September 5, 1548.

KATHERINE PARR was the eldest of three children of Sir Thomas Parr
and Maud Green of Kendal Manor of Westmoreland in northern England
near the Scottish border. The Parr family history claimed descent with
remote royal connections to Edward III through his youngest son Thomas
of Woodstock. Thomas Parr served as an attendant to King Henry VIII
when he was crowned in 1509, and was knighted at that time by the king,
who also gave Parr the title Baron William Parr of Kendal. Maud Parr was
briefly appointed lady-in-waiting to Queen Katherine of Aragon.

The date of Katherine Parr's birth is uncertain, but falls around
1512/15. She was named in respect for Queen Katherine of Aragon.
Katherine Parr's father died in 1517, when she was a small child of four or
five years old. Her mother did not marry again, but she took her children
to live in the stately home of her husband's uncle William Parr Marquess
of Northampton. Maud devoted her life to the education and instruction
in courtly manners of her three children: Katherine, William, and Anne.
Katherine's brother William Parr inherited a title from his uncle, and
became William Parr II Marquess of Northampton. Her sister Anne became
Dame Anne wife of William Herbert, Sheriff of Northhamptonshire.

Katherine's early education was adequate in English, but not classical.
Only later in life after her first marriage, she independently mastered

Greek and Latin, as a prerequisite for true scholarship. She had superior intelligence coupled with a desire to learn and understand fine points of religion and philosophy.

In appearance, Katherine Parr was taller than average. She was slender, had hazel eyes, reddish blond hair, and a small nose. Her alert inquiring appearance was attractive, but lacked notable beauty. She enjoyed dancing, fine clothes, and social encounters of all kinds. She was accomplished in womanly arts of needlecraft, music, and management of a manor house. By nature, she was witty, vivacious, outgoing, and enjoyed taking part in challenging intellectual argument. Her tolerant kindly good manners found favor with all she met in formal and informal encounters.

At age fourteen/seventeen, Katherine was contracted in marriage to Lord Edward de Burgh Baron of Gainsborough, who was sixty-three years old and in declining physical and mental health. Despite the forty-five year difference in their ages, Katherine served as his dutiful uncomplaining wife. In her two to three year marriage to aged Lord Edward de Burgh, Katherine learned patience and skills needed for care of an elderly sick husband, and how to manage a great stately home. No children were born of this marriage, but Baron Edward's grown children all approved of the way Katherine performed her domestic duties with competence and good humor.

When Katherine's first husband died in 1528, she was between sixteen and eighteen years old. She received a substantial life pension as the widow of Lord Edward de Burgh, which gave her financial independence. Her mother died the following year. Thereafter, Katherine was financially independent and free to determine her own destiny. At this time, she elected to begin a program of self-education that continued through the rest of her life

Lady Katherine (Parr) de Burgh in the summer of 1533 or 1534 was an attractive well-born widow of means in her early twenties. She accepted an offer of marriage from John Neville Baron Latimer of Snapes in Yorkshire. He was a widower about forty years old, and had two children by his first wife, Dorothy de Vere a daughter of the Earl of Oxford. John Neville was related at the highest level to powerful noble peerages in northern counties of England. The nine-year marriage of John and Katherine Latimer of Snapes was compatible, but no children came from their union. They spent time between their residences at Snapes Castle in Yorkshire and a townhouse in London. In London, they enjoyed respected positions on the outer fringe of court as Lord and Lady Latimer.

Little of importance affected the Latimer's lives before the autumn of 1536 when a local rebellion broke out at Lincoln and York. The rebellion was in opposition to consequences from outlawing Catholicism and creation of the new Church of England in 1534. The widespread lack of uniformity from diocese to diocese in the way rituals of worship were carried out by the new Church of England created much unease throughout England. Priests in local parishes overwhelmingly opposed any tampering with the form of worship in holy services, and the closing of abbeys. The new State Religion now banned all these former religious practices, because they were instruments of outlawed Catholicism.

The ancillary church agencies—abbeys, monasteries, cloisters, nunneries, and chanceries that were traditionally operated by friars and nuns—had provided public schools, orphanages, hospices, and hospitals for the aged and indigent poor. The defrocking of friars and nuns, which accompanied dissolution of monasteries, terminated but provided no alternatives for the public schools and hospices.

The rebellion in Lincoln and York (later called the *Pilgrimage of Grace*) quickly grew into a public protest against the new Church of England. Catholic practices were reinstated in churches in direct defiance of the king. The king's men confronted several thousand insurgents, and over two hundred insurgents were executed in the next several weeks. Katherine's husband Lord John Neville of Latimer was Catholic, and he played an active part in the rebellion. He was among the arrested lords, but along with most other titled insurgents, King Henry soon gave him a pardon. Katherine served as her husband's advocate in the adjudication of that altercation. In that capacity, Katherine became known to King Henry VIII.

It is almost certain that through the duration of her marriage to Lord John Neville (c. 1534-1543), Katherine did not openly depart from his Catholic religious conviction. However, by 1543 after he died, Katherine became sympathetic to Protestant views. Her change in religious orientation agreed with the gradual acceptance of Protestant thought in the English court. The growing English sympathy for separation from Rome occurred during years when Queen Jane Seymour (1536-37) and Queen Anne of Cleves (1540) reigned. Katherine probably weighed the philosophical and dogmatic elements in the prevailing religious controversy, and changed her original Catholic persuasion to tolerance of Puritanism.

King Henry paid no special attention to Katherine Parr's presence in court until after Queen Katherine Howard's fall and execution in February 1542. By then, Katherine was thirty-one and King Henry was fifty-one, and prematurely aged. Parliament persisted in pressuring King Henry to marry again, because his six year old heir Prince Edward of Cornwall was sickly, and all England expressed the hope that King Henry VIII would sire another son to assure his dynasty.

As early as February 1543, King Henry began to pay special court to Katherine Parr by privately sending her gifts of expensive clothing. As a married woman, Katherine recognized the impropriety of the gifts, but was fearful of returning them, and thereby, earning the king's anger. At that time, her husband Lord Latimer was near death as he approached his fiftieth year. He died on March 2, 1543, and his will left Katherine two manor houses and a substantial annuity.

Lady Latimer was now an independent widowed heiress of great wealth. She had a serene attractive personality, flawless manners, and an intelligent cultivated mind. She had also fallen in love with Lord Thomas Seymour Baron of Sudeley, a brother of former Queen Jane Seymour. He was handsome, personable, and was rising rapidly as a power in government. Thomas Seymour was in his mid thirties, six to eight years older than Katherine. They were mutually attracted to one another, and were considering marriage.

Parliament was determined that Henry should marry again, but Henry was equally determined never to be humiliated in another marriage, as his marriage to Katherine Howard had done. To protect him, Parliament passed an act designed to "protect the King from marriage to a woman of disrepute." The act made it treasonous, on pain of death, to recommend any candidate for marriage to the king who was not 'a pure clean maid.' However, who in Henry's court could be completely certain of any woman's chastity? The new law made sure that Henry would face a monstrous lack of candidates for his marriage bed.

Lady Katherine (Parr) Latimer was twice honorably married, was without children, and she could not be represented other than what she was. King Henry saw much about Lady Latimer that pleased him, and he lost no time in pursuing Lady Katherine (Parr) de Burgh-Latimer with marriage on his mind. Henry learned of Katherine's inclination toward marriage with Lord Thomas Seymour, so he resolved that problem by appointing Seymour ambassador to Brussels. That done, King Henry VIII proposed marriage to Katherine in early May 1543.

Henry VIII was an aging, senile, hugely fat, old man. Katherine's personal choice lay elsewhere. However, for the present, she bowed to the king's command. Bishop Stephen Gardiner married Henry VIII and Katherine Parr on July 12, 1543 at Hampton Court in a private ceremony with only a few courtiers present. Henry's fourth wife, Anne of Cleves was present as an invited guest, as were the king's three children by former wives: Prince Edward, Lady Mary, and Lady Elizabeth. Katherine was a caring faithful wife for King Henry's in his three remaining years of life.

Henry VIII was content to have a wife who was a comfortable companion, one who was willing and happy to engage in intelligent conversation on many subjects. He was deeply knowledgeable of religious Canon and Church history. Discussion of dogma was much to his liking. He enjoyed having a mental sparring partner who was able to carry her part in discussions of fact and theory on science and religion.

Only three months into their marriage, Queen Katherine obtained permission from the king to invite his three children to visit her in London. During most of their lives, the royal children had lived in separate residences, each with its own household and court.

Lady Mary and Queen Katherine were in their late twenties. They developed a sincere friendship that welcomed candid exchanges of opinions, but they tactfully avoided subjects allied to religion: Mary was a nondeviating Catholic; whereas, Katherine accepted the Church of England, and was tolerant of Puritan concepts of reformation and separation from the old dogma.

Lady Elizabeth was ten when she first went to visit Queen Katherine. Elizabeth had endured much privation and little love before meeting her new stepmother. The child was starved for affection, and immediately fell in love with kindly Queen Katherine who greeted her with a warm outpouring of affectionate understanding. Elizabeth faced a strict curriculum of classics, languages, and natural philosophy, as well as instruction in religion, dance, embroidery, and music. She excelled in every discipline, and exhibited an unquenchable thirst for knowledge, which was matched with a capacity for almost total recall. Queen Katherine employed Roger Ascham of Cambridge as tutor for Elizabeth. He extolled her prodigious capacity for learning languages. Elizabeth, as queen, was as fluent with French, Latin, and Greek as with her own English tongue.

Prince Edward had been reared by nurses and tutors in isolation far from court to protect him from contagious diseases. Soon after Prince Edward's sixth birthday, he came to Katherine's court. She gave Prince Edward, whose mother had died at his birth, his first experience of motherly affection. His visits to London were less frequent than those of his half-sisters, but he became devoted to his stepmother Queen Katherine.

Queen Katherine added yet another royal child to her palace school—Lady Jane Grey—the eldest grandchild of King Henry's younger sister Mary Tudor Duchess of Suffolk. Lady Jane was six, of nearly the same age as Prince Edward. She was exceptionally bright and thirsty for knowledge. Ascham later said of her that, on one occasion when all in the palace had gone out for a hunt, Lady Jane was found alone in her room reading Plato's *Phaedo* in original Greek.

King Henry approved Katherine's choice of Roger Ascham (pronounced, *Ask-am*) to be in charge of tutorial educations for Prince Edward, Lady Elizabeth, and Lady Jane Grey. Ascham was the primary scholar of Latin and Greek at Cambridge. He was unstinting in praise of his charges' abilities to learn quickly and retain fine points of classical grammar and vocabulary.

Queen Katherine supervised all aspects of Prince Edward and Lady Elizabeth's education. The schedules for learning were strenuously designed to meet King Henry's intent that his children excel. Fortunately, both Elizabeth and Edward were highly intelligent and strongly motivated to learn. They were paragons in studies of language, science, and history.

As an outgrowth of strengthening the family bonds, Katherine encouraged Henry to make his will to include an order of succession to the throne for Parliamentary approval, namely: *first*, Prince Edward; *second*, Lady Mary; *third*, Lady Elizabeth; *fourth*, Lady Jane Grey.

Neither the King, nor Parliament, had great enthusiasm for the long train of women lined up in his plan for succession, which included Lady Mary, Lady Elizabeth, and Lady Jane (also, possibly even Queen Mary of Scotland). In February 1544, Henry ordered Parliament to enact the new Act of Succession, which placed any offspring he and Queen Katherine might have, male or female, ahead of his daughters Mary and Elizabeth by his former queens Katherine of Aragon and Anne Boleyn. This was clearly an expression of his high regard for Katherine Parr, but it did little for the self-esteem of the two half-sister princesses.

Separately, Queen Katherine tried to, but was unable to convince the King Henry to legitimize his two daughters. Therefore, in strict conformity with previous court protocol, their official titles for his daughters remained simply, Lady Mary and Lady Elizabeth.

Katherine chose the motto *To be useful in all I do*. It is a window into her character as queen. She won approval from Archbishop Thomas Cranmer of Canterbury, with whom she exchanged arguments on matters of Gospel and religion. The court accepted their new queen as an amiable ambassador of goodwill with no particular agenda of religion or politics to promote. She was known and admired in court for her friendly honest outgoing nature. The public approved of her conservative virtuous propriety in managing the house of their king, and of her role as a loving stepmother for her three royal stepchildren. After many years of turmoil, England at last had a queen who was approved by all.

Katherine's primary intellectual interests revolved around understanding matters of religion, dogma, faith, and philosophy. However, she was not an original innovator of new ideas on such matters. Her interests ran close to those of King Henry, who, as a second son of King Henry VII, was at first educated with the likelihood that he would become a high prelate in the Church. With that end in view, Henry (then Duke of York) was educated in all maters of Catholic history and its ritual formalities. As a young king in 1521, he had written a scholarly apology entitled *In Defense of the Seven Sacraments*, which was a scathing rebuttal and denunciation of the *Ninety-nine Theses* Martin Luther's nailed to the Wittenberg Cathedral door on All Saints Day 1517. The dissertation by King Henry VIII was so highly regarded by High Church authorities as justification for ecclesiastical orthodoxy that Pope Leo X gave Henry the title, *Defender of the Faith*. The 'Defense' by Henry VIII is still available in print, and remains part of Catholic justification for traditional papal authority in matters of dogma for Christian belief (as opposed to Protestant reliance on faith in the truth that 'Biblical writings are the Word of God').

In July 1544, England went to war with France, and Henry showed great confidence in his queen's loyalty and judgment by making Queen Katherine his regent during his two-month absence on the Continent. In his absence to France, Katherine handled affairs of State with a sure hand. She sent forces to the Scottish border to quell an insurrection in the northern marches, and signed several Parliamentary proclamations that required royal approval. On the domestic side, she ordered the royal children to move out of London to the king's country estate at Oakham, so they would avoid infection from a usual summer flare up of plague.

Queen Katherine's acts as regent greatly impressed ten year old Lady Elizabeth who witnessed them. They may have set a model for her own actions when she later became the reigning queen. At Christmas 1544, Lady Elizabeth at age eleven gave the queen a book of prayers and devotions she had translated from French, which Elizabeth bound in an embroidered cover of her on making. The gift book was dedicated, "To The Most Noble and Virtuous Queen Katherine, [from] Elizabeth, her humble daughter wisheth perpetual felicity and everlasting joy."

During the following year, Katherine was engaged in scholarly efforts of her own. With the king's permission, she published her first book in November 1545, entitled *Prayers and Meditations*, and a second book entitled *Lamentations of a Synner*. Both volumes were well received by teachers of divinity and philosophy at Oxford and Cambridge Universities. The dons were astonished that a woman without scholarly instruction had written such intellectually challenging treatises. Oxford and Cambridge Universities asked her to become their patroness. For a woman, even a queen, to be so honored for scholarship was a groundbreaking novelty.

The brief war with France ended in victory for England on September 14, 1544. Henry's role as Commander-in-Chief of England's expeditionary force to France invigorated him. For a few weeks, his ulcerating thigh began to heal, and he was free of pain. Soon after his return to London from France in October, however, the ulcer erupted again, and he never again was free of constant agony from the festering sore. While at Windsor in 1545, the king was stricken with illness of undetermined nature. After recovery, his legs, already weekend with age, could no longer carry his great weight. A sedan chair was improvised by which servants carried him from place to place about the palace. By mid winter 1546 (in what is now known to be the last year of King Henry's life), pain and sobering thoughts of impending death were the king's constant companions.

Katherine willingly and dutifully spent days in his company trying to distract his mind from agony and depression. They enjoyed debates on fine points of religious doctrine and dogma, and friendly disputations on religion. Both enjoyed the intellectual jousting, which, like a game of chess, had the quality of equal minds testing ingenuity and cunning in the other.

Katherine often baited the king with arguments put forth by Puritans and Quakers, who advocated heretical challenge to traditional Catholic dogma for the king to rebut. Henry was still essentially of Catholic persuasion, even though he denied veto power by the Pope in Rome. Queen Katherine was innocently unaware that she was intellectually dancing at the edge of disaster in presenting these Protestant challenges to the king.

By summer 1545, Great Harry's health was poor, and all knew that he was mortal, and would not be king for long. His death, of which naught could be spoken, would bring great change to everyone throughout the realm. His successor, Prince Edward was a child of not quite ten who would be unable to assure a steady course for the Ship of State. Where would King Henry's great power go when he died? Would Parliament and Church stay the course Great Harry steadfastly set? Would freethinking radicals take command? Would tradition, or anarchy rule?

Those already in power (Chancellor Thomas Wriothesley and Bishop Stephen Gardiner), who shared the views of Henry VIII on Catholic orthodoxy, wanted to make sure that the Church of England survived the approaching storm. However, Thomas Cranmer Archbishop of Canterbury, who devoutly hoped the Church of England would move steadfastly away from Catholicism and join the Reformation movement on the Continent, opposed them.

By mid year 1545, Chancellor Thomas Wriothesley and Bishop Stephen Gardiner initiated a vigorous search for Protestant heretics (the Lollards, Puritans, and Quakers) who had become more outspoken in opposition to Catholic traditions still evident in the Church of England.

Wriothesley and Gardiner suspected that Queen Katherine secretly supported radical Puritan views.

The first serious challenge against the queen came indirectly through the shameful trial and execution of Anne Askew in February 1546.

> Anne Askew was a twenty-four year old devout Puritan-Quaker who, against her will, was given in marriage by her father to a Catholic husband. Anne rebelled and left her husband when he insisted that she must celebrate the Mass with him. She refused for reason of conscience, and went to London where she became an outspoken advocate of Puritanism. She defied law, read the Bible out loud in public palaces, and sold books that had been banned by Parliament.

To understand the severity of Anne Askew's crimes, one must understand that the central belief of the new Puritan-Quaker Protestant faith was the need for personal familiarity with the 'Bible as the fount of truth for Christian faith.' Puritan converts were expected to think for themselves. Reading Miles Coverdale's first translation of the Latin Bible of St. Jerome into English was a heretical criminal offense, because Parliament had passed the *Act for the Advancement of the True Religion*, which criminalized reading scripture by anyone but the ordained clergy, licensed scholars, and jurists in courts of law.

Anne Askew's intransigence came to the attention of a local magistrate, and she was apprehended, taken to the Tower of London for examination, and trial as a heretic. Chancellor Thomas Wriothesley and Bishop Stephen Gardiner's chose to use the Askew-case to implicate Queen Katherine as a conspirator in a subversive plot to alter the Church of England in ways contrary to King Henry's will. They fabricated rumors that Anne Askew was Queen Katherine's agent. Anne Askew was severely tortured on the rack, until her legs were broken at many joints. Anne never denied her Quaker faith, nor that she had committed the crimes of which she was charged. However, she steadfastly denied ever having had any contact with the queen. Queen Katherine survived the Askew trial unscathed.

Bishop Gardiner remained convinced that the queen and many ladies of her court were conspiring to redirect the king's mind toward Puritan heresies. Gardiner, as a confidant of the king, convinced Henry that, in a manner of Biblical speaking, he was, 'harboring a viper in his bosom.' Henry agreed to let Gardiner, Wriothesley, and the Privy Council secretly question several of the queen's ladies-in-waiting on the queen's religious persuasions, and whether any forbidden writings were in her possession. The interrogations revealed nothing, and, a search of the queen's apartment found no incriminating manuscripts or books.

As summer turned to autumn 1546, Katherine was unaware of the chain of circumstantial evidence being forged against her, and she innocently continued to enjoy lively arguments on religion and philosophy with the king.

Wriothesley witnessed one of these debates, and saw Queen Katherine challenge the king with arguments counter to those expressed as fundamental to the Church of England. In it, he saw a way of pleasing the king, while engineering the downfall of Queen Katherine Parr, and a means for advancing himself in the king's favor. He proceeded to play the part of Iago poisoning the mind of Othello against the virtue of his wife Desdemona.

The Lord Chancellor suggested to King Henry the possibility that his queen's arguments might actually have a sinister purpose of guiding the king into making fundamental changes in the Church of England. That is, to bring about changes foreign to the king's own will—*in fine*, to bring the English Church closer to heretical churches on the Continent. Wriothesley knew the king's vanity would not tolerate the thought of being tutored by a *mere woman*, no matter how learned she might be.

Henry did not believe that the criticisms of his queen were true. However, he agreed to have discussions with Katherine that could reveal an ulterior motivation, if such did exist. Katherine was not aware that she was being tested in later conversations. However, Henry was on guard to the possibility that Katherine might be attempting to manipulate his thinking. With that suspicion firmly planted in his mind, Henry soon became convinced of Katherine's guilt.

King Henry was an invalid in Whitehall Palace in August 1546 when he authorized Wriothesley and the Privy Council to draw up papers for Katherine's arrest. When the warrant arrived by courier, Henry signed it and gave it back to the courier for return to Wriothesley. King Henry then, in an offhand manner, informed his attending physician, also a friend of the queen, that Queen Katherine would be arrested.

By strange happenstance, delivery of the warrant was delayed, and was delivered instead into Queen Katherine's hands. On reading the damning nature of its contents, she was devastated. However, she had sufficient presence of mind to go immediately to King Henry, and convince him of her innocence of any intent to direct his thinking on any matter of religion or government. The king, at first, contested her arguments, until she explained that her motive was simply to benefit from his personal wisdom on the subjects they discussed. She mentioned that when they talked of religion he seemed forgetful of his constant pain. That had encouraged her to continue their discussions, which also rewarded her with better understanding on hearing his learned words of wisdom. She ended by saying that she would always heed his better judgment, for he was her lord and husband, "So God hath appointed you as Supreme Head of us all, and of you, next unto God, will I ever learn . . . for I have always held it preposterous for a woman to instruct her lord."

This convinced King that Queen Katherine was his loyal wife, and he accepted her arguments. He promised he would never doubt her again. He concluded by saying, "Then Kate, we are friends again."

The warrant was replaced where the currier was able to retrieve it, and return it to Wriothesley.

Next day, Wriothesley arrived at the king's quarters with forty armed guardsmen to arrest the queen, and take her to prison in the Tower of London. He was dumbfounded on finding the king and queen in the garden engaged in merry chatter. He was even more distressed when the king called him, "Arrant Knave and Fool," and ordered Wriothesley and his men to leave his presence without the queen in chains.

Katherine realized her precarious position—only the accident of a misplaced paper had saved her—she never again tested her wits against the king. She made sure nothing again would create gossip of her disloyalty to her husband. For Queen Katherine, King Henry's vanity was sacred, and it would be protected.

It is uncertain how far Katherine's religious beliefs had moved toward Protestantism. However, it is known that she had become a friend and confidant in Thomas Cranmer Archbishop of Canterbury, who was strongly of the Puritan persuasion. Therefore, Gardner and Wriothesley of the Catholic camp probably had good reason to fear the queen's influence on King Henry.

By November 1546, King Henry was rarely seen outside his private rooms at Greenwich Palace. His days were numbered, and he lost interest in control of government. He was aware that his nine year old son Prince Edward of Cornwall, who had spent much time in the care of his Seymour Puritan relatives, had leanings toward Protestant theology. When the boy became king, the Church of England would probably adopt Puritan heresies.

King Henry made a last speech to his Privy Council in December 1546 with advice that they avoid bickering argument, and instead, attempt to hear and work for the will of God.

Before the close of 1546, festivities for Christmas were cancelled. The king made his will at the end of the year, which reaffirmed the order for succession approved by Parliament earlier: *Prince Edward, Lady Mary, Lady Elizabeth, and Lady Jane.* The will also expressed his love for Queen

Katherine, and it made bequests that assured her great wealth as Dowager Queen after his passing.

King Henry moved court from Greenwich to Whitehall Palace after New Years 1546/47, where he remained to the end of his life. Rumors of impending death of Henry VIII filtered out of the palace beginning early in January. However, he clung to life in misery long after his physicians had given up hope that anything more could be done for him.

A week before he died Henry created a Regency Council of four who would rule for his son during the minority years of King Edward VI. The Regency Council included the prince's uncle, Edward Seymour Duke of Somerset, who would be chief with the title of *Lord Protector*, assisted by Thomas Cranmer Archbishop of Canterbury, John Dudley Duke of Northumberland, and Thomas Wriothesley Lord Chancellor. Henry knew that all in the Regency Council, even Wriothesley, would be amenable to reforming the Church of England.

So, be it. That was for them to decide.

It is thought that Katherine was offended by being omitted from the king's Regency Council. She probably hoped to have influence on the child-King Edward VI who loved her. However, in 1547, to have a woman with real power was the last thing male members of the Council desired.

On January 26, Henry suffered acute vascular respiratory distress. It possibly was caused by a blood clot from his ulcerated leg. Many historians suspect that syphilis may have been a contributing factor to his death. In keeping with prevailing custom, which maintained that 'death of a king is man's business,' some reports say that Katherine had no personal contact with Henry after January 10, and that no women were present in his last hours.

However, it is a matter of record that in King Henry's last hours, when Archbishop Cranmer administered Extreme Unction to Great Harry, Lady Mary was at his bedside. Dying King Henry showed affection for Queen Katherine by saying to her and others around him, "It is God's will that we should part . . . I order all these gentlemen to treat you as if I were living still, and if it should be your pleasure to marry again, I order that you shall have £ 7,000 for your service as long as you live, and all your jewels and ornaments."

Henry VIII, at age fifty-six, died a few hours before dawn on January 28, 1547 at Whitehall Palace. Prince Edward and Lady Elizabeth were brought to London, and Edward was acknowledged to be King Edward VI on January 31, 1547.

Preparations for the funeral of King Henry VIII required a fortnight to complete. During that time, the king's body lay in state at Whitehall. Then, beginning on February 14, two days were required to move his ponderous casket the twenty-plus miles from central London to Windsor Castle. Burial took place with great ceremony in St. George's Chapel on February 16. 1547. King Henry was placed in a tomb shared with Queen Jane Seymour. Legend says that during the overnight stop at Syon Abbey on the way to Windsor, his casket dripped blood, and dogs were seen licking it up the following morning.

Sic transit gloria mundi—Thus, passeth worldly acclaim.

Whether, as some say, Henry VIII was a monster in life, Great Harry has remained among the most colorful and most memorable personalities in English history.

Dowager Queen Katherine Parr occupied a high social position after King Henry VIII died. Her status in court was *First Woman in the Realm.* Etiquette ruled she would keep that position until Edward VI married, and had his own queen—however, he died at age sixteen without marrying.

Katherine had neither political influence after Henry VIII died, nor contact with child-King Edward VI, who was carefully isolated to prevent any influence from outside his Regency Council.

Katherine moved to her private estate Old Chelsea Manor in southwest London. Dowager Queen Katherine, as an attractive thirty-four year old matron of great status and wealth, possessed splendid qualifications for remarriage at the highest level. Forty-four year old Lord Thomas Seymour Baron of Sudeley returned to London after Great Harry died, and Katherine lost no time in letting him know that he was much in her favor.

Lord Thomas Seymour was consumed with ambition. Before he went to Dowager Queen Katherine, he first courted thirty-one year old Catholic Lady Mary, but she rejected him out-of-hand for being a convert to detested Protestantism. He then went to thirteen year old Lady Elizabeth. With sweet words of unmistakable intent, he asked, "Am I to be the most happy, or the most miserable of men?" Princess Elizabeth, with wisdom beyond her years, said that she was too young and innocent to understand such matters.

Only after having been rejected by a two princesses, Lord Thomas Seymour turned to the welcoming arms of Dowager Queen Katherine.

Katherine Parr and Thomas Seymour were secretly engaged in March 1547, but the Council of Regents would not grant permission for them to marry. In April, Thomas obtained direct permission to marry from King Edward VI who had great affection for Katherine, and for his Uncle Thomas. King Edward VI concluded with, "I do love and admire you with my whole heart. Wherefore, if there be anything wherein I may do you a kindness, either in word, or deed, I will do it willingly."

Katherine Parr and Thomas Seymour were privately married at Chelsea Palace near the end of April or early May 1547. Their marriage was kept secret for several weeks, but was known at court by the end of May. Lady Mary disapproved of the poor taste Queen Katherine Parr exhibited in marrying Thomas Seymour less than three months after the death of King Henry VIII—proper etiquette ruled that she stay in mourning for at least a year for her dead husband.

The married coupled remained at Chelsea Manor, and invited fourteen year old Lady Elizabeth to take up residence with them. She gladly accepted. Ten year old Lady Jane Grey also joined them as their ward. Dowager Queen Katherine supervised the education and activities of the two royal girls while they were in residence.

Soon after the royal wards entered the Chelsea household, Katherine's husband Lord Thomas Seymour began a seemingly playful practice of awakening Lady Elizabeth by tickling her with unsuitable familiarity that became evermore questionable. Elizabeth's chief lady-in-waiting testified at an inquiry by the Privy Council that Lord Thomas, who was often dressed scantily in only his nightshirt, would "enter Elizabeth's chamber in the morning, climb into her bed, and tickle her," She was so upset and shocked by his behavior that she "resolved not to leave Elizabeth alone with him."

Several months later in 1547, Dowager Queen Katherine surprised her husband and Lady Elizabeth embracing. Feeling betrayed in her own home, Katherine asked Lady Elizabeth to leave her household in the spring of 1548.

Elizabeth was devastated at losing the only 'emotional mother' she ever had. Elizabeth wrote a letter requesting forgiveness, but the former deep affection between Katherine and Elizabeth was never fully restored. Katherine replied to Elizabeth, "God has given you great qualities. Cultivate them always, and labor to improve them, for I believe you are destined by Heaven to be Queen of England."

Many believed that Thomas Seymour, as a means of enhancing his position in court, was actually courting Elizabeth with a hope of marrying her at some future date.

Lady Jane Grey remained at Chelsea Manor, and continued her education with Dowager Queen Katherine. Lord Thomas had purchased the title of wardship for Lady Jane from her parents. Thus, Lady Jane was an official resident at Chelsea Manor. Lord Thomas Seymour perused unsuccessful plans to marry Lady Jane to King Edward VI. They were of nearly the same age. The ulterior motive behind this scheme probably was to win an appointment at head of government as Chancellor after the young king reached his majority in about five years, and would then exercise his own full right to rule.

The remainder of Katherine Parr's life, which had expectation of great promise, soon ended in tragedy. At age thirty-five, some time after New Years Revels of 1548, Queen Katherine knew she was pregnant. That may have been her deciding factor to abandon court life, and move from London to her husband's estate at Sudeley Castle in Gloucestershire. She waited there for birth of her child. A daughter named Mary was born on August 30, 1548. At the christening, Lady Jane Grey served as godmother. However, Katherine Parr died from puerperal fever birth complications only a week later on September 5, 1548.

Katherine Parr was buried in St. Mary's Chapel at Sudeley Manor. Lady Jane Grey was chief mourner. Katherine Parr's tomb still exists; however, it is not the one in which she was buried. Late in the 19th century, St. Mary's Chapel on the Sudeley Manor estate was rebuilt, and a new marble tomb for Queen Katherine was placed in it near the altar, where visitors may see it today.

Queen Katherine Parr's will, which had been prepared months before her death, left everything she owned to Thomas Seymour. Her newborn daughter inherited nothing.

Lord Thomas Seymour Baron of Sudeley and Lord High Admiral, was more knave than noble. He returned to court in London after his wife Katherine died in September 1548. He was jealous of his older brother

Edward Seymour Duke of Somerset who had been named in the will of King Henry VIII to be Lord Protector and Chief of the Regency Council. Thomas Seymour was driven by political ambition, and was determined to replace his brother at the apex of power. However, his own dishonesty and the political maneuvering of others, with even more ambition, led to his imprisonment in the Tower of London in January 1549. He was accused of treason, condemned by Act of Attainder, and Thomas Seymour was executed by beheading on March 20, 1549.

The fate of Queen Katherine and Lord Thomas Seymour's infant daughter Lady Mary Seymour is tragic and uncertain. She was orphaned when only six months old after her father Lord Thomas Seymour Baron of Sudeley was beheaded for treason and his estate was confiscated to the crown. The infant Lady Mary Seymour was given as ward to a relative. Since she had no inheritance in her own name, no funds were available for her care. Being orphaned, even of parents at the highest social level, was hazardous for survival in the 16th century, an age of turmoil and greedy ambition. Reports differ in saying that the infant Lady Mary Seymour may have died in infancy (possibly at age two or three), or of living obscurely until mature. In that event, she may have married, and had children.

The life of Katherine Parr leaves an impression of a woman of superior ability and character. She was admirable for accepting responsibility for others above her own desires. She leaves her major mark on history in the guidance she gave to the education of Princess Elizabeth, and for the example of mature rectitude she provided as Elizabeth's mentor. For her time, Katherine Parr stands out as a person of true scholarly ability, and of ethical principle in public life that was far, far superior to her much more famous and notorious husband King Henry VIII.

REIGN 21

CHILD-KING EDWARD VI

Summary of the Reign of Edward VI (Reign 1547-1553)

> King Edward VI: life dates c. 16 years, b. October 12, 1537-d. July 6, 1553; King of England c. 6 years, January 26, 1547-July 6, 1553; not married, no queen consort.

KING EDWARD VI (1537-1553) before becoming king was known as Edward of Cornwall. He was the son of Henry VIII and Jane Seymour. His birth was difficult, and possibly required partial Caesarean section to complete his removal from her womb. His birth was fatal for his mother who died within a fortnight after his birth. The child was sickly from birth, and his father King Henry VIII insisted that the prince must be given utmost care in isolation from court.

Queen Katherine Parr, the last wife of King Henry VIII, supervised the prince's later schooling. She appointed leading Protestant scholars from Cambridge to be his tutors. His precocity in learning beyond his years was the occasion of much comment and admiration. Prince Edward was a child of barely ten when he came to the throne. As chief regent, Edward Seymour Duke of Somerset and Protector of the Realm immediately took steps to move the Church of England strongly into the Protestant camp.

Changes for the Church of England were first enunciated clearly in 1549 in Archbishop Cranmer's *First Book of Common Prayer*. For the first time, it gave a clear exposition of Anglican differences from the traditional Catholic dogma and order of service, and the qualities of the English Church that diverged uniquely from Protestant trends in Continental Europe. The Church of England kept the English monarch as head of the Church, and it retained the Catholic hierarchy of priesthood of Archbishops, Bishops, and Priests. However, the *Second Book of Common Prayer* specifically declared that, in raising the Host in Mass, transubstantiation was symbolic, and not a literal change of bread and wine into the body of Christ.

All manner of decorative imagery (saintly pictures, statues, stained glass windows) were ordered removed, or painted over in all chapels, churches, and cathedrals.

In the six and a half years of his reign, King Edward VI became ever more fanatically Protestant in his personal beliefs. Only with great reluctance, Edward approved the parliamentary dispensation that gave his half-sister Lady Mary the right to celebrate the Catholic Mass in the privacy of her own court. Edward was convinced that the crown of England, above all, should defend and spread the word of God. The first three years of the reign of Edward VI mark establishment of the Church of England as an authentic Protestant creation.

By Great Harry's will, which had been approved into law by Parliament, as surely as night follows day, Lady Mary would follow Edward to the throne. The fate and fortune of Protestants in power rested on the shaky foundation of the deteriorating fragile health of Edward VI.

King Edward was known to be dying by 1551. The struggle for power and the scheming for continuation of a Protestant government after Edward's death dominated the last two years of his brief reign. Political ambitions of Edward's regents quickly surfaced between Lord Protector Edward Seymour and John Dudley Earl of Warwick (later Duke of Northumberland). The former friends and compatriots became opponents in competing for parliamentary leadership. Dudley retained his authority over Parliament until the end of the reign of Edward VI. King Edward VI was a pawn of the powers that managed him, and he was not accountable for the evils surrounding him.

When it became abundantly clear that Edward had only weeks to live, he was persuaded by John Dudley Protector of the Realm, to choose his Protestant cousin Lady Jane Grey to be his successor. The king readily agreed, and King Edward used his waning powers to persuade the Protestant Privy Council to approve Lady Jane's right to reign. In this, Edward bypassed his half-sisters Princesses Lady Mary and Lady Elizabeth, and rejected the line of succession approved by Parliament in the will of his father Henry VIII: Great Harry had placed Lady Jane in the last place after Mary and Elizabeth, not in first position in his order of succession.

Rumors of his passing surfaced day by day, but they were not accepted as anything more than the usual speculations on the king's declining health. After a reign of barely six years, King Edward VI died painfully at age fifteen, probably from tuberculosis, and other complications. King Edward VI died at dusk on July 6, 1553 at Greenwich Palace.

King Edward VI, age 15, was unmarried, without issue, and he was buried in the Henry VII Chapel at Westminster Abbey. His second cousin, Lady Jane Grey succeeded him for nine days as the Queen Regnant Jane of England.

REIGN 22

QUEEN LADY JANE GREY

AND

HUSBAND GUILFORD DUDLEY

Narrative of Queen Lady Jane Grey
(Reign July 10-19, 1553)

Queen Lady Jane Grey: life dates c. 18 years, b. October 1537-d. February 12, 1554; married to Guilford Dudley 8 months, May 21, 1553-February 12, 1554; Queen Regnant of England 9 days, July 10-July 19, 1553.

LADY JANE Grey is known to history as *The 9-day Queen* when the start of her reign is calculated from July 10, the day she was proclaimed queen by John Dudley Duke of Northumberland. Less often she is called *The 13-day Queen* based on July 6 the day Edward VII died and his reign ended. Whatever the case, her reign ended on July 19, 1553. She was never crowned, and had no personal lasting influence on events that happened after her brief elevation to the throne. Many histories of the English monarchs do not credit her with ever being a queen regnant, but only with being a failed contestant for that honor. Those who consider

Lady Jane to be a true queen point out that Queen Lady Jane should be credited also as being the *First Queen Regnant of England.*

Lady Jane's proximity to the throne rested on her descent from her great-grandfather King Henry VII, by his youngest daughter Mary Tudor, a sister of Henry VIII. Mary Tudor married Charles Brandon Duke of Suffolk, and they were the parents of Frances Brandon, who was Lady Jane's mother.

Lady Jane Grey was the eldest daughter of Henry Grey III Marquess of Dorset and Frances Brandon Duchess of Suffolk. Most likely, she was born on an uncertain date in October 1537 at her parents' estate Bradgate Park north of London near Leicester. She was christened Jane in honor of Queen Jane Seymour, and was born only a few weeks before Jane Seymour died after giving birth to Prince Edward of Cornwall (later King Edward VI).

Jane's parents were rigidly authoritarian, and their children were expected to perform at near perfection without praise or commendation. Their mother Duchess Francis Brandon disapproved of overt expressions of affection, and almost sadistically favored beating her children often as an incentive for learning. Jane and her two sisters respected, but feared and did not love their parents. Jane sought refuge in books and study. She was intelligent, and had a gift for mastering languages. She received a good general education in history, science, religion, and became a staunch Protestant.

At the age of nine, Jane moved to London as a guest and ward of Queen Katherine Parr who acted as her guardian and mentor. Jane studied with scholars Queen Katherine employed for education of Princess Elizabeth and Prince Edward. When Jane was twelve, in addition to English, she could read, write, and speak French, Italian, Latin, Greek, and a little Hebrew. The tutor Roger Ascham of Cambridge University praised the royal girls, Lady Elizabeth and Lady Jane, as paragons of scholarship.

In contrast to life with her own parents, Lady Jane loved life in the palace with Queen Katherine Parr. Jane confessed to Ascham, " . . . when I am in the presence of either father or mother, whether I speak, keep silence, sit, stand, or go, eat, drink, be merry, or sad, be sewing, playing, dancing, or doing anything else, I must do it as it were in such weight, measure, and number, even so perfectly as God made the world; or else I am so sharply taunted, so cruelly threatened, yes [punished] sometimes with pinches, nips, and bobs, and other ways . . . that I think myself in hell."

Jane was a great favorite of her cousins, the royal children of Henry VIII (Lady Elizabeth and Prince Edward). After Henry VIII died early in 1547, Lady Jane continued to live with Dowager Queen Katherine when she married Thomas Seymour, and left court to live at Chelsea Manor. Lady Jane was an official resident at Chelsea Manor until Dowager Queen Katherine Parr died only a few days after birth of her only child in 1548. Lady Jane at age eleven was the chief mourner at Queen Katherine's funeral. The years Jane spent with Katherine Parr, from ages nine to twelve, were the happiest of her life.

After Queen Katherine's death, Jane returned to the home of her parents. However, in 1548, Lord Thomas Seymour bought wardship of Lady Jane from her parents with the possible political motive of arranging her marriage to her cousin King Edward VI who was of nearly the same age. It is thought that through their marriage, Thomas Seymour hoped to gain enough influence on the young king and queen to win appointment as Chancellor at head of government, when his nephew King Edward VI reached his majority in about five years. However, that never happened. Thomas Seymour fell afoul of the law, and was hanged for embezzlement and treason in 1549.

After Thomas Seymour's fall from favor, Lord John Dudley Duke of Northumberland the Lord Protector and head of Parliament bought Lady Jane's warship from her parents. Thereafter, Duke John Dudley had legal responsibility for Jane's future. His motive for getting control of Lady Jane as his ward was closely linked to the matter of royal succession after Edward VI died. However, Duke John Dudley's purpose in gaining control of Lady Jane was much different than that of Thomas Seymour—Dudley intended to make Lady Jane the reigning queen of England—not the Queen Consort of King Edward VI.

The will of Henry VIII approved of Parliament in 1546 placed Lady Jane as third in the line of succession for the crown after Prince Edward became King Edward VI: that is, first in place was Lady Mary, then Lady Elizabeth, and last Lady Jane Grey. This was the first time since the Norman Conquest that there was no male heir close in succession for the throne. Probability approached certainty that the next monarch of England would be a reigning queen.

The Protestants that ruled Parliament knew that when King Edward VI died, their only way to stay in power and preserve the Anglican Church would be to prevent Catholic Princess Mary from coming to the throne after her half-brother's death. Princess Mary was a devout Catholic; if she became queen, she was certain to restore the 'Old Faith of Rome' to England.

Protestant hope in the future rested on Lady Jane Grey—she was a child of royal birth; she already was approved for the royal succession—she was a strong Protestant. Some way must be found for Lady Jane to replace Princess Mary as the next ruling monarch of England.

Frances Brandon Duchess of Suffolk, Lady Jane's mother, was exceedingly ambitious. She resented the precedence Princess Mary and Princess Elizabeth had to the throne over that of herself and her daughter Jane. Parliament had declared both princesses to be bastards. Even their father King Henry VIII, although he had admitted paternity of them, had shown no inclination to declare Lady Mary or Lady Elizabeth legitimate after Prince Edward was born. In Lady Brandon's mind, her daughter Lady Jane had the clear right to follow King Edward VI to the throne. Lady Brandon was determined to have her eldest daughter Lady Jane become the reigning Queen of England.

In 1551, John Dudley Duke of Northumberland grasped the title Lord Protector as head of government, after which he had the power of the king himself, but his powers lasted only while King Edward was underage and still living—Duke Dudley's powers only acted 'for the King.'

In April 1552, sickly King Edward contracted measles and smallpox from which he barely escaped death. Thereafter his health steadily declined. Serious concern arose that he was not long for this world.

Early in 1553, Duke John Dudley and Lady Jane's parents began examining the advantages of a marriage between fifteen year old Lady Jane and seventeen year old Lord Guilford Dudley who was Duke John Dudley's youngest son. The advantages to the respective parents were that after King Edward died, which was imminent, Lady Jane Grey would be put forward as Queen Regnant. Then, John Dudley Duke of Northumberland would be the father-in-law of the Queen. If that happened, his place at the head of government would be secure. Parliament would remain Protestant, and the Church of England would be preserved.

King Edward's health steadily worsened after the New Year in 1553. Imperative plans for the Dudley-Grey wedding moved rapidly to final marriage vows. Jane's parents surprised Jane with news that she had just been promised in marriage to Guilford Dudley, the youngest son of John Dudley Duke of Northumberland who held Jane's warship.

Lady Jane knew Guilford Dudley, and disliked him. He was poorly educated, adolescently immature, devoid of intellectual curiosity, lacking in religious conviction, and had no depth of character of any kind. She told her parents she would not, and could not marry Guilford. He was a fifth son with no expectation of ever having a title of his own. Anyway, she was already promised to Lord Edward Seymour Earl of Hertford. Jane's parents informed Jane that they had canceled the Hertford premarital agreement, and she would, indeed, marry Guilford Dudley! Jane sullenly agreed to the marriage, but only after several beatings from her parents, and commands from Duke John Dudley who held her wardship. She knew that, when one is *royal*, one has no right to choose whom one marries.

Lady Jane Grey and Sir Guilford Dudley were married on May 21, 1553. She was sixteen, and he was almost eighteen years old. The wedding was at Durham House a London residence of the Duke of Northumberland. Ailing King Edward was invited to attend the grand affair. He sent regrets that he could not attend because of illness (after sight informs us that King Edward had only forty-seven days, a little less than seven weeks, to live). The wedding took place so precipitously that there was insufficient time for a suitable wedding dress to be made for Jane. Her wedding gown was borrowed from the Royal Master of Wardrobe. Jane and Guilford knew nothing of any underlying political purpose behind their union. The newlyweds did not immediately begin living together; after the wedding, the bride and groom returned to their own homes with their parents.

The wheels for John Dudley Duke Northumberland's *coup d'état* were turning. If all continued as planned, his son, Guilford would soon be King Consort, possibly even Co-monarch. Duke John Dudley's own social and political position as chief in government would be unassailable. For England, it would be a smooth transition of one Protestant monarch to the next. There would be no upheaval in government. Duke John Dudley was in a position of power to make it work. However, King Edward must live long enough to let it happen as planned—otherwise, Northumberland's power would vanish with death of King Edward, because Dudley was *only acting for the king*.

Dying King Edward was a fanatic Protestant, and the duke had no difficulty getting him to name his cousin Lady Jane to be his successor, for she also was a fervent Protestant.

The first evidence of trouble ahead came soon after the marriage of Lady Jane and Guilford Dudley took place in mid May. In addition to getting the king's approval of Lady Jane's succession, Northumberland learned that he also needed the Chief Justice for Courts of Law to rule that the change was legal.

Duke John Dudley secretly presented to the Chief Justice his plan to put Lady Jane on the throne. The Chief Justice examined the proposal with two associate judges. With regret and trembling in fear, they told Dudley that, without advance parliamentary approval, his plan would be treasonous.

Duke John Dudley frantically tried to get Parliament to approve Lady Jane as Queen. However, he had few loyal personal fiends in power. Everyone in high places knew the death of King Edward would cancel all Northumberland's power. At this perilously unsettled time, members in Parliament were unwilling to declare for either Lady Jane or Lady Mary, for fear later of being accused of treason. Dudley was only able to get parliamentary approval by acclamation for Lady Jane to be queen. Parliament would not be coerced into giving an official headcount vote. That was the best Dudley could do without more time.

In desperation at mid June with certainty that Edward had only a few more weeks to live, Dudley tried to complete his plans for the palace *coup d'état*. If his plan failed, John Dudley Duke of Northumberland had most to lose; he was the one who engineered the treasonous events to bring Protestant Lady Jane to the crown after Edward VI died.

John Dudley tried to lure Lady Mary and Lady Elizabeth to London on a pretext of seeing their dying brother. He needed to have them secure in the Tower of London to isolate them from the support of protesters, who were sure to arise, when Lady Jane was put forward as queen. However, friends warned the princesses to stay away from London, and Dudley failed to capture either Lady Mary or Lady Elizabeth.

Lady Elizabeth was at Hatfield House. She sent regrets to Dudley, which said that she was so ill "I expected to be in Heaven to greet him, when my brother Edward enters Paradise."

Lady Mary fled to Norfolk, and appeared ready for escape to France. However, she knew that if she left England, it would be taken as evidence that she had abdicated her right to rule.

King Edward VI died on July 6, but his death was kept secret and not proclaimed for days until July 10 when he was buried in Westminster Abbey with little fanfare.

On that same day, John Dudley Duke of Northumberland announced that an important proclamation would be made at a grand occasion at his Syon House Palace. All persons in high office and the peerage were ordered to attend. The assembled court expected that the new monarch would be presented. Most assumed that Lady Mary would be named queen. No one outside Duke John Dudley's Privy Council suspected that he was attempting to break Great Harry's will, which had the force of law supported by previous parliamentary approval.

That is also what Lady Jane expected when she entered the great hall at Syon House, with everyone dressed to the nines all around. When she entered, she had not yet learned that King Edward had died, for knowledge of it had been suppressed for four days. She was astonished and embarrassed as persons came up to her and kneeled, or kissed her hand. She was confused when even her parents showed honor by bowing to her.

Duke John Dudley came forward, and made a long speech that ended with a statement that King Edward, shortly before his death, had named Lady Jane to be his successor, and that Parliament had approved.

Lady Jane was then proclaimed queen, everyone knelt, and acknowledged her to be Queen of England. She was in shock as she was led to a throne at the end of the great hall. Her mother ordered her to take the seat of royal honor. Her husband Guilford Dudley, and his father and mother the Duke and Duchess of Northumberland took places at one side of the throne. Jane's parents Henry Grey and Frances Brandon the Duke and Duchess of Suffolk stood on the other side. She knew her destiny only seconds before she was proclaimed queen. Gradually the realization came, and she finally knew that she, not Lady Mary, was being honored.

At first, Jane broke into tears with sobbing. Finally, she was able to say, "The crown is not my right. It pleaseth me not. The Lady Mary is the rightful heir."

After her presentation as queen, she was carried by boat to the Tower of London for residence in the royal apartments in the White Tower, as was the custom for a monarch who awaited coronation.

A flotilla of private boats accompanied her down the Thames from Syon House to the Tower of London. The banks were crowded with onlookers, but most of them were strangely silent. They did not hail their new queen boisterously as was the usual way for Englishmen to greet their monarch. An observer described Jane, "[She was] very short and thin, but prettily shaped and graceful. She has small features, and a well-made nose, the mouth flexible and the lips red. The eyebrows are arched and darker than her hair, which is nearly red. Her eyes are sparkling, and reddish-brown in color . . . [her face with] freckled skin, and sharp white teeth . . . she wore a green velvet gown stamped in gold."

At first, Lady Jane repeatedly protested that Lady Mary was the rightful queen after her half-brother King Edward died, and that she did not want the crown. Therefore, Jane had to be convinced that she was *in fact* the rightful queen.

She was told truthfully that, although Henry VIII had given first and second positions to Lady Mary and Lady Elizabeth in the order of succession, neither King Henry nor Parliament had ever repealed the separate acts that declared them bastards. Therefore, in the eyes of the law, they were still bastards, and therefore both were ineligible to reign. Thus, since Jane was legally next in line for the crown, Parliament had declared by acclamation that she was the queen. Therefore, she legally, justly, honestly, truly was the queen!

On July 11, the day after Jane was proclaimed queen, the Privy Council sent orders to Princess Mary and Princess Elizabeth (addressing them as bastards and unfit to rule) that they must recognize Lady Jane as the true Queen of England. The Bishop of London echoed the same sentiments in his Sunday sermon in Westminster Abbey.

All went well that day, until a currier delivered a letter to the Privy Council from Princess Mary, which had been written in Norfolk two days earlier. In the letter, Mary announced that she was Queen of England, and "[We hope] to be accepted without rancor or blood shed."

The Protestants in Parliament, knowing that Princess Mary had never bowed to the will of Great Harry her father, also knew that she was far less inclined to take orders from any heretical Protestant lackeys in government. They had expected, and now they knew that the Protestants in power would be challenged in a struggle of 'winner takes all.'

In a futile gesture of false diplomacy, Duke John Dudley sent two of his sons (Ambrose and Robert Dudley) to meet Lady Mary on her way from Norfolk to London, in hope that they would be able to convince her to accept as *fait accompli Lady Jane was Queen,* or even better, to capture Mary. However, Dudley's sons were unable to meet Mary. She was forewarned, and took refuge in the walled fortress Framlingham Castle a stronghold of the Catholic Duke of Norfolk.

The failure of the Dudley brothers in their mission to accost Lady Mary, and to remove her from contention, probably saved their lives. If they had been successful in their purpose, they would surely have been accused of treason, and sentenced to death after Lady Mary became queen. If that had happened, English history would have been deprived of one of its great romances—Robert Dudley Earl of Leicester was fated to be the favorite great love of Queen Elizabeth I.

The next few days were a flurry of activity. Royal decrees went out that were signed by Queen Jane. They were written on recommendations by advisors around her. All her advice came from frantic Protestants who were desperate to protect their wealth, power, and lives from the wrath of Lady Mary, should she became queen. No concern was given for Jane's well being. As an innocent child, she was unable to recognize or sidestep the traps that soon destroyed her.

In her first days after she accepted her roles as queen, Jane recognized her need to look the part of a queen. She was slightly over four feet tall, and chose to wear chipines (a platform shoe that added about four inches to her height) to enhance her semblance of majesty. Because she was so petite, Jane was fitted for a crown, since all on hand were too large for her small head. She again protested, "But the crown has never been demanded . . . by me, or by anyone in my name." A remark was dropped that another crown would also be needed for her husband Guilford. When she learned that her husband expected to become the king, and that her approval was needed for him to receive that honor, Jane protested strenuously. She said she might create him a duke, but never a king—that would require Parliament to decide. Guilford started to cry, and said, "I will not be duke! I will be king!" He ran out crying to get reassurance from his mother.

In the next days, self-serving advisors persuaded Queen Jane to issue a proclamation to the people of London and all England. It read, "You will endeavor yourself in all things to the uttermost of your power, to defend Our just title to the Crown, but also assist Us to disturb, repel, and resist, the feigned untrue claim of the Lady Mary, a bastard daughter of Our Great-uncle Henry the Eighth of famous memory. "signed, *Jane the Queen.*

The proclamation would be a death sentence for treason after Queen Mary came to power.

On July 13, the Privy Council realized there was little public support for Lady Jane, and that the citizens of London overwhelmingly preferred Lady Mary to be their queen. Duke John Dudley decided to go out of London to raise militia in support of Queen Jane to confront and repel Mary, who was thought to be advancing on Westminster.

Dudley left London on July 14 intent on raising countrywide hue and cry support for Queen Jane to oppose Lady Mary. John Dudley faced public apathy, and he was unable to convince the common people to take up arms against Lady Mary, even though the religious sympathy of many of them was Puritan, and they opposed Catholicism. Instead, Lady Mary's declaration to be the true Queen of England received a spontaneous groundswell of support from the countryside, and in the City of London. As days passed, earls and dukes raised a great militia that grew in size from town to town as they moved on London.

Lady Mary remained at Framingham Castle, but she took time to meet, and encourage the growing number of persons who flocked to her cause. Some were those who were sent by Dudley to capture her, but then defected, and became her supporters.

On July 19—just nine days after Lady Jane was proclaimed queen—the Lord Mayor of London proclaimed Lady Mary to be Queen of England. Duke John Dudley was absent from London while he tried to raise support for Queen Jane. Without Dudley's leadership, and under pressure of public sentiment in support of Lady Mary, the Privy Council at first vacillated, but finally agreed to give Lady Mary its verbal approval.

When Queen Jane learned that the Lord Mayor had declared for Lady Mary, she ordered guards in the Tower to lock the gates, but they would not obey. When her father Henry Grey Duke of Suffolk told Jane that she must give up her crown, and return to private life, she said, "[I only] accepted the crown out of obedience to you and my mother . . . I most willingly relinquish it now." An apocryphal tale said that when Jane was told she was no longer queen, she asked, "Can I go home now?"

Lady Jane never left the Tower of London. She waited until evening of July 19 in the royal suite with a few of her ladies-in-waiting. Near dusk, jailors came to remove her from the royal apartment to a prison elsewhere in the Tower on July 19. She was deposed officially by act of Parliament on July 22.

Lady Mary left Framingham Castle for London on July 25, and entered London in triumph with a great assembly of titled peers on August 3. Her half-sister Princess Elizabeth and Dowager Queen Anne of Cleves accompanied Lady Mary to London when she became queen.

In a very short time, Jane's husband Guilford Dudley, most members of the Grey and Dudley families, and many others, who had conspired to deprive Queen Mary of her rightful crown, joined Jane as prisoners in the Tower of London. Most were charged with felonious treason for parts they played in advancing Lady Jane to the throne, but Queen Mary pardoned most of them later. However, John Dudley Duke of Northumberland, and a few other high conspirators in the *coup d'état* were executed in November after Mary was firmly in power.

Lady Jane and her husband Guilford Dudley were held in the Tower for about half a year in comfortable but separate living accommodations. Three ladies-in-waiting attended Jane, and she and Guilford were allowed to meet occasionally. Their common experiences of loneliness and desperation in prison, for the first time, brought them together in real affection. Both were charged with treason, and had received a sentence of death, but the sentences were suspended awaiting Queen Mary's direct approval. Their fates were uncertain until the abortive Thomas Wyatt Rebellion in January 1554 threatened to overthrow Queen Mary, and restore Lady Jane to the throne.

The Wyatt Rebellion was a strong protest to Mary's announced intention to marry King Philip II of Spain, and to make him co-reigning King of England. Jane's Father Henry Grey Marquess of Dorset and Duke of Suffolk was an active participant in the Wyatt Rebellion. After the rebellion was put down, he was charged with treason, and imprisoned. Queen Mary's advisors persuaded her to approve the execution of Lord Henry Grey, and also Lady Jane and Guilford Dudley, because Lady Jane, while still living, would always be a focus for insurgency, unrest, and a threat to Mary's crown.

Innocent though they were, the children's deaths were needed for tranquility of the realm. Less than a week after the Wyatt Rebellion was put down, Jane and Guilford were executed.

On the morning of February 12, 1554, eighteen year old Guilford Dudley was taken to Tower Hill, the usual place in London for execution of traitors by beheading. His head and body were carried back to the Tower of London in an open cart. Jane saw it pass by the White Tower for burial in the Chapel of St. Peter ad Vincula. She cried out his name, "Guilford, Guilford," and probably added a prayer of benediction for God to show mercy on his soul.

Jane's execution was scheduled for the same morning. Queen Mary gave permission that Jane's execution would be private inside the Tower walls on Tower Green in deference to her royal status.

Jane was sixteen or seventeen years old. She faced death with dignity, grace, and gave no evidence of terror or fear. On the scaffold, she made a statement that admitted her guilt by consenting to be made queen, but she pled innocence of wanting the crown, or of being part of the conspiracy to deprive Lady Mary of her throne. Jane said, " . . . touching the procurement and desire . . . [for the crown], I do wash my hands thereof in innocence, before God, and you, good Christian people . . . ." She then read Psalm 51:1, "Have mercy upon me, O God, according to thy loving kindness, and according unto the multitude of thy tender mercies, blot out my transgressions."

She then gave a prayer of forgiveness to her executioner who knelt before her. He tied a kerchief around her eyes. He then helped her kneel, and put her head on the block. She said to the axman, "I pray you will dispatch me quickly." She put her arms out and said, "Lord God, into Thy hands do I commend my spirit." Then her neck was severed with one blow of the ax.

Lady Jane and Guilford Dudley were buried within the Tower of London in the Chapel of St. Peter ad Vincula, where two of the queens of Henry VIII (Queens Anne Boleyn and Katherine Howard) were put to rest. A week later her father Henry Grey Duke of Suffolk was executed.

Lady Jane Grey, quasi-queen for only 9 days, is a tragic figure in England's royal history. Foolish ambitious parents exploited her, as did power-hungry Protestants in government, who justly feared a return of Catholic rule that followed the crowning of Princess Mary Tudor.

The present chapter has not labored the issue of whether Lady Jane Grey was a true reigning queen. It is content to outline events in Lady Jane Grey's short tragic life, and to place emphasis on the ruthless powers in court that used her heartlessly in attempts to advance their own goals. Lady Jane was innocent of willful pursuit of the crown in the attempted *coup d'etat* that destroyed her. Jane did not seek the crown. Lady Jane was a pawn used in a hopelessly failed ploy to defeat the coronation of imperiously determined Queen Mary.

Secular history credits Lady Jane with being a minor casualty of power politics. Protestant history, as presented in John Foxe's, *Lives of the Martyrs* (written in the reigns of Mary I and Elizabeth I) places Lady Jane as the first Protestant Martyr of Queen Mary's bloody reign. Almost three hundred lost their lives as heretics while Mary was queen.

REIGN 23

QUEEN REGNANT MARY I

AND

PRINCE CONSORT PHILIP II
OF SPAIN

Narrative of Queen Mary I
(Reign 1553-1558)

Queen Mary I: life dates 42 years, b. February 18, 1516-d.
November 17, 1558: married to Philip II of Spain, January 16,
1556-November 17, 1558; Queen Regnant of England 5 years,
July 19, 1553-November 17, 1558.

QUEEN MARY I was the fifth and only surviving child of six born to Queen Katherine of Aragon and Henry VIII. She was born at Greenwich Palace, Kent, on February 18, 1516, and christened *Mary* in honor of Mary Tudor Duchess of Suffolk, the younger sister of King Henry VIII and the grandmother of Lady Jane Grey. Queen Mary's elevation to the throne completely reversed the life of rejection she had known before in much of her life. Queen Mary is known to history as *Bloody Mary* for the execution of many Protestant heretics in her relentless efforts to nullify her father's Church of England, and return England to the Catholic Church.

In contrast with her parents, Queen Mary was of below average height, and had dark brown eyes and black hair. In her youth, she was considered beautiful 'in a Spanish sort of way.' Like her father Henry VIII, she was born strong willed and imperiously stubborn. Her eyes were piercing and her gaze intense. Her mother Queen Katherine of Aragon supervised her education. Mary was well educated and informed on many subjects. She was fluent in several languages and gifted in music. At the age of four, she played the virginal (a portable tabletop harpsichord) and was complimented in having a "light touch with much grace and velocity." Throughout her life, she enjoyed music and faithfully practiced to improve her mastery of several instruments including the lute and clavichord. From childhood throughout life, she showed a fondness for wild birds, flowers, and the open countryside.

As an adult, Mary had a deep, almost masculine voice, and a clear and forceful way of speaking that commanded attention. She earned respect for the intellect and knowledge that lay behind the words she spoke. Notwithstanding being small, Mary had great dignity and was a logical effective public speaker. She was a sickly child, and introspective to the point of being antisocial.

Mary was deeply offended by the humiliation her mother suffered when her father Henry VIII pursued Anne Boleyn. The shame was even worse when King Henry broke from the Catholic Church, and annulled his marriage to Queen Katherine. By that same action, Mary acquired bastardy for herself.

Princess Mary was betrothed at age six to her cousin Emperor Charles V of the Holy Roman Empire who was twenty-two years old. However, in 1525 when Mary was almost ten, her marriage contract to the Emperor was cancelled. In the same year, Mary was honored by being created Princess of Wales and given Ludlow Castle, the traditional residence of the Prince of Wales on the Welch border. She remained at Ludlow for a year and a half (1526-1527) until she was twelve. She was away from court while friction intensified between her father and mother, as King Henry VIII pursued Anne Boleyn. As time passed, he moved toward separation from Queen Katherine and became more remote from his daughter Mary.

However, King Henry did not neglect his parental responsibility of finding a suitable husband for Princess Mary. Francis I of Savoy and Henry of Orléans were considered, but were soon rejected. Queen Katherine proposed that Mary's groom might be Reginald de la Pole the son of Margaret Plantagenet Duchess of Salisbury. Reginald did not have a title, but he was of royal Plantagenet blood. Twelve year old Mary responded favorably to the thought of marriage to Reginald, but he was deeply religious, and currently was a student priest of Canon Law at the Vatican and had taken vows of chastity. Reginald was sixteen years older than Mary, and he was committed to a life in the priesthood and was not interested in marriage.

Mary's status as prospective Princess of Wales abruptly ended in 1531 when as Henry VIII became committed to getting a divorce from Queen Katherine. For the remainder of the reign of Henry VIII, Mary was excluded from plans for her to be the next reigning monarch of England. Instead, Mary lived outside London with a severely reduced staff of servants and with barely enough money for necessities.

King Henry was determined to have a wife who could give him a son. Anne Boleyn became Henry's queen in 1533, in the same year Princess Elizabeth was born. Princess Mary refused to recognize Anne Boleyn as Queen, or to call her infant daughter Elizabeth *Princess*. Mary's own title was reduced to *Lady Mary*, and her mother became merely *Katherine Dowager Princess of Wales*—that title was in reference to her first brief marriage to Arthur Tudor Prince of Wales, who was the elder brother of Henry VIII.

When Henry put Queen Katherine of Aragon aside, Mary was not permitted to visit or communicate with her mother. Their forced separation for almost six years was a severe penalty for Princess Mary and Queen Katherine. In her isolation from court, Mary continued to practice music, and she was praised for her mastery of the virginal and lute. She also became a proficient seamstress. She made lace, and was praised for fine needlepoint. Mary persisted in improving her command of French, Spanish, Italian, and Latin, and she began the study of Greek.

After Queen Anne Boleyn was executed in 1536, Princess Mary pledged loyalty to her father King Henry, and accepted his claim to be supreme head of the Church of England. Lady Mary did so with a mental reservation that satisfied herself—Great Harry's claim to be head of the Church, might well apply to the Church of England, but it did not apply to the Church of Rome, on which Mary's personal faith rested. Mary steadfastly insisted on having a Catholic Mass said daily in her own court. This expression of Tudor stubbornness imperiled her survival, but she persisted in celebrating the Catholic order of service for herself, and for the small court of loyal retainers and servants, she kept around her.

Lady Mary's lot improved in 1536 when King Henry married Queen Jane Seymour after Queen Anne Boleyn was executed. In a way, it also improved Mary's place in court, for with the execution of Queen Anne Boleyn, her three year old daughter Princess Elizabeth also fell from grace. The two rejected daughters of King Henry now consoled one an other. Mary gracefully accepted responsibility to be the surrogate mother to baby Elizabeth. The two half-sisters lived together in Hatfield House with Mary supervising baby Elizabeth's care and creature comforts.

When Jane Seymour became queen in 1536, she went out of her way to befriend Lady Mary, and she asked King Henry to give permission for Mary to be accepted again in court. The request was not immediately granted, but by 1537, Princess Mary was so well received in court that she was at Hampton Court when Queen Jane gave birth to Prince Edward, and Mary was the chief mourner at Queen Jane Seymour's funeral that came only a few days later.

Mary enjoyed her happiest time in court when Katherine Parr was queen (1543-1547). Queen Katherine was only about four years older than Mary, and they became close friends. At that time, Mary first had her experience of family life. King Henry VIII and his three children—Mary, Elizabeth, and Edward and Lady Jane Grey enjoyed good standing with one another. In his will, Henry VIII left Mary and Elizabeth properties that guaranteed an annual pension of £3000, and reinstated their title of *Princess*, but it did not legitimize them.

When King Henry VIII died on January 28, 1547, Mary was thirty-one, Elizabeth was fourteen, and Prince Edward was nine. They differed greatly in their religious persuasions. Edward was stoutly Protestant; Princess Mary was an undeviating Catholic, and Princess Elizabeth was of uncertain faith.

Prince Edward, now King Edward VI, firmly believed that his sister Mary should not be permitted to continue having private Mass said in her own residence. Around 1550 when Edward was thirteen and in the third year of his reign, he ordered Parliament to inform Mary that she could no longer celebrate Mass in the privacy of her own court.

Mary was ordered to appear in the Council Chamber before judges. Mary was told that her Mass must cease. Mary refused to yield. She demanded her right to worship in whatever way her conscience dictated. She said, "I shall continue to have Mass said every day, or I shall leave England, and go to Spain."

The issue was at impasse, until Mary finally got her way. That happened after the Ambassador of the Holy Roman Empire informed Parliament that, " . . . unless Princess Mary had freedom to celebrate Mass daily, and unless her religious harassment ended, I will leave England." Since his departure would be the equivalent of a declaration of war on England by the Holy Roman Empire, Parliament bowed to political necessity and relented. Mary was permitted to have a priest celebrate Catholic Mass in the privacy of her own court every day, whenever she pleased.

This did not please her brother King Edward VI. He rued the day England bowed to secular need, and did not follow conscience in matters of God's will.

Mary sent word to Edward that she would willingly die before denying her faith, but that in all things not related to religion, she was his obedient servant. Even so, she was punished. Her pension and staff were severely reduced for the remainder of the reign of her half-brother King Edward VI.

In April 1552, King Edward recovered from measles and smallpox that nearly took his life. Thereafter, his health rapidly declined. The court knew he would not long survive.

In May John Dudley Duke of Northumberland, who was chief in government, falsely told Lady Mary that her brother the king was recovering and wished to see her. Mary prepared to go to London from her country home at New Hall, but friends warned Mary to stay away from London. Mary took refuge with loyal Catholics in Norfolk, and escaped Lord Dudley's ruse to capture and imprison her in the Tower of London. Lady Mary took refuge in Franglingham Castle, a stout fortress surrounded by high stone walls, and three motes designed to frustrate invaders. The Catholic Howard family of the Duke of Norfolk quickly rallied around her, and recruited many supporters from the countryside.

Lady Mary was thirty-eight years old when her brother King Edward VI died on July 6, 1553. Most believed that Mary would succeed him to the throne. However, her succession was greatly feared by the established Protestants in control of Parliament. When Mary learned of King Edward's death, she sent word to Parliament that, as queen-designate approved by Parliament, she hoped she would be accepted as queen in good faith for the peace of England.

At this time, her cousin, frail tiny Lady Jane Grey, was going through her 9-day rehearsal to be queen.

On July 19, the Lord Mayor of London proclaimed Mary to be Queen of England. Three days later Parliament gave oral approval of Mary's succession.

On July 22, Lady Jane was officially deposed as queen. When Mary received that information, she left Franglingham Castle on July 24, and arrived in London on August 3. She came with a great militia that pledged loyalty to her. Mary orchestrated her entry into London carefully by insisting that Princess Elizabeth and Dowager Queen Anne of Cleves be part of her triumphal entry into the city. The people of London welcomed her with unrestrained enthusiasm. Parliament approved Mary as Queen of England on July 30, and she began her residence in the Tower of London awaiting coronation on August 3.

On the same day that Lady Mary arrived in London, Queen Jane was deposed, and imprisoned in the Tower of London with her husband Guilford Dudley. Guilford's father John Dudley Duke of Northumberland was taken a few days later. He had served as Lord Protector of the Realm during the last years of the reign of King Edward VI, and he was the primary leader in Parliament who tried to make Lady Jane Grey the Queen. Others, who had treasonously conspired to deprive Queen Mary of her right to reign, were imprisoned, but relatively few of them were later executed.

Deposed Queen Lady Jane Grey and her husband Guilford Dudley were declared traitors, and were held in the Tower. For a time, their fates were uncertain, even though Mary signed warrants for their execution.

In the first days of Mary's reign, she ordered the release of prisoners who were imprisoned for their Catholic belief. Among them was Thomas Howard Duke of Norfolk, the uncle of Queen Katherine Howard and Queen Anne Boleyn. The Duke of Norfolk had been in the Tower of London for almost a decade awaiting execution while Protestants were in power.

Citizens of London and outlying England greeted Queen Mary with guarded acceptance and fear. No one knew what she might do in reprisal against Protestants, or how she would reform of the Church of England, or how she would return England to Catholicism. The Protestant community trembled in apprehension for what the queen might do. In all instances, their worst fears would become reality.

As evidence of things to come, Queen Mary immediately took control of the Church of England. She declared that, like her father King Henry VIII, she alone was the head of the Anglican Church, and that she had supreme right to rule on doctrine for the English Church. Even so, English Common Law required that Parliament, alone, could reverse its prior restraints on celebration of the Mass. Clearly, another act of Parliament was needed to restore legitimacy for Catholicism in England.

Queen Mary's first political act was an order for Parliament to annul all religious laws that selectively favored Protestants and discriminated against Catholics, which had been enacted in the reigns of her father King Henry VIII and her half-brother King Edward VI. Then, as head of the Church of England, she ordered on her own initiative that:

> The Mass would be said in the Catholic manner in all Churches
> of England.
> The *Book of Common Prayer* was heretical and was outlawed.
> The *Act of Uniformity*, which outlawed worship in Catholic
> Churches, was annulled.
> Supremacy over the Church of England, and authority for
> dogma was delegated to the Papal Nuncio (ambassador)
> appointed by the Pope in Rome.
> Archbishop Thomas Cranmer, all other bishop, and priests in
> the Anglican Church were declared heretics.

Mary announced that, all persons who would not admit their heresy, and declare renewed loyalty to the Pope of Rome, would be burned at the stake. As a final act that precluded a whisper of tolerance for opposing her religious views, Mary removed Archbishop Cranmer, and sent him to the Tower to await trial for heresy. Mary then sent a letter to Rome, which requested that Cardinal Reginald de la Pole be made Archbishop of Canterbury and head of the Catholic Church in England

Overnight, England changed from being one of the most progressive Protestant nations in Europe, to one completely subservient to Rome. However, Mary had not yet initiated wide scale executions by burning for heresy.

On the secular side, Mary ordered Parliament to restore legitimacy of her mother's marriage to King Henry VIII, and by extension, to proclaim her own legitimacy. Nevertheless, Mary permitted her half-sibling, Lady Elizabeth, to keep all rights and privileges of bastardy.

Mary was the queen after her brother King Edward VI died in July 1553, but he was laid to rest in Westminster Abbey in rites of the Protestant Anglican Church officiated by Thomas Cranmer Archbishop of Canterbury, in his last official act before he was deposed, and later executed for heresy. Although, Edward was buried in the manner of his Protestant belief, Mary requested that a Catholic Mass be said for him in her royal suit in the Tower of London, to help speed him on his way to Heaven.

Mary's coronation in Westminster Abbey finally took place almost two months later on October 1. The delay in Mary's coronation was forced by her refusal to be crowned in a Protestant ceremony. She waited until Parliament revoked laws prejudicial to Catholicism, so she could be consecrated in the traditional Catholic way of crowning monarchs before her father Henry VIII created the Church of England twenty years before.

The ceremony was magnificent with the full court in formal regalia. Princess Elizabeth and Dowager Queen Anne of Cleves followed Mary from the Tower to Westminster with the remaining peers strung out in a long queue behind them. Mary was the first crowned Queen Regnant of England since Saxon time, a half millennium before. Queen Mary opened Parliament four days later, and asked Parliament to restore her mother Katherine of Aragon's title of Queen of England.

Almost immediately after Mary's coronation, the issue of her marriage became a pressing problem. She was almost thirty-eight years old, and could not hope for more than a few more childbearing years. Several groom nominations from the English nobility were suggested, but none of them was acceptable to Queen Mary.

Emperor Charles V of the Holy Roman Empire, on hearing of Queen Mary's predicament, nominated his son and heir Don Philippe d'Espagne (Prince Philip of Spain) to be Mary's husband.

Mary was overwhelmed with the honor he suggested. Don Philippe had full expectation of becoming the King of Spain with reasonable certainty that he would follow his father as Emperor. Mary had been engaged to his father when she was ten; what a strange world it was that now proposed marriage to his son who was almost twelve years her junior. Mary received a full-length portrait of Don Philippe painted by Titian and instantly fell in love with him. It is said that Mary prayed for guidance about marriage to Don Philippe, and that she had a revelation—*God hath chosen Don Philippe for you!*—thereafter, she was single minded in insisting that he was the only one she could ever marry.

At age twenty-four, Prince Philip was not enchanted with the prospect of marrying his elderly cousin Queen Mary of England. He had a hot, self-indulgent, Mediterranean temperament, and his middle aged diminutive cousin had little appeal for him. Philip's aversion to the marriage was in complete agreement with everyone in England, save the queen. From the highest noble to the lowest serf, no one in England liked or trusted Spain. They all abhorred the idea of having their queen married to a Spaniard.

To make the match much, much less acceptable to England, Mary insisted that her husband would be a Co-monarch—a King with equal power to rule with her. Even her major Catholic advisor Stephen Gardiner Bishop of Winchester stressed the folly of the match. Mary was as stubborn as her father Great Harry, so negotiations progressed briskly to finish the nuptial arrangements. Its provisions, among others, were:

> King Philip and Queen Mary would be co-monarchs of England and Spain.
>
> However, the two nations would be ruled independently.
>
> Only Englishmen would hold public office, or be in the queen's Privy Council.
>
> England would have no obligation to support Spain in foreign wars.
>
> Other complicated details set rules for inheritance by any offspring.

The proposed marriage of Mary Tudor of England to Philip of Spain was publicly announced on January 15, 1554. The announcement was greeted with dismay and anger throughout the land. Within a week, a Sir Thomas Wyatt organized a rebellion. He was a Catholic who strongly protested the Spanish marriage, and openly expressed desire to restore Lady Jane Grey to the throne, because "even an English Protestant was better than having a Spaniard as King Consort of England."

Mary was at Whitehall when Wyatt led his motley brigands into Charing Cross. Mary stoutly stood her ground, and said to loyal retainers around her, "If others durst not stand against the traitors, I shall go out into the field and face the quarrel, and die with those that would serve me."

Her bravery may have turned the tide. In any case, the rebellion was soon repressed. In less than a week, peace was restored. The rebels disbanded, and their leaders were secure in the Tower of London. Most of them would soon be executed for treason.

Lady Jane Grey had been securely confined in the Tower of London throughout the fracas. However, her father Henry Grey Duke of Suffolk openly supported the Wyatt Rebellion, and, being one of the leaders, was among those beheaded. His guilt was a death sentence for his daughter Lady Jane, even though she was innocent of any involvement in the rebellion. Mary's Chancellor Stephen Gardner Bishop of Winchester persuaded Queen Mary that Lady Jane and her husband Guilford Dudley would be a constant focus for insurrection. They were a real and present threat to Mary's very survival. The two innocent teenagers were beheaded on February 10, less than a month after the announcement of Mary's wedding to Philip of Spain, and only two weeks after the Wyatt Rebellion was put down.

Her advisors told Mary that the insurrection came from her own folly in the first months of her reign when she showed forbearance to those that opposed her. Mary resolved, "I shall not be guilty of the error of kindness again." Dozens of leaders in the Wyatt Rebellion were executed, and their heads and body parts were mounted on every gate to London, and at crossroads throughout the land.

More than anything else, her Spanish marriage alienated Queen Mary from her people. She began her reign with tolerance and forbearance, with the intention to be a good just queen, but her better nature never again emerged after her expressed intent to marry Philip precipitated the Wyatt Rebellion.

Mary was always certain that her half-sister Lady Elizabeth was actively involved in fomenting Wyatt's rebellion. Elizabeth was imprisoned in the Tower of London. Mary's fear and distrust of her sister Princess Elizabeth never died. Elizabeth was ordered to stand trial. She defended her innocence without aid of counsel, but Elizabeth could not be proven guilty of conspiracy, and her judges were unable to find her guilty of treasonous plotting against the person of the Queen. Only by the slimmest good fortune was she able to defend herself against charges of treasonous complicity in Wyatt's Rebellion.

Mary banished Elizabeth from court, and sent her to Woodstock near Oxford, and later to Hatfield House, where she was kept under guard to prevent any possibility that she could be involved thereafter in court intrigue. Elizabeth guarded her every act and word to avoid entrapment by anything that could be interpreted as disloyal or treasonous to her sister Queen Mary. Elizabeth was not again formally accused or brought to trial on any charge of disloyalty to the queen.

What may have saved Elizabeth was Mary's thought: Who would take her place in the royal succession, if she died without an heir? The thought of her cousin Mary Queen of Scots—now married to the Dauphin of France, and some day Queen of France, might also one day possibly the Queen of England—an unholy triple alliance of being simultaneously Queen of England, Scotland, and France was impossible to accept. That thought may have given Queen Mary of England sufficient pause to spare her distrusted half-sister Elizabeth's life.

The Wyatt rebellion had a lasting effect on Mary's reign. She never recovered the spontaneous devotion shown by her subjects that brought her to the throne. After the Wyatt Rebellion, she feared her subjects, and trusted no one who was not a Catholic and preferably a foreign Catholic with strong ties to Spain and Rome. Queen Mary developed a deep abiding personal fear and distrust of her subjects. She saw enemies and threat in every shadow that crossed her path. Her stubborn Tudor nature, however, was not diverted from her divinely ordained determination to return England to Catholicism, and to marry Philip of Spain. She was fearful that she was too old to bear children, but she was determined to give England an heir, and thereby deprive the bastard Elizabeth of a chance to rule.

Mary's next crushing disappointment came with her marriage to Philip of Spain. The Pope granted dispensation for the marriage in March 1554. Mary was anxious to move rapidly into marriage, because, she must have a child soon.

Queen Mary married Prince Philip by proxy on March 6 at Whitehall. Philip sent her a jeweled wedding ring, but no letter of affection or devotion. That, of itself, was warning of his lack of enthusiasm for their union. Prince Philip was expected to arrive in England by Pentacost-Whitsontide

(49 days after Easter commemorating descent of the Holy Spirit on the Apostles). He was much overdue, but he sent Mary no explanations for his delay. Finally, after a rough Channel crossing in a tempest of high wind and rain that harassed all southern England, Philip arrived at Southampton, the entry port for Winchester on July 20.

Noble emissaries knelt to greet queasy storm-tossed Philip, and to welcome him to English soil.

Philip thanked them in formal Latin, since neither he nor any in his retinue of grandees understood English. Philip was of average height, and strutted with austere haughty bearing. He had the long nose and face characteristic of the Spanish Habsburgs. His hair was medium brown, and eyes grey with hooded lids implied secretive cunning in the mind behind them. In keeping with court etiquette in Spain, Philip's face was frozen in aloof neutrality that revealed little of what he thought, or felt in a given situation. The twenty-four year old Prince of Spain made a better first impression than was expected, but he irritated his English hosts, by refusing food presented to him. He only ate dishes prepared for him by his own chef. Later, it was learned that he had been forewarned of his unpopularity in England, which made it likely that, eventually, he would be poisoned.

Queen Mary hastened to Winchester for their wedding, because London was considered unsafe and prone to riotous protest. The wedding took place on July 25, 1554 (the same day Philip unknowingly became King Philip II of Spain). Chancellor Stephen Gardner Bishop of Winchester officiated in place of the Archbishop Thomas Cranmer of Canterbury who was imprisoned in the Tower of London awaiting execution for heresy. The marriage was performed with appropriate splendor, and without civil protest. Mary ordered that Philip's name precede hers on the marriage document. They exchanged simple rings, as Mary said, "like any other maid." After a day, the bride and groom journeyed from Winchester to Windsor, and then, after a week, to Richmond Palace on the edge of London.

A full month after their marriage, Philip and Mary made their formal entrance into London on August 28, 1554.

Almost immediately after her return to London, Queen Mary was asked to meet with her Privy Council, and call Parliament to assemble. Public opposition to Mary increased when she announced that her marriage contract with Philip promised that he would be given the title,

Co-monarch King of England. She insisted that Philip's name be included on all State documents she signed. This permanently alienated Parliament from Queen Mary.

Parliament adamantly refused to authorize the title *King*, or give an official coronation for Prince (now King) Philip of Spain. History continues to dispute the fine point of whether Philip was once actually a King of England—Mary surely felt so, but England refused to crown him, and never accepted him as their king. In any case, he had no claim to the English crown himself, even though he was a descendant of John of Gaunt through his daughter Princess Katherine of Castile, who was Philip's grandmother. At best, Philip of Spain was the Prince Consort of Queen Mary I. Whatever his rights to the crown were, they died with Queen Mary.

In London, Queen Mary and Prince Philip took residence behind closed gates at Hampton Court. Mary sincerely wanted a child of her own to love and spoil. She also ardently desired an heir who, she said "should shut her contumacious, dissembling, heretical sister [Elizabeth] out of the succession."

No matter how much she strived to get his affection, and wanted to have his child, Mary never won Philip's love or desire for her.

The single way Mary pleased Philip was in her ability to speak flawless court Castilian Spanish, which the queen had learned at her mother's knee. In all other ways, Mary repelled him. Philip found her to be a repugnant withered relic lacking youth, and without appeal to his fancy. Even though, as Mary believed their marriage was the will of God, it was never more than a sterile contract with little comfort in it for either Mary or Philip.

Philip performed his husband function reluctantly. Mary was convinced she had conceived. Her belief was the first of two false pregnancies that dashed her hopes of ever being a mother. Without children, the only purpose for her marriage to Philip failed. Philip soon rebelled against his role as England's *Royal Stud*, and he returned to Spain to be the real King of Spain in his mother country. He set foot in England only once again, near the end of Mary's reign in 1557. Mary's second false belief that she was pregnant came when Philip returned to England to persuade Mary to have England join Spain in its war with France.

Mary's mission as England's ruling monarch was to save her people from damnation by returning England to Catholicism, which in her view was the only true path to salvation, and to ban the heretical Church of England that her father had created only to get rid of her mother.

Mary knew she could not reverse her father's despoiling of the monasteries, but she was determined to return England to the True Faith. A reign of terror followed, where more of the innocent than guilty were swallowed up. During the reign of Edward VI, Parliament had repealed the practice of burning heretics at the stake. Mary instructed Parliament to reissue the Papal act, *De Haeretico Comburendo* (For the Burning of Heretics), which legalized that form of punishment for those that held opinions counter to the Church in Rome.

> The Church of Rome has always raised a fine point of protest against the charge that, 'the Church, itself, burned heretics.' The nicety of law was that The Church *only persuaded* governments of Christendom to pass civil laws that called for the burning of people when the Church declared them heretics. Irrespective of where blame may lie, during religious confrontations of the 14th, 15th, and 16th Centuries, scores of heretics were burned throughout Catholic strongholds in Christendom. Previously, the number of executions for heresy in England was relatively small, compared with those carried out by the Inquisition in Spain, in the Spanish Netherlands, and in Huguenot massacres in France. In those countries, burning of heretics exceeded 100,000. In the twenty-four year reign of King Henry VII, 10 Lollards had been burned; 81 were burned on King Henry VIII orders in thirty-eight years; and only 2 heretics were burned in the six year reign of Edward VI just ended. Whereas, Queen Mary approved the burning of 287 heretics in her short reign of less than five full years. However, many more martyrs died in prison from neglect or torture.

In England, the burnings were always in the Smithfield district of London, and always were public. London liked a good execution—whether hanging and beheading, or drawing and quartering, or burning at the stake—London always celebrated executions in festive spirit. Even so, London and all England disapproved of executions for heresy. Englishmen understood the reasonableness of executions for traitorous acts of treason, but they disapproved executions for difference in thoughts on faith. They especially disapproved of burning good Englishmen merely to appease the hated queen and her Spanish advisors at the top of government. Mutual dislike and distrust characterized the relationship between government and subjects in Queen Mary's reign.

Queen Mary I felt she was being charitable in giving Protestants the opportunity to recant their heresies, and to renew their statements of faith to the Church of Rome. Her Spanish Catholic advisors felt that her Protestant English subjects should be burned for past idolatrous beliefs without an option for forgiveness and pardon. Many clergy and persons of wealth escaped to Geneva or Zürich to wait out Mary's reign. However, many others remained to face persecution and death.

Mary was relentless in opposing all who disagreed with her political goals and religious convictions. The Protestant cleric John Foxe (in his *Acts and Monuments,* usually called *The Lives of the Martyrs* documented the way almost 300 people lost their lives for refusing to deny their Protestant beliefs during Mary's reign. Among the most bitterly resented executions, were those directed against leaders of the Protestant Reformation in England. Chief among them was the greatly honored Thomas Cranmer, the first Anglican Archbishop of Canterbury, and the author of the *Book of Common Prayer*, which for the first time set forth the doctrinal uniqueness of the Anglican Church of England. He was burned at the stake with other Protestant leaders who would not recant, and accept the Pope of Rome as supreme head of the Church. Another high churchman, Hugh Latimer Bishop of Worcester's, dying words at the stake were, "In my death such a candle is lit, by God's grace, in England that it shall never be put out." His was a profoundly accurate prophecy.

Most historians have faulted Queen Mary more for being a religious zealot, than for being, like her father Henry VIII, inherently cruel and vindictive. In this light, her persecution of Protestants can be viewed more as concern for the their salvation, than as delight in their damnation. In fairness to Mary, as many died of religious persecution during Queen Elizabeth's long reign that followed, as in Mary's short one. Queen Elizabeth escaped the condemnation Mary received, possibly because Elizabeth openly loved her subjects, and they returned her affection with forgiveness, not censure.

The execution and burning of hundreds, who refused to change their religion from Anglican Protestantism to Catholicism, made Mary the most thoroughly despised monarch in English history. Her subjects called her *Bloody Mary*, a name that has followed her through time.

Mary was almost delirious with joy when, near the end of her reign, Philip of Spain returned to England in 1557, but only to get England's support for Spain's ongoing war with France. Mary was unable to deny her husband anything. England went to war, and became nearly bankrupt, before loosing its only Continental possession, Calais. The loss of Calais bothered Mary more than all other failures of her reign. At her death, she said, "When I am dead and opened, you will find Calais lying in my heart."

Despite her appearance of strength and resolve, Queen Mary was in poor health much of her life. Her last delusion of pregnancy came in March 1558, but its symptoms came from more sinister disorders that took her life a half-year later in November 1558.

In October, Mary knew she was dying, and knowing that Elizabeth would soon be queen, Mary invited Elizabeth to come to her. Mary hoped to persuade Elizabeth to pledge to keep the Catholic Faith as England's official religion. Elizabeth only pledged to follow her own conscience in what she would do.

Early in Princess Mary's adolescence, when her father King Henry VIII discarded her mother Queen Katherine of Aragon, Mary referred to herself as, "the most unhappy Lady in Christendom." This judgment aptly described her entire life. Except for her mother, Queen Katherine of Aragon, no one ever loved Mary. She repelled the man she married. She longed for children that were never born. Her uncompromising certainty in matters of faith earned hatred from subjects she never trusted. In truth, happiness was a stranger to Mary all her life.

Ironically, Mary's greatest legacy to England was undying animosity for Catholicism. The faith she so sincerely and devoutly wished to restore to England was thwarted by her actions. Over a century later, anti-Catholic fear and distrust was still sufficiently strong to force Catholic King James II to abdicate his throne in 1688. Restrictions against Catholics continued to exclude them from British politics and government until anti-Catholic laws were repealed in 1829. Catholics are still ineligible to wear the crown of England.

Queen Mary I died without an heir. She was tormented by her personal demons, and her towering evangelical religious zeal. Mary had been in declining health for months, before she succumbed at St. James

Palace on November 17, 1858. Death came from multiple complaints, possibly from influenza, pneumonia, and widespread visceral cancer. Next day, her despised confidant Cardinal Reginald de la Pole Archbishop of Canterbury also conveniently died.

Queen Mary I is buried in Westminster Abbey in a tomb she now shares with her half-sister Queen Elizabeth I.

Following the death of Queen Mary I, the crown passed to Lady Elizabeth, who succeeded to the throne on November 17, 1538 as the incomparable Queen Elizabeth I.

REIGN 24

QUEEN REGNANT ELIZABETH I

Narrative of Queen Elizabeth I
(Reign 1558-1603)

Queen Elizabeth I: life dates c. 70 years, b. September 7,
1533-d. March 24, 1603; Queen Regnant of England c. 45
years, November 17, 1558-March 24, 1603.

Q UEEN ELIZABETH I (Elizabeth Tudor, Gloriana, or The Virgin
Queen) was known to her adoring subjects as *Good Queen Bess*. She
was the only surviving daughter of Henry VIII and Anne Boleyn. Elizabeth
was born at Greenwich Palace on September 7, 1533, and Henry VIII was
so certain that the child would be his longed for son that announcements
were printed for the birth of a prince. The invitations were corrected by
hand to say *princes* (because there was no space to add 'ss'), before the
announcements were sent out to foreign dignitaries.

In the quarter century that separated her birth from coronation on
January 15, 1558, Elizabeth faced a kaleidoscope of changing fortunes.
Elizabeth lived in luxury as the 'Darling of Court' for the first three years
of her life. However, after her mother Queen Anne Boleyn fell from grace,
Princess Elizabeth lost favor, and was judged a bastard. As a three year

old when her mother was executed, Princess Elizabeth said, "How hap it yesterday [I was] Princess, and today but Lady Elizabeth."

Elizabeth soon fell on such hard times that her housekeeper made a desperate appeal to King Henry VIII for money, because the three year old child needed "muffs, caps, and kerchiefs . . . and had no gowns, nor petticoats . . . nor linens, nor sustenance." For a time, Elizabeth suffered from a lack of adequate clothes and creature comforts deemed necessary for any growing child.

Queen Jane Seymour took steps to reconcile King Henry with his daughter Elizabeth. Her lot greatly improved when she again came back to court at age four. Elizabeth always had a strong-willed outgoing nature that guaranteed she would test the patience of her father. Elizabeth was again banished from court after Queen Jane Seymour died. Elizabeth was not permitted to meet Queen Anne of Cleves during her short reign of only a half-year, from January to July 1540. Nor was Elizabeth seen in court in the eighteen months that Katherine Howard was queen (July 1540 to January 1542).

Elizabeth's lot improved greatly when she returned with high favor to the court of Queen Katherine Parr after 1543. Queen Katherine gave Elizabeth her first experience of affectionate care with motherly love. She supervised Elizabeth's education from the age of ten to fourteen. Queen Katherine took responsibility for Elizabeth's education in scholastics, language, and courtly manner suitable for a child of King Henry VIII. Elizabeth learned Italian, Greek, Latin, and the 'Godly ethics of Erasmusian tolerance.' She enjoyed and excelled in music, dancing, archery, and riding. She could converse easily in six languages, as well as, the dialects of Ireland, Wales, and Cornwall. Roger Ascham her tutor from Cambridge University was greatly impressed by Elizabeth's prodigious memory for total recall.

The will of Henry VIII left Elizabeth an annual pension of £3,000, and a £10,000 dower portion to be paid on her marriage. However, Elizabeth again faced difficult times in the reigns of her half-siblings King Edward VI and Queen Mary I. Her father placed Elizabeth third in line of succession behind a frail sickly brother, and an asthmatic sister in declining health. In the unlikely event that she ever might become queen, powerful persons in court tried to control Princess Elizabeth for their own personal gain. Thus, Elizabeth had a precarious existence up to the moment of her coronation.

During the reign of her half-brother King Edward VI, Elizabeth was at a marriageable age in late teens, and it is not surprising that she was the focal point of many court intrigues to capture her in marriage. Thomas Seymour, a brother of Queen Jane Seymour, was accused of improper familiarity with Elizabeth that implied he had designs on marrying her, but Elizabeth stoutly maintained that she was not a knowing party to the charges brought against him. Elizabeth protested that she was under the impression that his attentions were only 'pleasantries of courtesy,' but she could not deny testimony by one of her domestics that "[Lord Thomas often] entered her bed chamber, bounced her out of bed, and slapped her bottom in an unseemly familiar fashion." Thomas Seymour was tried and convicted on unrelated crimes of embezzlement and malfeasance in office, so the matter ended without great harm to Elizabeth. On hearing of the execution of her first suitor, Elizabeth is reputed to have said, "This day died a man with much wit, and very little judgment."

Elizabeth escaped with little more than censure. However, the fact that trusted members of her own household, under threat of torture, had fabricated lies that nearly cost Elizabeth her life, taught Elizabeth of the danger of over-familiarity with anyone in a court that thrived on destroying the lives others with lies and innuendo. Elizabeth, even as a teenage girl, showed remarkable gifts for escaping entanglement from skillful traps set to ensure her downfall. Elizabeth learned to guard her thoughts, acts, and comments. She became adept in practicing skills for dissembling, delay, and devious deception, which served her well in the rest of her life. Her intelligence, courage, political intuition, and an astute judgment of people were her armor for survival.

When her sister Mary came to the throne as Queen Mary I, Elizabeth's religious beliefs became a matter of concern to advocates for both Calvinism and the Papacy. Elizabeth disarmed both factions with the statement, "I profess only the faith which I have been taught at home, and a willingness to receive fresh instruction on matters expressed in Holy Writ."

Queen Mary was so delighted on hearing this that she promptly gave Elizabeth a jeweled rosary; whereas, Archbishop Thomas Cranmer, equally pleased, gave her a copy of his *Book of Common Prayer*—both were convinced that Elizabeth was willing to be a new convert to their own persuasion—two dogmas a world apart.

Elizabeth's closest encounter with death came in the aftermath of the Thomas Wyatt Rebellion, which occurred in January 1554 within months after the beginning of Queen Mary's reign. Lady Jane Grey and Elizabeth's names were used by the rebels in the Wyatt Rebellion as candidates to replace Queen Mary on the throne.

Elizabeth was summoned to Parliament to stand trial for treason. She arrived in London on February 23, and was taken to Whitehall Palace where a witness said she was "dressed in white [as a sign of innocence, with] her mien proud, lofty, and disdainful . . . to conceal her trouble." She immediately asked to have an audience with Queen Mary, but Mary refused to see her. Mary also refused several later requests from Elizabeth to see her, and swear to her innocence of treason.

The Council ordered Elizabeth to prison in the Tower of London, and she was taken by water to the Traitor's Gate, where she wept, and refused to enter the Tower. She said, "Here stands as true a subject . . . as ever landed at these stairs. Oh God, I speak thus . . . having no other friend than Thee above." Reluctantly, she entered her prison. Elizabeth was suspected of deep complicity in the Wyatt Rebellion, and she was held in the Tower for several months. Elizabeth was certain she would be executed, and share the fate of her mother Anne Boleyn who was beheaded eighteen years before.

Queen Mary and her Catholic Court believed that Wyatt's cause had Princess Elizabeth's approval, because Elizabeth would be one to benefit if Queen Mary were deposed. Queen Mary's chief advisors clamored for Elizabeth's death. Chief among them were Chancellor Bishop Stephen Gardner and Bishop Bonner of St. Paul's London. Heads of Catholic countries in Europe, even Emperor Charles V of the Holy Roman Empire advised Queen Mary "to remove the viper [Elizabeth] from your bosom."

Numerous courts of inquiry examined Elizabeth in detail. The best legal minds in England were determined to find a legal basis to have Elizabeth executed for treasonous collusion in the Wyatt plot. Elizabeth was still in her teens, and was denied legal council. However, she argued her case with such adroit skill that the best legal minds from Inns of Court were unable to find direct evidence of Elizabeth's treasonous involvement in the Wyatt affair. The Council for the Crown finally decided there was insufficient evidence for guilt of treason to stand up in a court of law. An Act of Attainder was considered as a means of bypassing due process of law, but, since Elizabeth previously had been approved by Parliament of her place in the royal succession, that path for conviction was abandoned.

Elizabeth miraculously escaped with her life.

To her surprise and relief after about two months, Elizabeth was released from the Tower of London. However, she was confined under guard, first at Woodstock, with her patient but steadfast warden Sir Henry Bedingfield. Later she was permitted to move on parole to her own manor, Hatfield House, on the northern edge of London, It is to Elizabeth's credit that she was able to leave her prison at Woodstock on amiable terms with Sir Henry Bedingfield, whom she had baited shamelessly throughout her confinement. Even so, for the rest of Mary's reign, Elizabeth was under a cloud of suspicion for disloyalty. She was required to observe Catholic ritual and take Mass each day, but she did so with such a show of reluctance that Puritans had hope that she would come to the throne as a Protestant queen.

In October 1558, Queen Mary knew she was dying. In a last futile effort, she implored her Privy Council to appoint her husband Philip of Spain to be King of England in his own right, since he already was co-monarch with her. That request died as the words were spoken.

When Mary knew that Elizabeth would succeed to the throne, she summoned Elizabeth to court. Queen Mary implored Elizabeth to keep the Catholic faith as the official religion of England. Elizabeth expressed sorrow in seeing Mary in ill-health, but she was noncommittal, and only said, "I hold myself as much at liberty to choose my councilors and faith, as Your Majesty has been to choose your own. I promise not to change the religion of our land, inasmuch as it can be approved by the Word of God."

Queen Mary died on November 17, 1558, and a deputation from Parliament arrived at Hatfield House a day later to tell Lady Elizabeth that Queen Mary died. Tradition says that Elizabeth was in the yard, under a tree, reading a book, when they informed her that she was queen. Elizabeth quoted from the 118th Psalm in Latin, "*Domino factum est istud est mirabile in oculis nostris.*" (This is the Lord's doing, and it is marvelous in Our eyes).

Throughout England, rejoicing greeted the proclamation of the new queen. Bonfires were lit. Singing and dancing filled the streets. All made merry with food and drink. Shouts rang out, "Hurrah! Hurrah! No mingled blood of Spain, no stranger here. Just a Queen borne of mere England is here among us."

A few days later, Elizabeth left Hatfield House and entered London on November 23, 1558. She passed through the city stopping at many crossroads to greet her jubilant subjects. At the entrance to the Tower of London, she stopped and spoke to the surrounding crowd, "I am raised from being a prisoner in this place to be a prince of the land . . . This advancement is a work of God's mercy . . . so I must be thankful to Him, and [I will] to all men be merciful."

Elizabeth met extravagant expressions of good will by the people of London on her arrival in London for her coronation and for her first meeting with Parliament. Elizabeth was crowned at Westminster Abbey on January 15, 1859. However, since Reginald de la Pole Archbishop of Canterbury had died only days before, the Church was still under orders to perform all rituals in the Catholic manner approved by Queen Mary. Catholic Bishop Owen Oglethorpe of Carlisle performed necessary religious aspects of the coronation ceremony. Elizabeth showed Protestant leanings by departing to a side chapel when the Host was raised during the Mass. This delighted Protestants, but angered Catholics. However, nothing could please both sects simultaneously.

A contemporary witness of the coronation of the young Queen Elizabeth, said "[She was] tall, complexion and hair fair . . . high-nosed; of limbs and features neat . . . of stately and majestic comportment . . . [in this way she was] more like her father than her mother . . . [she has] affable virtues which well suit with majesty . . . and did render her of more sweet temper, and endeared her more to the love and liking of her people."

Beneath the acclimation, Elizabeth's position was exceedingly grave. She had almost no personal contacts or friends in high places. Most of her immediate family had been eliminated, or disgraced, during the reigns of her father, half-brother, and half-sister. She was still under the stigma of bastardy, which had been set upon her by Parliament before the execution of her mother Queen Anne Boleyn. The official religion of the land was still that of Mary's Catholic decree. Elizabeth's religious persuasion was uncertain, concerning the pressing religious issues that divided England. Irrespective of which way she leaned, nearly half the nation would oppose her. Moreover, the French War, which her brother-in-law King Philip of Spain had persuaded his wife Queen Mary to wage in support of Spain, had just ended, and the public purse was bare.

It is hard to define Elizabeth's personal religious convictions. She was not evangelistic about any cause, but seemed to prefer Protestantism to Catholicism, and Luther's views on Heaven and God to those of Calvin.

She emphatically did not like John Knox and Presbyterianism, probably because she despised everything of Scotland.

Two weeks after she became queen, Elizabeth convened her first Council of State with a slate of persons who would administer power in the land. She appointed commoners of ability to her Privy Council, irrespective of Protestant or Catholic persuasion. Elizabeth's most astute decision in the first days of her reign was the appointment of William Cecil (later Lord Burghley) to be her official secretary and advisor. It is uncertain how Cecil came to Elizabeth's attention, but, since he was a student at Cambridge of Roger Ascham (Elizabeth's tutor when she was in court with Queen Katherine Parr), it is probable that Elizabeth knew Cecil personally from early days, or that Ascham recommended Cecil to her. He remained her most trusted confidant for forty years until his death in 1598—for all those years he was true to his pledge, "[My advice will always be] true to my best lights without seeking my own favor."

It is reasonable to suspect that Queen Katherine Parr as regent in the reign of Henry VIII greatly impressed ten year old Princess Elizabeth who witnessed Queen Katherine's style for ruling under difficult circumstances. It may be that her example served as the model for fairness in ruling that young Queen Elizabeth used as reigning queen.

The most controversial and colorful of Queen Elizabeth's appointments went to Robert Dudley whom she created Earl of Leicester. He was the youngest surviving son of John Dudley Duke of Northumberland, who had been executed for treason for his roles in engineering the brief reign of Lady Jane Grey. Robert's youngest brother Guilford Dudley was executed with his wife Queen Lady Jane Grey.

Throughout Elizabeth's reign, Robert Dudley was Queen Elizabeth's most favored courtier. Both were born on September 7, 1533. This gave them a bond of unity that was almost mystical. Robin and Elizabeth were prisoners in the Tower at the same time during Queen Mary's reign, but it is uncertain that they ever met on that forlorn occasion. Elizabeth often referred to Robert Dudley as 'Sweet Robin.' Much gossip speculated on a romantic relationship between them; whatever it may have been, it was deep and lasting. He was her court favorite until his death. Rumor named him as her lover.

Robin was a tall handsome athletic man with few special talents for leadership aside from his good looks, great charm, and affable manners. Not everyone in court shared Elizabeth's opinion of Robert Dudley. Indeed, he was disparaged and said to be "without courage, without talent, without virtue; merely a handsome sleek-mannered courtier, the direct opposite of the queen in intellect, in daring, and in loyalty to duty."

Sweet Robin was a clone of other favorites, who, from time to time, also enjoyed the queen's favor, including: Robert de Vere Earl of Oxford, Sir Walter Raleigh, and Robert Devereux Earl of Essex. Elizabeth appointed Sweet Robin to be her *Master of the Horse*: that is, the majordomo of her palace household. He had responsibility for making sure that all social events, entertainments, masques, tableaux, dances, dinners, musical events, and court amusement went smoothly for the queen. In this capacity, he performed admirably. Robin would have been the one who approved arrangements with the Lord Chamberlain's Company at the Globe Theater. He may have been acquainted with Shakespeare and Burbage by arranging performances of Shakespeare's early plays, which the queen greatly enjoyed. It is said that, *The Merry Wives of Windsor,* was written on command for the queen.

Soon after Elizabeth became queen, a minor matter of court gossip involved Lady Frances Brandon Duchess of Suffolk, the mother of Lady Jane Grey, whose father Duke Henry Grey had been executed for his involvement in the Wyatt Rebellion. Widowed Frances Brandon quickly married handsome young Adrian Stokes, a commoner in her household staff. The mismatch in social status of the royal bride and common groom caused much sniggering criticism. William Cecil reported word of the Stokes-Brandon marriage to Queen Elizabeth, who snidely remarked, "What? Hath the Duchess married her horse keeper?" Cecil replied, "Yes Madam, Lady Brandon said your majesty would like to do so, too (in reference to Lord Robert Dudley who was Queen Elizabeth's Master of Horse)."

For a time, Robert Dudley Earl of Leicester was the leading contestant in the long running suit for the queen's hand in marriage. However, when Robert's first wife died, after falling down a stair at their estate near Oxford, rumor inflated the accident into 'suspicious circumstances.' Robin was suspected, and accused of planning his wife's death. In his trial, Robin was found to be in court at Windsor at the time of the accident, and he was judged innocent on all charges, but even so, gossip thereafter destroyed his chance to be a serious contender for the queen's matrimonial affections.

Robert of Leicester fell from grace from time to time, but he was always recalled to favor with the queen. Their greatest tiff occurred when

Elizabeth learned that, without her knowledge and her required approval, Robin had secretly married again, this time to a great court beauty, Lettice Knollys (mother, by an earlier marriage, of Robert Devereux Earl of Essex, see below). Their marriage catapulted the queen into a simulated jealous rage. Later she invited Sweet Robin back to court, but Lettice was never allowed to return. Leicester died in the month after the defeat of the Spanish Armada in July/August 1588. The queen locked herself away, and would see no one for many days. In fear of her safety, at last, the door to her suit was forced open. She was found to be well, but in deep mourning. The abiding affection of the queen for Robert Dudley was not realized until after her own death thirteen years later. At that time, a letter from Robin was found among Elizabeth's treasured keepsakes in her vanity chest. On the note, in her own hand, the queen had written, "His last letter."

Upon recommendation of her financial advisor Sir Thomas Gresham, Elizabeth recalled the devalued currency of former reigns (many coins were clipped and did not have true weight), some of which went back almost three centuries to the reign of Edward I. Gresham advised the queen to issue a new coinage of true value. It immediately gained respect in foreign markets. This monetary revision enhanced the value of the English pound, which consequently led to a steady increase in the wealth of the entire nation. Gresham is remembered as founder of the Royal Exchange. He is the author of the First Law of Economics—Gresham's Law: *Bad money drives out good money.* Elizabeth knighted Gresham for his services.

England's economy boomed, and common men prospered. Vagabonds and ne'er-do-wells were treated harshly. As the work ethic grew, farmers and wool merchants thrived. The nation's ships were present in every port. Goods came to England, and even more went away for sale of English products on the Continent. Happy days were here again in 'Ye Merry Olde Anglesland.'

Elizabeth began to build her strength in her first meeting with Parliament by saying, "Nothing, no worldly thing under the sun, is so dear to me as the love and goodwill of my subjects. Have a care over my people . . . They cannot revenge their quarrels, nor help themselves. See unto them for they are my charge."

This set the pattern for her reign. Elizabeth's greatest joy lay in cultivating the love of her common English subjects. During numerous progresses through the country, she spoke to persons of all ranks, and accepted all gifts presented, valuing only sentiment to be of worth. On one occasion, she was given a sprig of rosemary by a peasant woman, and continued to hold it throughout the day. On Maundy Thursday (the Thursday before Good Friday and Easter) 1560, she washed the feet of twenty peasant women, and gave one of her gowns to each of them.

The other side of her condescension was shown in her insatiable passion for splendor in dress, for inordinately ostentatious display in courtly manners, for magnificent jewels by the bushel, for majestic spectacles at court, and, not least, for an Olympian vanity that thrived on extravagant flattery and praise. In public display, Elizabeth was lavish, but in her own apartment away from public view, she preferred food and dress of a simple and temperate kind.

Elizabeth's frequent public appearances and royal progresses through her realm were an important part of the way she built good will in her realm. The carefully planned spectacles reassured her people that their queen truly cared for their wellbeing, and that public justice was the chief purpose of her station as queen. By acclamation, she became the people's Good Queen Bess. She loved their adulation, and they loved her wit and common touch.

An anecdote that shows the depth of love her subjects had for their queen involved the fact that Elizabeth suffered from toothaches in much of her adult life—from childhood she could not curb a desire for sweets—a mouth full of rotten teeth was the price she paid for her obsession for confections. Some time after she became queen, another tooth ached severely. The queen wanted relief from pain, but she was fearful of an extraction. After days of agony, her spiritual mentor Puritan Bishop John Aylmer of St. Paul's London came to demonstrate that having a tooth pulled was no great matter. To prove his point, he had one of his own good teeth extracted. Wherewith, the queen permitted an apothecary-barber to pull her painfully decayed tooth. After the extraction, she upbraided the bishop for deceiving her—the pain had been beyond endurance—she resolved never to go through such an ordeal again.

Elizabeth made visits to both Cambridge and Oxford Universities, where she matched wits and linguistic skill in classical languages with the dons. In his private life, her secretary William Cecil was also Chancellor of Cambridge University. On the occasion of her visit to Cambridge, he was her host. Elizabeth was able to hold her own in disputations in Latin and Greek. She was clearly at ease in the group of scholars, and they recognized she had interests and understanding superior to all but a few academicians.

The Counter-Reformation in Rome (roughly 1540 to 1560) resulted in an internal religious reordering of the Catholic Church. Among many other things, it approved the *Society of Jesus* (commonly known as the *Jesuits*). The Order created by Ignatius Loyola had as its purpose: teaching, evangelizing, defending (if necessary, by militant means) doctrine, and dogma that had newly been reaffirmed by the Council of Trent.

After the Council of Trent, Pope Pious V proclaimed a papal bull that authorized Elizabeth's assassination. With that in mind, subversive Jesuits entered England bent on restoration of the Catholic faith, in England, and with determination to replace Queen Elizabeth with Mary Queen of Scots, an avowed Catholic who was next in line for succession to the English throne.

Mary Queen of Scots was captured, and held prisoner in England for almost eighteen years, before she was finally convicted of high treason in a fourth Catholic plot to assassinate Queen Elizabeth. Elizabeth reluctantly signed Mary's death warrant; whereupon, the execution was carried out so swiftly in the privacy of Fotheringhay Castle that the queen was not told until after the execution had taken place. On being informed of the execution, Elizabeth was incoherent with rage. However, since the entire Privy Council was involved in the act, she could not send all accomplices to the Tower for execution.

Elizabeth was by no means above holding a grudge, and on occasion of being vindictive. She was too proud to petition Parliament to repeal her stigma of bastardy. She just ignored that, but she could not forgive the entire family descended from her father's sister Mary Tudor Duchess of Suffolk, from whom Lady Jane Grey was descended. The entire Brandon-Dorset-Grey family always treated Elizabeth as a bastard usurper of the crown. Elizabeth hounded them with threats of imprisonment, and a few of them expired in the Tower.

Elizabeth was tightfisted to a fault. Francis Walsingham, Elizabeth's head of her secret service, worked tirelessly to entrap Mary Queen of Scots on charges of treason against the person of Queen Elizabeth. He complained that Elizabeth could not be trusted to keep a promise, especially when it was inconvenient or cost money. Elizabeth suffered for every penny that flowed out of the public purse. Walsingham spent his personal fortune on things that Elizabeth should have paid for from taxation. At death,

Walsingham he was buried at night to avoid the embarrassment of not being able to afford a public funeral.

Above all things, Elizabeth abhorred war. Elizabeth had used all her feminine and very considerable intellectual wiles, to avoid war with the Netherlands, Austria, France, and Spain. The execution of Mary Queen of Scots in 1587 united all Catholic Europe against England. England was viewed to be a renegade nation, and after the Council of Trent, Rome declared there was a moral obligation to depose England's heretical queen.

With the wrath of God as justification, Philip II of Spain (Elizabeth's brother-in-law by marriage to Elizabeth's half-sister Queen Mary I, and himself, nominal King of England during Mary's reign) declared war on the Island Country. His stated purpose was to remove Queen Elizabeth, and to claim the Kingdom of England in his own name.

Queen Elizabeth at last was cornered, and forced to fight invincible Spain. Philip expected all English Catholics to support him, but to his chagrin, they rallied to their queen. First, they were Englishmen. History repeatedly shows that, when a nation is attacked, all its factions will unite, because patriotic love of country always takes precedence over every internecine controversy. England was united against the coming onslaught from Spain.

A French diplomat warned Elizabeth that, since her case was hopeless against the insuperable might of Spain, she would do well to concede defeat, to flee to Ireland, and save whatever she could from her sinking Ship of State. To this, Elizabeth replied, "I think that, at the very worst, God has not yet ordained that England shall perish."

Captain Francis Drake on his ship *The Golden Hind* attacked Cadiz in 1587, and set fire to the harbor. The fire destroyed a sizeable part of King Philip's Spanish invasion fleet. Drake reported to the queen that he had just returned from 'singeing the King of Spain's beard.' It delayed the Armada by about one year.

At last, on July 29, 1588, sails of the huge galleons of the Spanish Armada were sighted off Plymouth, heading up the English Channel toward the Straits of Dover. Philip intended to control the narrows, and enable the invasion of England to follow. At the time, as everyone knows, Sir Francis Drake Vice Admiral of the Fleet was playing at boles. He calmly announced, "I have time to finish the game before engaging the enemy."

Francis Drake, Martin Frobisher, and John Hawkins were in command of naval strength of England. Robert Dudley of Leicester had authority over ground forces, which were readied, but were not used.

In that time of crisis, Elizabeth rose to her highest in calling for an all out effort to repel the invaders. She declared herself leader in a speech at Tilbury Camp. Englishmen learn it by rote, much as Americans memorize *Lincoln's Gettysburg Address,* or Jefferson's *Preamble to the Declaration of Independence.* In the greatest public address of all English monarchs, Queen Elizabeth said to Drake's assembled men at Tilbury Camp in her, *Let Tyrants Fear,* speech:

" . . . My loving people, We have been persuaded by some that are careful of Our safety, to take heed how We commit Our self to armed multitudes, for fear of treachery; but I assure you, I do not desire to live in distrust of My faithful and loving people. Let tyrants fear. I have always so behaved Myself that under God, I have placed My chiefest strength and good will in the loyal hearts and good will of My subjects; and therefore I am come amongst you, as you see, at this time, not for recreation and disport, but being resolved, in the midst and heat of the battle, to live or die amongst you all; to lay down for God, My kingdom, and for My people, My honor and My blood, even in the dust. I know I have but the body of a weak and feeble woman; but I have the heart and stomach of a King, and a King of England, too, and think it foul scorn that Parma, or Spain, or any Prince of Europe should dare to invade the borders of My realm; to which, rather than any dishonor should grow by Me, I Myself will take up arms, I Myself will be General, Judge, and Rewarder of everyone of your virtues in the field."

The sea battle with the Spanish Armada, July 28-29, 1588, was another Agincourt.

One hundred and thirty Spanish Galleons, like castles on the sea, lumbered in close formation majestically into the English Channel carrying upwards from 20,000 invasion troops. Less than thirty small English vessels, only lightly equipped for war, followed them. What the English ships lacked in size, they more than made up for in maneuverability, and skilled seamanship. The English ships raced about, like harrier hawks in a pen of chickens, striking a blow here, setting fire there, with a result that the great ships, in total confusion and disarray, collided, burned, sank, or limped on into the North Sea where an unseasonable storm battered them further. With masts shattered, sails in shreds, crews decimated, and in despair, only about fifty of the one hundred and thirty original Spanish galleons navigated between the Orkney and Shetland Islands, went around Scotland and Ireland, and then limped back to Spain with only one-third of their men still alive.

After the great victory over the Armada, England celebrated, and was united. However, Elizabeth was at fault that many of England's brave sailors, who carried the battle for England, were shamefully neglected, and allowed to die in poverty. Elizabeth was stingy, and always reluctant to dip into her own reserves. She always hoped something else would come up to defray expenses for her. However, the golden days of piracy against Spanish ships from the New World no longer bailed her out. The defeat of the Armada did not fatally diminish the power of Spain, but it gave great encouragement to Protestantism in Europe, and enormous prestige to England in the last decade and a half of Queen Elizabeth's reign.

Following the Armada's defeat, the country basked in being first among the nations of Europe. Commerce and industry prospered, and colonialism began in the New World. The period produced Shakespeare, Marlowe, Johnson, Sydney, Bacon, and Spencer. This is the time in her reign that we think of as, *The Elizabethan Age*. The age was the glory of England, largely because Elizabeth was tolerant of religious differences, she encouraged originality, and excellence at all ranks among her subjects, such that William Shakespeare, as we know him, and Samuel Johnson, and Christopher Marlowe could not have existed a century before, or a century after her reign.

Elizabeth contracted smallpox, and nearly died in 1562 when she was twenty-nine. At that time in the event that she might become incapable of ruling, Elizabeth appointed Robert Dudley Earl of Leicester to serve as Protector of the Realm. This warning raised pressure among her advisors that she must provide an heir for the crown. Throughout her nearly forty-five year reign, her advisers constantly pestered Elizabeth to marry. In reply, she pointed to her coronation ring, and said, "I am already married to the people of England."

She had a long list of suitors that she toyed with for political advantage, as cat-with-mouse. Among her suitors were: her brother-in-law King

Philip II of Spain, Archduke Charles of Austria, Eric of Sweden, Casimir of Poland, the two French Princes, sons of Queen Katherine d'Medici, Francis d'Anjou, and Henry d'Alençon (later Henry III of France)—the latter said to be the ugliest man in France. Among her English swains: Henry FitzAlan Earl of Arundel, James Hamilton Earl of Arran (Scotland), and of course, 'Sweet Robin,' Robert Dudley Earl of Leicester.

As an alternative to marriage, Elizabeth was asked to designate, by name, an heir to the throne. Elizabeth is reputed to have countered that annoying demand by saying, "Silly, silly man! Has anyone ever been designated second without his immediate desire to be first?"

However, behind all this sparring, Elizabeth was aware that she had failed to provide for continuation of the Tudor line. On hearing that her cousin, Mary Queen of Scots, had given birth to Prince James (later James VI of Scotland, and James I of England), Elizabeth said, "Alack, the Queen of Scots is lighter of a bonny son, but I am but of barren stock." In this, she acknowledged that, in the end, Mary Queen of the Scots line would win out.

Elizabeth never married, but she skillfully played her marriage availability as a diplomatic ace, which kept Continental rivals for her favor guessing, and disarmed. An understanding of her nature makes it clear that Elizabeth's vanity would neither have permitted her to marry anyone less than a king—that excluded all titled Englishmen, including her great favorite, Robert Dudley Earl of Leicester—nor could she ever share authority with another equal. That excluded all foreign kings.

It has been suggested that her fear of childbirth, and its all too frequent accompaniment, death, may have been a sizeable factor behind her antipathy for marriage. Thus, to the end, Elizabeth remained *Gloriana, The Virgin Queen*.

Although Elizabeth disdained marriage, she was in love with love. She demanded undying devotion from her male favorites. If their protestations of affection flagged, so did their position of favor decline in court. Queen Elizabeth childishly resented the marriage of men who once fluttered around her for favors, and then departed to build families of their own. That was the case for Leicester, Raleigh, Essex, and others. However, usually, with time, she was able to forgive them.

However, the infatuation of her old age Robert Devereux Earl of Essex, the stepson of her old favorite Robert of Leicester, went too far for forgiveness by his treasonous involvement in an abortive threat to her throne. Legend reports that, when Essex faced execution in the Tower, and requested an audience with the queen to profess his loyalty, Elizabeth refused him, even though Essex sent with his plea the jeweled ring she had given him as an expression of her unfailing love. Queen Elizabeth could forgive a perceived insult to her person, but she could never forgive anyone who reached out to touch her crown.

Elizabeth dominated a predominately masculine society for half a century. She charmed and created a court fantasy of herself as the Virgin Queen Bee who was surrounded by adoring dependent musicians, poets, composers, philosophers, scholars, artists, that buzzed around making it one of the most intellectually exciting courts of the late English Renaissance.

Her vanity was boundless. She delighted in extravagant dress and jewels. She would not admit to aging until near the end of her life. The charade of *Gloriana* continued long after she was only a caricature of deathless youth and beauty. She loved to be surrounded by handsome young men of good manners. It is said that what she liked most in a man was 'a well turned calf.' However, he also needed to play his proper part in an artificial atmosphere of courtly love, one in which the men, although unable to approach the queen, professed undying love for her. This produced scandalous speculation in London and all capitols of Europe, much to Elizabeth's amusement and delight.

She met her last Parliament in 1601, and gave what has been called her, *Golden Speech*. It epitomized the relationship that existed throughout her reign between herself as monarch and her people. In it, she said, " . . . There will never a Queen sit in my seat with more zeal to my country . . . and though you have had, and may have, many Princes more mighty and wise, sitting in this seat of State, yet you never had, nor shall ever have, any that will be more full of care and love than I."

Gradually the men died off who had supported her during her long reign, which reached almost forty-five years. Even though new ones took their place, the queen was not pleased. The queen became embittered and moody. She said, on the subject of all her old companions now dead, "I am tired of living, with nothing more to give content, or anything to give pleasure." When the bell tolled for Gloriana, she no longer had a will to combat intrigue, or even live.

After Christmas masques of 1602 and Twelfth Night Revels of New Year 1602/1603 at Whitehall Palace, Elizabeth began to fail rapidly. She was almost 70, an unheard of antiquity in those times in which natural causes ordinarily removed one from among the living before the age of fifty. She repaired to Richmond Palace, her favorite dwelling, built by her grandfather King Henry VII.

During her last week of life in late March, Queen Elizabeth refused to lie down, and, instead, only leaned against a bank of pillows. Her Chancellor Robert Cecil Earl of Salisbury (son of William Cecil Lord Burghley) said, "Your Majesty must now lie down." To which she roused, and whispered, "Little man *Must* is not a word one addresses to Princes!"

Although, taller than most women, and famous for her Plantagenet auburn hair, for piercing hazel eyes, and in spite of elaborate dress, she was never a great beauty. Even so, her presence was one of overpowering majesty. Her closets burst with over three thousand gowns. With age, her hair thinned, and was covered over with a flaming red wig that sparkled with fabulous jewels. Her teeth, those that were not pulled out, blackened as time passed. In all, at the end of her life, she was an awesome frightful harridan, a grotesque caricature of Gloriana.

In summing up the Great Queen as a woman, one wishes Shakespeare could have done it for us. He would have come up with, even better than, his—the best of all accolades for great ladies—'Time cannot wither, nor custom stale, her infinite variety.'

To the end, she refused to name her successor, but she knew plans were afoot to invite James VI of Scotland, the son of Mary Queen of Scots, to sit on her throne. At last, without speaking, Elizabeth nodded when asked if she approved of James Stewart to be heir to her throne, and England's King James I.

Elizabeth died on March 24, 1603. Elizabeth is buried in a common tomb with her sister Queen Mary I, at Westminster Abbey. The tomb has only one effigy over it, which is of Elizabeth, but the citation in Latin, translated, read:

> *Consorts both in Throne and Grave,*
> *Here rest we two sisters, Elizabeth and Mary,*
> *In hope of our resurrection*

Elizabeth is one of the great women of all time. She came to her throne, disparaged by birth, bankrupt in wealth, surrounded by enemies of great power and station, all wished nothing so much as her failure. Her

Englishmen were divided in their advocacy of many issues, but she held their loyalty in the hollow of her hand by bonds of love she cultivated with sincere devotion.

At the age of 25, Elizabeth inherited a divided bankrupt State from her father, brother, and sister. At the end of her reign at the age of 70, she left England the strongest power in Europe in an exciting age of exploration and expansion. At the close of her reign, England ranked first among nations of the Western World in wealth, prestige, power, and brilliance. Her reign is still remembered with envy for the luster of its creative achievements.

Following the death of Queen Elizabeth I, the son of her nemesis Mary Queen of Scots, James VI of Scotland, succeeded to the throne in 1603 as, King James I of England. His reign initiated England's journey into Modern Time.

Conclusion to the Tudor Dynasty

WHEN QUEEN Elizabeth I died on March 24, 1603, her death brought to a close the Tudor Dynasty in England. It had lasted for only 118 years, from 1485 to 1603. The founder of the Tudor Dynasty, Henry VII, was followed by is son, Henry VIII, and his three children: King Edward VI, Queen Mary I, and Queen Elizabeth I. The unfortunate 9-day queen, Lady Jane Grey (a granddaughter of Mary Tudor, the youngest daughter of Henry VII) completes the list of six Tudor monarchs.

The Tudor Dynasty years were outstanding in English History as a transitional period that connected Medieval and Modern Times. For England, King Henry VII restored sound economic practices in government. King Henry VIII initiated religious reformation and independence from Rome. Queen Elizabeth I, with tolerance and intuition, brought her realm into the High Renaissance, and by defeat of the Spanish Armada, made England the most powerful nation in the Western World. Thus, the Tudors ushered in the beginning of Modern Time.

The Tudor Age was a triumphant expression of the English spirit, but the Tudor Age was also was a time when monarchs with absolute power ruled the nation. Confused topsy-turvy religious acrobatics characterized the time, because England still subscribed to medieval unquestioned acceptance of the principle: *Cuius regio, eius religio* (meaning, *The religion of the Monarch determines the religion of the people*). Religious controversy would continue to be a controlling factor in politics for the Stuart monarchs who came after Elizabeth I.

For many generations, the Norman and Plantagenet kings were Saxon-Norman Englishmen who married French, Spanish, or native English wives. After the reign of Elizabeth I, it would be a long, long time, before English blood again entered the royal lineage.

King James Stuart I, founder of the Stuart Dynasty, and his Stuart descendants was primarily of Scottish-Danish-German-French descent. The Hanoverian Dynasty that followed the Stuarts were without exception all of German-Danish extraction. The Saxe-Coburg-Gotha—Windsor Dynasty was also German-Danish until present Queen Elizabeth II came to the throne with a transfusion of native British blood. That came by way of her mother, the beloved 'Queen Mum' Elizabeth Bowes-Lion, the mother of Queen Elizabeth II.

DYNASTY V

THE STUART DYNASTY
REIGN 25 THROUGH 30 (1603–1714)

Introduction to the Stuart Dynasty

THE TUDOR dynasty ended with the reign of Queen Elizabeth I for lack of heirs from Henry VIII. None of his three children (Edward VI, Mary I, and Elizabeth I) had offspring. Therefore, the right to sit on England's throne devolved by primogeniture to living descendants of Margaret Tudor, the older sister of Henry VIII.

Margaret Tudor was the eldest daughter of King Henry VII of England (Henry Tudor Earl of Richmond) and his consort Queen Elizabeth of York. Margaret was married three times. She had one offspring from each of her first two marriages, and none from the last.

Margaret Tudor first married King James Stewart IV of Scotland. Their only surviving child was King James Stewart V of Scotland. He first married Princess Madeleine de Valois of France (she died without issue); second, he married Mary of Guise Duchess de Longueville. James V and Mary of Guise had one child, a daughter named Mary. In her own right, Princess Mary became the reigning Queen of Scotland when her father James V unexpectedly died only six days after her birth. She is known in English history as *Mary Queen of Scots*.

Margaret Tudor's second husband was Archibald Douglas Earl of Angus. They had one daughter named Margaret Douglas. Margaret Douglas married Matthew Stewart IV Earl of Lennox, and they were the parents of Henry Stewart Lord Darnley.

Margaret Tudor's third husband was Henry Stuart Lord Methven; however, there was no issue from this union.

Mary Queen of Scots married her first cousin Henry Stewart Lord Darnley. They had an only child, James Stuart. The Scottish Presbyterian Kirk deposed Mary Queen of Scots, and her son became King James VI of Scotland in 1567 when he was a year old. After the death of Queen Elizabeth I of England, he became King James Stuart I of England in 1603, as the founder of the English Stuart Dynasty.

Note: The surname in Scotland is spelled 'Stewart', but in England, it is spelled 'Stuart.'

Mary Queen of Scots
Matriarch of the Stuart Dynasty

DESCENDANTS OF Mary Queen of Scots are the Stuart monarchs of England. Therefore, it is reasonable to spend a little time reviewing events in her life, even though she was not an English monarch herself.

Mary Stuart was the only surviving legitimate child of King James Stuart V of Scotland and Mary of Guise Duchess de Longueville of France. Mary was born on December 8, 1542. Six days later, her father unexpectedly died, and she became titular Queen of Scotland; nine months later she was crowned Queen of Scotland on September 9, 1543. Scottish regents governed for her, and at age six, to strengthen the 'Auld Alliance' between Scotland and France, Scottish regents arranged a diplomatic marriage of Mary Stuart to the Dauphin Francis of Valois (later, King Francis II of France). At the age of six, Mary was sent to live in the French court, where she remained from 1548 until 1561.

Mary Stuart's childhood years in France imprinted her strongly with French culture. Her French outlook was strengthened further by maternal Guise-de Longueville social connections at the highest court levels in

France. As the prospective bride of the Dauphin, Mary was coached meticulously in the court of Queen Catherine de Medici (the Dauphin's mother) for her position as *La Dauphine,* and in expectation of the role she was would play later as Queen of France. Mary Stuart received an excellent education supervised by Queen Catherine, who made use of the superlative opportunities provided in Paris, which then was at the apogee of late Renaissance learning. Mary became proficient in French, Spanish, Latin, and Greek. She was accomplished in music, and was well read in literature, history, and poetry. Portraits show clearly that she was an attractive child, and a beautiful adult woman of somewhat taller stature than was common at the time. Also, in religion, Mary was a devout undeviating Catholic.

When Mary Stuart was sixteen, she and Dauphin Francis (age fifteen) were married in Paris on April 14, 1558. It is relevant to point out that in the same year (after the death of Queen Mary I of England on November 17, 1558, and the coronation of Elizabeth I on January 15, 1559) Mary Stuart claimed her right to be the true Queen of England. Her claim rested on grounds that Elizabeth had been declared a bastard by Parliament after the execution of Elizabeth's mother Queen Anne Boleyn—therefore, Elizabeth was unfit to be Queen of England. Elizabeth was too proud to petition Parliament for annulment of the charge of bastardy, and her status, as bastard was never repealed.

When the Dauphin's father King Henry II of France died on July 10, 1559, Francis became King Francis II of France. Mary was Queen of France for only a year and a half, until her husband died on December 5, 1560. At eighteen, Mary was Dowager Queen of France. Mary remained in France for a few months before she returned to Scotland on August 19, 1561.

Regents ruled Scotland from 1542 until 1561, but on Mary Stuart's return, she became Scotland's *de facto* reigning queen. In the years that Mary had been in France (1548-1561), religious ferment had transformed Scotland into one of the most militantly conservative Protestant kingdoms in Europe. John Knox, the founder of Presbyterian Calvinism, held political power in the Scottish government. To him, Queen Mary's Catholicism was anathema; to her, his Presbyterianism was abomination. The queen and government were at an irreconcilable impasse. Even so, Mary was more willing to compromise on matters of religion, than was John Knox and the Scottish Kirk (Church). For them, all deviation from study of Gospel and the worship of God was idolatrous interference with the important business of dying—that is, the saving of one's soul in preparation for eternal life in the Hereafter—which required ascetic austere self-denial, as the straight and narrow path to salvation.

Mary Queen of Scots had no heir when she returned to Scotland from France, and the subject of her marriage was pressing. On July 29, 1565, she married her cousin Henry Stuart Lord Darnley. Both Mary and Henry had equally strong Tudor connections to the English throne and Stewart connections to the Scottish throne—therefore, any child of theirs would have strong claim on both thrones. Their only offspring, James Stuart, was born on June 19, 1566. He became King James VI of Scotland and King James I of England.

A half-year after his son was born, Henry Stewart Lord Darnley was murdered on February 10, 1567. He died under suspicious circumstances that involved the explosion of a palace bomb. Most believed that his wife Mary Queen of Scots and her lover James Hepburn Earl of Bothwell were part of a conspiracy to remove Darnley. After his death, Mary and Bothwell married with unseemly haste. The Calvinist head of the Scottish Kirk John Knox dominated the ultra-conservative Scottish Protestant court, and he immediately ordered the marriage of Queen Mary to James Hepburn annulled. Bothwell was convicted of treason for the murder of Lord Darnley, and was exiled to prison in Denmark until his death a decade later.

The less than year old Prince James was taken from Queen Mary, and he was soon proclaimed King James VI of Scotland. John Knox's Presbyterian clergy reared the prince in a severely simple Protestant manner free of luxury and courtly manners. Knox ordered Mary Queen of Scots to renounce her right to rule, but Mary refused to abdicate. On May 23, 1568, Mary escaped to England, where she requested sanctuary from her cousin Queen Elizabeth of England.

Elizabeth gave Mary safe haven, but kept her in custody. Mary of Scotland was the focal point for rebellion in England because Mary still claimed to be the rightful Queen of England. Everyone agreed that Mary was next in line for the English crown. Mary, being a Catholic, was the focus for simmering underground rebellion to remove Protestant Queen Elizabeth, and to reestablish Catholicism as the national religion of England.

For almost 18 years (1570 until 1587), Queen Mary of Scotland remained a captive of Queen Elizabeth I. On four separate occasions, Mary was the focal point for Catholic conspiracies to depose Elizabeth. Constantly, Elizabeth's Privy Council, including William Cecil Lord Burghley, tried to persuade Elizabeth to sign Mary's death warrant. Constantly, Elizabeth refused to order Mary's execution. Elizabeth was the only voice to stand between Mary and death.

In this light, Queen Elizabeth's forbearance and delay in approving Mary's execution was almost saintly. Neither her grandfather Henry VII nor her father Henry VIII would have put up for eighteen years with the meddlesome focal point for rebellion provided by Mary of Scotland's presence. They would have lopped off her head in an instant.

Early in her reign, Queen Elizabeth I was aware that James Stuart (Mary Queen of Scots' son) was the logical heir to the English throne. Yet, she never openly stated that he was her choice to succeed her. Immediately after Elizabeth's death, envoys from the English Parliament hastened to Scotland, and offered James VI of Scotland the crown of England. He accepted, and became the first Stuart King of England in 1603.

Several years after James became king, he ordered that the body of his mother, Mary Queen of Scots, be exhumed from Peterborough Cathedral, and reinterred in Westminster Abbey.

The Stuart Dynasty Lineage, Reign 25 through 30 (1603-1714)

Note: In Scotland the family name is spelled *Stewart*, but in England, it is spelled *Stuart*; the latter spelling is used here.

THE STUART Line includes Kings James I, Charles I, Charles II, James II, William III, and Queens Regnant Mary II and Anne. They were also ruling monarchs of Scotland, until the reign of Queen Anne when England and Scotland were united as a single nation called *Great Britain*.

James Stuart, England's King James I, by right of birth was James VI of Scotland. His Scottish lineage can be traced from the 9th Century through Houses of Macoupin, Duncan, le Bruce, to the House of Stewart, the last of which ruled Scotland throughout the 15th and 16th Centuries.

James Stuart's Scottish lineage is not given here. James I was a great-great-grandson of King Henry VII and Elizabeth of York, by their eldest daughter Margaret Tudor who was the great-grandmother of King James I.

The following Stuart lineage is traced only from Henry VII. In the lineage given below, the names of reigning monarchs are given in bold type with the number for each reign. Dates in parenthesis give duration of reigns. Queen Consort names are included when they are also mothers of a following reigning monarch. Numbers in parenthesis give offspring in chronological order; however, only offspring are shown who figure conspicuously in events discussed in the present treatment of English history.

Dynasty IV: the Tudor Lineage:
    Reign 19. Henry VII (reign, 1485-1509) married Queen Consort Elizabeth of York, parents of—
      Margaret Tudor:
      By her first husband James Stewart IV of Scotland, parents of—
        James Stewart V of Scotland married Mary of Guise, parents of—
          Mary Queen of Scots, married Henry Stewart Lord Darnley, parents of—
            James Stuart (VI & I) of Scotland and England
            Continue with the Dynasty V, The Stuart Lineage, James I of England.

      By her second husband, Archibald Douglas Earl of Angus, parents of—
        Margaret Douglas married Matthew Stewart IV Earl of Lennox, parents of—
          Henry Stewart Lord Darnley and wife Mary Queen of Scots, parents of—
          James Stuart (VI & I) of Scotland and England
          Continue with the Stuart lineage, Dynasty V, The Stuart Lineage, James I of England.

Dynasty V. The Stuart Lineage:

Reign 25. James Stuart I of England (reign, 1603-1625) married Queen Consort Anne of Denmark, parents of—

(1) Elizabeth Stuart Queen of Bohemia married Frederick Elector Palatine King of Bohemia, parents of—

Sophia Electress of Hanover married Prince Ernest Augustus Elector of Hanover, parents of—

> **Reign 32. George I of Great Britain** = Prince George of Hanover; continue with Dynasty VI. The Hanover Lineage.

(2) **Reign 26. Charles Stuart I** (reign, 1625-1649) married Queen Consort Henrietta Maria of France, parents of—

(1) **Reign 27. Charles Stuart II** (reign, 1660-1685) married Queen Consort Katherine of Braganza, no issue.

(James Fitzroy Duke of Monmouth, the eldest of 16 illegitimate children of Charles II and many mistresses.

(2) **Reign 28. James Stuart II** (reign, 1685-1688) married—

By James' first wife, Anne Hyde, parents of—

> (1) **Reign 29. Queen Regnant Mary Stuart II** (reign, 1689-1694), married to her co-monarch King William of Orange III, (reign, 1689-1702), no issue.

> (2) **Reign 30. Queen Regnant Anne Stuart** (reign, 1702-1714), married Prince George of Denmark, no surviving issue.

By James' second wife, Mary of Modena, parents of—

> (3) James Francis Edward Stuart, (the 'Old Pretender' self-styled, James III), married Maria Sobieska, parents of—

> > Charles Edward Stuart (the 'Young Pretender' popularly known as 'Bonnie Prince Charlie'), no issue.

(3) Mary Stuart married Prince William II of Orange, parents of—

Reign 29. William III (reign, 1689-1702), married to co-monarch **Mary II** (reign, 1689-1694), no issue, (see above, Reign 29. Mary Stuart II).

End of the Stuart Dynasty; continue with the Hanover Dynasty VI.

REIGN 25

KING JAMES I
AND
QUEEN CONSORT ANNE
OF DENMARK

Summary of the Reign of King James I
(Reign 1603-1625)

King James I: life dates, 58 years, June 19, 1566-March 27, 1625: King of Scotland reign 57 years, July 24, 1567-March 27, 1625; King of England reign 22 years, March 24, 1603-March 27, 1625.

KING JAMES I was the only son of Mary Queen of Scots and Henry Stewart Lord Darnley. His parents were first cousins; both were grandchildren of Margaret Tudor the eldest daughter of King Henry VII, and the eldest sister of King Henry VIII. James was born on June 19, 1566 at Edinburgh Castle. He was separated from his mother before he was a year old. He was reared and educated in a stark Scottish Presbyterian manner. James was Protestant in religion, but he stoutly objected to Puritan ascetic dogma. Otherwise, he was tolerant and well educated in most religious matters.

It is customary for English historians to disparage achievements in the *Jacobean Period* (that is, in the reign of James I, 1603-1625), and to contrast it unfavorably with the national glories of the *Elizabethan Age* that immediately preceded it. Some even belittle James' reign with the statement that "The only significant Jacobean contribution was the introduction of golf, the national sport of Scotland, to England."

The contentious relationship between King and Parliament was characterized more by stalemate than governmental progress throughout his reign, but other important developments cannot be denied. Most of Shakespeare's greatest plays were written and produced in the first decade of the reign of King James I, who licensed the Bard's theater company with the name *The King's Men,* and the king's patronage greatly enhanced the Shakespeare-Burbage player's position in the London Theater. King James was often hard up for ready cash. In the hope of gaining the riches of Croesus, he employed Sir Walter Raleigh to seek the mythical Eldorado in Caribbean Guiana, but Sir Walter found no gold, and he lost his head for failure in that enterprise.

Many who have evaluated the positive and negative aspects of the Jacobean period credit King James with having a sense of true scholarship, which encouraged continuation of the cultural advances of the Elizabethan Age. Evidence cited in his behalf, point to his appointment of Francis Bacon to be Attorney General in 1616, and Chancellor in 1618. Bacon is credited with providing the philosophical basis for the *Empirical Scientific Method*, which asserts that reason alone is not sufficient to reveal truth. True understanding of natural phenomena also requires observation, measurement, testing, and reproducible data from direct observation of controlled experimentation. Ever since, this has been the guiding principle of modern science. In this sense, modern science in England began in the Jacobean Age.

King James promoted colonial ambitions in the New World with the start of permanent colonies at Jamestown, Virginia (1603), and the Plymouth Colony in Massachusetts (1620). He detested Puritanism, but chartered the Puritan colony with freedom to practice religion in any manner they chose, but Plymouth would remain a property of the crown with its secular affairs approved and supervised by the English Parliament.

However, King James is remembered most for *The King James Authorized Version of the Bible*. The translation following the Conference of Hampton Court (January 1604) was first printed in 1611. James took great interest in the project, but although he had no part in its translation or composition, his hand is felt in the sound scholars he chose to complete the task. The King James Bible has stood the test of time as a jewel of the English language.

As king of both Scotland and England, James had a lifelong desire to unite the two kingdoms, for which he suggested the name *Great Britain*. This goal was not achieved until the Act of Settlement was passed a century later in the reign of his great-granddaughter Queen Anne. The British flag, which combines the crosses of St. George (of England) and St. Andrew (of Scotland), was authorized by James to be the official flag for his reign. It is now known as the *Union Jack*, and it has remained Britain's emblem ever since. He also ordered that all citizens of Scotland and England, by birth, enjoyed dual citizenship in the both kingdoms.

King James I died of kidney failure or a cerebral stroke on March 27, 1625. He was buried in Westminster Abbey with his Queen Anne of Denmark who died in 1619. They had seven or eight children, but only three survived to maturity. Prince Charles was their only surviving son.

After his death, King James I was followed to the throne in 1625 by his only son King Charles I.

Narrative of Queen Consort Anne of Denmark

Queen Anne of Denmark: life dates 44 years, b. December 12, 1574-d. March 2, 1619; Queen Consort of James VI of Scotland, 30 years, August 20, 1589-March 2, 1619; Queen Consort of James I of England, 16 years, March 24, 1603-March 2, 1619.

QUEEN ANNE of Denmark the Consort of King James I of England was the second daughter of King Frederick II of Denmark and Sophie of the Duchy of Mecklenburg-Güstrow. Anne was born on December 12, 1574 at Skanderborg Castle on the Danish peninsula of Jutland. Her father at the time was King of both Denmark and Norway. Anne's mother Queen Sophie was only seventeen when Anne was born. Sophie was greatly admired for her erudition and cultivated manners. She sent her children Elizabeth, Anne, and Christian (later Christian VI of Denmark) to her mother for their education at the ducal palace in Mecklenburg, Germany. After a few years, the children returned to Denmark, where Sophie supervised continuation of their education, which emphasized literature, science, history, and languages. When Anne was thirteen, Sophie initiated negotiations for Anne's marriage to King James VI of Scotland. The marriage contract involved a formal dowry of £150,000, and it conceded Scottish claims on the Orkney and Shetland Islands in the North Sea above Scotland. Ownership of the islands by Denmark and Scotland had been contested for over a century.

From the Scottish view, a royal marriage that united the royal houses of Scotland and Denmark was highly desirable. Both nations were Protestant, and closer Scottish ties to Scandinavia favored improved opportunities for trade. Scottish diplomats originally courted Anne's older sister Elizabeth; however, she was given in marriage to Henry Jules Duke of Brunswick. Thereafter, Scottish negotiations for a royal marriage focused on her younger sister Princess Anne.

King James VI of Scotland was twenty-three, and had shown only lackluster interest in previous marriage negotiations. His preference for male company convinced many that he possessed a deviant sexual orientation. However, the need for an heir, or heirs, in the Stewart line forced completion of a marriage contract for James.

Queen Sophie sealed the agreement for the royal marriage in July 1589. Anne was fourteen when the marriage took place in 1589. It is reported that three hundred tailors worked on her wedding dress. Fourteen year old Anne was delighted at the prospect of being a queen. She romantically fantasized that she was deeply in love with her prospective husband she had never met. She hand-embroidered monogrammed shirts for him, and she is reported to have said, "[I am] so far in love with the King's Majesty as it were death to have it broken off."

James and Anne were married by proxy on August 20, 1589 in the ancient citadel of Elsinore Castle, which overlooked the sea north of Copenhagen. Frederick II had restored and lavishly refurbished it as his favorite residence The proxy ceremony concluded when the groom's Scottish representative, Lord George Keith Earl Marischal, symbolically sat beside Anne on the marriage bed.

Anne lost no time in completing her preparations for departure to meet her husband, and be truly married at Holyrood Palace in Edinburgh. In September, her small leaky ship *Gideon* set sail from Copenhagen in company with several other vessels that carried her bridal paraphernalia. A powerful North Sea storm scattered the small fleet, and only one ship reached Leith the port city of Edinburgh on September 12. It carried the doleful news that the raging sea may have consumed Princess Anne and all others in her entourage. The other ships had been driven back to a Norwegian fishing village. The princess and her bridal party, with vast bridal accoutrements, finally arrived safely in Oslo with no loss of life.

James, with a suitable assembly of Scottish nobles, armed knights, servants, grooms, and priest-Presbyters of the Calvinist Scottish Kirk immediately sailed to Oslo to bring his queen to Scotland. They, too, were forced by stormy weather to land on the Norwegian shore and travel overland to Oslo.

James and Anne were married in Oslo by a Scottish Presbyterian minister at the Bishop's Palace on November 23,1589. The ceremony was in French, a language familiar to both James and Anne. The marriage was performed without ceremony, because arrangements had been quickly improvised with no advance notice.

Unseasonably heavy North Sea storms and leaky ships delayed the return of James and Anne to Scotland until May 1, 1590. Presbyters of the

Scottish Kirk concluded that witchcraft was responsible for the succession of severe storms that delayed the return of King James and his Queen Anne to Scotland. A witch-hunt quickly rounded up several hundred witches, who were executed to rid Scotland of agents of the Devil.

On May 6, Anne made her first official entry into Edinburgh. She rode in a Danish silver coach to Royal Holyrood Palace, while her husband King James rode beside her on a horse. Anne was crowned in a formal ceremony on May 17.

The coronation was novel in being the first Protestant coronation in Scotland, and one for which there were no presidents for propriety. Anne was Lutheran, and she objected on being crowned as a Calvinist Protestant. After a contentious seven-hour-long ritual, the Lord Chancellor Presbyter finally put a crown on Anne's head. She was too exhausted to protest any longer. She " . . . affirmed [did not swear] to defend the true religion and worship of God, and to oppose and despise papistical superstitions, and whatsoever ceremonies and rites are contrary to the word of God."

In the Scottish system of government, the king was merely the first among equal lords of the land. The Scottish Kirk exercised veto power over all personal, financial, and political actions of their king who was *sovereign* in-name-only. Royal living in Scotland was at a substantially lower level than Anne had been accustomed to in Denmark. The Scottish government was nearly bankrupt. James was forced to borrow formal clothes and table service for the paltry celebration that followed Queen Anne's coronation as Queen of Scotland. Soon after twenty-three year old King James and his fifteen year old Queen Anne settled into married life, the euphoria of initial truelove faded. James and Anne had very different temperaments, and shared few common interests.

James professed scholarly enlightenment. He had written and published books in Latin on witchcraft, demonology, and a diatribe on smoking tobacco, a practice Sir Walter Raleigh brought to London from the New World. King James despised the practice, and said, "[I find the] custom loathsome to the eye, hateful to the nose, harmful to the brain, dangerous to the lungs, and in the black stinking fume thereof, nearest resembling the horrible smoke from the bottomless pit of Hell."

Although James had a true gift for memory that permitted his mind to accumulate a huge clutter of facts, he had little ability to generalize, or derive any useful common sense from them. Contemporaries gave him faint praise in saying he was "The Wisest Fool in All Christendom."

Queen Anne's interests centered mainly on fancy clothes, music, theater, dance, and court gossip. Queen Anne had no interest in power politics, government, or religion, so long as they did not restrict her personal freedoms. After birth of her children, she also was a devoted mother.

Anne was a disappointment to the Scottish Kirk. Anne was not the defender of Protestantism, which the Scottish Kirk had hoped for in giving its approval of the royal marriage. Anne's frivolity set poorly with the Scottish clergy, who despised all worldly distraction from the serious business of worshiping God. Throughout her reign as queen consort of King James in Scotland, and later in England, Anne's personal religious beliefs were never evident. She always may have had Catholic sympathies.

Soon after Queen Anne's Scottish coronation in May 1590, she was under pressure from the Kirk to provide an heir for the Scottish throne. Her first child was born on February 19, 1564, four years after her marriage. Prince Henry Frederick was the first of seven or eight children born to Anne, who in addition had two or three miscarriages. On average, Anne produced a child at two-year intervals from 1560 to 1606. Of all the births, only three survived beyond adolescence:

> Henry Frederick Prince of Wales (February 19, 1594-November 9, 1612)
> Elizabeth Stewart of Scotland (August 19, 1596-Febuary 13,1662) married Frederick King of Bohemia Elector Palatine, the mother of Sophia of Hanover, and grandmother of King George I of England (see the Hanover Dynasty).
> Charles I of England (November 19, 1600-January 30, 1649)

The birth of her first child, Prince Henry Frederick, instead of giving maternal satisfaction, was the focus of intense frustration for Anne. Immediately after the child was born, the prince was removed from Anne, as was the custom for rearing the Scottish heir apparent. He was placed in care of the Earl of Mar for supervision and education for the throne. Anne protested vehemently for being separated from her child, but James was firm in supporting Scottish tradition. The Scottish manner of rearing the royal heir seemed completely reasonable to him. In his own case after he was six months old, James never had contact with his own mother Mary Queen of Scots.

Anne rarely saw Prince Henry during his childhood years, but Prince Henry was always the center of affection from both his parents. Anne unsuccessfully attempted to gain control of her son, but James ordered that Anne should not, under any circumstance, be given custody of the prince. Violent arguments continued, and one in 1595 was so stressful that it precipitated a miscarriage. After that, Anne no longer openly contested stringent Scottish customs, but the royal marriage was never again marked with affectionate cordiality. An observer at court said of them, "There is nothing but lurking hatred disguised with cunning dissimulation betwixt the King and the Queen, each intending by slight to overcome the other."

The king and queen continued to live together as estranged man and wife. James at first encouraged Anne to participate in manly sports of hunting. In her first, and only, excursion in the field, she accidentally discharged her fowling piece and shot James' favorite dog, Jewel, mistaking it for a rabbit or fawn. The king forgave her, but she never went fowling again. However, James regularly continued his effort to provide Scotland with additional heirs, as is shown by the succession of nine or ten pregnancies Anne endured from 1594 until 1606.

In late March 1603 after Queen Elizabeth I died in London, deputies sent by her Chancellor Lord Robert Cecil Earl of Salisbury notified King James Stewart VI of Scotland that he was invited to be King James I of England. His presence was requested in London to receive Parliament's approval, and to set a date for his coronation.

James received the English Parliament invitation to be King of England at the end of March 1603. He left Edinburgh for London in April with a sizeable company of Scottish lords and attendants. However, Queen Anne, being far advanced in pregnancy, was unable to travel and she remained in Edinburgh.

James was accustomed to Calvinist austerity and widespread poverty in his Scottish homeland. Therefore, when he passed Hadrian's Wall, and entered Carlisle, he was astonished to discover the wealth and superior standard of living enjoyed by nobility and the common folk of England. The prosperity of England became more evident as he travelled south toward London. He was delighted to learn that he would be king of so wealthy a land.

London and all England viewed the arrival of the Scottish king to be the inevitable working of God's will, nevertheless, he was a foreign invader from whom there was no escape—they did not like it, but they had to lump it—in this grudging manner, England accepted its first Stuart king.

A clash between discordant cultures met James and his Scottish attendants when they first encountered English customs. The English court was very different in formal etiquette from that at Holyrood House in Edinburgh where James had been the King of the Scots for thirty-six years. Edinburgh offered a crude no frills deportment that prepared James poorly for the ostentatious protocol Queen Elizabeth had fostered to glorify her own reign. James immediately offended the English nobility with his coarse language, vulgar oaths, oafish sense of humor, and shrill jarring laughter that irrationally punctuated his garrulous chatter.

Moreover, James was physically unattractive. He had a pear shaped body—large of rump, narrow at shoulder—set on spindly legs, and topped by a long face with a tongue too big to fit its mouth. James constantly slobbered and stuttered. His Scottish brogue uttered from his drooling mouth fell ill on English ears. His English subjects found him crude and uncouth, but the Scots who accompanied James were no better. They admired blunt frankness, preaching, and prayer. They repudiated the artificial ceremonial manners they encountered in the English court. They considered "all manners [to be] immoral hypocrisy unworthy of righteous men." The English and Scotts considered the others worthy only of ridicule and contempt.

A sizeable party of Quaker and Puritan petitioners, who hoped the new king would make wide-ranging changes in the Church of England, met James on his way to London. James was pleased to learn that, as king, he would have supreme authority over Church and State. Among other things, the Quaker petitioners wanted James to revise Church government along the lines of Presbyterian Calvinism; that is, they wanted to abolish the Episcopal hierarchy of bishops and archbishops in the Church of England, and have only ordained presbyters as advocates for doctrine. They also wanted a revised *Book of Common Prayer* that agreed in every detail with Holy Writ, but most important, they wanted a new edition of the entire Bible authentically translated from original Latin and Greek texts to assure purity of Christian doctrine.

James agreed to consider their petitions, for which he had great personal interest, but he privately resolved that, as head of Church, he would never again be the pawn of any clergy. He would prevent Calvinists and Puritans from dominating the Church of England.

> *King James Authorized Version of the Holy Bible:* Only six months after he became king, James personally selected representative participants for the historic Hampton Court Conference. It met in mid January 1604, and James played a direct role in supervising the conference. At the outset, he refused to abolish the Episcopal hierarchy of priests, with the flat statement, "No Bishops, No King!"
>
> He approved a study for revision of the *Book of Common Prayer* to bring it to conformity with the new Bible (but the prayer book would generate more dissension than unity). The major achievement of the Conference was approval of translation of the entire Holy Bible from original Latin and Greek texts. Over forty classical scholars performed the task, which took seven years.
>
> At last, in 1611, the first edition of the *King James Authorized Version of the Holy Bible* was printed with much critical approval. The King James Bible was by far the most ambitious and acclaimed work of biblical scholarship ever undertaken in English. James took great interest in the project, and he may have played some minor editorial role in its completion. The new Bible became the standard religious text for all Christians in England. It has stood the test of time, but differences in interpretation of its parts led to great diversity and contention among religious sects that arose in the late Reformation (see the summary at the end of this chapter entitled "The Rise of Protestant Sects During the Stuart Dynasty").

Queen Anne remained in Scotland for about three months after James arrived in London. Her pregnancy ended in miscarriage, and after a time for recovery, James ordered her to come to England in advance of their coronation, which was planned to take place at Westminster Abbey in August 1603.

Anne refused to leave Scotland, unless she was given custody of Prince Henry Frederick to bring with her to England. James did not want yet another public confrontation with his wife at the beginning of his reign, so he relented, and for the first time, Anne was given custody of the prince. Before leaving Edinburgh, Anne gave her personal belongings in Scotland to her Scottish ladies-in-waiting. Queen Anne never returned to Scotland, and the king returned only once, after they went to England in 1603.

Anne left for England in June with nine year old Prince Henry Frederick, seven year old Princess Elizabeth, three year old Prince Charles, and a coffin containing the body of her dead infant. They arrived at Windsor on July 2, 1603 for their first presentation to the English court. A great assembly of nobles greeted them. All wanted to meet their new queen, and they especially wished to see and appraise the heir apparent Prince Henry Frederick. The prince made a fine first impression that improved immeasurably with time.

James Stuart and Anne of Denmark were crowned King and Queen of England on August 24, 1603. The palaces and treasures of the English crown they inherited overwhelmed them. Parliament was generous in awarding them handsome annuities at State expense, and the royal couple responded by going on a spending spree of unprecedented dimensions. Neither Anne nor James ever understood finance—money was for spending, and for underlings to provide—to be in want for anything was not for kings and queens.

In the first two years of their reign in England, they resided in several great royal houses in and around London. For a time, Greenwich Palace (the favorite residence of Henry VIII) was preferred. Later, Queen Anne was delirious with delight at Richmond Palace to find that she had inherited almost six thousand gowns from Queen Elizabeth. The wardrobe was an inexhaustible treasure of rich fabrics, laces, and ornaments that would keep an army of needle workers busy for decades in fitting and redesigning apparel for fashion hungry Queen Anne. However, soon after their arrival in London, King James and Queen Anne chose to live apart at separate residences. This allowed two courts to arise; each would have very different influences on social customs and patronage during the reign of James I.

The personal relationship between the king and queen was formal, cool, but not contentious. Their deportment was always appropriate for State occasions. As one person in court said, "[The king and queen] . . . did love as well as man and wife could do [when living apart and] not conversing together." Anne rarely involved herself in matters of government. An Italian diplomat said of her, "She is intelligent, prudent, and knows the disorders of the government, in which she takes no part . . . She is young and averse to trouble; she sees that those who govern desire to be left alone, and so she professes indifference . . . She is full of kindness for those who support her, but on the other hand, she is terrible, proud, and unendurable to those she dislikes."

After the Guy Fawkes Affair on November 5, 1605, in which a plot was foiled in a Catholic attempt to blow up Parliament and the king, James chose to live away from London in the security of his Theobalds hunting lodge about twelve miles north of the city near Royston. There, protected by his brawny Scottish guards and served by Highland cooks, he felt safe and got fat eating bland barley soup, game and beef in rich gravy, bannock, haggis, and clootie dumplings (sweet or savory puddings wrapped in cloth and boiled for several hours).

Anne, instead, chose to live at the city center. She set up her own court at Somerset House located off the Strand at Waterloo overlooking the Thames. It was remodeled for her at great expense by Inigo Jones and renamed *Denmark House*. It was the location for staging extravagant social and theatrical events for which Queen Anne's court became famous.

Queen Anne's last child Sophia was born on June 23, 1606, and almost cost Anne her life. For the remainder of her life, she and the king no longer shared any marital intimacy. Queen Anne deliberately avoided involvement in any matters that embroiled King James in his interminably contentious dealings with the Church and Parliament.

When James first came to London, he wisely asked Queen Elizabeth's able Chancellor Robert Cecil Earl of Salisbury to remain and lead his government. Cecil would remain James' head of State until Cecil's death on May 16, 1612. For about two years, management of government affairs went reasonably well. However, King James and Queen Anne always overspent the annuities Parliament awarded them. Unlike previous English kings, James did not have rich personal estates in England to provide him with a source of independent revenue. Parliament resisted requests to vote the king and queen more money for the increasingly lavish life styles they chose to live.

After Robert Cecil died in 1612, King James decided to manage national affairs himself. That decision was disastrous, for he had no competence in economics, or diplomacy, or personal relationships. He was ineffectual in getting the Parliaments of 1611 and 1612 to do his wishes, but he went on with his spending without concern that no money came in to pay his debts. He doubled the national debt left by Queen Elizabeth. The Spanish war had been sputtering on since the Spanish Armada threatened England in July 1588, and had exhausted the Exchequer. James solved that pressing problem with a stroke of diplomatic genius—he simply declared England to be the victor, and signed a treaty of peace with Spain.

King James was criticized for wastefulness in the operation of his court, but he was censured even more severely for favoritism in making appointments to young men of little ability for whom he was sexually attracted. The acquisition of noble titles and wealth by these favorites was a major underlying factor in Parliament's obstruction of the king's will.

Few historians now doubt that King James was actively homosexual. His sexual inclination was well known before he came to England. At the age of fourteen when he was King James VI of Scotland, he was involved in a scandalous affair with his older cousin Esmé Stewart Duke of Lennox. In England, the involvement of King James with male inamorata became public knowledge by 1606. The king's most notorious English favorites were Robert Carr (whom he raised to Earl of Somerset), and George Villiers (raised to Duke of Buckingham).

King James met Robert Carr in 1606 when Carr was an attractive youth of seventeen. The king was transfixed when he saw Carr fall off his horse, and break his leg, after which the king personally insisted on nursing and caring for the boy. Carr remained the king's favorite until 1615. He was a Scot of very limited ability, but the king gave Carr important appointments in government. Carr even became Chancellor after Robert Cecil died in 1612. Carr eventually fell from power for malfeasance in office, and for an intrigue involving the murder of Carr's former lover, Sir Thomas Overbury, another handsome young man who at the time was Carr's prisoner. The scandal led to Carr's removal from office, and to his imprisonment in the Tower of London. King James I later pardoned Carr, but by then, George Villiers had replaced Carr as the king's lover.

George Villiers, who was said to be the handsomest man in all England, had more natural ability to govern than Robert Carr. King James was open in expressing his deep affection for Buckingham. On one public occasion he said, "I, James, am neither a god nor an angel, but a man like any other. Therefore I act like a man and confess to loving those dear to me . . . You may be sure that I love the Earl of Buckingham more than anyone else." He also tactlessly compared his affection to Villiers with that of Jesus for the 'Beloved Disciple' John.

George Villiers' influence on the king was decisive, and he was the chief intermediary between the king and Parliament until the end of James' reign in 1625. Villiers stayed in power well into the reign of James' son Charles I, until his political intrigues and personal ambition led to his own assassination in 1628.

King James' indiscrete relationships with younger men was a subject of common gossip that further tarnished an otherwise undistinguished reign. Oxford and Cambridge students smirked and said, *"Rex fuit Elizabeth, nunc est regina Jacobus"* (Yesterday King Elizabeth, Today Queen James)."

Court conjecture and ridicule soon led to contempt for perceived depravity and corruption at the highest levels of government. The king's proven inability to rule and his reliance on self-serving male favorites to lead his government undermined public respect for his reign at a time when the people of England were becoming evermore conservative and intolerant of corruption.

Anne showed little concern for her husband's dalliances with young men. She despised Robert Carr, but actively supported the rise of George Villiers to prominence. Queen Anne's place in public opinion was little affected by the king's feckless inept management of personal and national affairs.

Anne was entirely free to pursue a cultural agenda that brought her fame through support of art, music, and theater. She chose to be isolated in her own court at Denmark (Somerset) House in the heart of London, where she became the preeminent patroness of manners and arts in England. Hers was the most magnificent court in Europe. She was an enthusiastic devotee of the theater, and went to every play presented in London. She often had the plays presented in her palace salon. Many of Shakespeare's major plays were written in the Jacobean Period, including *All's Well that Ends Well, Othello, King Lear, Macbeth, Measure for Measure, Anthony and Cleopatra, Coriolanus, Timon of Athens, Pericles, Cymbeline, Winter's Tale, The Tempest,* also a few later plays in collaboration with John Fletcher.

Records show that Queen Anne requested to have earlier plays of Shakespeare, Marlow, and Sydney presented at State events in which she entertained foreign diplomats. However, her *Salón del Arte* at Denmark House was best known for bringing quasi-theatrical *Masques* to their highest form.

Masques had antecedents in entertainments arranged for Queen Elizabeth by her favorite Robert Dudley Earl of Leicester. He brought together, what today we would call *variety acts,* that incorporated a mélange of "pretty poetry pieces, dance with timbrels, heavenly noyse of all kynde of musicke" that were much admired by the Elizabethan court. Present day descendants of *Jacobean masques* persist today in citywide *Carnivals* in Venice and Monte Carlo, or *Mummers* parades in Philadelphia and Baltimore, or in the famous extravagantly costumed private *Krew Balls* of Mardi Gras in New Orleans. Faces were uncovered in Jacobean masques; only later, the observers of carnival balls also wore facemasks.

In Queen Anne's day, masques were prepared for court entertainment in elaborate form. They united instrumental music, choruses, dance, soliloquies, elaborate costumes, and fantastic stage sets. Costumed professional performers and suitably dressed invited guests all participated in grand balls, which were designed to recreate some real or imaginary religious, historical, or mythological event. Queen Anne paid important authors, such as Ben Johnson, to write scripts, and great architects, such as Inigo Jones, to design sets for her masques. Months were required to prepare costumes and scenery that cost a king's ransom. The splendor of Queen Anne's Denmark House masques and entertainments in London surpassed anything in other capitals of Europe. These elaborately costumed and staged pageants were for invited guests, and they were performed only once. Masques were not for the public, and the increasingly austere Puritan climate in England doomed the Queen Anne Masque art form to an early death.

In Puritan England, Queen Anne was strongly criticized for active participation in several masques. In one of them, she appeared costumed as the heathen infidel Pallas Athena dressed in a tunic so short that it revealed her ankles. In another, she put on 'black face makeup' and appeared as a Moor on stage when she was six-months pregnant with her last child Princess Sophia.

Little merit is seen in the surviving written stage directions and monologues for Jacobean masques. Their great popularity lay in dazzling spectacle, music, and the opportunity for the noble audience to participate with royalty in miming and dance. Queen Anne's masques were scheduled at a frequency of about one per year. They usually coincided with a regular Church holiday, such as, Candlemas (February 2), Shrovetide Mardi Gras (February/March), Easter (March/April), May Day, or All Saints Day

(November 1), but, most often, it was the Christmas-New Year Twelfth Night Revel of the Epiphany on January 6.

Anne was a patron of many arts. She greatly enjoyed music and dancing, and was generous in promoting careers of accomplished musicians and painters. It is a credit to her that the pictures she acquired to decorate her palace walls are the foundation for the first royal gallery of art. The commissioning and accumulation of works by major painters was continued and significantly expanded and improved by her son when he became King Charles I.

Important writers of English literature, such as William Shakespeare, Ben Johnson, Thomas Kyd, John Donne, Francis Beaumont, and John Fletcher, prospered handsomely in the Jacobean period. Usually, King James is credited for the burst of creative writing that graced his reign. However, there is little evidence that he had any appreciation for fine points of art, music, writing, or theater, since he usually fell asleep at plays and concerts. Queen Anne had enthusiasm for all arts, and she spent generously to support them. It is probable that she, more than the king, deserves credit for providing the environment for all arts to prosper in the first quarter of the 17th century.

The decade 1604 to 1614 covers the years of Queen Anne's importance to Jacobean culture. Queen Anne's public life leaves one with the impression of a vain superficial Dueña of inexhaustible wealth who scattered gratuities around with abandon to acquire reflected glory from the creative genius of common persons with true talent, which she personally lacked. In her private domestic life, Queen Anne was an ordinary mother who loved her children.

Queen Anne's decline to final irrelevance began when her eldest son Prince Henry Frederick suddenly died from typhoid on November 6, 1612. From birth, the prince had been trained to be the King of Scotland, and was expected some day that he would also be King of England. As a growing boy, he was strong, athletic, intelligent, handsome, studious, well mannered, affable, but distant and aloof. As Prince Henry grew to manhood, he showed a flair for learning languages, sciences, literature, history, and philosophy. He enjoyed sports, and was proficient in use of hand weapons for war and tournament. He was a strong Protestant, with a clear sense of ethical responsibility that brooked no compromise of principle. He was a natural leader of men. He was all a prince should be. Prince Henry became the hope of all England—a later day Galahad or Harry of Monmouth—who was expected to give England another Agincourt. Suddenly, as winter approached in 1612, he contracted typhoid fever, and died at the age of eighteen on November 6.

All England and Scotland mourned. The hopes of England then fell despondently on the Golden Prince's twelve year old younger brother, Prince Charles Duke of York, who was now the heir apparent. Prince Charles was a small, weak, sickly child with negligible qualifications suitable for governing a village, much less a nation.

Prince Henry Frederick death was a cruel blow to King James and Queen Anne, who were united in holding the prince most dear. Queen Anne, in spite of her many trivial interests, deeply loved and grieved for her eldest son.

That loss was followed only three months later by the long planned marriage of her daughter Princess Elizabeth Stuart to King Frederick V of Bavaria the Elector Palatine. The marriage at Whitehall Palace on February 14, 1613 was a suitably grand affair, but her departure to her own court in Heidelberg, left Queen Anne with only one remaining child, Prince Charles.

Charles was considered by his father King James to be a deformed monster. As a child, Charles suffered from rickets, and his growth was permanently stunted, such that as an adult, he was only five feet four inches tall, but his mother loved dwarf-like Charles. She lavished protective attention on him, and he returned her devotion.

Queen Anne never fully recovered from the death of Prince Henry Frederick. Thereafter, she never showed the great enthusiasm she formerly lavished on arts, theater, and entertainment. She became withdrawn, quiet, and indolent. After her last great masque was given in 1614, her health visibly began to fail. Two years later, she moved from Denmark House to Hampton Court Palace, which was her last residence.

By 1612 Queen Anne had used up her huge dowry of £150,000. Thereafter, she was dependent on the king's generosity to maintain her household and courtly ways of life. However, King James had long since exhausted their official State pensions. The Puritan Parliament resented the unremitting extravagance of King James and Queen Anne. The government felt that maintenance of their royal courts was a pointless sinful waste of public taxes that could better be spent to relieve rampant poverty, or better still, to build houses for the worship of God.

King James had an ongoing prickly relationship with his Puritan government. He was contemptuous of it, and said, "I am surprised that my ancestors ever allowed such an outlandish institution as Parliament ever to come into existence." As time went on, James avoided calling Parliament, but he continued to irritate his officers in government by constantly telling them, as he said, " . . . of my divine right to rule." James reminded Parliament that his wisdom was superior to theirs on all matters concerning the realm. He expressed the opinion, "Kings are not only God's lieutenants, and sit upon God's throne with God himself; they can even be called Gods." King James' outspoken claim for his divine authority to rule set poorly with his English subjects.

By 1614, the king and queen were totally out of money. Parliament was called to approve new taxes to support the bankrupt government. Parliament was completely insensitive to King James' pleas for money. It only lectured him on the wasteful operation of his court. When he saw that nothing would be accomplished, James disbanded Parliament after only two months. History has called it the *Addled Parliament* of 1614.

James and Anne had no ability to cope with poverty. King James cleverly solved their financial problems in a novel way. He created a new *Order of Baronet*, a noble rank between Knight and Baron. He then put noble titles up for sale (give or take a little as each case would determine): the title of Baronet sold for £1,000, Baron for £5,000, Viscount for £10,000, and Earl for £20,000. King James I felt the titles of marquess, duke, and prince could not, with propriety, be put on the open market for sale. Opportunities for social advancement were now available to any successful businessman able and willing to pay for the right to brush shoulders with nobility, and to sit in the House of Lords.

However, the English people deplored the practice of selling hereditary titles. They referred collectively to the new noblemen as the 'Lousy Lords.' Many of them were of uncouth common stock, with little learning, with dirt under their fingernails, with no sense of style, and abysmally deficient in manners and a sense for the fitness of things.

In the last four years of Queen Anne's life, she no longer maintained a noble court, or sponsored lavish entertainments, as had been her custom. She had a cordial relationship with George Villiers after 1615. She encouraged his advance, as he rose to heights of power in King James' government. However, increasingly, she was ignored and abandoned to a lonely existence. By 1617, she only rarely left her palace. She suffered from recurrence of a disabling malady of undetermined nature, which did not respond to any treatments or remedies. Her physicians could not agree whether her malaise was caused by gout, or dropsy, or "of indisposition through her whole body."

She continued to weaken to the end of her life. King James visited her only three times during her last year of illness, but the king's favorite George Villiers Duke of Buckingham was solicitous for her condition, and Prince Charles stayed faithfully by her side to the end.

After her death, accountants discovered that her personal debts were over £84,000, but her personal possessions were valued at nearly half a million pounds. However, almost none of her jewels or other tangible property was ever discovered in any of her residences after her death. Her trusted servants probably had absconded, like thieves in the night, with all valuable articles their queen possessed.

Queen Anne died at Hampton Court Palace on March 2, 1619 at age 44. Her body was moved to Somerset House to lie in state until May 13 for her burial in Westminster Abbey. King James at no time came to show his respect, or bid her leave. Instead, he sent a currier (possibly George Villiers) with a four line sentimental verse he composed, which scanned and rhymed poorly:

> *So did my Queen from hence her court remove*
> *And left off earth to be enthroned above.*
> *She's changed, not dead, for sure no good prince dies,*
> *But, as the sun, sets, only for to rise.*

Her funeral was a dreary affair. A throng of attending nobility dressed in black accompanied the catafalque bearing her body from the Strand to Westminster Abbey. In deference to Anne's native Denmark, banners of Goths and Vandals preceded the casket on its somber way. Midway in progress, a great storm broke, and the entire cortège was drenched. The noble ladies in great gowns and many petticoats were so overburdened in wet clothes that many of them could not walk, and were dragged to the Abbey in Westminster. The Archbishop of Canterbury led the Anglican funeral ceremony, which included the king's poetic eulogy.

Elaborate decorations were later installed over Anne's burial place in Westminster Abbey, but they were removed during the Republican

Government of Oliver Cromwell (1648-1660), in retribution for Queen Anne's "profligate squander on vanity."

King James lived for six years after Anne died. He faced an evermore difficult and contentious Puritan government. The reign of King James I ended in great frustration for the king, and with little progress for his realm. Death mercifully deprived Parliament of his impeachment. King James died at age 59 after a sudden attack of dysentery at Theobalds House on March 27, 1625. The great love of his life, George Villiers, was at his bedside, and arranged for his burial in Henry VII Chapel of Westminster Abbey with Queen Anne.

Queen Anne of Denmark the Queen Consort of James I is usually written off as an intellectual lightweight who was concerned only with trivial superficial matters of no real substance for cultural advance in England. However, the personal appearance of respectable women of high social status in her famous masques set a president for women to be cast in theatrical productions. An important day for a woman's rights came when Queen Anne appeared on stage in shocking costumes, in facial makeup, while pregnant. Her presence in court masques came at a time when, otherwise, only well coached boys, whose voices had not yet changed, read the lines Shakespeare wrote for *Juliet, Ophelia, Portia, Cordelia, Rosalind, Cleopatra, Desdemona,* and *Lady Macbeth.* One is in awe at Shakespeare's skill in writing so well for women, when he only heard his lines spoken by preadolescent boys.

King James I was succeeded to the throne in 1625 by his only surviving son King Charles I.

The Rise of Protestant Sects During the Stuart Dynasty

AT THE time James I came to the English throne, the Bible, itself, was a source of contention. William Tyndale's translation of the Bible, published over fifty years before, was in many ways inadequate, and a source of irritation to all religious sects. Tyndale's belief in the necessity for 'passive obedience to the monarch' expressed in his biblical text was rejected out of hand. Pacifists in Scotland and England all preferred revolutionary violence, to any governmental authority in matters of faith. They were firm in belief that, to preserve purity of their faith, rebellion was justifiable against anointed monarchs. That right became an obligation, when secular laws supported actions contrary to their own understanding of the 'revealed truth of God.'

Although the Lutheran *Augsburg Confession* was the starting point for all Protestant sects, other doctrinal differences prevented the new Protestant sects from uniting under a unified set of beliefs. Dogmatic intolerance of one another made Protestants a contentious lot. On grounds of fundamental principle, they rarely could work effectively together. In an oversimplified way, major Protestant groups in England in the 17th and 18th Centuries may be broadly characterized as follows:

> *Lutheranism*: Luther's goal was to reform the Catholic Church, and cleanse it of errors that had crept in during the long history of the Catholic Church. Luther felt that, when doctrine was true to Scripture, any other associated ceremonials that accompanied worship were acceptable. It mattered little whether persons chose to observe, or ignore traditional Church rituals or paraphernalia of worship including holy water or oil, shrines, graven images, rosaries, chants, hymns, paintings, statues, candles, etc. These were all viewed as unnecessary, but nevertheless acceptable accompaniments of worship.

> *Anglican Church of England*: The English Church, like the Lutheran Church, retained many ritual features in the order of service from Catholicism. During the reign of Edward VI, Archbishop Thomas Cranmer moved the English Church strongly toward Lutheranism. Chief among these was rejection of transubstantiation of the Host when it is elevated and consecrated by the priest. The *Book of Common Prayer* considered raising the Host to be merely symbolic of the presence of Christ in communion. The Anglican Church differed significantly from other Protestant sects in retaining an Episcopal hierarchical order of authority involving priests, bishops, and archbishops, as was traditional in the Catholic Church.

Methodism: In the early 18th Century, John Wesley an Oxford student who worked in the Anglican Church initiated a movement motivated by evangelism and revivalism. It separated from the Anglican Church as the High Church moved back closer to Catholicism in its form of service after the restoration of Charles II. Methodism retained the Anglican system of an Episcopal hierarchy of bishops that have authority over conference priests (now called ministers or preachers). In other respects, Methodism resembles other Protestant sects.

Calvinism: The chilling Doctrine of Predestination was at the heart of belief in this sect. Calvinism was strongly anti-humanist and put great weight on the doctrine of original sin. The concept held that man is born totally depraved. Salvation is entirely a gift in the hands of Christ as God. Those who are chosen (called the *elect*) will be forgiven their sins, and they will enjoy a life everlasting as a Saint in Heaven. Those not chosen (called the *reprobates*) will be damned to eternity in Hell.

Presbyterianism: John Knox was a Scottish Protestant religious leader, and at first, he was a strict follower of John Calvin of Geneva. Knox, on invitation from Lords of the Kirk, returned to Scotland to establish a Calvinist Church as the official religion of Scotland. A major theme of this sect was that The New Testament gives no special status to a hierarchy of priesthood above ministers who are called *presbyters*. All priest-presbyters are of equal rank with no superiors above them. Presbyterians, like many other Protestants, approved retention of a clergy, but elimination of bishops and archbishops.

Separatists: Anabaptists (Baptists), *Quakers, and Puritans* (formerly Wycliffe's Lollards, later Baptists and Foxe's, Levellers): The outer fringe of radical Protestantism felt that reformation of the Catholic Church was impossible. Total separation from all practices of the Church of Rome was the only course consistent with their beliefs. Most Separatist sects shared common doctrinal convictions on pacifism, and the elimination of formalism in church services, and they denied the significance of infant baptism. Separatist Puritans in England and the New England Colonies removed all elements of Catholicism and formalism from their form of worship. Thereby, they *purified* their faith to include only teachings specifically approved in the New Testament Gospels.

Protestant churches did not give the priesthood authority to assign penance, forgive sins, and provide absolution by extreme unction for the comfort of common man. In their stead, Protestants sought lonely solace through faith, study of scripture, endless prayer, and unrelieved guilt from real and imagined sins. All sects were dogmatically intolerant of all other sects. They gloried in their own dogmatic righteousness. They condemned as heretical all disagreement. The only thing individual Protestant sects could all agree on was willingness to go to war, rather than budge from dogmatic principles in their own religious persuasions—compromise was evil—just the Devil's name spelled backwards.

The religious leaders had all forgotten, or ignored, Christ's Seventh Beatitude from the Sermon on the Mount: *"Blessed are the peacemakers for they shall be called the children of God."* Their forgetfulness led to turbulent times in the Stuart's 17th Century England that we now examine.

REIGN 26

KING CHARLES I

AND

QUEEN CONSORT HENRIETTA MARIA OF FRANCE

Summary of the Reign of King Charles I
(Reign 1625-1649)

King Charles I: life dates c. 49 years, b. November 19, 1600-d. January 30, 1649; King of England 24 years, March 25, 1625-January 30, 1649.

KING CHARLES I of England was the only surviving son of James I and Anne of Denmark. He was born in Fife, Scotland in 1600. His reign of 24 years began when he succeeded his father James I on March 25, 1625, and it ended with his execution at Whitehall Palace on January 30, 1649.

Charles I inherited the worst of his father's many faults, to which was added his own pigheaded stubbornness. His imperious characteristics led to a steadfast irrational pursuit of folly that led to a Civil War, in which the people's Parliament of Puritan Roundheads was pitted against the Royalist Cavaliers, who supported their king. Charles's defense of himself admitted no argument, and rested solely on the imperious uncompromising statement, "My royal powers came from God himself, and, therefore, Parliament has no right to question my will on any matter whatsoever!"

In the end, Charles I was tried by the Roundhead Parliament, condemned, and finally beheaded in 1649. Charles met his death with the grace and dignity of a martyr. The English people were horrified by his execution, and Parliament no longer represented the will of the majority. His Catholic Queen Henrietta Maria escaped to Paris with most of the royal children.

Little of merit is found in the life and reign of Charles I. He was out of step with his time. He was an adamant advocate of the *Divine Right of Kings* in an age when the people of faith in England were resolute in deciding their own religious convictions, irrespective of what their monarch might believe. However, despite his lackluster reign, his face today is one of the most readily recognized of all English kings. This contradiction arises from the fact that King Charles was the patron of the Flemish painter Anthony van Dyke who painted him many times. King Charles preserved these portraits in the expanding collection of excellent painting that he added to the Royal Gallery. King Charles was far more able as a connoisseur of art than was his ability to rule England.

Charles' Queen Consort Henrietta Maria de Bourbon was the youngest daughter of Henry of Navarre, the first Bourbon King of France. As a Catholic, she refused to be crowned in the Anglican manner, and she and her husband were never popular in Puritan England.

After his execution, King Charles I was buried in St. George's Chapel at Windsor. The Interregnum or Protectorate Government of Oliver Cromwell followed the death of Charles I in 1649. The Puritan government lasted as a republic from 1649 until 1660.

In that year, the monarchy was restored, and the eldest son of Charles I, Charles the Prince of Wales, ascended the throne in 1660 as King Charles II.

Narrative of Queen Consort Henrietta Maria of France

Queen Henrietta Maria of France: life dates c. 59 years, b. November 25, 1609-d. September 10, 1669; Queen Consort of King Charles I 24 years, June 13, 1625-January 30, 1649; Dowager Queen of England 20 years, January 30, 1649-September 10, 1669.

QUEEN HENRIETTA Maria de Bourbon-Navarre of France was the youngest of six children born to King Henry IV of France and his second wife Marie de Medici. Henrietta Maria was born in the Louvre Palace on November 25, 1609. She was only six months old when a malcontent assassinated her father on May 14, 1610. Henrietta's mother Dowager Queen Marie de Medici became Regent of France within hours after the murder of her husband. However, her total lack of political ability led to her banishment from Paris in 1617. Her six year old son Louis began his rule as King Louis XIII with assistance from Cardinal Richelieu who was his Prime Minister. Richelieu's diplomatic genius brought France to unprecedented heights of prestige.

Princess Henrietta Maria accompanied her mother to exile in Fontainebleau in 1617. Her mother sent Henrietta Maria to be educated in the strict Catholic traditions provided by a Carmelite convent. Henrietta Maria's religious training permanently imprinted her with a lifelong undeviating Catholic religious conviction. Henrietta's mother supervised her training for court, much of which was spent in the Fontainebleau Palace, which her mother expanded and lavishly refurbished as her personal extravagance. In that setting outside Paris, Henrietta Maria enjoyed riding, singing, and dancing. She was literate in French, Italian, and Latin, and mastered excruciatingly correct French court etiquette. However, she was never praised for having any qualities of intellectual distinction of her own.

Henrietta Maria was painted many times by famous painters including Anthony van Dyke, and was always portrayed with a sweet aristocratic feminine countenance. Her contemporary, Queen Sophia of Hanover (the mother of King George I), said, "Her arms were long and lean, her shoulders uneven, and some of her teeth came out of her mouth like tusks . . . She did, however, have pretty eyes, nose, and a good complexion."

By 1620, Henrietta was back in Paris with her own court of several hundred retainers. She was thirteen in 1622 when diplomatic negotiations for her marriage to Prince Charles of England began. It would end in marriage on June 13, 1625 when Henrietta was fifteen, and Charles was twenty-four. However, circumstances that preceded their marriage were unfavorable for a happy union. Henrietta was not Charles' first choice; he hoped to marry a Spanish princess. However, Charles was rejected by the Spanish king, so Henrietta Maria of France would have to do.

Mechanics for the royal marriage presented difficulties. Appeal to Pope Urban VIII for special dispensation was denied, because a royal marriage between a Protestant Prince and Catholic Princess was impossible. Nevertheless, England and France approved a secular marriage of State, after which Charles and Henrietta were married by proxy in a Catholic ceremony in Paris on May 11, 1625. They were married again in person in Anglican manner at St. Augustine's church in Canterbury, Kent on June 13. A joint coronation was planned for an Anglican ceremony in Westminster Abbey, but Henrietta Maria refused to be crowned by a Protestant bishop. She observed the crowning of her husband from a distance, while screened from the congregation in the Abbey. Henrietta Maria requested a private coronation by the Catholic Bishop in the retinue she brought with her from France, but George Abbot Archbishop of Canterbury denied her request.

Henrietta Maria transported her entire Parisian ménage to England. Her personal duffel included a huge collection of dresses, a great store of jewelry and gems, whole sets of porcelain dishes, silver service, bedroom and salon furniture, chandeliers, and an entire library of books. In addition, over four hundred French attendants accompanied her to England, including one bishop, nineteen priests, many ladies-in-waiting, equerries, maids, laundresses, seamstresses, cooks, pages, courtiers, cobblers, *ad nauseam*, all of whom spoke only French, and had assurance they would all be supported handsomely by Parliament. By faith, they were deeply committed Catholics, and her wedding contract gave them freedom to celebrate the Catholic Mass daily.

The Puritan Parliament was outraged to learn that the secret marriage contract permitted daily Catholic Mass in the queen's personal court. Henrietta Maria's unwillingness to be crowned in the Anglican manner and her steadfast Catholicism was a barrier to her being accepted with favor by her English subjects. The English government and people strongly supported European Protestantism, and even gave aid to the persecuted Huguenots in France.

The young queen Henrietta Maria's religious intransigence created Puritan protest. The Puritan Parliament rebelled at the thought of paying for her heretical idolatry. Most of the Queen's attendants were sent back to France in June 1626, but Henrietta Maria was steadfast in insisting on her right to have freedom to worship in the Catholic manner. A Catholic priest and a small domestic staff of her French attendants were permitted to remain in personal service to the queen.

Henrietta Maria was ordered to appoint all her ladies-in-waiting from the English nobility and gentry. She was given Somerset House as her personal palace in central London. It had been designated 'The Queen's House' for Charles mother Queen Anne of Denmark, who had furnished, and decorated Somerset House lavishly for court functions and entertainment. Later, Henrietta was given other grand residences including Richmond Palace, and Oatlands (the favorite Royal Hunting Lodge of Henry VIII) located a few miles north of London, where Henrietta kept kennels for her hunting beagles, and a menagerie for caged wild animals, monkeys, and birds.

In the first three years of their marriage, Charles I and Henrietta Maria were barely on speaking terms. When they met at court, violent arguments and personal recriminations followed, which ended in angry separation. Weeks would pass before they met again and then only to have the painfully strained behavior recur. Henrietta Maria was a product of excessively correct French court etiquette, and she was too imperious to show any concern for the wounded feelings of her husband's barbaric inferior English subjects.

Henrietta spoke no English when she arrived in London, and she made little effort to master the language in later years. She refused to speak the barbaric tongue, except when necessary and even then only with difficulty, but she never became idiomatically proficient in understanding spoken English. Her spoken English was always with a strong Gallic accent.

Henrietta Maria was an outspoken spoiled brat with little inclination, or experience, in holding her tongue to repress expression of divergent opinions that would offend sensibilities of powerful dukes, earls, archbishops, and bishops in England. She never failed to contrast

England with the superior French standards for propriety with which she was familiar from childhood. She was shocked when she first arrived in London to see the boundaries of parks at Whitehall and St. James Palaces ringed with gallows on which were hung the putrid heads and body parts of executed criminals and heretic Catholics.

The first act by the new queen to outrage all London occurred when she went in peasants clothing, barefooted, and head uncovered to the gallows where a Jesuit priest had been put to death without trial. She knelt in the mud to pray for his salvation. Her charitable act earned her a storm of public protest. Henrietta Maria was militantly individualistic, and was never apologetic in defending her own points of view.

In contrast with his queen, Charles I always tried to create the impression that he was omnisciently master of all he surveyed. However, at heart, he was insecure, and had low self-esteem. As a child, Charles was small, weak, sickly, and failed to speak until he was four years old. He suffered from rickets, and only walked well after he was seven. His growth was permanently stunted, such that as an adult he was only five feet four inches tall. He was the shortest of all English kings. Charles always preferred to appear in public riding on horseback—in that way he could appear regal, and he was able to look down on others with hauteur. Like his father James I, Charles stammered when he talked, and was shy, withdrawn, humorless, and arrogant. He welcomed no argument. He was confident that his exalted station in life came straight from God. None of his personal qualities endeared him to his courtiers or subjects.

Although he was not mentally retarded, Charles always depended on others for reassurance of his judgment. For this reason, he retained his father's chief advisor George Villiers Duke of Buckingham, as his own confidant and advisor in the first three years of his reign.

King James I had openly recognized Villiers to be his homosexual lover, as well as his chief of state. King Charles retained Villiers in the latter capacity, but court gossip never impugned a deviant private relationship between Charles I and Villiers. Queen Henrietta Maria detested Villiers, and she resented his dominating advisory relationship with her husband. Villiers' powerful place in court was central to the alienation of the king and queen during the early years of the reign of Charles I. George Villiers' end came in August 1628, when a resentful army officer, who had been passed over for advancement, assassinated him. Almost immediately after Villiers died, the relationship between King Charles and Queen Henrietta

Maria improved when she took over the dominant advisory role Villiers formerly filled.

Henrietta Maria first became pregnant in 1628, and the royal marriage may not have been consummated before that year. Six surviving children born to Charles I and Henrietta Maria:

> Charles Prince of Wales (May 29, 1630-February 6, 1680), later Charles II
>
> Mary Princess Royal (December 18, 1635-September 8, 1650), later Princess of Orange, and mother of King William III
>
> James Duke of York (October 14, 1633-September 16, 1701), later James II, and father of Queen Mary II and Queen Anne
>
> Elizabeth Stuart (December 28, 1635-September 8, 1650)
>
> Henry Duke of Gloucester (July 8, 1640-September 18,1660)
>
> Henrietta of England, later Duchess of Orléans (June 16, 1644-June 30, 1670)

Henrietta Maria enjoyed great favor with the king throughout the 1630s. She received many expensive gifts from him, and she showed little restraint in spending lavishly on every whim of dress, ornament, palace, and entertainment. The London Court of King Charles I and Queen Henrietta Maria was soon recognized throughout Europe as a model for sophisticated good taste. Music, theater, and dance were encouraged. The Royal Gallery was enriched by paintings of Anthony van Dyke, Guido Reni, and Peter Paul Rubens.

However, the royal court was completely out of touch with the prevailing mood of the Puritan Parliament. The trivial pursuit of pleasure in court was an outrage. The Puritans were offended, and outspoken in criticism of the " . . . immorality of the queen who openly performed 'like a common whore' in theatrical events."

As Henrietta grew in favor with the king, she soon became a real power behind the throne. Increasingly, she took an active part in persuading the king to oppose all parliamentary attempts to curb his hereditary power as king. Consequently, secular leadership moved steadily toward open conflict between the king and Parliament through the 1630s.

Many believed that Henrietta Maria's strong, almost evangelistic Catholicism, if not actually converting Charles, led to his sympathetic toleration of Catholicism. Charles' aloof relationship with the English Church was shown by his grant of a Royal Charter for creation of the Colony of Maryland, which served as a refuge for Catholic exiles and immigrants to the New World. The colony was named for Queen Henrietta Maria, whom King Charles and the English people all called *Queen Mary*.

Queen Henrietta Maria religious intransigence surely alienated her from leaders in the Church of England such as George Abbot Archbishop of Canterbury. She was blamed for persuading Charles to introduce Catholic rituals into services of the Anglican Church. The appointment of William Laud as Archbishop of Canterbury, following the death of George Abbot, was very unpopular. Laud, although not a Papist, was a vigorous opponent of Puritanism. Moreover, he approved reinstatement of vestments, crucifixes, and ceremonial rituals, which suited the queen and king's taste perfectly. However, this 'Papistry' was anathema to the Puritans, who continued to increase in number throughout Charles's reign, and who felt that "all ornamentation in worship was pure idolatry."

At each new conflict, the King and Parliament became ever more estranged. Like his father James I, Charles was a strong believer in 'The Divine right of Kings' as expressed in the Latin phrase, *Cuius regio, eius religio* (The monarch's religion is the religion of his people) He irrationally used military force in an attempt to make the Presbyterian Church of Scotland adopt all the new ritual formalities of the English Church. The religious outrage in Edinburgh resulted in the king's forces being decisively defeated and expelled from Scotland. In one stroke, Charles alienated his strongest hereditary support in the realm.

Charles and the Puritan leaders in the English government were equally incapable of compromise. The king resisted all parliamentary interference on his right to control political appointments, and approve doctrine in the Anglican Church. He totally rejected remaking the Anglican Church into a Presbyterian or Puritan form of worship.

Parliament, in retaliation, asserted its right to nominate, and approve, or veto, all members of the king's Privy Council, all his ministers, all military officers, and even the right to approve those involved in education of the king's children. Parliament believed that the king was increasingly a pawn of his Catholic queen."

Before 1635, the queen showed little concern for public affairs. However, in 1637, she privately appointed an agent to represent the

English court in Rome. Moreover, she invited the Pope to send a Papal Legate as ambassador to England for the first time since Henry VIII separated the English Church from Rome. This created fear in Parliament that the queen conspired to make the Anglican Church subservient to Rome. In 1641, as an attempt to silence public criticism that he might be a Catholic, King Charles approved marriage of his seven year old daughter Mary Princess Royal to Protestant Prince William of Orange of the Netherlands who was eleven.

Charles' most egregious breach of English custom occurred, however, in 1642 when Parliament was scheduled to meet with intent to impeach Queen Henrietta Maria for her presumed role in persuading the king to reinstate Catholic practices in the Church of England. In open defiance of Parliament, Charles led a militia into the House of Commons to arrest its leading members. The queen was believed to have persuaded the king to take this reckless action.

Parliament was forewarned, and all its members escaped. Even so, the damage was done. The king had crossed a threshold in egregiously challenging the power of Parliament. The threat of imminent civil war was apparent to all.

Queen Henrietta Maria recognized the perilous situation, and in February 1642, she took steps to escape Puritan wrath by fleeing to Flanders with her personal jewels. She hoped to sell them, and buy guns and military support for Charles, in the event open hostilities broke out. Henrietta Maria spent almost a year in Holland and Flanders.

Civil War began in October 1642. The people's Parliament (the *Roundheads* or *Levellers*) was pitted against the King's Men (the *Cavaliers* or *Royalists*) who supported the crown. Cavaliers were largely composed of nobility and landed gentry. Levellers were Puritan religious fanatics; their name expressed their belief that all men were created equal, and that there could be no distinction in secular government between king, nobility, or commons.

Geographically, England was divided. The southeast supported Parliament, and the northwest supported the king. Thus, two-thirds of the population, and three-quarters of the wealth of the nation supported Parliament. It was foregone that, in the end, the king would lose.

Henrietta was successful in raising two million pounds from sale of her jewels, which she used to buy supplies, guns, and hire mercenaries to fight for the Royalist Cause. At first, the Royalists prevailed with superior military leadership in the Civil War. In a climate of optimism, Queen Henrietta Marie returned to England in February 1643. The monetary and military support she brought with her played a significant part in raising hopes for an eventual royalist victory. However, as time passed and military supplies ran out, the royal successes were short-lived. The king's militia was decisively defeated at the Battle of Marston Moor on July 2, 1644.

With collapse of Cavalier hopes, the queen knew she must flee again to France. On July 14, 1644, she chartered a Dutch ship to take her to Brest. She took three of her younger children with her to Paris. The youngest child, Princess Henrietta, however, was less than a month old, and she remained with nurses in Exeter. Two years later, she was spirited out of England dressed as a peasant child, and was carried to her mother in France by her nurse.

The two older princes, Charles Prince of Wales and James Duke of York, remained in England, because their flight would be taken as the equivalent to abdication of all claim to hereditary rights in England. Prince Charles was fourteen, and he remained in England for two more years as nominal leader for King Charles' dwindling Cavalier forces. However, he was finally forced to take sanctuary in France in July 1646. The second son, James Duke of York, was eleven years old and confined at St. James Palace in London, until he also was able to escape to France in 1648.

When Henrietta Maria arrived in Paris in May 1644, her six year old nephew was King Louis XIV and Cardinal Mazarin acted as regent of France. He authorized apartments in the St. Germain Palace for the expatriate English royal family. A small stipend for living expenses was also provided. The queen worked tirelessly to get funds and military support for King Charles I, but her success was limited and insufficient to change the course of events in England.

Henrietta Maria frequently wrote to Charles I. At first, she encouraged her husband to accept nothing but total surrender without compromise in any negotiations with Cromwell and Parliament. Later, after his total defeat in 1645, she changed, and tried to convince Charles that compromise was the only way in which he could keep his crown. However, Charles' was as unswerving in defense of his omniscient Divine right to rule, as Henrietta was in her Catholic faith. He could not be moved to accept any compromise that Parliament later offered, which could have spared his life.

The decisive defeat of the king at Marston Moor in 1644 was a turning point from which the Cavaliers never recovered. A year later, King Charles I retreated north to the Scottish border where he surrendered in expectation that the Scots would support him against English Parliamentary forces. However, the Scots distrusted the Charles' religious faith, and turned him over to English Roundheads led by Oliver Cromwell.

With the king in custody, Cromwell presented him with a constitutional contract that clearly set out the rights and responsibilities of Crown and Parliament. Charles would not sign it. His unalterable view on his Divine right to rule made meaningful compromise impossible.

Therefore, the civil war broke out again. Cromwell's parliamentary forces quickly and decisively put down the Cavaliers. Puritan army leaders closed the House of Lords, and purged the people's Parliament of all members who favored compromise with the king. The remaining rump Parliament voted to put the king on trial for declaring war on Parliament and his own people.

A special high court of inquiry composed of 135 judges tried the king at Westminster Hall in January 1649. King Charles would not recognize legality of the court, and he refused to make any defense in his own behalf, except the statement, "My Royal powers come from God alone and, therefore, Parliament has no right to question my will on any matter whatsoever!"

Charles I was tried by the rump Puritan Parliament, and was condemned to death by beheading for having committed treasonous attacks against his own subjects during the Civil War. In the decision to execute the king, the final tally was 67 to 67. Cromwell cast the additional deciding ballot for execution. Charles' sentence read:

> Charles Stuart, for levying war against the present Parliament and people therein represented, shall be put to death by beheading as a tyrant, traitor, murderer, and public enemy of the good people of this land.

The Princess Elizabeth and Prince Henry Duke of Gloucester, who had been detained as State prisoners, were permitted to see their father before his execution. Prince Charles in France sent a *carte blanche* letter to his father, in which he bound himself to any terms that could assure that his father's life would be spared. King Charles I burned the letter to prevent any improper use of it, and he did not attempt to bargain with Parliament for a reprieve.

The execution of Charles I took place on January 30, 1649. The day was very cold. As the king dressed for his execution, he calmly requested an additional warm shirt, "For the weather is sharp, and probably may make me shake. I want no suggestion of fear, for death is not terrible to me. I thank God I am prepared. Let the rogues come whenever they please."

The executioner was dressed in the coarse garments of a butcher; a black mask covered his face, all but his eyes. The parade ground at Whitehall Palace was nearly filled with guardsmen. Only few people of London were admitted to the far edge of the green. When the ax man kneeled, and asked forgiveness of the king, Charles said, "No! I forgive no subject of mine who comes bent on shedding my blood."

The Bishop of London assisted the king in binding up his hair, which was the king's custom to wear long. King Charles removed his cloak, and knelt before the block. He gave a silent prayer, put his head down, then his last spoken words were, "I go now from a corruptible to an incorruptible crown."

Charles met his death with the grace and dignity of a martyr. When his head was severed with a single blow of the ax, a great groan arose from the assembled multitude of men-at-arms, common tradesmen, and peasants. A witness in recalling the event said, "The sound that broke from the crowd, such a groan as I never heard before, and desire I may never hear again; that sound shall I remember for the rest of my life."

King Charles' head was sewn back to his body, and he was then buried at St. George's Chapel, Windsor, but no religious observance was permitted at his interment.

The people of England were appalled by the execution of their consecrated king. News of Charles's execution was greeted in Europe with horror and revulsion. Except for a few Swiss Cantons, no countries in Europe gave diplomatic recognition to the new English Republic headed by Oliver Cromwell.

Henrietta Maria received word of Charles' execution in the Louvre Palace. Charles' execution was a shattering blow to her, who for a time took refuge and comfort with Carmelite nuns at the Convent Rue St. Jacques in Paris. She grieved for several days, and then stoically returned to her apartments in St. Germain en Laye, but thereafter, Henrietta dressed in black mourning to the end of her life. It is reported that she said, "I have lost a crown . . . [It is] one I have long ceased to regret. It is for my husband that I grieve. [He was] a good, just, wise, virtuous Prince, worthy of my love, and the love of his subjects. My existence now is a succession of pain."

At about that time, her second son, James Duke of York escaped from England, and joined his mother at St. Germain.

Henrietta Maria was in desperate financial straits after the execution of Charles I in 1649. Her charitable stipend from the French government ended when the civil war of the 'Fronde' (which challenged the authority of Cardinal Mazarin) broke out in 1647. Henrietta appealed to Cromwell for a parliamentary pension to support herself and her destitute royal children in exile.

Cromwell refused her request with the cold explanation that " . . . since you refused to be crowned in England, you are not considered a legitimate English queen at all."

The English royal family remained in France through most of the period known to history as, the *Republic*, the *Interregnum*, or the *Protectorate* under parliamentary leadership of Oliver Cromwell. Henrietta Maria was neither recognized as Dowager Queen, nor as a person of any English status or importance. She was only a Princess of France and the mother of Prince Charles, the Pretender to the Throne of England.

Her small loyal court in St. Germain Palace was noted for its strict observance of Catholic formalities. In total frustration, Henrietta openly attempted to convert all her children back to the Catholic faith. However, Edward Hyde (the person most responsible for bringing about the restoration of Charles II) counseled Charles Prince of Wales and James Duke of York that they could never expect to regain their inheritances in England, if they ever appeared to be Catholic, as would be implied if they remained in their mother's court in Paris. Thereafter, Henrietta Maria had little influence on either of her elder sons Charles Prince of Wales or James Duke of York.

Prince Charles heeded the warning, and left Paris. He established his own expatriate court in 1654: first in Cologne, and then near Den Haag, Holland. James chose a military career, and creditably served sequentially in armies of France and then Spain.

After the Restoration of Charles II, Dowager Queen Henrietta Maria returned briefly to England in 1660. Her somber arrival clad darkly in mourning was met with profound indifference. Pepys diary recorded that "[She was] a very little plain old woman, and nothing more in her presence in any respect or garb than an ordinary woman." She took residence again in Somerset House with a generous federal pension of £30,000, matched by an equal amount from her son King Charles II.

Henrietta Maria returned to France in 1661 to complete arrangements for the marriage of her youngest daughter, Henrietta Anne to Philippe Duc d'Orléans, the younger brother of Louis XIV. After the wedding, Dowager Queen Henrietta Maria returned to England in 1662 with intent to remain permanently in London. However, the damp English climate exacerbated her chronic bronchitis, so she returned to France in 1665. Her health improved slightly, but she never regained enough strength to return to England.

In her last years, as an heiress of substantial means, Henrietta Maria founded the Carmelite Convent of the Visitation at Chaillot outside Paris. Her life ended in great physical pain from throat cancer. She died on August 21, 1669 from an overdose of palliative morphine while in residence at the Châteaux de Colombes near Paris. She was buried in the royal mausoleum at the Basilica of St. Denis in Paris, but her tomb was destroyed a century later during the French Revolution.

Immediately after the execution of Charles I on January 30, 1649, England entered a decade that is popularly called the Puritan Republic. It annulled the Monarchy and the House of Lords. At the same time, Charles Prince of Wales became the Pretender Expatriate King of England. He would wait for eleven years (until his thirtieth birthday on May 29, 1660) to claim his crown in what is known as the Restoration of Charles II.

After eleven years of righteous Puritan rule, England was ready to return to a monarchy with the Pretender Expatriate as their King Charles II.

REIGN 27

KING CHARLES II

AND

QUEEN CONSORT KATHERINE
OF BRAGANZA

Summary of the Reign of King Charles II
(Reign 1660-1685)

King Charles II: life dates c. 55 years, b. May 29, 1630-d. February 6, 1685; King of England 25 years, May 29, 1660-February 6, 1685.

KING CHARLES II was the eldest son of Charles I and Henrietta Maria of France. He was born in St. James Palace, London, and his twenty-five year reign 'officially' began at the death of his father in 1649, but it 'functionally' began with the restoration of the monarchy following termination of the Cromwell Republic of 1649-1660. Charles Prince of Wales returned from Holland to London on his 30th birthday May 29, 1660. His coronation came almost a year later on April 23, 1661. His death from a stroke at Whitehall Palace, London in 1685 ended his life, and he was buried in Westminster Abbey.

Charles II was known as *The Merry Monarch* for the libertine ways he acquired as an expatriate prince in France, Germany, and The Netherlands during the decade of Cromwell's Republican Protectorate. His reign is called *The Restoration Period,* a time characterized by hedonistic manners brought in from France by the king. His reign was in astonishing contrast to the stark Puritan years preceding it. The Restoration was a time of explosive English creativity in architecture, arts, letters, theater, and sciences, made famous by Christopher Wren, Henry Purcell, John Dryden, Alexander Pope, William Congreve, and above all, Sir Isaac Newton. In addition, his host of notorious mistresses, including Nell Gwynne, brought color to his reign.

The great fire of London in 1666 permitted the city to be rebuilt, and take on its character of modern times. Charles II had no strong conviction in matters of faith, and the Parliamentary Bill of Amnesty and Oblivion, which promised to forgive and forget past traitorous crimes and errors, show his tolerance and magnanimity. It permitted the land to get on with life without rancor. The Civil War and Interregnum, however, forever reversed the relationship between the king and Parliament. After the Restoration, Parliament ruled and the crown was required to persuade to get its way.

For the English colonies in America, both Charles II and his father Charles I, are honored in naming the Carolina Colonies (1629 and 1663). Charles II granted the charter to William Penn for the colony of universal religious freedom, which became Pennsylvania (1664). The Dutch colony of New Amsterdam was annexed, and called New York (1662 & 1672) in honor of the king's younger brother James Duke of York.

Charles II married his Queen Consort Katherine of Braganza in 1662. She was eldest daughter of the King of Portugal. Katherine was born in 1638; she survived Charles until 1705, and died at Belém Palace near Lisbon, Portugal, where she is buried. Although Charles II had over a dozen illegitimate children by various mistresses, he had no legitimate heir by his Queen Katherine of Braganza.

Following the death of Charles II, his younger brother James Duke of York succeeded to the throne in 1685 as King James II.

Narrative of Queen Consort
Katherine of Braganza

Queen Katherine of Braganza: life dates 67 years, b. November 25, 1638-d. December 31, 1705; Queen Consort of Charles II 23 years, April 16, 1662-February 6, 1685; Dowager Queen of England 20 years, February 6, 1685-December 31, 1705; Regent of Portugal, 1704-1705.

ENGLAND'S HISTORICAL relationship with Portugal: The western part of the Iberian Peninsula, known as Portugal, was part of land dominated by the Kingdom of Castile until 1385. In that year, John Duke of Avis won temporary independence of Lisbon from Castile, and became King John I of Portugal. In the next year, he signed a treaty of alliance with England for support in the event of future aggression from Spain. Thus, Portugal became one of the oldest allies of England against Spain in 1385 when John Duke of Avis married John of Gaunt's daughter Philippa of Lancaster and signed a treaty for mutual support with England.

Their son Henry (known to history as Henry the Navigator) followed his father as King Henry I of Portugal. With its new national freedom, and under the energetic leadership of King Henry the Navigator, Portugal became a leader in Old World exploration of the South Atlantic and Indian Oceans. Bartolommeo Dias circumnavigated Africa, and found a way to the Indian Ocean around the Cape of Good Hope in 1488; Vasco de Gama proved that ships could sail around Africa directly to Bombay (now, Mumbai, India) in 1498. By these, and other adventures, Portugal immediately became a competitor with Venice for trade with the Far East.

In 1581, King Philip II of Spain (the previous husband of England's Queen Mary I) succeeded in making Portugal again a subordinate Duchy of Spain. Portugal remained a province of Spain for sixty years. However, in 1640, a civil war began that would eventually sweep Spain out of Portugal, and restore Portugal's independence. The rebellion was led by Duke John VI of Braganza who was rewarded by election as King John IV of Portugal.

Duke John IV of Braganza was the father of Katherine of Braganza, with whom the present narrative is concerned.

Queen Katherine of Braganza the third child of Duke John of Braganza and his wife Luiza Maria de Gusmão de Medina-Sidonia. Katherine was born on November 25, 1638, and her name at birth was Catarina Henriqueta de Bragança. She was born at the Ducal Palace of Braganza at the village of Viçosa located near the Spanish border in the southern Portuguese province of Alentejo, which was the major county south of the Tagus River.

Katherine's birth came at a time when Portugal and her parents were deeply involved in preparations for a civil war of liberation from Spain. Two years later on December 1, 1640, the Duke and Duchess of Braganza were Portugal's leaders who declared independence from Spain. Her father was chosen to be King John IV of Portugal. The fierce Portuguese Civil War of Restoration continued intermittently until 1668, when Spain finally acknowledged independence of Portugal, and the legitimacy of its royal Braganza Dynasty.

King John IV moved his family from Vila Viçosa to Lisbon in 1642 when Katherine was four years old. Katherine thrived in the cultured intellectual environment luxuriously provided by the Palace Ribeira on Lisbon's harbor. Her father was a noted patron of music and scholarship. He possessed one of the largest private collections of books in Europe, and he was a recognized composer of polyphonic church music in the style of the Italian master Giovanni da Palestrina. The new musical form created sounds never heard before with use of several melodic themes in harmony with multiple instrumental and choral voices.

Katherine was educated in the palace convent school. Her mother strictly supervised every aspect of her education, which placed strong emphasis on Catholic dogma, cultural history, languages, and music. Katherine was only seldom removed from her mother's presence for even a day. She possibly was not away from the palace more than a dozen times in as many years and then only to visit holy shrines, abbeys, and cathedrals. Katherine grew up happily in a conservative cloistered world in which she was unaware of the tawdry world of intrigue and vice outside the Palace Ribeira.

King John of Portugal was a military strategist as well as scholar. He knew that Portugal's independence from Spain would require foreign assistance. In 1644, his ambassador approached King Charles I of England with a proposal for marriage of England's Charles Prince of Wales (then 14 years old) and his six year old daughter Infanta Catarina de Bragança.

Unfortunately, Charles I and his Cavalier militia in England had just experienced decisive defeat from Oliver Cromwell's Puritan army in the Battle of Marston Moor on July 2, 1644. King Charles I of England was in no position to sign a diplomatic binding agreement with a foreign power, so long as he was unable to control his own government.

The matter of a royal marriage for Portugal and England ended when Charles I was executed by Parliament on January 30, 1649, and Parliament terminated the English monarchy with installation of a Republican form of government. At that point, King John of Portugal explored the possibility of strengthening Portugal's foreign diplomatic ties with France—Spain's traditional competitor. The Dauphin Louis (later Louis XIV) became the object of King John's pursuit of a husband for his daughter Princess Katherine; the dauphin and princess were of the same age. Katherine became the Infanta of Portugal (the heiress to the throne of Portugal) after an older brother and sister died in 1653. Her father King John IV of Portugal pursued the goal of Katherine's marriage to Louis XIV of France until 1656, when King John died at age fifty-three.

All Europe never faced more uncertain times of change and transition than it experienced between 1656 and 1660. France, Spain, the Low Countries, and Austria were embroiled in build up to, or consequences of, the Franco-Dutch War, the League of Augsburg War, and onset of the War of the Spanish Succession. England had tired of its experiment with Puritan Republicanism, and was seeking a way to restore the monarchy without losing autonomy for Parliament.

Regent Luiza Maria of Portugal learned in 1660 that Louis XIV of France had married Maria Theresa of Spain, and that Charles Prince of Wales would soon become King Charles II of England with restoration of the monarchy in England. Luiza then renewed negotiations for a royal marriage of the restored Prince Charles as the King of England to her daughter Katherine the Infanta of Portugal. The calculated political move for the marriage contract hoped to gain English support as an ally in Portugal's protracted civil war with Spain.

Charles Prince of Wales signed the Declaration of Breda on April 4, 1660, which cleared way for restoration of the monarchy in England, and for his return to England as King Charles II on May 29, 1660. The Declaration approved pardons for all who had participated in the English Civil War, provided they pledged loyalty to the new king and government.

The House of Lords was restored, and other concessions assured peace and tranquility in the hastily restored shaky English monarchy.

Charles II inherited many debts from his miserly Puritan Parliament. Charles needed to marry with a handsome dowry from a foreign princess. Queen Luiza enticed Parliament with the richest dower package ever proposed: £ 300,000 and full free trading rights with Tangiers (opposite Gibraltar), Brazil, the Portuguese East Indies, and with full autonomy over the harbor islands in the port of Bombay, India (the last was of enormous later value to England as its access to the Indian Subcontinent). The dower offer from Portugal outbid all others. The impoverished Puritans disapproved of having a Catholic Queen, but Parliament was pleased to have the foreign princess foot the bill for restoring the monarchy to England.

The marriage contract for Charles and Katherine was signed on June 23, 1661. Some reports say that a marriage by proxy took place in Lisbon on April 23, 1662, but other reports say that, contrary to custom, no proxy marriage occurred, because no Papal approval could be obtained for the marriage of a Protestant prince to a Catholic princess. The marriage contract gave Katherine of Braganza £30,000 a year, and "a private chapel in her residence with the right to practice her Catholic religion freely."

Katherine departed from Lisbon for England on April 13, 1662. The people of Portugal were delighted with the marriage of their princess to the King of England, which gave recognition of legitimacy to their infant country. Katherine accepted her fate with calm obedience to her mother. She arrived in Portsmouth on May 13/14, 1662, and was married a week later first, in a private Catholic ceremony with a priest provided by King Charles' mother Dowager Queen Henrietta Marie, and second, on May 21, in a public Anglican ceremony with the Bishop of London presiding. On May 24, the king introduced his new queen to the English public at Hampton Court, and he appeared well pleased with his queen consort.

Charles II was an experienced roué with practiced skills and seductive powers over most women. Katherine was a mature woman of twenty-four in 1662, but her sheltered past made her as vulnerable to masculine charm as any inexperienced teenage girl. It is hardly surprising that court gossip reported that, at first sight of the king, Katherine fell immediately and permanently in love with her husband. All Katherine's future deportment affirmed her affection for Charles.

Gossip was the lifeblood of London's court. Prying curiosity about every detail relating to the new queen received attention. Queen Katherine spoke no English. She was inclined to paint her face in the Mediterranean fashion. She was slim and short. Her large, dark eyes were angelic. Her teeth 'wronged her mouth' by sticking out too much. Her ladies-in-waiting insisted on wearing Portuguese national dress with vast skirts known as farthingales. Nothing about Queen Katherine escaped attention, gossip, and evaluation.

Favorable comments included reference to her intelligence, amiable disposition, deep religious devotion, and perfect courtly etiquette in the manner of Lisbon. In speech, she was discrete and reserved. She demurely tried to please, and did not disparage the English court, but once she did remark "[The ladies of the English court] . . . spend so much time in dressing themselves, I fear they bestow but little time on God."

Katherine's reception in her husband's libertine London court was muted by her modest manner, and her lack of linguistic competence in English. Only rarely was Katherine described as a beautiful or handsome woman. However, King Charles II, an acknowledged connoisseur of beautiful women, said of her, "She has as much agreeableness in her looks altogether as ever I saw . . . and if I have any skill in physiognomy, which I think I have, she must be as good a woman as ever was born. In a word, I think myself very happy."

The truth probably is that Katherine was of average appearance, possibly better than plain, but no great beauty by any ordinary standard. Although Katherine spoke no English, the king and queen conversed freely in Spanish, a language in which both were idiomatically proficient.

Queen Katherine's happy introduction to the London court was short-lived. Five weeks after her arrival in England, Lady Barbara Villiers Countess Castlemaine, the royal 'favorite' of King Charles II, gave birth to a son on June 18. The king immediately acknowledged the infant to be his own. The infant Charles FitzRoy was ennobled as Duke of Southampton. Lady Barbara his mother immediately demanded that the king order his queen to appoint her *Chief Lady of the Queen's Bedchamber*, which was the highest ranking social position for a woman in court—below only the queen herself.

Queen Katherine had been informed before she left Lisbon of Barbara Villiers' illicit relationship with King Charles. Her mother advised

Katherine that she should refuse to have any socially approved relationship with Barbara Villiers, or with any other mistress of the king. Therefore, Katherine at first refused to obey the king's demand that she admit Barbara to her own court. However, the king commanded Katherine to honor his concubine Barbara Villiers with the official title *Chief Lady of the Queen's Bedchamber.*

At their first command meeting, Queen Katherine was so shocked at seeing the infant Charles FitzRoy in Barbara's arms that she fainted, and was carried away without greeting her rival. When Charles applied more pressure, the queen threatened to return to Portugal. Katherine finally bowed to the unswerving will of Charles II to have his mistress receive all social honors the court could bestow. In August, notwithstanding the humiliation it entailed, Queen Katherine relented, and dissembled acceptance of Countess Barbara as a ranking person in her own court. Thereafter, their personal interactions were models of correct formal etiquette, but the chill of their individual feelings remained palpable.

Her patriotic understanding of Portugal's need for its English ally motivated Katherine's bending to the king's will. The whole point of her marriage, from the point of view of Portugal, would vanish if she alienated the English when its backing was needed. Portugal's war of independence against Spain continued to be fiercely contested until 1668 when Spain finally signed the treaty that recognized Portugal as an independent nation.

A view into the shallow tawdry court favored by Charles II is given by John Evelyn's account of an average evening at Whitehall, "[One is surrounded by] inexpressible luxury and profaneness, gaming, and all dissoluteness . . . [in] total forgetfulness of God. The King sits and toys with his concubines; a French boy sings love songs in that glorious gallery; whilst about twenty of the great courtiers and other dissolute persons were at Basset [cards] 'round a large table, with a bank of at least £2,000 in gold before them . . . [the new Queen sat] untaken notice of, whilst a large crowd of courtiers surrounded her rival [Countess Barbara Villiers]."

Katherine's acceptance of humiliation from her husband's inability to deny his doxy Barbara Villiers everything she demanded, set a pattern for lesser persons in court to disparage and ignore the queen's rightful place as moderator of propriety in court etiquette. Thus, Katherine's life became increasingly isolated, lonely, and ignored. Two years after her marriage in 1662, most of her Portuguese attendants were ordered to return to Lisbon.

Only a half-dozen priests, friars, and a score of her personal staff remained. Katherine had no official court of her own, and she moved from palace to palace with her husband, often to Whitehall, which was most favored by Charles II. Somerset House, the traditional *Queen's Court*, continued to be held by the king's domineering mother, Dowager Queen Henrietta Maria until her death in 1669. After that date, Queen Katherine was given Somerset House for her own court.

Queen Katherine was a dutiful wife who stoically accepted the succession of her husband's favorites. She found each substitution to be less acceptable than its predecessor. Shabby ostentation flaunted poor taste and flouted propriety at social occasions in the reign of Charles II.

Katherine of Braganza failed in her primary roles as Queen of England to provide a legitimate heir for the throne. On several occasions between 1662 and 1665, Katherine was ill from other causes, and was thought to be pregnant. However, in February 1666 she had her first known miscarriage. Another occurred in 1668, and her last pregnancy ended in like manner in 1669. After that time, many assumed that the queen was incapable of carrying a conceptus to full term. This perception further eroded Katherine's significance in court.

In July and August 1671, court rumors surfaced that the king planned to divorce Katherine to be free to marry a wife who could provide a legitimate royal heir. It came as a surprise to everyone when Charles II denied the gossip, and steadfastly refused to consider the possibility of separation from his queen. It suddenly became apparent that he had a sincere affection for his Portuguese princess, and had no thought of abandoning her for failing to provide him with an heir. King Charles II apparently was blessed with the fundamental polygamous nature of an Oriental Potentate in his ability to love, respect, honor, and defend all wives and quasi-wives in his harem.

King Charles II put lie to rumors of a royal divorce by taking Queen Katherine 'on progress' in September 1671 to Norfolk, and then through Yorkshire. In the countryside, the people responded to their queen enthusiastically. She enjoyed participating in informal picnics, in festive local entertainments, and she received favorable comment for her common touch by wearing rustic peasant attire that showed off to advantage her slender well-shaped legs. A report on the progress said, "[The queen was] infinitely gracious . . . [and] the whole of our inhabitants sing nothing but her praises."

In the same year, 1672, England stabilized its claim on the Dutch colony of New Amsterdam in the New World. Under English rule, the colony was renamed New York in honor of the king's brother James Duke of York, who led the English naval armada that attacked, and took command of New Amsterdam. The Long Island Borough of Breukelen (now Brooklyn) was named 'King's Borough' in honor of Charles II, and the adjacent Borough of Nassau was named 'Queen's Borough' in honor of Queen Katherine of Braganza.

The king's loyalty and the public response marvelously restored the queen. Although she never became proficient in spoken English, or had much impact on events of her time, the spontaneous show of genuine affection melted her stilted formal nature, such that she was transformed into an outgoing gracious social hostess. She enjoyed informal court activities such as cards, archery, country fairs, and riding to the hounds. She held her own place in official court activities where she attended theatrical events, and enjoyed dancing at balls. In her own court at Somerset House, she introduced the uniquely English practice of having daily formal 'High Tea' at four o'clock. The hot tea beverage used savory leaves of a camellia plant fetched at great expense from her Bombay estate in India.

Katherine of Braganza was accepted and admired by ladies of the English nobility who appreciated the queen's respect for propriety and courtly decorum. In the later years of his reign, King Charles always insisted that Katherine be accorded all respect due the royal station of his wife. He even defended her when his unruly mistresses (in particular Barbara Villiers Countess Castlemaine and Louise de Kéroualle Duchess of Portsmouth) got out of hand.

King Charles II was an acknowledged intellectual lightweight. Contemporaries said of him, "He is a Prince of many virtues, and many great imperfections." Another remarked "He never said a foolish thing, nor ever a wise one either." Yet, Charles II is credited with providing the impetus that many historians of the Natural Sciences consider to be beginning of 'real science' in England.

His erudite queen gave intellectual support to his approval of a charter for the *Royal Society* (name in full: *The Royal Society of London for Improvement of Natural Knowledge*) on April 23, 1663. Seventeenth Century founding members of the Royal Society included Christopher Wren (architect), Edmund Halley (astronomer), Robert Hooke (microscopist-biologist), Christian Huygens (astronomer-lens maker),

Nicholas Mercator (logarithm mathematician), Robert Boyle (chemist), Isaac Newton (mathematician-physicist), and about a dozen more. The goal of the Royal Society was emancipation from the stultifying view of Puritan universities that "the important goal of science is to verify Holy Writ as given in the Holy [King James] Bible."

The king had numerous openly acknowledged male illegitimate offspring who had been generously awarded high noble titles by the king. The lack of a legitimate heir for King Charles was of chronic concern to the realm. Without a legitimate heir, James Duke of York would succeed Charles II. That created a serious problem for the Puritan Parliament because James had secretly converted to Catholicism in 1668 or 1669. He openly declared his Catholic faith in 1673, and in the same year, he married his second wife Maria Beatrice d'Este de Modena (known in English history as Mary of Modena), who was a confirmed Italian Catholic. If they had a surviving male child, England could anticipate having a Catholic King as head of the Anglican Church in England for the foreseeable future.

To thwart that unacceptable possibility, Puritan members of Parliament explored the possibility of legitimizing one of King Charles' Protestant bastard sons. This began the so-called *Lucy Walters Black Box* search. Lucy Walters was a mistress of Charles Prince of Wales (later Charles II) when he was in exile in Holland in 1657/58 before his restoration. His illegitimate son with Lucy named James Scot was born in Rotterdam on April 9, 1649, and he was later ennobled as James Duke of Monmouth who became a popular favorite in his father's Whitehall Court. Members in Parliament embroiled in the royal succession problem, envisioned a simple solution: if they could find a marriage certificate, or even a precontract for marriage of Lucy Walters to Charles Prince of Wales, then the Duke of Monmouth would be *prima facie* legitimate. Lucy died in 1658, but rumor said that she kept a 'Black Box' with personal documents in it. Therefore, a search for Lucy Walter's Black Box began, but no black box was ever found. To the distress of Parliament, search for it ended abruptly when King Charles said there never was any thought of his marriage to Lucy Walters. Charles even made a legal entry in Privy Council minutes that denied Monmouth's legitimacy. Lucy Walter was promiscuous before and after her liaison with Charles, and she died a courtesan prostitute in Paris in 1658.

Following 1670, the Catholic problem posed by the royal succession steadily fed Puritan intolerance for Catholicism. Parliament passed the

Test Act of 1673, which required all government employees to deny belief in transubstantiation of the Host, to deny other articles of Catholic faith, and swear loyalty to the Anglican Church. All who refused to sigh the Test Act would be denied government appointment. James Duke of York refused to sign, and openly avowed his Catholic faith; he then resigned his official position as Admiral in the English Navy.

By 1678, prejudice ran sufficiently high that a radical Anglican priest named Titus Oats was able to fabricate a rumor that Catholics were about to assassinate King Charles, and replace him with his Catholic brother James Duke of York. This notorious *Popish Plot* (without a word of truth in it) was accepted by Parliament as 'gospel truth.' The Popish Plot led to a hysterical anti-Catholic outburst of witch-hunts and executions. The inventor of the Popish Plot Titus Oats accused Queen Katherine of being part of a conspiracy to poison her husband, but King Charles scoffed at the idea.

At this time, the king's younger brother James Duke of York (a humorless autocratic antisocial malcontent) expressed concern over the lax security measures surrounding his brother the king. However, Charles with characteristic *sang-froid*, said, "Never fear dear Jamie. They'll never assassinate me to make you King."

Even though the Popish Plot lacked any valid evidence, and was later proven entirely false, the House of Commons voted to banish the queen and her entire staff from court, but King Charles protested, and the ban was dropped. However, Katherine's Catholic attendants were reduced to less than ten, even though the queen's huge dower had financed Charles' profligate court for many years.

Riotous street gangs threatened the queen's very existence. In April 1679, the Portuguese envoy advised Katherine to return to Portugal for her own safety. Even so, she remained in England. In July, dying confessions from perpetrators of the Popish Plot proved that all charges against the queen were bogus fabrications, as were all allegations made in Titus Oats' scare tactics that brought on reprisals against Catholics. Even so, as an aftermath of the Popish Plot, the aging King Charles was again pressured to divorce his Catholic queen, and marry "a Protestant lass who would . . . bring contentment to the troubled land with birth of a proper Protestant bairn."

Again, Charles II adamantly refused to consider divorce and remarriage. King Charles knew he had been inconsiderate in forcing his queen to accept his many mistresses and their ill-begotten children. Katherine had failed to provide an heir but, otherwise, she had been exemplary in every way. When divorce from her was again proposed, the king said, "They think I have a mind to take a new wife, but, for all that, I will not see an innocent woman so abused."

Thereafter, so long as Charles II lived, Katherine's place in court was secure. Katherine wrote to her younger brother Peter, who was regent of Portugal, with praise for Charles, "[Who] every day shows more clearly his purpose and goodwill towards me, and thus baffles the hate of my enemies [in court]."

After the tempestuous hysteria of the Popish Plot subsided in 1681, Queen Katherine wisely chose to live inconspicuously away from public controversy in her apartments at Hampton Court and Somerset House. With stoic resolve, Katherine tolerated the procession of brassy royal concubines who passed through court. She liked none of the 'Mesdames,' but she accepted the king's children with unbiased affection. Private records indicate that Queen Katherine gave an annuity to Nell Gwynne's son, Charles Beauclerk Duke of St Albans, until her death in 1705.

After the new year of 1685, while apparently in good health, Charles II experienced a series of attacks that are believed to have been cerebral strokes. The last one (four days after the first) on February 9 at Whitehall caused his death at age fifty-four. When the king's death was near, the corridor to his apartment was crowded with his mistresses, bastards, Privy Councilors, Parliament members, bishops, surgeon-barbers, and servants. Katherine attempted to see Charles, but she was unable to gain access to her husband.

She sent him a note that begged his pardon for failing him as a wife; to which Charles made the famous reply, "Alas poor woman, she asks my pardon? I beg hers with all my heart; take that answer back to her."

Charles, a master of manners to the very end, graciously apologized for taking so " . . . unconscionably long a time in dying." Charles then listed by name his many mistresses and children, and asked his brother James Duke of York (who would soon be King James II) to pledge that he would look out for them, His reference to Nell Gwynne said, "Let not poor Nelly starve." His last public request was, "Draw the curtain, and open the window . . . that I may behold the light of the sun for the last time before I die."

Charles II requested Catholic last rites of Extreme Unction. He probably was a closet Papist all his life, or possibly, guilt and faith intermingled as the curtain fell to close his hour on the stage. England was a happier land than when he came to it as its king a quarter century before. Charles II was sincerely mourned by his people, and he was buried with honor at Westminster Abbey.

When Charles II died, James Duke of York succeeded as King James II on February 6, 1685. He was a Catholic king in a militant Protestant country. During the reign of James II, although Dowager Queen Katherine was favored in court as a Catholic, she maintained a low public image. Katherine stayed in mourning in Somerset House for a year. She was rarely seen in public, and played no part in political events. Katherine's place in the court of Catholic King James II was more highly favored than she ever enjoyed in the reign of her husband Charles II. However, in the Monmouth Rebellion (1685) that faced King James II early in his reign, she tried without success to moderate King James' wrath at his nephew's insurgency. The Duke of Monmouth was beheaded at Tower Hill on July 15, 1685.

Katherine's favored position with King James II and his Queen Mary of Modena was shown in her being named the godmother for the infant heir James Edward Prince of Wales, who was born on June 10, 1688. The birth of the infant prince gave him precedence in the succession over his two Protestant half-sisters, Princess Mary Stuart and Princess Anne Stuart (daughters of James Duke of York and his first wife Anne Hyde). The birth of Prince Edward was anathema to the Puritan Parliament, because he would be reared a Catholic. His birth was the proximal cause for the Glorious Revolution that impeached and exiled his father King James II only six months later and brought King William III and Queen Mary II to the throne on February 13, 1689.

Dowager Queen Katherine lived quietly, and carefully avoided expression of any partisan views during the Glorious Revolution that exiled James II, and led to the succession of the Protestant co-monarchs King William III and Queen Mary II in 1689. Katherine's circumspect behavior earned friendship from the new king and queen from Holland. However, as a Catholic of gentle breeding in a Protestant court, her place of respect soon faded to irrelevance.

Queen Katherine of Braganza left little mark on events in the turbulent years from 1685 to 1693. In 1691, she petitioned her younger brother King

Pedro II of Portugal for permissions to return to Lisbon, but permission was denied until 1692. Dowager Queen Katherine left England in March 1692, and travelled leisurely through France and Spain until she finally arrived in Lisbon on January 20. 1693. Her departure from England was welcomed as a reduction in the Catholic presence in court.

On her return to Portugal, Katherine of Braganza was greeted in Lisbon as *The Guardian Angel of Portugal.* Katherine's marriage to Charles II was seen as "a personal sacrifice for her native land" to guarantee that England would be allied with Portugal in its long struggle for independence from Spain.

While Katherine was away from her native land (1662-1693), the two countries maintained free trade ties, in which English wool was exchanged for Portuguese wine to mutual advantage for working people in both countries. After Katherine returned to Portugal, she continued to work for stronger diplomatic ties between England and Portugal. She worked actively for passage of the Treaty of Methuen that was signed in 1703. It assured continuation of mutual trade advantages for the two nations, agreements that have lasted to the present time.

On Katherine's return to Portugal, she built the Palace of Bemposta near Lisbon where she lived until 1705. In 1701 and 1704/5, her brother King Pedro II was ill, and incapable of ruling. Katherine was persuaded to serve as regent until she died on December 31, 1705. During her brief time in public service, Katherine showed exemplary judgment and leadership. However, few data are readily available on her life after her return to Portugal, because the great Azores earthquake-tsunami of November 1, 1755 destroyed the royal archives and library of the Palace Ribeira in Lisbon.

Katherine of Braganza died at age sixty-seven on December 31, 1705 at her Bemposta Palace. She was buried at nearby Jerónimos Monastery, Belém, Lisbon. She won the love and appreciation of her Portuguese subjects, who showed their respect by honoring her with a magnificent funeral.

Today, Katherine of Braganza (*Catarina de Bragança*) is more highly regarded in her native land than in England where as queen she lived for thirty years. She is honored as a Matriarch of Portugal Independence with a life-size statue on the Tagus River Walk in the Parque das Nações (Park of the Nation), Lisbon.

Mistresses and Illegitimate Offspring of Charles II

KING CHARLES II the licentious *Merry Monarch* insisted on keeping his numerous brassy courtesans and common whores on center stage in his London court. They were so intrusive that history often forgets to mention that King Charles had a true wife, Katherine of Braganza, approved by holy matrimony in Catholic and Anglican ceremonies. Through no fault of her own, Katherine of Braganza is one of the most forgotten of all Queens of England, because her husband's many uppity mistresses command center stage in histories of England in the seventeenth century.

Charles II had more than fifteen mistresses, and as many illegitimate children. However, not all mistresses had his child, and some had substantially more than one. Charles acknowledged at least eleven children to be his own, and as many more were claimed to be of his royal parentage by their courtesan mothers. The growing number of royal bastards was sufficiently well-known for the Duke of Buckingham to remark that "[King Charles II is] the father of his people . . . [at least] father of a good number of them."

By the age of fourteen, Prince Charles had been instructed in ways of sex by maids in the Palais St. Germain en Laye, while he lived in exile with his mother Queen Henrietta Marie in Paris. It is unlikely that Charles was ever out of earshot of one or more of his mistresses for the rest of his life. Barbara Villiers was Prince Charles Stuart's chief mistress before his coronation as King Charles II in 1660, and she retained her position as arbiter of court manners until 1671. Barbara finally exhausted the king's patient acceptance of her demanding ways until Louise de Kéroualle, a French maid-in-waiting to Charles' sister Henrietta Duchess of Orléans, replaced her. Louise came to London in 1670, and her coquettish ways quickly captivated the receptive king. Hortense Mancini Duchess of Mazarin came later from the Parisian court of Louis XIV in 1676 as Charles' last *maitresse en titre*.

Throughout his life Charles II was a democratic admirer of talented lower class young wenches of the theater. Two of these were Moll Davis and Nell Gwynne. Both rose to be the king's favorite and, in time, became the mother of at least three of his children. Moll Davis attracted the king's attention by singing a plaintive ballad at Duke's Theater that ended with, "My lodging is on the cold, cold ground." Samuel Pepys reported that "[The King] raised the fair songstress from her bed on the cold ground to the royal couch . . . [Pepys prudishly added] She is the most impertinent slut in the world."

Charles II met Nell Gwynne in 1668 when she sold oranges, and was an occasional actress at the Duke Theater. Samuel Pepys called her 'pretty, witty Nell', and she soon became a companion of the king. Nell Gwynne was the most appealing of all King Charles' mistresses. She came from the Drury Lane slums of London, and was without affectation or pretence during her rise to fame on the London stage, and in winning the affection of the king. She also was probably the only one of his many mistresses who truly loved him. Charles acknowledged his affection for Nell with a pension of over £5,000 a year. Nell did not receive a title of her own, and she never put on airs beyond her own common station in life. She earned eternal fame from one occasion in which her carriage was threatened by an unruly mob that mistook her for Louise de Kéroualle; Nell cried out, "Pray good people, be civil. I am not the Catholic one, I am the Protestant whore."

History also records a charming domestic scene of King Charles and Nell with their infant son Charles. Nell called, "Come here you little bastard." King Charles reprimanded her use of such harsh language against his son. Nell asked, "What should I call him? Is not 'bastard' what he truly is?" On the spot, King Charles II created their son Charles Beauclerk Duke of St. Albans. Nell Gwynne was not acquisitive or personally ambitious. The requests she made of the king were often for the benefit of others, as was the case when the king was persuaded to charter the *Royal Soldiers Hospital* at Chelsea, after Nell told the king of an aged soldier begging on the street.

The Puritan Parliament was well aware of their king's philandering. The king was accused him of being "The great enemy of chastity and marriage." During much of his reign as King of England, it is said that his favorite courtesan at a given time knew of her status when she enjoyed the king's company for "four or more nights a week." Charles II was probably the most oversexed king England ever had. However, twelfth century King Henry I admitted fatherhood of more bastards than Charles II—Henry I recognized twenty-six bastards as his own.

Charles II acknowledged that ten or eleven illegitimate offspring where his own. The male children were usually given noble titles; six were created duke, four of the dukedoms persist today with living heirs. His daughters usually married wealthy or titled husbands. The biographies on the mistresses of Charles II are richly documented in other annals of English history.

REIGN 28

KING JAMES II

AND

FIRST WIFE ANNE HYDE

AND

QUEEN CONSORT MARIA BEATRICE OF MODENA

Summary of the Reign of King James II (Reign 1685-1688)

King James II: life dates c. 67 years, b. October 14, 1633-d. September 16, 1701; King of England 3 years, February 6, 1685-December 11, 1688.

JAMES STUART Duke of York later King James II was the second son of King Charles I and Henrietta Maria of France. He was born in 1633 at St. James's Palace, London. For most of his life, he was styled Duke of

York. He succeeded his brother Charles II in 1685, but three years later, he was forced to abdicate on December 11, 1688. He was deposed following the so-called Glorious Revolution, which was led by his son-in-law Prince William of Orange who replaced him on the throne in 1689. James II died in 1701 at Palace St. Germain en Laye in Paris. He was buried in the English Benedictine Church in Paris, but his tomb was destroyed later during the French Revolution.

James II was staunchly Catholic. As king, he was evangelistically committed to returning the Catholic religion to equal status with the Anglican Church in England. James issued a Declaration of Indulgence on his own initiative without approval of Parliament, which, in effect, repealed the Test Act, and permitted Catholics to hold positions of authority in government. James proceeded to make many Catholic appointments to high courts, to the Exchequer, and to his Privy Council without approval from Parliament.

A Scottish invasion with James Duke of Monmouth (the illegitimate son of Charles II) at its head was bent on removing James II from the throne. However, the Monmouth Rebellion was resoundingly defeated. In reprisal, a reign of terror called the 'Bloody Assizes' followed shortly thereafter. The Monmouth Rebellion led to religious persecution against Protestants in Scotland and England.

James Duke of York married his first wife Anne Hyde in 1659/60. She was the eldest daughter of Lord Chancellor Edward Hyde Earl of Clarendon, who played an important role in restoring Charles II to the throne in 1660. James and Anne had eight children, but only two daughters survived; both succeeded as Protestant Queen Mary II and Queen Anne. His first wife Anne Hyde died in 1671.

Two years later, James married his second wife Maria Beatrice of Modena who was Catholic. Their only son to survive was James Francis Prince of Wales who was born on June 10, 1688. His birth and Catholic rearing complicated matters immeasurably for James II. Protestant Whigs in Parliament immediately moved to remove James II from the throne, and replace him with his son-in-law Protestant Prince William of Orange and his wife Mary Stuart (the eldest daughter of Charles I). They were crowned King William III and Queen Mary II on February 13, 1689. James II escaped to exile in France, which was taken to be his abdication. The deposition of James II and the coronation of William III and Mary II are known in English history as the 'Glorious Revolution.'

Descendants of James Duke of York (later James II) and his first wife Anne Hyde, parents of—

Princess Mary married her first cousin Prince William III of Orange; after the abdication and deposition of James II, they became co-monarchs of England: Queen Mary II and King William III, no heir.

Princess Anne, after the death of Mary II and William III, she became Queen Anne in 1702; she married Prince George of Denmark, no surviving heir.

Descendants of King James II and Queen Consort Maria Beatrice of Modena; parents of—

Prince James Francis, known to history as 'The Old Pretender,' self-styled James III of England, but not accepted by the English people; father of—

Prince Charles (son of James, the Old Pretender and grandson of James II) known to history as, the Young Pretender (in Scotland as Bonnie Prince Charlie), self-styled King Charles III, but not accepted by the English people.

Following the deposition of James II in 1688, his son-in-law Prince William of Orange-Nassau, and his daughter Princess Mary succeeded to the throne in 1689 as co-monarchs King William III and Queen Mary II.

Narrative of Anne Hyde
first wife of James Duke of York

Anne Hyde: life dates c. 33 years, b. March 22, 1638-d. April 10, 1671; Duchess of York 11 years, September 3, 1660-April 10, 1671.

ANNE HYDE was the first wife of James Duke of York. She died before he became King James II; therefore, she was not a queen consort. Her exalted place as Duchess of York in the mid seventeenth century derived directly from the long loyal service her father Edward Hyde gave to Kings Charles I and Charles II. Edward Hyde from 1640 to 1667 served the two kings in the English Civil War. During Cromwell's Protectorate, he was the diplomat that made possible the Restoration of King Charles II. For Hyde's many services, King Charles II created him Earl of Clarendon and Lord Chancellor.

Anne Hyde was the youngest of five children of Edward Hyde and his second wife Frances Aylesbury. Anne was born on March 22, 1638 at Windsor Park, England. Her parents were of lower nobility/upper gentry stock. Anne's mother Frances (Aylesbury) Hyde was the heiress daughter of baronet Sir Thomas Aylesbury. Anne's father was Edward Hyde was of common gentry birth, which boasted no noble family connections.

Anne Hyde at age fifteen made her first appearance in high court social life in 1654 when she was appointed maid-of-honor to Princess Mary Stuart who had married Prince William of Orange, and was Queen of The Netherlands. Anne adapted quickly to life in court at Teylingen Palace located midway between Den Haag and Amsterdam. Although she was without title, Anne created a place for herself as a witty and attractive addition to the group of young persons who hoped to find titled husbands in court. She was praised for cheerful gay enthusiasm that won many admirers.

After New Years 1655/56, Princess Mary Stuart Queen of The Netherlands went to visit her mother Dowager Queen Henrietta Maria in Paris. Anne Hyde was among the attendants who accompanied Queen Mary to France. Anne possibly met James Duke of York at that time. However, not until two years later were Anne and James romantically entangled. That happened when James came to stay at his brother Charles

Prince of Wales' court in Breda near Den Haag in 1658/59. Twenty-five year old Prince James and nineteen year old Anne Hyde had an affair that resulted in Anne's pregnancy. Anne Hyde was in an 'advanced family way' in May 1660 when Prince Charles returned to England as King Charles II.

A marriage between Prince James Duke of York (the heir presumptive) and commoner Anne Hyde faced fierce opposition from all levels of society. The marriage was most strongly protested by James' mother, the Dowager Queen Henrietta Maria who returned to London from Paris expressly to prevent the wedding. She referred to Anne as 'that obnoxious Nan Hyde.' In defense of the honor of his trusted aid Chancellor Edward Hyde, King Charles II ordered his brother James to marry, and 'make an honest woman' of Anne Hyde.

The marriage was ordered at a time when royalty never married commoners, and when one would hardly expect Charles II to be a champion of marital fidelity. Charles, nevertheless, ordered his brother James to marry Anne Hyde, a common lass whose paternal grandmother was a 'tub woman', who earned her keep honestly by carrying buckets of ale from brewery to pubs and taverns in Wiltshire.

James stoutly protested the marriage, but his brother Charles said, "Jamie, as you have brewed, so now must you drink [in reference to Anne's paternal grandfather being a brewer]."

The wedding ceremony was performed privately in the residence of Edward Hyde in London on September 3, 1660. After the marriage, the bride and groom moved into St. James Palace in London, the traditional residence for the Duke of York in London. Chancellor Edward Hyde gave his daughter Twickenham House in Windsor Great Park as dowry. It became the country home of the Duke and Duchess of York, and it has been called 'York House' ever since. Anne's ill-begotten first child, a son, was born on October 22, 1660 only two months after the wedding; however, he died at birth. James and Anne Duke and Duchess of York had eight children. Only daughters Mary and Anne survived childhood. *They became reigning Queen Mary II and Queen Anne:

Charles (October 22, 1660-May 5, 1661), died at birth
* Mary (April 30, 1662-December 28, 1694), Queen Mary II
James (July 11, 1663-June 20, 1667), died in early childhood
* Anne (February 6, 1665-August 1, 1714), Queen Anne

Charles (4 July 4, 1666-May 22, 1667), died in infancy

Edgar (September 14, 1667-June 8, 1671), died in childhood

Henrietta (January 13, 1669-November 15, 1669), died in infancy

Catherine (February 9, 1671-December 5, 1671), died in infancy

The marriage also gave Anne Hyde the title Duchess of York. Anne's social status as Duchess of York made her the second highest-ranking woman in the realm; only Queen Katherine of Branlza outranked her. Her personal court in London was only slightly less grand than the royal court of King Charles II.

Anne had a quick wit, and an acid sense of humor, which, taken with her common origin, rankled her noble associates who considered her to be an upstart with poor manners and little to admire. She was not beautiful, but she was astute and clever enough to hold her own in a society that was proud of its cutting wit. She soon had many spiteful enemies in court. She was criticized for many things, and received exaggerated censure from licentious social climbers who were notorious for immorality. Anne's critics sniped at her extravagant poor taste, but nothing she did could ever have earned their praise.

One court observer said of Anne Hyde, "[She had] courage, cleverness, and energy almost worthy of a King's blood." Another said, "She was a woman of exceptional talents and accomplishments, and was gifted with discretion and tact, together with a certain innate grandeur of both manner and spirit." Other contemporary descriptions of Anne were less flattering—Duchess Anne had wit without personal charm; in Anne Hyde there is much to admire, but little to love; Anne possessed dignity without grace.

Anne Hyde is credited with being a patron of the celebrated Dutch painter Peter Lely, who gained fame for painting nearly everyone of breeding and wealth in mid seventeenth century England. He painted Anne Hyde several times in the splendidly draped fleshy voluptuous manner of Titian and Rubens that was popular at the time. The fashion in art was particularly appropriate for Anne as she gained weight in her later years. A critic of several pictures of Anne Hyde by Lely observed, "They represent for the most part a large, heavy woman, with an abnormally wide mouth, and we know from contemporary evidence that she became very fat early in life." She enjoyed rich foods, and was very heavy at age thirty-three when she died in 1671. Pepys' Diary said she was " . . . plain and glutinous."

James Duke of York, like his brother King Charles II, was involved in the endless pursuit of amours with maids-of-honor and titled ladies of the court. Anne's husband's many infidelities irritated, but were tolerated by her. The court gave Duchess Anne little sympathy or comfort for her husband's cheap vulgar affairs.

Before 1668, Duke James and Duchess Anne outwardly professed obedience and loyalty to the Church of England, but in that year, they both exhibited growing sympathy for the Church of Rome. When King Charles II heard of their change in faith, he immediately ordered that their two daughters (six year old Mary and three year old Anne) be educated in the Anglican Protestant way. The girls were removed from their parents' authority to Richmond Palace to avoid later conflict with Parliament over their future eligibility to accede the throne.

Anne Hyde Duchess of York joined the Catholic Church in August 1670, but this was not generally known until after her death in April a year later at age thirty-three. She died from cancer of the breast a few weeks after the birth of their youngest child, who was christened Catherine in honor of the queen, but the child died in infancy when less than a year old.

Anne Hyde received final rites in the Catholic faith from Bishop Walter Blandford of Worcester in the presence of her husband James Duke of York and Queen Katherine of Braganza. In the conclusion to her absolution, Anne asked the bishop, "What is truth . . . truth, . . . truth, . . . truth.?" as her last words before she died. This raised questions about Anne's conversion to Catholicism: was it spiritual redemption, or was it motivated only by her desire to retain control over her husband, who had professed Papist inclinations previously?

Anne Hyde died in St. James Palace on April 10, 1671, and was buried on April 15 in the Henry VII Chapel of Westminster Abbey in the Stuart vault with Mary Queen of Scotts.

As the mother of future Queen Mary II and Queen Anne, Anne Hyde has an assured place in chronology of the English monarchy; however, in other ways, she had little effect on any later event in English history.

A little over two years after his first wife died, James Duke of York married Maria Beatrice d'Este the daughter of the Duke of Modena, a small province north of Bologna, Italy.

Narrative of Queen Consort Maria Beatrice of Modena

Queen Maria Beatrice d'Este of Modena (Mary of Modena): life dates c. 59 years, b. October 5, 1658-d. May 7, 1718; Duchess of York as second wife of James Duke of York c. 12 years, September 30, 1673-February 6. 1685; Queen Consort of King James II c. 3 years, February 6, 1685-December 11, 1688; exiled deposed Dowager Queen of England 30 years, December 11, 1688-May 7, 1718.

JAMES DUKE of York's conversion the Catholic faith was publicly known soon after the death of Anne Hyde in 1671. The Test Act passed by Parliament in 1673, required a declaration of allegiance to the Anglican Church by all persons in government. The Test Act required James, who as a Catholic and heir presumptive to the crown, to resign his position as Lord High Admiral of the English Navy.

The Whigs in Parliament were enraged by the thought of a Catholic monarch on the throne who would be in conflict with the Protestant Parliament. The possibility of a repetition of Bloody Mary's reign of terror frightened everyone. Therefore, a number of so-called *Exclusion Acts* were proposed between 1679 and 1683 that would have removed James from succession to the throne. However, none of them won parliamentary approval.

James Duke of Monmouth, the eldest illegitimate son of Charles II was deeply involved with those who supported the Exclusion Acts. Clearly, he was the primary one to benefit, if James Duke of York was judged unfit to serve as king.

In this climate of religious tension and intolerance, James Duke of York chose to marry an Italian princess with resolute bonds of faith in the Catholic Church. His choice of Maria Beatrice d'Este of Modena to be his duchess, in a manner of speaking 'threw fat into the fire' of religious dissent that divided England in the last decade of King Charles' reign.

> Note: Maria Beatrice d'Este of Modena is usually called 'Mary of Modena' in English histories. However, in the following account, the name *Maria Beatrice*, or *Maria*, is used to avoid confusion by mistaking her with other persons named 'Mary' that abound at this time in England's 17th century.

Maria Beatrice d'Este of Modena was the only daughter of Alfonso IV d'Este Duke of Modena and Laura Martinozzi of an ancient noble Roman family with high connections in the Catholic Church. Maria was born at the Ducal Palace in Modena on October 5, 1658. Duchess Laura, who was regent of Modena after her husband died in 1662, supervised Maria's strict and classic education. Maria learned to speak and write Italian, French, and English, and read Latin. As a child, Maria travelled with her mother, and became well known in Rome and Paris. Maria was a grandniece of Cardinal Mazarin Grand Chancellor of Louis XIV. By frequent visits to Paris, Maria became a favorite of the Sun King.

However, the glitter of court life held little charm for Maria. She was deeply religious and inclined toward a life of contemplation in a convent or cloister. Her greatest wish was to join the order for nuns in the priory for the Sisters of the Visitation in Modena. She never abandoned this goal, and throughout life, she was, above all, a devout pious Catholic. She came from a heritage that had produced four Cardinals of the Church.

Fourteen years old Maria was described as " . . . tall and admirably shaped; her complexion was of the last degree of fairness, her hair black as jet; so were her eyebrows and her eyes, but the latter so full of light and sweetness that they did dazzle and charm, too."

When an envoy from James Duke of York approached Duchess Laura with an offer of marriage for her daughter Maria, neither mother nor daughter thought well of the proposal. Duke James, even though he had become a recent convert to the 'True Faith,' was notorious throughout Europe to be a dissolute roué like his brother King Charles II. The duchess hoped for a better and more suitable match for her sheltered daughter.

On her part, Maria was horrified by the thought of life in the licentious Protestant Restoration court of London where Catholics were persecuted as criminals.

However, Pope Clement X personally intervened with a letter written in Latin to Maria that said, "We therefore . . . earnestly exhort you . . . to reflect upon the great advantage that would come to the Catholic faith [in England] through your marriage [to James Duke of York]." Maria took this to be a command that must be followed. Maria of Modena was the only Italian queen England ever had.

The marriage agreement was signed, and a wedding by proxy took place on September 30, 1673 in Modena. Since Modena bore a subordinate seigniorial relationship with France, Maria stopped in Paris on her way to England to pay respect to Louis XIV. She already was a favorite of Louis XIV, and he gave her his blessing and a jeweled heirloom brooch valued at £8,000 as a bridal present.

Maria's mother accompanied Maria to England, and she was present when Maria and James were married first in Dover in a secret Catholic service on November 21 in which James gave her a ruby wedding ring of great value. They were married again in a public Anglican ceremony in London on November 23, 1673.

Their wedding was greeted in England with alarm. The membership of Parliament was Protestant. It strongly disproved of the heir presumptive James Duke of York marrying a Catholic. Parliament prepared a bill to annul the wedding, but King Charles II disbanded Parliament before a vote was taken.

Pope Gregory X gave public approval to the union. Maria Beatrice then was commonly referred to as "The Pope's Daughter." Gossip asserted that she was an advance agent of the Pope, and was part of a plot to restore Catholicism in England. Even the Puritans most tolerant of Catholics expressed the view that James should have chosen 'a less-*Papist*, *Papist* as his bride.' Maria was never forgiven for her close ties with the Court of Louis XIV in Paris, or for her support of Jesuit militant evangelism in England.

Maria Beatrice met her husband for the first time in Dover just before their Catholic marriage vows were exchanged. His aging smallpox marred face shocked her. For weeks, she broke into tears each time she saw him. However, with time, Maria accepted her husband, and she was very loyal and supportive in all his political ventures, even though she was always offended by his many continuing infidelities.

When they married, he was forty years old and she but fifteen—only a few years older than his eleven year old daughter Lady Mary (later

Queen Mary II) and eight year old Lady Anne (later Queen Anne) whose mother was Anne Hyde. James introduced his daughters to their new mother-in-law by saying, "I have brought you a new play-fellow."

Maria attempted to win the children's affection with games and conversation. Lady Mary responded well and became very friendly, but Lady Anne resisted all attempts Maria made to win her affection. Anne always disdained showing affection for her mother-in-law.

King Charles II approved of Maria Beatrice, and said, "She is much better than my brother deserves."

The Protestant Parliament disapproved of her simply because she was a Catholic. The English public was ambivalent in its acceptance of Maria Beatrice Duchess of York. The people of England soon warmed to her beauty, grace, and good manners, such that she became admired and loved by many. By comparison, Duchess Maria Beatrice was better liked than her husband James Duke of York.

As the Duchess of York, Maria Beatrice had a social position second only to that of Queen Katherine of Braganza, As Catholics, the duchess and queen might have developed a close supporting relationship, but for the fact that Maria was a cousin of Hortense Mancini the mistress of King Charles II. That was an impossible barrier to friendship between the queen and duchess.

Maria Beatrice's court was organized along the same lines as the royal court. She had a substantial annual domestic budget of around £5,000 to manage York House, St. James' Palace, and other ducal residences. James selected her ladies-in-waiting, including a number of his past and present mistresses. Maria strongly disapproved of the morals and manners of most of the female associates forced upon her. Maria preferred a life in modest surroundings with much tranquil time for contemplation and devotions. Her ladies-in-waiting wanted none of that. They insisted on filling days with parties, dancing, gambling, and gossip.

The only physical mark Queen Maria Beatrice left in England was the splendid private chapel she commissioned for worship in her private apartments at Westminster Palace. The chapel renovation cost £13,000. It was her only known extravagance, and it is a monument to her taste.

Maria Beatrice and the entire nation knew of her husband's many mistresses. The only criticism James received from his brother King Charles II on the matter of mistresses was that James " . . . should try to improve his unfailing fascination for ugly women." Mary knew in advance of James' long affair with Catherine Sedley, and of the children, she had borne for him.

When James became King in 1685 and created Mrs. Catherine Sedley Countess of Dorchester, Maria rebelled. The humiliation and insult were too much for Maria to bear. She threatened to renounce her marriage, return to Modena, and become a nun. She said to James, "Give her my dower; make her Queen of England, but let me never see her again." James II reluctantly banished her from the Whitehall court. However, she remained in London, and continued to have frequent contact with the king. The 'Madam Sedley Matter' did not end until James' priest pointed out that his " . . . flagrant adultery with Protestant whores besmirches your Catholic image, and makes you appear no better than your disreputable brother Charles II." King James at last banished Countess Sedley to Ireland with a rich pension.

King James II was accepted as king, because no one wanted either a renewal of civil war, or the bloody purges that followed the crowning of Queen Mary I in 1553. James was grudgingly tolerated in belief that a Protestant queen would follow his reign. The Protestant Parliament allowed Catholic James II to wear the crown, in belief that he would be followed by one of his Protestant daughters Mary or Anne Stuart. They were firm Protestants, and had married Protestant Princes.

However, the sequential birth of Maria Beatrice's five infants over a period of eleven years always placed her at the center of parliamentary concern on the question of the succession. The idea was intolerable of him having a surviving son reared as a Catholic. A male child would instantly supersede James' Protestant daughters by Anne Hyde—Princesses Mary and Anne. It was impossible to accept the permanent alienation of a Catholic King from his Protestant Parliament.

Maria Beatrice's first pregnancy ended in miscarriage, and she had four normal births between 1675 and 1682, but they all ended in infant death. The repetition of infant deaths lulled Parliament into thinking that Queen Maria could not produce a viable heir. Even so, religious tension increased sufficiently by 1678 for the Puritan extremist Titus Oats to fabricate a rumor that Catholics were conspiring to assassinate King Charles II in order to put his brother James Duke of York on throne.

The so-called 'Popish Plot' inflamed irrational fears, and led to false accusations and executions. Catholic Queen Katherine of Braganza, Duchess Maria Beatrice of Modena, and Duke James were said to be involved in the plot that was later found to be entirely false. Even so, Charles II ordered the Duke and Duchess of York to flee to safety in Europe, and then to Scotland.

The Puritan Parliament was faced with two abhorrent choices for their next king: would it be a Catholic, or a bastard for king?

Despite all the furor of the Popish Plot, and the Exclusion Acts in the years before King Charles II died on February 6, 1685, the transition to the reign of his brother James was calm and without protest. The Duke and Duchess of York became King James II and Queen Maria Beatrice on April 23, 1685. Their coronation was in Westminster Abbey; however, a Catholic priest also secretly crowned them the night before. James and Maria Beatrice had the first joint coronation since Henry VIII was crowned with Katherine of Aragon on June 11, 1509.

In the trying times to come, Queen Maria Beatrice was not involved in the political turmoil. As queen, she promoted elegance in court life by inviting excellent Italian artists and craftsmen to England.

At his coronation, James pledged to defend the Church of England, but after his coronation, he immediately embarked on a mission to make Anglican and Catholic forms of worship equally acceptable in England. James issued a Declaration of Indulgence that repealed the Test Act, and permitted Catholics to hold high positions in government. James, on his own initiative without approval of Parliament, proceeded to make many Catholic appointments to Courts, to the Exchequer, and to all his Councils of State.

The Presbyterians in the Church of Scotland rebelled at the Declaration of Indulgence, which legitimized filling government appointments with Catholics. They immediately moved to impeach James II, but were faced with the offensive choice of a Catholic or Bastard King. The Scottish Kirk reasoned that, since God forgives the ill begotten, a bastard was preferable to a Papist. Scotland replaced Catholic King James Stewart with Protestant James Duke of Monmouth, the eldest bastard son of Charles II.

The Scots then invaded England in the naïve expectation that all 'right thinking Englishmen would rise to remove Popish King James.' The Scottish invasion, with James Scott Duke of Monmouth leading it, was resoundingly defeated under expert military leadership of James II.

Monmouth was captured, taken to the Tower of London, imprisoned, and was beheaded without trial. Many Monmouth supporters were captured and executed by Act of Attainder. A reign of terror called, the

'Bloody Assizes' followed in reprisal against the Monmouth Rebellion. Many were executed, or imprisoned, or perished in jail, or were sold into slavery in Caribbean Colonies. Then, James initiated persecution against Protestants by making illegal any outspoken opposition against Catholic doctrine by Anglican clergy. James removed the Bishop of London from his office at St. Paul's Cathedral. He appointed Catholics to his Privy Council. He then attempted to pack Parliament with unelected Catholics of his own choosing.

The Duke of Monmouth, while in the Tower of London awaiting execution, requested Queen Maria Beatrice to intercede on his behalf for his life to be spared. She replied, " . . . had you offended against myself alone, I would gladly forgive, but since you are a traitor to both king and country, I can not, and ought not interfere." This was the single event in which Maria Beatrice participated in the controversy.

At New Year 1687/88, Maria new she was again pregnant. The child born on June 10, 1688 was a healthy boy christened James Francis Edward Stuart and titled Prince of Wales. The infant's birth and good health complicated matters for the realm immeasurably. The infant prince now was heir apparent. He replaced his two half-sisters, Princesses Mary and Anne in the succession. His parents, who were steadfastly Catholics, would rear the child in that faith. England had gone through too much during Cromwell's Interregnum, and in the recent Monmouth Rebellion to risk having another religious war.

Protestant Whigs in Parliament moved immediately to remove James from the throne. At first, false rumors were circulated that the so-called Princeling James Francis was, in fact, a foundling babe who had been smuggled illegally into the queen's bed, in a hidden warming pan, to replace yet another stillborn royal infant. The rumor was widely believed, because four of the queen's previous births had ended in early death. Princess Anne was a strong advocate of the 'foundling bedpan' myth of the prince's birth. However, almost immediately, many witnesses of the birth denied the 'bedpan rumor', and the child was soon accepted as the true Prince of Wales son of King James II.

Prince James Francis' birth quite naturally created a breach in the cordial relationship Maria previously had with Princesses Mary and Anne. They were half-sisters of the prince who now preceded them in the royal succession. Princess Mary had married to Prince William of Orange in 1677. Puritans in Parliament now courted him as the next king of England.

King James' final act that brought the crisis in government to a head was the arrest of seven bishops, including the Bishop of London and Archbishop of Canterbury. The bishops had petitioned the king to withdraw his Declaration of Indulgence. James ordered the bishops to stand trial for seditious treason against the crown. Seven noble lords (later called the Immortal Seven) acquitted the bishops on July 10, 1688. On the same day, a small group of Church and Parliament leaders sent a secret invitation to William Prince of Orange, and his wife Princess Mary Stuart (the eldest daughter of James II) to accept the crown of England. The message invited them to come as co-monarchs " . . . to protect liberty, property, and rights of succession to the crown . . ."

William of Orange landed in England in November 1688 with an army of over 15.000 men. King James's army and navy defected to William. James realized that, without military support, all was lost. Queen Maria escaped to France on December 10, 1688 dressed as an Italian washerwoman carrying the infant Prince James Francis camouflaged as a bundle of dirty bed linen.

King James attempted to flee, but he was captured, and then was allowed to make good his escape. Parliament ruled that by fleeing England, he had abdicated, and King James II was declared deposed on December 23,1688, the day he fled England.

A brief interregnum followed the deposition of James II. After two months, William of Orange and his wife Mary Stuart were declared joint sovereigns on February 13, 1689. They were crowned William III and Mary II on April 11, 1689. The deposition of James II and Coronation of William III and Mary II is known in English history as, the Glorious Revolution. It denied all possibility of James Francis Prince of Wales ever being crowned King of England.

King James II, his Queen Maria Beatrice, and Prince James Francis stayed in permanent exile in France. Louis XIV received them royally. He gave them as residence his Palace St. Germaine en Laye, and a generous pension on which to live.

James insisted to the end of his life that he was still King James II of England. He denied Parliament's right to depose him. James set up a quasi-government in exile in Paris that became known as the 'Jacobin Court'—its title was derived from the English name 'James' being derived from the Biblical name 'Jacob.' James' life in exile was spent in plotting, without success, to recover his English throne. Jacobin major support came from Scotland and English expatriates; however, Catholics in England also secretly supported plans to return James to his throne in England.

Attempts for James' restoration began as early as 1689, and continued sporadically through the 1690s. Military tactics included plans for prior domination of Ireland, from which invasion forces and loyalists in Wales and Scotland would conquer England. The most serious effort between French and English naval forces, called the Battle of Bantry Bay in 1691, was rebuffed by King William III men, but English suffered severe loses before the French were driven from Ireland. Much of the expense for the invasion attempt came from the sale of jewels Queen Maria carried in her escape from England.

The collapse of James's invasion of Ireland in 1691 set a pattern for the failure of future Jacobin attempts to reclaim the English crown.

Maria Beatrice lost her status as Queen of England when her husband James was deposed, but she continued to be honored by the title of 'Queen' in the Parisian court of Louis XIV where she was very popular at Versailles. She was admired for flawless manners, piety, and intelligent conversation. Maria became a close friend of Madame de Maintenon, the all-but wife of Louis XIV. However, James was never accepted in highest social circles in Paris. He was disliked for endless boring monologues on how his royal prerogative had been flouted. A wit summed James up with faint praise by saying, "He is a silly man with no interests in arts or science; he is over-sexed, and a poor judge of men, but I don't believe he is actually mentally defective."

James II died of a cerebral stroke at the age of sixty-seven on September 16, 1701. He was buried at Chateau St. Germain, Paris. For a time his supporters hoped he could be reinterred at Westminster Abbey, but his body disappeared during the French Revolution and its fate is unknown.

When James II died in 1701, the Jacobites in Paris announced that Prince James Francis was King James III of England. This claim was given international credence when Louis XIV gave James Francis official French recognition that he was the true King James III of England and James VIII of Scotland. However, the claim was never approved in England, where Prince James Francis is better known as the 'Old Pretender,' and his son Charles as the 'Young Pretender.'

Prince James Francis was thirteen when his father died. His mother Dowager Queen Maria Beatrice acted as his regent in the ongoing Jacobite cause while he was a minor until he reached the age of sixteen. She faced a difficult problem when diplomats from Scotland approached her with the proposal:

> If Prince James Francis came to Edinburgh, renounced Catholicism, and become a Presbyterian, he would immediately be crowned King James VIII of Scotland, and crowned King James III of England after the death of William III who then was King of England.

Maria was ill-prepared for practical matters of diplomacy, and her profound religious convictions did not permit her to jeopardize the eternal salvation of her son's soul, so she refused to let James Francis become King of Scotland and King of England. She continued to support the Jacobite cause with all the wealth she could give, but her resources were insufficient to halt the steady decline of her fortunes.

The same offer was renewed by Scotland for James Francis to become king after William III died in 1702, but Maria again would not approve her son's conversion to Protestant faith, and the offer was declined.

France and England were in bitter conflict for eight years from 1689 to 1697 (called *King William's War* in England, the *First French and Indian War* in America, and the *War of the Grand Alliance* in Europe). At its conclusion, William III defeated Louis XIV, and France was impoverished. Queen Maria Beatrice's pension from the French king was gravely reduced, and the Jacobite Cause in Paris fell on hard times.

All hope for the expatriate Jacobins collapsed in 1713 with the Treaty of Utrecht that set rules for arbitration of the interminable War of the Spanish Succession. Among its many provisions, the treaty stipulated that French recognition of Prince James Francis as King James III of England must be ended, and that he would be exiled from France.

James Francis left Paris, and went briefly to Scotland, but later settled permanently in Rome with a pension from the Vatican. The Jacobite nucleus died in France, but fragments continued to work for restoration of the prince in various countries, especially in Scotland and Ireland. The prince, without title, was thereafter known as The Old Pretender.

Queen Maria Beatrice remained in Paris, but was destitute when her pension ended after Louis XIV died in 1715. Without family or money, she entered the Convent of the Sisters of the Visitation in Paris, and became a nun. Thus, at the end of her life of many honors and disappointments, Dowager Queen Maria Beatrice of Modena finally achieved her childhood goal to be a Sister of Poverty in a priory convent.

Maria at last was free to enjoy pious meditation to the end of her days, not in Modena, but in the cloister of the same Order in environs of the Bois de Boulogne, Paris. The priory preserved her records and letters; in one of them she wrote, " . . . a heart full of divine love is at peace . . . it is the one thing necessary . . . [in spite of the world's misfortunes] that cannot cause unhappiness." Another record said, "The good and pious Queen of England . . . Surely must be in heaven. She kept nothing for herself, and gave all she had to the poor . . . she is . . . regarded as a saint . . ."

Maria Beatrice of Modena died from breast cancer on May 7, 1718 at the Palace of St. Germain en Laye. She was buried at the Convent of the Sisters of the Visitation that had given her refuge and comfort. Her tomb was destroyed in the French Revolution.

Queen Maria Beatrice is a footnote in English history that often cites only her name—Mary of Modena. However, in a sense, Maria was responsible for terminating the Stuart Dynasty. The birth of her son Prince James Francis was the proximal cause for the Glorious Revolution, which cost King James II his throne. By Maria's intransigent unyielding Catholic faith, she prevented her son from regaining the throne as King James III of England, after the reign of King William III in 1702.

REIGN 29

KING WILLIAM III

AND

QUEEN REGNANT MARY II
CO-MONARCHS OF ENGLAND

WILLIAM AND Mary were grandchildren of Charles I. Theirs was a marriage of State made during the reign of Charles II as part of a diplomatic agreement for ending a war between The Netherlands and England. In it, England acquired the Dutch New Amsterdam Colony, which was renamed New York in honor of King Charles's younger brother James Duke of York (later James II). The marriage assured England's support of Holland in its long war with France. William and Mary were first cousins. They were invited to reign as co-monarchs when the 'Glorious Revolution' of 1588 deposed King James II.

Summary of the
Co-Reign of King William III
(Reign 1689-1702)

King William III I: life dates c. 52 years, b. November 14, 1650-d. March 7/8, 1702; Stadtholder of the Netherlands 52 years, November 6, 1650-March 8, 1702; King of England 13 years, February 13, 1689-March 8, 1702.

KING WILLIAM III was the only son of William II Prince of Orange-Nassau Stadtholder of Holland and The Netherlands. He was born in 1650 at Binnenhof Palace, Den Haag in Holland. William's mother was Princess Mary Stuart a sister of England's Kings Charles II and James II. William's wife Mary was his first cousin and the eldest daughter of James II. She was heiress presumptive to the crown of England.

William III was born on November 14, 1650, just a week after his father Prince William II of Orange died of smallpox. At birth, Prince William inherited the title Prince William III of Orange-Nassau Stadtholder of Holland and The Netherlands. He was the only child by his mother Princess Mary Stewart. William was reared by State appointed governors, and throughout life, he only rarely had contact with his mother. He was painted by Jan van Wyck, and was described as having a " . . . thin hunched body, extremely long face with a large aquiline nose, and piercing eyes." He was described as " . . . asthmatic, short of stature, by nature introspective, and generally expressionless and distant in personal associations. However, he was intelligent, ambitious, and resolute in pursuit of his goals."

William was educated at the University of Leiden in military history and sciences, but he showed little interest in arts, humanities, or philosophy. William was a stubborn patriotic Dutchman, and above all, he was an effective military leader with primary concern for his native Holland and The Netherlands. He was often admired, but rarely liked, and he never was popular with those he ruled.

On an invitation from English Parliamentary leaders, William entered England with armed force in November 1688, and forced King James II to flee to France. James flight into exile was taken to be his abdication, which permitted William and Mary to takeover of the monarchy without bloodshed. The regime change is referred to in English history as the *Glorious Revolution*.

William of Orange's relationship with his father-in-law James II was complex and contradictory. During King James II reign, William supported his father-in-law by giving armed assistance in putting down the Scottish Monmouth Rebellion of 1685. This support placed William in the awkward position of being, at the same time, the Protestant leader of Europe, but one who helped to defeat Scottish Protestants in their efforts to remove the Catholic King of England. Not surprisingly, William was strongly criticized in Protestant Europe for his role in suppressing the Monmouth Rebellion. Moreover, William had no desire to increase Catholic strength in England. To do so, would only bring England closer to Holland's implacable foe, France. William had nothing to gain from giving military aid to King James. Moreover, the only interest James II had in Holland was that his son-in-law William was willing to lend support in James' desire to repeal anti-Catholic laws in England.

Two months following the deposition of James II in December 1688, William succeeded as King William III to the English throne in February 1689. He was crowned as co-monarch with his wife Mary Stuart. Before William was offered the crown, Parliament required him to agree to a *Declaration of Rights*, which included major items in English Common Law, which required him to be governed by laws passed by Parliament.

England was primarily useful to King William as a military resource in his continuing war with Louis XIV of France (called King William's War, 1689-1697). William showed diplomatic genius in creating the so-called *Grand Alliance of Protestant Nations*, which included England, Sweden, Holland, and the Holy Roman Empire as his allies for the defeat of France. France admitted defeat in the Peace of Rijswijk in 1697, which reestablished William as the most effective Protestant leader in Europe. The Treaty of Den Haag in 1701 blocked Louis XIV ambitions to dominate all Europe.

Not everyone approved of the new co-monarchy in England. Many in Scotland, Ireland, England, and France believed that a consecrated king had a divine right to rule, which could not be revoked by any secular government. They believed that deposed King James II was still the ordained King of England. These so-called Jacobites worked for restoration of James to the throne. As early as July 1689, Jacobite uprisings with military support from France erupted in Scotland, and soon after in

Ireland. The rebellions required military repressions led by William III. By 1692, the Jacobites were repressed, but William had additional conflicts in Europe with France that kept him occupied from spring to autumn of most years from 1692 until 1697. In the final year, William broke the power of France with armies recruited in his Grand Alliance.

William's reign of thirteen years lasted until he died following a fall from his horse in 1702. He was buried at Westminster Abbey.

After William III died in 1702, the younger sister of his wife Queen Mary II came to the throne as Queen Anne.

Narrative on the Co-Reign of Queen Mary II (Reign 1698-1694)

Queen Mary II: life dates 32 years, b. April 30, 1662-d. December 28, 1694; Princess of Orange wife of William III of Orange c. 17 years, November 4, 1677-December 28, 1694; Queen Regnant of England c. 5 years, February 13, 1689-December 28, 1694.

LADY MARY Stuart was born on April 30, 1662 at St. James Palace London (but some say at York House in Windsor Great Park). She was the eldest daughter of James Duke of York (later King James II) and his first wife Anne Hyde who was the daughter of Lord Chancellor Edward Hyde Earl of Clarendon the trusted aid of Charles II. James was the younger bother of Charles II, and so long as Charles had no heir, James was heir presumptive to the throne.

Lady Mary and her younger sister Lady Anne were the only surviving children of the Duke and Duchess of York. Much of the girls' childhood was spent in St. James Palace in London. However, when it became known that the duke and duchess had converted to Catholicism in 1668/69, Charles II ordered that his two nieces be removed from their parents' household to Richmond Palace where they were educated in the Anglican manner under the supervision of bishops of the Church of England.

Charles II ordered this done to preserve his niece's acceptability to the Protestant Parliament in England, if they ever were in direct line to inherit the throne.

Lady Mary Stuart had a winning outgoing manner that assured her popularity in court. She was a favorite of King Charles II, and of her father James Duke of York. At first, Charles II planned a marriage for Lady Mary to the Dauphin Louis of France. Charles saw the French marriage as a way to reinforce the favorable ties between England and France that existed in the 1660s and 1670s when Charles II was King of England. Charles II favored a strong friendship with France. However, the hostility of Catholic France against Protestant northern Europe alarmed and alienated the Puritan Parliament in England. Finally, political necessity took precedence over Charles's personal preference, and he ordered his niece Lady Mary Stuart to marry William III Prince of Orange Stadtholder of The Netherlands. The marriage contract gave assurance that England would continue to give support to Holland in its ongoing struggle against Louis XIV and the mighty power of France.

Mary Stuart and William of Orange-Nassau were betrothed in October, and they were married a month later in November 1677. Her father James Duke of York disapproved of the match, but he finally gave his consent when he thought that the marriage of his daughter to a Protestant prince might improve his own shaky position as a Catholic in the eyes of the Puritan Parliament. However, this hoped for benefit to James public image was an illusion never realized.

Lady Mary was fourteen years old when she learned that her husband would be her first cousin Prince William of Orange. In disappointment, she cried for two days. Prince William was twelve years older than Mary, and she was four and a half inches taller than William. He was short, stocky, with a hunchback, and had long horse-like face. Mary's sister Lady Anne called the groom 'Caliban' in reference to the ugly deformed savage monster of Roman mythology.

Henry Compton the Bishop of London officiated at the wedding in Westminster Abbey on November 4, 1677. The wedding was a gloomy affaire. Mary sobbed through the ceremony. The groom was sullen and morose in a Dutch military uniform that was ill tailored and fit poorly. King Charles II, who was the host, tried to lift the doleful spirit of the occasion, with witticisms and cheerful chatter as he mingled with the guests.

Soon after the wedding, Prince Willliam returned to Holland with his bride. Mary suffered from homesickness for weeks. She soon became pregnant, but miscarried, and although she may have had two more conceptions, she never was blessed with a living child. William usually treated Mary with cold indifference. He was absent from the Den Haag court for long periods on military matters.

After a time, however, Mary's optimistic resilient nature overcame her early distress. She accepted life as she found it, and tried to become a devoted loving wife. She dutifully learned the Dutch language and the customs of Holland, and she soon developed a profound affection for her Dutch subjects. They returned her honest love. In all things, Mary worked to be an obedient subservient helpmate to her surly distant husband. Mary even accepted as a lady-in-waiting Lady Elizabeth Villiers who was William's only known longtime mistress. After its unpromising start, the marriage of the Prince and Princess of Orange settled into one of marital affection and success.

In the first decade of their marriage (1677-1687), William of Orange as Stadtholder of The Netherlands was constantly occupied with his military responsibility to defend The Netherlands against France. Although he was not always victorious, William was successful in maintaining the independence of his country, and by so doing, he reinforced the high opinion he had with Puritans who were a majority in the English Parliament.

In early fall 1687, a delegation of officials high in Parliament and the Church of England privately approached Prince William of Orange and asked for his opinion: If his wife Mary was invited to be Queen of England, would he be willing to be the Prince Consort of England while retaining sovereign control of Holland and The Netherlands?

William replied, "Unless I am king, on an equality with the queen, I shall remain in Holland."

However, William had experienced serious recent military losses, and he badly needed reinforcement and allies. His interest in the English monarchy was that England could be an inexhaustible resource in his defense of The Netherlands. However, William was adamantly opposed to any offer from Parliament that did not include his being given equal rank with his wife Mary.

His dutiful wife Princess Mary Stuart said, "I am the Prince's wife, and will never be other than what she should be in conjunction with him and under him; and that I will take it extremely unkindly, if any, under a pretext of care for me, would set up a divided interest between me and the Prince."

In February 1688, King James II irreparably alienated Parliament by issuing a *Declaration of Indulgence* without Parliamentary approval. It revoked the Test Act so that Catholic and Anglican religions were equally acceptable in the government England.

On June 10, 1688, to increase immeasurably the friction between Crown and Parliament, King James' wife Queen Maria Beatrice gave birth to a healthy male child named James Francis Stewart. The infant was immediately entitled *Prince of Wales*. He was *heir apparent*, the next following his father King James II in line for the throne. In that position, the infant took precedence over his half-sister Princess Mary Stuart the wife of William III of The Netherlands. The birth of James Francis Prince of Wales hugely exacerbated the religious tensions that had been building in England for over a decade.

Three weeks later on June 30, a secret deputation from Parliament went to Holland and invited William to come to England with armed force to depose King James.

Princess Mary faced a difficult choice. Where did her loyalties lie? Should she support her father or her husband?

Mary convinced William of her loyalty, and calmed his jealousy with assurance that she had no interest in ruling England herself. She said to others, "I will be no more than the Prince's wife, and shall do all that lies in my power to make him King of England for life."

In September 1688, William was invited to come to England and assist in removing King James II. William secretly gave assurance that he would invade England with military force to depose King James. William said he desired only to give Englishmen " . . . a lawfully elected Parliament free of control by a dictatorial king."

William's invasion force of nearly 15,000 men landed in southwest England in Devon on November 5, 1688. In William's progress to London, most of England's military and naval leaders, and many common Englishmen who were disillusioned by their autocratic Catholic king, joined William and his militia.

With neither a shot fired, nor a drop of English blood shed, King James fled to sanctuary in France on December 23, 1688. Parliament ruled that his flight was the equivalent of abdication.

The series of events that led to the regime change in England is called the *Glorious Revolution*. England was without a king or queen for a brief interregnum that lasted for less than two months following James' flight to France. On January 22, 1689, William summoned a Convention Parliament to settle legal matters associated with authorizing a co-monarchy, and to spell out conditions of the monarch's relationship with Parliament.

A co-monarchy had never existed in England before. Only two approximations of joint rule existed in English history:

> The first occurred in 1170 when Henry II permitted his eldest surviving son to be crowned 'The Young King'.
> The second instance came in 1553 when Queen Mary I insisted that her husband Philip II of Spain be named King of England. In the latter instance, Parliament refused to authorize a coronation for Philip II, and historians still debate whether Philip II actually was ever a King of England.

With this uncertainty, the Convention Parliament improvised rules for the co-monarchy. Parliament decided that both William and Mary would be crowned in identical regalia—two crown, orbs, scepters, robes, thrones, and whatever. In the event one died, the other would continue to reign until his or her death. However, Parliament indicated that, in the present case, real power of the crown lay with William, who would have "The sole and full exercise of the regal power will be only in and executed by the said Prince of Orange in the names of the said Prince and Princess during their joint lives."

Mary, the ever-dutiful wife, agreed that her husband would rule, and that she was content with being only his wife.

On William's insistence, Parliament agreed that he would remain Prince of Orange and Stadtholder of The Netherlands after he became King of England. A Declaration of Rights (a precursor of 'The Bill of Rights') required William to agree to rule under English Common Law as defined by Parliament. These restrictions on the royal prerogative were formalized later in the historically important Parliamentary 'Bill of Rights' of December 1689.

It required the monarch to obtain Parliamentary approval in making appointments, and the levy of taxes. Additional stipulations also stated that the royal succession would first go to Mary's children, then to children of Princess Anne. Only if both of them failed to have viable issue, would the succession go to offspring of William and a later wife. Other conditions denied Catholics a right to rule. These conditions had approval from Princess Anne.

William and Mary were decreed king and queen of England on February 13, and they were crowned in Westminster Abbey on April 11, 1689. Mary was distraught by the deposition of her father, but William ordered her to refrain from tears, and to wear a happy face during the coronation ceremony before the full court in Westminster Abbey.

Henry Compton Bishop of London performed the coronation ceremony, because the Archbishop of Canterbury refused to accept the legality of the deposition of James II by Parliament. James II (James VI in Scotland) was a much more popular king in Scotland than in England. Only with difficulty, was he deposed, and replaced by William and Mary. Their coronation finally took place in Edinburgh, Scotland a month later on May 11, 1689.

The new king, queen, and Parliament were divided in their interests, and personal loyalties. William was indifferent to the needs of England, and had concern only for the wellbeing of Holland and The Netherlands. Thus, as long as Parliament paid for his militias he was content.

Mary was loyal to her husband, and was willing to be subservient to his will and interests. She had little desire to wield authority, and her political loyalty remained with England.

A majority of Englishmen supported the reign of William and Mary. Parliament was jealous of its newly asserted power to depose and elevate its monarch. It preferred to have only Mary, as the reigning monarch, a woman easily controlled, but Parliament was content to expand authority without conflict from its co-monarchs.

As events unfolded, all parties were well pleased in gaining their goals. With England's resources behind him, William was able to defeat Louis XIV. Mary as reigning monarch earned the love and respect of her English subjects, while her husband fought battles on the Continent. Parliament dispensed absolute power in England with the Bill of Rights, which put an end to 'Royal Prerogative.' It is true, Parliament would have preferred that Mary be the only monarch, but Mary's regency in William's absence served Parliament's wishes well.

Parliament's Puritan members were pleased to have a Protestant Queen who delighted most in trying to please and earn the love of her subjects. When Mary first served as reigning queen, she received strong criticism for supporting her husband instead of her father King James II in the revolution that dethroned him. She met the criticism by convincing Parliament and Church leaders that her only desire was to do what was best for England. In all things, she respected and supported her husband King William III who was the true authority on the throne. She wished only to be a good wife of the king, and a good steward for the realm.

Despite her protest that she had no interest or ability for governing, she intuitively proved to be a wise unbiased ruler when authority of Government and Church became her responsibility. With advice from the Privy Council, she arrested and imprisoned her uncle Henry Hyde II Earl of Clarendon and John Churchill I Earl of Marlborough (the favorite of her sister Princess Anne). Both of them were charged with treasonous conspiracy to restore her father James II to the throne.

When William returned to London from his foreign battles, Mary immediately returned powers of the crown to him. From the beginning of their co-reign, William was known to be the one who ruled.

However, throughout her reign, Mary was directly involved in Anglican Church matters that required crown approval. Mary played a dominant role as the Supreme Governor of the Church of England, because, her husband William III was a Reform Calvinist, and he had no concern for the Church of England.

On her personal initiative, Queen Mary granted a charter for endowment for the College of William and Mary in the Colony of Virginia on February 8, 1693. It was the second college (after Harvard University) created in English Colonies in New World. She also created and endowed the Royal Hospital School at Greenwich, often called 'The Cradle of the English Navy,' which was a public boarding school for training seamen.

When William was in England, Mary was content to manage the palace, and organize social receptions. In that capacity, Mary II was often depicted as a colorless drudge, but she improved court manners greatly following the libertine ways of her uncle King Charles II, and of her father King James II. Mary II contributed significantly to the popularity of William III by providing a social setting in which he was viewed with favor.

By English standards, William was poorly educated in classics and courtly courtesy. A contemporary said "He was ill-natured, surly, and so little polished that neither in great nor small things had he the manners of a gentleman. On many instances he had worse than vulgar behavior at table." However, both William and Mary were Protestant in faith, and their marriage probably worked out as well as, or better than average.

Their favorite residence was Hampton Court, which had been greatly improved by Sir Christopher Wren after being damaged the Great Fire of London in 1666. Whitehall, a favorite London residence of many Tudor kings, also burned in the London fire, but it was rebuilt in the reign of William III. Mary II acquired Nottingham House, and had it completely redesigned and rebuilt into Kensington Palace, which to this day is one of the grand homes continuously in use by members of the royal family.

Over most of Mary's life, she expected some day to become queen in her own right, or to share rule with her husband William of Orange-Nassau. She seriously educated and prepared herself for the roles she was expected to play. Mary's brief reign of five years came at a time of national upheaval and uncertainty. Those distractions denied her an important place in the cavalcade of English queens.

At age 32, Mary contracted smallpox in early winter of 1664. The disease was a major scourge of the time. Those who contracted the disease, and survived usually suffered horribly with pockmarked faces. William stayed with Mary as her condition worsened. She died at Kensington Palace on December 28. William mourned deeply for Mary on whom he came to depend and trust.

Queen Mary II died on December 28, 1694, and was buried in Westminster Abbey. Henry Purcell an early master of Baroque music and the first English composer of major rank wrote a somber work for the occasion, *Music for the Funeral of Queen Mary,* which is still respected and occasionally heard in concert. After Mary's death, William said, " . . . from being the happiest [I will now] be the miserablest creature on earth."

King William III continued to rule alone as King of England, and as Stadtholder of The Netherlands for eight years after 1694. William and Mary had no surviving children. A few months after her death, Parliament encouraged William to marry again to provide a Stuart heir for the throne.

William refused, saying, "You can well imagine the state of my feelings, loving her as I do. Though I am pressed to do so, I cannot marry again."

After Mary's death, William's popularity declined greatly when her courtly social affairs ended. He disliked England, and much preferred to live in Holland with his men-at-arms. The damp chilly fog of London aggravated his chronic respiratory distress. He was never popular with his English subjects, nor did he inspire their loyalty. They always perceived him to be a dour arrogant distant wheezing Dutchman.

February 21, 1702 was a rare sunny winter day when King William left Kensington Palace for a brisk ride in the park. His horse Sorrell stepped into a mole hole and fell, throwing William to the ground with a broken collarbone. The trifling accident would not mend, but it aggravated his chronic asthma. Pneumonia set in, and William died in Kensington Palace on March 7/8, 1702. On his deathbed, William said, "My only regret is that I have not lived to see defeat of Louis XIV' of France." The sincerity of his affection for Queen Mary was proven when a sprig of her hair and her wedding ring were found on a chain on his breast when his body was prepared for burial with her in Westminster Abbey.

England wasted little time mourning William's passing, but Jacobites throughout Europe initiated a tradition of raising a glass of wine or stout at the beginning of each meal, with a toast 'To the Little Gentleman in the black velvet coat' in reference to the lowly mole that made William's horse Sorrell stumble, and bring King William down.

Queen Mary II was a thoroughly admirable person. She was without personal ambition, yet she accepted and exercised authority with wisdom and justice when she was forced to accept the regency. She showed unswerving affection and loyalty to her husband. Her private life was a model for propriety and good taste. She loved her subjects, and they respectfully praised her efforts to bring ethical behavior and good manners back to the court, which had been noted for shabby banality and bad taste in the reigns of her uncle and father, Charles II and James II.

After the death of King William III, English crown went to Mary's sister Queen Anne, The Netherlands's crown passed to male descendants in the House of Orange-Nassau.

REIGN 30

QUEEN REGNANT ANNE

AND

PRINCE CONSORT GEORGE OF DENMARK

Narrative of Queen Anne
(Reign 1702-1714)

Queen Anne: life dates 49 years, b. February 6, 1665-d. August 1, 1714; wife of Prince George of Denmark 25 years, July 28, 1683-October 28, 1708; Queen Regnant of England c. 12 years, March 8, 1702-August 1, 1714; Queen Regnant of Great Britain (England, Ireland, Scotland, and Wales) 7 years, May 1, 1707-August 1, 1714.

LADY ANNE Stuart, who would become Queen Anne, was born on February 6, 1665 at St. James Palace London (some say at York House in Windsor Great Park). She was the fourth of eight children born to James Duke of York (later James II) and his first wife Anne Hyde.

James was the younger brother of Charles II who had no offspring; thus, James was heir presumptive to the crown, and his two daughters followed him in the succession to the throne. Lady Anne was the younger of only two children to survive early childhood. Her older sister Lady Mary (later Queen Mary II) was second in line to the throne, and Anne was third. Since, all assumed that her father and sister would have surviving offspring, Anne was not expected be a reigning queen.

Lady Anne's education was standard for noble women with emphasis on languages, music, and manners. She was not instructed in history, government, diplomacy, or military affairs that would ordinarily be part of the training for an heir who expected to inherit regal power. Anne Stuart's modest natural abilities and education made her a poor candidate to be Queen of England.

Princess Anne had black hair, blue eyes, and exceptionally fair complexion. The early childhood years of Lady Mary and Lady Anne were spent in St. James Palace the Duke of York's London residence. When she was three, Anne was sent to Paris to live with her grandmother Dowager Queen Henrietta Maria in the Château de Colombes near Paris. Anne remained with her grandmother until her death in 1669. Anne stayed in France in care of her aunt the Duchess of Orléans until Anne returned to London at the age of five as a charge of the State in 1670.

When it became known that the Duke and Duchess of York had converted to Catholicism in 1668/69, King Charles II ordered that his two nieces be moved to Richmond Palace where they were reared and educated in the Anglican manner under the supervision of bishops of the Church of England. This was done to preserve the acceptability of their positions in succession, which was demanded by the Protestant Parliament in England.

When Anne was eighteen, her uncle King Charles II ordered her to marry her distant cousin Prince Jørgen (George) the second son of Prince Frederick III of Denmark. Anne's father James Duke of York (later James II) and Louis XIV of France arranged the marriage in a devious conspiracy designed to generate English opposition to William of Orange's defense of Protestantism in the Low Countries. For that reason, Anne's marriage to George of Denmark was unpopular with Parliament, because it suggested a strengthening of ties with France (a strongly Catholic nation, said to be 'the Pope's Goliath'), while Parliament's sympathies favored alliance with Protestant nations of Central Europe and the Low Countries.

For the marriage, Prince George gave up his candidacy to be King of Poland, but he gained the English titles Earl of Kendal and Duke of Cumberland. Princess Anne and Prince George were married in the Chapel Royal at St. James Palace, London on July 28, 1683. George was a pleasant buffoon with no strong political views or ambitions. He was said to be the 'handsomest blond Norseman, but the stupidest dull crashing bore in England.' He never did anything, good or bad, that influenced national affairs in England.

Charles II said of George, "I've known him drunk and I've known him sober, but either way there is nothing in him." Asthma afflicted Prince George, and an unkind court observer maintained, "He has to breath heavy lest he be taken for dead and be removed for burial." Charles II often tried, but was never able, to drink Prince George under the table. The regal ability to hold his liquor was the only admirable trait regularly attributed to George of Denmark.

Their marriage was a source of great happiness to Princess Anne and Prince George. They were a well-matched pair that sincerely loved each other. They were dull mediocrities with shared temperaments that found contentment in simple things—rich food, playing cards, and good brandy. Princess Anne was noted for her ability to consume quantities of whiskies, for which she was popularly called 'Brandy Nan.'

Within a few months after the marriage, Anne was pregnant. However, the infant was stillborn. Anne was pregnant most of her married years (1683-1708), but she left no living heir. She tried hard enough to provide a successor for the throne. Anne had eighteen pregnancies, all of them ended in stillbirth, infant, or adolescent death. Only William Duke of Gloucester survived his earliest years, but he suffered from hydrocephalus, was mentally retarded, and died five days after his eleventh birthday.

Anne was deeply religious. She saw in the repetition of deaths of her children, God's wrath, and His punishment for abandoning her father James II in his time of need at the Glorious Revolution, when he was deposed, and sent into exile in 1688.

As a sickly child with strict Anglican upbringing, Anne was emotionally and intellectually insecure, and needed close friendship with dominant personalities to lead her. While at Richmond Palace, Anne met Sarah Jennings (later the Countess then Duchess of Marlborough) who would figure as a friend and councilor during much of Anne's life. Sarah and Anne developed an adolescent 'best friend' relationship that lasted for years. Anne wrote, "[Sarah] let me beg of you not to call me your highness at every word, but to be free with me as one friend ought to be with another; you can never give me any greater proof of your friendship than in telling me your mind freely in all things, which I do beg you to do."

Anne then proposed that in writing to each other, Sarah and Anne use secret names that would not reveal their rank; thus, Anne was 'Mrs. Morley' and Sarah was 'Mrs. Freeman.' Anne initiated this practice, which has persisted in raising questions about sexual impropriety in the relationship between Anne and Sarah. The subterfuge clearly was designed only to remove class distinction from their personal relationship, and nothing more.

Sarah Jennings became Princess Anne's closest confident in a friendship that lasted from 1673, when Anne was only eight years old, until 1707, when she was forty-two, and had been queen for five years. When they first met, Sarah Jennings was a thirteen year old maid-of-honor in the court of Anne's stepmother Maria Beatrice of Modena. Sarah was Protestant, and the friendship of the two girls was promoted as a way of making sure that Anne would not become Catholic, as were her father James Duke of York and his second wife Maria Beatrice.

Sarah Jennings possessed a decisive domineering managerial nature. She was ecstatic when Princess Anne chose her to be her Lady-of-the-Bedchamber, an appointment that immediately elevated Sarah far beyond her former station in court. On her part, Sarah was romantically infatuated with a young common squire in service to Anne's father James Duke of York. His name was John Churchill. Sarah and John were married in Princess Anne's apartments sometime in the winter of 1677/78.

Sarah (Jennings) Churchill's rise in court through favored intimacy with Princess Anne immediately brought John Churchill to the attention of the Duke of York who gave Churchill a military appointment in his palace guard. When James Duke of York became King James II in 1685, John Churchill, as a junior lieutenant in the king's militia, served James well in helping to put down the Monmouth Rebellion, which challenged King James' reign. However, in the Glorious Revolution, John Churchill defected from King James, and helped to depose him by joining the forces of Prince William of Orange. For his service, William elevated Churchill to Earl of Marlborough. With John's title of earl, his wife Sarah Churchill became the Countess of Marlborough.

Soon after his coronation, King William III faced challenges from Jacobites who desired a return of exiled James Stuart to his throne. As early as August 1689, Jacobite uprisings in Scotland and Ireland required William's intervention with military force. When William was in Ireland in 1690, John Churchill was given command of all homeland military arms in England. However, Churchill, ever sensitive to winds of change, did not sever all ties with those who supported exiled King James.

Queen Mary did not trust John Churchill Earl of Marlborough who on, several occasions, opposed her judgment. In the spring of 1692 when a Jacobite invasion from France threatened England, Queen Mary ordered the imprisonment of Churchill in the Tower of London on suspicion of treason and treachery. Mary believed that Churchill had leaked information to the enemy that enabled the Jacobites to avoid total defeat.

Sarah Churchill persuaded Princess Anne to ask for her husband's pardon from the life-threatening charges of disloyalty to the crown. Anne confronted her sister Mary, and demanded that Churchill be released from the Tower. This so infuriated Queen Mary that she dismissed John Churchill from all his official duties in government, and banished Sarah Churchill from court. Princess Anne in high temper followed Sarah to the London residence of the Earl of Marlborough.

In retaliation, Queen Mary stripped her sister Princess Anne and her husband Prince George of Denmark of all honors of social respect. Mary and Anne were estranged and only rarely ever exchanged even words of greeting again.

King William ordered the release of John Churchill from the Tower on June 15, 1694 when he returned from Ireland. William recognized Churchill's military ability, and he needed his services. Six months later, Mary died of smallpox at the end of 1694.

Parliament named Princess Anne the heir apparent to the throne. It had previously ruled that any children William might have by a second wife would have precedence inferior to that of Anne. Princess Anne was given St. James Palace as her official residence for the remainder of William's reign. An uneasy truce of distrust between Anne and William marked the eight remaining years of his reign following the death of Queen Mary II in 1694. John Churchill bided his time. He would play a decisive role in commanding England's armies in *Queen Anne's War* after Anne became queen in 1702.

The reign of William III ended with his death on March 7/8, 1702, which came from pneumonia after he fell from his horse on February 21, and broke his collarbone. When William III died, many felt that the crown should pass to Anne's half-brother, James Francis Stewart (the Old Pretender), but he was firmly Catholic and Parliament would not countenance his becoming king.

Anne was thirty-seven years old when she was crowned Queen of England on April 13, 1702. At her coronation, Anne used diplomatic skill to ingratiate herself with the English public by saying, "I know myself to be entirely English. I can very sincerely assure you there is not anything you can expect or desire from me that I shall not be ready to do for the happiness and prosperity of England."

In this way, she indirectly made contrast with her predecessor William III, who was always perceived to be a dour alien Dutchman.

At the time of her coronation, Anne was grossly over weight, and suffered from gout for consuming vast amounts of rich food. She thoroughly detested exercise, and she customarily was dragged around St. James palace on chairs with wheels and pulleys. At her coronation, she was carried, like an Oriental Potentate, to the throne in a sedan chair with a twenty-foot train dragging behind.

Immediately after being crowned, Anne faced a national emergency that required a declaration of war on France on May 4, 1702. She appointed John Churchill Earl of Marlborough to lead English troops against Louis XIV. John Churchill became one of England's greatest generals for his part in winning the Battle of Blenheim (August 13, 1704), in which Louis XIV lost hope of ever dominating all Europe. The battle was a grand slaughter with deaths of over 32,000 for both French and English armies. Anne rewarded John Churchill (great-great-great-grandfather of Winston) by elevating him to Duke of Marlborough. She gave him the ancient royal estate at Woodstock near Oxford (the royal estate at Woodstock went back to Henry Plantagenet's reign, when he created the 'bower' for his Fair Rosamond Clifford). The Dukes of Marlborough's Blenheim Castle at Woodstock is, possibly the grandest private home in England.

Anne was deeply religious and possessed very conservative views on behavior. She was praised for kindness and consideration in her dealings with persons of all social ranks. Her first domestic order declared that her court would not countenance vice, immorality, or crude behavior. The essayist and wit Philip Stanhope Lord Chesterfield said, "[I] . . . regret the decline of sin at the hands of strict morality in Queen Anne's court."

Anne's minimal education and shallow interests were inadequate for her role as a ruling monarch. She had uncultivated tastes, eschewed literature, learning, music, arts, and cultural things in general. Instead, she preferred a stiff belt of brandy, card games, gambling, and stag hunting. Her chief passions were food, dominoes, and playing whist (the ancestral card game that gave rise to the ever popular card game *Bridge*). Her major cultural contribution came in creation of the annual *Races at Ascot* when she became to fat to ride with the hounds. Anne was a good-natured kindly person with no pretensions. The people were fond of her, and they soon would immortalize her as their second 'Good Queen Anne' (the first was Anne of Bohemia the child-wife of King Richard II).

As queen, Anne was more a figurehead than in any sense a ruling monarch. Friends and persons in government manipulated her for their own gain. Anne was interested in little but court gossip. She was unconcerned with the brilliant achievements of English writers, artists, architects, scientists, and philosophers, who graced her reign: Daniel Defoe, Jonathan Swift, Isaac Newton, Joseph Addison, Richard Steele, and Alexander Pope.

Jonathan Swift described her at court: "The Queen sits in a circle of twenty illustrious visitors, with her fan in her mouth, saying no more that three words a minute . . . then, hearing that dinner is served, she goes out at once."

The French ambassador said, "I am constantly astounded by the volume of food she consumes at each meal, and, like Aesop's frog, I fear she might burst."

Anne had no gift for organization or administrative authority. At the beginning of her reign, she tried to govern with a nonpolitical Privy Council that she chose with intent to represent all factions in government. She exercised no authority over the contentious group. It soon became known as, the *House of Squabbles*. In hope that members of the Houses of Parliament would honor her presence, and be more respectful of one another, Anne, on rare occasions, went to Parliament to act as peacemaker—to no avail. Anne's political understanding was limited primarily by personal likes and dislikes of members in Parliament.

Parliament became entirely modern. The concept of political parties was still a novelty for elected public servants who maneuvered for personal prestige. The Tory (republican conservatives for king and nobility) and Whig (democratic liberals for gentry and commons) were driven entirely to gain personal power. Whigs and Tories would agree on nothing, lest, by doing so, one party might give prestige to the other. Anne's natural inclination was to favor the Tories, but her friend and mentor Sarah Churchill played a decisive role in persuading the queen to support Whig opposition to France in what was now called *Queen Anne's War*. As time went on, Anne became more committed to the Tories, and came to dislike all Whigs intensely.

The overriding political issue of the time was the royal succession: Who would follow Queen Anne to the throne? The Whigs were unanimous in supporting the Act of Succession choice of Protestant Sophia of Hanover, and her heirs. The Tories were divided and weakened by factions who had Jacobite tolerance for a Catholic Stuart monarch.

The succession issue was further complicated by Queen Anne's ambivalent support of her half-brother James Francis Stuart, The Old Pretender, and her refusal to let the German Hanoverians become personally involved in English affairs so long as she lived.

The year 1707 was notable in England and Scotland for passage of the Acts of Union, whereby the Kingdom of Great Britain was created with Queen Anne as its first monarch. The Crowns of Scotland and England had been united since 1603 when James VI of Scotland also became James I of England following death of Queen Elizabeth I. However, both countries retained independent Parliaments. Part of the pressure to sign the Acts of Union in 1707 came from fear in England that the independent Kingdom of Scotland would not agree to accept a Hanoverian monarch, as was prescribed in the Act of Settlement. Many in Scotland preferred James Francis the Old Pretender to a German prince.

England emphatically did not want an independent Kingdom of Scotland on its northern border—that would restore the Auld Alliance with France—it would be a disastrous diplomatic threat to English security and economics.

At mid point in Queen Anne's reign (1708), public elections replaced the Tories, and put the Whigs in power. Parliament demanded that the queen's advisors reflect the party in power. She objected strenuously to parliamentary intervention into her personal choices for the Privy Council and other advisory offices. The Whigs adamantly insisted that she accept their nominees for political appointments. When Parliament removed crown rights to name bishops for the Church of England, Anne became even more alienated against her Whig government, but she accepted Parliament's superior power.

For years, Anne's closest confidant was Sarah Churchill, the wife of John Churchill the Duke of Marlborough. By nature, Sarah was a bullying person who was unable to see that the *persona* of Anne as Queen was vastly different than Anne had been as just a friend. Sarah was insultingly rude to the queen, and once, in St. Paul's Cathedral where the court was assembled to celebrate a military victory, Sarah ordered the queen, "Be quiet!" The court was stunned in expectation that a bolt from heaven would immediately strike Sarah dead. On other occasions, Sarah pressed the queen to make appointments in government that were clearly designed to advance the status of her husband John Churchill. Anne resented the impropriety of Sarah's demands, and she shifted her affections to Sarah's cousin, Abigail (Hill) Masham, who was a maids-in-waiting who Sarah had recommended for Anne's service.

Sarah was not aware that Abigail had replaced her in the queen's affection until 1707 when Sarah learned that Anne had sponsored Abigail's wedding to Samuel Masham who was a page in Prince George's court. Abigail remained Anne's friend and companion to the end of Anne's reign in 1714.

The relationship between the Duchess of Marlborough and Queen Anne deteriorated until it ended permanently in 1708, shortly after the death of Anne's husband Prince George of Denmark. The twenty-five year marriage of Prince George, and Queen Anne was exceptional in its devotion and fidelity. At age forty-three, Queen Anne was devastated by the loss of her husband on October 28, 1708. A court order cancelled social functions, and requested privacy for a half-year until April 1709 for the queen's official period of grieving and mourning.

Sarah Churchill presumed that she was exempt from the court order, and she forced her way into the queen's presence at Windsor a few weeks after Prince George died. Anne begged to be left alone at least until after Easter. However, Sarah persisted in intruding with querulous demands and criticisms of the queen's neglect of her previous requests. Sarah persuaded Anne, against her will, to return to London, and resume social audiences. Sarah's persistent intrusions earned Anne's growing displeasure. Early in 1709, they had a severe argument, after which Anne informed Sarah that their friendship was ended. A year later, Sarah wrote a long letter that outlined the many ways Anne was indebted to her. Anne granted Sarah a final audience in which Sarah criticized the queen, and concluded by saying "I wish no answer." Anne responded tartly, "You desire no answer and you shall have none." Sarah was banished, and they never met again.

Acid tongued Sarah Churchill responded to banishment by publicly saying, "Queen Anne is the quintessence of ordinariness; she also has more than her fair share of small mindedness, vulgarity, and downright meanness."

After Prince George died in 1708, the question of succession again became prominent. After the death of her son William Duke of Gloucester in 1700, Anne had no surviving children. With no heir of her own, Anne personally favored the hereditary claim for the crown of her half-brother James Francis (the Old Pretender). That also was the goal of all Jacobites in England, Scotland, and France. However, the Old Pretender steadfastly refused to consider a Protestant conversion, and Parliament adamantly refused to have him as a Catholic king.

The Act of Settlement of 1701 specified that at the end of Queen Anne's reign, Protestant Electress Sophia of Hanover (or her son Prince George of Hanover) would rule England. One recalls that Sophia was a granddaughter of James I descended from his daughter Elizabeth. In choosing Sophia of Hanover, dozens of Catholic descendants of James I with closer hereditary ties to the crown were bypassed by Parliament in choosing the next English monarch.

The end of the Stuart Dynasty and the arrival of Hanoverian monarchs to England became a certainty by 1708.

Anne detested her Hanoverian cousins. However, in 1706, she approved award of the title Duke of Cambridge to Prince George of Hanover. He had previously been nominated for the Order of the Garter. However, when Electress Sophia also requested that her son George be given English citizenship with permission for him to attend House of Lords meetings. Queen Anne refused.

In 1708, Queen Anne rejected a parliamentary request for a royal invitation for Sophia of Hanover to visit London. Queen Anne, like Queen Elizabeth I, could not bear the thought of meeting her successor.

In 1714 at age forty-nine, Anne's health deteriorated rapidly in the last year of her life. She dined alone, and was bedridden much of the time. She received the best medical treatment available, but the bloodletting, burning poultices, and induced sweating did more to hasten death than affect a cure. She suffered from gross overweight, dropsy (a malaise characterized by abnormal subcutaneous retention of body fluids), and other ill-defined complications. Her death on August 1, 1714 in Kensington Palace came after a series of strokes and coronary attacks. Her attending physician said, "Sleep was never more welcome to a weary traveler than death was to her."

At the time of Queen Anne's funeral, Jonathan Swift spoke for many of his contemporaries, "[Queen Anne] ever glorious, immortal, and of truly pious memory . . . [is] the real nursing mother of her kingdoms."

When she died, Anne was so much overweight that her casket was almost square. She was buried in the Henry VII Chapel at Westminster Abbey with her husband Prince George of Denmark. Seventeen small caskets surrounded them with their infant children, and the separate casket for Prince William Duke of Gloucester who died at the age of eleven.

Sophia of Hanover died on June 8, 1714 two months before Anne died on August 1, 1714, so Parliament's notice of Queen Anne's death went to Sophia's eldest son Prince George Elector of Hanover with an invitation for him to be King George I of England.

It is difficult to quantify the effect Anne's reign had upon English law, government, and history. A wit summed up the years 1689 to 1714 by saying:

> King William III thinks all;
> Queen Mary II talks all;
> Prince George drinks all;
> Queen Anne eats all.

A fair, but meaningless, assessment is that her reign did less harm than good. Anne's reign was a time when Parliament tested its power to rule with minimal crown leadership.

During her reign, England and Scotland signed the Acts of Union in 1707, which created the Kingdom of Great Britain.

The Treaty of Utrecht in April 1713 ended the War of the Spanish Succession, and established England as the major military power in Europe, but England got little more than Gibraltar for its efforts in Queen Anne's wars.

Queen Anne is usually described as a person, who had pedestrian tastes, and was stultifyingly dull, but, even so, excellence flourished in works of writers, scientists, and artisans. The *Age of Good Queen Anne* is now usually thought of as a time of grace, elegance, and refinement.

Conclusion to the Stuart Dynasty

THE CENTURY of the Stuart Dynasty began with the death of Elizabeth I in 1603 and included reigns of James I, Charles I, Charles II, James II, co-monarchs Mary II & William III, and Anne.

All told, the Stuarts were not notably successful or admirable monarchs. Kings Charles I and James II were forcefully removed from office. The others provided little direct leadership. They merely allowed developments to blunder on without direction.

Religious turmoil characterized the Stuart period. Wide swings in parliamentary approval of different brands of Protestantism were authorized by passage of Acts of Uniformity that, from time to time, gave legitimacy to one, and then another form of worship. In the Civil War that deposed Charles I, those who hoped for establishment of Calvinism with its restrictive dogma of predestination and the elimination of bishops were disappointed. For a time, the Puritans prevailed with adamant rejection of all formalism in worship. They maintained that God's grace was freely available to everyone.

With the Restoration of Charles II, the Anglican Church was back again with all its priestly paraphernalia. The Methodists disapproved of High Church practices, and split off from the Anglican mother church, but the Methodists retained its bishops. The Interregnum permanently weakened authority of an established State Church. At the end of the Stuart period, Parliament grudgingly passed an Act of Toleration. It disapproved all forms of worship, other than that of the Anglican Church, but it did not criminalize alien forms of worship.

During the latter part of the Stuart period, thousands of English citizens immigrated to the American Colonies for freedom to believe and worship in any manner they wished. However, the individual Colonies usually preferred a particular form of worship, and would not permit total religious tolerance. Pennsylvania came closest to the ideal of full freedom of religion. However, even there, Catholics were rejected, but they were welcome in neighboring Maryland.

Most Puritan Colonies in New England viewed their Colonial neighbors, from New York to Georgia, as zoos of Protestant religious heresy. This Colonial religious diversity demanded the separation of Church and State, as a prerequisite for ratification of a Constitution following the American Revolution in 1783.

The transformation of England during the Stuart century of stewardship was enormous, and mainly to the good. Gone were tactics of the Star Chamber and Acts of Attainder, the darlings of the Tudors that enabled their kings to be real kings with unlimited power. Gone was absolutism in religion that permitted only one faith to be recognized as acceptable by government.

A Parliament of the people ruled. With the invention of political parties (the Tories and Whigs), government recognized that there could be legitimate differences in opinions on how the nation should be governed, and how its citizens worshiped.

The Industrial Revolution had begun, and the Age of the Common Man soon would follow on its heels.

In agreement with the Act of Settlement passed by Parliament in 1701, following Queen Anne's death, her second cousin, Prince George of Hanover, succeeded to the throne without protest in 1714 as, King George I.

DYNASTY VI

THE HANOVER DYNASTY
REIGN 31 THROUGH 36 (1714–1901)

Introduction to the Hanover Dynasty

BEFORE THE death of Queen Anne, and in anticipation of problems concerning the royal succession, Parliament passed *The Act of Settlement* (1701). In it, Parliament claimed the right to determine who the monarch will be, and that it must be a Protestant member of the Anglican Church of England. When necessary, it gave Parliament freedom to depart from principles of primogeniture. The Act of Settlement, still in effect today, permitted Parliament to sidestep James Stuart (the Old Pretender), and his son Prince Charles (the Young Pretender), both of whom were Catholic, and closer to the royal line than any other descendants of James I.

Following death of Queen Anne in 1714, Parliament selected a Protestant monarch descended from Princess Elizabeth Stuart, the older sister of Charles I, who married Frederick V of Bohemia. Elizabeth Stuart's grandson was Prince George of Hanover who became King George I of England.

Although the rise of the House of Hanover in England was a bloodless takeover, it nevertheless was revolutionary in the sense that these monarchs were considered by common English subjects to be, and they considered themselves to be Germanic invaders of England. The surname of Princes of Hanover was *Guelph*, so the technically correct name for this period in English history should be the *Guelph Dynasty*, but that has always sounded too Germanic for the English ear to bear. The Hanoverian kings always married German princesses. Even Queen Victoria, the last Hanoverian, considered herself to be German.

The Hanoverian King George I and King George II were treated by English historians of the 18th and 19th Centuries with patronizing condescension. Hanoverians came to the throne in England with primary support of a Whig Parliament made up chiefly of middle class Puritans. A majority of the noble and aristocratic classes were Tories, and many of them belittled the thought of a German royalty in England.

Thus, through the first third of the Hanoverian Dynasty, the traditional alliance between king and upper social classes was broken. The English titled houses played along with the politics of court, but showed arch disdain for the new regime. The kings and their foreign courtiers and courtesans responded in kind and found all traditions in the Island Nation to be incomprehensibly irrational and alien. The invading German court distrusted the English nobles, and held them at arm's length.

The English upper classes, being the ones most likely to record events in the 18th and 19th centuries, consistently slanted the historical record of the time toward disparagement of the ruling house. The Hanoverians were resented, ridiculed, and despised by many of their English subjects. The only exception was the last Hanoverian, Queen Victoria, the most popular monarch England ever had.

A lingering troublesome matter in reigns of early Hanover kings came from persistent attempts by supporters of James Francis Stuart (the son of James II) to put him on the throne—these supporters in England, Scotland, Ireland, and France were called *Jacobites*. The first so-called Jacobite Rebellion after the death of Queen Anne in 1714 occurred in 1715, and was quickly put down. Several hundred Jacobites were killed in battle, many were captured, executed, or were sent to slavery on Caribbean plantations. The most important Jacobite Rebellion occurred in 1745/46 in an attempt by the son of James Francis Stuart to dethrone King George II. However, Charles Stuart (The Young Pretender, 'Bonnie Prince Charlie' in Scotland) was decisively defeated at the massacre of Culloden Moor on April 16, 1746. Soon thereafter, many Scottish and Irish Jacobite loyalists emigrated to Georgia and Carolina Colonies in the New World. No later Jacobite uprising posed a serious threat to the monarchy in England.

The Hanover Dynasty Lineage
Reign 31 through 36 (1714-1901)

THIS LINE includes Kings George I, George II, George III, George IV, William IV, and Queen Regnant Victoria. All except Victoria were also the Prince/King/Elector of Hanover, Germany.

Lower Saxony in the eighteenth century consisted of city-states in what is now northwestern Germany. They were constituent dukedoms of the Holy Roman Empire. Prince George Ludwig Guelph, who became King George I of England, was the Duke of Brunswick-Lünburg and Elector of Hanover. His mother Princess Sophia of Hanover was a granddaughter of King James I of England, and it is through her that George Ludwig Guelph came to the throne as King George I of England after Queen Anne died in 1714.

Only his Stuart connection to the English crown is given here. One is referred to other genealogies for his German ancestry. The lineage below shows descent from King James I to his only surviving daughter Elizabeth Stuart who married Frederic V of Bohemia. For other lines of Stuart descent, see Dynasty V, The Stuart Kings and Queens,

In the lineage given below, the names of reigning monarchs are shown in bold type with the number for each reign, which date in sequence back to the Norman Conquest in earlier dynasties. Dates in parenthesis give the duration of reigns. Queen Consort names are included when they are also mothers of a following reigning monarch. Numbers in parenthesis give offspring in chronological order; however, only offspring are shown that figure conspicuously in events discussed in the present treatment of English history.

Dynasty V. The Stuart Lineage:
Reign 25. James I of England (1603-1625) married Queen Consort Anne of Denmark, parents of—

Elizabeth Stuart married Frederick V of Bohemia, parents of—

Sophia of Hanover married Ernest Augustus of Hanover, parents of—

Reign 31. George I of England

Dynasty VI. The Hanover Lineage:

Reign 31. George I of England and Prince of Hanover (1714-1727) married Sophia Dorothea of Celle, parents of—

Reign 32. George II (1727-1760) married Queen Consort Caroline of Brandenburg-Ansbach, parents of—

Frederick, Prince of Wales (died before reigning) married Augusta of Saxe-Gotha, Parents of—

Reign 33. George III (1760-1820) married Queen Consort Charlotte of Mecklenburg-Strelitz, parents of—

(1) **Reign 34. George IV;** Prince Regent (1811-1820); King George IV (1820-1830), married Queen Consort Caroline of Brunswick, parents of—

Charlotte Augusta married Leopold of Saxe-Coburg-Saalfeld, no issue

(2) **Reign 35. William IV** (1830-1837) married Adelaide of Saxe-Meningen, no issue.

(3) Edward, Duke of Kent married Victoria of Saxe-Coburg-Saalfeld, parents of—

Reign 36. Queen Regnant Victoria (1837-1901) married Albert of Saxe-Coburg-Gotha, (end of Hanover Dynasty) parents of—

Reign 37. King Edward VII

End of the Hanover Dynasty; continue with Dynasty VII: The Saxe-Coburg-Gotha—Windsor Lineage—Reign 37. Edward VII.

REIGN 31

KING GEORGE I

AND

WIFE SOPHIA DOROTHEA OF CELLE

Summary of the Reign of King George I
(Reign 1714-1727)

King George I: life dates 67 years, b. May 28, 1660-d. June 11, 1727; Elector of Hanover, c. 1698-June 11, 1727; King of Great Britain (England, Ireland, Scotland, and Wales) reign 13 years, August 1, 1714-June 11, 1727.

As a child in Hanover, Germany, George I was known as Prince George Ludwig Guelph. He was the eldest son of Prince Ernest Augustus Guelph Elector of Brunswick-Lüneburg. George's mother was Sophia Stuart of Bavaria. Through his mother Sophia, George was a great-grandson of James I, and grandson of his daughter Elizabeth Stuart. George was born in 1660 at Osnabrück, Hanover. He became the Elector of Hanover on the death of his father in 1698. George Ludwig succeeded to the throne in England as George I following the death of Queen Anne in 1714. He was the first King of Great Britain, because the Act of Union, which was passed in Queen Anne's reign, united England and Scotland as a single nation. Throughout his life, Prince George also continued to be the ruling Prince of Hanover.

Prince George of Hanover was German in upbringing, outlook, and preference. He could barely speak English, even though he had known he was heir apparent for twenty years before he was crowned King George I of England in 1714. His reign of thirteen years was inauspicious. In 1715 only a year after coming to the throne, George I faced a Jacobite Rebellion. In it, James Francis Stuart 'The Old Pretender', a half-brother of Queen Anne, tried to take the crown, but he was easily defeated.

Somewhat later, a financial embarrassment called the *South Sea Bubble* collapsed in 1719-1720. The pyramid fraud snared a vast number of private and public individuals who invested in a scheme with no inherent product of value in it, and it created a nationwide panic. The government was implicated in the swindle. Riots ensued, and civil war to overthrow the government was feared. The South Sea Bubble scandal was occasion for yet another Jacobite Rebellion, which was put down decisively.

George I spent much of the time during his English monarchy in Hanover. He left the operation of government in England to parliamentary representatives, who would later be called *Prime Ministers*. They advised and essentially ran English affairs of State for him.

Before he came to the throne in England, Prince George of Hanover was married to Sophia Dorothea of Celle, who was the mother of his only son George Alexander (later George II). Sophia Dorothea was later put aside for adultery, and imprisoned before George I became King of England. She was never presented in England as the queen consort of King George I.

After the death of George I, his son George Alexander ascended the throne as King George II.

Narrative of Sophia Dorothea of Celle
Wife of King George I

Sophia Dorothea of Celle: life dates 60 years, b. September 15, 1666-d. November 13, 1726; Princess of Hanover by marriage to Prince George of Hanover 12 years, November 22, 1682-December 28, 1694; divorced and imprisoned in Schloss Ahlden at Celle c. 32 years, December 28, 1694-November 13, 1726; she was never the queen consort in England.

SOPHIA DOROTHEA was born in 1666 in Celle, a town located about sixty miles northeast of Hamburg, Germany. She was the only child of George William Duke of Brunswick-Lüneberg and his mistress Countess Eleanor of Esmiere-Olbreuse. Her parents had a 'Contract of Intent to Marry' when Dorothea was born, and they were formally married when she was ten years old in 1676. At that time, she was fully legitimized. As an only child, Dorothea was the heiress of Brunswick-Lüneberg with Celle its provincial capital.

Dorothea's mother Countess Eleanor was an expatriate of France. She was a Protestant Huguenot who fled from Paris when the persecution of Huguenots intensified after 1661. Countess Eleanor was responsible for transforming Celle from a farm village into a center for culture. She supervised renovation of the ducal residence Schloss Celle in the Italian Renaissance style with in a formal garden surrounding it.

Dorothea's childhood until marriage was with her mother in the enlightened court of Celle. She was literate, and her education in manners, music, and domestic arts were appropriate for a noble woman of her time. In addition to being a wealthy heiress, Dorothea was widely acclaimed for beauty and grace, which added to her desirability in the noble marriage market.

In 1680 when Dorothea was fourteen, Princess Sophia of Hanover persuaded Countess Eleanor of the advantage for her daughter Dorothea in marrying her son Prince George Ludwig of Hanover. He was six years older than Dorothea, and in addition to being the Crown Prince of Hanover, he was also designated to be King of England—as his wife, Dorothea could expect one day to be the Queen of England.

Countess Eleanor saw the advantages of the union, and to finalize the wedding contract, she agreed to a dower of 100,000 thalers annuity for her daughter's privilege to marry Prince George of Hanover.

The only thing about the marriage that appealed to Prince George was the size of the dowry he would receive—1 thaler had the value of 25 grams of pure silver; a German *thaler* was worth nearly ten times more than a French *livre*, Dutch *guilder*, or English *pound*.

Dorothea had a teenage tantrum when she was given a portrait of Prince George Ludwig, and learned that he would be her husband. Dorothea screamed, "Ich will nicht heiraten das Schweinschnauze (I will not marry that pig snout)." She fainted, and fainted again when she first met Prince George Ludwig shortly before their marriage on November 22, 1682.

The marriage of these two 'star crossed lovers' was doomed from its start. The bride and groom shared mutual contempt, and the mothers-in-law despised each other.

The bride Dorothea always received praise for her appearance, manner, and charm. Sophia of Hanover falsely criticized her new daughter-in-law Dorothea for bad manners, poor taste, and bastard origin.

George was despised for his chronic cruel and selfish bad manners. His mother Sophia of Hanover described her son "George Ludwig, is the most pigheaded, stubborn boy who ever lived. He has around his brain such a thick crust that I defy any man or woman ever to discover what is in it. He does not care much for the marriage itself, but one hundred thousand thalers a year have tempted him as they would have tempted anyone."

The beginning of George and Dorothea's married life together in Hanover was marked by endless argument and recrimination. Even so, their first child was born almost precisely a year later on November 10, 1683. Prince George Augustus was their only son. Their only daughter Princess Eleanor was born four years later on March 26, 1687, and was named for Dorothea's mother. At a public celebration of the birth of their daughter, George and Dorothea fought so violently that Dorothea feared for her life. Thereafter, they lived apart, and only rarely communicated.

In his best behavior, George ignored his wife entirely, but when court occasions required their presence together, he made a point of insulting Dorothea by denying her honors her station in court deserved.

Prince George soon acquired a mistress, Mélusine von Schulenburg, who remained his constant companion for the remainder of his life. He created her Duchess of Munster with whom he had three children, but he did not acknowledge them to be his own. Madam Mélusine was given the honors in court that Dorothea should have received. Dorothea requested permission to leave Hanover and return to Celle, but George refused to let her go for fear her departure would result in cancellation of her annual dower payments.

Under those conditions of extreme restraint and despair, Dorothea sought comfort from a childhood friend Count Philip Christoph von Königsmarck of Brandenburg. They became lovers, and after two years, they planed to flee Hanover. However, on the eve of their planned flight, Philip Christoph suddenly disappeared under suspicious circumstances discussed at the end of this chapter: "*The Mystery of Count Philip Christoph von Königsmarck.*"

Immediately following the disappearance of Philip Christoph Königsmarck, his affair with Dorothea became common gossip in Hanover. Prince George reacted poorly to being publically named a cuckold. He despised his wife, and cared little about whom she slept with, but George could not stomach public ridicule. The current humiliation could not be endured.

He wrathfully upbraided Dorothea with the accusation of infidelity. She returned the charge against him. A shouting match began. He pulled out much of her hair, tried to strangle her, and finally beat her so violently that her maids-in-waiting had to pry them apart.

Dorothea departed for Celle, and vowed never to return to Hanover. George Ludwig sued of divorce on grounds of 'desertion' because that charge would not void the annual dower payments from Celle.

The marriage was dissolved on December 28, 1694 with a final statement from Dorothea, "[I resolve] . . . never to cohabit matrimonially with my husband, and . . . desire nothing so much as the separation of marriage requested [by him] . . ." Part of the ruling denied Dorothea the right to marry again, and she was banished from Hanover to house arrest at Schloss Ahlden on the outskirts of Celle.

Dorothea was given the title Duchess of Ahlden, but her travel outside the Ahlden estate was severely restricted. She was denied contact with her children, and only rarely was free to have guests from outside her residence. However, she enjoyed a life of ease with an adequate expense account in a stately country home staffed by maids, servants, gardeners, and guards. Dorothea's name was removed from all State records, and her name was deleted from the list of the royal family who routinely received benediction at religious services.

However, George, even as King George I of England, continued to receive and bank 100,000 thalers annually from Dorothea's dower.

Dorothea of Celle was never the Queen Consort of George I, nor did George ever marry again, and have an official queen consort. Dorothea remained a prisoner of Ahlden for thirty-two years until her death on November 13, 1726, fully thirteen years after Queen Anne Died in 1714 when her former husband became King George I of England.

Dorothea's son and daughter, George Alexander (later King George II of England) and Sophia Dorothea (later the Duchess of Brandenburg) were never again permitted to have contact with their mother. Responsibility for their rearing and education was given to the children's grandmother Princess Sophia of Hanover, who made sure they could speak idiomatic English.

Prince George of Hanover landed at Greenwich on September 18, and was crowned King George I of England in Westminster Abbey on October 20, 1714. The people of England greeted him in silence. His German entourage to London included his long time mistress Mélusine von Schulenburg Duchess of Munster, whom he promptly created Duchess of Kendal in England. He also brought Sophia Charlotte von Kielmansegg who was given the English title Countess of Darlington. She was the daughter of his father's mistress Baroness Clara Meysenburg von Paten, but since Clara had numerous lovers, Sophia Charlotte possibly had a different father than Prince George—if they indeed shared the same father, she would have been George's half-sister.

The English court of George I, ever happy to find cause for disparagement of their new king, assumed that Sophia Charlotte von Kielmansegg was King George's incestuous mistress, but the actual nature of the personal relationship of King George and Sophia Charlotte was uncertain.

The Duchess of Kendal was so tall and thin that, behind her back, she was called the *Maypole*; whereas, the Countess of Darlington was so short and fat that she was called the *Elephant*. Both were constantly mimicked for their lack of linguistic competence in English. A crowd jeered the

'Maypole' for saying, "Goot people why you abuse us? We come for all your goots." A heckler called back, "Yes, and for all our chattels, too."

King George's 'German Ladies' occupied exalted places in the English court. They were useful in political circles for the ease by which they could be bribed to obtain an audience with the king. They behaved like tarts, selling influence for access to the king at great financial advantage to themselves. By English standards, their German manners were atrociously boorish.

George I was unpopular with his English subjects, and he had little but contempt for England. He spoke and understood English poorly, as was also true of all German attendants George brought with him from Hanover. They were resented and ridiculed by prominent Englishmen in court, and by leaders in government who considered them all to be stupid bores.

As his reign stumbled on, George I chose to spend more and more of his time in the peace and serenity of his beloved palaces of Leineschloss and Herrenhausen near Hanover. In his small Hanover court, Prince George was an absolute monarch. His subjects gave him complete authority over all matters down to approval of all public expenses that cost over twenty pounds.

When George was in Hanover, administrative power in England was delegated to Robert Walpole who is credited with being the first real English Prime Minister. His Cabinet Council became the central agency by which policy decisions were made. The Cabinet (made up of secretaries of different offices of government) gradually took over duties of the king's Privy Council, which formerly performed those functions. This set in motion the method of government recognized as the beginning of the English 'parliamentary system' as we know it today. Thus, by royal neglect, George I strengthened and encouraged democratization of Parliament. As an anachronism, the King's Privy Council continues to exist today, but it meets only for formal approval of State matters already passed by Parliament and the Prime Minister's Cabinet.

The single glowing act that distinguished the drab reign of George I was his support of George Frideric Handel, who left his position as Kapellmeister at Herrenhausen, and came to England, where he lived out his life, and enriched the world with masterful creative inventions in music.

Literary classics produced in the reign of George I included Daniel Defoe's *Robinson Crusoe,* and Jonathon Swift's *Gulliver's Travels.* The reign of George I was singularly free of the strife over dogmatic religious beliefs that dogged reigns of the preceding Stuarts.

Duchess Sophia Dorothea of Celle, who had been long ignored and nearly forgotten for a quarter century, became bedridden in August 1726 from various ailments including liver failure, strokes, and cardiac problems that took her life on November 13, 1726 at age sixty-one. Half of her life was spent nearly alone in house arrest at Schloss Ahlden. Before dying, Dorothy wrote a damning letter to her former husband King George I of England that included a curse that misfortune would follow him for the rest of his life, and a prediction that he would die within a year of her death.

George I denied State funeral rites and burial for Dorothea. Her casket was unceremoniously stored for a half-year in a cellar at Leineschloss in Hanover. In May 1727, her casket was secretly moved for burial with her parents at the St. Mariankirche in Celle. No recognition or mourning for her death was permitted in Hanover or London. George I was enraged when he learned that his daughter Sophia Dorothea Queen of Prussia ordered her court to wear black in mourning for her mother.

Those who wish to repair Dorothea's besmirched marital reputation, assert that there was no legal proof of her infidelity with Philip Christoph von Königsmarck. However, a correspondence of over a thousand letters they exchanged is convincing evidence that a torrid intimate affair went on between Dorothea and Philip Christoph for about two years.

Dorothea's defenders say that the letters are fabrications written after her death to destroy her good name and justify her imprisonment—but one wonders, why would anyone fabricate a thousand letters when one or two damming notes would suffice?

Prophetically, less than a year after Dorothea's death, George I died on June 11, 1727 at age 67. He was returning to Hanover, and on the way, he stopped for rest and refreshment at the estate of a friend in Delden, Holland. In the evening, he enjoyed a banquet that ended with a rich baked desert of pastry and fresh fruit. Indigestion kept him awake most of the night, but he insisted on continuing toward Hanover next morning. Before he reached Hanover, he had an apoplectic attack and died in Osnabrück. He was buried, first in the chapel at Leineschloss, but reinterred later at Schloss Herrenhausen.

After his death in Hanover, no request was made in England for a return of his body for burial in Westminster Abbey, or at Windsor, or Canterbury, as was customary for almost all previous English monarchs. A news release of his death was entitled 'The Devil has caught him by the throat at last.' It expressed the indifference all England shared on learning of his passing.

Without controversy after the death of George I, George Augustus, the only son of George I and Sophia Dorothea of Cell was crowned King George II of England on October 11, 1727. George II came to the throne with little previous knowledge or understanding of government processes in England, He had been strongly alienated against his father for the imprisonment of his mother, and he only rarely communicated with his father during much of their lives.

The Mystery of
Philip Christoph von Königsmarck

COUNT PHILIP Christoph von Königsmarck of Brandenburg was a military officer employed in the army of Prince Ernest Augustus Duke of Hanover Elector of Brunswick-Lüneburg. Philip Christoph was a frequent visitor in the Duke of Hanover's court where he became a mentor of the duke's sons who hoped to make their fortunes as military men. In his association with the duke's family, Philip Christoph met and renewed an acquaintance with Sophia Dorothea of Celle who was Prince George's wife, and they became lovers. Usually, it is said that Philip Christoph secretly met Sophia Dorothea of Celle who was Prince George's wife for the last time on the evening of July 1, 1694. At that time, they made plans to escape next day from Leineschloss in Hanover, and escape to some secret rendezvous where they 'could live happily ever after.'

However, Dorothea did not meet Philip Christoph on July 2, 1694 as planned, and he was never seen again anywhere by anyone with knowledge of his activities. It was assumed then, and was reported as fact by many later historians, that her husband Prince George ordered his palace guards to capture and murder Philip Christoph as he left the palace on the night of July 1, and that his body was thrown into the Leine River that flowed by the palace. Unreliable court gossip said that George bribed four of his guardsmen to do away with Königsmarck—but the 150,000 thalers amount of bribe money is too great to be credible, and it throws into doubt the entire statement.

Prince George protested that he knew nothing, and cared less of Philip Christoph's disappearance and fate. However, he was not believed. However, Prince George probably was truthful in saying that he knew nothing about the disappearance of Philip Christoph.

Evidence that surfaced many years later suggested that what actually happened was veru different than the above account.

After the death of George I in 1727, his son George II gave orders for the Leineschloss palace in Hanover to be renovated. When floorboards in what had been Dorothea of Celle's dressing room were removed, a skeleton was found of a young man who had been garroted, and left to decompose. The skeleton of the strangled man was almost surely that of Count Philip Christoph von Königsmarck, the lover of Dorothea of Celle.

I now seems most likely Duke Ernest Augustus of Hanover arrested, and imprisoned Philip Christoph on the night he left Dorothea's bedchamber on the evening of July 1, 1694. In addition, that Philip Christoph was held for several months until after Dorothea was placed in house arrest at Schloss Ahlden in Celle.

Then, with her apartment in Leineschloss vacant, Duke Ernest Augustus decided to get rid of Philip Christoph by murder, and his body was hidden beneath the floor in an unoccupied part of the huge Leineschloss palace in Hanover. His motive was to avoid family scandal when he was a candidate to be Emperor.

The Duke's mistress Baroness Clara Paten supported this explanation on her deathbed. She said that out of spite, when Philip Christoph abandoned her for Dorothea, she informed Duke Ernest Augustus of the affair between Dorothea and Philip Christoph. The duke knew he must resolve the matter secretly to protect his own reputation while he was a candidate for election to Emperor of the Holy Roman Empire. Duke Ernest Augustus was elected Emperor, but he died in 1698 before taking office.

Although, this resolution of the mystery is reasonable, it is not positive proof of what happened. The mystery of Count Philip Christoph von Königsmarck of Brandenburg is such that it will surely continue to attract romantic speculation.

REIGN 32

KING GEORGE II

AND

QUEEN CONSORT CAROLINE
OF BRANDENBURG-ANSBACH

Summary of the Reign of King George II
(Reign 1727-1760)

King George II: life dates c. 77 years, b. November 9, 1683-d. October 25, 1760; King of Great Britain (England, Ireland, Scotland, and Wales) and Elector of Hanover 33 years, June 11, 1727-October 25, 1760.

GEORGE II was named Georg August at his birth in Herrenhausen Palace on October 30, 1683 at Hanover. He was the only son of Prince George of Hanover (later George I of England) and Sophia Dorothea of Celle, and he succeeded his father George I in 1727. His reign of thirty-three years was outstanding for military success, and for English colonial expansion in Asia and the New World.

George Augustus Prince of Wales was alienated from his father during much of the reign of George I. The prince despised his father for the way he had imprisoned his mother Sophia Dorothea of Celle, and for excluding him from any involvement in government. Throughout their lives, the father and son, lived apart, and rarely spoke to each other.

George II was the last King of England born outside Great Britain After he came to the throne, England enjoyed general prosperity, and colonial expansion under parliamentary leadership of Robert Walpole and William Pitt, Sr. Aggressive colonial growth included founding the Colony of Georgia as a buffer zone between Spanish Florida, and more northern English colonies on the eastern coast of North America. The Georgia Colony was named in honor of George II.

The War of the Austrian Succession (1739-48) and the Seven Years War (1756-1763) were fought primarily between England and France. English victories determined English colonial dominance in the Orient and North America. The last phases of the French and Indian War in English American Colonies ended with General James Wolfe's decisive defeat of General Louis Montcalm at Quebec in 1759. Louis XIV of France ceded to England all French colonial lands east of the Mississippi River, and the entire St. Lawrence River basin. These gains initiated English expansion west of the Eastern Continental Divide in North America.

A Jacobite Rebellion broke out in Scotland in 1745, and was finally and resoundingly put down at the Battle of Culloden Moor in 1746 by the king's army under leadership of his second son, William Duke of Cumberland. The aftermath of this Jacobite uprising was a massive immigration of Scottish Highlanders into the New World Carolina colonies. The last year of the reign of George II (1759) saw great military triumphs with complete defeat of French power in the American Colonies, Canada, India, and the Caribbean West Indies. No English monarch's reign ended on a more victorious note than the reign of George II. His death came at age seventy-six from an aortic aneurism in 1760 at Kensington Palace, London.

The Queen Consort of George II was Caroline of Brandenburg-Ansbach, who was the mother of nine children; she died in 1737 at St. James Palace, London, and was buried at Westminster Abbey.

Frederick Louis Prince of Wales was the eldest son of George II. The prince died in 1751 from a sporting accident, and his eldest son George William Duke of Cornwall succeeded to the throne in 1760 as King George III.

Narrative of Queen Consort Caroline of Brandenburg-Ansbach

Queen Caroline of Brandenburg-Ansbach: life dates 54 years, b. March 1, 1683-d. November 20, 1737; Princess of Wales on marriage to George Augustus Prince of Wales 22 years, August 22, 1705-June II, 1727; Queen Consort of King George II 10 years, June II, 1727-November 20, 1737.

QUEEN CAROLINE of Brandenburg-Ansbach was the sixth of eight children of Johann Frederick Margrave of Brandenburg-Ansbach, and the first child by his second wife Princess Eleanor of Saxe-Eisenach. Caroline's full name was Margravine Wilhelmina Charlotte Caroline von Hohenzollern of Bavaria (Margravine was the German equivalent of the English title marchioness). She was born on March 1, 1683 at Grafresidense, Ansbach in south central Germany near Munich. Her father died in 1686 when Caroline was three years old. The margrave's first wife and her children contested their father's will, and his second wife (Caroline's mother) was reduced to poverty relieved only by generosity from her own family. Therefore, the childhood of Caroline and her younger brother Johann was a frugal existence until 1692, when their mother Princess Eleanor married again—this time to Johann George IV Elector of Saxony. The union was arranged for political expediency with no sentimental attachment between the wife and husband. Indeed, on one occasion, Johann George attacked Eleanor with his sword, and would have murdered her, except for physical intervention by his brother, which saved Eleanor's life.

Caroline's mother died in 1696, and Caroline was orphaned at the age of thirteen. At that time, her godmother Queen Sophia Charlotte of Prussia the Electress of Brandenburg invited Caroline to live at her court in Berlin. Sophia Charlotte supervised Caroline's education, and introduced her to court. Her move to Berlin was a determining change in fortune for Princess Caroline.

Queen Sophia Charlotte was a learned person who was a patron of the great mathematician and philosopher Gottfried Leibnitz and of other leaders in intellectual thought at the dawn of the Age of Enlightenment. Her soirées were envied throughout Europe for the brilliant guests she attracted to them. She was recognized as a cognoscenti and intellectual equal of anyone in her age. On her deathbed in 1705, Sophia Charlotte said, "Don't grieve for me. I am about to satisfy my curiosity about things that even Leibniz cannot explain—space, existence, the infinite, even nothingness. And for the king my husband [Frederick the Great], I provide a funeral spectacle to display his pomposity and splendor." The luster of Sophia Charlotte's salon had a lasting effect on the awakening mind of Princess Caroline of Ansbach.

Despite the vicissitudes of her early life, Caroline matured into a remarkably amiable person who was much sought after as an intelligent, attractive, and cultivated young lady of fashion at the highest level of society. She refused to accept a proposal of marriage from Charles VI von Habsburg Archduke of Austria-King of Bavaria who later became Emperor of the Holy Roman Empire. For Caroline to accept him would have required her to denounce Lutheranism, and become a Catholic.

At the age of twenty-two, Princess Caroline of Ansbach met Prince George Augustus of Hanover, and they were married at Herrenhausen Palace in Hanover on August 22, 1705. They remained in residence in Hanover until George Augustus's father became King George I of England in 1714. They then moved to London where they were given apartments at Hampton Court Palace. At that time, George Augustus and Caroline of Ansbach became the Prince and Princess of Wales. Caroline immediately sponsored a salon that entertained intellectual, social, and political celebrities of creative genius of a caliber not seen in the London court since the reign of Charles II.

As Princess of Wales, Caroline was the preeminent woman in England, because there was no Queen Consort to supersede her rank. George I had annulled his marriage with Sophia Dorothea of Celle, and all the king's mistresses were common to the core.

George Augustus and Caroline had nine (some say ten) children, seven of whom survived; four were born in Hanover before George I became King of England; the remaining children were born at St. James Palace or

Leicester House in London. The children of George II and Caroline of Ansbach were:

> Frederick Louis, Prince of Wales (February 1, 1707-March 31, 1751), died without reigning; his son Prince George William Duke of Cornwall became King George III.
>
> Anne, Princess Royal (November 2, 1709-January 12, 1759)
>
> Princess Amelia (July 10, 1711-October 31, 1786)
>
> Princess Caroline Elizabeth (May 30, 1713-December 28, 1757)
>
> Prince Augustus George (November 9, 1716) Stillborn
>
> Prince George William (November 13, 1717-February 17, 1718)
>
> Prince William, Duke of Cumberland (April 26, 1721-October 31, 1765)
>
> Princess Mary (March 5, 1723-January 14, 1772)
>
> Princess Louise (December 7, 1724-December 19, 1751)

Prince George Augustus resented his father for imprisoning his mother Sophia Dorothea of Celle, and for preventing him from having contact with his mother while she was in house arrest at Schloss Ahlden in Celle. The prince was only nine years old when he was separated from his mother, and she was little more than a romantic fantasy in his mind. Alienation of the king and prince reached a breaking point in 1717. The final break came when King George I ordered the Prince and Princess of Wales to leave their three month old child in care of the St. James house staff, and accompany him on progress through the realm. Regrettably, the infant died of unknown causes while the parents were away. George Augustus accused his father George I of responsibility for the loss of their son. A major argument of condemnation and recrimination followed; after which, the Prince and Princess of Wales left the court of George I at St. James Palace in Westminster, and other royal palaces in and near London.

The Prince and Princess of Wales set up their personal residence in Leicester House, a grand private manor on what is now Leicester Square, London. They sponsored a lavish court, called the 'Leicester House Set.' The social circle at Leicester House was noted for having a livelier intellectual atmosphere than the court of King George I, which was notorious for the king's tawdry courtesans who had no regard for proper discourse or manners. Caroline always supported her husband, but she constantly tried to use diplomatic tact to reduce the antagonism between the royal father and son, but she had little success in reconciling them.

Prince George Augustus and Princess Caroline were happily married, and shared deep affection for one another. Although she had a flirtatious manner, and occasional bawdy sense of humor, Caroline was a vivacious, intelligent cultivated woman who was a distinct asset to her husband. Caroline probably was never unfaithful to her husband. She accepted his constant philandering with good humor. When she was informed that her husband had an ongoing relationships with one of her English maids-in-waiting, Caroline matter-of-factly remarked, "Mrs. Edwards will undoubtedly improve George's English." Caroline calmly accepted that George had an illegitimate son named Graf Johann Ludwig von Wallmoden-Gimborn by Countess Amalie of Yarmouth.

Caroline cultivated a good relationship with Robert Walpole the Prime Minister of George I, and through him, she was able to assure continuation of a generous pension from Parliament for Leicester House. The amount of £800.000 was far in excess of the amount previous Princes of Wales were awarded from the Civil List. After Caroline became queen in 1727, she continued to enjoy an influence on the government through tactful pressure she used to convince her husband when he became king George II to keep Robert Walpole as his Prime Minister.

Prince George Augustus and Princess Caroline were crowned King George II and Queen Consort Caroline of Ansbach in a splendid ceremony at Westminster Abbey on October 11, 1727. Caroline's coronation robes were so heavy with gold and jewels that a pulley was used to lift her skirts, as one lifts a window shade, so she could kneel at scheduled intervals during the ritual. George Frideric Handel composed anthems that have been sung at nearly all coronations since theirs.

Prince George Augustus, in spite of having a heavy German accent, was fluent in English, and was well informed on English history. When he became king, he won the loyalty of his English subjects by saying, "Above all, I am a British king, not an expatriate German prince . . ." as his father George I had been.

After Princess Caroline became queen in her own right, she made a conscious effort to bridge the gap between the German and English elements at court. She made all her appointments for ladies-in-waiting to English women of title and excellent breeding. However, when the Prince became king, he continued to prefer the company of large buxom German women.

As queen, Caroline followed the model set by her mentor Queen Sophia Charlotte of Prussia. Caroline encouraged the work of artists, writers, musicians, scientists, and philosophers. Among those she sponsored were the writers Alexander Pope, Joseph Addison, Richard Steele, the mathematician and physicist Isaac Newton, and astronomer Edmund Halley.

On the more feminine side, she was a patroness for enlarged gardens at Hampton Court, Kensington, and Richmond Palaces. She loved fine clothes, and expensive jewels. She had a personal fondness for fine works of art showing refined craftsmanship, such as cameos, intaglios, miniatures, and fine porcelain.

Above all, she had a great appetite for reading and self-improvement. However, she always read in privacy of her own salon. Her husband the king hated books, and criticized her for "wasting time by dabbling in all that lettered nonsense." However, George was not totally opposed to learning. He chartered 'King's College' in New York City in 1754, which became Columbia University after the American war of rebellion of 1776-1783.

It was hoped that on the prince's ascension as George II, the royal court would continue to be brilliant in the manner established by the Leicester House Set. That hope was never realized. George II had all the pedestrian tastes of his father George I. Parliament knew of the lack of affection of George I for his son George II, and they feared that when George II came to the throne all persons previously in positions of authority during his father's reign would be removed. Much to everyone's surprise, and for the good of the realm, that was not the case. With only minor changes, the old regime was retained, largely because Caroline had a favorable synergistic ability to influence King George II and Prime Minister Robert Walpole. The king continued in much the same manner of benign governmental neglect that had worked well for his father.

George II did not care for the business of government, but as a military man, he was obsessed with observance of court etiquette and punctuality. Court occasions under George II were repetitious, tiresome, boring events with carefully prepared lists for receiving lines that went on forever. Court events were endured with exquisite pain. Court events were described "No mill horse ever walks a more constant track, or a more unchanging circle than that at the Court of St. James." The king never failed to dominate all conversations with endless repetitions of the way he had successfully conducted military events over which he had personally presided.

Caroline was far more intelligent and intellectually alert than her husband. She maintained a long time correspondence with Gottfried Wilhelm Leibniz the mathematical genius who, like Isaac Newton, independently developed *The Calculus*, an analytical tool of immense importance. Leibniz was in the court of George I in Hanover, while Newton was in the Royal Society in London. Caroline was instrumental in stimulating the correspondence between the two giants of natural philosophy that resulted in the *Leibniz-Clark Papers* (Clark was a confidant of Newton), which is one of the all time great person-to-person debates in science and mathematics.

King George II sincerely loved his wife, and he had great confidence in her ability. When he was in Hanover, or while he attended to military matters on the Continent, Caroline served as regent of England. This infuriated his eldest son Friedrich Louis who felt that he should be given that honor and responsibility. However, George II never placed any confidence in his son's ability to do anything but swing a cricket bat.

It is largely through Caroline's influence on the king that George II continued patronage of George Frideric Handel whose best known, and most frequently performed composition, *The Messiah*, was first heard in London in 1743. George II was so moved during its "Hallelujah Chorus" that he rose and stood throughout the movement—it has been customary ever since for audiences to do the same whenever *The Messiah* is performed in concert.

Queen Caroline played a greater part in the government of her spouse than any other queen consort since Philippa of Hainault was the wife of Edward III. Caroline's influence was felt in many ways, but she used her power tactfully, so that George II always was convinced that he alone was the author of all decisions in government. Her influence behind the throne was widely known, and was acknowledged in a popular jingle of the time:

> *You may strut, dapper George, but 'twill be in vain.*
> *We know 'tis Queen Caroline, not you that reign.*

Much of the middle third of the reign of George II was taken up with the War of the Austrian Succession (1741-1748). The dynastic dispute eventually embroiled all Western Europe when Emperor Charles VI died in 1740 without a male heir. His will designated his daughter Maria Theresa to inherit Greater Austria (Austria, Hungary, Bohemia, and Croatia), but Salic tradition held that only males could rule. The antagonist nations were: *on one side*—England, Austria, Hanover, Holland, and others; *on the other side*—France, Prussia, Spain, Bavaria, and others. England's side was victorious in 1747. The final resolution of the war in 1748 recognized Maria Theresa to rule as Archduchess of Austria.

King George II was criticized in England for wasting taxes without any perceived benefit to England in order to keep his small Principality of Hanover from being swallowed up by Frederick II (the Great) of Prussia. However, at the Battle of Dettingen (1743), King George II led a joint army of British, Hanoverians, Austrians, and Dutch to a victory over the French. In that battle, George II was the last British sovereign to risk his life with his soldiers in war. For this bravado, the popularity of George II briefly reached the highest point of all Hanoverian monarchs, except Queen Victoria who was, without question, the most popular monarch England ever had.

England's victories in the War of the Austrian Succession in Europe, and the French and Indian War in North America gave England enormous colonial gains: *in Asia*, England won hegemony over India; *in the New World*, England acquired colonial rights to all the Continent east of the Mississippi River, and all the St. Lawrence River basin. George II was informed of the victories in the Orient and New World, but he died before the Treaty of Paris (1763) was signed that made England the greatest colonial power the world had ever known.

The most striking similarity between the reigns of the first two Georges was repetition of the animosity that arose between fathers and first sons. From the moment of his birth, George II and Caroline irreconcilably detested their first son Crown Prince Frederick Louis. The king and queen also took an immediate dislike to their daughter-in-law Princess Augusta, whom Caroline had personally chosen to be the wife of her son, the Prince of Wales. The depth of this parent-child animosity was manifest in a comment of George II made on meeting his son's prospective bride, "I do not think that ingrafting my half-witted coxcomb son upon a mad woman will improve the breed." Queen Caroline attacked in kind, "Our first-born is the greatest ass, the greatest liar, the greatest peasant, and greatest beast in the whole world, and we heartily wish he was out of it!"

The king and queen had as little to do with Prince Frederick Louis and Princess Augusta of Wales as possible. Queen Caroline was in disbelief when she learned that her daughter-in-law Augusta of Saxe-Gotha was pregnant. Caroline was determined to be present at the child's birth to attest to the legitimacy of the heir to the throne. However, Prince Frederick and Princess Augusta did not want Queen Caroline to be present. The pregnancy ended two months prematurely. When Augusta's labor began, the palace guard took her from Hampton Court to Norfolk House where the baby was born. The infant was George William Frederick, who would be King George III.

Queen Caroline was furious at the deception, which denied her presence at his birth. Even after Frederick and Augusta had other children, there was no family reconciliation. In most matters Caroline was a model for restraint, self-control, and good judgment. It is difficult to account for her irrational negative rejection of those of her own family.

Prime Minister Robert Walpole, in evaluating the national importance of Queen Caroline, said, "Oh, my lord! If this woman should die, what a scene of confusion will be here! Who can tell into what hands the king will fall?"

Queen Caroline died at age fifty-four at St James Palace on November 20, 1737. The immediate cause was blood poisoning following a botched operation without anesthesia, and an ignorance of bacterial infection. The primary cause most likely was from a ruptured uterus for which she suffered without complaint for over a decade after her last pregnancy in 1724.

On her deathbed, she told her husband that he must marry again, but he famously said that he loved her too much, "No, I will only have mistresses."

Queen Caroline of Ansbach was by far the most admirable of the Hanoverian Queens Consort. She was an affectionate and loyal helpmate for her husband King George II. Queen Caroline was an intelligent, charming, blond, blue-eyed charmer with style and grace. She had sincere concerns for learning, art, literature, history, government, and philosophy. She was intelligent and used her high social position to promote what she believed was to the good of the nation. Her subjects admired and loved her. She had flaws of personal vanity, of favoritism, and the burden of a highly dysfunctional family. However, taken all together, she wore the mantle of queenship exceedingly well.

Queen Caroline was buried in Westminster Abbey. Handel composed a ten-part *Funeral Anthem for Queen Caroline* for her. King George II ordered a two-part marble sarcophagus to accommodate both of them in the Royal Hanover burial site in the Henry VII Lady Chapel at Westminster Abbey.

George II was heartbroken, and sincerely mourned Caroline. Until his death twenty-three years after Caroline died, he did not marry, but true to this word, George II took only mistresses. The principal one was one of Caroline's ladies-in-waiting Henrietta Howard Duchess of Suffolk. She became his official *maitress en titre*. After Caroline died, Henrietta Howard was the dictator of manners in London. Under her leadership, etiquette devolved into the very model for banality, bawdry, and boredom.

Although his realm prospered as the years passed, George II became progressively more disillusioned with England and he imported his last mistresses from Hanover. The German language again became *lingua franca* in court. His German mistresses alienated him against everything English. He complained, "No English cook can cook; no English coachman can drive; the superiority of English nobility, horses, and roast beef are all in doubt." On one occasion he blurted out, "I am sick to death of all this foolish English stuff, and with all my heart hope that the devil may take all your Bishops, your Ministers, your Parliament, and your whole Island, provided I can get out in time to get back to Hanover."

The fact that he was the first king to receive the fanfare, *God Save the King*, hardly made up for all the irritations he suffered as he approached his seventy-seventh birthday. Although his reign ended on a grand victorious note, George's German mistresses alienated him against everything English.

George II died at Kensington Palace of an aortic aneurism that took his life almost instantly on October 25, 1760. He is buried beside Queen Caroline in Westminster Abbey with a small paving slab on the floor of the Lady Chapel marking the location. The burial of George II was the last royal interment in Westminster Abbey. Following sovereigns were buried at Windsor.

Crown Prince Frederick Louis, the eldest son of George II, did not reign; he died in 1751 from an abscess resulting from a cricket accident. He was buried at Westminster Abbey. Following the death of George II, his grandson, Prince George William Duke of Cornwall, the eldest son of Prince Frederick Louis, ascended the throne in 1760 as King George III.

REIGN 33

KING GEORGE III

AND

QUEEN CONSORT CHARLOTTE
OF MECKLENBURG-STRELITZ

Summary of the Reign of King George III
(Reign 1760-1820)

King George III: life dates c. 82 years, b. June 4, 1738-d. January 29, 1820; King of Great Britain (England, Ireland, Scotland, and Wales) and Elector of Hanover reign 60 years, October 25, 1760-January 29, 1820.

KING GEORGE III was the eldest son of Frederick Louis Prince of Wales (eldest son of George II) and Caroline of Brandenburg-Ansbach. His father died before George II, so George III ascended the throne following the death of his grandfather in 1760. The sixty-year reign of George III is the second longest in English history, and is surpassed by only that of Queen Victoria who reigned for sixty-four years. George III is best remembered in America as the King of England during America's War of Independence—The Revolutionary War (1776-1783). For that reason, American historians generally treat him poorly. Actually, George III was a reasonably good king with sensitive feelings for his subjects. He supported liberal and creative efforts in humanities and science. This is shown by his personal collection of books, which is the nucleus for the Royal British Library in London. He paid out of pocket for the telescope used by William Herschel in his demonstration that Uranus was a planet in 1871.

George III was determined to recover the powers lost from the crown by indifference of kings George I and George II. George III was willfully unrealistic in handling his American colonies, which he treated as though they were his private property devoid of the common rights accorded his subjects in England. In his misguided attempts to recover sovereign powers, George III and his Prime Minister Lord Frederick North so angered Parliament that he and all subsequent English sovereigns lost veto power over government actions.

George III was troubled, not only by loss of the English Colonies in the American Revolutionary War, but also by the extreme threat to the entire concept of monarchy by the French Revolution, in which the French royalty and nobility were decimated. Later the imperial ambitions of Napoleon threatened the survival of English independence itself.

The end of the reign of George III was seriously marred by periods of extreme mental failure. He lived to the age of 82, but during the last decade of life, he was senile, blind, and incapable of judgment or communication. During his last and most severe madness that lasted for nine years (1811-1820), his eldest son George Prince of Wales served as regent for the realm.

George III and his Queen Charlotte of Mecklenburg-Strelitz had fifteen children. Two reigned as King George IV and King William IV. Queen Charlotte died at Kew Palace in 1818, and George III died at Windsor in 1820. They were buried in St. George's Chapel at Windsor Castle.

Following the death of George III, his eldest son the Prince Regent George Prince of Wales succeeded to the throne in 1820 as King George IV.

Note: The most severe madness of George III lasted for nine years (1811-1820). In those years, George Prince of Wales was created the Prince Regent. The years 1811 to 1820 are treated here as part of Reign 34. King George IV.

Narrative of Queen Consort Charlotte of Mecklenburg-Strelitz

Queen Charlotte of Mecklenburg-Strelitz: life dates 74 years, b. May 19, 1744-d. November 17, 1818; Queen Consort of King George III 57 years, September 8, 1761-November 17, 1818.

QUEEN CHARLOTTE was the eighth child, and fifth daughter of Duke Charles Louis Frederick of Mecklenburg-Strelitz, and his wife Princess Elizabeth Albertine of Saxe-Hildburghausen. Lady Charlotte was born on May 19, 1744 at the modest family estate Schloss Mirow. The manor house was on an island near the shore of lake Mirowersee located somewhat south of Rostock in northern Prussia. Although the noble titles of Charlotte's parents were impressive, the history of the family over many generations had few royal connections—indeed, royal descent was restricted to only one distant link with each of the ruling houses of Sweden and Norway. In the main, the traditional way of daily living for the Mecklenburg-Strelitz family in Schloss Mirow was unpretentious and parochial.

Charlotte's father Duke Charles briefly attended the University of Griefswald in Pomerania. He had a modest gift in music, and for a time served in the army of the Holy Roman Emperor Charles VI. Otherwise, he was undistinguished in personal achievements or influence. Charlotte's mother Princess Elizabeth Albertine was the ninth child of Duke Ernst of Saxe-Hildburghausen, and she was so far down the line in inheritance that little unusual effort was expended on her education or marriage.

All siblings of Charlotte were born in the modest country manor Schloss Mirow. They were educated under supervision of their mother Lady Elizabeth Albertine in a manner suitable for domestic life in a provincial province, but not suitable for the pretentious style needed in an imperial court. A Lutheran priest tutored the children. He was well grounded in Protestant belief, but only modestly learned in humanities, history, mathematics, or natural sciences. Lady Elizabeth Albertine personally instructed her children in court etiquette, and her daughters in modest domestic skills of embroidery, dancing, drawing, and music. The duchess was a confirmed believer in the adage, "Idle hands are the Devil's workshop." Every minute of every day had the name of a duty written on it—whether they liked it or not—she was determined that her children would be properly trained for a provincial princely station in life.

Charlotte's father Duke Charles of Mecklenburg-Strelitz died in 1751. The family then moved from Mirow to the court of Charlotte's brother Adolph Friedrich who became the Duke of Mecklenburg-Strelitz when their father died. In Strelitz, Lady Elizabeth Albertine employed the service of a learned governess, Madam de Gabrow, for advanced instruction of the children. Charlotte mastered reading and writing Latin, French, and Italian, but gained no knowledge of English language or history. A priest taught her elements of natural science: geography (maps and map making), mineralogy (crystals and fossils), and botany (native and exotic plants).

Charlotte's mother and brother hoped they would find a titled husband for Charlotte. However, they admitted that Charlotte's features were plain—she was not ugly—but by all standards, she was not beautiful. She possessed a good mind, an independent spirit, and was suitably qualified to be the mistress of a manor house for a baron or even a count of a provincial German town. No one thought that an offer of marriage one day would create Charlotte the Queen Consort of England—the magnificence of such a proposal was far beyond anything that the Mecklenburg-Strelitz family had ever experienced before.

On October 25, 1760 the day that George II died, his grandson Prince George William Duke of Cornwall at age twenty-two became King George III of England. He was poorly qualified, and ill prepared for his inherited station in life. His father Frederick Louis Prince of Wales died in 1751 when George was thirteen. His mother Dowager Princess of Wales Augusta of Saxe-Gotha was autocratic. She dominated her children, and supervised their education and training. However, she had been *persona non grata* in the court of George II, so she and her children had little participation or contact with the royal court. Prince George William never challenged his mother's authority as a teenage youth, and the same held true in the first years of his reign after he became king George III.

In his late teenage years, Prince George was deeply attracted to Lady Sarah Lennox a great-granddaughter of Charles II and his mistress Louise de Kéroualle Duchess of Portsmouth. Although Lady Sarah Lennox was well received in court, the possibility of marriage of Prince George to her was considered inappropriate, because the royal bastardy in Lady Sarah Lennox's lineage was not suitable for her to be the Queen of England.

Immediately after Prince George William became King George III in 1760, his marriage became a matter of national concern. His mother Dowager Princess August was determined to play a pivotal role in the marriage of her docile son who had just become king. She favored a Prussian princess for George's royal bride. All Hanoverian Kings of England married German princesses, and Prussia was preeminent among German principalities. However, England and Prussia had only recently been opposed in the War of the Austrian Succession (1741-1748). The war had ended, but the Treaty of Paris (1763) had not yet been signed to conclude the war, so the idea of a Prussian princess as the next Queen of England was unpopular throughout England. Augusta examined all the dukedoms of northern Germany in search of a suitable heiress. She finally settled on sixteen year old Lady Charlotte of Mecklenburg-Strelitz. The two mothers of the young couple engaged in a preliminary secret correspondence on the possibility of marriage of George III and Lady Charlotte.

At the same time in England, the flourishing romance between Lady Sarah Lennox and young King George III was quashed for complex political reasons. When the king's father Prince Frederick Louis died in 1751, Dowager Princess Augusta appointed John Stuart Earl of Bute to be the tutor of her son Prince George William. Princess Augusta and Lord Bute soon developed a close personal relationship that was suspected of being sexually intimate, but it is not certain that there was any impropriety in their friendship. Nevertheless, Bute, who was a Scottish Tory member of the House of Lords, hoped to rise quickly in political power when his royal student became king. Bute feared that his Whig rival, Henry Fox Baron of Holland who was a bother-in-law of Sarah Lennox, would gain advantage, if the king married Sarah. Therefore, Dowager Princess Augusta and Lord Bute vetoed the idea of a marriage of Sarah Lennox to George III. King George dutifully accepted the decision of his mother and former mentor without protest, and gave up thought of marrying Lady Sarah Lennox.

Lord Bute chose Colonel David Graeme as an envoy to go to Germany for information on the suitability of Lady Charlotte of Mecklenburg-Strelitz to be the king's queen consort. Colonel Graeme had minor military experience, some familiarity with German geography, and an ability to speak the German language. Graeme went in June 1761 to Strelitz to interview Lady Charlotte. He was instructed to make an honest first hand evaluation of all her qualities.

Graeme's initial report after meeting seventeen year old Lady Charlotte said, "Her countenance is expressive and shows intelligence . . . she is not tall, but has a slight rather pretty figure . . . her eyes sparkle with good humor; her mouth is large, and her teeth are white and even . . . her hair is a beautiful light brown color . . ." The report, although generally favorable, did not extol her beauty, and by that omission, implied that, in truth, she was plain.

King George was pleased with Graeme's report, and on July 8, 1761, the king informed his Privy Council in London, "I now, with great satisfaction, acquaint you, that after the fullest information and mature deliberation, I am come to a resolution to demand in marriage the Princess Charlotte of Mecklenburg-Strelitz."

His decision was sent immediately to England's Paris ambassador Lord Simon Harcourt, with instructions for him to proceed secretly to Strelitz, and to secure a royal marriage contract. He was told, "It need not have any significant dower demands."

Lord Harcourt arrived in Strelitz in late July. The city was still in mourning for the death of Charlotte's mother Dowager Duchess Elizabeth Albertine who had died at the end of June. Charlotte's brother Adolph Friedrich Duke of Mecklenburg-Strelitz was dazzled in learning for the first time that his sister was invited to become Queen of England. Papers for the marriage were quickly drawn up, and approved by August 15. Among its provisions were statements to the effect:

> The Princess would depart immediately for England.
> She would join the Church of England.
> She would be married in Anglican rites.
> As queen, she would never be involved in any government matters whatsoever.

The last codicil helps to explain why Queen Charlotte's reign was forever free of political involvement and intrigue.

Only two days after the marriage contract was signed, a Strelitz citywide celebration for the coming royal wedding was hastily organized in the manner of a county fair. On August 17, garlands decorated all houses. A triumphal arch was constructed on the city square with banners that extolled the historical splendors of England and Strelitz. A city guard led a parade down the main street. After the guard came Lady Charlotte in a Coach of State (actually an open wagon) decorated with pine boughs, banners, and flowers. Wine and sweetmeats of all kinds were available for all to partake.

It was the best a small town could throw together on short notice for an honor they never expected and could ill afford.

On the next day, August 18, Charlotte set out on her journey across northern Germany to England, never to return. Lord Harcourt made all arrangements for the entourage that travelled quickly with excellent ostentation. On August 26, they arrived at Cuxhaven at the mouth of the Elbe River, where a flotilla of British warships awaited Charlotte. Her naval escort was under command of Captain George Anson Lord High Admiral of the Fleet, who was famous for circumnavigating the globe, and capturing rich Spanish galleons. One of the naval vessels had been hastily renamed *The Royal Charlotte* to carry her to England.

The small armada departed next morning from Cuxhaven in bad weather. It took nine days (instead of the usual three days) to complete the crossing. They arrived at Harwich on September 6 and went on to London next day. They arrived at St. James Palace on September 7, and for the first time, she met King George III and the royal family. Neither King George III nor his mother Dowager Princess Augusta was overwhelmed by the appearance of the recently seasick travel worn Princess Charlotte.

Twenty-two year old King George III married seventeen year old Princess Charlotte of Mecklenburg-Strelitz at nine o'clock on the evening of September 8, 1761. Archbishop Thomas Seeker of Canterbury presided over the ritual at the Chapel Royal in St. James Palace. It is of minor interest that on King George's personal invitation, Lady Sarah Lennox was one of ten bridesmaids at his wedding to Queen Charlotte. At that time, Lady Sarah told a friend, "Luckily for me, I did not love him; I only like him."

As an additional consequence following this royal marriage, Colonel David Graeme was employed as Queen Charlotte's personal secretary. She later promoted him to General for "The Queen's Own Royal Regiment of Scottish Highlanders." In addition, Lord James Stuart Earl of Bute, a Tory, became the first Prime Minister for George III in 1761-1762. However, he soon was replaced by the Whig Prime Minister George Grenville, who became notorious in American history for sponsoring the *Stamp Act*, which would ignite revolution in the English colonies of North America in 1775.

The public response to the coronation of Queen Charlotte was overwhelmingly condescending, but not entirely unfavorable. A printed description of the new queen after the joint coronation on September 22, 1761 said, "She is of middling stature, rather small, but her shape is fine, and carriage graceful; her hair auburn; her face round and fair; the eyes light blue and beaming with sweetness; the nose a little flat and turned up at the point; the mouth rather large with rosy lips and very fine teeth . . . The Queen cannot certainly be pronounced an absolute beauty . . . [But] by her affable manner to all who approach her, she evidences a mind elevated above the dazzling eminence of a throne, and thus she endears herself to the people by the sweetness of her temper. He has so completely won the heart of the king, that every day is witness to his increasing affection for her."

King George quickly adapted to married life. Although Queen Charlotte was not his first choice, he soon became devoted to her. George may have had one mistress before he was married named Hannah Lightfoot, but unlike all other Hanoverian Kings of England, George III had no more mistresses, and he was faithful to his Queen Charlotte during the forty-seven years they were married.

After the wedding, the primary residence of the young king and queen was St. James Palace; however, they also enjoyed stays at Dowager Princess Augusta's Leicester House, Kew Manor, Richmond Palace, and enjoyed outings to Windsor.

The only person who never warmed up to Charlotte's modest charm was the king's mother Augusta Dowager Princess of Wales. Early years of Charlotte's marriage were complicated by the domineering presence of her mother-in-law who, before the marriage, had enjoyed the highest rank for a woman in court, but now she was subordinate to Queen Consort

Charlotte, a teenage girl with little knowledge of court intrigue or formal protocol.

At first, Queen Charlotte was bullied and misinformed of her true status in court. Charlotte was not aggressive, self-promoting, or confrontational. Dowager Princess Augusta tried to retain her dominant place in court as the mother of the king, and as the power behind the Prime Minister James Stuart Earl of Bute. The king, long accustomed to accepting maternal domination, did not intercede on his wife's behalf. Charlotte was led to believe that her mother-in-law had veto power on all persons whom the queen could meet.

Friction soon arose in the queen's court among English and German factions of her ladies-in-waiting as they sparred among one another for preference in the queen's favor. Charlotte brought to London from Strtelitz her childhood nurse and maid, Madam Juliane von Schwellenberg, who defended Charlotte like a tigress, and earned hate and contempt from all the queen's English ladies-in-waiting. Charlotte's domestic problems were as troubling to her, as was the infighting in Parliament and the Privy Council was to her husband the king. However, after her mother-in-law Dowager Princess Augusta died in 1772, Queen Charlotte's supreme place in court was uncontested.

Queen Charlotte enjoyed music and dancing, and these became standard elements of entertainment at St. James Palace. That differed greatly from somber State occasions in the preceding court of George II. In her own court, she enjoyed playing card games with her ladies, and with the king. However, as compared with fashionable royal palaces on the Continent, the London court was thought to be a wasteland of cultural poverty, and intellectual mediocrity. St. James Palace was notorious for being the most frugal, dullest, plain, pious, royal court in Europe.

Early in his reign, George III bought Buckingham House in 1763 as a private London residence for his queen. The residence was first referred to as Queen's Palace, and it served as the royal nursery for their growing family. Fourteen of their fifteen children were born at Buckingham House. It would later be extensively enlarged, and remodeled into Buckingham Palace on designs prepared by the architect John Nash in 1826 during the reign of George IV.

Kings and queen consorts in most European capitals often occupied separate palaces, and sponsored separate courts. George III was a natural family man. He and Queen Charlotte had a harmonious marriage, and they occupied a single dwelling, which was a model of contented domesticity.

Children soon came. The first was George Prince of Wales (later George IV) who was born about eleven months after the king and queen were married. Children followed at the rate of about one birth every fourteen months—a total of fifteen infants were born between 1762 and 1783 (in all, 9 sons and 6 daughters); two sons died in infancy; thirteen children survived to maturity; over half of them lived past seventy years. Their children were:

> George Prince of Wales (August 12, 1762-June 26, 1830), Prince Regent and King George IV
>
> Frederick Duke of York (August 16, 1763-January 5, 1827)
>
> William Duke of Clarence (August 21, 1765-June 20, 1837), King William IV
>
> Charlotte Princess Royal (September 29, 1766-October 6, 1828)
>
> Edward Duke of Kent (November 2, 1767-January 23 1820), the father of Queen Victoria
>
> Augusta Sophia (November 8, 1768-September 22, 1840)
>
> Elizabeth (May 22, 1770-January 10, 1840)
>
> Ernest Augustus Duke of Cumberland (June 5, 1771-November 18, 1851), later King of Hanover after 1837
>
> Augustus Frederick Duke of Sussex (January 27, 1773-April 21, 1843)
>
> Adolphus Frederick, Duke of Cambridge, (February 24, 1774-July 8, 1850), the grandfather of Mary of Teck Queen Consort of King George V
>
> Mary Duchess of Gloucester (April 25, 1776-April 30, 1857)
>
> Sophia (November 2, 1777-May 27, 1848)
>
> Octavius (February 23, 1779-May 3, 1783) died in infancy.
>
> Alfred (September 22, 1780-August 20, 1782) died in infancy.
>
> Amelia (August 7, 1783-November 2, 1810)

Unlike most titled great ladies, Queen Charlotte spent part of each day with her children. As a devoted mother, she once said in astonishment to a duchess, "What? Do you leave your children entirely in care of their attendants? That is more than I dare to do, for it is impossible, no matter how true, or affectionate they may be, servants can never have the responsible feelings of a parent."

The queen watched over her children with as much concern as if they had no other person to look after them, even though they had abundant carefully selected nurses, attendants, and tutors.

Visitors from foreign courts could not believe that the lack of ostentation and splendor in the English court could be the voluntary choice of the King and Queen of England. However, George and Charlotte truly preferred to enjoy a simple life. The pedestrian simplicity of the royal household is shown in an anecdote in which King George politely inquired about the health of a deputy's children. The clerk replied that the children were doing well since " . . . they began eating a hearty breakfast of excellent oatmeal porridge." The king then asked for the name of the miller who supplied the ground oats. King George immediately engaged the miller to provide oatmeal, which the royal brood dutifully ate for several years.

In every way, the royal marriage was a successful union of mutual respect, and affection between a man and wife with thoroughly middle class tasters. George had a profound interest in agriculture. Palace grounds were constantly replanted as vegetable garden plots. The royal family was soundly criticized for running St. James Palace, more like a country farm than a properly maintained imperial palace. The nobility disapproved of King George's unpretentious peasant ways, and he soon acquired the name 'Farmer George.'

Education of the royal brood was a serious concern to their parents. The daily regimen for their children's activities and education was demanding. They rose at six o'clock; dressed, then had breakfast with their parents at eight. By nine in the morning, they were with tutors. Except for a midday break for refreshment, instruction continued until after four in the afternoon. Studies included history, languages, literature, natural science, philosophy, and religion. King George had great respect for 'learning by doing'; once, he ordered twelve year old Crown Prince George and his younger brother Frederick Duke of York to grow, harvest, and process wheat that was grown in a garden plot behind Buckingham House. The boys dug the plot, planted the seed, then grew, reaped, harvested, threshed, and milled the grain; finally, they baked loaves of bread from the wheat flour. The king then told the princes, "Now you know how much work goes into giving you your daily bread."

Queen Charlotte was equally concerned for the education of the young princesses. She employed Mrs. Sarah Siddons (the most acclaimed tragic actress of the 18th century) to give elocution and public speaking lessons to her daughters. Mrs. Siddons' performances as Lady Macbeth, Portia, Ophelia, Desdemona, and Rosalind, with David Garrick at the Drury Lane Theater played an important part in establishing Shakespeare as the preeminent English author for female roles. A statue of Sarah Siddons is in Westminster Abbey, and the 'Sarah Siddons Award' is given each year for the most distinguished female stage performance, attest to the lasting regard for Sarah Siddons' acting talent.

The marriage of King George III and Queen Charlotte was exceptionally amiable with not a whisper of impropriety attached to the behavior of either the king or queen. However, their seven surviving sons were notorious lechers. Many of the royal princes fathered numerous illegitimate children. The first three sons had no surviving legitimate children. Queen Victoria was the only legitimate grandchild by their fourth son Edward Duke of Kent.

George III held very conservative conventional views on personal morality. He was troubled by the licentiousness of his brood. In hope of curbing their willful ways, he forced Parliament to pass the Royal Marriage Act in 1772. It ruled that members of the royal household could not marry before the age of twenty-five without the King's approval, and all royal spouses must be Protestant; otherwise, a royal heir would void the right to rule, and would forfeit a pension from the Civil List. Instead of having its desired effect of protecting legitimate marriage, the Royal Marriage Act fostered an explosion in clandestine liaisons with royal bastards popping up everywhere. It soon led to the court of George III and Queen Charlotte being misnamed 'The Nunnery.'

In keeping with the proscription in her marriage contract against involvement in government affairs, Queen Charlotte kept her actions free of political involvement. The closest she came to meddling with national affairs came with her introduction of Norse paganism into the English celebration of Christmas. In Norse mythology, 'Lucia Tag' (The day of Light) celebrates the winter solstice with evergreens, and candles in recognition that daylight begins to get longer and anticipates the greening of the earth in spring. For her children's delight, Charlotte introduced the use of an evergreen tree with lighted candles for Christmas at Buckingham House around 1780. With the passage of time, the Norse 'Lucia Day'

(Christmas) with a 'Kerzetannenbaum' (a candle lit fir tree), 'Christkindl' (the Christ Child), and 'Weinachtsmann' (Santa Claus) were incorporated into the Christmas seasonal festivities familiar today.

George III and Queen Charlotte enjoyed classical music, and they preferred the works of German composers. George I and George II employed Kapellmeister George Frideric Handel as their State musician in London. Handel died before George III came to the throne. The void created by Handel's death was filled when Queen Charlotte persuaded George III to offer the position of State musician to Johann Christian Bach (the youngest son of Johann Sebastian Bach, the master of counterpoint music). Johann Christian Bach departed from his father's musical style, and was the first major composer to exploit the superiority of the pianoforte over the harpsichord. He also pioneered the new melodic-harmonic styles in opera, and symphony that anticipated the acclaimed works of Joseph Haydn and Wolfgang Amadeus Mozart.

Queen Charlotte invited the eight-year-old prodigy Wolfgang Mozart to come to England in April 1764, and stay for a year. His musical talent dazzled, and delighted the court. In addition to his technical virtuosity, the child amazed everyone with his ability to sight-read and play complex compositions by Purcell, Handel, and Bach that he had never seen before. Queen Charlotte demonstrated her modest competence as a flutist to Mozart's accompaniment on the harpsichord (note: 'flutist' is English; 'flautist' is a pretentious imported Italian term).

Although the king and queen were not notable intellectuals, the long reign of George III (1760-1820) was singularly fertile for the expression of creative ability in many fields by his British subjects; some were:

> *Moralist-philosophers,* Jeremy Bentham, Edmund Burke, David
>   Hume, Joseph Priestley, Adam Smith, John Wesley;
> *Dramatists,* Oliver Goldsmith, Francis Sheridan;
> *Painters,* William Blake, Thomas Gainsborough, Thomas
>   Lawrence, Allan Ramsay, Joshua Reynolds, George
>   Romney;
> *Writer-authors,* Jane Austin, James Boswell, Edward Gibbon,
>   Samuel Johnson, William Hazlitt;
> *Poets,* Robert Burns, Lord Byron, Samuel Coleridge, William
>   Cowper, John Keats, Walter Scott, Percy Shelley, William
>   Wordsworth;

. *Explorer-naturalist-scientists,* Sir Joseph Banks naturalist, Thomas
     Malthus sociologist, Captain James Cook navigator, William
     Herschel astronomer, and many others.

George III chartered The Royal Academy of Arts, and his concern for
science was practical and sincere. From his own pocket, he gave £4,000 to
build a fine Newtonian reflecting telescope for the astronomer Sir William
Herschel, who thereupon, proceeded in 1781 to prove that the star Uranus
was a planet—the first trans-Saturnian planet known to man.

George III also had a profound interest in navigation, and he gave
a prize to John Harrison for producing the first chronometer that could
accurately be used to determine longitude. The clock mechanism worked
at sea, and was tested by Captain Cook; the chronometer lost only five
seconds on a voyage from England to the Caribbean Sea.

Royal patronage was important for the success of creative scientists,
artists, musicians, and craftsmen. A case in point was Thomas
Gainsborough who was the queen's favorite painter. He painted many
members of the royal family, and he quickly became the most popular
portraitist in England.

Another person to benefit from the queen's patronage was Josiah
Wedgwood, a young potter who had just opened his kiln a year before
George III became king. Wedgwood received a commission from Queen
Charlotte for simple everyday table service at Buckingham House. After
filling the order for the queen, Wedgwood continued producing the simple
pattern of dishes called *Queens-Ware.* The simple pale cream-colored dishes
were immediately popular with gentry, and nobility throughout England.
Queens-Ware made Josiah Wedgwood rich and famous. Wedgwood
Queens-Ware is still available for people of good taste at $50 for a place
setting of 5 pieces.

Another example of the value of royal patronage came many years
later after Johann Christian Bach died, and Queen Charlotte paid for his
funeral and established a pension for his widow. In 1790 the composer
Joseph Haydn's patron Prince Nikolaus Esterházy died, and his son,
who inherited the estate in Eisenstadt, Austria, promptly discharged all
house musicians, but he gave Haydn a pension that allowed him to seek
patronage elsewhere. In the same year, Queen Charlotte invited Joseph
Haydn (often called the 'Father of the Symphony') to settle in London.
Haydn arrived in London in 1790 and stayed until 1792, then returned

for the years 1794-1795. In his London years, Haydn created his most enduring works: the *Surprise, Military, Drumroll,* and his thee great *London Symphonies.* Through Haydn's genius, London became a major center for creative music.

In 1788-1789, the reign of King George was impaired for the first time by a period of madness brought on by what is now believed to have been *porphyria*, a rare hereditary metabolic disease of the liver, with symptoms that suddenly come and go. Attacks were accompanied by extreme change in temperament and behavior: such as, convulsions, foaming at the mouth, blood red eyes, incoherent babbling, talking to inanimate objects, and totally unwelcome sexual advances upon ladies in court. Medical treatments of the time were cruel, useless, and only delayed his recovery. Over ensuing years, he had increasingly severe relapses. Finally, in 1810, he became permanently blind, and unable to fulfill governmental duties. In 1811, Parliament appointed George Prince of Wales regent with sovereign power for the rest of his father's life.

During the periods of madness of George III, the king was confined at Windsor Castle where Queen Charlotte was her husband's legal guardian. She gave him devoted care, except for times when he was irrationally violent and needed restraint. In 1792, the queen acquired the country estate of Frogmore located between Windsor Park and Windsor Forest. Frogmore became her favorite residence near Windsor Castle where she would be close to the king during his periods of madness.

The royal family for years had rented Kew House north of Richmond as an alternative to St. James Palace, which was their official London residence. In 1797 after the king's illness began, Charlotte, on her own initiative, bought the Kew manor and grounds for her personal use. From childhood, Queen Charlotte had strong interests in botany. Explorers and naturalists such as Sr. Joseph Banks, Robert Brown, Captain Cook, and others brought exotic plants to London from around the world to Queen Charlotte. She decided to use Kew as a horticultural haven. Kew became her favorite London dwelling, and its gardens soon became the repository for rare plants from remote romantic places around the earth.

After her death, the Kew estate became the center for the present Royal Botanic Gardens at Kew; it is possibly the most prestigious botanical research institute in the world. Botanists named the flamboyant 'Bird of Paradise' flower, *Strelitzia reginae,* for Queen Charlotte; it is a member of the 'Ginger' family of flowering plants.

Queen Charlotte of Mecklenburg-Strelitz reigned for fifty-seven years (1761-1818). Throughout her reign, she avoided court controversy. Most of her life was devoted to the rearing, education, and benefit of her numerous children. The last fifteen of her years as queen were overwhelmed by responsibilities for the care of her husband King George III. Even so, she sponsored numerous charities, which included support for hospitals, several orphanages, and a home for expectant mothers.

The queen aged rapidly after King George became mentally impaired following 1810. She became severely depressed and ill in July 1818, and moved from Windsor to Kew, where her health continued to worsen through the summer and fall. She expressed a desire to return to Windsor to see the king, but her condition failed to improve sufficiently to make that journey of twenty miles possible.

By the end of October 1818, the queen spent most days in sleep and comatose repose. She died at Kew House on November 17, 1818. Her son the Prince Regent and several of her daughters were by her side.

Queen Charlotte was buried in St. George's Chapel at Windsor Castle on December 2, 1818. King George III lived for fourteen more months, until January 29, 1820. He was in a pitiable state of blind deaf madness, and was never aware that his queen had departed.

A court report summed up the queen's life, "Our Queen is neither a wit nor a beauty. She is prudent, well informed, has an excellent understanding, and is very charitable . . . [Her Majesty] is full of good sense and good temper. She loves domestic pleasures . . . is extremely affable, very pious, and is praised by all at home and abroad . . . The Queen of England does not affect splendor in her apparel; she seldom wears jewels except on public ceremonies . . . above all, she favors neatness and simplicity." All told, Queen Charlotte was a loving wife, a devoted mother, and an excellent queen, who, in good conscience, used her abilities with grace, wisely, and well without malice for the benefit of her subjects and family, which is as much as one may wish from any queen.

Following the death of George III, his eldest son Prince Regent, George Prince of Wales, succeeded to the throne in 1820 as King George IV.

The Strange Matter of 'Madragana the Moor'

The Allan Ramsay portrait of Queen Charlotte referred to in the following discussion can be seen on the Internet by referencing *Queen Charlotte of Mecklenbiurg-Streilitz* on Wikipedia. This painting is the most frequently reproduced picture of Queen Charlotte, but it is unlike other portraits of her by major contemporary artists, which can be viewed on the Internet by referencing *Portraits of Queen Charlotte of Mecklenbiurg-Streilitz* on *Google*.

IN THE United States before the Civil War, abolitionists of the 19th century created a myth that Queen Charlotte was of African Negro descent. The basis for this idea came indirectly by way of a popular portrait of Queen Charlotte by the painter Sir Allan Ramsay an abolitionist in England. It is believed that he deliberately inserted 'mulatto' characteristics into his painting of Queen Charlotte—features that are not present in portraits of her by other reputable painters such as Thomas Gainsborough who painted her several times.

It has been proposed that Allan Ramsay fabricated the picture of Queen Charlotte for abolitionists in the American Colonies to advance the argument that enslaved African Negroes should not be considered inferior, because the Queen of England was one of them.

Efforts have been made to find hereditary evidence in support of the suggestion that Queen Charlotte was in part a Negro. Historical research discovered that her attending physician, Baron Christian Friedrich von Stockmar, wrote a note that described Queen Charlotte as having "ein wahres Mulattengesicht" ("true mulatto features").

It then was necessary to seek additional proof of Negro ancestry in her genealogy. That search discovered a mistress of King Afonso III of Portugal (1210-1279) whose name was *Madragana*, who was called a 'Moor' three centuries later in a chronicle by Duarte Nunes de Leão in the 16th century.

It is impossible to know exactly what Duarte Nunes meant by *Moor* in the ancient chronicle. In Medieval usage, the word *Moor* usually referred to the Arabic Islamic invaders of Iberia (Spain and Portugal) who ruled from the Alhambra Palace at Granada. However, *Moor*, without ethnic specificity also generically included all North African Berbers (Tunisians, Moroccans, Algerians), Hindus of Southern Asia, as well as black African races. Thus, the word *Moor* did not specifically or exclusively imply Negro ethnicity.

Genealogical connection between Queen Charlotte and Madragana the Moor shows a lineage of nine (possibly more) generations that separate Madragana from Queen Charlotte. All intermediates are Nordic Caucasian wives of Charlotte's male ancestors.

If Madragana had been a full 100% African Negro, then her nine-generation distant descendant Queen Charlotte would be expected to have only one one-thousandth of Madragana's genes; the remaining 999/1000 parts of Charlotte's genetic makeup would be Caucasian. Madragana's black African ethnic characteristics could not possibly suddenly reappear in Charlotte to make her a true mulatto after nine generations of Nordic Caucasian inbreeding. Known genetic mechanisms make it inconceivable that Queen Charlotte could be a "true mulatto" (that is, 50% African Negro) after nine generations of Caucasian inbreeding.

The consensus among scholars is that, since paintings of Queen Charlotte by Gainsborough and others are hardly recognizable as the same person painted by Sir Allan Ramsay, he probably purposely falsified his painting of Queen Charlotte for the previously stated *abolitionist* reasons. As well intentioned as the original motive may have been for Sir Allan Ramsay to represent Queen Charlotte as half-Negro (mulatto), that myth is not supported by known genetic mechanisms.

It is now thought that 'Madragana the Moor' was an *Iberian Moor* living in Spain—that is, a Mozarab Christian, or a Sephardic Jew, or an Arabic Muslim—in which case, she probably was a full Caucasian of Semitic origin. Notwithstanding these facts, Queen Charlotte's alleged Afroethnicity continues to be an important issue for some persons of Afrocentric persuasion.

REIGN 34

KING GEORGE IV

AND

WIFE MARIA ANNE FITZHERBERT

AND

QUEEN CONSORT CAROLINE OF BRUNSWICK

Summary of the Regency (1811-1820) and Reign of King George IV (1820-1830)

King George IV: life dates c. 68 years, b. August 12, 1762-d. June 26, 1830; Prince Regent of England c. 11 years, February 5, 1811-January 29, 1820; King of Great Britain (England, Ireland, Scotland, and Wales) and Elector of Hanover c. 10 years, January 29, 1820-June 26, 1830.

PRINCE GEORGE Augustus, who would become George IV, was the eldest son of George III and Charlotte of Mecklenburg-Strelitz. During much of his life, George Augustus was known as the Prince of Wales, later as the Prince Regent, before he became King George IV. He was created Prince Regent to serve as sovereign during the last decade (1811-1820) in the reign of his father George III who was in senile dementia.

George Prince of Wales was intelligent and had a gift for learning languages. He was precise in use of English, and fluent in French, German, and Italian. He had a good command of history. He loved the theater of Sheridan and Shakespeare. He was famous for setting fashions of rich elaborate dress, and in his youth, he was called 'The First Gentleman of Europe.'

George IV was the first Hanoverian monarch to be considered completely English. He was handsome, and possessed great charm. His admirable qualities were offset by willful stubbornness, indolence, and insensitivity to all that was not self-serving. His father George III tried to curb his extravagant excesses, and that led to a permanent alienation of father and son; the relationship was usual for Hanoverian kings and their crown prince.

Prince George's love of extravagant ornamentation was reflected in *The Regency Style* of 19th century English dress, architecture, and interior design. Above all, he was determined to make London equal to, or surpass the most magnificent capitals in Europe. Prince George was regent during the final defeat of Napoleon, which marked a high point in England's prestige.

On a personal level, Prince George was impulsive, and not given to thinking through to see consequences from hasty decisions. He had no political convictions, or interest in the public weal. During his ten year personal reign (1820-1830), he was a weathercock with no sense of purpose. He never sponsored any act of government that can be regarded as beneficial for his realm. His only political efforts were to delay, or block measures that were in the best interests of his subjects. Public favor turned against him for his self-indulgent and profligate waste of public money. His ostentatious frivolity and monumental architectural renovation of London increased during his regency and reign. George IV lost favor in Parliament to such a degree that political power never returned to royal hands.

George as Prince of Wales was twice married. Both marriages, although never actually annulled, failed to provide an heir. The first marriage was to Maria Anne (Smythe) FitzHerbert, a Catholic widow in 1785, but the union was never approved by English law. His second marriage was to Princess Caroline of Brunswick in 1795, but she was queen consort in name only.

George IV and Caroline of Brunswick had one child Princess Charlotte Augusta who died in childbirth and left George IV without a legitimate heir. George IV reigned for ten years from 1820 until 1830 when he died from a heart attack or aortic aneurism. He is buried at St. George's Chapel, Windsor.

Following the death of George IV in 1830, his younger brother William Duke of Clarence succeeded in 1830 as King William IV.

Narrative of Maria Anne FitzHerbert Wife of George Prince Regent

Maria Anne Fitzherbert: life dates c. 80 years, b. July 26, 1758-d. March 27/29, 1837; wife of George Weld c. 3 months, July-October 1775; wife of Thomas Fitzherbert c. 3 years, June 1778-May 7, 1781; wife of George Prince of Wales-Prince Regent-King/George IV c. 45 years, December 15, 1785-June 26, 1830; widowed 7 years, June 26, 1830-March 27, 1837.

MARIA ANNE (née Smythe) Fitzherbert was the eldest child of Walter Smythe and Mary Anne Errington of Bambridge, Hampshire. Her parents were without title, but her father was the younger son of Baron John Smythe of Acton. She was born on July 26, 1756 into a well-to-do Catholic family. Catholic education was not then permitted in England, but her parents were able to afford a superior education for Maria in a convent in Dunkirk, France.

In July 1775 at age eighteen, Maria married Edward Weld a wealthy Catholic landowner of Lulworth Castle in Dorset. At the time, Catholic marriages had no legal standing in England; only Jews and Quakers were exempt from the Marriage Act of 1753. Edward Wald was several years older than Maria, and just three months after their marriage, he died from injuries after falling from his horse. Maria was widowed at eighteen, and she returned to live with her parents.

Three years later in 1778 at age twenty-one, Maria married Thomas FitzHerbert a younger son of Baron Stafford of Swynnerton in Staffordshire. The Smythe and FitzHerbert Catholic families had long been friends. Thomas was almost ten years older than Maria. Their only child, a son, died in infancy. Thomas was frail and suffered from pulmonary distress said to be tuberculosis, of which he died on May 7, 1781. He left Maria an estate that earned £2,500 annually, and a residence at Mayfair in central London, and another at Brighton on the shore south of London. After an appropriate period of mourning for her husband Thomas FitzHerbert, Maria said to a friend, "I am almost ashamed of being happy again."

She was now twenty-three years old, twice married, twice widowed, and a wealthy heiress with residences in the two most fashionable places in England. As a beautiful young matron of means, Mrs. Maria FitzHerbert entered social life in court with confident good manners in the spring of 1784.

George Prince of Wales, who then was nineteen and bursting with defiance against his pedestrian parents King George III and Queen Charlotte, already dominated social life in London. Prince George was intelligent, clever, charming, superbly educated, and possessed exquisite taste and manners. However, by nature he was lazy, profligate, and insensitive to the feelings of others. He also lacked a moral sense, and was driven by self-gratification. Prince George possessed the Hanoverian preference for older women who possessed, as was said, 'ample matronly bosoms.'

Mrs. Maria FitzHerbert first met the Prince of Wales by accident at a concert in London in 1784. He was smitten by Mrs. FitzHerbert's beauty and elegant bearing. He pursued her affection with invitations to court events. He sent expensive gifts, and contracted Gainsborough to paint her portrait. Maria acknowledged his favors, but held him at arm's length, and refused to be anything more than an acquaintance. Maria's friend Anne Lindsay the Duchess of Devonshire summed up the early phase in their relationship, in saying, "Mrs. FitzHerbert is at present the Prince's favorite, but she seems, I think, rather to cut him than otherwise."

Maria's sense of propriety excluded any possibility of becoming his mistress. She was an undeviating Catholic. She knew marriage was out of the question. King George III would need to give his consent for the Crown Prince to marry, and that would never happen. Before getting further involved with the Prince of Wales, Maria left England to travel in Europe to let Prince George cool off.

However, on the day before her departure, July 8, 1784, a message was delivered to Maria that said the Prince had attempted suicide by stabbing himself and that " . . . only your immediate presence will save me."

Maria persuaded her friend the Duchess of Devonshire to accompany her to the Prince's bedside. They found him with bloody bandages on his chest. He protested that he had no desire to live unless Maria promised to marry him. He put a ring on Maria's finger before the ladies left. Maria did not think her reluctant agreement to marry him was binding because it had been made under duress.

On July 9, 1784, Maria left England, and stayed in Europe for a year. She only returned then because legal matters affecting her properties required her return to London. During her year away from London, King George III denied permission for Prince George to join Maria in Holland.

The Prince was steadfast in his pursuit of Maria. Maria relented and agreed to wed the Prince on December 15, 1785. They were married secretly by an Anglican priest in Maria's parlor at Mayfair. Witnesses of the event were her brother John Smythe and her uncle Henry Errington.

The marriage would not be legal in secular courts of English law; however, Pope Pious VII later gave Maria assurance that, although not married in the Catholic Church " . . . in the eyes of God, [you are married] . . . according to every other law both human and divine." In the religion that was important to her, Maria FitzHerbert knew she was married. Thereafter she lived openly and honorably as the true wife of George Prince of Wales, also later when he was George Prince Regent, and when he was King George IV.

Socially, Prince George honored her, and treated her with all respect due his wife. He insisted that Maria be accorded royal respect and deference. They lived separately: he in Carleton House; she at a new home the prince provided for her in Mayfair. In social functions at court, Maria enjoyed the honor of being seated beside the Prince of Wales. In this way, they lived for about two years. Their marriage was widely suspected, but the prince did not officially acknowledge it, because to do so would jeopardize his right to be King of England.

In 1787, Prince George was forced to ask Parliament to give him a grant to cover a huge personal debt to pay for renovation of Carleton House, and other incidental extravagances, including the new home for Maria. Before Parliament would agree to pay the prince's debts, the attorney representing the prince declared emphatically "Prince George and Mrs. FitzHerbert were not, and never had been married." If they ever had been married, Parliament would never have come to the prince's aid, and his right to reign would have been revoked.

Prince George did not protest the denial of their marriage. Parliament gave the prince of about £160,000 (equal to ten fold as much today) to pay his debts.

Maria was deeply wounded by Prince George's passive acceptance of what, in her opinion, amounted to 'annulment of their marriage.' For a time, Mrs. FitzHerbert left London, and took refuge at her home in Brighton. For weeks, she would have nothing to do with the prince. Finally, however, the prince was able to convince her that his representative in Parliament testified without his personal approval. They were again reconciled. Maria returned to London, and, they continued their man and wife relationship as before. During that period until 1794, the prince gave her an annual pension of about £3,000 in addition to her own inherited income.

Throughout their continuing relationship, the prince had a succession of mistresses. Maria accepted his infidelity with equanimity as merely a royal prerogative for any 'prince of the blood.' His brief byplays included Grace Dalrymple (who produced an illegitimate daughter Georgina Elliot), and Elizabeth Milbanke (who produced an illegitimate son George Milbanke). A much longer more notorious relationship began in 1782 with Frances Villiers Countess of Jersey. His relationship with her lasted until 1803. During that time, she exercised a great influence in court. Lady Jersey selected the future wife of Prince George by convincing King George III and Queen Charlotte that Princess Caroline of Brunswick would be the perfect wife for the Crown Prince. Lady Jersey hoped, however, that the marriage would be a failure, so she could keep her dominate place in court.

A special problem of State arose for the first time in 1788, which would become increasingly serious in following years. In that year, King George III had his first debilitating attack of madness that raised the possibility of a need to appoint the Prince of Wales regent. King George temporarily recovered in February 1789 before Parliament acted on the matter.

By 1794, Prince George's was again deeply in debt. His father King George III refused to pay his bills. Prince George again went to Parliament for aid. However, in 1894, Prince George was thirty-two years old, and officially unmarried. With no prospect for an *heir presumptive* to follow his reign, Parliament refused to cancel his debts unless he would agree to marry a suitable Protestant princess to provide an heir.

Three acts of Parliament denied Catholic Maria FitzHerbert the right to be the mother of a crown prince: the Act of Settlement of 1701, the Royal Marriage Act of 1772, and the Marriage Act of 1753. Prince George's Catholic marriage to Mrs. FitzHerbert had no legal standing, and was void in English law. Prince George was officially seen to be entirely unencumbered in his freedom to make a legal marriage commitment elsewhere.

Prince George agreed to marry anyone Parliament approved, if Parliament would pay his debts that amounted to £630,000, and in addition, Parliament must double his annuity of £60.000.

Princess Caroline of Brunswick was chosen to be Prince George's bride. She was a Protestant first cousin of the prince; her mother was a sister of King George III. Negotiation for the marriage of the Prince of Wales to Princess Caroline of Brunswick began in July 1794, and was complete by November.

The relationship between Prince George and Maria FitzHerbert steadily deteriorated as plans for the royal marriage progressed. Early in 1794, Maria FitzHerbert left London, and remained away for a period of two years. She was deeply wounded by implication that George did not consider their prior vows to be valid. When she was in England, she avoided London and spent most of her time in Brighton.

Prince George married Princess Caroline of Brunswick on April 8, 1795. Early in his first year of his official marriage to Caroline of Brunswick, Prince George began overtures for reconciliation with Maria FitzHerbert. She saw the impropriety of his advances, and refused to have any contact with him.

Nine months after the Prince and Princess of Wales were married their only child Princess Charlotte Augusta, was born on January 7, 1796. Shortly after Princess Charlotte Augusta's birth, Prince George separated permanently from his wife Caroline of Brunswick, and again invited Maria to return to London. She accepted, and they renewed their relationship, which was amiable, but possibly no longer intimate. A letter that Maria FitzHerbert wrote to a friend around 1800, said, " . . . I did not consent to make it up with the Prince to live with him either as his wife or as his mistress . . . but rather like brother and sister . . ."

The prince treated Maria respectfully as his wife on all social occasions. Maria FitzHerbert resumed her former place in court beside the Prince, and maintained a friendly relationship with Lady Frances Villiers Countess of Jersey, who was the prince's mistress and manager of his social affairs.

However, in 1803 after twenty years as the prince's favorite, Lady Jersey lost her place to Lady Isabel Seymour-Conway Marchioness of Hertford. When Lady Jersey vanished from court, Lady Hertford moved rapidly to undermine Mrs. FitzHerbert's wifely position with the prince. Her opportunity to oust Mrs. FitzHerbert came at a great State occasion during the Napoleonic Wars when exiled King Louis XVIII of France was fêted at Carleton House by Prince George.

Prince George left responsibility for all banquet arrangements to Lady Hertford. When Mrs. FitzHerbert arrived at the banquet and expected to take her usual place beside the prince, the major domo informed Mrs. FitzHerbert "You will find your place at the foot of the table with other common persons without title."

Mrs. FitzHerbert was publicly humiliated, and personally wounded by Prince George who failed to defend her. She was his true wife of many years, and the prince showed preference for his most recent whore! Maria departed in icy fury, and refused to see Prince George ever again.

In 1804 without making any further contact with the prince, Maria FitzHerbert moved permanently from London to Brighton, where she built a new home that would be her major residence for thirty-three years until the end of her life in 1837. In those years, she traveled freely around England and on the Continent, but she never again was part of London court life.

In 1811, King George III descended into permanent madness, and the Prince of Wales became Prince Regent with sovereign powers of the king. The regency lasted until George III died in 1820, wherewith the Prince Regent became King George IV on January 29, 1820 in a reign that lasted ten years until 1830.

Mrs. FitzHerbert had no contact with her husband during his nineteen years as prince regent and king. It is uncertain whether George attempted reconciliation with her during that time. However, he authorized an annual pension of £10,000 for her, but usually only about £6,000 was paid each year. Even so, her pension, together with income from her own estate, assured her a comfortable living.

Mrs. Maria FitzHerbert made a notable departure from Brighton to Holland in the month of July 1820 to be absent from England during the scandalous trial of Caroline of Brunswick that took place shortly after the Prince Regent finally became King George IV. The trial of Queen Caroline called *The Queen's Trial* began on July 5, 1820.

The trial was designed to eliminate Caroline as King George's wife and queen consort, by showing that she was guilty of "acts highly unbecoming of her rank and station, and of a most licentious character." Maria FitzHerbert went to Europe during the trial, as a precaution against being subpoenaed to testify before Parliament that King George was just as guilty of infidelity as was charged against Queen Caroline.

Maria FitzHerbert was informed on King George's sixty-seventh birthday in August 1829, that his health was failing, and in May 1830, she learned that the king was near death. She wrote with an expression of concern for his wellbeing, but she received no reply, possibly because he was too ill to dictate an answer.

An aortic aneurysm suddenly burst in King George's chest on June 26, 1830. In a few minutes, he died. His death came after a lifetime of overeating, and alcoholic excess. A locket was found around his neck with a picture of Maria FitzHerbert in it. He is buried in St. George's Chapel, Windsor.

When George IV died, his younger brother William Duke of Clarence came to the throne as King William IV. He offered to give Maria the title of Duchess, as a long overdue recognition of the honored place she occupied in the royal family. However, Maria refused the title and said, "I have borne through life the name of Mrs. FitzHerbert. I have never disgraced it, and I do not wish to change it."

In 1833, Mrs. FitzHerbert wrote a will that, among other things, provided for storage of personal papers, including her marriage certificate. It proved without question that she and Prince George had been married in Anglican rites on December 15, 1785. Another record of the marriage, believed to be written by George IV, was found in Windsor archives.

The bulk of the considerable wealth in Maria FitzHerbert's estate went to two daughters of dear friends in Brighton, for whom she had acted as guardian and surrogate mother when they were young. Her note about them said, " . . . this paper is addressed to my two dear children . . . I have loved them both with the . . . affection any mother could do, and I have done the utmost in my power for their interests and comfort . . ." The beneficiaries were: Mary Ann Stafford-Jerningham and Mary Georgina Emma Dawson-Damer.

After Mrs. FitzHerbert's death, gossip raised suspicion that the girls named in her will were her own children, with George IV being their father. The bequests in her will are simple truthful expression of concern by an elderly person without heirs, who loved and cared for the two girls named in her will.

Maria FitzHerbert lived into her eighty-first year, and died on March 27, 1857 (some records give March 29) of uncertain causes associated with old age. She was buried in the Catholic Church of St. John the Baptist in Brighton. In life she had contributed generously to rebuilding the church, and in death, she endowed it handsomely. A mural in the chapel honors her memory.

Narrative of
Princess of Wales and Queen Consort
Caroline of Brunswick

Queen Caroline of Brunswick: life dates, 53 years, May 17, 1768-August 7, 1821; Princess of Wales wife of George Prince of Wales, 15 years, April 8, 1795-January 29, 1820; Queen Consort of King George IV, 18 months, January 29, 1820-August 7, 1821.

CAROLINE AMELIA of Brunswick was the third child, and second daughter of Karl Wilhelm Ferdinand Duke of Braunschweig-Wolfenbüttl and Princess Augusta Frederika of England the eldest sister of King George III of England. Therefore, Caroline was a first cousin of her future husband George Prince of Wales.

Caroline was born on May 17, 1768 in Wolfenbüttl, the small provincial capital of the Prussian county of Braunschweig (in English,

Brunswick), which borders on Hanover. Caroline's mother Princess Augusta haughtily distained being demoted to mere duchess by her forced diplomatic marriage to the Duke of Brunswick, because England needed German allies in its ongoing war with France. Throughout her life, Princess Augusta wanted to return to London. She paid little attention to a proper education of her children that would be suitable for court life in a major European capital. Thus, her daughter Caroline Amelia, by nature and for lack of suitable training, was a colossal failure in her efforts to cope with life when she was thrust into high London society as wife of the Prince of Wales. The Prince was the very embodiment of sophisticated learning and elegant manners. Whereas, Caroline was intellectually impoverished, and the essence of tasteless tawdry banality.

However, Caroline possessed two essential qualifications for a Queen of England: she was of royal birth, and she was a Protestant. Suddenly in the summer of 1794, Lady Caroline found herself engaged to Prince George of Wales a cousin she had never met. The prince had agreed to marry whomever the Parliament and Privy Council chose in exchange for payment of his monumental debts, and for doubling of his allowance.

Caroline knew that the Prince of Wales had a 'favorite' named Lady Frances Villiers Countess of Jersey, and a 'wife' named Mrs. Maria FitzHerbert. However, *royal favorites* and so-called *wives* did not concern Caroline. She understood that princes married for politics and had mistresses for pleasure.

On November 20, 1794, Lord James Harris Baron Malmsbury of England's diplomatic staff went to Wolfenbüttl to make marriage arrangements for Lady Caroline and the Prince of Wales. Lord Malmsbury previously informed Prince George of his reservations on Caroline's suitability to be his Princess of Wales. His pointed out that Lady Caroline " . . . lacked judgment, decorum and tact; she spoke her mind too readily, acted indiscreetly, and often neglected to wash, or change her underclothes . . . and had no acquired morality, and no strong innate notions of its value and necessity." He suspected that Caroline was not a virgin.

By the end of March 1795, the bridal party was prepared to embark on the British naval vessel *Jupiter* at Cuxhaven to cross the North Sea. They completed the passage to Greenwich on April 5, and were met at the pier by a welcoming party headed by Lady Jersey who escorted Lady Caroline to London. The Duke of Wellington explained that Lady Jersey deliberately chose Caroline of Brunswick to be Prince George's bride because she knew that Caroline's " . . . indelicate manners, indifferent character, and not very inviting appearance, from a hope that disgust with his wife would secure constancy to his mistress [Lady Jersey]."

Three days after Lady Caroline arrived in England, she met and married the Prince of Wales in London on April 8, 1795. He was thirty-two years old, and she was twenty-seven. At their first encounter in St. James Palace, both Prince George and Lady Caroline disliked one another intensely for reasons of appearance and behavior.

Prince George found Caroline to be short, fat, vulgar spoken, ill-mannered, and dressed in atrocious taste. He requested brandy to steady his nerves before the wedding could proceed.

Lady Caroline's opinion was "[The Prince] was a fat fancy dandy, and not nearly as handsome" as she thought he would be.

The wedding ceremony took place in the Chapel Royal at St. James Palace on the evening of April 8 as a State occasion with the court in full attendance. The Archbishop John Moore of Canterbury performed the long ceremony. A report described Caroline to be " . . . a short, very fat, elderly maid, with an extremely red face, and wearing a frock cut disgusting low at the neck."

After the ceremony, the groom went to his apartment, and spent much of the evening lying on the floor in a drunken stupor. Later, when his bride Caroline joined him, the marriage was consummated, and once again on the next night. The Marine Pavilion in Brighton was the honeymoon get away for the bride and groom, and their invited guests. Later, Caroline described the disgusting experience, " . . . the disreputable Lords were constantly drunk and filthy, sleeping and snoring . . . in bouts that resembled a bad brothel much more than a palace."

After the honeymoon, the Prince and Princess of Wales lived in separate residences, and never again lived together as man and wife.

Exactly nine months after the Prince and Princess of Wales were married, their only child, Princess Charlotte Augusta, was born on January 7/8, 1796. The infant's parents despised each other, and Prince George felt that his wife was an unsuitable mother for his daughter. To emphasize his absolute separation from Princess Caroline, he wrote a new will two days after Princess Charlotte Augusta was born. It read, " . . . she who is called the Princess of Wales, the mother of my daughter, should in no way be concerned in the education or care of the child, or have possession of her person . . . To my daughter, I leave my jewels, which are mine, having been bought with my own money, and to her [Caroline] who is called the Princess of Wales I leave one shilling . . ."

The infant was taken from Caroline, and given to caretakers chosen by Prince George. Princess Caroline was permitted to see her child several times a month under strict supervision that severely limited her ability to have influence on the child's rearing and training. Princess Caroline had only fleeting contact with her daughter, except when she stayed with her grandmother Queen Charlotte of Mecklenburg-Strelitz who always welcomed her daughter-in-law Caroline. The grandmother, mother, and daughter Charlotte Augusta developed a close affectionate relationship. Her father Prince George did not like Caroline's access to their daughter, but there was little he could do to thwart the female conspiracy of two noble women to outwit him.

The disgruntled prince felt that he had been swindled by Parliament in the marriage. He had only agreed to get married, if Parliament would pay his debts and double his annual allowance. True, his income had been raised to £125,000, but £75,000 was garnished to pay past debts, which left only £60,000 for living expenses as a married man—it was less than his allowance of £78,000 for himself alone.

Caroline was banished from Carleton House and the Court of St. James in central London. In 1799, set up her own rowdy ménage in a manor house rented from Lord Edward Montagu Earl of Sandwich near Greenwich east of London. Her boisterous parties were compared with Roman orgies. In her private residence, she entertained whomever and whenever she pleased at vulgar parties that soon were the talk of London. Gossip impugned her character with tales of her easy virtue with anyone who would cast a lecherous eye in her direction. Among the names associated with her were young and mature swains who were the heirs to great estates, or army officers, or members of Parliament. A frequent visitor was Admiral William Sidney Smith (second in the British Navy only to High Admiral of the Fleet Horatio Nelson).

It was widely known that she opened a 'charitable foundling home' for children of unwed mothers. However, many suspected the home was a means for concealing a product of her own indiscretions. Gossip impugned a so-called 'orphan' named William Austin, born in 1802, to be Princess Caroline's own natural son, and that his father, most likely was Admiral Smith of the Royal Navy. However, Caroline insisted that her 'orphanage' was set up only to care for "unfortunate parentless children, who were given food, lodging, care, and education, without which they would have perished on the street."

By 1804, gossip about Princess Caroline's unseemly behavior was a national scandal. When the *William Austin Matter* became common knowledge, it created a storm of national concern—if William Austin were indeed Princess Caroline's son, and if his father was George Prince of Wales, then the infant William Austin was second in line of succession to the throne of England.

In 1806, two brothers of the Prince of Wales (Frederick Duke of York and William Duke of Clarence) demanded that an investigation into the paternity of William Austin be made to decide the question of his legitimacy, since it directly affected their own places in the succession. In that year, the Privy Council and Parliament started a 'Delicate Investigation' of the *William Austin Matter*.

The Prince and Princess of Wales both emphatically denied parentage of the infant. A common woman named Sophia Austin testified that the child was her own, but many believed she had been bribed to testify falsely. Servants of Caroline's household refused to testify against her, and they would neither confirm nor deny that she had several lovers, or that she had ever been pregnant.

The commission report to King George III concluded, "We are happy to declare to your Majesty our perfect conviction that there is no foundation whatever for believing that the child now with the Princess is the child of Her Royal Highness, or that she was delivered of any child in the year 1802 . . ." However, that did not end the matter.

Prince George, motivated by a desire to rid England of Princess Caroline's presence, asked the commission to extend its investigation into improprieties in the Princess of Wales' behavior. In pursuing its investigation of Caroline's unseemly deportment, the commission called many witnesses; many names were named; political careers were jeopardized; a huge body of conflicting testimony was gleaned, and the press had a field day.

In the end, the examiners decided that evidence was conflicting and impossible to separate fact from hearsay, so the whole matter was dropped without any final resolution to the charges that impugned Princess Caroline's character. The final report in December 1806 stated, "[In the opinion of the court] . . . no evidence had been produced to justify any legal proceeding . . ."

Therefore, the 'Delicate Investigation' collapsed for lack of reliable legal evidence of Princess Caroline's wrong doing. However, Princess Caroline's reputation was in tatters. Many believed that the so-called 'orphan' named William Austin born in 1802 was Princess Caroline's own natural son, and that his father was Admiral William Sidney Smith of the Royal Navy.

Prince George banned Caroline from London, and denied her all official court recognition. He had no personal contact with her after 1807.

Princess Caroline's personal following at Montagu House dwindled to insignificance after her husband was created Prince Regent in 1811. For his investiture as Prince Regent in 1811, George designed costumes so sumptuously grand that peacocks, had they attended, would have looked like crows. Prince George fumed at the press when it described him at the investiture as " . . . a fat Adonis of loveliness."

The *Regency Period* in English history lasted specifically from 1811 to 1820, when George Prince of Wales was the Prince Regent. However, in a cultural sense, the Regency Period refers to the entire period when George wielded influence as the Prince of Wales, Prince Regent, and King George IV: namely, from 1790 to 1830. In the latter sense, the Regency Period encompasses the entire time when Prince George of Hanover played a transforming role in the rise of English Baroque art, literature, architecture, fashion, and language, all of which were imprinted with opulent excess.

The Regency Period also was a time of brilliant English military success over the French at Trafalgar and Waterloo. Those sea and land battles brought the curtain down in the final defeat of Napoleon. The Battle of Waterloo on June 18, 1815 was an event that marked a high point in England's prestige and power in Europe.

Prince George was forty-eight when he became Prince Regent in 1811. The Prince Regent responded like a child in a candy shop. His extravagance spent on royal functions and projects knew no bounds. In the last decade of his father's reign, the Prince Regent took London as his stage. With help from the architect, John Nash, central parts of the city were torn out to create present Regent Street and Regent's Park to enhance access and views to his palaces.

After the regency began in 1811, everyone seeking power, influence, or fame ignored Queen Caroline. Caroline remained in London until 1814, but she finally agreed to be exiled from England with a bribe of an annual pension of £35,000. She travelled widely in Europe without returning to London for six years. She took William Austin with her, and went first to Brunswick, Germany to visit her mother on August 8, 1814. From there, she went to Switzerland, then to Italy.

In Milan, she hired Bartolomeo Pergami, to manage Villa d'Este on Lake Como, which she purchased in 1815. Caroline and Bartolomeo were inseparable for many years. They travelled leisurely around the Mediterranean Sea with lengthy stops in Elba, Sicily, Tunis, Malta, Milos, Athens, Constantinople, Jerusalem, Venice, and in Rome, she had an audience with Pope Pious VII.

In 1816, Caroline sold the Villa d'Este, and moved to Villa Caprile on the Adriatic Sea north of San Moreno. Caroline and Bartolomeo shared adjoined bedrooms, ate their meals together, and gave every appearance of being man-and-wife. Gossip in courts and spas throughout Europe speculated on the nature of their relationship. Lord Byron informed his London publisher that 'he knew for sure they were lovers.' Scandal sheet cartoonists illustrated their supposed illicit relationship with ribald nude drawings of them splashing together in baths and public fountains of Rome.

On May 2, 1816, Caroline's daughter Princess Charlotte Augusta at age twenty married Prince Leopold of Saxe-Coberg-Saalfeld in London. Prince Leopold of Saxe-Coberg-Saalfeld was an impoverished prince with little land and less money. The marriage ceremony was a lavish affair in the Crimson Parlor at Carleton House. The stilted ritual was briefly broken when Charlotte giggled as penniless Prince Leopold promised, "With all my worldly goods, I thee endow."

The marriage, although congenial, was very brief. Charlotte Augusta died one year after her marriage following the stillbirth of a son on November 17, 1817.

The tragedy of Charlotte Augusta's death deprived her father Prince George of a legitimate heir to the throne. Charlotte Augusta's death also moved William Duke of Clarence to second place in the royal succession. The Prince Regent ordered his brother William to marry, and have legitimate offspring who would be acceptable in the line of succession. However, William Duke of Clarence had a long time common law wife, the actress Dorothea Bland, who was the mother of his ten illegitimate children.

By Charlotte Augusta's death, Caroline of Brunswick, who had been the mother of the next prospective Queen of England, lost all significance in the English court. The Prince Regent lost no time in his attempt to remove her from England.

For years, the Prince Regent's secret agents had followed Caroline around Europe to collect damning evidence, as Caroline created scandal wherever she went. The best evidence against her was a testimony that said, "[Caroline and Pergami] . . . are to all appearances man and wife; never was anything so obvious." In November 1818, the Prince Regent moved to obtain sufficient proof of Princess Caroline's infidelity that could be used against her in a court of law.

Early in 1819, the Prince Regent sent spies to Milan to question and bribe Caroline's servants, associates, and friends to give salacious information on Caroline's daily behavior. George's spies collected bales of hearsay information that suggested misbehavior. However, no witnesses with firsthand information gave solid evidence that Caroline had illegally violated her marriage vows. In autumn of 1819, the Prince Regent offered Caroline a bribe of £50,000 to stay abroad permanently, and to accept the lesser title Duchess of Cornwall. That would imply that she abdicated all later right to be titled Queen of England when the Prince Regent eventually became King of England. Princess Caroline refused the offer, but she remained in Italy.

Everything changed on January 29, 1820 when aged King George III died after a decade of progressive senile dementia. On that date, George the Prince Regent at age fifty-eight finally in his own right became King George IV. At the same time although she had been separated from the Prince Regent for a decade, Princess Caroline became his titular Queen Consort of England.

Caroline was determined to claim all rights implied by her new title. She let it be known that she would return to London. Caroline bid adieu to her Italian household, including Bartolomeo Pergami, and went to France to finalize plans for her return to England. The fate of her adopted son William Austin is uncertain.

Caroline arrived in England on June 6, 1820. She was welcomed with extravagant public approval as Queen of England. However, George IV was determined to block Caroline's efforts to regain royal recognition. In July 1820, the king began divorce proceedings against his detested wife.

He requested Parliament to declare his previous marriage to Caroline of Brunswick "forever wholly dissolved, annulled, and made entirely void."

Parliament charged Caroline with illegal "acts highly unbecoming to her rank and station, and of a most licentious character." The House of Lords examined the damning information collected in Milan against Caroline, and submitted a *Bill of Pains and Penalties* on July 5, 1820. The bill in the House of Commons was known as *The Queen's Trial.* Its stated purpose was to deprive Queen Caroline " . . . of the title, prerogatives, rights, privileges, and exemptions of Queen Consort . . . and to dissolve the marriage between His Majesty [George IV] and the said Caroline . . . for adultery with Bartolomeo Pergami, a foreigner of low station, . . . [by which] she forfeits her right to be queen consort."

Debate began in August and ended in November 1820. Testimony and arguments were long and replete with sordid details that embarrassed many persons in high office.

On November 6, 1820, a vote of condemnation finally passed the House of Lords. However, the House of Commons never considered the bill, for fear of inciting a riot because Caroline's English subjects still loved her. When the Bill against her failed to pass, Parliament again offered Caroline £50,000 a year, but this time without any restrictions, and she accepted it.

In spite all his efforts, George IV failed to get the divorce he so greatly desired. Nominally, Caroline remained the Queen Consort for a year and a half, until the end of her life in 1821. As in the 'Delicate Investigation' sixteen years before, the English public saw the lack of a conviction of guilt as equivalent to a declaration of her innocence. Accordingly, Caroline spent over a year in anticipation of being an active participant in the upcoming coronation of George IV, which was planned to take place in July 1821.

The vanity of George IV was never revealed more clearly than in his coronation. It took eighteen months from his ascension to the throne in January 29, 1820 to complete preparations for the event that took place on July 19, 1821 in Westminster Abbey. George's ambition was to achieve even greater heights of splendor in his crowning, than the standard set by Napoleon when he crowned himself Emperor of France in 1804 at Notre Dame cathedral.

King George IV supervised every step in the most costly and elaborately choreographed coronation ever held. Almost £240,000 (equal to nearly ten million pounds today) was spent on ornate coronation costumes and decorations.

A description of the event reported that "[The coronation] . . . procession was led by 'Herb Women' who (in the Medieval manner to ward off plague) sprinkled herbs and flower petals on the ground; followed by government officials (with the symbols of state: crown, orb, scepter, etc.); then came high Church officials (with Holy Writ and chalice); the King followed in a gold, silver, jeweled, and ermine coronation robe with a twenty-five foot train, and on his head was a four-foot high ostrich plume bedecked hat; Lords of the Cinque Ports carried the Coronation Canopy; Lords of the Realm followed in order of rank; last, came the Lord Mayor of London and officials of the City of London; everyone was dressed-to-the nines (as best they could ill afford) in the style the king decreed."

Caroline asked for advice on how she should be dressed for the role she would play in the coronation. She was rudely informed that she would neither be crowned, nor would she have any part to play, nor would she even be permitted to attend the ceremony in Westminster Abbey. She refused to accept her expulsion, and continued with plans to dress magnificently, and take her rightful place in the event. Friends and advisors cautioned her to accept the king's decision with grace, but she paid no heed, and pursued her goal.

When the coronation day July 19, 1821 came, a huge crowd gathered around the Abbey to witness the magnificent pageantry that included everyone in England able to afford a crown and gown. Caroline arrived in a carriage, and tried to enter Westminster Abbey through one after another of its doors. However, she was barred entry by stout armed guards. Finally, in shame and humiliation, she departed through the lowborn crowd who scoffed in derision as she entered her carriage and drove away.

The fickle public of England turned against Caroline after that hour of public shame. Common Englishmen had supported her throughout 'The Queen's Trial' a few months before, when she was seen as a persecuted noblewoman possessing the common touch. However, the unproven sordid evidence made public by her trial, sullied her reputation beyond repair. Her battle at the coronation to gain entry to the Abbey seems to have turned the public against her, because she lacked queenly good taste on an occasion of great national celebration. The public perception changed.

Caroline became *persona non grata* in England after the coronation. The following doggerel expressed the public attitude:

> Most gracious Queen, we thee implore
> To go away and sin no more;
> Or, if the effort be too great,
> To go away at any rate.

On the day of the coronation, after leaving grounds of the Abbey, Caroline returned to Brandenburg House on the outskirts of London. Dowager Queen Charlotte gave her the residence when Queen Caroline returned to London the year before. Queen Caroline survived for only twenty days after the coronation on July 19. As is always the case for an unexpected royal death, poisoning was suspected. However, in Caroline's case, no evidence was proven, or even seriously considered creditable, but Caroline was convinced she had been poisoned.

On the evening of the coronation day, when she arrived in Brandenburg House, Queen Caroline collapsed from nervous exhaustion, digestive complaint, nausea, and vomiting. Her condition steadily worsened with great pain in days that followed. She died at age fifty-three in Brandenburg House on August 7, 1821. Her will, written a few days before her death, ordered that all her private correspondence be burned, and that there would be no autopsy. Therefore, no medical evidence explains the cause of her death. Caroline's will also requested that she be buried with members of her family at Wolfenbüttl in Braunschweig, Germany. All her requests were honored. Her body was returned to Brunswick, and she was buried in Braunschweig Cathedral on August 25, 1821. Her memorial reads:

Here lies Caroline, the Injured Queen of England

Caroline of Brunswick was the mother of Princess Charlotte Augusta, who would have reigned after her father George IV. However, she tragically died in childbirth. The death of her daughter Princess Charlotte Augusta denied Dowager Queen Caroline of Brunswick any important part in the history of England.

To be sure, no court of law ever convicted her of illegal impropriety, but Queen Caroline steadfastly courted scandal throughout much of her life. She never refuted outrageous tales of improper behavior with many swains. Judgmental English historians often title her *The Immoral Queen of England.*

King George IV lived for nine years after Caroline died. During the regency years of his reign, his renovation of central London transformed it into the city one recognizes today. He spent lavishly on building and renovation of many famous landmarks including Buckingham Palace, Windsor Castle, and the Brighton Pavilion. The exuberant excesses of his regency dwindled in the final years of his own reign. He was intelligent enough to realize that his life—blessed with great ability, opportunities, wealth, and position—had been wasted on trivial matters. His main claim to fame as arbiter of elegance for *The Regency Style* of a bygone age was even castigated as outlandish bad taste.

King George IV died on June 26, 1830, and was buried in St. George's Chapel, Windsor.

When King George IV died, his younger brother William of Clarence followed, and became King William IV.

REIGN 35

KING WILLIAM IV

AND

COMMON-LAW 'FAVORITE' DOROTHEA BLAND

AND

QUEEN CONSORT ADELAIDE OF SAXE-MEININGEN

Summary of the Reign of King William IV (Reign 1830-1837)

King William IV: life dates c. 72 years, b. August 21, 1865-d. June 20, 1837; King of Great Britain (England, Ireland, Scotland, and Wales) and Elector of Hanover 7 years, June 26, 1830-June 20, 1837.

KING WILLIAM IV was the third surviving son of George III and Charlotte of Mecklenburg-Strelitz. He was born in 1765 at Buckingham Palace. For most of his life, he was styled William Duke of Clarence. As a third son, it was not expected that he would reign. Therefore, he entered a personal career in the Royal Navy where he rose through the ranks to become an admiral. He was a friend of Admiral Horatio Nelson of the Battle of Trafalgar fame.

Little of importance occurred during the seven-year reign of William IV, other than passage of the Reform Bill of 1832. This Parliamentary Act gave voting rights to middle class men. The revolutionary act created a constitutional change that was the beginning of the transfer of major power in the House of Commons from landed gentry to common working class citizens. Without William's effort, the Reform Bill almost certainly would not have passed.

William IV is remembered mainly as a plain man with the common tastes of a sailor on shore leave. For many years, William IV enjoyed a common-law relationship with a London actress named Dorothea Bland whose stage name was Mrs. Dorothy Jordan. She was the mother of his ten illegitimate children. The children were later acknowledged, and given the surname FitzClarence. After Mrs. Jordan died in 1816, William was required by his older brother King George IV to make a suitable royal marriage, and have an heir who might solve the problem of royal succession. He married Adelaide of Saxe-Meiningen in 1818, but they had no surviving children. After King William died in 1837, Dowager Queen Adelaide lived for twelve more years. She died in 1849, and was buried in St. George's Chapel, Windsor.

After a reign of seven years, William IV died on June 20, 1837 at age seventy-one, and was buried at St. George's Chapel, Windsor.

King William IV lacked a surviving legitimate heir, and his niece Princess Victoria, the daughter of his deceased younger brother Edward Duke of Kent, succeeded him. She reigned for sixty-four years as Queen Victoria.

Narrative of Common-law 'Favorite' Dorothea Bland

Dorothea Bland (stage name Mrs. Dorothy Jordan): life dates c. 54/55 years, b. November 21/22, 1761-d. July 5, 1816; common-law 'favorite' of William Duke of Clarence c. 20 years, 1791-1811.

DOROTHEA BLAND was born on November 21/22, 1861 near the ancient Irish seaside city of Waterford. She was the sixth and last child of her father Francis Bland and his mistress Grace Phillips. Her illegitimacy and family background made little claim on respectability. Her parents were 'theater people' who traveled widely in Ireland, and were professionally involved in a variety of stage productions. Her father was a stage manager, and her mother was a performing musician and actress. Around 1774 when Dorothea was thirteen, her father departed with a new actress-mistress named Catherine Mahoney, They moved to County Kerry, and had a son and daughter who were Dorothea's half-brother and half-sister. On rare occasions, Dorothea's father sent small amounts of money for his family of six children with Grace Philips in Waterford.

Times were hard. By the age of ten, all the children began to work. When Dorothea was thirteen, her mother saw that Dorothea had winsome beauty and acting talent that promised success on the stage. Little is recorded of Dorothea's first few years on the stage. By the time she was eighteen, she had become sufficiently experienced and skilled as an actress to be hired as a performer-actress by Richard Daly manager of the Theater Royal in Cork. He recognized her talent, and was captivated by her youthful beauty. He cast her in a number of ingénue parts in productions in which he acted her lover. He was married, but he seduced Dorothea, and was the father of her illegitimate daughter Frances Daly born in 1782 when Dorothea was twenty.

At about that time, Dorothea and her mother left Ireland bound for a stage career in London. Dorothea took the stage name *Mrs. Dorothy Jordan*. Theatrical legend maintains that, during her crossing the Irish Sea from Dublin to Anglesey, Dorothy Bland chose her stage name. She explained "[I felt I] was crossing the Jordan River to the Promised Land." As was customary at the time, she added 'Mrs.' to her name, to lend middle class respectability—that is, so actresses could avoid scandal in case one became pregnant while acting on the London stage. There was no *Mr. Jordan*, and Dorothea, although she had over a dozen children by several fathers, never married anyone during her entire life.

Dorothea Bland's first English theatrical employment was in a Leeds theater managed by Tate Wilkinson with whom she became intimate to advance her career. In Leeds, she had additional affairs; the first was with a young army officer Charles Doyne, whose offer of marriage was declined because Dorothea did not wish to abandon her theatrical ambitions. She then fell in love with Master George Inchbald the leading man in the Leeds Company. She would have married him, but he never proposed marriage.

The Leeds Company often went on tour to towns in the provinces where Dorothea perfected her theatrical skills. Dorothea arrived in London in 1785, and had great success in her first appearance at the Drury Lane Theater. She was cast as 'Peggy' in the smash hit *A Country Girl*. At the end of the season, she was the toast of London nightlife.

In 1786, she met Sir Richard Ford of the London constabulary, and with his promise of eventual marriage, she moved in and lived with him for about four years. During this time, she gave birth to three of his children: a son who died early, and two daughters, who survived to maturity. Her stay as a regular actress at the Drury Lane lasted from 1786 until 1801, and intermittently thereafter until 1809. In that year, the Drury Lane Theater burned down, but she continued acting by performing at the Covent Garden and Haymarket theaters until the Drury Lane was rebuilt in 1811.

Mrs. Jordan played many roles, but she was most admired as a comedienne. She excelled as Lady Teazle in Sheridan's *A School for Scandal,* and in Shakespeare plays as the nurse in *Romeo and Juliet,* as Rosalind in *As you Like It,* and as Imogene in *Cymbeline.*

As a bright light in offstage London sporting life, Mrs. Jordan was acclaimed as a beautiful witty clever companion who 'possessed the most beautiful legs clad in knit stockings in London.' Titled young swains competed for dazzling Mrs. Jordan's company and favors. She was at the peak of her professional fame in the years between 1786 and 1789. She was thirty years old in 1791 when she became the official 'favorite' of Prince William Duke of Clarence. He was a 'navy man', and the third son of King George III and Queen Charlotte, who would eventually become

King William IV of England in 1830. However, during most of his life, he did not expect to reach the throne.

Duke William was neither schooled in court manners, nor given anything remotely resembling a classical education suitable for a ruling monarch. When he was thirteen, his father King George III decided that his third son would find a career in the Royal Navy. George III instructed the Admiralty that his son, Billy, should receive no special preferment. The career in the Royal Navy was much to the young William's liking. He became a first class seaman without any royal privileges. He learned his craft: climbed the rigging, ate, drank, swore, gambled, and had a tart in every port—just like any other naval recruit. On his own merit, William advanced to a captaincy in the Royal Navy. In times of both war and peace, he commanded two ships of the line, *HMS Pegasus* and *HMS Andromeda*. Prince William was a tasteless bombastic eccentric. He never gave a fig about ceremony. Washington Irving, on visiting his Court at St. James Palace when William was king, remarked of William, "His Majesty has an easy and natural way of wiping his nose with the back of his hand, which, I fancy, is a relic of his midshipman days." All his life, William hated formal manners, and court protocol. He had simple taste in food, dress, friends, and mistresses.

Prince William, after ten years in the Royal Navy, returned to London at the age of twenty-three, and was created Duke of Clarence on May 16, 1789. Thereafter, when he was not serving in the Royal Navy, he enjoyed his prerogative of being a member of the House of Lords, and of receiving an allowance from the Civil List that permitted him to participate in the fashionable social life of London.

Thus, around 1790, twenty-four year old Prince William Duke of Clarence saw Mrs. Jordan at the Drury Lane. In the blink of an eye, she captured his heart.

Mrs. Jordan knew that nothing honorable could come from an association with Duke William, so for a time, she held him at arms length, with lingering hope that Richard Ford, her long time live in friend and the father of her three children, might eventually marry her. Prince William was on his rise to a captaincy in the Royal Navy in 1791 when Mrs. Jordan finally realized that Richard Daly would never marry her. She decided the next best course of action would be to lodge with Prince William, even though that, too, would never end in respectability.

William and Dorothea began living together in 1791 in a prolonged amiable association that lasted for twenty years. Dorothea gave up her acting career during pregnancies after she joined William in his London residence at Ranger Lodge near Hampton Court. Publically, she presented herself as William's housekeeper, but everyone knew, and accepted their relationship for what it was. In that capacity for the first time, Dorothea met William's mother Queen Charlotte, who greeted, and accepted her with grace and kindness. Queen Charlotte also affectionately received the succession of bastard grandchildren Dorothea presented to her, as she had also done for the mistresses, and grandchildren of several of her other four sons who also enjoyed living arrangements that lacked blessings of the Church.

William enjoyed the simple domesticity of life with his mistress Dorothea Bland. London society found William to be dull witted and crude. So, notwithstanding his royal rank, he was thought lucky to have acquired one of the most clever, attractive, and admired women of the *demimonde* to be his one-and-only 'favorite.' He was not known to have had another mistress in the twenty years he lived with Dorothea Bland.

Dorothea was entirely a creature of the stage. She had little interest in government, politics, or royal court intrigue. She was a simple good-hearted country girl who was intelligent enough to realize good fortune when it came her way. Duke William was devoted to her. He said to a friend, "Mrs. Jordan is a very good creature, very domestic and careful of our children. To be sure, she is absurd sometimes, and she has her humors. But, there are such things more or less in all families." On her part, Dorothea said, "We shall have a full and merry house this Christmas, 'tis what the dear Duke so delights in." In all ways, save in lacking the blessings of Law and Church, they enjoyed for two decades what may be thought of as an ordinary married life. Dorothea bore William ten children (5 sons and 5 daughters). The babies appeared at a rate of about one every sixteen months: the first child was born in January 1794, and the last one in March 1807. They were later legitimized with the surname 'FitzClarence':

George Augustus (FitzClarence) Earl of Munster (1794-1842)
Henry Edward (FitzClarence) (1795-1817)
Sophia (FitzClarence)-Sidney (1796-1837)
Mary (FitzClarence)-Fox (1798-1864)

Frederick (FitzClarence) (1799-1854)

Elizabeth (FitzClarence)-Hay (1801-1856)

Adolphus (FitzClarence) (1802-1856)

Augustua (FitzClarence)-Hallyburton (1803-1865)

Augustus (FitzClarence) (1805-1854)

Amelia (FitzClarence)-Cary (1807-1858)

Sometime after the birth of their last child in 1807, and after he and Dorothy Bland separated in 1811, Duke William of Clarence acknowledged the ten children he sired with Dorothea Bland. However, Parliament was not asked to legitimize them as royal heirs eligible to inherit the throne. After William became King William IV, his eldest son George Augustus was ennobled as the Earl of Munster in 1831. All FitzClarence children enjoyed social prominence, and they married well. Their numerous FitzClarence descendants have since risen to positions of prestige, service, and authority throughout the British Empire.

While Duke William and Dorothy Bland lived together as man and wife, his income was barely adequate for a prince of the realm. His pension was far too little for maintenance of a fashionable residence in London. His eldest brother, the profligate George Prince of Wales, always spent wildly beyond his allowance, and he was constantly petitioning Parliament to pay off his huge debts. Accordingly, Parliament was ill inclined to make financial commitments to the fourteen other children of King George III and Queen Charlotte.

Out of necessity, William and Dorothea lived in modest style. William and Dorothea were required to make ends meet, as best they could, on William's income as an officer of the Royal Navy, supplemented by a modest stipend from the Civil List approved by Parliament for living expenses of members of the royal family. Therefore, William was severely in debt much of the time, Dorothea often returned to the stage as Mrs. Jordan to supplement William's income. Friends wondered if Prince William or Mrs. Jordan paid household bills.

In 1796 after birth of Sophia their third child, William was deep in debt, and he asked his father King George III to petition Parliament for an addition to his stipend from the Civil List. In 1797, he received a modest rise, also the use of a manor house at Bushy Park for his growing family. He was appointed Ranger of Bushy Park, which provided a slight addition to his annual income. William bought the Bushy Park Manor in 1801, and kept it for thirty-six years until his death in 1837. Bushy Park Manor was the London home for the ten children of William and Dorothea as they grew to maturity. At the end of his reign in 1837, the house was willed to his Queen Adelaide for her London residence as Dowager Queen.

In 1811, William was made Admiral of the Fleet. He greatly enjoyed the official duties it created, and it substantially improved his income. Finally, in that year, William and Dorothea amicably agreed to end their domestic relationship. Debts and a lack of means were at the root of their separation. Dorothea said, "Money . . . has, I am convinced made . . . [the Duke] at this moment the most wretched of men . . . With all his excellent qualities, his domestic virtues, his love for our lovely children, what must he not at this moment suffer?" Their separation agreement gave all sons to their father Duke William, and the daughters went to their mother Dorothea Bland. She was given a generous annual pension and an additional £1,500 each year for the care of their daughters, if she did not return to the stage as Mrs. Jordan.

After their separation, Dorothea was constantly pestered for money by her relatives and her children of previous liaisons, all of whom were in debt. She agreed to pay off debts of the husband of her illegitimate daughter Frances Daly born before Dorothea met William. Her generous attempts to pay the family debts finally exhausted her financial means. In 1815 at age fifty-three, Dorothea made her final return to the stage at the Duke Theater as Mrs. Jordan. Her success as yesteryear's faded comedienne was brief, and financially unrewarding. In 1815, Duke William reclaimed custody of his daughters, and terminated the pension of £1,500 to Mrs. Jordan for their care and maintenance.

Dorothea Bland was deeply in debt, and she fled from her creditors to France. Hearsay claimed that she died in poverty on July 3, 1816 in Saint Cloud near Paris. Neither the cause of her death at age fifty-four/fifty-five, nor her place of burial is known. Other rumor exists that she survived beyond that date by several years, and that she returned to England, and was an actress under a different assumed name. As a memorial for her, King William IV commissioned a bronze statue of Dorothea Bland, which is part of royal artifacts in Buckingham Palace.

During much of his life, Duke William of Clarence was third or fourth in the line of succession, and too far removed to expect that the crown would ever descend to him. Therefore, the succession had not been a matter of concern to William before 1816, the year Mrs. Jordan was reported dead in France. However, the matter of William having a legitimate heir became nationally important in 1817, when Princess Charlotte Augusta, the heiress presumptive, died following stillbirth of her only child.

With Princess Charlotte Augusta's death, the Privy Council suddenly realized that, although King George III had over a dozen grandchildren, not one of them was legitimate. The Prince Regent ordered two of his brothers (William Duke of Clarence and Edward Duke of Kent) to marry suitable princesses who could provide legitimate heirs to perpetuate the Hanover Dynasty.

A double royal wedding was celebrated on July 11, 1818 at the Royal Palace of Kew in London:

> Prince William Duke of Clarence married Princess Adelaide of Saxe-Meiningen (it produced no viable heir).
>
> Prince Edward Duke of Kent married Princess Victoria of Saxe-Coberg-Saalfeld (it produced one viable heir, Princess Alexandrina Victoria, later Queen Victoria).

Narrative of Queen Consort Adelaide of Saxe-Meiningen

Queen Adelaide of Saxe-Meiningen: life dates c. 57 years, b. August 13, 1792-d. December 2, 1848; Duchess wife of William Duke of Clarence 12 years, July 11, 1818-June 26, 1830; Queen Consort of King William IV 7 years, June 26, 1830-June 20, 1837; Dowager Queen Consort 12 years, June 20, 1837-December 2, 1849.

ADELAIDE OF Saxe-Meiningen was born on August 13, 1792 in Meiningen a minor city in the free state of Thuringia in central Germany. She was the eldest of three daughters of George Frederick Duke of Saxe-Meiningen and Louise Eleanor of Hohenlohe-Langenburg. Saxe-Meiningen was one of the smallest, and politically least important of the German principalities. However, it allowed a free press to criticize the ruling regime, and was recognized to be one the most intellectually liberal of the German States. Adelaide spent her childhood in the provincial court at Meiningen. Her father Duke George Frederick died when Adelaide was eleven years old, after which her mother carefully reared her in expectation that she would marry into another German Protestant principality of similar modest tradition and circumstance.

Nothing in Adelaide's twenty-five years of life before 1817 anticipated the information, that she was third on a list of German princesses Duke William of Clarence of England was considering for marriage. Duke William was the fifty-three years old son of King George III, and he was twenty-seven years older than Adelaide. She bordered on being an Old Maid, so she needed to think of the future, and to be an English duchess surely was better than nothing.

William agreed to get married in exchange for Parliament's payment of his personal debts, and for a substantially greater pension than he formerly enjoyed. William canvassed the royal houses of Germany for a suitable bride. Several that he preferred rejected him; others were rejected by the Prince Regent. Finally, Adelaide of Saxe-Meiningen was judged a suitable bride. However, at that late point in the negotiation, Parliament failed to meet the duke's demand for an increased pension. Duke William refused to go through with the wedding plan, until Parliament finally voted an addition to his annuity.

In a double wedding, William and Adelaide were married in London on July 11, 1818 at Kew Palace, and William's brother Edward Duke of Kent married Victoria of Saxe-Coberg-Saalfeld. The English court snubbed the new Duchess Adelaide of Clarence. She was criticized for being plain, thin, and for a lack in taste in dress. However, she was respected for having good manners, good character, and for loyalty to her husband.

In spite of all problems that preceded their union, William and Adelaide soon settled into contented domesticity. William was unable to afford life in London, so they moved to Hanover for a year where living was less expensive than in England. Adelaide possessed a gentle nature, and was a willing homemaker for Duke William who was old enough to be her father. He soon became very fond of his young wife Adelaide. He wrote to his eldest son George Augustus, " . . . she is doomed, poor dear innocent young creature, to be my wife." The marriage was William's only legal marriage after over twenty years of common-law cohabitation with his actress-mistress Dorothea Bland 'Mrs. Jordan' who had given him ten children. Adelaide willingly accepted them as part of her family, and two of William's children that were under twelve years old lived with them. They all accepted and honored Adelaide as a loving mother-in-law.

William and Adelaide presented to the world the appearance of being a mutually devoted couple. Adelaide improved William's argumentative nature, which was a carryover from his life in the Royal Navy. His ordinary speech "became less profane; he drank less, eschewed insulting his associates, and he even made attempts to be tactful." Adelaide efficiently managed his domestic affairs on their limited budget. Their lifestyle was described as "simple, almost miserly, but withal, good natured, and happy."

After their marriage, William and Adelaide attempted to provide a royal heir. However, over a period of four years, with six births or stillbirths, they had no surviving offspring:

> Charlotte Augusta, a premature birth and death on March 21, 1819, born in Hanover.
> Unnamed infant, a miscarriage on September 5, 1819, born in Calais.
> Elizabeth Georgina, born on December 10, 1820, born in St. James Palace, London, died when four months old.
> Unnamed stillbirth, in 1821, born in London.
> Unnamed twins, stillborn on April 22/23, 1822, born in London.

Queen Adelaide's deportment as queen in London court life showed that she favored the customs appropriate for a conservative provincial court. She refused to receive persons who flaunted infidelity in marriage. In the absence of any children of her own, Duchess Adelaide of Clarence poured motherly affection on her royal niece Princess Alexandrina Victoria of York. However, her mother the Dowager Duchess of Kent resisted the familiarity of Duchess Adelaide with her daughter. The Duchess of Kent on many occasions refused to recognize Adelaide's precedence in court, and even kept Kensington Palace that Adelaide should have received. The Duchess of Kent's aggressive and condescending treatment of Adelaide infuriated Duke William of Clarence, who never forgave the Duchess of Kent for her disrespectful treatment of his wife.

On June 26, 1830, King George IV died, and Duke William became King William IV. He inherited the throne from an older brother who was thoroughly loathed and hated by his subjects. The decade 1820-1830, in which George IV was king, was a time when the English monarchy fell to its lowest level of public esteem. Although the reign of King William IV lasted only seven years (1830-1837), the favorable transformation he and his Queen Adelaide brought about in the public perception of the monarchy was profound.

William Duke of Clarence was sixty-four years old when he became the king on June 26, 1830. He was the oldest person to ascend to the throne of England. William and Adelaide were crowned king and queen in a simple ceremony on September 8, 1831 at Westminster Abbey. There was never a greater contrast between the coronations of two brothers, than between George IV and William IV. George's coronation was so lavish and ostentatious that it nearly bankrupts the nation in 1820. King William's coronation in 1830 was puritanically simple—no robes, only ordinary dress was permitted—even the traditional banquet for peers was canceled.

William was publically criticized for his unbecoming mockery of religious formalities in the coronation. He openly compared the coronation 'to characters in a comic opera performing a ridiculous charade.' In contrast with her husband, Adelaide received high praise for showing appropriate 'dignity, repose, and grace for the occasion.' Both of them would soon receive accolades for being accessible with common touch, honest affection, and unaffected good humor in dealing with the public.

The public approved of Queen Adelaide for her modest piety. She was accused of being a prude when she ruled that dress must be circumspect without décolletage, She later gained public respect and affection for the novelty of being a queen who gave much of her household allowance to charities and goodly causes.

By personal nature and his Naval background in youth, William was coarse, crude, and had no interests in learning, arts, or culture. On the subject of art, he said, "I wouldn't know a picture from a window shade." On the subject of scholarship, he said, "I know of no person so perfectly disagreeable, even dangerous, as an author." William was a stubborn irascible old man, who enjoyed obstinacy for its own sake. He was a Tory at heart, and he believed in the inherent right of the titled classes to rule the inferior masses. Even so, he approved of abolishing of slavery during his reign in 1833.

Queen Adelaide is not known to have expressed any interest in political matters. However, she was suspected of pressuring William to withhold his support for the Reform Act of 1832. The Reform Act was a liberal piece of legislation designed to modify voting laws in a manner that would permit members of the House of Commons to be elected by the male population at large. With the king's persuasion, the act passed the House of Commons and House of Lords. Adelaide was a conservative, but even if she ever tried to influence King William, it is unlikely she could have swayed his stubborn will. With the king's moderating intervention, civil mutiny was averted, and unexpectedly, the public perception of the crown was greatly enhanced.

Public gossip against Queen Adelaide claimed that she was having an affair with her chamberlain Lord Richard William Howe. However, her known fidelity to her husband, and all else in her pious nature made the assertion laughable. King William always gallantly defended his wife when she was criticized or shown disrespect. King William nursed a smoldering resentment for Duchess Victoria of Kent for her repeated insults to Queen Adelaide. The Duchess of Kent was the mother of Princess Victoria, for whom King William and Queen Adelaide had a great fondness. In 1836 at a State dinner, William ended his long list of criticisms of the Duchess of Kent with the statement, "I trust to God that my life may be spared for nine months longer . . . I should then have the satisfaction of leaving the exercise of the Royal authority to the personal authority of that young lady [Princess Victoria], heiress presumptive to the Crown, and not in the hands of a person now near me [the Duchess of Kent], who is surrounded by evil advisers, and is herself incompetent to act with propriety in the situation [as Regent] in which she would be placed."

The court was silenced by the vehemence of the king's attack. The Duchess and Princess left the banquet in tears.

King William suffered from respiratory and cardiac problems from a lifetime of excessive drinking and smoking. Queen Adelaide cared for him as his health worsened in the last year of his life. In his will, written a few months before his death, King William named Princess Victoria as his successor.

William IV clung to life with Adelaide by his side until the age of seventy-two. King William IV ordered his physician to keep him alive, at least until June 18, so he could celebrate the anniversary of the Battle of Waterloo, and if possible, let him live until Princess Victoria's eighteenth birthday on August 26, 1837. King William died on June 20, 1837, just two days after the date for the Battle of Waterloo. He died peacefully from heart failure at Windsor Castle where he was buried.

The London Times obituary of William IV said, "He was not a man of talent or of much refinement . . . But he had a warm heart, and an English heart, too."

King William IV was succeeded by Princess Alexandrina Victoria of York who was crowned Queen Victoria of Great Britain. However, she did not inherit the title Queen of Hanover. Hanover, Germany did not recognize female inheritance of their crown. On the death of King William IV, who was also King of Hanover, the Crown of Hanover reverted to his younger brother Ernest Augustus Duke of Cumberland.

When William IV died in 1837, Dowager Queen Adelaide was forty-five years old. She retired from court on a dowager queen annual income of £100,000, and was given Marlborough House, a grand home near St. James Palace that was originally designed by Christopher Wren as the London home of John Churchill First Duke of Marlborough during Queen Anne's reign.

Dowager Queen Adelaide lived at Marlborough House until 1842, and remained a close friend of young Queen Victoria. She was a guest at Victoria's coronation on June 28, 1838, and was present at Victoria's wedding to Prince Albert of Saxe-Coburg-Gotha on February 10, 1840. A year later, Adelaide was godmother of Queen Victoria's first child Princess Victoria. Adelaide remained a great favorite with Queen Victoria's growing family, but she had little contact with court after King William IV died.

In 1846, Dowager Queen Adelaide was in frail health when she leased Bentley Priory in Middlesex as a convalescent nursing home. She travelled briefly to Malta and Madeira in search of a warm dry climate, but she did not recover from her general malaise. She returned to the priory, where she died at age fifty-seven on December 2, 1849.

Dowager Queen Adelaide was buried with her husband William IV at St. George's Chapel, Windsor. She was put to rest with simplicity in the manner she requested in a will that said:

> "I die in all humility; we are alike before the throne of God, and I request therefore that my mortal remains be conveyed to the grave without pomp or state . . . [I desire] as private and quiet a funeral as possible. I particularly desire not to be laid

out in state . . . I die in peace, and wish to be carried to the fount in peace, and to be free from the vanities and pomp of this world."

The royal family and nation mourned Queen Adelaide as a pious, kind, and generous queen. Her name is memorialized in the name *Adelaide* for the Capital City for the State of South Australia.

REIGN 36

QUEEN REGNANT VICTORIA

AND

PRINCE CONSORT ALBERT
OF SAXE-COBURG-GOTHA

Summary of the Reign of Queen Victoria
(1837-1901)

Queen Victoria: life dates 81 years, b. May 24, 1819-d. February 2, 1901; Queen Regnant of Great Britain (England, Ireland, Scotland, and Wales) c. 64 years, June 20, 1837-February 2, 1901; wife of Prince Albert of Saxe-Coburg-Gotha c. 21 years, February 10. 1840-December 14, 1861.

Note: Unlike other Hanover monarchs of Great Britain, Queen Victoria was not also the reigning Monarch of Hanover, Germany. The German State of Hanover followed Salic law, which did not recognize female rule. Therefore, the Prince of Hanover that followed after death of William IV was his younger brother Prince Earnest Augustus the fifth son of George III.

P RINCESS ALEXANDRINA Victoria of Kent was a granddaughter of George III, and the only child of his fourth son Prince Edward Duke of Kent and Victoria of Saxe-Coburg-Saalfeld. Princess Victoria was born at Kensington Palace, London on May 24, 1819. At age eighteen on June 20, 1837, she became queen of Great Britain on the death of King William IV. Her name at birth was Alexandrina Victoria of Kent. The name *Alexandrina* was in respect for her godfather, Czar Alexander I of Russia. Her reign lasted sixty-four and a half years until February 2, 1901—the longest reign in English history.

The first four sons of King George the III (namely, George Prince of Wales, Frederick Duke of York, William Duke of Clarence, and her father Edward Duke of Kent) all had illegitimate male children, but Princess Alexandrina Victoria was the only surviving legitimate offspring of any of them. None of her aging uncles would have legitimate issue late in life. Thus, from her birth, virtual certainty predicted that Princess Alexandrina Victoria would someday become Queen of England.

Victoria's mother the Duchess of Kent supervised her rearing and education with the near certainty in mind that someday she would be the reigning queen. Victoria's instruction emphasized learning court manners, more than the acquisition of any real knowledge, or cultural appreciation above the most ordinary. Victoria had a natural, but minor, talent as a graphic artist. She loved music and dance, and possessed a better than average capacity for intuitive evaluation of issues and persons. At the age of only eleven, on being explained the complexity of her relation to cousins (almost all of them illegitimate) within the descendants of her grandfather George III, she recognized her own position by saying, "I am nearer to the throne than I ever thought."

Victoria's father Edward Duke of Kent died when Victoria was an infant. Throughout life, she showed a compulsive need for a male arm on which to lean. In her childhood, her maternal uncle Prince Leopold of Saxe-Coburg-Saalfeld, who later became King of the Belgians, filled this need. He was her mother's brother, and had been the husband of Crown Princess Charlotte Augusta, the only legitimate child of King George IV, who would have been Queen of England, had she not died in childbirth.

When King William IV died on June 20, 1837, eighteen year old Princess Victoria of York became queen. Thereafter, she chose to use only the name Victoria. On acceding the throne, Victoria immediately severed relationships with her domineering mother the Duchess of Kent, and moved from Kensington Palace to Buckingham Palace where she set up her own court. The palace had been extravagantly remodeled during the regency and reign of her uncle George IV.

From the start of her reign, Victoria had strong ideas on how a queen should be treated. She created for herself a formal protocol for the way in which she would be served by her palace staff, by the government, and by members of the royal family.

Although Victoria probably had decided to marry her first cousin Prince Albert of Saxe-Coburg-Saalfeld and Gotha before she became queen in 1837, the marriage was delayed for about three years. Victoria and Albert were twenty years old when they married on February 10, 1840. Prince Albert was the second son of Duke Earnest III of Saxe-Coburg-Saalfeld, and he had no landed title of his own. The marriage of Victoria and Albert is always described as an idealized union of true affection. It lasted for twenty-one years until the death of Albert on December 14, 1861. They had nine children (4 sons and 5 daughters) born between 1840 and 1857:

> Victoria Princess Royal (November 21, 1840-August 5,1901), Empress of Germany
>
> Edward Prince of Wales (November 9, 1841-May 6, 1910), King Edward VII of England
>
> Alice (April 25, 1843-December 14, 1878), Grand Duchess of Hesse
>
> Alfred (August 6,1844-July 20,1900), Duke of Saxe-Coburg and Gotha
>
> Helena (May 25-June 9, 1923), Princess of Schleswig-Holstein
>
> Louise (March 18, 1848-December 3, 1939), Princess of Argyll
>
> Arthur (May 1, 1850-January 16, 1942), Duke of Connaught
>
> Leopold (April 7, 1953-March 28, 1884), Duke of Albany
>
> Beatrice (April 14, 1857-October 26, 1944), Princess of Batttenburg

The marriages of the nine royal princes and princesses, and their children later saturated the ruling houses of Europe. Consequently late in her reign, Victoria was called, *The Grandmother of Europe.*

Early in Victoria's reign, Albert bought and rebuilt Osborne House on the Isle of Wight on the English Channel as a gift to Victoria. She did the same for him with Balmoral Castle in Scotland. He was the primary architect for redesign of both estates. These dwellings remained the personal properties, and favorite vacation residences for the royal family through Victoria's reign to the present.

Throughout her life when Victoria made up her mind, there was little chance her opinion would later change. However, when Victoria came to the throne, she intellectually accepted as natural the shallow banality of the Hanoverian court surrounding her. It is certain that Prince Albert's views on government were important in molding Queen Victoria's ideas on the function and purpose of the monarchy in government.

Albert was a person of wisdom, culture, and taste. He had enlightened views far in advance of those held by ruling classes in the 19th century. Victoria revered Albert, and his philosophies on government became hers as well. Even after his death, Albert continued to be such a power behind the throne that he justly can be considered a co-monarch with Queen Victoria.

A crisis in government occurred only two years after Victoria came to the throne. Tory Prime Minister Robert Peel replaced Whig Prime Minister Lord Melbourne in 1839. Peel demanded that Tory wives replace the Whig wives among her ladies-in-waiting, as had been the practice with a change of government since the reign of Queen Anne. Victoria refused to accept the Tory ladies, until the Privy Council and Prime Minister firmly informed Victoria and Albert that they must conform to government policy.

A succession of Tory (conservative) and Whig (liberal) governments came and went during Victoria's sixty-four year reign, and, with them, different casts of Prime Ministers and their Secretaries of This-'n-That briefly strutted across the stage, like a well choreographed variety act. The queen liked some, and detested others.

England's involvement in the Crimean War (1853-1856) was an almost Crusade-like altercation between Orthodox Christian Russia and the Islamic Turkish Sultanate over emancipation of Christian ethnic groups within the Turkish empire. England's interests in supporting the Turks was motivated, more by a desire to embarrass and weaken Russia, than by any perceived moral or economic principles. Little was gained for efforts that cost England almost twenty-five thousand lives, and twice as many more wounded. England gained little more than a fantasy of heroism in *The Charge of the Light Brigade*, and of Florence Nightingale—*The Lady with the Lamp*—whose inspired service created the profession of modern nursing. History of the Crimean War records it as the most wasteful, purposeless, mismanaged, incompetently executed military venture in England's history.

In the period of the American Civil War (1860-1864), the British government sympathized with the South. The Confederacy believed that, because it supplied cotton essential for factories in the Midlands, Britain would support the Confederacy. However, England did not support the principle of slavery (which had been abolished in the entire Empire in 1833), but political wisdom saw separation of a Southern Confederacy as weakening the United States. Two small nations, instead of one unified large one, would be easier to dominate in world trade.

Prince Albert died in 1861 when Victoria was forty-two. His death, at the time, was attributed to typhoid fever (currently, the cause of his death is suspected as being of cancer). Victoria went into a prolonged mourning that lasted for over twenty-five years. During that time, she had rare contact with her subjects, and minimal consultation with her succession of Prime Ministers: mainly, Melbourne, Peel, Palmerston, Gladstone, and Disraeli. During the prolonged absence of the queen from public functions, a growing republican demand to abolish the monarchy was expressed. Evidence of social unrest at the time is shown by seven attempts to assassinate the queen between 1840 and 1882. However, when Victoria again was seen in public, the republican movement died out.

Victoria had not a shred of social or racial prejudice. She carried on a cordial correspondence over many years with Queen Liliuokalani, the last native ruler of the Sandwich Islands (Hawaii). The islands had been a British protectorate after their discovery in 1778 by Captain Cook. The two queens treated each other as equal reigning monarchs: one was the sovereign of one-sixth of the Earth—the other was a chieftainess of a minute volcanic speck, all but lost out there somewhere in the vast expanse of the Pacific Ocean.

During her period of mourning for Albert in her Scottish Balmoral Castle, Victoria formed a close friendly relationship with a Scottish yeoman, John Brown, who took care of her horses, and looked out for the health and welfare of the queen. She was grateful for the presence of a masterful man at her side. She spent many hours with him riding over highland moor and heath. Victoria's relationship with Mr. Brown was a source of much gossip and speculation. Behind her back, Victoria was called *Mrs. Brown*, but there is no evidence for impropriety between them.

Victoria's reign coincided with remarkable industrial invention, economic growth, and colonial expansion, which gave the average Englishman hope for advancement and deep national pride in being British. Growth of Empire was a dominant theme of her reign. British trade needed goods and markets; the expanding population needed food and living space; colonial expansion was essential for England's economic wellbeing. Conquests in Africa brought in enormous new wealth with colonial opportunities for individual fame, fortune, and social advancement. The mutiny in India made governmental intervention essential. Authority over the Indian Subcontinent was transferred from the East India Company to the Crown. By her own statement, the high point in Victoria's reign was her coronation as Empress of India in 1877. She said India was the 'Jewel in the Crown.' Other great occasions were her Golden Jubilee, which celebrated the 50th year of her reign in 1887, and the Diamond Jubilee ten years later in 1897.

The British Empire doubled in size, principally by acquisition of colonial holdings in India, Africa, New Zealand, Burma, and Oceanic Islands. The Boer War (1899-1902) climaxed Victoria's years of colonial expansion. At its start, the war went poorly, but the queen ordered that there would be no defeatist talk in court. Before her death, England would prevail. British colonies from *Cape Town to Cairo* became a fact when the Transvaal Republic was annexed in 1899/1900.

At the height of Empire, one person out of four on Earth was Victoria's subject; one-sixth of the land mass on earth was British; the British navy ruled the seas; her children and grandchildren sat on the thrones of Germany, Russia, Sweden, Denmark, Spain, Greece, Romania, Yugoslavia, as well as, Britain.

The apogee of British prestige and colonial expansion occurred by the end of the 19th century when one could truly say, 'The sun never sets on the British Empire.' At the end of her reign, Victoria Regina was the most popular monarch England ever had.

However, she also was a dowdy frump, a middle class German hausfrau, and a short square person, who was said to have " . . . no sense of style, and the personal majesty of an overfed meadow mouse." She was a well-intentioned monarch with a profound sense of duty, and a refined sense of the fitness of things.

On January 22, 1901, Queen Victoria died peacefully at Osborne House on the Isle of Wight, at the age of 82, after a reign of sixty-four and a half years. She outlived Prince Albert by forty years. Queen Victoria and her Prince Consort Albert of Saxe-Coburg-Gotha are buried at the Frogmore Royal Mausoleum at Windsor, which Victoria ordered built for them, and which is now the preferred burial place for members of the royal family.

Memorials for Victoria and Albert in London include: the Victoria and Albert Museum, the Royal Albert Concert Hall, the Royal Albert Memorial Art Museum, the Victoria Monument at Buckingham Palace, the Imperial College of Science and Technology, the Royal College of Music, and many others.

Following the death of Queen Victoria on January 22, 1901, her eldest son Albert Prince of Wales ascended the throne as King Edward VII. He was first in the Saxe-Coburg-Gotha—Windsor Dynasty.

Narrative of Prince Consort Albert of Saxe-Coburg-Gotha

Prince Albert of Saxe-Coburg-Gotha: life dates 42 years, b. August 26, 1819-d. December 14, 1861; husband of Queen Victoria, February 10, 1849-December 14, 1861; Prince Consort June 26, 1857-December 14, 1861.

PRINCE FRANCIS Albert Augustus was the second son of Duke Earnest III of Saxe-Coburg-Saalfeld and his first wife Princess Louise of Saxe-Gotha-Altenburg. Albert's older brother Ernest Alexander was heir to the estates of their parents; accordingly, Albert did not inherit a title to any noble estate. Albert was born on August 19, 1819 at the summer manor Schloss Rosenau outside Coburg in Bavaria, Germany. A month later, Albert was baptized as a Lutheran Protestant. Albert was a half-year younger than his first cousin Princess Victoria, whom he would marry twenty years later—his father and her mother were brother and sister.

Prince Albert's parents separated, and were divorced when he was five years old. His childhood rearing was disrupted, and his education was under tutors at home, then in Brussels, and later at the University of Bonn. He studied law, but also received a sound education in political history, natural sciences, economics, philosophy, art, and music. He had a natural gift for music, and became a competent pianist, organist, and the composer of minor works of classical music for the keyboard. He spoke German, English, and French, and easily read Classical works in Latin and Greek. He was tall, handsome, enjoyed physical competition, gymnastics, fencing, and equestrian sports. Many would say that Albert was the paragon of what a prince should be.

Prince Albert's education at the University of Bonn made him familiar with prevailing philosophies of government expressed by Voltaire, Montesquieu, and Rousseau, which, although, not exactly advocating revolt by the canaille, certainly had applied grease to the wheels of revolution against despotism in America and France. Albert knew of evolving thought on social problems of the working classes, such as ideas expressed in the extreme thinking of Thomas Paine, Adam Smith, and Jeremy Bentham. Thus, he appreciated what a monarchy should be in a time of change. He saw the sovereign in a Constitutional Monarchy—not as the advocate for the privileged classes, nor as the agent of a single political party—but as a benevolent parental custodian for the nation. In his view, the monarch had responsibility to see justice administered impartially to all its subjects. Albert was not a social egalitarian. He believed in proper roles for all class ranks. However, he was opposed to slavery, which during the mid 19th Century was a major social issue in Europe and America.

Albert's personal accomplishments and breadth of understanding surpassed the parochial standards accepted as adequate by England's previous Hanover monarchs. His manner of cool aloof contempt suited the highest standards for courtly etiquette, and proclaimed the fact that, even lacking a title of his own, he was, 'borne to the purple,' and destined to be the ruler of men.

As early as 1832, after Princess Victoria entered her teenage years, plans were afoot to marry her to a German prince for political advantage, but without special concern for Princess Victoria's personal desires. She was determined to delay marriage until she became queen, when no one could force her into a marriage she did not approve.

The Duchy of Saxe-Coburg-Saalfeld and Gotha was among the smallest of the German States, yet the ruling House of Coburg had enhanced its prestige by marriage into the royal houses of Russia, Portugal, Belgium, and many German principalities. Its highest achievement would come in a takeover of the Royal House of England with the marriage of Albert Coburg to Queen Victoria of England.

Albert's father was a brother of Prince Leopold of Saxe-Coburg-Saalfeld who, one recalls, married Crown Princess Charlotte Augusta of England, the only child of King George IV. Following her death in childbirth in 1818, Leopold was chosen to be King Leopold I of Belgium when Belgium gained independence from The Netherlands in 1831. The next step in the Coburn climb to eminence came when Leopold's sister Victoria of Saxe-Coburg-Saalfeld became the Duchess of Kent, and soon became the mother of Crown Princess Victoria, who soon would be Queen of England. Leopold orchestrated events that led Princess Victoria (after she became Queen Victoria) to marry his nephew Prince Albert of Coburg. That union elevated the Coburg family to the highest level of royalty in Europe.

That is, reigning Queen Victoria of Britain and her husband Prince Consort Albert were first cousins, both of Saxe-Coburg-Saalfeld-Gotha lineage.

For a time, Leopold of Saxe-Coburg-Saalfeld's stratagem for taking over the royal house of England was frustrated by King William IV, who planned to have Crown Princess Victoria marry a prince of the House of Orange to strengthen ties between England and the Netherlands. William IV also despised Princess Victoria's mother the Duchess Victoria of Kent. As long as he lived, King William would never approve the marriage of Princess Victoria to anyone of the House of Saxe-Coburg-Saalfeld-Gotha.

In 1836, Princess Victoria's mother the Duchess of Kent invited her nephews, the two sons of her brother Duke Earnest III of Saxe-Coburg-Saalfeld, to visit her in London. The visit was carefully planned to appear like an innocent family gathering, but its real purpose was to provide an opportunity for Princess Victoria to meet her Coburg cousins, Ernest Alexander and Francis Albert, in hope that she might favor one of them for marriage.

Princess Victoria did not care for the 'very plain appearance' of the older brother Ernest Alexander who would inherit his father's title and estates. However, she immediately responded positively to the younger brother Francis Albert. Of him she said, "[Albert] is extremely handsome; his hair is about the same color as mine; his eyes are large and blue, and he has a beautiful nose and a very sweet mouth with fine teeth; the charm of his countenance is his expression, which is most delightful." Victoria's reaction on meeting Albert was so positive, that the family understood that Albert would be Victoria's choice for marriage.

William IV died, and Victoria ascended the throne on June 20, 1837. She delayed for three years in making any formal statement of her intent to marry Albert. After an extended correspondence with Victoria, Albert returned to England in October 1839. Since an untitled man could not presume to request marriage from a reigning queen, Victoria proposed marriage to Albert on October 15, 1839. He was granted British citizenship, and they were married on February 15, 1840 at St. James Palace in London.

Those in authority with titled social status treated Albert as a pretentious social climber of little worth. Parliament awarded him an annual allowance of £30,000, the equivalent of little more than half of what was usual for a titled royal spouse. For seventeen years, Parliament refused to grant him an official title other than *His Royal Highness Prince Albert*. Finally in June 1857, Queen Victoria was able to get Parliamentary approval for Albert to receive the official title *Prince Consort*, after which, he was permitted to view official State documents, and to serve as the personal secretary for Her Majesty Queen Victoria. The lingering resentment and unpopularity of Prince Albert with the people and government of England may have been caused by his rigid sense of social proprieties that made him seem distant, unapproachable, and lacking in a common touch necessary for one in high office to win public affection.

Throughout their marriage, Albert had a constant profound impact on the queen's attitudes and opinions. Albert's influence was so ubiquitous that his detractors often referred to Victoria's reign as the 'Albertine Monarchy.' In all but name, Albert was the king. He had advanced liberal views on slavery, child labor, agriculture, and public education. He recognized the cultural importance of support for music and arts. His liberal social opinions were far in advance of his time. Albert, in his opening address as chairman of the *Society for the Improvement of the Condition of the Laboring*

Classe, said, "[We must have] sympathy and interest for that class of our community who have most of the toil and fewest of the enjoyments of this world . . . [It is the] duty of those who, under the blessings of Divine Providence enjoy station, wealth, and education . . . to assist those less fortunate than themselves."

One of Albert's great personal prides came from his formal election as Chancellor of Cambridge University in 1847. In that role he was able to stimulate curriculum revision that led to the addition of many new programs in the natural sciences, social philosophy, and political history, as was the practice in progressive German institutions such as his Alma Mater the University of Bonn.

Albert took over management of palace financial affairs with a view toward increased efficiency and economy. His acceptance of the principle of 'living within one's means,' instead of 'spend, spend, spend, and ask Parliament to pay debts,' as had been the royal practice for decades, was an unheard of novelty. Albert was sufficiently successful as a home economist that in only four years he saved enough from his own allowance to buy Osborne House and farm on the Isle of Wight, which became the summer home for the royal family in years to come. Essentially the same course of events occurred in the acquisition of Balmoral Castle in Scotland. Balmoral was purchased from independent funds, and it would be Victoria's primary residence in the years after Albert died in 1861.

Albert achieved his greatest popularity for sponsoring the *Great Exhibition of 1851*—it was the ideological ancestor of World Fairs. Its purpose was to display and advertise English ingenuity in industry through applications of science and technology. His opponents to the fair included a majority of the House of Lords and every conservative voice in the nation: the fair was wasteful; it would cost too much; it would undermine morals by advocating new ideas; science would destroy faith; it would attract thieves and whores to London; who needs more radicals and revolutionaries in an unsettled time?

In 1843, Albert began seven years of work on the Exhibition. He was sure that it would have a long-term favorable effect on British industry by contrasting the best qualities of home products with those of foreign nations. Queen Victoria opened the Exhibition on May 1, 1851, which was set up in a newly constructed glass enclosure in Hyde Park called the *Crystal Palace*. It entertained the world through the summer of 1851, and was a huge financial success. Among other cultural and educational projects, profits from the fair paid for construction of the Victoria and Albert Museum, which became one of the world's greatest collections of art, history, and antiquities.

Albert spoke for English moderation and noninvolvement in the American Civil War. An international incident arose in 1861 that threatened English involvement in the war. The northern Union States blockaded Confederate ports, and a Union naval vessel in open sea stopped and boarded a British blockade runner. Two Confederate diplomats were captured who were travelling to England on the merchant ship *Trent*. The British government demanded the release of the Southern diplomats. Lincoln's State Department refused to honor the British request. Indignation in England over the, so-called, *Trent Affair*, almost led to British entry into the war on the side of the Confederacy. Prince Consort Albert, who was on his deathbed, persuaded Prime Minister Lord Palmerston to be conciliatory; so, a diplomatic release of the two Confederate diplomats was achieved. The outcome of the American Civil War might have been quite different without Albert's diplomatic effort. The Confederacy could have prevailed with aid from England, and the United States nation might have been divided.

Victoria and Albert had nine children (4 sons and 5 daughters). Albert ordered strenuous six-hour-a-day instruction programs for them, but family relationships between parents and children remained respectful and affectionate. However, none of their children had the love for scholarship that characterized their father.

Albert was only forty in 1839 when his vitality and energy notably declined. Two years later he died at age forty-two of what was said to be typhoid fever contracted during a visit to Cambridge University to see his son Crown Prince Edward. However, it is now suspected that his death was complicated by kidney failure, or a more systemic condition such as cancer.

Queen Victoria gave her name to *The Victorian Age*. In most minds that is synonymous (as Shaw would put it in *Pygmalion*) with 'stuffy middle class morality.' Victoria's married life with Prince Albert was a model of rectitude in sharp contrast with all the hopping in and out of beds that characterized all previous Hanoverian reigns. Victoria's father and all other sons of George III were notorious womanizers. Almost none of Victoria's cousins were legitimate. Scandal at court was legion. Albert laid down the law: 'No one with a hint of scandal would be welcome at

Windsor.' Albert believed that the royal household should set standards of behavior for the nation. Albert's *middle class morality* became the stiff backed model for propriety in the Victorian Age. It came from rinky-dink Saxe-Coburg-Gotha, not Victoria's libertine London.

Prince Albert died on December 14, 1861 at Windsor Castle, and was buried in the Frogmore Royal Mausoleum at Windsor. Victoria withdrew almost totally from public life, and remained away from London in residence at Balmoral Castle in Scotland until 1886. His death devastated Queen Victoria who entered a twenty-five year period of mourning, during which she wore only black.

Conclusion to the Hanover Dynasty

THE DEATH of Victoria in 1901 ended the Hanover Dynasty, which included Kings George I, George II, George III, George IV, William IV, and Queen Victoria.

The Dynasty lasted for almost 200 years. The crown passed from generation to generation without political controversy. It is surprising, therefore, that the relationship between parent and offspring in the succession was, almost without exception, one of resentment, distrust, dislike, or naked hate between father and son—between king and crown prince. The royal family commonly received public criticisms on grounds of adultery, illegitimacy, immorality, and for behavior considered unsuitable for a ruling house. Courts became so licentious by 1772 that a Royal Marriages Act by Parliament set strict standards for eligibility to reign, but even that was not sufficient to stop flagrant hanky panky from going on behind palace doors.

Victoria was in sharp contrast to her Hanoverian predecessors. However, Victoria was far more tolerant of indiscretions early in her life, than the image she projected following her marriage to her Prince Consort Albert. He imposed his own 'Victorian standards' of propriety on Victoria.

During the Hanoverian Age, Parliament continued to appropriate powers of the crown. Gradually, monarchs ruled less, and, eventually, they merely reigned as an anachronistic figurehead, but often with surprising powers of persuasion. At the end of the Hanoverian Dynasty, Britain reached its highest level of national and colonial power. By the start of the 20th century, Britain was the envy of the world.

The 20th Century would begin with the death of Queen Victoria. Her son Edward Prince of Wales came to the throne on February 2, 1901 as King Edward VII of the Saxe-Coburg-Gotha—Windsor Dynasty.

DYNASTY VII

THE SAXE-COBURG-GOTHA— WINDSOR DYNASTY
REIGN 37 THROUGH 41 (1901–PRESENT)

Introduction to the
Saxe-Coburg-Gotha—Windsor Dynasty

AT THE turn of the 20th Century, the British Empire was at its apogee, second to none in the world. However, world events, including the Russian Revolution and two World Wars, foretold an unsettled fate for monarchies. The British Empire became a Commonwealth of Nations following the Second World War, after which independent member nations shared the same sovereign, but some parts of Victoria's Empire severed all ties to the Empire, and no longer had any link with Britain.

The name of the reigning house in England changed from Saxe-Coburg-Gotha to Windsor during World War I (1914-1918). King George V decided that an English name, rather than a decidedly German one, was desirable at a time of war when all things German generated extreme animosity in England. At that time, there was renewed republican talk of doing away with the monarchy entirely.

The Hanover family name *Guelph* was rejected as being no improvement over *Saxe-Coburg-Gotha*, for existing reasons. The name King George V chose for the family (suggested first by his secretary Lord Stamfordham) with approval of the Privy Council was *Windsor*. The name of Windsor Castle had been associated with English royalty ever since William the Conqueror established a fort at its promontory on the Thames following the Conquest in 1066. Edward III was born there, and was known by the name Edward of Windsor. With these and other examples, the Windsor name was chosen for the present Royal Family. It is now officially designated, *The House of Windsor*.

When the name change was approved, children, and grandchildren of the English monarch thereafter would bear the title, *Prince (name) or Princess (name) + Windso*r. However, the more distantly removed great-grandchildren would be styled *Lord (name) or Lady (name) + Windsor*. The traditional laws of primogeniture created in the Middle Ages would continue to determine the rank of precedence in succession to the throne.

The Windsor name will continue to apply to the British Royal House after the reign of Queen Elizabeth II ends. The paternal family name of Charles Prince of Wales is *Mountbatten,* from his father Prince Philip Mountbatten. Prince Charles and his direct descendents will carry the surname *Mountbatten-Windsor.*

The Saxe-Coburg-Gotha— Windsor Dynasty Lineage Reign 37 through 41 (1901-present)

THIS LINE includes all British monarchs of the 20th Century, namely: Kings Edward VII, George V, Edward VIII, George VI, and Queen Regnant Elizabeth II.

These are descendants of Prince Consort Albert of Saxe-Coburg-Gotha and his wife Queen Victoria of Hanover. The connection between Hanover Dynasty and Saxe-Coburg-Gotha—Windsor Dynasty through Queen Victoria is shown here.

Reigning monarchs are given in bold type with the number for each reign beginning with Reign 37 and continuing to Reign 41. Dates in parenthesis give the duration of reigns. Queen Consort names are included when they are also mothers of a following reigning monarch. Numbers in parenthesis give offspring in chronological order; however, only offspring are shown that figure conspicuously in events discussed in the present treatment of English history.

Dynasty VI. The Hanover Lineage:
Reign 36. Queen Victoria (1837-1901) married Albert of Saxe-Coburg-Gotha, parents of—**Reign 37. Edward VII**

Dynasty VII. The Saxe-Coburg-Gotha—Windsor Lineage:
Reign 37. Edward VII (1901-1910) married Queen Consort Alexandra of Denmark, parents of—

> **Reign 38. George V** (1910-1936) of Saxe-Coburg-Gotha (name later changed to Windsor) married Queen Consort Mary of Teck, parents of—

>> (1) **Reign 39. Edward VIII** of Windsor (1936), after abdication, Duke of Windsor, no issue.

>> (2) **Reign 40. George VI** of Windsor (1936-1952) married Queen Consort Elizabeth Bowes-Lyon, parents of—

>>> **Reign 41. Queen Regnant Elizabeth II** of Windsor (1952-present) married Philip Mountbatten, parents of—

>>>> Charles of Mountbatten-Windsor Prince of Wales married Dianna Spencer, parents of—

>>>>> Prince William of Mountbatten-Windsor.

REIGN 37

KING EDWARD VII

AND

QUEEN CONSORT ALEXANDRA
OF DENMARK

Summary of the Reign of King Edward VII
(Reign 1901-1910)

King Edward VII: life dates c. 69 years, b. November 9, 1841-d. May 6,1910; Prince of Wales c. 59 years, November 9, 1841-January 10, 1901; King of Great Britain (England, Ireland, Scotland, and Wales) c. 9 years, January 10, 1901-May 6, 1910.

KING EDWARD VII was the second child and eldest son of Queen Victoria and Albert of Saxe-Coburg-Gotha. He was born in 1841 at Buckingham Palace, and was christened Albert Edward, but always in the family, he was known as 'Bertie'. However, he chose to use only his second name Edward when he became king.

As Prince of Wales, Edward was denied experience in government while his mother Queen Victoria lived. He expressed few political opinions, but he disliked David Lloyd George his Chancellor of the Exchequer for pointing out that "It costs the government more to pay for the Prince of Wales's trivial entertainments than to buy a battleship for the Royal Navy."

Edward's genuine fondness for France enabled him to play a decisive role in negotiating the *Entente Cordial* between England and France in 1904. That alliance gave hope that war with Germany could be averted, by blocking Germany's program of aggression against neighboring countries. On the international scene, Edward was credited with being the *Peace Maker of Europe*, and "There will be no war as long as there's good King Edward to look out for us." Edward died in 1910 and World War I began in 1914. However, the Entente Cordial made England and France allies in World War I.

His reign is called the *Edwardian Age* (in France, *La Belle Époque*). The decade was a period of manners and privilege epitomized by the self-indulgent king. He was immensely popular. His love of frivolous amusement was legendary, as were his openly acknowledged liaisons with ladies of fashion and position: namely, the *Divine* Sarah Bernhardt, the *Lovely* Countess Daisy of Warwick, the theatrical *Jersey Lily* Lillian Langtry, the socialite *Elegant Patsy* Cornwallis-West, and the *Honorable* Mrs. Alice Keppel, to name a few of his mistresses.

None of the political maneuvering of the time changed the course of history. The frivolous age had outlived its usefulness, and failed to recognize the social and political warnings of the wars and revolutions soon to come. In short, Edward VII, lived a life of luxury to the full, and accomplished nothing.

His Queen Consort, Alexandra of Denmark was born in 1844 in Copenhagen. They were married in 1863. Edward VII and Queen Alexandra had six children, of whom one son and three daughters survived to maturity. Alexandra died in 1925 at Sandringham House, Norfolk, and was buried at St. George's Chapel, Windsor.

Following the death of Edward VII, his only son Prince George Duke of York succeeded to the throne in 1910 as, King George V.

Narrative of Queen Consort Alexandra of Denmark

Queen Alexandra of Denmark: life dates c. 82 years, b. December 1, 1844-d. November 20, 1925; Princess of Wales wife of Edward Prince of Wales 42 years, March 10, 1863-January 10, 1901; Queen Consort of King Edward VII c. 9 years, January 10, 1901-May 6, 1910; Dowager Queen Mother c, 15 years, May 6, 1910-November 20, 1925.

PRINCESS ALEXANDRA of Denmark was the second of six children, and the eldest of three daughters of Prince Christian Oldenburg of Schlieswig-Holstein-Sonderburg-Glücksblurg and Princess Louise of Hesse-Cassel. Both of her parents had close ties with the royal house of Denmark. King Frederick VII of Denmark had no heir; when he died, the crown of Denmark was offered to Alexandra's father to solve the crisis in succession. Prince Christian of Oldenburg became King Christian IV of Denmark in 1863.

Alexandra was born on December 1, 1844 in the Yellow Mansion in Copenhagen. The fine manor home was adjacent to the royal Amalienborg Palace. Although her father Christian was a prince of Denmark, there was little likelihood in her childhood that he would ever be the King of Denmark. During Alexandra's childhood, the family was not wealthy. Her father's official pension was about £1,000 a year, about average for upper middle class families, but their residence was provided by the state, and was rent-free.

The style of living enjoyed by the Oldenburgs was unpretentious, and not greatly different than that of common families with similar financial resources. They rarely participated in court events. The children shared unheated upstairs bedrooms that they were required to keep orderly. Hans Christian Anderson was a popular occasional visitor who was persuaded to tell the children bedtime stories.

The children received appropriate training in courtly manners, and were educated in the usual range of subjects to qualify them for lives of privilege in court: history, literature, languages including English, and especially music. Alexandra was notably proficient as a pianist. Throughout her life, it remained important to have a piano available to play for personal enjoyment. The boys were tutored in military arts, and the girls learned many domestic arts. They were taught " . . . to bake and brew, to sew and knit . . . to manufacture bonnets and gowns."

Alexandra and her sisters became competent seamstresses. They prided themselves in making their own clothes. Thus, childhood in the Yellow Mansion was unremarkable except for the fact that four of the six children eventually became crowned heads in Europe: in order of age—King Frederick VIII of Denmark, Queen Alexandra of England, Empress Dagmar of Russia, King George I of Greece.

Alexandra married Edward Prince of Wales on March 10, 1863. He was twenty-two and she was nineteen. She became the Princess of Wales in the same year her father became King Christian IX of Denmark.

Negotiation for the marriage began in 1861 under pressure of circumstances that now seem trivial. In 1861 at age nineteen, the Prince of Wales was sent to Ireland as part of his curriculum on military tactics. While on military maneuvers, his superior officers discovered Edward in his tent with an actress named Nellie Clifton. Victoria and Albert were scandalized when they were informed of the *Bertie-Nellie Affair.* They were sure that the Prince of Wales was on his way to become a philandering wastrel like many of his Hanover ancestors.' In their fear, they were not far from anticipating what would actually be a distinguishing characteristic of their eldest son's life. A hasty palace conference decided that the wayward Prince of Wales must get married immediately (not to Nellie Clifton of course), but someone suitable to be a queen consort.

After considering many royal princesses, Victoria and Albert decided that Princess Alexandra of Denmark was an ideal choice to be Edward's wife. Prince Albert went to Cambridge to explain that arrangements for Prince Edward's marriage to Princess Alexandra of Denmark were under way. During this Cambridge visit, Albert contracted his fatal infection of typhoid fever that led to his death later that year.

Edward's older sister the Crown Princess Victoria of Prussia arranged for Alexandra and Edward to meet on September 24, 1861 at the ancient city of Speyer on the Rhine. The formal meeting was agreeable, but Edward made no proposal of marriage at that time. After Prince Albert died in December 1861, Queen Victoria ordered Edward to obey his father's wishes, and marry Alexandra. Nine months later on September 9, 1862, Edward finally proposed, and Alexandra accepted.

The ship *HMS Victoria and Albert* of the Royal Navy brought Alexandra from Copenhagen to England. It docked at Gravesend at the mouth of the Thames on March 7, 1863. A military band greeted Alexandra's arrival with a stirring fanfare written for the occasion by Sir Arthur Sullivan (the same Sullivan as in *Gilbert and Sullivan*), and Poet Laureate Alfred Lord Tennyson read a poem.

The welcoming party on the pier saw a pretty, modestly dressed, shy girl who seemed frightened by the crowd who greeted her. The titled lords and ladies who met beautiful Princess Alexandra were shocked by the plain style of her dress. Runners ran pell-mell to London to fetch a fashionable bonnet and gown from the Royal Wardrobe that would be suitable for Alexandra's first appearance later in the day before the crowds who waited to get a glimpse of their new Princess of Wales as she entered London. Of the borrowed 'fine feathers' she wore that day, Alexandra later said, "[They] cost more than my sister Dagmar and I had ever spent on clothes in all our lives put together."

She passed through London in a carriage with the Prince of Wales beside her. A thunder of boisterous cheering from the crowded streets followed them. She was told to bow and wave to the crowd to assure public affection. They finally arrived at Marlborough House in central London, which Queen Victoria had given to the Prince of Wales in anticipation of his marriage. The old stone mansion soon would be the center for an exuberant junior court very different than Buckingham Palace with the somber entertainments Queen Victoria favored.

Crown Prince Edward and Princess Alexandra of Denmark were married in St. George's Chapel, Windsor on March 10, 1863. Victoria decreed that dress for the marriage of the Prince of Wales would be respectful of Prince Consort Albert had died over a year previously: men would dress in black or grey, and women were limited to taupe, lilac, or mauve. These color restraints for dress remained *de rigueur* in Victoria's court through her twenty-five year period of mourning for Albert.

Aside from that somber decree, the wedding for Edward and Alexandra was a grand occasion in which the renowned opera diva, Jenny Lind (the Swedish Nightingale), movingly sang the anthem *This Day with Joyful Heart and Voice*, which Prince Consort Albert had composed just before his death. The cream of Europe's royalty attended the wedding at Windsor. After the ceremony, all ranks of nobility, heads of government, common pickpockets, and unsavory East-End roughs packed the train back to

London. The third class carriages had 'standing room only.' Millions of pounds worth of jewels, coronets, and *haute couture* dresses were exposed to vandals and toughs; cut-purse sneaks made a heyday of it; no crowns, but several jeweled brooches and gold watches with heavy chains carrying handsome fobs were pinched.

The Prince and Princess of Wales honeymooned at Queen Victoria's Osborne House summer retreat on the Isle of Wight. Almost immediately, the Prince and Princess of Wales were known in London society as *The Wales*. Alexandra's unaffected sincerity, gentle humor, good manners, and youthful beauty won all England. One description of her said, " . . . her wonderful bloom and youthful loveliness . . . like some fair pale flower . . . her eyes soft and lustrous, her hair profuse and wavy . . . and the carriage of her head and shoulders are perfection."

Although Alexandra had been instructed in English from early childhood, and was thoroughly proficient linguistically in grammar, she had a unique accent that set her off from those of native English birth.

Although it began as a 'Marriage of State,' the Wales's union became one of sincere affection and mutual respect. Their six children (3 sons and 3 daughters) were born between 1864 and 1871. The first and last sons were born with impaired mental limitations. Only one son survived who became King George V. The children of King Edward VII and Queen Alexandra were:

> Albert Victor Duke of Clarence (January 8, 1864-January 14, 1892), died before his father.
>
> George Duke of York (June 3, 1865-January 20, 1936), King George V
>
> Louise Princess Royal Duchess of Fife (February 20, 1867-January 4, 1931)
>
> Victoria of Wales (July 6, 1868-December 3, 1935)
>
> Maude Queen of Norway (November 26, 1869-November 20, 1938)
>
> John (died at birth, April 6/7, 1871)

Early in 1864, Alexandra gave birth to her first child Albert Victor. He was two months premature and weighed only four pounds at birth. He was mentally deficient, possibly due to oxygen poverty from poorly developed lungs at birth.

Unlike Queen Victoria and Prince Consort Albert, Edward and Alexandra were affectionate permissive parents who loved and spoiled their children. In turn, the children adored them. Soon after the marriage, Queen Victoria and Prince Albert purchased Sandringham House for £22,000, and gave it to the Edward Prince of Wales as a wedding present. The manor was surrounded by generous farming land, and was far from London near the Wash northwest of Norfolk. Sandringham was the favorite escape refuge for Edward, Alexandra, and their children.

The Sandringham manor house had been altered over many years. The house was a jumble of wings, dormers, towers, porches, bay windows, and architectural novelties added higgledy-piggledy from time to time. Edward hired builders to modify the monstrosity further to suit the growing family needs. Alexandra delighted in turning the spacious grounds into a grand menagerie for free ranging animals: horses, sheep, cats, dogs, chickens, geese, and whatever wild creatures chose to accept her hospitality. She loved flowers; so grounds surrounding the manor were planted with a view to provide the house with an abundance of floral decorations throughout the year.

The Walses loved to entertain. Social events at Sandringham were frequent and informal. Life at Sandringham was bucolic, but in its own way whimsically grand—by example, a stuffed baboon at the entry of the main hall accepted calling cards as an invitation for merriment, but it disappeared into a closet when Queen Victoria was expected to visit.

Alexandra's name in the family was Alix. She was notable for charm, and the ability to win affection from every one she met. She enjoyed many social activities including dancing, ice-skating, and horseback riding. However, in her mid twenties, she began to experience two physical problems that increased as the years went on. Rheumatic fever impaired her stamina, and ability to walk. She also had a hereditary hearing problem that finally rendered her almost entirely deaf. These impairments limited her social activities, and led to her spending more time within the circle of family and friends.

Not withstanding these handicaps, Alexandra was always gracious, cordial, approachable, and nonjudgmental. She enchanted everyone and was exceedingly popular with the public. She was unique in the royal family for never being humiliated by criticism from the English press. However, once on a visit to Ireland in 1885, she faced open hostility in Cork. An angry street crowd of black shirted nationalists booed her and

Prince Edward. The animosity of the crowd was not personal, only an expression of usual Irish displeasure with everything English.

Alexandra's only intolerance focused on the Emperor Wilhelm II of Germany, first cousin of Edward—she never forgave Germany for invasion of her beloved Denmark in the Schleswig-Holstein War of 1864, and again in World War I.

After their last son was born, and died only a few hours after birth in 1871, it is believed that Edward and Alix ceased to live together as man and wife. Nevertheless, they continued an amiable, understanding, acceptance of life together to the end of Edward's reign when he died in 1910. Part of their understanding was that they would be respectful of each other, and be devoted parents to their children, and grandchildren. In addition, Crown Prince/King Edward VII was unfettered in making whatever social entanglements with ladies of fashion he might choose. Their arrangement seemed to work out reasonably well. They never criticized or demeaned one another in public.

Alexandra kept her youthful appearance into advanced years. Her natural beauty and modest taste in clothes set standards for fashion in England. Women in court always followed styles worn by royalty. Alexandra's preference for pastel lace dresses with high necklines, and multi-strand choker necklaces put a chill on décolletage at court. Rumors claimed that the fashion craze for high neckline dresses was not an evidence for modest good taste, but that Alix was simply hiding a disfiguring mole, scar, or birthmark on her throat. Alix added a refinement to existing customs by wearing special afternoon teatime frocks that were relatively simple, but elegant. Her taste in clothes earned her praise for being the best dressed woman in England.

Much of Alexandra's time was taken up with domestic duties associated with the rearing of her children. She enjoyed bathing the babies, dressing them, and putting them to bed at night. Alexandra's typical day began with a trip to the nursery, and ended at night with another visit to see that her children were safely sleeping in their beds. Throughout the day, she made sure to know what was being done for the children, and how her orders were carried out. The nurseries at Marlborough House in London and Sandringham House at Norfolk were cluttered with all needed for the care and amusement of children.

When the children were older, Alexandra had time for other duties. She endeared herself to Queen Victoria by sponsoring numerous civic charitable tasks of nonpolitical nature for the aging queen. The queen expressed her appreciation by saying, "[Alix] . . . spares me the strain and fatigue of functions. She opens bazaars, attends concerts, visits hospitals [for me] . . . She not only never complains, but endeavors to prove that she has enjoyed what to another would be a tiresome duty."

Alexandra was never unfaithful to Edward, and no gossip ever touched Alexandra's behavior. However, Edward's libertine behavior repeatedly created scandal and serious problems outside the palace. Edward's illicit affairs created a storm in the London press. As the Prince of Wales and as King, Edward, he deserved his rakish reputation, but his sins merely enhanced his immense popularity. Some of his escapades dealt with adultery, or illegitimacy, or gambling, but in all cases they were resolved without threatening the monarchy.

Edward was a frequent visitor to Paris, and a connoisseur of its food and nightlife. On one occasion, he was dining with a dancer from the Follies Bregère when the restaurant chef presented him with a new desert that Edward enjoyed. The chef then asked permission to name the confection Crêpe Prince of Wales, but Edward demurred, and said, "Name it for my charming companion." The desert was called *Crêpe Suzette*: a thin pancake sautéed in buttery sauce, of caramelized sugar, orange juice, lemon zest, Grand Marnier liqueur, and served en flambé.

Edward travelled more widely than any preceding King of England, but Alexandra rarely accompanied him on his worldwide ranging visits to the United States, Canada, India, Palestine, Turkey, Egypt, or on his hunting expeditions to India and Africa. However, the two frequently travelled together to European capitals and spas of fashion. Edward and Alexandra had been married for 38 years before Edward became king at the age of fifty-nine. Alexandra was Princess of Wales longer than anyone else in English history.

Queen Victoria died on January 22, 1901, and Edward Prince of Wales became King Edward VII. Edward and Alexandra were crowned in a joint ceremony on August 9, 1902. His reign lasted less than ten years, only until May 6, 1910. Victoria wanted Edward to use the double name, *Albert-Edward*, to honor his father, but Edward (who had been called Bertie by the family all his life) declined, and said that both his mother and father should share the distinction of being the only ones to bear the official name *Victoria* or *Albert*. Edward's coronation was delayed for a year and a half, while he recovered from severe appendicitis. He underwent the operation when methods for anesthesia and aseptic surgery were primitive.

Aside from congenital tardiness, only good reports accompanied Alexandra all her life. Alexandra was notable for being late—frequently for hours—to every single event in her entire life. Her tardiness was legendary. She appeared oblivious of inconvenience and annoyance it created. Of Edward's impatience with her, Alix merely said, "Let him wait; it will do him good." Often after a delay of several hours, she would make an elegant stately entrance, and calmly ask, "Am I late? Please, do forgive me." Queen Victoria, always a stickler for punctuality, constantly reprimanded Alexandra with, "Promptness is the courtesy of kings and queens!"

Alexandra was late even for her coronation in 1902. Edward threatened to leave Buckingham Palace for Westminster Abbey in the Royal State Coach without her. He threatened that she would have to call a cab, if she didn't get a move on. Even so, the Coronation was delayed for over fifteen minutes. On that occasion, she petulantly expressed the view, "There is little point in being a queen if you can't get to the party whenever you choose."

A worldwide influenza epidemic in 1892 took the life of their eldest son Crown Prince Albert Victor on January 14, 1892. Their eldest son, commonly called Eddy, died of pneumonia at the age of twenty-eight and created a family crisis for the succession. Edward and Alexandra sincerely mourned his death, in spite of the fact that his intellect was severely limited, and he was unsuited for the throne. Alexandra nursed Albert Victor faithfully in Sandringham House until his death. It seems she never fully recovered from losing her first child. She kept his room as a shrine in which Albert Victor's personal belongings appeared to be waiting on his return.

Anti-British sentiment from the Boer War at the turn of the century inspired the only attempt upon Edward and Alexandra's lives. In that incident, a Belgian boy fired several shots from about six feet away into their rail carriage as it left the Paddington station in London. Neither Edward nor Alexandra was injured. With royal equanimity, the Prince remarked, "It is fortunate that anarchists are almost always poor shots." The Prince was an excellent shot. He enjoyed aristocratic *shoots* on estates in England, Scotland, and on foreign safaris to India and Africa.

Queen Victoria died on January 22, 1901, and Prince Edward became King Edward VII, and Alexandra his Queen Consort. They moved from

Marlborough House to Buckingham Palace, but kept Sandringham House as their favorite refuge away from London.

In private, Alexandra continued as a student of piano. Her instructor from the London Conservatory evaluated her in saying, "Her Majesty is fairly well trained in most things . . . she is an excellent theorist in music, reads well, and is quick and intelligent in practice . . . but not a professional." In the growing silence of her deafness in later years, her music was an increasing source of pleasure and contentment.

At age sixty-eight, Edward VII suffered from overweight, from too much good brandy, too many cigars, and asthma. He developed a persistent bronchitis in Paris in March 1910, and returned for convalescence to Sandringham House. Alexandra was in Athens visiting her brother King George I of Greece when word reached her in April that Edward was severely ill. She hurried back to England, and arrived at Sandringham House to be with Edward.

King Edward VII died from a terminal heart attack on May 6, 1910, and was buried at St. George's Chapel at Windsor. His only son Prince George Duke of York ascended as King George V.

Dowager Queen Alexandra moved to Marlborough House as her London dwelling, but she kept Sandringham House in Norfolk as her favorite residence for the remainder of her life. As Dowager Queen Mother, she had little interest or involvement in political affairs during the reign of her son George V. Her public activities dealt mainly with sponsorship of charities, but as her deafness increased, her activities centered mainly on her growing family of grandchildren. She delighted in spoiling the six children of her son George V. Their mother Queen Mary of Teck was dismayed at freedom the princes and princesses were given at Sandringham. Alexandra's daughter Victoria never married, and stayed as her mother's companion in her later years.

In 1917, the Bolsheviks overthrew the Russian government, and killed Tsar Nicholas II and all the royal Romanov family. However, Alexandra's sister, the Tsar's mother Tsarina Dagmar of Denmark was spared. She was rescued in 1919 when Alexandra persuaded her son George V to rescue her sister by sending the British naval vessel *HMS Marlborough* to bring Tsarina Dagmar from the Crimea to England.

Dagmar stayed with Alexandra for a few years in London, but, after having been the Empress, she found it intolerable to be third in court precedence in England. Her place came after Queen Consort Mary of Teck, and after her sister Dowager Queen Alexandra; then third, Dagmar was only the *Former Empress Tsarina of All the Russias*. When Alexandra died in November 1925, Dagmar's brother King Frederick VIII of Denmark invited Dagmar to return to Copenhagen where she lived out her life, and died at age eighty.

After the end of the Great War in 1918 when Alexandra was seventy-four, her health began to decline. In 1920, a broken blood vessel in an eye resulted in partial blindness, and the family noted that she had occasional lapses of memory, and difficulty in completing rational sentences. However, she retained her perfect posture, and the warm gentle dignity in her manner of greeting everyone.

As years passed, Alexandra's appearance seemed to escape the passage of time. Even as an old woman, she retained an appearance of youthful beauty. Jealous ladies-in-waiting and courtiers said her apparent youth was all due to often repeated henna rinses whenever a grey hair appeared, and to skillful masking with petit point lace veils, or to an abundant use of unguents, and to heavy makeup that gave her the appearance of an imperishable lacquered oriental mannequin.

Without notable previous illness, Alexandra suffered a heart attack, and died at Sandringham House on November 20, 1925. She was buried beside her husband Edward VII in St. George's Chapel at Windsor.

Dowager Queen Alexandra of Denmark was an admired and loved member of England's royal family. She was a person of modest abilities, yet possessed altogether admirable human qualities. Alexandra moved with ease and grace into the company of the most respected women in history.

Following the death of Edward VII, his only surviving son, George Prince of Wales succeeded to the throne in 1910 as, King George V.

REIGN 38

KING GEORGE V

AND

QUEEN CONSORT MARY OF TECK

Summary of the Reign of King George V (Reign 1910-1936)

King George V: life dates c. 70 years, b. June 3, 1865-d. January 20, 1936; King of Great Britain (England, Ireland, Scotland, and Wales) 26 years, May 10, 1910-January 20, 1936.

GEORGE V was the second son of King Edward VII and Queen Alexandra of Denmark. He was born at Marlborough House, London on June 3, 1865. As the second son and Duke of York, he did not expect to be king. At first, he pursued a career in the Royal Navy, but that ended when his older brother Albert Victor died in 1892, and George became the heir apparent. During the reign of his father Edward VII (1901 to 1910), George was Prince of Wales. When Edward VII died, he became King George V on May 10, 1910.

George V was an able but colorless monarch who served well in the trying years of World War I, and in the postwar Great Depression. He married his cousin Princess Mary of Teck. They had six children, two of whom later became King Edward VIII and King George VI.

The reign of twenty-six years was a time of turmoil and decline for the British Empire. King George V was unable to prevent or control the course of history. As early as 1911, the House of Lords lost its ancient power to veto acts of the House of Commons, which then became the only real power in England. The King and Lords thereafter had only powers of persuasion and delay—the people ruled, and the nobility had to grin and bear it.

Possibly the most memorable action of George V was his choice of the name *Windsor* for the royal family to replace the surname *Saxe-Coburg-Gotha* of his father. This change in dynastic name was in response to intense anti-German sentiments in England during World War I. At that time, there was strong republican public opposition to the monarchy itself.

Victoria's Empire was the culmination of land acquisitions by colonialism, conquest, annexation, and adoption. Following World War I, many components of the empire sought greater independence, and some began slipping away toward total separation. Ireland led in the move by dominions and colonies to seek independence.

The Great Depression and the rise of European totalitarian nationalism in the 1930s weakened the authority of monarchies throughout Europe. The rise of Nazism with Hitler in Germany, and of the Fascists with Mussolini in Italy created an axis of militant aggression that threatened democracy everywhere. Neither leadership nor diplomacy was able to block the steadfast march of nations into World War II.

King George V died At Sandringham House, Norfolk on January 20, 1936, and was succeeded by his eldest son who became King Edward VIII.

Narrative of Queen Consort Mary of Teck

Queen Mary of Teck: life dates c. 85 years, b. May 26, 1867-d. March 31, 1953; Duchess of York as wife of Prince George Duke of York, 8 years, July 6, 1893-November 9, 1901; Princess of Wales as wife of George Prince of Wales, 9 years, November 9, 1901-May 6, 1910; Queen Consort of King George V, 26 years, May 6, 1910-January 20, 1936; Dowager Queen Mother and Grandmother of King Edward VIII, King George VI, and Queen Elizabeth II, 17 years, January 20, 1936-March 31, 1953.

PRINCESS VICTORIA Mary of Teck was the only daughter and eldest of four children of Francis Duke of Teck-Württemberg and Princess Mary Adelaide Duchess of Cambridge. Mary of Teck was born in Kensington Palace, London on May 26, 1867. Before she became queen consort, she was known in the family by the name *May* in recognition of the month of her birth.

By birth, Mary Victoria was a princess of Württemberg, Germany. By maternal descent, she was a member of the English royal family as a great-granddaughter of George III through his eleventh child Prince Adolphus Duke of Cambridge, whose only daughter Mary Adelaide of Cambridge was Mary of Teck's mother. Princess Mary of Teck's father Francis Duke of Teck was related maternally to the Royal House of Württemberg, but his title was at an inferior Morganatic level that lacked succession right to the throne of Württemberg.

Mary of Teck's mother Duchess Mary Adelaide of Cambridge was a happy popular member of the British royal family in London, but she was without a personal inheritance of significant monetary value. From childhood, she had become much over weight. Many overtures for marriage failed, and she remained single to the age of thirty. Queen Victoria was fond of her cousin, and she conspired to find Mary Adelaide's husband and settled on Prince Francis of Teck. He had the title *Prince of Württemberg* in Stuttgart, Germany, but he, too, was without an official annuity, taxable property, or means of employment.

Prince Francis and Princess Mary Adelaide were married on June 12, 1866. The royal pair was penniless. Queen Victoria persuaded Parliament to add Princess Mary Adelaide to the Civil List, with a stipend of £5,000 per annum. The amount was adequate for basic survival, but insufficient for a royal family that aspired to prominence in the London court. Parliament denied later petitions for supplementary income. Wherewith, Mary Adelaide's mother Princess Augusta of Hesse-Kassel (née, Duchess of Cambridge) is reported to have given her an additional £4,000 per annum from her own allowance. Additional assistance came when Queen Victoria gave them free occupancy to a Kensington Palace apartment in London, and another in the country at White Lodge in Richmond Park.

Between the years 1867 and 1874, four children (1 daughter [Mary of Teck] and 3 sons) were born in London, and brought up in England. Tutors taught the children in a relaxed undemanding domestic environment at home. However, for reasons of economy, the family often chose to live for extended periods as uninvited guests with relatives in Germany.

As is common for most royalty, Mary of Teck's mother Princess Mary Adelaide of Cambridge had little concern or knowledge as to how bills were paid. She had expensive taste, and lived far beyond her means. She dressed in fashionable clothes; she gave extravagant parties, and she was usually drowning in debt. Her eldest child Mary of Teck, as an early teenage girl, sensed the chronic financial disaster facing the family. Mary of Teck constantly but futilely tried to curb her mother's wasteful ways, but her mother continued to plan parties they could not afford.

In 1883 when Mary was sixteen, the family fled to Germany to avoid a legion of creditors in England. For two years, they traveled in Europe through Germany, Austria, and Italy. While in their self-imposed exile, they traveled as the family of Count and Countess von Hohenstein (the family name of Prince Francis) to avoid detention by bill collectors. They shamelessly invited themselves to stay for extended periods with relatives along the way. Mary of Teck was later credited her lifelong interest in art, architecture, music, and history to the opportunity her travels gave for enhancing her modest education through many days spent in museums, conservatories, and galleries in cultural centers of Europe.

In 1885, Mary of Teck was eighteen years old, a marriageable age. Her mother knew that her daughter's name must be high on the list of available maidens in the London marriage market. Mary Adelaide of Cambridge wanted her daughter to marry no less than Prince Albert Victor the eldest son of the Prince of Wales. If that happened, her daughter some day could be Queen of England.

The 'Hohensteins' returned to London in 1885, and resumed occupancy of White Lodge in Richmond Park. Mary Adelaide of Cambridge determined to convince Queen Victoria and Edward Prince of Wales that her daughter was the best choice of bride for Prince Albert Victor who was second in line for the crown. After six years of careful planning, the plot to marry Princess Mary of Teck to Prince Albert Victor Duke of Clarence resulted in their engagement early in December 1891.

Mary of Teck knew her cousin Prince Albert Victor well. She was no fool, and knew there was a real price to pay in becoming Albert Victor's wife. Theirs would be a marriage of State, and it made little difference that Albert Victor was an illiterate, imbecilic, profligate lecher. Mary knew she would have the royal duty to produce heirs for the crown. Albert Victor contracted pneumonia, and died in mid January 1892, only six weeks after their engagement was announced. Mary was dressed in black for mourning at his funeral, and she may have experienced real grief, but she soon recovered.

Queen Victoria had fondness for Princess Mary of Teck. She suggested that Mary would be a desirable bride for Prince George Duke of York, Albert Victor's younger brother, who was now the heir presumptive following his father the Prince of Wales.

Prince George proposed marriage to Princess Mary of Teck, but she refused. Her sensible mother, Princess Mary Adelaide of Cambridge, told her to think it over. The advantage of being the Queen of England was substantial. Mary of Teck reconsidered, and when George proposed again, they became engaged. George Duke of York and Mary of Teck were married on July 6, 1893 in St. James Palace. Mary's mother Princess Mary Adelaide was right; the gifts for the royal marriage equaled almost £8,000,000 in present worth.

The young Duke and Duchess of York were given apartments at St. James Palace in London, and the guest house York Cottage on the Sandringham estate in Norfolk while George's parents the Prince and Princess of Wales, Edward and Alexandra, occupied the great house at Sandringham.

Although the York Cottage was cramped for the accommodation of their household staff of almost thirty, George and Mary preferred country life at Sandringham to the royal court in London. York Cottage was emotionally their *home*, and the home where most of their children were borne.

From all appearances, George and Mary Duke and Duchess of York enjoyed a successful marriage. No shabby gossip tarnished either of their lives. Unlike all his immediate male predecessors, George never took a mistress. Between 1894 and 1905, they had six children (5 sons, and 1 daughter); all but the last son survived to maturity:

> Edward Prince of Wales (June 23, 1894-May 28,1972), in the
>   family always called David, later King Edward VIII.
> George Duke of York (December 14, 1895-February 6, 1952),
>   in the family always called Bertie, later King George VI.
> Mary Princess Royal (April 25, 1897-March 28, 1965)
> Henry Duke of Gloucester (March 31, 1900-June 10,1984)
> George Duke of Kent (December 20, 1902-August 25, 1942)
> John (July 12, 1905-January 18, 1919), retarded epileptic, died
>   in adolescence.

History does not record Queen Mary of Teck to be a model for excellent motherhood. The young children were placed in the care of nannies with little parental supervision for their happiness and wellbeing. That was the custom for royal and noble families at the time. At least one of the children's nurses was almost sadistic in her abuse of her young charges. King George and Queen Mary of Teck were oblivious of much that went on over long periods in their nursery. Their youngest child Prince John was removed at age eleven from court to a private residence at Wood Farm near Sandringham, possibly to avoid the embarrassment of his epileptic seizures. Prince John died at age fourteen shortly after the end of World War I.

In public life, Mary of Teck's appearance and deportment were flawless. She was without affectation, guile, vindictiveness, or conceit, but her outward appearance, although perfect in grace and bearing, was aloof and unapproachable. Her subjects always saw her as a mannequin of cool stately grace. An observer at a parade described her perfectly, "Her Majesty is the one with the pillbox hat level on her head, and a choker of big pearls tight around her neck."

That trademark of her public appearance continued down through the years. Queen Mary's costume was invented around 1905, when it met the approval of George V (then Prince of Wales). He did not like change, and his wish was Mary's command. Therefore, in this 1905 manner, her appearance became frozen in time. Her appearance, like an ornate confection, made it completely understandable that, later on, at a wedding reception at court, a nearsighted octogenarian bowed to the wedding cake, mistaking it for Her Royal Highness Queen Mary. Her appearance and impeccable manners created an unforgettable picture of all a queen should be.

To the public, King George and Queen Mary were colorless effigies of propriety with the appearance of stiff unyielding caricatures. This may have been the only appearance they were capable of presenting even behind palace walls. Their sons, Prince David (later Edward VIII), Prince Bertie (later, George VI), and the other three surviving children, all reported that life in the palace was grimly military. King George ran the palace and his family as though they were midshipmen on a battleship. The household lacked both affection and understanding.

King George and Queen Mary disliked demonstrations of affection even with their children. Regulations were strict, and punishments severe. King George V intimidated his eldest child Prince David (who became Edward VIII), and he terrorized his second son Prince Bertie (who became George VI). The children always received criticisms, and never praise. None of the children remembered their mother Queen Mary ever to have expressed the warm affectionate compassion all children need, and should have as a natural right, whether born in a hovel or a palace.

Many years later after Queen Mary's death, her son King Edward VIII/Duke of Windsor spoke of the inability of his mother Queen Mary to express affection, or to compromise principles with respect to his wife Wallis Warfield Duchess of Windsor. He said, "My sadness was mixed with incredulity that any mother could have been so hard and cruel towards her eldest son, for so many years, and yet so demanding at the end without relenting a scrap. I'm afraid the fluids in her veins have always been as icy cold as they are now in death."

The stoic parenting by King George V and Queen Mary is hard to comprehend, considering that both King George V and Queen Mary of Teck were reared in homes in which merriment and expression of affection were commonplace.

Uncertainty exists concerning what the king and queen's private personal lives were like. From all appearances, they were content with the lives they shared. King George was described as a person with an intellectual range of interests " . . . as small and orderly as the quarters he occupied when he served on shipboard during his years in the Royal Navy." Aside from the Navy, George's only true love throughout his life was stamps. At the end of his life he had over 300 notebooks filled with them, the largest stamp collection in the world.

Mary of Teck had a superior intellect. Her memory never ceased to astound all who knew her. She rarely forgot details of any personal experience. She remembered every fact she read, and all that was reported to her. When she evaluated problems, her analysis usually proved to be correct. Her mental competence, as compared with the rest of the royal family, placed her in a class alone. She was known to give her husband assistance in understanding complex matters of government, and she probably held the pen that drafted many of his government replies to Parliament. Neither George nor Mary had a natural gift for oral communication. On a daily basis, they sent each other written notes, but they only rarely engaged in detailed discussions on any topic.

However, in their own inexpressive ways, George and Mary were sincerely devoted to one another. Their evenings at Buckingham Palace involved King George V working on stamps, and Queen Mary of Teck knitting. Infrequent forays to concerts, theater, and State banquets broke the routine. On the subject of classical music, George commanded that the bombastic music of Richard Strauss should never be played in court. His preference of *La Bohème* over all operas was because it was the shortest. The king and queen both gave the appearances of being almost without emotion.

In their defense, one must remember that, at that time, "any public display of affection was always common, and in bad taste."

George Duke of York had an excellent relationship with his father King Edward VII. During his reign (1901-1910), George and Mary were the Prince and Princess of Wales. They served as goodwill ambassadors for the crown by traveling widely over the empire in lengthy visits that took them to Canada, Ceylon, Egypt, Gibraltar, Malta, Mauritius, New Zealand, Singapore, South Africa, and Australia. In Australia, George represented the crown in the opening of Parliament for the newly created Commonwealth of Australia in 1901. When they returned to London Edward VII gave them Marlborough House as their London residence.

They soon were involved in more travel for the empire that took them to Greece, Norway, Spain, Egypt, and India.

On the death of Edward VII on May 6, 1910, George Prince of Wales became King George V and Mary of Teck became Queen Consort Mary. Deceased King Edward's wife became Dowager Queen Alexandra. Intricacies of royal protocol created a tempest in a teapot at the funeral of Edward VII. Dowager Queen Alexandra felt that she should have precedence at her husband's funeral, but rules of protocol gave first place to the active queen (Mary of Teck), which demoted Dowager Queen Alexandra to second place. However, Alexandra stubbornly refused to bow to custom. She insisted on her right of top billing at her husband's funeral. The two queens remained on friendly terms. Alexandra soon vacated Buckingham Palace to King George and Queen Mary, and went into semi-retirement on the Sandringham estate in Norfolk, but she kept a London residence in Marlborough House.

When George V became king, he asked his wife to use only the name *Mary* as her official name as queen, and not her first name Victoria, which he felt should be reserved for his grandmother the great Queen Victoria.

Soon after the coronation of King George V and Queen Mary on June 22, 1911, they went to Delhi, India to be crowned Emperor and Empress at the Great Durbar of December 12, 1911. All maharajas, rajas, and many lesser government officials were present. The Durbar was a magnificent event in a country of great poverty. King George wore the priceless Imperial Crown of India containing over six thousand large diamonds, set off by innumerable rubies, sapphires, and emeralds. As a token of the grand affair, Queen Mary was given a magnificent diamond tiara and an enormous emerald and diamond necklace with a detachable pendant for either, a huge solitary emerald or diamond. The Great Durbar of 1911 was the last of its kind. Soon thereafter, India moved toward independence with increasing momentum led by Mohandas Gandhi. No longer was there enthusiasm in India for subservience to the English Crown. The king and queen returned to England in February 1912.

King George V and Queen Mary were conscientious monarchs. Queen Mary never inserted her opinion into government or diplomatic affairs, but many strongly suspected that she interpreted State papers for George, who was slow in comprehension of complicated matters. The king only injected himself into matters of political contention in a conciliatory peace-making way. The first four years of his reign were beset with the problem of Irish independence, but with start of World War I (1914-1918), the conflict with Germany became the dominant national issue that swept all other matters aside. The young king and queen supported national morale in the war efforts by the king visiting his armed forces in Flanders, and by the queen visiting arms factories and veterans hospitals at home.

The Russian Revolution (1917-1918) contributed to growing republican demands for termination of monarchies in many nations of Europe, including Germany, Greece, Italy, Rumania, and Russia, where monarchy was replaced by a republic or dictatorship. In 1917, King George received criticism from most royalty in Europe for refusing to give sanctuary for the Russian Royal Family, that later was massacred by the revolutionaries. Civil unrest in England followed the Great War, as the entire social system of monarchy and peerage was challenged.

The most memorable action of George V at the end of the war years involved the choice of the name, *Windsor,* for the Royal House of England. *Windsor* replaced the Germanic name *Saxe-Coburg-Gotha.* This change in dynastic surname came in response to strong anti-German sentiments in England during World War I. The choice of the name, Windsor, was accepted by the Privy Council, and was received with overwhelming approval by the British subjects. The dynastic name for the English ruling family became the *House of Windsor,* whereas the surname for descendants of present Queen Elizabeth II and Prince Philip Mountbatten is *Mountbatten-Windsor.* Other noble families followed suit; *Battenberg* became *Mountbatten,* and *Teck* became *Cambridge.*

Queen Mary had an inflexible sense of propriety for formal court events. Her views on manners still govern royal protocol for correct court behavior today. In public, she was always impeccably dressed, and magnificently bedizened with her personally acquired splendid jewels. Queen Mary was attentive to the public image of the monarchy as something of importance to the realm, and she helped to establish the tradition for members of the royal family to be sponsors and champions of goodly works. She and others in her household were constantly in the news at openings of hospitals, schools, libraries, parks, and support of charity drives, veteran care, christening ships, and endorsing all manner of manufactured articles.

Queen Mary is credited with setting in motion a plan for the royal family to acquire private fortune through financial investment in the Windsor Family Trust. Financial needs of the royal family, since the reign of William III in the latter half of the 17th Century, had been paid by the Civil List from public tax revenues approved annually by Parliament. From pinchpenny childhood experiences, Queen Mary knew all too well, what domestic poverty was like when Parliament chose to withhold payment of annuities to members of the royal family. She did not relish a return to bare-bone economy for the House of Windsor. During World War I, when there was talk of terminating the monarchy, Queen Mary recommended that the crown begin an investment program for acquisition of independent family wealth. The royal family's precautionary investment plan that started during World War I, and now having been in effect for almost a century, has made present Queen Elizabeth II one of the richest persons in the world.

Queen Mary had an intense interest in all aspects of history of the English Royal Family. She embarked on a mission to regain lost, loaned, and misplaced properties of art, jewels, and personal property of former kings and queens of England. Articles in her 'Royal Collection' were housed in numerous palaces around the realm. When she tracked down an item of past royal generosity, she was relentless in her effort to recover it. She would point out to the present owners the provenance of the item, in hope that they would be proud to give it back to the crown. Many noble houses resented being coerced into giving up family treasures under the pressure of losing Queen Mary's favor. The aloof imperious manner of the king and queen led them to be secretly called *St. George and the Dragon.*

Queen Mary was particularly aggressive in her personal acquisition of gems and jewelry. During the turbulent years of revolution following World War I, during the Great Depression in the 1930s, and World War II, she acquired a world-class collection of jewelry. From her own wealth, she was willing to spend more than market value to obtain items of spectacular worth.

Perhaps, Queen Mary is most remembered today for the famous *Queen Mary Doll's House* on display at Windsor Castle. It is a replica in miniature of many rooms of the royal suite at Windsor, all done to the scale of *1 inch to 1 foot.* Its construction and collection was begun in 1921, and was shown in the Empire Exhibition of 1924-25. The house includes replicas of staterooms in the royal apartment, bathrooms, servant's quarters, and the garage complete with motorcars. Wall hangings, chandeliers, paintings, rugs, furniture, dishes, table settings, tea service, *ad infinitum,* are all done as works of art in miniature. Light fittings work, faucets run, toilets flush,

Rolls-Royce doors and windows open, and wheels turn, and the wine cellar has tiny labeled bottles filled with wine. Artists, artisans, craftsmen, and model makers across the nation made the doll's house furnishings as gifts to the queen.

King George's health noticeably began to fail in 1928 from respiratory distress brought on by excessive smoking. His condition continued to worsen through 1935, which was memorable for celebration of his twenty-fifth year as king. The Silver Jubilee was celebrated throughout the empire, and in his speech to the nation, the king acknowledged his indebtedness to Queen Mary for her selfless support in all he did during his reign.

The health of King George V, which never was robust, declined as his excessive smoking augmented chronic pulmonary distress. By 1935, King George required oxygen to assist ordinary breathing. He was in residence at Sandringham House for New Years 1935/36, and by mid January 1936, he became bedridden in his final illness. On January 20, one of King George's last statements was, "How is the Empire?" To which was replied, "All is well, Sir, with the Empire." His final words were to a nurse who gave him a sedative, "God damn you!" After which, he lapsed into final unconsciousness with deep labored breathing.

Shortly before midnight, King George V died on January 20, 1936 just before midnight at Sandringham House. Injections of cocaine and morphine eased his passage into death. His eldest son Edward Prince of Wales who became King Edward VIII succeeded King George V.

Prince Edward was a nonconformist who was in rebellion against the strict rules of propriety advocated by his parents. He was a leader of fashion in *The Roaring Twenties*, and his rapport with his parents was always strained. The king and queen disapproved of his informality, of his liberal socialist views, and particularly of his demimonde friends among the popular extremists of the Jazz Age. Before his death King George V prophetically said of Edward, "After my death, the boy will ruin himself in twelve months . . . I pray to God, my eldest son will never marry and have children, so nothing will come between Lilibet and the Throne ['Lilibet' is present Queen Elizabeth II]."

Queen Mary detested the American socialite Wallis Warfield, who, as early as 1933 had captivated the affections of Edward Prince of Wales. She saw Wallis to be a scheming social climber of the most sordid kind—a twice-divorced adventuress who consorted openly with the Prince of Wales for personal notoriety, monetary gain, and social prestige. In 1934 when he was Prince of Wales, Edward presented Wallis Warfield to Queen Mary at court, but Queen Mary never permitted Wallis to be in her presence again.

Soon after King George V died on January 20, 1936, Queen Mary left Buckingham Palace for Marlborough House, which was often the residence for a dowager queen. When Prince Edward became king in January 1936, it soon became abundantly evident that he intended to make Wallis Warfield his queen. That was anathema to every element of authority and power in the realm. Prime Minister Stanley Baldwin (with strong support from Queen Mary, the nobility, the British public, and heads of government in every corner the empire) informed King Edward VIII that he could not be king and marry Mrs. Wallis Warfield-Spencer-Simpson. King Edward VIII abdicated his throne on December 10, 1936—he had been king for six weeks short of one full year.

The abdication of Edward VIII caused a constitutional crisis in government, which resulted in Edward's younger brother being crowned King George VI on May 12, 1937. He was married to Lady Elizabeth Bowes-Lyon, and they were the parents of two daughters Princesses Elizabeth and Margaret Rose.

During World War II, Queen Mary moved from Marlborough House in London to the Gloucestershire countryside with her niece the Duchess of Beaufort, but after the war in 1945, she returned to her London residence.

Queen Mary gave unstinting support to her second son George VI during his reign of sixteen years from 1936 to 1952. During that time, she was also the mentor who prepared Princess Lilibet for her long successful reign as Queen Elizabeth II. Her formal court education had been neglected during childhood when her parents did not suspect that she would ever be queen. George VI died on February 6, 1952, but Queen Mary did not live to see her granddaughter crowned Queen Elizabeth II on June 2, 1953.

At the end of her life at age eighty-five Queen Mary died of lung cancer at Marlborough Houses, in London on March 24, 1953. She was buried with King George V in St. George's Chapel, at Windsor Castle.

Queen Mary was one of the least colorful, but most memorable royal personages of the 20th Century. She had been in succession: Princess of

Württemberg, Duchess of York, Princess of Wales, Queen Consort of England, Empress of India, and finally Dowager Queen Mother of King Edward VIII and King George VI, and grandmother of Queen Elizabeth II. As part of her legacy, she set a national standard for manners, propriety, and good taste. Her funeral was an occasion for unprecedented national mourning.

REIGN 39

KING EDWARD VIII

AND

WALLIS WARFIELD DUCHESS OF WINDSOR

Summary of the Reign of King Edward VIII (January 20 to December 10/12, 1936)

King Edward VIII: life dates c. 78 years, b. June 23,1894-d. May 28, 1972; King of England and United Kingdom c. 1 year, January 20-December 10/12, 1936; Duke of Windsor, 36 years, December 10/12, 1936-May 28, 1972.

KING EDWARD VIII was the eldest son of George V and Queen Mary of Teck. He was born in 1894 at Richmond, Surrey, and was created Prince of Wales when his father came to the throne in 1910.

Edward VIII succeeded his father in 1936, but his reign lasted less than a year before he abdicated on December 10/12, 1936.

The abdication and events leading up to it totally eclipsed all other aspects of the reign of Edward VIII. The abdication was a major crisis for the monarchy, and it emphasized the fact that to be a ruling monarch in England is not a right of birth, but is a privilege approved by Parliament. He accepted the parliamentary decision that, to remain king, he could not marry twice divorced Mrs. Wallis (Warfield) Spencer-Simpson.

King Edward VIII announced his abdication on December 10, 1936, and Parliament ratified it two days later on December 12. Shortly after his abdication, Edward was created Duke of Windsor, and after Wallis divorced her second husband Earl A. Simpson on May 3, 1937, she married Duke Edward and became the Duchess of Windsor.

Although she became the Duchess of Windsor, she was not honored with the title *Her Royal Highness*. The Royal Family, Parliament, and English public despised Wallis. They would not countenance her being given royal status

After their marriage, the Duke and Duchess of Windsor lived in exile and only rarely were permitted to return to England. The duke briefly held an honorary position in British armed services, when he served as Governor General for the Bahamas Islands in most years of World War II. His remaining life with Wallis was in retirement at their chief residence in Bois de Boulogne, Paris. Following his death from cancer in 1972, Duke Edward of Windsor was buried at the Royal Mausoleum, Frogmore at Windsor.

Duchess Wallis Warfield of Windsor was almost ninety years old when she died in senile old age at her Paris home in 1986. She was buried at the Frogmore Royal Mausoleum with her husband. There was no issue from their marriage.

After the abdication of Edward VIII in 1936, his younger brother Albert succeeded to the throne as King George VI.

Narrative of Wallis Warfield
Duchess of Windsor

Wallis Warfield: life dates c. 89 years, b. June 19, 1896-d. April 24, 1986; wife of Earl Winfield Spencer, Jr. 11 years, November 8, 1916-divorced December 10, 1927; wife of Ernest Aldrich Simpson 11 years, July 21, 1928-divorced May 3, 1937; Duchess of Windsor wife of Edward Duke of Windsor 36 years, June 3, 1937-May 28, 1972; Dowager Duchess of Windsor 17 years, May 28, 1972-April 24, 1986.

BESSIE WALLIS Warfield was the only child of Traeckle Wallis Warfield and Alice Montague, both came from modest family affluence and social prominence in Baltimore, Maryland, USA. Wallis was born at Blue Ridge Summit, Pennsylvania a summer resort community in the Appalachian Mountains that was favored by Baltimore's elite who wished to escape the humid heat of a coastal summer. The date of Wallis's birth was not officially recorded, but June 19, 1896 is usually accepted. A question also exists concerning the date for the marriage of her parents, which also was not recorded, but was said to be November 19, 1895, which would be just early enough for Wallis to be legitimate.

Her father Traeckle Warfield died of tuberculosis on November 15, 1896 when Wallis was barely six months old. Thereafter, her mother Alice Montague Warfield carefully reared Wallis in the genteel manner of the 'Old South.' However, they enjoyed few comforts money could bring, and were dependent for livelihood on the generosity of her unmarried uncle Solomon D. Warfield.

From early childhood, 'Wallis' was the only given name she used. In 1908, Wallis's mother married her second husband John F. Rasin, Jr., who was active in Maryland politics, but Solomon Warfield continued to give financial assistance to his niece by paying for her education at fashionable Oldfield School, an academy for young ladies of 'Good Baltimore Families.' Her mother could not afford to buy the uniforms required for girls at the school, so Wallis's mother made the uniforms Wallis wore. At Oldfield School, Wallis met girls from prestigious families of Pennsylvania, Maryland, and Delaware. One of her closest friends was Renée DuPont of the wealthy Wilmington, Delaware chemical family.

Wallis always pushed herself to excel, and was meticulous in dress, even though she could not afford expensive clothes. A classmate said, "Wallis was brighter than the rest of us. When she decided to go for something, she did it."

Donald Spoto in, *The Decline and Fall of the House of Windsor,* describes Wallis at the end of her formal education and late teenage years, "[Wallis was] . . . clever rather than profound, she had a quick sense of humor, a sharp memory, an irrepressible vitality, an unerring poise, and all the right social skills . . . She knew how a canny choice of color, wardrobe, makeup, and costume jewelry could compensate for her essentially plain features . . . She also had the give-and-take of bright conversation, and she knew better than many prettier girls how to attract and keep the attention of boys she wanted to meet."

Wallis's first husband was Earl Winfield Spencer, Jr., whom she married on November 8, 1916, and divorced on December 10, 1927. In May 1916 while visiting with friends in Pensacola, Florida, twenty year old Wallis met Earl Winfield Spencer, Jr., a pilot at the Naval Air Station, who was eight years her senior. As a young Commander with promise for a career in the Naval Air Force, he was a handsome attractive catch. Wallis and Winfield were married in Baltimore on November 8, 1916.

Theirs was a typical navy marriage, in which Spencer was assigned duties that required their frequent separation for extended periods. He was given several land based posts on the east and west coasts of the United States. Later, he received a long assignment in the Orient. After a period of separation, Wallis joined Winfield in Shanghai, China, which was noted for its fast paced social life with few restraints for foreigners with military and diplomatic connections.

Persons who knew the Spencers in China recalled of Wallis that "Her conversation was brilliant, and she had a way of bringing up the right subject for conversation with anyone . . . and entertaining them on that subject." She had no gift for languages. Her Mandarin was limited to "Boy, pass me the champagne."

China gossip linked Wallis romantically with foreign diplomats when Winfield was away from his post for extended periods. Without validation, gossip asserted that Wallis experienced a botched abortion that permanently prevented her from ever conceiving again.

As years went by, Winfield Spencer became a compulsive alcoholic, and physically abusive to Wallis; even so, they remained married for eleven years. In September 1925, they returned to the United States, but in 1927, after Wallis was severely beaten, she left Winfield and sued for divorce, which was granted on December 10, 1927.

Wallis married her second husband Ernest Aldrich Simpson on July 21, 1928; they divorced on May 3, 1937. Ernest was born in New York City and graduated from Harvard University. He then moved to London, renounced his American citizenship, and became a naturalized British citizen who served in the British Coldstream Guards in World War I. He was a wealthy partner in a British shipping company founded by his father. Ernest was only a year older than Wallis, and *The New York Times* described him as "a tall, blue-eyed, fastidiously dressed charmer, with blond curly hair."

In 1926, Wallis spent Christmas in New York City with an old friend from school days. By chance, she was introduced to Ernest and Dorothy Simpson from London. They were vacationing in New York in an attempt to forestall their marriage breakup by going on a seasonal shopping spree to the city. Ernest gallantly volunteered to squire Wallis around town. After a few forays to points of interests, Dorothy declined to accompany her husband and Wallis to additional museums, concerts, to historic landmarks around Manhattan, and up the Hudson River to view the Palisades. Wallis's divorce was pending, so she refused to encourage Ernest when he asked Wallis if she would consider marriage when divorce freed them both. After the Simpson's return to London, Ernest divorced Dorothy, and after her divorce was final, Wallis married Ernest Simpson on July 21, 1928 in London.

Ernest Simpson had a comfortable income, but he was not by any measure truly wealthy. The Simpsons rented a furnished house on Preston Road at the northern edge of fashionable Mayfair in London. They hired four servants: a cook, butler, and an upstairs and a downstairs maid. Wallis carefully planned her attack on London society to be within her financial means. However, their resources were insufficient to assure entry into the British world of real fashion and power.

Wallis Simpson was soon recognized in the outer fringe of society to be a hostess of rare ability. She created a small salon noted for its formal dinners with excellent food served in high style, at which about a dozen guests were careful chosen for social status, personal achievement, and possession of wit, sophistication, and a gift for bright brittle chatter.

The Simpson's efforts were rewarded by entry into an expanding circle of social climbers, known at the time as the 'Posh Mayfair Set,' all whom were bent on achieving goals identical with those of Wallis. They hoped to rub shoulders with lesser and possibly even higher nobility. Mayfair was one of the slave markets in London where wealthy Robber Barons of the New World purchased respectability by marrying their daughters to penniless Old World nobles in exile from recently created European republics. From past experience with Vandals and Tartars, the destitute nobles knew that loss of elegance is a price one must expect to pay for world wars and great depressions.

In the summer of 1929, Wallis returned to Baltimore to be with her mother whose health was failing. The New York Stock Market crashed on Tuesday October 29. Her mother was wiped out, penniless, and she died four days later on November 2. Wallis also lost all her personal divorce settlement from Winfield Spencer. However, her second husband Ernest Simpson survived the crash with little loss. The shipping business was a bread-and-butter trade for England. Therefore, Wallis was able to carry on during early years of the depression much as before.

With time, the Simpsons met friends with ties to the nobility and royalty. Their first contact of real importance was with the American Pittsburg heiress Countess Consuelo Morgan de Maupas Thaw (Consuelo's mother was a railroad-Vanderbilt and her father was a steel-Morgan) who was married to Count Jean de Maupas du Juglart of the ancient French nobility. Consuelo's title and money gave her access to the highest levels of London society. Consuelo's closest friend of high station was Russian Princess Nadejda Mikailovna Romanov-Mountbatten Marchioness of Milford Haven—her husband Lord Louis Mountbatten Marquess of Milford Haven was (depending on how one figures those things) the first-cousin-once-removed of King George V. Princess Nadejda was a 'mover and shaker' in Mayfair. She gained personal fame for once winning a *Charleston Dance Competition*, and for other eccentricities. By her friendship with Princess Nadejda, Consuelo Morgan de Maupas Thaw had access to the court of St. James and Buckingham Palace. However, an even closer tie with high society came to Consuelo through her elder sister Viscountess Thelma Morgan Furness (a twin sister of Gloria Morgan Vanderbilt) who married Viscount Marmaduke Baron Furness (of the Furness-Withy Shipping Line fortune). Thelma was the constant companion (i.e., mistress) of Edward Prince of Wales from 1929 until 1932-33.

Edward (known to first name friends as David) was the 'Golden Prince' of the age. He enjoyed occasional slumming with the *hoi polloi* in Mayfair. The prince had a natural taste for rebellion against the stodgy stiffness that characterized his admirable parents: the impeccably correct King George V and his glacially imperial mother Queen Mary of Teck. David was a constant embarrassment to the king and queen when he became the icon for the 'Flapper Years' of the 1920s. David was enormously popular, and was a pace setter for styles and fashion, the likes of which had not been seen since days of the Prince Regent and Beau Brummell a century before. Any remote contact with his person was cause enough for a claim to fame. Lyrics of a popular song of the time expressed this well in the refrain lines:

> "I danced with a man, who danced with a girl,
> Who danced with the Prince of Wales."

However, his estimate of his own ability was candidly realistic; he said, "My place at the British apex is unearned. It demands leadership I do not have."

Wallis met Viscountess Thelma Morgan Furness at a birthday party Countess Consuelo gave for her sister in August 1930, to which the Simpsons were invited. Wallis and Thelma soon became close friends. Eventually, the Simpsons met the Prince of Wales at a social event sponsored by Thelma Furness.

The story comes down that, at the first introduction of Wallis to Prince Edward in the winter season of 1930/31 (possibly January 10, 1931), Prince Edward made a vapid comment, "As an American, do you miss central heating in English homes?" Wallis replied, "I am sorry, but you have disappointed me. Every American woman who comes to your country is always asked that question. I had hoped for something more original from the Prince of Wales."

Edward was probably taken aback by Wallis—a common American with presumption to criticize a royal prince—but he was noted for liberal democratic views, so her disdain of rank possibly piqued his interest in a way that an obsequious response would have failed to be memorable.

In the years 1931-1933, Edward specifically requested that the Simpsons be included in many social events to which he was invited. Independently without formal invitation, he visited the Simpsons at their unpretentious residence on Preston Road adjacent to Mayfair. Prince Edward enjoyed the Simpsons company, but Wallis was the loadstone that made him return.

The social level in which the Simpsons now moved created major financial expenses that were far in excess of Ernest's income. His personal debts created a crisis for the Simpsons.

The turning point for the Edward-Wallis affair came in the winter season of 1932/33, when Thelma Furness returned to New York City for an extended stay. Following Thelma's departure, Wallis was seen alone with Prince Edward at many social events. She was known to travel with the prince without her husband Ernest Simpson. It is believed that she left Ernest and became the prince's mistress early in 1933. Wallis was so firmly in possession of Edward's affection by May that, when Lady Thelma Furness returned to London, she never attempted to reclaim her former place with the Prince of Wales. However, Lady Thelma divorced Viscount Marmaduke Furness in 1933, and moved on to be, for a time, the mistress of the Ali Khan, heir to Saudi Arabian oil billions, but he left her for the ultimate Hollywood sex goddess, Rita Hayworth.

By most standards, Wallis was not beautiful, but she was frequently complimented for having striking lavender blue eyes. She had a refined sense of style, and was famous for elegant dress and manners. She was a vivaciously interesting conversationalist, and Prince Edward was madly infatuated with her. She captivated him—that, of itself, was neither a moral sin, nor a civil crime—but she was never forgiven in England for meddling in royal affairs.

Wallis possessed a domineering manner that offended many of her associates. However, Wallis captivated Edward, and he became dependent on her guidance. By 1934, Edward was obsessed with Wallis, and he could deny her nothing. He was lavish in the gifts of jewels and clothes he gave her. On one social occasion, a person spoke disparagingly of Wallis saying, "She has wonderful taste in clothes, but why does she clutter herself up with all that dreadful costume jewelry?"

To which the reply was, "It's not 'costume', it's the real thing. Edward gives jewels to her hand over fist." A single emerald broach he gave her at the depth of the Depression in 1935 was evaluated at $500,000, but it would be worth ten fold that today. King George V and Queen Mary of Teck objected strenuously to Edward's gifts to Wallis of jewels from the Royal Collection.

Over the years from 1934 to 1936, the Prince of Wales and Wallis were frequently seen in gossip generating and even compromising circumstances in their travels together in Scotland, Switzerland, and places of fashion on the French Riviera. In 1934 without advance notice, Edward presented Wallis to his parents King George V and Queen Mary of Teck at a social event in Buckingham Palace. The king and queen were outraged at having to acknowledge the presence of a divorced woman in court.

By 1934, the Simpson marriage was dissolving, and by 1935, Wallis was the acknowledged *maitresse en titre* of the Prince of Wales. The English court and government was alarmed by the increasing influence Wallis had over Prince Edward at a time when King George's health was rapidly failing.

King George died, and Prince Edward became King Edward VIII on January 20, 1936.

The event that brought matters to a head in late spring of 1936 was word that Wallis had filed for a British divorce from her second husband Ernest Simpson. This was taken as a declaration that she intended to marry King Edward, and that the king agreed that she would be his queen. Her divorce was granted on October 26/27, 1936, but it would not be final until May 4 1937.

The British press had been silent on King Edward's infatuation with Wallis through the summer of 1936. However, gossip about the royal affair was rampant throughout Continental Europe and America.

Finally, in November, everyone in England knew that the king planned to marry a common American divorcée with two living former husbands. The entire Commonwealth went into shock. Dowager Queen Mary expressed the sentiment within the royal family, "It is of course impossible that We (speaking of herself) should ever become acquainted with Mrs. Simpson for Her Majesty (again, referring of herself) would not even for her son alter her decision—no divorced woman can ever be admitted to conversation with the Queen (again, herself) . . . for she (Wallis) is an adventuress!"

Every corner and remote island in the Empire despised Wallis. The English aristocracy hated Wallis because she was an American commoner. English working masses hated her because she was not ashamed of being twice divorced. The British government hated her because she did not fit tidily into English tradition of kings marrying royalty, or at the very least, nobility.

Tradition-conscious social journalists pointed out that there was no exact precedence for an English king to marry a divorced commoner:

> Henry II Plantagenet had married divorced Eleanor of Aquitaine, but Eleanor was noble, a duchess in her own right, and she had been Queen of France.
> Edward IV married commoner Elizabeth Woodville, who had been married with children, but she was widowed, not divorced, before her marriage to the king.
> Anne Boleyn, Jane Seymour, and Katherine Howard all were common, but were neither married nor divorced—anyway who could have stopped Great Harry, once his mind was set to do anything.
> Anne Hyde was common, but she married James II when he was just the Duke of York, not yet a king.

No royal precedent could be found (not that anyone wanted to find one) to save Wallis in the eyes of British subjects.

More to the point for legal minds, the reigning sovereign was also the *Supreme Governor of the Church of England*, and Church tradition adamantly opposed divorce. For the King of England to marry a twice-divorced woman, with two previous husbands still living, was unthinkable. The opposition of the Establishment (*which included Dowager Queen Mary, the entire Windsor family, all career politicians, the old aristocracy, higher clergy, heads of colonies, territories, dominions, and everyone canvassed for an opinion on the suitability of the king's intent to marry Wallis*) found Wallis to be an unacceptable queen. The consensus was unanimous: Wallis could not be Queen of England!

Parliament clearly had every right to approve all royal marriages. The Privy Council adamantly refused to approve of the King's choice of Wallis to be his wife and queen. Prime Minister Stanley Baldwin, with the 1772 Royal Marriages Act of George III gripped firmly in his fist, informed King Edward that he had only three options: *he could either give up the idea of marriage to Wallis altogether and retain the crown, or he could marry*

Wallis in opposition to the will of government and be deposed, or he could abdicate and marry Wallis later. Edward chose the last option.

With his thorough grounding in English history and parliamentary law, it is incredible that Edward could have expected anything other than this Parliamentary ruling. However, as Prince of Wales and then King, Edward was so accustomed to accolades of praise and approval as a popular idol and trend-setter of fashion in the 1920s and '30s, it appears that he was totally unprepared for the opposition he received with regard to desire to make Wallis his queen.

Until November 1936, King Edward and Prime Minister Stanley Baldwin pursued a bluffing game. Neither one thought it would ever come to a marriage, or an abdication. The present perception is that Edward was obsessed with Wallis, and he was unwilling to yield. Baldwin was equally set in his defense of English tradition.

Thus, implacable resistance faced immovable resolve.

In November 1936, Wallis left England to escape constant efforts by the press to interview her. She went to Cannes to wait out finalization of her divorce from Ernest Simpson on May 4 1937. A diplomatic negotiator from 10 Downing Street, Baron Peregrine Cust of Brownlaw, went to Cannes to persuade Wallis to give up Edward in order to avoid a crisis in government that would surely ensue. If she insisted on marrying the king, the government would fall, and a new Parliament would then demand the king's abdication.

Wallis could afford to leave the London social scene with a clear unambiguous title to a fortune in gems from the Crown Collection that Edward the king had given her. She was very well off, and could have survived as a private citizen in a life of great ease. Wallis appears to have been 'an adventuress' (as Queen Mary declared), but apparently, she was not the devious seductress *femme fatale* bent on destroying the British monarchy she was painted to be.

Numerous documents to her friends exist that clearly indicate that Wallis wanted to leave England, and not force the abdication. She possibly proposed to Edward that a 'morganatic marriage' (a marriage between a titled person and a commoner that would be legal, but the common wife would not receive the title rank of her husband) would be acceptable to her. Reports also indicate that Edward may have made a compromise proposal for a morganatic marriage in which Wallis would not be queen, and that none of their children would inherit the throne.

However, at the time, Edward refused to consider the morganatic alternative. Everyone believed that he was determined to marry Wallis and make her his wife and queen!

Prime Minister Baldwin ruled that morganatic marriage was not possible by English Common Law, so that option did not exist.

On December 7, Lord Cust read to the London Press a statement from Wallis that expressed her willingness to give up the king, and return to Baltimore. However, with no willingness to compromise by either the King or Prime Minister, the momentum for abdication moved on, and became a fact.

On December 10, 1936, King Edward VIII signed a document of abdication and made his worldwide shortwave radio speech that announced his decision to give up his throne. His voice (as it came with squeaks and howls of short-wave radio reception from London to the USA) was unexpectedly high, thin, asthmatic, indeed, very British, when he said:

> " . . . But, you must believe me when I tell you that I have
> found it impossible to carry the heavy burden of responsibility
> and to discharge my duties as King, as I would wish to do,
> without the help and support of the woman I love . . . ."

It was very moving and romantic. The abdication played well with much sympathy in America for both Edward and poor Wallis. However, in England the abdication, from beginning to end, was a disaster. The rattle of teacups in Mayfair was deafening. The abdication of Edward VIII was a major crisis for the monarchy. It further emphasized the fact that to be a reigning monarch in England is not a right of birth, but a privilege conferred by Parliament.

Parliament specified that the former king Edward VIII would be exiled from England, and that his name would be deleted from the Civil List. That meant he would need to survive on his own wealth, which was considerable. It included among many other trifles, the great homes of Sandringham and Balmoral that he inherited from his father George V. These two estates he sold to his brother King George VI, and the proceeds became the core for his personal wealth.

Simultaneously with Edward's abdication, his younger brother Albert (known to all as Bertie) became king, and chose to be called King George

VI. He had a timid gray mouse persona, as contrasted with the gilded Galahad image of his deposed brother.

The first official act of George VI was to create his brother Edward, the Duke of Windsor. Edward initially hoped that he could be mentor to help his brother learn his duties as king. However, that role for the deposed king was resoundingly vetoed when he was ordered into exile.

George VI generously restored from his own pocket, Edward's former annuity from the Civil List. It carried the provision that Edward could not return to England without an invitation approved by King George VI or his government. Edward as Duke of Windsor was informed that he would retain the honor of being addressed HRH (His Royal Highness). However, if he married Wallis Warfield, she would be styled only, the Duchess of Windsor. She was denied the right of address as *Her Royal Highness*. The establishment adamantly opposed giving Wallis royal recognition.

The Duke and Duchess of Windsor never forgave this arbitrary ruling, which in essence, denied Wallis full membership in the Royal Family. Wallis never was given royal status, and it would be many years before she entered England, or was received by King George VI and Queen Elizabeth (The Queen Mum).

Immediately after his abdication in December 1936, Edward of Windsor left England, and went to Austria where, as a guest of Baron Eugen de Rothschild at his estate Schloss Enzesfeld in the hills south of Vienna, Edward remained until Wallis's divorce was final in May 4, 1937. The divorce legally expunged names of her first two husbands; thereafter she was simply Wallis Warfield, with no recognition of past marriages.

Edward and Wallis were married in Paris on June 3, 1937 at Château de Candé lent them for the occasion. The English Royal Family was invited, but none of them chose to attend. With her marriage to Edward, Wallis became the Duchess of Windsor. The childless marriage lasted for thirty-six years until the death of Edward in 1972.

In the two years leading up to open hostilities of World War II in autumn of 1939, the Duke and Duchess of Windsor were strongly criticized for their frequent friendly associations with persons of power and influence in Germany. In 1937, they were guests of Hitler himself. They were strongly suspected of being Nazi sympathizers. Their loyalty was distrusted in both England and America.

When war finally broke out in October 1939, Edward was given a military appointment as British Army Field Marshall in France. With the invasion and fall of France in May and June 1940, the Windsors fled with aid from German sympathizers to Spain, and then to Portugal. It is reputed that they requested and were given German guards to protect their properties in Paris and the Riviera during the German occupation of France from 1940 to 1944.

In August 1940, Edward was appointed Governor of the Bahamas Islands, where he served in Nassau for five years until the fall of Nazi Germany in 1945. His appointment was motivated by the desire of Winston Churchill and Franklin Roosevelt to isolate Edward where he could do little damage to the Allied war effort by leaking information of value to the German government in the time of war. Heads of government and many diplomats suspected that Hitler planned to restore Edward (who was assumed to be pro-German) as King of England after the Battle of Britain defeated the Island Nation. Fortunately, that never came about.

In his autobiography, *A King's Story* (1951), Edward explained his views on Germany, "It was in Britain's interest, and in Europe's too, that Germany be encouraged to strike east and smash Communism forever . . . I thoughts the rest of us could have been fence-sitters, while the Nazis and the Reds slogged it out."

Wallis apparently shared Edward's views on Germany, but she also was embittered against England for its lack of acceptance of her as queen. She had little concern for what might befall the stuffy little island.

Edward and Wallis despised their assignment to Nassau, and referred to 1940-1945 as their 'St. Helena Years' (in reference to Napoleon's final imprisonment on that island). Whilst in the Bahamas, the Windsors made occasional highly criticized shopping trips to Miami and New York, where Wallis bought extravagant clothes at a time of great austerity and bombing in London.

Edward was a patronizing governor in the Bahamas. Edward was admired for his efforts to improve the standard for living of working classes in the Bahamas, but at the same time, he was outspoken in racist contempt for the Bahamian natives.

After the fall of Berlin, Edward resigned his Bahamas governorship on March 16, 1945. The Windsors returned to Paris to live out their lives at their estate in the Bois Boulogne at 4 Rue du Champ d'Entraînement, Neuilly-sur-Seinne. Their residence was provided at reduced rate by the City of Paris. The French government gave them income-tax-free status, and the British government provided tax-free privilege for purchase of items through the embassy commissary. The English and French generosity suggests that the Duke and Duchess of Windsor were charity cases, but in fact, their wealth was enormous.

The Duke and Duchess of Windsor were the most widely recognized celebrities in the world in the 1950s and 1960s. As world celebrities, they travelled aimlessly in Europe and America, and were seen at the right places in correct seasons as guests of the rich and powerful in Europe and America. However, their individual accomplishments were modest. The Duke received praise for promoting pug dogs as desirable house pets, and the Duchess was always listed among the ten best dressed women in the world.

The return of the duke and duchess to England was infrequent, and at discretion of the Royal Family. Edward attended some invited occasions, but Wallis generally refused invitations to England in protest against her being denied HRH status, and for her knowledge that she would never be accepted as a member of the Royal Family. Edward's mother the Dowager Queen Mary made clear that she would never under any circumstance receive Wallis; she irritated Edward by saying to him, "[How could you] give up all this for that [Wallis]!"

In 1952, Edward was in London for the funeral of his brother King George VI, but Wallis stayed in Paris. However, in 1967 the Duke and Duchess of Windsor accepted an invitation from Queen Elizabeth II to attend the unveiling of a portrait of Queen Mary of Teck (who died in 1853) to commemorate the hundredth anniversary of her birth. It is reported that, when Wallis was presented to Queen Elizabeth's mother the 'Queen Mum,' they shook hands, and the Queen Mum said, "How nice to see you." They exchanged a few pleasantries. Then the Queen Mum said, "I hope we meet again." to which Wallis blurted, "When?" The Queen Mum smiled, raised her eyes, and walked away to greet other guests.

On that occasion, Wallis did not curtsy to the Dowager Queen Mum. Later, when asked why she failed to bow, Wallis said, "She stopped people from curtsying to me. Why should I curtsy to her?"

Neither the Duke nor Duchess was a person of great ability or originality. Guests at Bois de Boulogne were constantly astonished by the narrow interests, and banality of opinions expressed by the Duke and Duchess of Windsor. Both Wallis and Edward put out 'ghostwritten' autobiographies that attempted whitewash their lives into flattering romances (i.e., Edward's, *A King's Story,* 1951; Wallis's, *The Heart Has Its*

Reasons, 1977). However, sighs were muted and tears were few when Wallis said, "You have no idea how hard it is to live out a great romance."

In the late 1960s, some members of the Royal Family visited the Duke and Duchess of Windsor at their Bois de Boulogne estate near Paris. Among them were Queen Elizabeth II and Prince Charles who went shortly before Edwards's death in 1972.

Edward Duke of Windsor turned seventy in 1964, and multiple medical problems surfaced that sapped the duke's vitality, and his desire for social activity. He was diagnosed for throat cancer in 1971. It resisted radiation treatment, and was the immediate cause of his death at age seventy-seven at their home in Paris on May 28, 1972. His body was returned to England for burial. Wallis was an invited guest of Queen Elizabeth II at Buckingham Palace to attend Edward's funeral at St. George's Chapel, and for his burial at the Frogmore Royal Mausoleum at Windsor.

Wallis was rarely seen in public after Edward's death. She lived in her French mansion for fourteen more years in increasingly frail senile health until almost the age of ninety. Around 1970, she developed arteriosclerosis, after which associates reported frequent memory lapses. During those years, Queen Elizabeth II continued to pay Wallis's annuity, which had first been given to Edward by her father George VI in 1936. During the last five years of her life, Wallis was a bedridden invalid who gradually lost all awareness of her surroundings.

Wallis died on April 24, 1986 two months before her ninetieth birthday. She was given a State funeral in St. George's Chapel, followed by burial beside Edward at Frogmore. Queen Elizabeth, Prince Philip, Prince Charles, and Princess Diana were present at her funeral and burial. Her grave memorial says only:

Wallis, Duchess of Windsor

After her death and the auction of her estate, Wallis's monetary wealth was revealed. Historically important 17th and 18th century furniture and house decorations were given to the French State Office of Antiquities The rest was sold at auction and earned £14 million. Her personal jewelry raised an additional £45 million. Almost all her estate went to French charitable foundations, with the major benefactor being the Pasteur Institute for

Medical Research. Her generosity revealed a charitable concern that was never suspected by those who knew her.

No important part of her estate went to any British person or institution. That omission confirmed a statement she made many years before to Edward when King George VI died and Elizabeth II became queen in 1952. Wallis said, "I hate this country, and shall hate it to my grave."

Wallis Warfield Duchess of Windsor is an enigmatic person, who has endlessly fascinated authors. Wallis's private world revolved around self-promotion and gratification of social ambition. Her life story is of little importance today. At the time of the abdication of Edward VIII in 1936, *Time Magazine* named her *Woman of the Year* for 1936. The magazine predicted that the *Edward-Wallis Romance* would be the *Signature Event of the 20th Century*.

After Edward gave up his crown, Wallis had no intrinsic importance. Her aimless self-promotion was of little concern in a world threatened by a succession of crises beginning with World War II.

In the 21st century, the *Edward-Wallis Romance* is all but forgotten. After a tempestuous three-quarter century, the romance is merely a footnote to history. However, in its day, the abdication was a blinding meteoric event that eclipsed everything for a dazzling moment in 1936.

REIGN 40

KING GEORGE VI

AND

QUEEN CONSORT ELIZABETH BOWES-LYON

Summary of the Reign of King George VI (Reign 1936-1952)

King George VI: life dates 56 years, b. December 14, 1895-d. February 6, 1952; King of Great Britain c. 16 years, December 12, 1936-February 6, 1952.

KING GEORGE VI was the second son of King George V and Queen Mary of Teck. He was born in 1895 at York Cottage on the Sandringham estate at Norfolk on December 14. He was named *Albert* on Queen Victoria's request, because his birth fell on the anniversary of the death of Queen Victoria's Prince Consort Albert. Throughout his life, his family called him Bertie.

The education of George VI was with a view of a career in the Royal Navy. However, following the abdication of his older brother Edward VIII, he ascended the throne in 1936 as King George VI. He was not a likely candidate to be king, and for a time, it was even proposed that he be bypassed for his younger brother Prince George Duke of Kent who had two sons, but that was soon rejected.

Albert Duke of York had little preparation for, and no desire to be the King of Great Britain. The growing threat of Hitler overshadowed everything in the late 1930's. The reign of George VI covered the span of four years before the beginning of World War II, the war itself, and the six years following it. The names of Hitler, Mussolini, Tojo, Stalin, Churchill, Roosevelt occupied center stage for the political and military battles, and crises that went on around the world following the Munich Crisis of 1938 until 1945. As a figurehead with no power, he did his best to support worthy causes, and provide an example of 'stiff upper lip' courage to the people of England during World War II. George VI had no responsibility or control over progress of the war.

Following the War, the Empire began to crumble. India moved toward national independence under leadership of Mohandas Gandhi. Ireland, African Colonies (Egypt, Rhodesia, Tanganyika, South Africa, etc.), even Australia and Canada wanted more independence. As the Empire disintegrated, members of the Commonwealth sought independent status among world nations as autonomous dominions or republics.

In spite of his shy retiring nature and with unremitting effort to serve his subjects, King George VI earned the love and respect of his people. At the age of fifty-seven after a reign of sixteen years (1936-1952), He died quietly in sleep at Sandringham House, Norfolk. He is buried at St. George's Chapel Windsor.

His Queen Consort Lady Elizabeth Bows-Lyon was born in 1900, and was affectionately known as *The Queen Mum*. They were married in 1923, and had two daughters: Princess Elizabeth and Princess Margaret.

Queen Elizabeth Bowes-Lyon died at Windsor on March 30, 2002 at age 101, and was buried at St. George's Chapel, Windsor with King George VI.

Following the death of her father George VI, Princess Elizabeth ascended the throne in 1952 as Queen Elizabeth II.

Narrative of Queen Consort Elizabeth Bowes-Lyon

Queen Elizabeth Bowes-Lyon: life dates 101 years, b. August 4, 1900-d. March 30, 2002; Duchess of York wife of Albert (George) Duke of York 13 years, April 26, 1923-December 12, 1936; Queen Consort of King George VI 16 years, December 12, 1936-February 6, 1952; Dowager Queen Mother (The Queen Mum) 50 years, February 6, 1952-March 30, 2002.

QUEEN ELIZABETH Bowes-Lyon was the ninth of ten children born to Lord Claude George Bowes-Lyon of Glamis and Lady Cecilia Nina Cavendish-Bentinck. Her father later became the 14th Earl of Strathmore and Kinghorne of the Scottish nobility. Her hereditary background had many ancient noble connections, but she was far down among siblings in her own family, so she had no title of her own. Therefore, technically, she was a 'commoner.' She was born on August 4, 1900, and registered at the village of Hitchin-Waldon Bury north of London.

Her childhood was divided between residences of relatives in England and Scotland. However, most often, she lived at her father's Strathmore country estate at Walden Bury, England, or at Glamis Castle, Scotland (the same castle named in Shakespeare's *Macbeth*). Governesses and tutors taught Elizabeth at home in a manner usual for aristocratic families. Her learning was sufficiently sound by the age of thirteen for her to pass entrance examinations to Oxford University, but she did not attend any institution of higher learning.

World War I began in 1914 on her fourteenth birthday. Glamis Castle was converted into a convalescent hospital for injured Scottish soldiers, and Lady Elizabeth earned high praise for her assistance in nursing wounded service men. In this experience, she learned, and never forgot how to respect and deal with persons from all cultural levels with empathy and understanding—it was a gift that won the hearts to her subjects when she became queen.

After the war ended in 1918, Lady Elizabeth spent much of her time in London, where she enjoyed being part of the young aristocratic court life. In that setting, she met Prince Albert Duke of York the second son of

King George V. Prince Albert was next in line for the throne after his older brother Edward Prince of Wales.

Prince Albert Duke of York, who would become her husband and King George VI, was known to all as 'Bertie.' He had been a weak sickly child. His father King Edward VII required him to wear splints to correct his knock-knees, and for a time he wore braces to correct his posture. He was naturally left-handed, but was required to write with his right hand. That ill-advised restraint may account for the pronounced stutter that characterized his speech over much of his life. His speech problem rendered him almost incoherent in social address.

Albert served honorably in World War I as a young naval officer in the important Battle of Jutland that demonstrated superiority of the British Navy over the highly acclaimed ships of the Kaiser's fleet. After the war, Bertie transferred to the air arm of the navy and earned his wings as a pilot. He kept his appointment in the Royal Naval Air Service, which required frequent assignment to Portsmouth and other naval posts. He was conscientious in doing his best in everything he attempted, but he was never a scholar, or accused having more than a mediocre intellect.

Albert had brown eyes, and he grew up to have medium height and a slender military build with perfect posture. He was painfully shy, and lacked social confidence to such a degree that, even as a prince second in line to the throne, he could hardly bring himself to converse with fashionable young ladies in court. Bertie was so socially insecure that it took over a year for him to find enough courage to declare his love for Lady Elizabeth Bowes-Lyon in 1921. His first stammering proposal of marriage to her was refused. Elizabeth's reason was, "[I was] afraid never, never again to be free to think, speak, and act as I feel I really ought to."

Prince Albert was not deterred by Elizabeth's first refusal. He informed the Royal Family of his determination to marry her, even though she was without a noble title. He persuaded his stratospherically correct mother Queen Mary of Teck to meet Lady Elizabeth Bowes-Lyon in hope of getting her essential approval for Elizabeth's acceptance into the Royal House of Windsor. Such a miss match in the status of a bride and groom was almost unheard of. It would also require government approval.

Queen Mary made a special visit to Glamis Castle in Scotland as a guest of the Earl and Countess of Strathmore and Kinghorne for the express purpose of meeting their youngest daughter Elizabeth Bowes-Lyon. Queen Mary came away convinced that Lady Elizabeth was an acceptable bride for her son Bertie. She informed King George V "[Lady Elizabeth] is the one girl who can make Bertie happy." Therefore, the courtship was allowed to continue without family interference. Several noble swains courted Lady Elizabeth, but after two years, Bertie was able to persuade her to marry him in January 1923.

With the King, and Queen, and the Privy Council's approval, the royal marriage was permitted to proceed, even though the bride was a commoner. In this, the Privy Council prided itself in being politically up-to-date for winking at the breach in propriety they approved. The liberal ruling on the wedding was based on an assumption that Bertie of Windsor and Elizabeth Bowes-Lyon would never sit on the throne as king and queen. Everyone knew that Bettie's flashy older brother Edward Prince of Wales would be the next sovereign.

With family and government approval, Prince Bertie Duke of York married Lady Elizabeth Bowes-Lyon at Westminster Abbey on April 26, 1923. On her way into the Abbey, either by accident or with an intuitive sense of grace, Lady Elizabeth briefly rested her bridal bouquet on the Tomb of the Unknown Soldier. For this simple act, Elizabeth immediately won high favor in the realm. After the marriage, the young couple lived modestly in Mayfair. Duke Albert continued in his employment in the Royal Naval Air Service. Between 1926 and 1930, the Duke and Duchess of York had two daughters:

> Elizabeth (April 21, 1926-present), now Queen Elizabeth II.
> Margaret (August 21, 1930-February 9, 2002), Countess of
>   Snowdon.

The two princesses were educated at home by tutors in a permissive environment that avoided high standards for breadth or depth of learning. No one expected that either child would require learning beyond that needed for the give-and-take of well-bred ladies in court.

The Duke and Duchess of York from 1924 through 1927 were involved as travelling royal emissaries to nations and remote corners of the British Commonwealth. Elizabeth had an easy democratic way of meeting everyone, which earned her the name, 'The Smiling Duchess.' On a visit to the Fiji Islands she earned laughs and affection by shaking hands with everyone in a long receiving line that included a wandering dog that held up its paw, which she also graciously shook.

Bertie found the necessity to give public greetings and speeches trying. Elizabeth patiently assisted him in years of speech lesions that eventually corrected his major stammering problem, but to the end of his life, an ingrained tendency to stutter rendered his oral communications labored and almost without expression.

In the early 1930 years of the Great Depression, the family of the Duke and Duchess of York lived quietly in their London residence away from most court activities. Their daily life was prosaic for a young married couple with small children.

With the death of King George V, Edward Prince of Wales ascended the throne as King Edward VIII. His reign began on January 20, 1936, and ended in abdication less than a year later on December 10 of the same year. The abdication crisis dominated his entire reign, and involved his mistress Wallis (Warfield) Spencer-Simpson. King Edward was determined to marry her, and make her his queen. This was unalterably opposed by all segments of the British government.

With King Edward's abdication on December 10/12, 1936, the monarch's duties fell on Edward's younger brother Prince Albert Duke of York, who chose to be called King George VI in honor of his father George V. He was the most reluctant monarch in England's history. However, his strong sense of duty forced him to accept his unwanted new duties, and to do his best to serve.

George VI had no inkling of the impending abdication by Edward VIII until just a few days before it occurred. When he heard that he would be king, he was horrified. He said to his cousin and mentor Lord Louis Mountbatten, "This is absolutely terrible. I never wanted this to happen. I'm quite unprepared for it. David (Edward VIII) has been trained to reign all his life. I've never even seen a State paper. I'm only a Naval Officer, it's the only thing I know about."

Lord Louis replied, "George, you're wrong. There is no more fitting preparation for a King, than to have been trained in the Royal Navy."

The recent abdication of Edward VIII hung over the opening reign of George VI like a lowering thunderhead. At the coronation, it is said, "King George and Queen Elizabeth felt like stand-ins called at the last minute to take center stage, because the star performer had taken ill."

George VI and Queen Elizabeth Bowes-Lyon were crowned in Westminster Abbey on May 12, 1937. The ceremony was filmed, but not simultaneously broadcast. The delay was felt necessary, because the king's stuttering might present difficulties. However, the film was released with little editing, and received worldwide viewing and approval.

The British monarchy was at its lowest level of approval when George VI ascended to the throne. The reign of George VI covered a span of sixteen years: four years before the beginning of World War II in 1939, through the end of the war in 1945, and the six and a half years following it until 1952. His subjects would soon be forced to accept the hardship of four years of war.

King George VI had no ability to alter the course of events during his reign. By parliamentary dictatorial fiat, he was denied any right to criticize, and was required to endorse all government policies. Thus, as King, he was irrationally criticized for supporting Neville Chamberlain's 'appeasement policy' in the Munich Pact of September 30, 1938 that authorized Germany to swallow Czechoslovakia in exchange for 'peace in our time.' Momentum for war rapidly accelerated in Europe after capitulation brought on by the Munich agreement, which gave Hitler encouragement for unrestrained aggression.

King George, with Queen Elizabeth at his side, set a standard for loyal service that stabilized the throne, and energized stout Englishmen, Scotsmen, and Welshmen to sustained commitments for victory at a time when there was little cause for hope of survival. Queen Elizabeth's motto from her mother, "*Duty is the rent you pay for your life*" helped her to sustain the king and the nation.

In an effort to strengthen ties with the United States, which at the time was overwhelmingly isolationist, King George and Queen Elizabeth made a highly successful goodwill tour to the United States. Theirs was the first visit to the United States by a crowned King or Queen of England. They were fêted in State dinners in Washington D.C., and famously at President Franklin Roosevelt and Eleanor's country estate on the Hudson River in New York State. At a cookout on the lawn at Hyde Park, 'hotdogs,' Virginia ham, cranberry sauce, strawberry shortcake, coffee, and beer were served *alfresco*. Queen Elizabeth charmed everyone with her indomitably cheerful acceptance of every surprise with good humor and grace. Eleanor Roosevelt said after the royal visit, "[Queen Elizabeth] was perfect as a Queen, gracious, informed, and kind in saying the right thing, but a little self-consciously regal."

The American people and government enthusiastically accepted the king and queen. The visit was of major diplomatic importance, because shortly thereafter Roosevelt signed an agreement approved by Congress to give England aid in the looming conflict with Germany.

Hitler's Wehrmacht invaded Poland only thee months later on September 1, 1939.

Lady Elizabeth Bowes-Lyon, as the Duchess of York and later as Queen Elizabeth, was always a great asset to her husband. Her natural easy social manner was crowned by a flawless sense of the right thing to do at the time. She enhanced the status of the crown with her decision about what the royal family would do when Germany bombed London. Strong pressure was expressed to have the two princesses (Elizabeth and Margaret) sent to Canada for their safety. The queen said simply, "The Princesses will not go without me. I will not go without the King. The King will not leave his people. You will find us at Buckingham Palace or Windsor."

King George VI, Queen Elizabeth, and the young princesses Elizabeth and Margaret quickly endeared themselves with the English public. They created a new image of the royal family as one of domestic serenity, much like any ideal ordinary middle class folk of England. For family safety, the Royal Family at night usually retired to Windsor about twenty miles from central London. However, in the morning, like many other out-of-town workers, they regularly returned to London to face their work schedules. From Buckingham Palace, they forayed out on morale building visits to military bases, munitions factories, and convalescent hospitals.

As wave after wave of night bombers from Germany devastated parts of London and surrounding cities in the Battle for Britain, much of the queen's time was spent in visiting disaster areas. She always dressed carefully and only wore muted pastel colors. She never wore black or dark colors to avoid emphasizing the depressing times that faced the nation. Her stated desire was to give England " . . . a rainbow of hope." However, early in the war, she was criticized for dressing expensively at a time when many citizens of London had lost everything from air raids. She silenced her critics by explaining "If you visited me out of respect, you would wear your best. So, out of respect for you, I am doing the same in visiting you."

The Queen never lost her intuitive social touch. When several bombs landed on Buckingham Palace, she said on radio to the people of London, "Now we can look you in the East End in the face. We can understand."

In the darkest hours of the Battle for Britain, the King and Queen represented the national resolve to withstand defeat. Hitler denounced Queen Elizabeth, "She is the most dangerous woman in Europe" for her intransigent patriotism, which prevented Englishmen from accepting inevitable defeat.

Through World War II, the King George played virtually no part in determining government policy. He loyally supported the succession of Prime Ministers: first was Stanley Baldwin, who had engineered the abdication of Edward VIII. Next came Neville Chamberlain, whose *Munich Agreement* with Hitler was naïvely believed would bring *peace in our time*. However, instead, it allowed Hitler to take Czechoslovakia, Poland, and Norway. Then came Winston Churchill, who guided England through the war to victory in 1945. Disillusion after the war led to rejection of Churchill, and his replacement by Clement Attlee, who headed the first Labor Government, which nationalized service industries, and created the National Health Service.

King George VI served as a Constitutional Monarch without criticism from contemporaries in public life, or from subsequent historians. King George VI was not among the leaders of events during his time. However, he was admired for doing his duty faithfully as a figurehead with no power. He provided a personal example of the expectation that 'every Englishman will do his duty.' At the end of his reign of almost sixteen years, he had earned respect and affection from his subjects. His presence strengthened the monarchy at a time of great stress. England was grateful for his quiet devotion to service.

Shortly after the war ended, his eldest daughter Princess Elizabeth married her cousin Prince Philip Mountbatten in 1947. Their first child, Prince Charles, was born the following year. Queen Elizabeth was delighted in becoming the grandmother of the four children of her daughter Queen Elizabeth II and Prince Philip: Charles Prince of Wales, Anne Princess Royal, Andrew Duke of York, and Edward Earl of Wessex.

In September 1951, King George was diagnosed with lung cancer caused by many years of excessive smoking, and his left lung was removed, although, he was not expected to recover. He died peacefully in his sleep four months later at Sandringham House, Norfolk early on February 6, 1952.

Following the death of her father, Princess Lilibet, came to the throne as Queen Elizabeth II, and her mother Elizabeth Bowes-Lyon became the Dowager Queen Mother. After Dowager Queen Mary of Teck died on March 24, 1953, Queen Elizabeth Bowes-Lyon was the uncontested matriarch of the House of Windsor.

In 1958, a Canadian newscaster felicitously referred to the Dowager Queen Mother Elizabeth, as *The Queen Mum*. The name immediately resonated as an appropriate expression of the deep public affection for the queen mother, a love that had been earned throughout the Commonwealth. For the next half-century, until her death at almost 102 years, Elizabeth Bowes-Lyon was affectionately known as the one-and-only *Queen Mum*.

Uncharacteristically for her usual irrepressible optimistic nature, she fell into a deep depression in 1952 following the death of her husband George VI. She took refuge from the world by going to her Castle of Mey on the coast at the northern tip of Scotland. To occupy her time, she renovated the ancient structure, and rebuilt its surrounding gardens.

After an appropriate time for mourning, Winston Churchill visited her at the Castle of Mey, and prevailed upon her to return to public life in 1953. They had the mutual admiration of one conservative for another. Soon, Dowager Queen Elizabeth was as busy sponsoring worthwhile public endeavors, as had been her custom as queen. In the next forty years of her life, she lent her name to over three hundred goodly causes. Among the first was as sponsor for creation of the University College of Rhodesia-and-Nyasaland (now the University of Zimbabwe), created as a multiracial institution, among the first of its kind. She was inaugurated as its first Honorary President when the university opened in 1957.

It was during her dowager years, as goodwill ambassador for the British Commonwealth, that she invented the image of how a queen should appear in public. Her costume included a hat with upturned brim to reveal her face, dresses always muted floral, expensive tasteful jewels, a wave of hand, and nod of head to the passing throng. The style is preserved by her daughter Queen Elizabeth II, and by her caricature, Mrs. Bucket, in the television series *Keeping up Appearances*.

The Queen Mum made over one hundred public service appearances each year until after she was ninety years old. She was regal-with-a-common-touch that permitted her to react with persons of every social background, and endeared her to the English people. Although she was deeply conservative, she was without bigotry or bias against any social class, religion, or gender preference. Two friends from theater and films were the gifted gay writers Noël Coward and Summerset Maugham. She enjoyed with them an exchange of wit and a stiff belt of gin, as was usual with her favored acquaintants.

The Queen Mum was famous for her unquenchable good humor and possession of an ability to cope with difficult social situations with originality and grace. The admired actor Sir Peter Ustinov added luster to the Dowager Queen's image by reporting on her response to a ribald greeting she received from Scottish students at the University of Dundee in 1968, "As we arrived in a solemn procession, the students pelted us with rolls of toilet paper. They kept hold of one end, like streamers at a ball, and threw the other end at us. The Queen Mother stooped and picked them up [she returned them to the students and said] 'Was this yours?' Or, 'Could you take this?' as though someone had carelessly misplaced them."

The Queen Mum was a collector of French Impressionist and English art, and of Fabergé artifacts, all of which were given to Elizabeth II as additions to the Royal Collection. However, she is also remembered for active interest in steeplechase horse racing. She acquired a stable of horses, and they competed against those of other stables, including the horses that belonged of her daughter Queen Elizabeth II. The Queen Mum made substantial winnings from the performance of her horses, but, as a rule, she did not also place bets on races.

The Queen Mum had enormous vitality, and remained active until only a few months before the end of her life at the age of 101. In 1995, she had a cataract operation, and another surgery to replace her left hip, which was broken in a fall at her stable in Sandringham. In the same year, she insisted in standing for hours to show respect for a parade in London that commemorated the fiftieth anniversary of the end of World War II.

At a banquet in celebration of her hundredth birthday in 2000, the Archbishop of Canterbury reached for a glass of wine to make a toast to her, but he was stopped when the Queen Mum protested and said, "That's mine!" Which made the occasion especially memorable.

In spite of falling several times and breaking bones, the Queen Mum appeared to be indestructible. In December 2001 at age 101, she fell and broke her hip, but two months later she stood through the national anthem at a 50th year memorial service for the death of her husband George VI on February 6, 2002. Three days later her youngest daughter Princess Margaret died in London on February 9. On February 13, 2002, the Queen Mum stumbled and injured her arm at Sandringham House. She was carried by wheelchair to St. George's Chapel for Princess Margaret's private family funeral. The Queen Mum requested that no pictures be taken to show her as an invalid.

She remained at the Royal Lodge, Windsor until March 30, 2002 when she died peacefully in her sleep without recovering entirely from her previous fall at Sandringham. At 101 years of age, the Queen Mum had been Dowager Queen for fifty years, the longest anyone had been dowager queen in English history.

The Queen Mother's personal estate was worth nearly £70 million. Aside from personal charities, most of her wealth established trusts for her great-grandchildren—the eight grandchildren of Queen Elizabeth II and the four grandchildren of Princess Margaret. About one-third of the Dowager Queen's estate went to the private Windsor Family Trust in the name of her daughter Queen Elizabeth II.

A quarter-million people passed her casket as she lay in state at Westminster Hall. At her request, her funeral wreath was placed on the Grave of the Unknown Soldier in Westminster Abbey, as a grace note reprise of her placing her wedding corsage on the monument at her wedding seventy-nine years before. The twenty-three miles from Westminster to Winsor was lined by silent crowds who watched the catafalque carry the Queen Mum's casket for burial at St. George's Chapel with King George VI.

As the Queen Mum, Elizabeth Bowes-Lyon was the most highly admired member of the Royal Family through times when other royalty cavorted in less than regal ways. Until her death in 2002, just four months shy her 102nd birthday, she was profoundly respected as a credit to her noble origins and for service to her subjects. A bronze statue of Elizabeth Bowes-Lion stands in The Mall in front of the statue of her husband King George VI; both are dressed regally as Knights of the Order of the Garter.

REIGN 41

QUEEN REGNANT ELIZABETH II

AND

PRINCE CONSORT PHILIP MOUNTBATTEN

Narrative of Queen Elizabeth II
(Reign 1952-present)

Queen Elizabeth II: life dates 2011 85 years, b. April 21, 1926-present [2011]; Queen Regnant of Great Britain 59 years, February 6, 1952-to present [2011].

QUEEN ELIZABETH II is the eldest daughter of King George VI and Queen Elizabeth Bowes-Lyon, the Queen Mum. She was born by Caesarean section on April 21, 1926 at her maternal grandfather's home in Mayfair, London. As a child, her family called her *Lilibet*. Her younger sister Princess Margaret was born in 1930, and the sisters were privately educated at home before her father came to the throne. Detailed instruction was neglected on matters of court manners and protocol, as unnecessarily restrictive for children of the Duke of York.

As a small child, Elizabeth was described as "a jolly little girl, but fundamentally sensible and well-behaved." However, on the abdication by her uncle King Edward VIII in 1936 when Elizabeth was ten, a high level of certainty predicted that some day she would be queen. She was the *heir presumptive to the crown*—'presumptive' because there was still a possibility that the king and queen, her parents, might have a son. In which case, he would replace her as first in line of succession to the throne. It is reputed that Elizabeth prayed fervently for a younger brother.

After her father George VI came to the throne in 1936, when Lilibet was ten and Margaret six, the children spent much time with their grandmother Dowager Queen Mary of Teck, who became their instructor on correct behavior in court. With their grandmother as teacher, they were taught everything that could be known about aristocratic manners and the decorum required of royalty. The children were drilled in history of the royal family, in manners, and etiquette for greeting persons of all ranks. They were also instructed in formal protocol for behavior and address for State occasions. Tutors were brought in for a standard program of studies on literature, arts, humanities, and sciences. In addition, the princesses received in-depth instruction from specialists on English Common Law, Parliamentary government, and conversational French by native teachers.

The sisters had very different temperaments and personalities. Elizabeth liked and wanted to learn everything that would be needed when she reigned. She was a willing intelligent perceptive student but, for amusement, she preferred horse riding to intellectual pursuits. Once during her tutoring, Princess Lilibet criticized someone by saying, "When I am Queen we will do that very differently." Whereupon, Queen Mary chided her by saying, "Before one becomes a Queen, my dear, one must first learn to be a Lady."

Princess Margaret's exposure to Queen Mary's instruction was less seriously endured. Her merry rebellious nature found as much to laugh about, as to take seriously in the formal acrobatics of court manners. It is reported that when the young princesses first heard that their father, the Duke of York, would become king, Princess Margaret asked Lilibet, "Does that mean you are going to be the next Queen?" To which Lilibet seriously replied, "Yes, someday, I guess." Margaret sadly said, "Poor you."

As a teenager during the World War II years, Elizabeth was on the home front in the Auxiliary Army. She served mainly as a lorry (truck) driver. The royal family respected wartime restrictions by living austerely at Windsor and Buckingham Palace when social display was cut back to a minimum.

After the war, Princess Elizabeth met, became engaged to, and eventually married her cousin Prince Philip Mountbatten of Greece & Denmark. His parents were Prince Andrew of Greece & Denmark and Princess Alice Mountbatten (née Battenberg).

Princess Elizabeth and Prince Philip are third cousins through descent from their great-great-grandparents Queen Victoria and Prince Albert, and they are also second cousins once removed through the Royal House of Denmark. Elizabeth's great-grandmother Queen Alexandra of Denmark was the elder sister of King George I of Greece, who was Prince Philip's grandfather. Prince Philip chose to adopt his mother's surname *Mountbatten*, after the Greek monarchy was terminated by civil war in 1923.

Philip moved to England as the favored nephew of his mother's brother, Lord Louis Mountbatten Marquess of Milford Haven. Lord Louis was Philip's advisor and mentor, who suggested that Philip follow a career in the Royal Navy. Lord Louis Mountbatten was held in high esteem in the British court and government for his many services to the crown. Among other things, he was the last Viceroy of India at the time India acquired independence in 1947.

When Prince Philip moved to England and became an English citizen, he renounced his royal titles, and his Greek and Danish nationalities. As a commoner, Philip became simply Mr. Philip Mountbatten when he entered the Royal Navy as a cadet with the intention to make that his career.

Family tradition says that thirteen year old Princess Elizabeth fell in love with her cousin Philip Mountbatten when they met in 1939. That happened when King George VI and his royal family were on a tour of inspection at the Royal Naval College in Dartmouth, and Philip was an eighteen year old naval cadet. Elizabeth and Philip corresponded frequently, and became engaged in July 1947 when she was twenty-one.

Their wedding four months later on November 20, 1947 was televised and filmed in Westminster Abbey. The event was an international theatrical triumph seen around the world. At the time of his marriage to Elizabeth,

Philip was created His Royal Highness Duke of Edinburgh. He was raised to the rank of prince in 1957, when he was given precedence over his children and the living sons of George V.

Following their marriage in 1947, the young couple first rented a dwelling near Windsor Castle, but later, they were given Clarence House as their London residence. Philip's naval service often required him to be away from England, often in Malta, during the years before Elizabeth became queen. After she became queen, Prince Philip continued to serve as an officer in the Royal Navy, and later he became Admiral of the Fleet and Marshal of the Royal Air Force.

From 1948 to 1950, Elizabeth was called upon to assume social responsibilities for her father as his health continued to decline. In October 1951, Elizabeth and Philip left England on a long planned goodwill tour around the world. They visited Canada, were guests of President Harry S Truman in Washington, D. C., and were in Kenya en route to Australia and New Zealand when they were informed that King George VI died on February 6, 1952. Princess Elizabeth was now Queen Elizabeth II. The travelling party returned immediately to London.

Elizabeth came to the throne two months before her twenty-sixth birthday. Her coronation on June 2, 1953 was televised alive, and was watched by millions round the world. At the time, the new title, Head of the Commonwealth, was added to the many titles the British sovereign carries.

A small matter of concern to the Commonwealth was the surname of the new queen. Most people assumed that Queen Elizabeth would carry her husband's name, and she would be known as Queen Elizabeth Mountbatten. However, on Prime Minister Winston Churchill's recommendation, Parliament ruled that the name *Windsor* would still apply as the name of the Royal Family—so, it has remained *Windsor*. Prince Philip strenuously objected, and said, "Am I the only man in this country that is not allowed to give his name to his wife and to his own children?"

In 1960, a compromise was reached: male-line descendants of Queen Elizabeth II and Prince Philip Mountbatten can use the surname Mountbatten-Windsor.

Queen Elizabeth II and Philip Duke of Edinburgh have four children with birth dates spread from 1948 to 1964; as of the present (2011), all are living:

Charles Prince of Wales (born November 14, 1948)
Anne Princess Royal (born August 15, 1950)
Andrew Duke of York (born February 19, 1960)
Edward Earl of Wessex (born March 10, 1964)

The present Royal Succession by primogeniture in descendants of Queen Elizabeth II and Prince Philip Mountbatten is shown by bold numerals 1 to 12 in parentheses:

1st child. **(1)** Crown Prince Charles Prince of Wales, married Lady Diana Spencer; their two children are: **(2)** Prince William Arthur and **(3)** Prince Henry Charles.

2nd child. **(10)** Anne Princess Royal, married Capt. Mark Anthony Philip; their two children are: **(11)** Peter Mark and **(12)** Zara Anne.

3rd child. **(4)** Prince Andrew Duke of York, married Sarah Ferguson; their two children are: **(5)** Princess Beatrice Elizabeth and **(6)** Princess Eugènie Victoria.

4th child. **(7)** Prince Edward Earl of Wessex, married Sophie Ryhs-Jones; their two children are: **(9)** Lady Louise Windsor and **(8)** James Viscount Severn.

Prince Philip Duke of Edinburgh had major responsibility for approving the plan for education of the four royal children. As young children, they were educated at Buckingham Palace by governesses. Princess Anne did not attend public school for any later education, but the three princes all spent time at Gordon Academy in Scotland in their teenage years. Like King George V, Prince Philip used the autocratic manner of a 'navy man' as his model for educating his royal sons. Philip's judgment in these matters was not always successful. Prince Charles responded poorly to the severe pedantry that served to intimidate individuality more than inspire individual excellence. Prince Andrew and Prince Edward adapted more readily to their Spartan schooling at Gordon Academy. Only Edward went on for a university education; he received an MA degree in history from Cambridge University.

Queen Elizabeth II kept in her own hands the control of her dwindling prerogatives as the monarch. She has allocated to others few duties associated with the crown. Among the queen's regular functions in government is her prerogative to open and address Parliament. She has the right 'to be consulted, the right to encourage, and the right to warn,' but she does not have the right to initiate political change, or to show partisan preference while parliamentary debate is on-going. She meets regularly each week to be briefed on matters of government with her Prime Minister and members of the Privy Council.

She has a tight agenda of State visits, overseas tours, sponsorship of official court and government events, and innumerable public appearances for press and media throughout her worldwide realm. Queen Elizabeth has faithfully travelled throughout her realm to maintain a personal touch with her subjects. She is the most widely travelled public figure in the world, and has logged hundreds of thousands of miles in her visits to many remote corners of the earth.

Queen Elizabeth II is the Supreme Governor of the Church of England—an anachronism that goes back to King Henry VIII the founder of the Anglican Church.

Most notably, Queen Elizabeth II is the nominal Head of the British Commonwealth of Nations. The Commonwealth's charter says that the British monarch is a " . . . symbol of the free association of its independent member nations." The Commonwealth consists of over fifty member states, of which over a third are sovereign nations. Most Commonwealth members were part of Queen Victoria's past British Empire, but some parts of the former Empire (most conspicuously Ireland and India) no longer have any ties with the Commonwealth. The composition of the Commonwealth constantly changes as individual states seek greater independence. Between 1960 and 1980, almost two dozen members of the Commonwealth voted to be self-governing republics.

In her long reign as queen since 1952, Queen Elizabeth II has become the most experienced political figure in the English-speaking world. She has been served by eleven different Prime Ministers: Winston Churchill, Anthony Eden, Harold Macmillan, Alexander Douglas-Home, Harold Wilson, Edward Heath, James Callaghan, Margaret Thatcher, John Major, Tony Blair, and Gordon Brown.

Anecdotes are legion of her amusing, thorny, hilarious, and chilly encounters with the great and near great in fifty years of British government. Her relationship with Prime Minister Margaret Thatcher was a bit prickly: one encounter was described as, " . . . Margaret was very queenly and the Queen was all business." Following another meeting when the queen and Mrs. Thatcher wore identical dresses, Prime Minister Margaret sent a note to the queen, suggesting that some arrangement might be made to avoid the social blunder of wearing similar clothes. The queen replied, "For goodness sake, never mind. I don't ever notice what others wear."

Military events were scattered through her reign. In 1956 Britain and France lost prestige for an unsuccessful invasion of Egypt designed to regain control of the Suez Canal. Queen Elizabeth was silent at the time, but personally opposed the aggression. From April to June 1982, Britain and Argentina were involved in the Falkland Islands War, which established British sovereignty over the remote islands in the extreme South Atlantic. The Invasion of Granada by the United States in 1993 was strongly resented by Queen Elizabeth. The invasion was authorized by President Ronald Reagan to force regime change in the tiny British Caribbean Island. The Persian Gulf War lasted from August 1990 until February 1991. Britain and a coalition of over thirty United Nation countries participated in protecting the oil-rich country of Kuwait from invasion by Iraq. The second Iraq War precipitated by the United States in 2003 was supported by Britain, but did not have approval or support from the United Nations. These events, although memorable as footnotes in history, have done little to enhance the luster of England's past.

Queen Elizabeth's public popularity has risen and fallen over the years, but in general, she has enjoyed approval by her subjects during her long reign of over a half century. In 1977, her Silver Jubilee celebration of twenty-five years on the throne, affirmed Commonwealth approval of her work well done, as did her Golden Jubilee in 2002, which celebrated her half-century reign. In 2007, the sixtieth wedding anniversary of Queen Elizabeth and Prince Philip was celebrated as the longest marriage of any previous monarch in English history. Her Diamond Jubilee of sixty years as queen is planned for 2012.

Queen Elizabeth at present is the second longest reigning monarch in English history. She is surpassed only by her great-great-grandmother Queen Victoria, who reigned for over sixty-three years. Queen Elizabeth's health is good and, in light of the fact that her mother The Queen Mum lived for a little over 101 years, it is probable that Queen Elizabeth II will live for many more years, and will be the longest reigning sovereign in English history.

Low points in Queen Elizabeth's popularity have surfaced from time to time. In 1981 during *Trooping the Colors* at Buckingham Palace, the queen was on horseback when several shots were fired at her as she rode in The Mall, but her skillful control of her mount earned her public praise.

Public approval of the crown reached its lowest point at the time of the death and funeral of Princess Dianna in 1997. The queen was in Scotland at the time Diana was killed in an automobile accident in Paris on August 31. The queen remained at Balmoral Castle in the days before the funeral, and she was strongly criticized by the press and public for staying in seclusion while the nation grieved. However, after the queen returned to London and made a public show of sorrow with a public statement of condolence and admiration for the mother of her grandchildren the Prince William and Prince Harry, she regained public approval.

Queen Elizabeth has often been criticized for being an individual of great personal wealth, but who also received a huge annuity from Civil List public money to support the lavish style in which the royal family lived. The amount of her wealth in personal fortune and that of the Windsor Family Trust has been a subject of curiosity without resolution. Estimates of its worth range from over a billion pounds to less than one hundred million. The problem of arriving at a reasonably accurate estimate of the queen's wealth centers on how to separate individual personal ownership from Crown properties, Crown properties go with her official position as queen, but they are government owned (like many royal palaces, grand estates, the Crown jewels, and the Royal Collection of art and artifacts) they cannot be sold or invested by the monarch. The collected items in the so-called *British Crown Estate* or *Windsor Family Trust* is believed to yield income upwards from £6.5 billions a year, but most of it is returned to the general funds of the Commonwealth nations.

Criticism of financial outlay for the Royal Family declined after 1992-93 when the queen surrendered her tax-free status in response to growing public resentment of costs for support of the Royals from the Civil List. The queen agreed to take on support of many of the royal family, and their names were then removed from the Civil List at a saving for the public purse of over one million pounds annually. The Queen was exempt from paying tax on capital gains until 1994. In that year, she agreed to pay income tax on profits from her private investments. However, even with these concessions, the queen is still thought to be one of the richest women in the world.

Queen Elizabeth II does very well to uphold the dignified traditions of her office. It is difficult for an outsider to discover what, if any, crown duties are necessary for survival of the realm. From all appearances, the queen has a strong sense of duty, and does very well in whatever her tasks may be. One thing is certain; she has a feeling of responsibility for continuation of the monarchy, even if it has little obvious purpose. It is equally certain that her offspring are not nearly so strongly committed to the noble purpose of setting superior standards for personal behavior in the realm.

The threat of a royal marriage to a divorced woman in the 1930s was so unthinkably shocking that it led to the abdication of King Edward VIII, who refused to give up the idea of marriage to Wallis Warfield. Twenty years later, beginning in the 1950s, and accelerating in the 1980s and '90s, divorce became so frequent in the Royal Family as to generate a response no greater than an occasional, "Ho. Hum." The Queen's sister Princess Margaret was divorced in October 1955 and again in 1978. Three of the Queen's children were divorced in 1992 when divorce ended the marriage of Charles Prince of Wales to Princess Diana Spencer; Princess Anne divorced Mark Phillips; Prince Andrew Duke of York divorced Sarah Ferguson Duchess of York. The year 1992 certainly was not notable for any conspicuous good it did for the public perception of the crown.

Queen Elizabeth has performed admirably as a representative for the entire Commonwealth. She has twice addressing the United Nations (1957 and 2010), and on many other occasions, she expressed good will in the government houses of foreign nations, including the joint houses of Congress of the United States in 1991. Among the queen's most treasured personal prerogatives are the awarding of State honors and peerage titles. She also appoints Governors-General for the Crown Colonies (of course, with advice and approval of leaders in their governments). She is known to be the patron of hundreds of charities and service institutions.

As a residue of her strict childhood instruction, Queen Elizabeth II always appreciates being surrounded by people who behave properly in all circumstances. She is annoyed by breaches in courtliness, by those who break with custom and know better. Usually a stare of blank disapproval is her reprimand. That is part of her makeup, which earns her the name *The Great Stone Face* (only said, of course, behind her back). The name attests to the unflappable majestic calm with which she customarily greets all occasions.

Her preference in dress and hats is conservative, in good taste, and not greatly different than that of her mother the Queen Mum (hats with upturned brim, and dresses in light cheerful patterns). She is famous for the affection she lavishes on her Welsh Corgis, and she keeps a fine stable of racing horses, but she has given up riding following knee surgery in 2005.

The queen goes through a seasonal routine of living in her royal homes, does the usual public service expected of her, but remains aloof from her public most of the time. From the outside, it appears there is a calculated goal of perpetuating a *Royal Mystique* of unapproachable majesty, which keeps the monarch far above the masses. This arch posture extends even to those in her immediate family, from whom she expects deference suitable to her position at the head of the Windsor clan.

In spite of being endlessly photographed, caricatured, and gossiped about, Queen Elizabeth is intensely private, often withdrawn, or distant. Since she rarely gives impromptu interviews, press statements about her personal views are unreliably subjective opinions of third parties, as is the case with the present account.

Queen Elizabeth II did not acquire her aloof manner from her parents King George VI and Queen Mum who had a great knack for interacting in a warm personal way with their subjects—subjects who returned their full love. Queen Elizabeth is in debt to her grandmother Dowager Queen Mary of Teck, whose royal manner was an anachronistic throwback to Hanoverian days, a time when the German Royals in England kept the English masses at arms length.

At the time of the coronation of Elizabeth II, general optimism predicted the beginning of a 'New Elizabethan Age.' Her first Prime Minister Winston Churchill was particularly impressed with her promise for leading Britain to new heights of grandeur. However, most observers of political events will agree that the past fifty years have been more a decline, than a burst of new glory for the crown. Repeated murmurs said her English Crown was an anachronism in a time of change. A columnist critic wrote, "She is out of touch with the modern world and her advisers are a tweedy entourage who know nothing of life outside the restricted circle of the *Establishment*." The critic who wrote those lines got his nose punched for saying it. Nevertheless, it expressed the view of a substantial percentage of subjects in her realm who pray that a republic will soon erase the monarchy.

A public opinion pole in 1992 indicated that almost seventy per cent of the British public favored an end to the monarchy after the reign of

Queen Elizabeth II. However, only ten years later, a similar pole indicated that almost seventy per cent of the British public wants to see the monarchy continue into an indefinite future.

Queen Elizabeth II has reigned in a difficult time for a half-century with determined dedication to her queenly duties. No fifty years has seen more change than the one just past. She has been a remarkably able steward in protecting the monarchy. She has made hundreds of personal appearances and public speeches, yet she never caused embarrassing blunders to injure the crown. On her twenty-first birthday in 1947, while on a trip to South Africa with her parents King George VI and the Queen Mum, she made a notable radio broadcast to the Commonwealth with a pledge that she has faithfully kept:

> " . . . I declare before you all that my whole life, whether it be long or short, shall be devoted to your service and the service of our great imperial family to which we all belong. But I shall not have strength to carry out this resolution alone unless you join in it with me, as I now invite you to do. I know that your support will be unfailingly given. God help me to make good my vow, and God bless all of you who are willing to share in it."

As of the present (2011): The House of Windsor (successor for the House of Saxe-Coburg-Gotha) has had six reigning monarchs: Edward VII, George V, Edward VIII, George VI, and the present Queen Elizabeth II.

Whether the monarchy continues into the reign of the present Prince of Wales Charles Mountbatten-Windsor is subject to the will of the British Parliament and people. Barring unforeseen events, it is expected that Charles Prince of Wales will ascend the throne at the end of the reign of his mother Elizabeth II. In that event the name of the Windsor Dynasty will continue, possibly as the *House of Mountbatten-Windsor*.

EPILOGUE

THE REIGNING

AND

CONSORT QUEENS OF ENGLAND

T**HIS NARRATIVE** includes fifty short chronological biographies (with an average of ten pages per person) of women who took turns at the summit of power and prestige in England from the Norman Conquest of 1066 to the present 2011.

The biographical portraits started at the close of the Dark Ages and continued into Modern Time. The book gives a view into life as daily living and courtly customs moved from a distant age to the way of life we know today. Although the narratives are brief, they bring individuals to life as unique personalities. Through the lives of these women, one sees England's history unroll.

Of the fifty personalities, 7 were reigning queens, 38 were queen consorts of monarchs, and 5 were wives or 'favorites' who did not reign, but who played a significant role during the life of a ruling king.

Among the forty-five queens are 6 named Anne; 5 named Elizabeth and Katherine; 4 named Mary; 3 named Eleanor, Isabelle, and Matilda; 2 named Adela-Adelaide, Caroline, Jane, Joan-Joanna, and Margaret-Marguerite; 1 named Alexandra, Berengaria, Charlotte, Henrietta, Philippa, and Victoria.

The fifty narratives of women on the throne, or close to the throne is too large to expect that any single quality can characterize them all. Some served as exemplary reigning queens, or as consorts who actively supported a sovereign husband or son. Some assertively played the part of regent as a significant power behind the throne. Some served chiefly as supportive mothers and wives. Some influenced historic events for religious reasons. Some avoided political involvement, but had great influence on culture and custom. Some were pawns manipulated by historic events of the time. Some had personal qualities that made them inherently interesting and deserving of admiration and friendship. A relatively small number of the queens were entirely unsuited to fill their role as queens. Some queen consorts resisted familiarity and remain enigmatic effigies.

It has taken some time to assemble this running tale of women of virtue and vice, leadership and ineptitude, bravery and cowardice, idealism and depravity, and gifts to charm or repel.

The author's intent was to make this a factual informative good read.

ABOUT THE AUTHOR

H. EUGENE Lehman is a native of Kentucky; he received the BA degree from Maryville College, Tennessee; the MA degree from The University of North Carolina-Chapel Hill, and the Ph.D. degree from Stanford University. He spent a year in post-Doctoral studies at the University of Bern-Switzerland and the University of Naples-Italy. For a year, he was a guest exchange professor at the University of Vienna-Austria.

During over four decades of university teaching at the University of North Carolina-Chapel Hill, he authored several college tests, wrote scholarly papers on a variety of topics, and twice received awards for excellence in undergraduate teaching. His lifetime of scholarship and teaching is reflected in an ability to explain even the most complex issues with clarity and whimsical perception.

The present book, ***Lives of England's Reigning and Consort Queens***: *England's History through the Eyes of its Queens* is a companion for the author's book, ***Lives Of England's Monarchs:*** *The Story of Our American English Heritage*, published by AuthorHouse in 2005.

INDEX

K

Plantagenet, Margaret (Duchess of Salisbury) 381
Plantagenet, Richard (Richard of York) 208-9, 211, 220, 241, 243, 246, 266
Plantagenet Dynasty (Plantagenet Dynasty lineage) 2-3, 28, 71-4, 174-5, 177-8, 204, 217-18, 220-1, 253, 261
Pole
　Katherine de la 200, 258
　Reginald de la 222, 381, 385, 395, 401
　William de la (Duke of Suffolk) 206-7, 260, 263, 296, 319, 367, 375-7, 388
Pope 8, 10-11, 19, 64-5, 81-2, 102, 146, 162, 185, 281, 286, 288-92, 298, 300, 385, 487
Popish Plot 471-2, 489-90
Presbyterian (Presbyterianism) 416-18, 423, 427, 431, 453, 494
Prime Minister 531, 540-1, 544, 548, 554-5, 604, 612, 642, 653-5, 676, 678-9, 682
Primogeniture 17-19, 56, 75, 88, 102, 174, 217-20, 266, 415, 521, 616, 677
Prince Albert (Albert, Albert of Saxe-Coburg-Gotha) 284, 599, 601, 603-5, 607-10, 612-13, 621, 624, 627, 633-4, 663-4, 666, 675
Prince Henry Frederick 429, 432-3, 438-9
Prince of Wales 127, 142-3, 276-7, 458-60, 491-2, 536-7, 547-50, 566-9, 571-2, 574-6, 578-9, 616-22, 626, 634-6, 641-2, 650-2
Princes in the Tower 224, 230, 233, 237, 239, 241, 244, 250-1, 266, 268, 271
Privy Council 53, 123, 319, 322, 324-5, 330, 337, 339-40, 343-5, 355-7, 360, 372-3, 375, 514-15, 531, 665

Protectorate (Interregnum, Republic) 447, 458, 461, 481
Protestant (Protestantism, Protestant sects) 348, 354-5, 363-5, 369-71, 385-7, 393, 400-2, 417-18, 442-5, 470-1, 473, 479, 484-91, 498, 500, 520-1
Provisions of Oxford 113, 118, 122-3
Puritan 350, 354-5, 357, 375, 424, 437, 439-40, 447, 449-50, 452-4, 456, 459, 464-5, 470, 489-90, 500

Q

Quaker 328, 340, 354-5, 431
Queen Adela of Louvain 59
Queen Adelaide of Saxe-Meiningen (Adelaide) 2, 57, 60, 63, 524, 587, 593-600, 632-4, 685
Queen Alexandra of Denmark (Alix, Alexandra) 620, 629-30, 675
Queen Anne (Anne Stuart) 421, 473, 489, 508-9
Queen Anne Boleyn 282, 294-5, 300, 305-10, 313, 324-5, 327, 381-2, 384, 396, 401, 417
Queen Anne Neville (Anne Neville of Warwick) 245, 252, 266, 269
Queen Anne of Bohemia 160, 169, 172, 186, 276
Queen Anne of Cleves 282, 314, 324-6, 334-5, 348, 376, 384, 386, 397
Queen Anne of Denmark 425-6, 442, 450
Queen Berengaria of Navarre 92
Queen Caroline of Brandenburg-Ansbach 537
Queen Caroline of Brunswick 574, 584
Queen Charlotte of Meckenburg-Strelitz (Queen Charlotte) 548-9, 553-6, 558-64, 568, 570, 589, 591-2